The Latino/a Condition

The Latino/a Condition

A Critical Reader

EDITED BY

Richard Delgado

AND

Jean Stefancic

New York University Press

NEW YORK AND LONDON

NEW YORK UNIVERSITY PRESS
New York and London

Library of Congress Cataloging-in-Publication Data
The Latino/a condition : a critical reader / edited by Richard Delgado
and Jean Stefancic.
p.   cm.
Includes bibliographical references (p.   ) and index.
ISBN 0-8147-1894-9 (acid-free paper). — ISBN 0-8147-1895-7
(pbk. : acid-free paper)
1. Hispanic Americans—Social conditions. 2. Hispanic Americans—
Politics and government. 3. Racism—United States. 4. United
States—Race relations.   I. Delgado, Richard.   II. Stefancic, Jean.
E184.S75L355   1998
305.868—dc21   98-13514
                         CIP

New York University Press books are printed on acid-free paper,
and their binding materials are chosen for strength and durability.

Manufactured in the United States of America

10 9 8 7 6 5 4 3 2 1

To Carlos Delgado

Contents

Acknowledgments

We owe special thanks to Michael Olivas, Gerald López, Leslie Espinoza, Kevin Johnson, Margaret Montoya, Juan Perea, Berta Hernández, Frank Valdes, Rachel Moran, and George Martinez for their support and inspiration. They give new meaning to the term colleague. Rodolfo Acuña, Derrick Bell, Ronald Takaki, and Ian Haney López, by their example, encouraged us to strive for excellence. Diana Stahl prepared the manuscript with care and precision. Kristen Kloven provided steadfast and superb research, editing, and production assistance. Magen Griffith, Kevin Cain, and Ida Bostian assisted with editing and proofreading. For continuing support of our work, we thank Dean Harold Bruff.

As always, we are grateful to our editor, Niko Pfund, for his support of innovative scholarship.

Introduction

Richard Delgado and Jean Stefancic

If you are a Latino, how much do you know about your own group, and especially about the new generation of writers (sometimes called "Lat-Crits") who analyze the Latino condition from a critical perspective? If you are a non-Latino—a member of the majority race, for example—how much do you know about our nation's second-largest minority group of color? Do you realize, for example, that since the 1980 Census—the first ever to attempt to count persons of Spanish/Hispanic origin—the number of Latinos has grown an astonishing 53 percent? The 1980 Census counted a little over 14 million Latinos; that number today stands at around 29 million, making up about 11 percent of the U.S. population. At its current rate of growth, the Latino group in the United States will double by the year 2020, surpassing African Americans as the nation's largest minority. Nearly two-thirds of the Latino group are Mexican Americans, who comprise the largest subgroup. Next come Central and South Americans, who account for 13 percent, then Puerto Ricans, about 11 percent, and Cubans, about 5 percent. The total U.S. Latino population is larger than the entire population of Canada and has an annual purchasing power of $300 billion.

In this volume, you will learn about the struggles of this multifarious group for identity, recognition, and legitimacy. Do Latinos constitute a single cohesive group or a collection of warring factions? You will encounter America's quest for a just immigration policy. You will read about the unremitting racism Latinos faced in this country's early years and still do, to some extent, today. Some of the lawyers and activists who put their lives on the line for social change tell their stories here. You will read about the furious battles that rage within the group over affirmative action and bilingual education and whether these programs are good or bad for Latinos. You will also read about Latino and Latina attorneys who have waged legal battles challenging discrimination in schools and jobs and language-based exclusion. Some chapters discuss demeaning stereotypes, such as the greaser, the bandito, the sleepy Mexican dozing under a cactus, and the romantic Don Juan of legend and myth. You will discover how legal scholars and film critics respond to these images and narratives, interposing ones of their own that are closer to the truth. You will read about interracial marriage and the experiences of Latinos who could pass for white but choose not to. The debate about assimilation has been going on for over a century.

Should Latinos and Latinas try to fit in, or preserve their differentness, language, and culture? Can they do both? And you will read of Latinos, like many from Latin America, who have Indian blood or are dark-skinned. Do they face racism at the hands of their own compatriots?

Black-brown and brown-Asian tensions have been building. In some cities blacks and Latinos are at swords' points over political representation and jobs. In other areas, Korean shopkeepers, blacks, and Latinos exist in uneasy tension: All compete for affirmative action. Is the traditional civil rights coalition breaking down and, if so, is this to be deplored? Or do the various groups have legitimate, genuine differences with each other that need to be identified and threshed out, not glossed over? Suppose a black engages in racial discrimination against a Latino or vice versa. Should the means of redress be the same—a suit under the nation's civil rights laws—as it would if the discriminator had been white? That is the paradigm for which the nation's antidiscrimination laws were designed, but does this paradigm break down when minority groups discriminate against each other? And what of Latinas? Do they not face a different set of hurdles from those that confront Latino men? Are Latino men sometimes part of the problem? What is the attitude of the Latino culture toward gays and lesbians? Can one be an openly gay person in that community, or is homophobia too deeply entrenched?

The world is sliced up into nation-states separated by borders. The border between the U.S. and Mexico is a special case—heavily armed and patrolled, with many desperately poor people trying to cross it to a land of better opportunity. Is the border a metaphor for much of life? For most of our identities? Is it, as one writer in this collection puts it, an "open wound"? If so, what will heal it?

Chapters by leading historians, sociologists, essayists, and law professors offer probing analyses of these and many other issues related to the Latino community. Berta Esperanza Hernández-Truyol's satirical essay "Building Bridges" doubts whether that community exists, as she recounts what happened when she, a Cuban Puerto Rican, moved to the U.S. Southwest and ordered a tortilla. Gloria Anzaldúa's pathbreaking essay "Borderlands" explores borderlands and their meaning. Rodolfo Acuña's dazzling analysis of the Latino condition concludes that, in the early years at least, the Latino community was for all intents and purposes a colony. Ian F. Haney López's incisive critique concludes that race (including the Latino race) is a social construction without any foundation in biological reality, and that it ought to be dismantled because of the harm it does. Other chapters explore the history and resurgence of nativism, the system of virulent pressures and attacks that make Latinos feel unwelcome. Writers such as Kevin R. Johnson, Linda S. Bosniak, Reginald Horsman, and Gilbert Paul Carrasco show how nativist, anti-Latino attitudes are rooted both in American history and the economic self-interest of U.S. elites.

Legal scholar George A. Martinez analyzes whether Mexicans have been regarded as white or nonwhite for purposes of the law, concluding that the answer is both, depending on what was at stake and who benefited from the result. Michael A. Olivas shows how American society has sold out the rights and well-being of Latinos and Asians as often and as readily as it did those of blacks in Derrick Bell's famous fictional chronicle of the "Space Traders." Margaret E. Montoya, an evocative writer, challenges the reader to explore the role of racial masks and disguises—Are we sometimes not what we really are, but another racial persona? Several scholars write about the "black/white" binary of race relations, which accustoms American society to thinking of race only in terms of black and white. What does this approach leave out, and how does it exclude and marginalize Latinos? Does it even, as Juan F. Perea suggests, make Latinos *los olvidados,* invisible people? Ruben Navarrette, Jr., Linda Chavez, and Richard Rodriguez say, in effect, "Not so fast." The leftist, liberal, or critical view is not the only one, and perhaps not even the one most likely to bring payoffs for Latinos. Is the only legitimate Latino voice a radical, urgent one? The Latino community has a traditional, Catholic, family-loving, and respectful side. Who speaks for that community?

One thing all the writers in this book seem to agree upon is that poverty is a key issue for the Latino community. The number of Latino-owned businesses has grown rapidly in recent years, as has the number of Hispanic professionals. Despite these gains, however, Latinos were the only ethnic group to experience a drop in average income between 1990 and 1995; the group's statistics in such areas as health, infant mortality, longevity, school drop-out, and ownership of medical insurance today rival, and sometimes are worse than, those of blacks. Despite poverty, Latinos have made and continue to make headway in sports, culture, music, cuisine, and many other areas. In sum, Latinos/as are leaving their mark on American society while not always reaping the gains one might expect from it.

Following are ninety-four tightly edited chapters—some excerpted from previously published works, some appearing here for the first time—grouped into twelve parts corresponding to major Latino/a-Critical themes. We have tried to be as broad as possible, presenting material from many disciplines and perspectives. Our authors range widely in age, political perspective, sex, and sexual orientation. General topics that affect all or most Latinos, such as identity and immigration, are placed early in the book, with more particular topics covered later. We make a special effort to include the dissenting voices of those who take issue with many of the insurgent writers whose work forms the body of this book. Each part begins with a brief introduction setting out its general content, and ends with a short bibliography of suggested further reading, as well as questions and issues for discussion. Those interested in reading more will find a lengthy bibliography at the end of the book.

What do we hope to accomplish with this volume? Even as we have tried to include as broad a range of materials as possible, we recognize that many important authors and works are not found on these pages. Indeed, it would be highly unusual if one volume could include the many and varied voices of a group as complex and diverse as that of U.S. Latinos/as. Rather, we aim to provide a readable but scholarly overview of the Latino community and its issues at the end of the century. We believe this book will be of use to the general reader wishing to keep informed of cultural currents, minority affairs, and civil rights, as well as to the specialist wishing to gain an insight into the new critical scholarship. Above all, we hope to reach readers and policy makers receptive to the idea of broadening and enriching the ongoing discussion of race in America and to taking into account the many perspectives and textures that latinicity can bring. It is with these hopes in mind that we prepared this book.

Part I

The Shape of the Latino Group

Who Are We and What Are We Talking about Anyway?

Most readers know that Latinos—persons who trace their ancestry to Latin America or, in some cases, the Caribbean or Spain—are one of the country's fastest-growing minority groups. Constituting about 11 percent of the population (precise numbers are difficult because of the unknown number of undocumented immigrants), Latinos will overtake African Americans as the nation's most numerous minority group of color early in the next century. About two-thirds of U.S. Latinos are Mexican Americans (sometimes called Chicanos), with Cubans, Puerto Ricans, and Central Americans making up substantial groups as well. Most Mexican Americans reside in the Southwest and California, most Cubans in Florida, and most Puerto Ricans in New York and other East Coast cities. A relatively young group, Latinos also suffer from poverty and a high rate of school drop-out. The chapters in Part I, written by some of the leading scholars of the Latino condition, raise key issues regarding the contours of the Latino group and how it sees and defines itself. Are Latinos a race, an ethnic group, or neither? What are the group's defining characteristics, as seen by itself or by others—federal law, for example? Are Latinos white? Can one be a Latino or Latina as well as something else—for example, black, or Irish, or gay or lesbian? And if so, what is one, really?

Chapter 1

Hispanics? That's What They Call Us

Suzanne Oboler

> A person is of Spanish/Hispanic origin if the person's origin (ancestry) is Mexican, Mexican American, Chicano, Puerto Rican, Dominican, Ecuadoran, Guatemalan, Honduran, Nicaraguan, Peruvian, Salvadoran; from other Spanish-speaking countries of the Caribbean or Central or South America; or from Spain.[1]

In the past two decades, the term *Hispanic* has come into general use in the United States to refer to all people in this country whose ancestry is predominantly from one or more Spanish-speaking countries. As a result, millions of people of a variety of national backgrounds are put into a single "ethnic" category, and no allowances are made for their varied racial, class, linguistic, and gender experiences. The term ignores, for example, the distinct and diverse experiences of descendants of U.S. conquest, such as the Chicanos, and those of the Puerto Rican populations, colonized by the United States at the turn of the century. Its users often neglect to contextualize the specific histories and cultures that differentiate these two groups, both from one another and from more recent immigrant arrivals, whether from Mexico, Central or South America, or the Spanish-speaking Caribbean nations. In so doing, they combine longtime native-born U.S. citizens and residents with more recently arrived economic immigrants who may have crossed the U.S. border yesterday.

The term *Hispanic* also lumps together recent political refugees from El Salvador with past political exiles like the first wave of Cubans who arrived in the early 1960s. The latter's upper- and middle-class status and racial composition in turn masks the differences between their entry process and experiences and those of the nonwhite working-class Cuban Marielitos, for example, who arrived in 1980. Moreover, some exiles have today become economic immigrants like the contras and upper- and middle-class Nicaraguans who originally left their country soon after the Sandinista victory of 1979.

While most scholars limit their policy-related research on Latinos to populations with ties to Latin America, the U.S. government census definition that begins this chapter also includes European immigrants from Spain. In addition, the perceptions of the general population compound the sources of definitional confusion about the term *Hispanic*. Unlike government agencies and scholars, many are not aware of the political and cultural implications of the diverse backgrounds of those whom public opinion also unofficially classifies as Hispanics. Among these are the Brazilians who, because of their Portuguese heritage, share neither the language nor the culture of Spanish America, and hence rarely self-identify as "Hispanics."

In addition, the term homogenizes class experiences and neglects many different linguistic, racial, and ethnic groups within the different nationalities themselves: various indigenous populations; the descendants of enslaved Africans; waves of immigrant populations from every country in Europe, Asia, the Middle East. Members of these populations too are increasingly making their way to the United States, ensuring the growing visibility of Latin America's heterogeneity within the Latino populations in this country.[2]

In the current usage by the U.S. census, government agencies, social institutions, social scientists, the media, and the public at large, then, the ethnic label "Hispanic" obscures rather than clarifies the varied social and political experiences in U.S. society of more than 23 million citizens, residents, refugees, and immigrants with ties to Caribbean and Central and South American countries. It reduces their distinct relations among themselves and with U.S. society to an ethnic label that in fact fails to do justice to the variety of backgrounds and conditions of the populations to whom it has been applied. As Martha Giménez put it, the term *Hispanic* "strip[s] people of their historical identity and reduc[es] them to imputed common traits."[3]

Like other ethnic labels currently used to identify minority groups in this country, the term *Hispanic* raises the question of how people are defined and classified in this society and in turn how they define themselves in the United States. It points to the gap between the self-identification of people of Latin American descent and their definition through a label created and used by others. . . .

Given the diversity of the various population groups both in Latin America and in the United States, how *did* the culturally homogeneous representations of people identified as Hispanics become commonplace among scholars, government agencies, the media, and the public at large in this country? Popular reasoning about the origin of the term *Hispanic* usually locates it within the legacy of the Spanish conquest and colonization of the New World.[4] After all, the justification goes, Spanish colonial rule lasted for over three centuries, certainly long enough for the social, ethnic, linguistic, racial, and national experiences of the populations of Latin America and the Caribbean to establish a homogeneous heritage.

But in Latin America itself, the role of the Spanish legacy in shaping a common cultural identity on the continent has been the subject of ongoing debates since that region's independence in the early nineteenth century. Underlying these discussions is the recognition that in spite of the shared Spanish colonial heritage, profound differences mark the various nations' postindependence histories and populations, often overriding cultural or linguistic commonalties they may also share. In many ways, then, the issue of the creation of a unified cultural—and even political and economic—"Hispanic identity" in the United States actually transports to this country a debate that Latin American intellectuals have themselves waged since the nineteenth century in historical essays, social science texts, and their respective national literatures.[5]

NOTES

1. U.S. Bureau of the Census, Population Division, Development of the Race and Ethnic Items for the 1990 Census 51 (New Orleans: Population Association of America, 1988).

2. J. Jorge Klor de Alva, *Telling Hispanics Apart: Latino Sociocultural Diversity,* in The Hispanic Experience in the United States: Contemporary Issues and Perspectives (Edna Acosta-Belén & Barbara R. Sjostrom, eds.) 107–36 (New York, Praeger, 1988).

3. Martha E. Giménez, *"Latino/Hispanic"—Who Needs a Name? The Case against Standardized Terminology,* International Journal of Health Services 19, no. 3 (1989), p. 41.

4. Discussing the confusion raised by the definition of *Hispanic,* Carl Mora (in a letter to the editor) remarks: "What do our statisticians and government officials do? They refer to all these people as being 'of Spanish origin' (except the Brazilians) when it is obvious that a great many Spanish-speaking Latin Americans have no ancestral connection at all to Spain (but some Portuguese-speaking Brazilians do). . . . The term 'non Hispanic white' is . . . used to denote one of European origin; but where then, did the 'Hispanic whites' originate if not also in Europe?" Carl J. Mora, *Americans of Hispanic Origin,* New York Times, February 25, 1985.

5. Simón Bolivar, Para Nosotros La Patria es América (Caracas: Biblioteca Ayacucho, 1991); José Martí, Páginas Escogidas (Robert Fernández Retamar, ed.) (Havana, 1985); La Identidad Cultural de Hispanoamerica: Discusión Actual (J. Giordano & D. Torres, eds.) (Santiago de Chile: Monografias del Maitén, 1986); Angel Rama, Transculturación Narrativa en América Latina (Mexico City: Siglo XXI Editores, 1982); Gabriel García Márquez, El General en su Laberinto (Madrid, Mondadori, 1989); Julio Cortázar, Rayuela (Buenos Aires: Ed. Sudamericana, 1967); América Latína en sus Ideas (Leopoldo Zea, ed.) (Mexico City: Siglo XXI Editores/UNESCO, 1987).

Chapter 2

Welcome to the Old World

Earl Shorris

We are ordinary people,
we are subject to death and destruction,
we are mortals;
allow us then to die,
let us perish now,
since our gods are already dead.

—Colloquies of 1524, transcribed by
Fray Bernardino de Sahagún

A small group of Dominican artists and intellectuals met in Manhattan in the closing days of 1989 to plan the attack. It seemed less than serious at first, an idea born over drinks and a little smoke in a dark room, whispered, enjoyed, explored over the sound of drums and an old piano. They laughed. Later, the next day and the day after, it became more than an amusement. They hated the imperialists, their whiteness, the soft dough feel of them, their thin hair hanging. And they hated Christopher Columbus most of all.

This was the plan: When the ships arrived to recreate his landing in celebration of the five hundredth anniversary of the discovery of Hispaniola, and all the weaklings, all the ass-lickers, rushed out to greet them, the true Dominicans, hundreds of them in native dress, would rise up out of their hiding places and attack the white invaders. With spears and stones, they would drive the Europeans back to their ships and away from the island of Hispaniola forever.

The Dominicans had overlooked history; they had permitted the symbolism to become confused. No one remembered that by 1570 only the imperialists and their African slaves were left; the genocide of the native population of Hispaniola was virtually complete. It did not occur to the little group of angry romantics in Man-

hattan that it was themselves they planned to drive away, for the Columbus Day conspirators were the children of conquest, doomed to a life of unendurable irony—Latinos.

Any history of Latinos stumbles at the start, for there is no single line to trace back to its ultimate origin. There are many Edens, a thousand floods, discoveries and conquests in numbers beyond the capability of human memory. Only the smallest fragment of this history survives. We shall never know the Olmecs or read the Mayan books the Spaniards burned; no more is known of the mind of Chief Hatuey of Hispaniola than what a Spanish friar heard; the grandeur of the Yoruba pantheon was not recorded during its reign.

Latino history has become a confused and painful algebra of race, culture, and conquest; it has less to do with evidence than with politics, for whoever owns the beginning has dignity, whoever owns the beginning owns the world. So every version has its adherents, for every human being wishes to be at least equal in his own mind: the African to the Spaniard, the person of mixed blood to the fair-haired descendant of Europeans, the Indian to the person of mixed races, the darker to the lighter, the one with kinky hair to the one with the softly curled hair of Europe to the one with the straight black hair of the Americas.[1]

For some the choice of beginnings is obvious. Imagine a family descended directly from Indians who lived in the Mexican state of Oaxaca: If the family concedes that Columbus "discovered" a New World, they accept the notion that whites (Europeans) come from a superior civilization. On the other hand, if the descendants of Indians say that Latino history began with the Toltecs or the Maya or with the emergence of people from the earth in a place called Aztlán, they raise the value of their own ancestry, making themselves at least equal and possibly superior to the whites.

The choice becomes more difficult for a person of mixed ancestry for whom those small conceits of identity, which are the ordinary rules of chauvinism, do not apply. Should a woman in Chicago who traces her family back to both Chihuahua and Castile identify with Europe or the Americas? According to the rules of conquest, the blood of the conquered dominates, but the rules are not profound; they are written on the skin. If the woman in Chicago appears to be European, she will have to choose where Latino history began, who were the subjects—the ones who acted, the dignified ones—and who were the objects—the people whom the forces of history acted upon.

Her decision will not be frivolous; it will determine her vision of herself, the face she sees in the mirror as well as the one she presents to the world. Her politics, left or right, Democrat or Republican, may be affected by what she considers the beginning of history; she may even choose to speak and dress and cook according to how and where she thinks Latino history began. The name by which she identifies herself—Hispanic, Latina, Spanish, chicana, Mexican, *Mejicana,* Mexican American—will depend upon her understanding of the past.

The history of Latinos was not always a difficult one. Until 1920 it was understood that Columbus had discovered the "New World" and begun the process of civilizing its savages and exploiting its natural resources. It was also understood that other savages had been imported from Africa, enslaved, and used to replace the American natives who died in such enormous numbers in the fields and mines of the Caribbean. But the end of the Mexican Revolution of 1910, after almost ten years of war, brought with it the need to integrate the rural Indians into the political economy of the nation. The task was given to one of Mexico's leading intellectuals, José Vasconcelos, who was appointed minister of education. With three words, he proclaimed the integration of the Indian into Mexican society at the most profound level: *la raza cosmica*.

To explain the notion of this cosmic race to people who could not read, Vasconcelos turned to Mexico's painters. He commissioned Diego Rivera, José Clemente Orozco, and David Alfaro Siqueiros, among others, to paint murals depicting Mexican subjects, and he gave them complete artistic freedom, which they used to attack the government, the colonialists, the capitalists, and the Spanish conquerors. A new version of Mexican history appeared on the walls of public places. For the first time in four hundred years a large number of people began to see the conquest in a different light: Instead of the discovery of a dark, savage continent by intellectually, technologically, morally superior white men, the muralists portrayed the destruction of the glorious civilizations of the Americas by the brutal Spaniards.

After Vasconcelos and his muralists, the victory of the Indianists would seem to have been assured. But there were doubts, even in the mind of the minister of education himself. Vasconcelos wrote that the "blood and soul" of Mexico were Indian, but the language was Spanish. And even more pointedly, the civilization, he said, came from Spain.

NOTES

1. In 1990, Kirkpatrick Sale offered a fascinating revision of the European version of the history of the Americas in *The Conquest of Paradise*. His humanistic, thoughtful work contrasts sharply with a restatement of the old ethnocentric white European view published a year later by Mario Vargas Llosa. As the quincentennial celebration of the Voyage of Columbus drew closer, books, films, television programs and articles appeared in ever-increasing numbers. The Sale and Vargas Llosa books remained at the opposite poles of opinion.

Chapter 3

███████████

Chance, Context, and Choice in the Social Construction of Race

Ian F. Haney López

The Mean Streets of Social Race

The literature of minority writers provides some of the most telling insights into, and some of the most confused explorations of, race in the United States. Piri Thomas's quest for identity, recorded in *Down These Mean Streets*,[1] fits squarely within this tradition of insight and confusion. Thomas describes his racial transformation, which is both willed and yet not willed, from a Puerto Rican into someone Black. Dissecting his harrowing experiences, piercing perceptions, and profound misapprehensions offers a way to disaggregate the daily technology of race. In the play of race, chance, context, and choice overlap and are inseverable. Nevertheless, I distinguish and explain these terms in order to explore the thesis that a race is best thought of as a group of people loosely bound together by historically contingent, socially significant elements of their morphology and/or ancestry.

Chance

The first terms of importance in the definition of race I advance are "morphology" and "ancestry." These fall within the province of chance, by which I mean coincidence, something not subject to human will or effort, insofar as we have no control over what we look like or to whom we are born. Chance, because of the importance of morphology and ancestry, may seem to occupy almost the entire geography of race. Certainly for those who subscribe to notions of biological race, chance seems to account for almost everything: one is born some race and not another, fated to a particular racial identity, with no human intervention possible. For those who believe in biological race, race is destiny. However, recognizing the social construction of

From "The Social Construction of Race: Some Observations on Illusion, Fabrication, and Choice." 29 Harv. C.R.–C.L. Rev. 1 (1994). Originally published in the *Harvard Civil Rights–Civil Liberties Law Review*. Reprinted by permission.

race reduces the province of chance. The role of chance in determining racial identity is significantly smaller than one might initially expect.

The random accidents of morphology and ancestry set the scene for Piri Thomas's racial odyssey. Seeking better prospects during the depression, Thomas's parents moved from Puerto Rico to Spanish Harlem, where Piri and his three siblings were born. Once in the United States, however, the family faced the peculiar American necessity of defining itself as White or Black. To be White would afford security and a promising future; to be Black would portend exclusion and unemployment. The Thomas family—hailing from Puerto Rico of mixed Indian, African, and European antecedents—considered themselves White and pursued the American dream, eventually moving out to the suburbs in search of higher salaries and better schools for the children. Yet in their bid for Whiteness, the family gambled and lost, because even while the three other children and Piri's mother were fair, Piri and his father were dark skinned. Babylon, Long Island, proved less forgiving of Piri's dark skin than Spanish Harlem did. In the new school, the pale children scoffed at Piri's claim to be Puerto Rican rather than Black, taunting Piri for "passing for Puerto Rican because he can't make it for white,"[2] and proclaiming, "[t]here's no difference . . . [h]e's still black."[3] Piri's morphology shattered not only the family's White dream, but eventually the family itself.

While the family insisted on their own Whiteness as the crucial charm to a fulfilling life in the United States, Thomas, coming of age amid the racial struggles of the 1950s and himself the victim of White violence, fought the moral hypocrisy he saw in their claim to Whiteness. Piri unyieldingly attacked the family's delusion, for example challenging with bitterness and frustration the Whiteness of his younger brother José:

> José's face got whiter and his voice angrier at my attempt to take away his white status. He screamed out strong: "I ain't no nigger! You can be if you want to be . . . . But—I—am—white! And you can go to hell!"

But Piri persisted in attacking the family, one at a time:

> "And James is blanco, too?" I asked quietly.
> "You're damn right."
> "And Poppa?"
> . . . "Poppa's the same as you," he said, avoiding my eyes, "Indian."
> "What kinda Indian," I said bitterly. "Caribe? Or maybe Borinquen? Say, José, didn't you know the Negro made the scene in Puerto Rico way back? And when the Spanish spics ran outta Indian coolies, they brought them big blacks from you know where. Poppa's got *moyeto* [Black] blood. I got it. Sis got it. James got it. And, mah deah brudder, you-all got it. . . . It's a played-out lie about me—us—being white."[4]

The structure of this painful exchange casts a bright light on the power that morphology and ancestry wield in defining races. In the racially charged United States, skin color or parentage often makes one's publicly constructed race inescapable.

Piri's dark features and José's light looks are chance in the sense that neither Piri nor José could choose their faces, or indeed their ancestry. Still, what we look like is not entirely accident; to some extent looks can be altered in racially significant ways.

In this respect, consider the unfortunate popularity of hair straightening, blue contact lenses, and skin lighteners. More importantly, however, though morphology and ancestry remain largely matters of chance, those aspects of identity gain their importance on the social, not the physical, plane. Consider, now, the operation of context.

Context

Given Piri's status as a Puerto Rican with ancestral ties to three continents, there is a certain absurdity to his insistence that he is Black. This absurdity highlights the importance of context to the creation of races. Context is the social setting in which races are recognized, constructed, and contested; it is the "circumstances directly encountered, given and transmitted from the past."[5] At the meta level, context includes both ideological and material components, such as entrenched cultural and customary prejudices, and also maldistributed resources, marketplace inequalities, and skewed social services. These inherited structures are altered and altered again by everything from individual actors and community movements to broad-based changes in the economic, demographic, and political landscape. At the same time, context also refers to highly localized settings. The systems of meaning regarding morphology and ancestry are inconstant and unstable. These systems shift in time and space, and even across class and educational levels, in ways that give to any individual different racial identities depending upon her shifting location. I refer to context in order to explain the phrases "historically contingent" and "socially significant" in the definition of race proffered at the start.

Changes in racial identity produced by the shifting significance of morphology and ancestry are often profoundly disconcerting, as Piri Thomas discovered. In Puerto Rico, prevailing attitudes toward racial identity situated the Thomases, as a family not light enough to be Spanish but not so dark as to be black, comfortably in the mainstream of society. They encountered no social or economic disadvantages as a result of their skin color, and were not subjected to the prejudice that usually accompanies rigid racial constructs. However, the social ideology of race in the United States—more specifically, in New York in the late 1950s—was firmly rooted in the proposition that exactly two biological races existed. Such an ideology forced the Thomas family to define themselves as either White or Black. In the context confronting Piri, "[i]t would seem indeed that . . . white and black represent the two poles of a world, two poles in perpetual conflict: a genuinely Manichean concept of the world."[6] Once in the United States, Thomas came to believe that he and his family were Black as a biological fact, irrespective of their own dreams, desires, or decisions. Yet, Thomas was not Black because of his face or parents, but because of the social systems of meaning surrounding these elements of his identity.

Consider how Thomas came to believe in his own Blackness. In a chapter entitled "How to Be a Negro without Really Trying," Thomas recalls how he and his fair-skinned Puerto Rican friend Louie applied for a sales job. Though the company told

Thomas they would call him back, they hired Louie to start Monday morning. Thomas's reflections bear repeating:

> I didn't feel so much angry as I did sick, like throwing-up sick. Later, when I told this story to my buddy, a colored cat, he said, "Hell, Piri . . . a Negro faces that all the time."
> "I know that," I said, "but I wasn't a Negro then. I was still only a Puerto Rican."[7]

Episodes of discrimination drove Piri toward a confused belief that he was Black. Aching to end the confusion, Piri traveled to the South, where he hoped to find out for sure whether his hair, his skin, and his face somehow inextricably tied him, a Puerto Rican, to Black America. Working in the merchant marine between Mobile, New Orleans, and Galveston, Piri experienced firsthand the nether world of White supremacy, and the experience confirmed his race: Bullied by his White bosses, insulted by White strangers, confronted at every turn by a White racial etiquette of violence, Thomas accepted his own Blackness. "It was like Brew said," he reflected after his time in the South, "any language you talk, if you're black, you're black."[8] Suffering under the lash of White racism, Thomas decided he was Black. Thomas's Blackness did not flow from his morphology but from traveling the mean streets of racial segregation. His dislocations suggest a spatial component to racial identities, an implication confirmed in Thomas's travel from Spanish Harlem, where he was Puerto Rican, to Long Island, where he was accused of trying to pass, to the South, where he was Black.

Piri and his family were far from the first to face the Manichean choice between White or Black. The Chinese, whose population in the United States rose fifteenfold to 105,465 in the twenty years after 1850, were also initially defined in those stark terms. Thus in Los Angeles circa 1860 the Chinese area downtown was called "Nigger Alley." During their first years in the United States, as Ronald Takaki observes, "[r]acial qualities that had been assigned to blacks became Chinese characteristics."[9] Not only were the supposed degenerate moral traits of Blacks transferred wholesale to the Chinese, but in a fascinating display of racist imagination, Whites also saw a close link between Black and Chinese morphology. Takaki cites a commentator who argued that Chinese physiognomy indicated "but a slight removal from the African race,"[10] and he reprints a startling cartoon contrasting Anglo Uncle Sam with a Chinese vampire replete with slanted eyes, but also with very dark skin, woolly hair, a flat nose, and thick lips.

In California, where the racial imagination included Mexicans and Indians as well as Blacks, Chinese were considered not only in terms of Blackness but also in terms of every non-White race, every rejected and denigrated Other. This point furnishes yet more evidence for the theory that racial identity is defined by its social context. Consider the 1879 play *The Chinese Must Go* by Henry Grimm of San Francisco. Notice the language Grimm ascribes to the Chinese characters, discussing, predictably, their nefarious anti-American plot to destroy White labor through hard work:

> *Ah Choy:* By and by white man catchee no money; Chinaman catchee heap money; Chinaman workee cheap, plenty work; white man workee dear, no work—sabee?
> *Sam Gin:* Me heep sabee.[11]

The Chinese in this Grimm play speak in the language that Whites associated with Indians and Mexicans, making Sam Gin sound remarkably like Tonto playing out the Lone Ranger's racial delusions. Thus, the Chinese were assigned not only their own peculiar stereotypes, like a fiendish desire to work for low wages, but also the degenerate characteristics of all the minorities loathed by Whites. Not coincidentally, three years after Grimm's play, the United States passed its first immigration law: The 1882 Chinese Exclusion Act. In a telling example of law reifying racist hysteria, the Supreme Court upheld the Chinese Exclusion Act in part by citing the threat posed by the Chinese to White labor.[12] The first Chinese, like the Thomas family nearly a century later, entered a society fixated on the idea of race and intent on forcing new immigrants into procrustean racial hierarchies.

The racial fate of Piri and the Chinese turned to a large extent on the social setting into which they immigrated. That setting provides the social meanings attached to our faces and forebears, and for this reason I write that races are groups of people bound together by historically contingent, socially significant elements of their morphology and/or ancestry. A race is not created because people share just any characteristic, such as height or hand size, or just any ancestry, for example Yoruba or Yugoslav. Instead, it is the social significance attached to certain features, like our faces, and to certain forebears, like Africans, which defines races. Context superimposed on chance largely shapes races in the United States.

Choice in Context

Piri's belief that he is Black, and his brother José's belief in his own Whiteness, can in some sense be attributed to the chance of their respective morphology and the context of their upbringing. Yet, to attribute Thomas's racial identity only to chance and context grossly oversimplifies his Blackness. Thomas's father shared not only his social context, but his dark looks as well, making context and chance equal between them. Nevertheless, his father insisted on his Whiteness, and explained this decision to Piri as follows:

> I ain't got one colored friend . . . at least one American Negro friend. Only dark ones I got are Puerto Ricans or Cubans. I'm not a stupid man. I saw the look of white people on me when I was a young man, when I walked into a place where a dark skin isn't supposed to be. I noticed how a cold rejection turned into an indifferent acceptance when they heard my exaggerated accent. I can remember the time when I made my accent heavier, to make me more of a Puerto Rican than the most Puerto Rican there ever was. I wanted a value on me, son.[13]

Thomas's father consciously exaggerated his Puerto Rican accent to put distance between himself and Black Americans. Thomas himself also made conscious and purposeful decisions, choices that in the end made him Black. As Henry Louis Gates argues, "one must *learn* to be 'black' in this society, precisely because 'blackness' is a socially produced category."[14]

Choice composes a crucial ingredient in the construction of racial identities and the fabrication of races. Racial choices occur on mundane and epic levels, for example in terms of what to wear or when to fight; they are made by individuals and groups, such as people deciding to pass or movements deciding to protest; and the effects are often minor though sometimes profound, for instance, slightly altering a person's affiliation or radically remaking a community's identity. Nevertheless, in every circumstance choices are exercised not by free agents or autonomous actors, but by people who are compromised and constrained by the social context. Choice, explains Angela Harris, is not uncoerced choice, "freely given, but a 'contradictory consciousness' mixing approbation and apathy, resistance and resignation."[15] Nevertheless, in racial matters we constantly exercise choice, sometimes in full awareness of our compromised position, though most often not.

Perhaps the most graphic illustration of choice in the construction of racial identities comes in the context of passing. Passing—the ability of individuals to change race—powerfully indicates race's chosen nature. Not infrequently someone Black through the social construction of their ancestry is physically indistinguishable from someone White. Consider Richard Wright's description of his grandmother in *Black Boy:* "My grandmother was as nearly white as a Negro can get without being white, which means that she was white."[16] Given the prevalent presumption of essential, easily recognized phenotypical differences, light-skinned Blacks exist at an ambiguous and often unacknowledged racial border between White and Black. Those in this liminal space often respond along a range from some few who cross the established color line by "passing" to those who identify strongly with their Black status.

For most people, the pervasive social systems of meaning that attach to morphology ensure that passing is not an option. Moreover, for those who do jump races, the psychological dislocations required—suspending some personal dreams, for example childbirth; renouncing most family ties, for instance forgoing weddings and funerals; and severing all relations with the community, for example ending religious and civic affiliations—are brutal and severe. In addition, because of the depth of racial animosity in this society, passing may only succeed in distancing one from her community, not in gaining her full acceptance among Whites. In this sense, recall the words of Thomas's father: "I noticed how a cold rejection turned into an indifferent acceptance when they heard my exaggerated accent."[17] Nevertheless, some people do choose to jump races, and their ability to do so dramatically demonstrates the element of choice in the micromechanics of race.

Passing demonstrates not only the power of racial choice, however, but the contingency of the choices people make, thereby reinforcing the point that choices are made in specific contexts. Choices about racial identity do not occur on neutral ground, but instead occur in the violently racist context of American society. Though the decision to pass may be made for many reasons, among these the power of prejudice and self-hate cannot be denied. Thomas's younger brother José reveals the racist hate within him in the same instant that he claims to be White. José shouts at Piri: "I ain't black, damn you! Look at my hair. It's almost blond. My eyes are blue, my nose is straight. My motherfuckin' lips are not like a baboon's ass. My skin is white. White, goddamit! White!"[18]

José's comments are important, if painful to repeat, because they illustrate that a person's choice in the matter of race may be fatally poisoned by ambient racist antipathies. Nevertheless, notice that the context in which passing occurs constantly changes. For example, it may be that in the contemporary context passing as White increasingly does not in fact require that one look White. Recently, many Anglos, committed to the pseudo-integrationist idea that ignoring race equals racial enlightenment, have seemingly adopted the strategy of pretending that the minorities they are friendly with are White. Consider the words of a White Detroit politician: "I seldom think of my girlfriend, Kathy, as black. . . . A lot of times I look at her and it's as if she is white; there's no real difference. But every now and then, it depends on what she is wearing and what we're doing, she looks very ethnic and very Black. It bothers me. I don't like it. I prefer it when she's a regular, normal, everyday kind of person."[19] Even so, passing may be far less common today than it was a hundred years ago. One observer estimates that in the half-century after the Civil War, as many as 25,000 people a year passed out of the Black race. The context in which passing occurs constantly changes, altering in turn the range of decisions individuals face.

Despite the dramatic evidence of choice passing provides, by far the majority of racial decisions are of a decidedly less epic nature. Because race in our society infuses almost all aspects of life, many daily decisions take on racial meanings. For example, seemingly inconsequential acts like listening to rap and wearing hip hop fashion constitute a means of racial affiliation and identification. Many Whites have taken to listening to, and some to performing, rap and hip hop. Nevertheless, the music of the inner city remains Black music. Rapping, whether as an artist or audience member, is in some sense a racial act. So too are a myriad of other actions taken every day by every person, almost always without conscious regard for the racial significance of their choices. It is here, in deciding what to eat, how to dress, whom to befriend, and where to go, rather than in the dramatic decision to leap races, that most racial choices are rendered. I do not suggest that these common acts are racial choices because they are taken with a conscious awareness of their racial implications, or because they compel complete shifts in racial identity. Rather, these are racial choices in their overtones or subtext, because they resonate in the complex of meanings associated with race. Given the thorough suffusion of race throughout society, in the daily dance of life we cannot avoid making racially meaningful decisions.

NOTES

1. Piri Thomas, Down These Mean Streets (1967).

2. *Id.* at 90.

3. *Id.* at 91.

4. *Id.* at 145.

5. Karl Marx, The Eighteenth Brumaire of Louis Bonaparte (1963), quoted in Renato Rosaldo, Culture and Truth: The Remaking of Social Analysis 105 (1989).

6. Frantz Fanon, Black Skin, White Masks 44–45 (1967).

7. Thomas, at 108.

8. *Id.* at 187–88.

9. Ronald Takaki, Iron Cages: Race and Culture in 19th Century America 217 (1990).

10. *Id.*

11. Quoted in Takaki, at 221.

12. The Chinese Exclusion Case: Chae Chan Ping v. United States, 130 U.S. 581, 595 (1884).

13. Thomas, at 152.

14. Henry Louis Gates, Jr., Loose Canons: Notes on the Culture Wars 101 (1992).

15. Angela P. Harris, *Race and Essentialism in Feminist Legal Theory*, 42 Stan. L. Rev. 581 (1990) (quoting T. J. Jackson Lears, *The Concept of Cultural Hegemony: Problems and Possibilities*, 90 Am. Hist. Rev. 567, 570 [1985]).

16. Richard Wright, Black Boy 48 (1966).

17. Thomas, at 152.

18. *Id.* at 144.

19. Kathy Russell, Midge Wilson & Ronald Hall, The Color Complex: The Politics of Skin Color among African Americans 120 (1992).

Chapter 4

Latino/a Identity and Multi-Identity
Community and Culture

Leslie G. Espinoza

American society forces individuals to label themselves by race and gender. Not surprisingly, race and gender are the categories that correlate to power. A person's race and gender correlate to the likelihood that one will have educational opportunity, be in a particular income class, be in prison, or be the victim of a violent crime. Race and gender identity are the ways in which we are taught to articulate ourselves.

Multi-identity is not an accepted concept in dominant discourse. That discourse is about being "for us or against us," a cowboy or an Indian, an American or an alien, a woman or one of the boys, black or white, Mexican or white, Asian or white, Other or white. The politics of dichotomous categorical identity[1] require individuals to be placed into or to be forced to choose one particular defining identity. Once placed in that category, the individual is assumed to possess all the characteristics of that category, good and bad. Furthermore, that category is understood by its opposition to another category.[2]

Understanding personal identity, however, often requires the expression of multiple and distinct defining categories and the recognition of a unifying concept—the individual person. Identity may thus seem a paradox. How can there be group identity where each individual is an amalgam of unique characteristics, where each community and culture is a mix? The tension between group and individual difference has caused trouble between those with the power to put others into categories such as race, gender, or sexual preference, and those individuals pushed into socially constructed group identities that are both overinclusive and underinclusive. The choice is to assimilate or to be pushed into some distinct category of "other," whether it fits or not. This neat, blanket packaging of people both reflects and perpetuates current power structures. Of course, in reality, most individual outsiders are comfortable with the messy ambiguity of identity—when we are not thinking about it. When we try to counter the socially imposed categories and the oppression they represent, we

From "Multi-Identity: Community and Culture." 2 Va. J. Soc. Pol'y & L. 23 (1994). Originally published in the *Virginia Journal of Social Policy and the Law*. Reprinted by permission.

find that we lack a language to express that which we have learned through experience.

I am a Mexican, Irish, Jewish, Woman, Heterosexual, Aunt, Law Professor, Californian, Bostonian, Tucsonian, middle child, professional; multi-identity is something I have thought about at length. So much so that often when I try to talk about it, my thoughts seem to all come out in an analytical jumble—a potpourri of personal anecdotes and generalized theory. Yet in all my formulations of self, whether geographical, educational, professional, or familial, the major categories that override all else are race and gender. For me, race and ethnicity should be more complicated; but they are not. The politics of race in America define me as Mexican. It is the identity of social hierarchy. It is the politics of being pushed to the bottom. It is the erasure of the richness of my Mexican/Irish/Jewish mix, and a white-washing of the colorful complexity of meaning in each of my ethnic roots.

Let us explore multi-identity by focusing on two examples — the classroom and the courtroom.

Learning Law, Learning Assimilation

I am a teacher, as was my grandmother. Maria Espinoza Cisneros taught in the town of Pitiquito, Sonora, Mexico, at the turn of the century. The oldest of eight children, she fled the Mexican revolution in 1912, settling with her family in Chino, California. My grandmother was the matriarch of her extended family until she died in 1967. Her husband died when he was still young and my grandmother raised her five children through the Great Depression. I never heard my grandmother speak a word of English.

When we were small, she would sit us in her yard and tell us of the Mayan and Aztec kings. She would start sometime around 700 A.D. and recite their names and year of ascension. She would tell us of the Spanish conquest. She would proudly tell us that we were Mexican. The Mayan, Aztec, and Spanish, however, were only part of our heritage. Being Mexican meant to be mixed, to have Indian blood, to be Mestizo. Our Indian ancestors were from three tribes: the Pima, the peaceful poets of the desert; the Tarahumara, the mystics of Northern Mexico; and the Apaches, the warriors of the plains and mountains. Each separate identity combined to create a unique composite. We were a mosaic, each tile separately colored and textured, piecing together a whole identity.

I knew my grandmother, my Nana, in the last years of her life. She was a bent, tiny woman, with well over eighty years behind her. Her hair was like her ideas, always neatly folded in braids and carefully contained in what looked like a frail hairnet. The braids wove a pattern that gave every strand a sense of structure and a knowledge of place and belonging. The hairnet was invisible, and seen, all at the same time. When she was in the kitchen or crocheting in the living room, it was hard for me to imagine her a "schoolteacher." Yet, she easily assumed her teaching persona when it was time to instruct her grandchildren in their legacy. She had a confidence and assurance that, just as her braids and her ideas fit together with a puzzling strength, her own sense of self would not unravel.

My own hair is short, cropped, and a mess of curls. Like my ideas, it moves every which way. No pattern of braids folds neatly around my head; no organizing net holds everything in place. I find my role transitions equally disarrayed. I am the carefully assimilated, accentless law professor. I move in and out of my other identities, but not smoothly. Like my grandmother, I want to teach my students a legacy. I want to teach them how they can take the pieces of their past and meld them with their developing lawyer persona. This is difficult to do when the discourse of law requires a single hegemonic voice.[3]

I teach law students the language of law—the vocabulary of torts, jurisdiction, procedure, nuisance, equity and remedy. Beyond the individual words and concepts, they are learning a whole new way of thinking, of categorizing and conceptualizing information. They learn to think of problems as issues, divorced from emotion; of justice in terms of economic cost-benefit analysis; of judging as the application of preset rules. They learn to evaluate power and to speak in the language that will be heard by the law.

Most of us learn to speak a number of different languages and still call it one language. Consider the language of law, for example, or that of the academy—pedagogical, doctrinal, rigorous, traditional, narrative, fem-crit, race-crit, intersectional—or that of family and close personal relationships, careless in precision with an assumed understanding: "you know what I mean," "the whatchama-call-it," "OK," "Ya." There is also the language of gender, race, ethnicity, and sexual preference.

We recognize our various identities in our different languages. Language is the vehicle by which others know us and by which we know ourselves. We give labels to our external and internal thoughts and experiences. Through this process of naming, we define our reality. Words are symbols for knowledge. Learning to speak is learning to attach the "right" symbol to the "right" knowing in the "right" context. This is a cultural, political, and personal process.

The problem, however, is that not all of us can learn new languages and keep our fluency in past languages. The story of social hierarchy has been one where the language of social power reinforces that power by muting other languages. Trying to hold on to disempowered identities causes dysfunctionality in the use of the newly learned language of power and assimilation.[4] When race equality means color-blindness that bleaches the concept to mean "the same as white," or when gender equality means "same as men" resulting in language categories like "non-pregnant persons,"[5] then socially-imposed bias makes those of us with certain identities outsiders. Our consciousness, our way of knowing, through our overlapping identities, cannot coexist with the new language. Our earlier cultural voice is dominated and silenced.

Gender differences provide a concrete example of this type of domination. Women use a special socialized style of speech which Robin Lakoff calls "women's language." This language includes "hedges," "tag questions," and "qualifiers." For example, when asked, "What time is dinner?" women will tend to respond indirectly: "I think that it should be around seven" or "Perhaps seven would be a good time." Alternatively, women will look for affirmation, "Would seven be good?" or "Dinner is at seven, if that's OK?" or "Seven, isn't it?" They might even try to qualify their response: "Assuming you'll be home, seven." Women tend not to respond directly: "Dinner is at seven."

This style of speech is both deferential and subordinating, reflecting women's historical lack of power and economic dependency, but it is also empowering. Women's use of this language was a strategy of survival in the private sphere and of manipulation for power in a world where women lacked the power for direct confrontation and demand. It empowered women within the confines of their subordinated position. It also enhanced a gender communication between women that was premised on listening and developing language by looking for reaction within the interrelationship of communication.

Women's traditional language has hurt them in law school. It does not mesh well with the language of Socratic response and positioning. The law school classroom experience is pedagogically designed to force a certain kind of interchange between the student and teacher. The "pure" Socratic method begins with the teacher describing a problem (e.g., case) and then asking a question regarding the basis for resolving the problem. The student responds by taking a position. The teacher challenges that position by posing a change in facts.

Women are socialized not to answer questions directly. Thus, women law students will usually begin their response with a hedge: "I think" or "Perhaps" or "One way of looking at it." Women are socialized not to interrupt. The quick back and forth of classroom questioning can make women uncomfortable. Women will qualify their answer or seek approval with a transition question: "Isn't it?" Furthermore, women communicate with a greater concern for the relationship between the listener and the speaker. Thus, they tend to take longer to respond and will respond in a way designed to increase communication rather than create an impregnable argument.

In the law school classroom, women students are deprived of the ability to speak in the language that they have been socialized to speak. It is not true that learning to speak the language of law in a more direct, categorized articulation will solve the problem. Much of women's language stems from experience in communicating where stating one's position was not nearly as important as enhancing the communicative relationship with the listener. Denying women the ability to use their language suppresses their gender identity and excludes their experience from the classroom.

For women of color, the strategies for survival within the languages of race and ethnicity are particularly challenging. Women of color are expected to channel their experience either through the discourse of race or of gender. Women of color are thus forced to divide themselves. They are forced to think of themselves as having only the language and experience of either men of color or white women. The category "women of color" is given a label acknowledging its existence, but it is not given a substantive voice. This forced channeling not only fragments women of color, it exhausts them. They end up having to do the work of suppressing whichever aspect of their identity disrupts the accepted discourse of gender or race.

In the classroom, women of color often engage in the divide and suppress strategy. For example, imagine a discussion of the O. J. Simpson trial in a criminal law class. How do women of color begin to articulate the complexity of their perspective? Nicole Simpson's murder raises issues regarding interracial marriage. It is complicated standing in a world where you understand and live the plague of domestic violence and also understand and live the race discrimination of the criminal justice system. But the world of women of color is not two worlds, each separate and distinct. It is a world of whole identity, two composites of the oppressions shared with white women and those shared with men of color. Many additional tiles make up the mosaic of their world. Only when women of color are forced to choose between being "women" or "of color" must they then divide their consciousness.

For law teachers, the challenge is to teach legal language in a way that incorporates and supports women's language. For women of color, an additional dimension of discourse must be developed that allows us to develop a legal language that keeps us functional in all of our identities. As the new language develops, it may well require the emergence of a new concept of legal discourse in the classroom and the courtroom.

Legal Doctrine, Reinforcing Hierarchy

I am intrigued by my grandmother, the teacher. To be a great teacher, she must have had a love for learning. Yet she never learned, or rather admitted to learning, English. She embraced all the different and often warring cultures of her Mexican identity. To the day of her death, she called herself a Mexican—never an American. She seemed to understand the difference of multi-identity in a culture where acceptance means assimilation, and assimilation means the uni-identity, the uni-lingualism of the dominant culture.

Linguistic assimilation has served as a particularly effective instrument in cultural suppression and eventually obliteration. Language domination means that English must be learned in order to participate in the society. More important is the pressure to disuse, and even unlearn, other languages. In 1991, the United States Supreme Court in *Hernandez v. New York*[6] reinforced uni-lingual, cultural domination. The Court held that the prosecutor's use of peremptory challenges during jury selection to exclude all Spanish-speaking, Latino jurors was constitutional—even if the exclusions resulted in all potential Latino jurors being excluded. Of course, all the excluded jurors spoke English. Their infirmity was that they also spoke Spanish. They had taken the first step toward "American identity," but they were not yet trustworthy. The government argued that its challenge to Latino jurors was justified because one of the witnesses at the trial would be testifying in Spanish. The government did not believe that bilingual, Latino jurors would adhere to the official English interpretation.

In *Hernandez,* the jurors were asked if they would abide by the official English translation. They answered that they would. The prosecutor argued, however, that the individual jurors questioned could not be believed. They hesitated and looked away when answering the question. The Supreme Court relied on this notion of individual exclusion to justify its decision. Bilingual Latinos could not be per se excluded. Indeed, bilingual, Latino jurors who promised to rely on the official translation could not be peremptorily challenged—unless they were not believed. As the prosecutor in *Hernandez* testified:

> I believe that in their heart they will try to follow [the official translation], but I felt there was a great deal of uncertainty as to whether they could accept the interpreter as the final arbiter of what was said by each of the witnesses.[7]

In *Hernandez,* the Court tears away the mask of inclusive justice. Ours is not an adjudicatory system where judgment includes the views of peers who speak the same language of multi-identity. Members of the Latino community must not only speak English to be jurors, they must cease to speak Spanish.

It is difficult to imagine that any bilingual juror could really and absolutely ignore inconsistencies in interpretation. It would be like asking them to step outside of their own head. Worse, unlike other kinds of evidentiary exclusions that jurors are asked to ignore, mistakes in interpretation would be an injustice uniquely perceived by the bilingual juror. In the usual case, an objection to evidence presented is sustained and the jury instructed to ignore the evidence. With interpretation errors, the bilingual juror is complicitous with the injustice. They have the ability to shed light on the truth, to perhaps aid a misunderstood Latino witness. Yet in order to be part of the dominant culture's power process, the court system, they have to agree to abandon their Latino language identity.[8]

The lure to trade our identity for power is strong. We want to be jurors; we want to be lawyers; we want to be law professors. I have this dream. My grandmother and I are speaking Spanish. I wake up but cannot understand what we said. Over the years, I have lost my ability to speak Spanish.

It takes a lot of energy to hide our accents, our idioms, our language. We have to learn to shift between identities, without an overlap. And then comes a time when we feel secure enough in the mastery of the dominant language to experiment with transformative speech—to create a new combination of languages. But can we remember that original language of culture and community? Have we lost all authenticity? I think not. We can try to stay connected to each of our identities. If we become fragmented, if we lose memory, we can endeavor to recapture it. I now understand why my grandmother never spoke English. She wanted to make certain that if we lost our ability to speak in Spanish, we would not lose our ability to dream in Spanish.

NOTES

1. Michele Lamont & Robert Wuthnow, *Betwixt and Between: Recent Cultural Sociology in Europe and the United States,* in FRONTIERS OF SOCIAL THEORY: THE NEW SYNTHESES 287, 298–99 (George Ritzer ed., 1990).

2. Angela P. Harris, *Race and Essentialism in Feminist Legal Theory,* 42 STAN. L. REV. 581, 583–84 (1990); see also Lisa C. Ikemoto, *The Code of Perfect Pregnancy,* 53 OHIO ST. L.J. 1205, 1294 (1992).

3. Richard Delgado, *When a Story Is Just a Story: Does Voice Really Matter?* 76 Va. L. Rev. 95, 103 (1990).

4. See, e.g., Leslie G. Espinoza, *Masks and Other Disguises: Exposing Legal Academia,* 103 Harv. L. Rev. 1878, 1884–86 (1990); Margaret E. Montoya, *Mascaras, Trenzas, y Greñas: Un/Masking the Self While Un/Braiding Latina Stories and Legal Discourse,* 17 Harv. Women's L.J. 185, 210–15 (1994); Robert A. Williams, Jr., *Taking Rights Aggressively: The Perils and Promise of Critical Legal Theory for Peoples of Color,* 5 Law & Ineq. J. 103, 106 n.6 (1987).

5. See, e.g., Martha Minow, *The Supreme Court, 1986 Term—Foreword: Justice Engendered,* 101 Harv. L. Rev. 10, 40–43 (1987); Robin West, *Jurisprudence and Gender,* 55 U. Chi. L. Rev. 1 (1988).

6. 500 U.S. 352 (1991).

7. *Id.* at 356 (quoting App. 3–4).

8. As Perea observed:

The overwhelming popularity of these [official English] laws proves what most Hispanics have already learned: that many people either dislike or ignore Hispanic culture and the Spanish language. The popularity of official English laws only proves, as Congress recognized in its 1975 amendments to the Voting Rights Act, that Hispanics are an unpopular minority that has suffered a long history of discrimination implemented in part through language discrimination.

Juan F. Perea, *Demography and Distrust: An Essay on American Languages, Cultural Pluralism, and Official English,* 77 Minn. L. Rev. 269, 362 (1992).

Chapter 5

Building Bridges
Latinas and Latinos at the Crossroads

Berta Esperanza Hernández-Truyol

Can one lump persons in a generic "hispanic" category? Only by ignoring the diversity of the latina/o population. For example, federal forms usually provide the following options: black (not of hispanic origin); white (not of hispanic origin); hispanic. As the forms seek information in the conjunctive, implicitly recognizing that ethnic identity and racial identity are two separate, co-existing traits, it is particularly ironic that latinas/os are deprived of the opportunity to identify as ethnic, i.e., latina/o, including subcategory identification such as Cuban, Mexican, Puerto Rican, as well as to identify by race. As multiple-layered selves we are denied part of our personhood when we have to deny part of who we are. Our experience simply cannot be sanitized to fit a mold in the creation of which we were not considered.

Two specific points are noteworthy. First, the disjunctive nature of the categories with which latinas/os are expected to identify collapses and simultaneously excises latina/o ethnicity from the black or white races and places latinas/os as separate from both. Second, it prevents latinas/os from claiming their racial identification, black or white, and renders invisible latinas/os of other racial and ethnic backgrounds such as Asian, Indios, Mestizos, and so on. Certainly, the insensitivity and the under- and over-inclusiveness of any generic latina/o categorization and the homogenization it engenders further the myth of a monolithic latina/o identity. What is tragically wrong with this picture is that latinas/os, in reality, are a racially and culturally diverse group. These experiences inform our perceptions differently. Consider who we are.

I moved to Albuquerque back in the summer of '82. That is the year when I started teaching at the University of New Mexico. I had been out there to find a place to live in the spring. I fell in love with New Mexico when I first visited the university to interview for the teaching slot. It felt like home, the familiar Spanish influence, the rice and beans, the sunlight and the bright clothing. That summer I arrived the day before my house closing—late, with my dog in tow, and hungry. Starving, really. And when I am hungry I have to eat. But with being in a new place and all, and the ex-

From "Building Bridges—Latinas and Latinos at the Crossroads: Realities, Rhetoric and Replacement." 25 Colum. Hum. Rts. L. Rev. 369 (1994). Originally published in the *Columbia Human Rights Law Review*. Reprinted by permission.

citement of the closing, the furniture arriving, etc., I figured a light meal would do. So I went into the only place I found open and ordered a tortilla, a plain tortilla. There, I was so happy, I could even order food in Spanish. The waitress looked at me kind of funny and asked, simply, "Are you sure all you want is a tortilla?" "Yes," I said. "Plain?" she asked. "Yes," I said, "it's late." So with a shrug of the shoulders she disappeared and promptly returned and put this plate in front of me. Sitting on the plate was this flat thing, white, warm, soft. My turn to ask, "And what is this?" "Your order ma'am." And we stared at each other. I ate this thing, although I did not quite know how I was supposed to do that. I got funny looks when I went at it with fork and knife. I ate, I paid, I left—still hungry and now confused. Clarity occurred several days later when I was formally introduced to the tortilla—that Mexican tortilla anyway, one that I learned to love even plain (well, with some melted butter). But that was not the tortilla I had in mind. That first night I wanted my tortilla, a simple omelette to those of us from the Caribbean.

This is a simple story about complex and diverse peoples. Here we were dealing with the same word: tortilla, and the same language: Spanish. Yet our different cultures give the word different meanings. The existing approach, one that would consider us both the same notwithstanding our common "language" and other cultural similarities, excludes. It denies the different cultural experiences of latinas/os and falsely homogenizes by making us the "same" when we are not. It creates a generic "hispanic" that in reality does not exist. Such a single-trait perspective (and whose point-of-view is it anyway?) does everyone a disservice by misinforming. A latina/o can be black, and no less latina/o, just as a woman can be latina/o and no less woman. Prevalent single-trait, uni-perspective methodologies prevent the constructive bridge-building that could occur if the focus were on universality. Yet, our differences need not make us adversaries. A multiple-perspective approach promotes understanding among different peoples by affording them the comfort to talk with each other armed with the knowledge that they will have different perspectives based on their life experiences. A multiple-perspective approach therefore promotes understanding instead of generating conflict.

Typecasting

Stereotyping is one of the greatest problems latinas/os must battle to debunk the myth of a monolithic latina/o. Stereotyping puts people in boxes and creates images that result in false presumptions accepted as incontrovertible truths. To be sure, we have seen how this problem plagues all women and men of color. Latinas/os can not escape its trap.

The Meat Market

I had an interview I will never forget. It was back in 1981, my first participation in the recruitment conference, back in the days when it was held in Chicago. I had been running around, up and down, a day full of thirty-minute interviews scheduled back to back. My 2:00 P.M. interview was with one of the good, progressive schools. My interviewers were four, what I would then have described as older (but today would describe as middle-aged), white men in lawyer uniform: wing-tips, pin-striped suits, white shirts, red and blue striped ties, dark socks, grey hair parted to the side, and wire-rimmed glasses. I arrived at the door, wearing my costume: a camel hair suit, blouse, pumps, leather briefcase. I knocked. El Jefe (read: dean) answered my knock. There was a pause as el Jefe and his three colleagues first looked at each other and briefly stared at me, in silence. Then they looked me up and down once, twice, three times. Silence. "Uh," said el Jefe as he proceeded to the door, "you must be at the wrong room. We are scheduled to see a Miss Ber . . . uh Ber . . . uh . . . Ber (mumble, groan) HERnandez." (Unpronounceable name indeed!) My turn. Pause. Extend hand, grip firmly. "I am Berta Esperanza Hernández," I introduced myself and proceeded to enter the interview suite and shake hands with the other three interviewers. Once everyone was seated we engaged in the usual obligatory preliminary chit-chat. We talked law, how exactly would I teach labor law, as I recall. Some ten or fifteen minutes into the interview (which considering its beginnings was proceeding unexpectedly smoothly) el Jefe asked, "Excuse me, do you mind telling us if you are from an academic background?" Young, yes; naive, yes; I still had radar. So I pointed to their hands (each one was holding a copy of my resume), and noted that the resume fully covered my educational experience. "No, no," el Jefe said, speaking for all of them, "we mean are you from an academic (emphasis here with arched eyebrows) background?" I too can play, I thought. "I am afraid I don't understand. I went to law school at . . ." Again the question (with very arched eyebrows). Again my answer, adding, "High School I attended in San Juan, Puerto Rico. St. John's Prep." Until finally el Jefe asked, "Well, er, I, what we mean, is, er, well is your father a professional"? There it was, he said it. "My father is a banker, my mother is a lawyer," I replied. Pause. Long Pause. Very Long Pause. "Um. Er. Well," said el Jefe, "I am afraid that with your background our Chicano students would not be able to relate to you. We are afraid they would consider you elite." Pause, again; long pause again, but this time it was mine. At which point I calmly (I think) stood up and, while shaking their startled hands and doing goodbye I said, "Well, I guess we do not have anything else to talk about then."

I can only speculate why the four interviewers concluded, erroneously, first that I was not me; and second, that their Chicano students would be unable to relate to me or I to them. However, it is plain that their conclusions, incorrect as they may have been, were driven initially by their pre-conceived image of what a latina law professor should look like and by their presuppositions as to what her family should be like. One thing was clear to me: their view depended upon coded ethnicity-gender and class assumptions. First, their image of latinas was one that did not look like me, and I hate to disappoint any who might infer I look "different," I am really rather typical looking, if a bit on the tall side: 5'8", dark hair, dark eyes, olive skin. Maybe it was my lawyer uniform that threw them off; although, I must confess, almost everyone who goes to the recruitment conference wears some variant of this uniform. Moreover, latinas/os from educated, professional families did not quite fit their image of who latinas/os are supposed to be. And perhaps because

I did not fit their image on either count they decided my "difference" was that I was not Chicana. This is the tragic flaw of homogenizing and stereotyping: somebody else's image of who we are, what our families are like, what we do and what we look like makes us the image. It is this imagery—gender, race, ethnic, color and class stereotyping—that falsely imprisons all of us. And I mean all. Latinas/os too. Read on. . . .

Counting

At a meeting, latina/o colleagues were trying to put together a list of who we were. Because the "final" list was so thin, we started combing available records to see if we had missed someone. I looked at the list carefully and noticed a name missing. The name skipped was someone I knew rather well; we had been in undergraduate school together. In fact our parents had known each other from their university days. So I volunteered, "We failed to include Maria." The chair of that meeting recognized but failed immediately to place the name. So the chair took a moment to collect her/his thoughts and said, "Yes, I know who that is. But she doesn't count, she's Cuban." Not knowing whether to laugh or cry I sat in shocked silence and thought, "And ain't I a Cuban?"

Again, as with the interviewers, a Cuban was deemed not to be one of "us," even among a group of latinas/os. This, of course, is the result of the diversity present even among latinas/os. For example, sometimes the first wave of Cuban refugees, because of their education and professional status, are viewed more like the majority, the privileged.

Thus, one can see that inter-latina/o presumptions about subgroups—subgroups that the majority denies by virtue of the notion of the monolithic latina/o—also exist. Such stereotyping, I fear, is the product of this country's divisive race-relations outlook, which, consciously or not, minority groups adopt too often. This model is one that we would be better off changing. Significantly, the majority does not care one bit if you are Cuban, first wave or not, or Mexican or Puerto Rican or anything else. The funny name, the accent, the different culture, and the brown skin are enough— you are an "outsider."

Latinas/os and Language

This predicament is hard to avoid. Language is harmful when it stereotypes in a destructive and isolating way. The poisonous nature of this "you do not belong there" is exacerbated because it comes not in terms of a dichotomy of black-white relations but rather in terms that touch deeply on latinas/os' multi-dimensionality. Latinas/os are continually bombarded with the "you are not us" message. The myth tells latinas/os: you are not white, not black, not Asian, not Indian. The reality is that latinas/os can be all of the above.

The result of the complete "otherness" perspective is a silencing of latina/o voices by all, a total banishment. On the one hand, so-called NLWs [non-Latino whites—

Eds.] perceive latinas/os as "minorities"—the "other," an "other" who speaks a different language to boot.

On the other hand, non-latina/o blacks see latinas/os as "not black," and perhaps even as white. Professor Derrick Bell, for example, in a recent address noted that "there is every reason to believe that Spanish-speaking . . . immigrants, like their European predecessors, will move beyond the bottom of the society and leave blacks in the role society has designated for them."[1] Certainly Professor Bell does not, as he cannot, believe the myth that all latinas/os are of European heritage or that they are all white. The history of intermarriages in, for example, the Southwestern states, Puerto Rico, Cuba, and the Republica Dominicana attests otherwise. It is plain that there are many latinas/os of African heritage, Asian heritage, and Indian heritage. Nor can, or should, recent latina/o immigrants be likened to "their European predecessors" even if they are of distant European heritage. As Professor Bell surely knows, dramatically different issues are at play today than existed in the colonial period or the earlier twentieth century European immigrations. Nevertheless, the perception exists that because latinas/os are not black, latinas/os and blacks do not share issues and concerns. In reality, this is a great misperception. For example, employment and education are two major concerns shared by the black and the latina/o communities. Nevertheless, the existence of the misperception as a reality—the view that these communities do not share issues and concerns—strengthens oppositionality.

A June 27, 1993, *New York Times* article provides a specific example of the tensions engendered by the scripting of latinas/os as adversaries of blacks. The piece, entitled "As Hispanic Presence Grows, So Does Black Anger," noted the growing resentment of blacks in Miami against latinas/os who "take their jobs."[2] The article suggests that the tension is aggravated as the city's latina/o population grows to dominate the economic and political life. As one black woman interviewed put it, "They are taking over, and I am a victim of that."[3] This echoes the complaints of her white counterparts about the evils of "affirmative action programs" (code: "minorities," meaning blacks and latinas/os) because they take jobs away from deserving whites.

The tragic flaw of the approach that drives the normative-driven oppositionality is that rather than trying to find a novel solution for a new dilemma—the existence of peoples in this society who do not fit squarely into the dichotomous black-white model's structure—it merely seeks to use the pre-existing model. The black or white model does not fit latinas/os, just as the black or woman model does not fit the black woman. Latinas/os bring different issues into play. Slavery is not the issue; that was theoretically solved by the Thirteenth Amendment. Nor is the problem the consequence of slavery, one that still lacks a solution. Nor is formal equal access to public accommodations, housing, employment, and education the issue. Technically, the 1964 Civil Rights Act crafted the tools to solve that problem, although making these wonderful paper rights a reality is a struggle latinas/os share with the black community. On the other hand, latinas/os need to grapple with the present-day issues of language and immigration. Latinas/os must do battle in order to work—either prove you have a green card when you are a citizen/legal resident or find a way to live without one and still be labeled lazy or a welfare cheat. Additionally, we must face the problems caused by the inhuman conditions in which migrant workers live as well as those that result from the creation of an uninsured, underclass of persons who provide domestic help, such as nannies, housekeepers, and gardeners. To be sure, this is not an issue unique to latinas/os, as we may well see analogous problems arise among some of the new groups of immigrants to the United States; so much the more important it becomes that latinas/os who have a long history in this country start working on building bridges.

Latinas/os' racial diversity also presents a novel issue, often unspoken, certainly as unresolved and complicated as the intersection of race and gender. Their racial diversity injects yet another layer to the essentialism/intersectionality[4] discourse. Latina/o blacks, for example Afro-Cubans, may identify more with the racially mixed Cuban population than with the racially homogeneous (but culturally diverse) English-speaking black population. Rather than identify solely on the basis of race, Afro-Cubans also identify with their linguistic and cultural heritage. This identification, however, does not, as it cannot, render Afro-Cubans "not black."

Yet another angle to latinas/os as "others" is that some appear "white" in the "Anglo" sense. Of course, this "white look" does not make one bit of difference if the initial interaction is on paper, as are most applications for employment or to institutions of higher education. Given that there appears to be a very clear image in our society of what a latina/o looks like, such initial paper contact may well conjure up the stereotypic images of what an applicant should look like. This is very likely the reason a good progressive law school's four interviewers once thought I was not me—not that I look "white" in the NLW sense by any stretch of the imagination; but there must have been something about me in my lawyer "costume" that threw them off. And then, of course, because my parents are educated professionals—much, I might add, like the parents of most colleagues I have had in my sixteen years in the legal profession—in the eyes of the four interviewers, I somehow did not fit the mold, which I imagine requires having pulled myself out of the working class by being the first in my family to enjoy the privilege of higher education.

These are particularly difficult issues without easy answers. If the law has difficulty understanding the concept of a "blackwoman," what can it do with a "black-Cubanwoman" concept? Or a Puertorriquena triguena? By restricting analysis to a single-trait approach, the law isolates and disempowers latinas/os by creating a landscape where both NLWs and (non-latina/o) blacks see latinas/os as "other." Yet the myth—the sham image—proliferates. Latinas/os are reduced to race-less homogeneity belonging nowhere. The reality of a culturally and racially diverse people is invisible. Rather than have us "torn between two colors," with alienating, isolating consequences, the diverse experience of latinas/os can be used to bridge gender, racial, ethnic, cultural, and linguistic differences to translate experiences and expressions. Let us consider how latinas/os can play a role in enhancing communication and understanding between and among groups that perceive each as the "other."

Building Bridges

I always have started out as the only latina lawyer or law professor in a workplace. Often, the women emerged as my support group—as if the gender commonality provided the necessary bridge. I remember in one of my myriad careers, I arrived as usual—the only latina. I could sense the otherness with which I was viewed by both black and white. One colleague directly asked once, "You don't really consider yourself hispanic, do you?" This changed when one day I had a close friend come to the workplace to put on a special event. Unbeknownst to all, my friend was African American. Once he arrived it was kind of obvious he was black. After the event, a smashing success, the black colleagues for the first time saw me as me as one of "them"—a person of color.

We can, and should, do better than this. Building bridges is a suggested replacement for oppositionality. This replacement demands a total reconstruction, one that debunks the old cast which only sculpts Dr. Kildares or Doogie Howsers as doctors, and Perry Masons or Douglas Brackmans as lawyers. The reconstruction, the replacement, has to be accomplished with a new universalist image. This image should be a multi-dimensional one informed by the variety of experiences that describe the realities of a fully diverse people. This approach uses multiple- rather than single-trait perspectives. It needs elasticity but not inflexibility or infirmity.

We need to decode the language so that we start calling things by their right names—names that can accommodate diversity and be changed if they cease to work. Two items are critical to this endeavor's success. First is the need to recognize and accept that the language we use carries a lot of baggage—coded messages that fail to portray reality accurately. Second, everyone must participate in the renaming. We must avoid a system whose appellations are designated by "founding fathers," who fail to reflect the diversity of our society. A replacement, including a decoding of language, creates meaningful classifications: relevant ones that do not operate in a vacuum. Classifications must be contextually legitimate. Latinas/os can reveal and lay claim to their multiple selves and fit corrective lenses on the myopic view of difference as a deviation from the "norm." Continuum, a concept that latinas/os can help by virtue of their diversity, must replace the illegitimate hierarchical norms that measure worth based on the degrees of separation from the so-called normative and depend on an inapplicable dichotomy.

Here is how latinas/os can help. We can build bridges as we have been doing for years. We are used to being black, white, brown, and every other color and shade. We can help create an understanding within the color spectrum, for we have been doing it among ourselves for years. We speak Spanish, English, Spanglish, regional dialects, and indigenous tongues. We can translate—we have been doing it among ourselves for years. We can promote an understanding of differences by engendering understanding of commonalities—we have been doing it among ourselves for years. The lesson to learn is that people, a composite of their race, gender, ethnicity, class, religion, sexual orientation, ability, and color, are complex. Rarely can we find the best answer (at least for a time) by asking only one obvious question, such as "What is the effect of a practice on an ethnic group?" Rather we will reach the better resolution by asking many questions, including ones that address the conflation of traits. To be sure, undertaking such a course is ambitious, difficult, and likely to be painful as we force ourselves to confront prejudices we would just as soon ignore. Such a multi-layered methodology is certain to result in mistakes. But as long as the mistakes are honest and made in a quest to learn, they will be forgiven and corrected, and we will all grow. Latinas/os, because of our many components, have lived multi-dimensionally, and thus know the multi-layered approach although we have not necessarily translated it into actual proposals for change. Let us now share it with the rest of society and get on with building bridges to a new place where respect and understanding reign.

NOTES

1. Derrick A. Bell, Jr., *The Permanence of Racism*, 22 SW. U. L. REV. 1103 (1993).

2. Larry Rohter, *As Hispanic Presence Grows, So Does Black Anger*, N.Y. TIMES, June 20, 1993, at A1.

3. *Id.*

4. Essentialism is the critique by feminists of color of white feminists who talk only of gender and not race. The idea of "intersectionality" analyzes the intersection of race and gender.

Chapter 6

Life in the Hyphen

Ilan Stavans

What if *yo* were you and *tú fueras* I, Mister?

Born in 1885 in Jalisco, Mexico, the painter Martín Ramírez spent most of his life in a California madhouse, in a pavilion reserved for incurable patients. Since his death in 1960 he has become a symbol in Hispanic immigrant experience and is considered today a leading painter with a permanent place in Chicano visual art. As a young man, Ramírez worked first in the fields and then in a laundry; he later worked as a migrant railroad worker, relocating across the Rio Grande in search of a better life and to escape the dangers of the violent upheaval sweeping his native land. He lost the power to talk around 1915, at the age of thirty, and wandered for many years, until the Los Angeles police picked him up and sent him to Pershing Square, a shelter for the homeless. Diagnosed by doctors as a "deteriorated paranoid schizophrenic" and sent to the Dewitt Hospital, Ramírez never recovered his speech. But in 1945, some fifteen years before his death, he began to draw. Ramírez was fortunate to be discovered by a psychiatrist, Dr. Tarmo Pasto, of the University of California, Sacramento, who, as the legend claims, was visiting the hospital one day with a few pupils when Ramírez approached him, offering a bunch of rolled-up paintings. The doctor was so impressed with Ramírez's work that he made sure the artist had plenty of drawing materials to use. Soon Pasto began collecting Ramírez's work and showed it to a number of artists, including Jim Nutt, who arranged an exhibit of Ramírez's paintings with an art dealer in Sacramento. Other exhibits soon followed—in New York, Chicago, Sweden, Denmark, and Houston, among other places—and Ramírez, the perfect outsider, was a dazzling revelation at the exposition *Outsiders* in London's Hayward Gallery.

In a controversial text written in June 1986 to commemorate the exhibit *Hispanic Art in the United States: Thirty Contemporary Painters and Sculptors* at the Corcoran Gallery in Washington, D.C., Octavio Paz, the 1990 winner of the Nobel Prize in literature, claimed that Ramírez's pencil-and-crayon drawings are evocations of what Ramírez lived and dreamed during and after the Mexican Revolution. Paz com-

Pp. 7–10, 21–22 from The Hispanic Condition: Reflections on Culture and Identity in America by Ilan Stavans. Copyright © 1995 Ilan Stavans. Reprinted by permission of HarperCollins Publishers, Inc.

pared the artist to Richard Dadd, a nineteenth-century painter who lost his mind at the end of his life. As Carlos Fuentes, the Mexican novelist and diplomat, claimed in his book *The Buried Mirror,* the mute painter drew his muteness, making it graphic. And Roger Cardinal, the British author of *Figures of Reality,* argued that the artist's achievements should not be minimized as psychotic rambling and categorized him as "a *naïf* painter." To make sense of Ramírez's odyssey, Dr. Pasto concluded that Ramírez's psychological disturbances were the result of a difficult process of adaptation to a foreign culture. Ramírez had left Mexico at a turbulent, riotous time and arrived in a place where everything was unfamiliar and strange to him.

Ramírez's plight is representative of the entire Hispanic cultural experience in the United States. Neither a diluted Mexican lost in a no-man's-land nor a fully rounded citizen, Ramírez symbolizes the voyage of millions of silent itinerant *braceros* and legal middle-class immigrants bewildered by their sudden mobility, furiously trying to make sense of an altogether different environment. But Hispanics are now leaving his frustrated silence behind. Society is beginning to embrace Latinos, from rejects to fashion setters, from outcasts to insider traders. New generations of Spanish speakers are feeling at home in Gringolandia. (Etymologically, *gringo,* according to *Webster's Dictionary,* is derived from *griego,* stranger, but it may have been derived from the Spanish pronunciation of a slang word meaning fast-spender, *green-go*). Suddenly the crossroad where white and brown meet, where "yo soy" meets "I am," a life in the Spanglish hyphen, is being transformed. Many of us Latinos already have a Yankee look: We either make a conscious effort to look gringo, or we're simply absorbed by the culture's fashion and manners. And what is more exciting is that Anglos are beginning to look just like us—enamored as they are of our bright colors and tropical rhythms, our suffering Frida Kahlo, our legendary Ernesto "Che" Guevara. Martín Ramírez's silence is giving way to a revaluation of things Hispanic. No more silence, no more isolation. Spanish accents, our *manera peculiar de ser,* have emerged as exotic, fashionable, and even enviable and influential in mainstream American culture.

However, just as Ramírez's art took decades to be understood and appreciated, it will take years to understand the multifaceted and far-reaching implications of this cultural transformation, the move of Hispanics from periphery to center stage. I believe that we are currently witnessing a double-faceted phenomenon: Hispanization of the United States, and Anglocization of Hispanics. Adventurers in Hyphenland, explorers of El Dorado, we Hispanics have deliberately and cautiously infiltrated the enemy, and now go by the rubric of Latinos in the territories north of the Rio Grande. Delaying full adaptation, our objective is to assimilate Anglos slowly to ourselves.

Indeed, a refreshingly modern concept has emerged before American eyes—to live in the hyphen, to inhabit the borderland, to exist inside the Dominican-American expression *entre Lucas y Juan Mejía*—and nowhere is the debate surrounding it more candid, more historically enlightening, than among Hispanics. The American Dream has not yet fully opened its arms to us; the melting pot is still too cold, too uninviting, for a total meltdown. Although the collective character of those immigrating from the Caribbean archipelago and south of the border remains foreign to a large segment of the heterogeneous nation, as "native strangers" within the Anglo-Saxon soil, our impact will prevail sooner, rather than later. Although stereotypes remain commonplace and vices get easily confused with habits, a number of factors, from population growth to a retarded acquisition of a second language and a passionate retentiveness of our original culture, actually suggest that Hispanics in the United States shall not, will not, cannot, and ought not follow paths opened up by previous immigrants.

According to various Chicano legends recounted by the scholar Gutierre Tibón, Aztlan Aztlatlan, the archetypal region where Aztecs, speakers of Nahuatl, originated before their itinerant journey in the fourteenth century in search of a land to settle, was somewhere in the area of New Mexico, California, Nevada, Utah, Arizona, Colorado, Wyoming, Texas, and the Mexican states of Durango and Nayarit, quite far from Tenochtitlán, known today as Mexico City. Once a nomadic tribe, the Aztecs settled and became powerful, subjugating the Haustec to the north and the Mixtec and Zapotec to the south, achieving a composite civilization. Latinos with these mixed ancestries, at least six in every ten in the United States, believe they have an aboriginal claim to the land north of the border. As native Americans, we were in these areas before the Pilgrims of the *Mayflower* and understandably keep a telluric attachment to the land. Our return by sequential waves of immigration as wetbacks and middle-income entrepreneurs to the lost Canaan, the Promised Land of Milk and Honey, ought be seen as the closing of a historical cycle. Ironically, the revenge of Motecuhzoma II (in modern Spanish: Moctezuma; in its English misspelling: Montezuma) is understood differently in Spanish and English. For Anglos, it refers to the diarrhea a tourist gets after drinking unpurified water or eating chile and arroz con pollo in Latin America and the West Indies; for Hispanics, it describes the unhurried process of the penetration of and exertion of influence on the United States—*la reconquista,* the oppressor's final defeat. Yesterday's victim and tomorrow's conquistadors, we Hispanics, tired of a history full of traumas and undemocratic interruptions, have decided to regain what was taken away from us.

There is no doubt that the attempt to portray Latinos as a homogenous minority and/or ethnic group is rather recent. Within the various minorities, forces have always pulled unionists apart. As Bernardo Vega, a Puerto Rican social activist in New York City, wrote in his *Memoirs* in the 1940s:

> When I came to [New York] in 1916 there was little interest in Hispanic culture. For the average citizen, Spain was a country of bullfighters and flamenco dancers. As for Latin America, no one could care less. And Cuba and Puerto Rico were just two islands inhabited by savages whom the Americans had beneficially saved from the clutches of the Iberian lion. Once in a while a Spanish theater company would make an appearance in New York. Their audiences never amounted to more than the small cluster of Spaniards and Latin Americans, along with some university professors who had been crazy enough to learn Spanish. That was it!
>
> The constant growth of the Puerto Rican community gave rise to riots, controversy, hatred. But there is one fact that stands out: at a time when there were no more than half a million of us, our impact on cultural life in the United States was far stronger than that of the 4 million Mexican-Americans. And the reason is clear: though they shared with us the same cultural origins, people of Mexican extraction, involved as they were

in agricultural labor, found themselves scattered throughout the American Southwest. The Puerto Ricans, on the other hand, settled in the large urban centers, especially New York, where in spite of everything the circumstances were more conducive to cultural interaction and enrichment, whether we wanted it that way or not.

. . . Idiosyncratic differences puzzle me: What distinguishes us from Anglo-Saxons and other European immigrants as well as from other minorities (such as blacks and Asians) in the United States? Is there such a thing as a Latino identity? Ought José Marti and Eugenio María de Hostos be considered the forefathers of Latino politics and culture? Need one return to the Alamo to come to terms with the clash between two essentially different psyches, Anglo-Saxon Protestant and Hispanic Catholic? The voyage to what William H. Gass called "the heart of the heart of the country" needs to begin by addressing a crucial issue: the diversity factor. Latinos, no question, are a most difficult community to describe: Is the Cuban from Holguín similar in attitude and culture to someone from Managua, San Salvador, or Santo Domingo? Is the Spanish we all speak, our *lingua franca,* the only unifying factor? How do the various Hispanic subgroups understand the complexities of what it means to be part of the same minority group? Or do we perceive ourselves as a unified whole?

Culture and identity are a parade of anachronistic symbols, larger-than-life abstractions, less a shared set of beliefs and values than the collective strategies by which we organize and make sense of our experience, a complex yet tightly integrated construction in a state of perpetual flux. To begin, it is utterly impossible to examine Latinos without regard to the geography we come from. We are, we recognize ourselves to be, an extremity of Latin America, a diaspora alive and well north of the Rio Grande. For the Yiddish writer Sholem Aleichem's Tevye the milkman, for instance, America was a synonym of redemption, the end of *pogroms,* the solution to earthly matters. Russia, Poland, and the rest of Eastern Europe were lands of suffering. Immigrating to America, where gold grew on trees and could easily be found on sidewalks, was synonymous with entering Paradise. To leave, never to look back and return, was an imperative. Many miles, almost impossible to breach again, divided the old land from the new. We, on the other hand, are just around the corner: Oaxaca, Mexico; Varadero, Cuba; and Santurce, Puerto Rico, are literally next door. We can spend every other month, even every other week, either north or south. Indeed, some among us swear to return home when military dictatorships are finally deposed and more benign regimes come to life, or simply when enough money is saved in a bank account. Meanwhile, we inhabit a home divided, multiplied, neither in the barrio or the besieged ghetto nor across the river or the Gulf of Mexico, a home either here or within hours' distance. José Antonio Villarreal's 1959 novel *Pocho,* for example, called by some critics "a foundational text" and believed to be the first English-written novel by a Chicano, is precisely about the eternal need to return among Chicanos: a return to source, a return to the self. And Pablo Medina's meticulous Cuban-American autobiography *Exiled Memories,* along the same lines, is about the impossibility of returning to childhood, to the mother's soil, to happiness. But return *is* indeed possible in most cases. Cheap labor comes and goes back and forth to Puebla and San Juan.

One ought never to forget that Hispanics and their siblings north of the border have an intimate, long-standing, love-hate relationship. Latinos are a major source of income for the families they left behind. In Mexico, for instance, money wired by relatives working as pizza delivery boys, domestic servants, and construction workers amounts to a third of the nation's overall revenues. Is this nothing new, when one ponders previous waves of immigration? Perhaps. Others have dreamed of America as paradise on earth, but our arrival in the Promised Land with strings attached underscores troublesome patterns of assimilation. Whereas Germans, Irish, Chinese, and others may have evidenced a certain ambiguity and lack of commitment during their first stage of assimilation in the United States, the proximity of our original soil, both in the geographic and metaphorical sense, is tempting. This thought brings to mind a claim by the Iberian philosopher José Ortega y Gasset, author of *Rebellion of the Masses*, among many other titles, in a 1939 lecture delivered in Buenos Aires. Ortega y Gasset stated that Spaniards assumed the role of the New Man the moment they settled in the New World. Their attitude was the result not of a centuries-long process, but of an immediate and sudden transformation. To this idea the Colombian writer Antonio Sanín Cano once mistakenly added that Hispanics, vis-à-vis other settlers, have a brilliant capacity to assimilate; unlike the British, for instance, who can live for years in a foreign land and never become part of it, we do. What he forgot to add is that we achieve total adaptation at a huge cost to ourselves and others. We become the New Man and Woman carrying along our former environment. Add the fact that we are often approached as traitors in the place once called home: We left, we betrayed our patriotism, we rejected and were rejected by the milieu, we aborted ourselves and spat on the uterus. Cubans in exile are known as *gusanos,* worms in Havana's eyes. Mainland Puerto Ricans often complain of the lack of support from their original families in the Carribean and find their cultural ties tenuous and thin. Mexicans have mixed feelings toward *Pachucos, Pochos,* and other types of Chicanos; when possible, Mexico ignores our politics and cultural manifestations. . . .

Chapter 7

Masks and Identity

Margaret E. Montoya

Let me show you my wounds: my stumbling mind, my
"excuse me" tongue, and this
nagging preoccupation
with the feeling of not being good enough[1]

Masking and unmasking ideas have been used to examine embedded truth and to expose ideas that lurk behind other more accessible and more conventional conclusions. Professor Mari Matsuda has written that "[t]he work of feminists, critical legal scholars, critical race theorists, and other progressive scholars has been the work of unmasking: unmasking a grab for power disguised as science, unmasking a justification for tyranny disguised as history, unmasking an assault on the poor disguised as law."[2]

Stories too can be unmasked to reveal their potential for challenging the dominant discourse. Personal narratives, and in this particular case Latina autobiography, are more than stories. They are an important site of resistance. Furthermore, they invent, reform and refashion personal and collective identity. The recounting of my personal stories in two languages is an individual exercise in resistance against cultural and linguistic domination.

In deciding to use an autobiographical narrative format, I am seizing literary space that has rarely been occupied by Latinas in either Spanish or English. Autobiographical works by Latino males have been published in the United States since the mid-1960s. There is, however, no significant body of contemporary autobiography written by Latinas in the United States. Autobiographical essays can be found in anthologies, but few autobiographical books by Latinas have been published.

That I am writing autobiographically as a Latina is unusual; that I choose to do so in the context of legal scholarship is even more so. My purposes resemble some of the goals ascribed to African-American autobiography. Autobiographical writing by

From "Mascaras, Trenzas, y Greñas: Un/Masking the Self while Un/Braiding Latina Stories and Legal Discourse." 17 Harv. Women's L.J. 185 (1994); 15 Chicano-Latino Law Rev. 1 (1994). Originally published in the *Harvard Women's Law Journal* and the *Chicano-Latino Law Review*. Reprinted by permission.

African Americans has been described as serving descriptive and persuasive functions that are distinct from White autobiography. African-American autobiography "looks not backward over a completed career, but forward to what the black writer is doing and intends to do in the future."[3]

Feminist method has been inextricably linked to consciousness-raising and the primacy of women's experience. One of the central issues of feminism is the cultural construction of subjectivity. In de/constructing myself and rendering myself as a speaking subject, I "dismantle the representation of stereotypes of [my] Self constructed, framed, and projected by the dominant ideology."[4] Language, images, and masks are key factors in that de/construction. For Latinas this endeavor entails the use of Spanish with English. My story requires that I use both languages. Writing about my experiences, as a child and as a law student, will hopefully contribute to a new critical understanding of what it means to be a Latina and increase the discursive space for the telling of stories from the Latina perspective. Telling my stories about my everyday experiences and capturing those experiences through two languages challenge the societal indifference that has isolated and marginalized Latinas. [see chapters 39 and 61 for additional treatment—Eds.]

Partly because of its bilingual character, Latina writing, whether fictional, autobiographical or traditionally academic, continues to be marginalized within the literary canon. Consequently, our individual stories and our collective her/story are lost. New narrative forms have enabled Sandra Cisneros, Gloria Anzaldúa, and others to explore the cultural borderlands where Outsiders engage and evade the oppressive weight of the dominant culture.[5] Anzaldúa's writing epitomizes the power inherent in the *mestiza*'s [*mestiza* refers to a woman whose identity is a product of at least two cultures—Eds.] stories, the power to fashion a new authentic identity, an identity made stronger and more resilient because it braids together the disparate. As Renato Rosaldo has noted:

> Gloria Anzaldúa has further developed and transformed the figure at the crossroads in a manner that celebrates the potential of borders in opening new forms of human understanding. . . . In rejecting the classic "authenticity" of cultural purity, she seeks out the many-stranded possibilities of the borderlands. By sorting through and weaving together its overlapping strands, Anzaldúa's identity becomes ever stronger, not diffused.[6]

Autobiographical writing and other forms of bi/multilingual expression in the legal academy and in legal scholarship legitimize multiple perspectives and validate personal experience. The writing of *mestizas* continues to expand the meaning of scholarship by including voices that "speak without the accents of ancestral power."[7] Through shared language, goals, and visions, *mestiza* scholarship also connects us to those poets of latinoamericana who "speak from the margins of the world system and from a position of exclusion."[8] Like them, we are engaged in a struggle to find ourselves as we reconstruct the world. The exploration of personal agency through autobiography and the seizure of discursive space formerly denied to Latinas are regenerative acts which can transform self-understanding and reclaim for all Latinas the right to define ourselves and to reject uni-dimensional interpretations of our personal and collective experience.

The law and the practice of law are grounded in the telling of stories. Pleadings and judicial orders can be seen as stylized stories. Legal persuasion in the form of opening statements and closing arguments is routinely taught as an exercise in storytelling. Client interviews are storytelling and story-listening events. Traditionally, legal culture within law firms, law schools, and courthouses has been transmitted through the "war stories" told by seasoned attorneys. Narrative laces through all aspects of legal education, legal practice, and legal culture. In these various ways the use of narrative is not new to the legal academy.

Only recently however, has storytelling begun to play a significant role in academic legal writing. In the hands of Outsiders, storytelling seeks to subvert the dominant ideology. Stories told by those on the bottom, told from the "subversive-subaltern" perspective,[9] challenge and expose the hierarchical and patriarchal order that exists within the legal academy and pervades the larger society. Narrative that focuses on the experiences of Outsiders thus empowers both the storyteller and the story-listener by virtue of its opposition to the traditional forms of discourse.

Understanding stories told from different cultural perspectives requires that we suspend our notions of temporal and spatial continuity, plot, climax, and the interplay of narrator and protagonists. Telling and listening to stories in a multicultural environment require fundamental re-examination of the text, the subtext, and the context of stories. The emphasis of critical scholarship (critical race theory, feminist jurisprudence, critical legal studies) on narrative affirms those of us who are Outsiders working within the objectivist orientation of the legal academy and validates our experimentation with innovative formats and themes in our teaching and in our scholarship.

> Because I, a *mestiza,*
> continually walk out of one culture
> and into another,
> because I am in all cultures at the same time,
> *alma entre dos mundos, tres, cuatro,*
> *me zumba la cabeza con lo contradictorio,*
> *Estoy norteada por todas las voces que me hablan*
> *simultaneamente.*[10]

> Because I, a *mestiza,*
> continually walk out of one culture
> and into another,
> because I am in all cultures at the same time,
> a soul between two worlds, three, four,
> my head buzzes with the contradictory,
> I am disoriented by all the voices that talk to me
> simultaneously.

The Euro-American conquest of the Southwest and Puerto Rico resulted in informal and formal prohibitions against the use of Spanish for public purposes. So by inscribing myself in legal scholarship as *mestiza,* I seek to occupy common ground with Latinas/os in this hemisphere and others, wherever situated, who are challenging

"Western bourgeois ideology and hegemonic racialism with the metaphor of transculturation."[11]

As Latinas/os we, like many colonized peoples around the globe, are the biological descendants of both indigenous and European ancestors, as well as the intellectual progeny of Western and indigenous thinkers and writers. As evidenced by my names, I am the result of Mexican-Indian-Irish-French relations. I am also the product of English-speaking schools and a Spanish-speaking community. Claiming our mixed intellectual and linguistic heritage can attentuate the subordinating forces implicit in the monolinguality and homogeneity of the dominant culture. While I reject the idea that personal narratives can or should be generalized into grand or universalistic theories, our stories can help us search for unifying identifiers and mutual objectives. For example, the deracination of language purges words of their embedded racism, sexism, and other biases.

Using Spanish (or other outlaw languages) in legal scholarship could be seen as an attempt to erect linguistic barriers or create exclusionary discursive spaces, particularly among Outsiders with whom Latinas share mutual ideological, political, and pedagogical objectives. Personal narratives of alienation or subordination present additional challenges when used in the domain of critical legal writing. Being a member of the legal professoriate, even if one is a member of several traditionally oppressed groups, means having a significant amount of social and cultural power and privilege. Personal accounts of humiliation, bias, or deprivation told from within the academy may sound to some like whining or may be perceived as excessive preoccupation with the self rather than with the real needs of the Outsider communities. Optimistically, linguistic diversity will be recognized as enhancing the dialogue within the academy by bringing in new voices and fresh perspectives. For this reason, incorporating Spanish words, sayings, literature, and wisdom can have positive ramifications for those in the academy and in the profession, and for those to whom we render legal services.

So, towards this goal, I tell one of my stories:

I am seated in the back of the auditorium on the first day of a three-day conference in Mexico City. The conference, entitled "Encuentro Chicano Mexico 1993," brings together Mexican and Latina/o academics to examine the conditions of Chicanos in the United States. The first roundtable is on historical issues and features a presentation on the history of Spanish-language radio in the United States. Toward the end of the question-and-answer period that is taking place in Spanish, I raise my hand. I want to discuss FCC v. Metro Broadcasting:[12] *not only for its potential to expand license ownership opportunities for Latinas/os, but also to discuss how Justice Brennan's opinion emphasizes that Latina/o licensees comprehensively change and enhance the business of radio broadcasting.*[13]

As I begin to speak and faces turn to the back of the room, I hear myself. My Spanish sounds pinched; I'm fumbling for words; I hear the American intonations and the English constructions forcing themselves on my Spanish. It feels dreamlike; I am aware of two dialogues—one is audible; I am talking to an audience. The other is inaudible; I am talking to myself. I am "on stage." What are they thinking behind their faces? Only this time the faces look like my face. Still I feel different, tongue-tied, childlike. I leave the conference feeling disturbed and nervous. I am scheduled to present a version of this paper on the following day. But what language do I use? I want to speak in Spanish, so as to be understood by the largest number, but to do so puts me at psychological risk: using a limited vocabulary, fractured syntax, and accented tones.

Like my trenzas *["braids"—Eds.] and my grade school uniform, I have long adopted a head-to-toe mask, to help me become the person I am when I am functioning in an Anglo and/or male environment. I think of this sometimes as I stand in front of the mirror to put on my make-up (as I "make myself up" or invent myself anew), as I apply mascara. Our word mascara comes from the anglicized pronunciation for the Spanish word meaning mask. Mascara reveals another level of meaning if we separate it into* mas cara, *which means "more face," as does* mascaras, *which separates into "more faces."*

In different situations, I have constructed my public face through make-up, clothes, vocabulary, and selective identification with my past. Ironically, this all seems even more relevant now as I am thrust into what should feel like home territory. The next day I apply my make-up and dress carefully. I wear a white suit, a cobalt blue silk blouse and matching suede heels.

I begin my presentation with a short introduction written in Spanish, but then I switch to English. I am compelled to switch. As a child I was forced to use English; now it is my language of choice. It has become my public voice—it lends me identity, authority, credibility. I deliver the narratives about my childhood and law school experiences. This is familiar terrain, my voice is confident. I continue with a short synopsis of the expository sections on masking. As I am standing there, I am aware of an internal voice urging me to listen to my own words; I am increasingly aware that my words spoken in English to this Mexican audience capture the very inauthenticity I am describing.

With great trepidation, I say: Masks can be sartorial, ideological, cognitive. Masks can also be lexographic, rhetorical, or linguistic. I stand before you with my linguistic mask. Aqui estoy ocultada por mi mascara linguistica con sus aspectos subtextuales. Desde nina, he entendido el significado de accentos, vocabulario, pronunciacion, sintaxis. En ingles estos elementos idiomaticos estan relacionados con mi psique, con la persona quien soy. Por la primera vez entiendo que espanol tiene el mismo poder, a pesar de estar donde no soy parte de una minoria cultural o racial. Para mi, hablar espanol afuera de la casa me hace sentir vulnerable. Sobre todo, hablar espanol donde la mayoria lo habla mucho mejor que yo, tiene algun aspecto de como me sentia cuando era nina, cuando me sentia vulnerable antes de los gringos. Por eso es dificil quitarme la mascara que me presta el ingles y hablarles en espanol. Asi es la locura de la discriminacion.[14]

The emotion could be heard in my voice. I continued into the next section, but now I persisted in speaking both languages, weaving English with Spanish, the personal voice with the academic.

I knew it wasn't neat and orderly: my greñas *["untidy" or "messy" hair—Eds.] were showing for all to see. I shrugged off my mother's concern about how others*

*might judge me, and there I stood "sounding grenuda." But this new identity, this
contradictory and ambiguous identity, was my own. I felt authentic. My public persona, like my private face and private speech, no longer reflected only those who had
dominated me and my people. I found my voice, mis voces.*

New discursive formats, including the use of Latina autobiography in legal scholarship, enable us to reinvent ourselves. We can reject the dualistic patriarchal masks
that we shrank behind and seize instead our multiple, contradictory, and ambiguous
identities. As we reinvent ourselves we import words and concepts into English and
into academic discourse from formerly prohibited languages and taboo knowledge.
The disruption of hegemonic tranquility, the ambiguity of discursive variability, the
cacophony of polyglot voices, the chaos of radical pluralism, are the desired by-prod-
ucts of transculturation, of *mestizaje.* The pursuit of *mestizaje,* with its emphasis on
our histories, our ancestries, and our past experiences can give us renewed appreciation for who we are as well as a clearer sense of who we can become.

Our conceptual *trenzas,* our rebraided ideas, even though they may appear unneat
or *grenudas* to others, suggest new opportunities for unmasking the subordinating
effects of legal discourse. Our rebraided ideas, the *trenzas* of our multicultural lives,
offer personally validating interpretations for the *mascaras* we choose to wear. My
masks are what they are, in Santayana's words, merely "arrested expressions and
. . . echoes of feelings," the cuticles that protect my heart.[15]

NOTES

1. Lorna D. Cervantes, *Poem for the Young White Man Who Asked Me How I, an Intelligent Well-Read Person, Could Believe in the War between Races,* in EMPLUMADA 35 (1981).

2. Mari J. Matsuda, *Voices of America: Accent, Anti-Discrimination Law, and a Jurisprudence for the Last Reconstruction,* 100 YALE L.J. 1329, 1394 (1991).

3. Jerome M. Culp, Jr., *Autobiography and Legal Scholarship and Teaching: Finding the
Me in the Legal Academy,* 77 VA. L. REV. 539, 542 (1991).

4. Eliana Ortega & Nancy S. Sternbach, *At the Threshold of the Unnamed: Latina Literary Discourse in the Eighties,* in BREAKING BOUNDARIES: LATINA WRITING AND CRITICAL READINGS 2, 14
(Asuncion Horno-Delgado et al. eds., 1989).

5. Gloria Anzaldúa, BORDERLANDS/*La Frontera:* THE NEW MESTIZA (1987); Sandra Cisneros,
THE HOUSE ON MANGO STREET (1985).

6. Renato Rosaldo, CULTURE & TRUTH: THE REMAKING OF SOCIAL ANALYSIS, 216 (1989).

7. Mike Gonzalez & David Treece, THE GATHERING OF VOICES: THE TWENTIETH-CENTURY POETRY
OF LATIN AMERICA, xv (1992).

8. *Id.*

9. Gita Rajan, *Subversive-Subaltern Identity: Indira Gandhi as the Speaking Subject,* in
DE/COLONIZING THE SUBJECT: THE POLITICS OF GENDER IN WOMEN'S AUTOBIOGRAPHY, 196 (Sidonie Smith
& Julia Watson eds., 1992).

10. Anzaldúa, at 77.

11. Françoise Lionnet, *Autobiographical Voices: Race, Gender Self-Portraiture* 15–16
(1989).

12. 497 U.S. 547 (1990).

13. See *id.* at 581–82.

14. Here I am, obfuscated by my linguistic mask with its subtextual aspects. Since I was a child, I've understood the meaning of accents, vocabulary, pronunciation, syntax. These linguistic elements of English are related to my psyche, to the person I am. For the first time I understand that Spanish has the same power over me, even though here I am not part of a cultural or racial minority. For me, speaking Spanish outside of the home makes me feel vulnerable: especially speaking Spanish where the majority speak so much better than I. All of this has some aspect of how I used to feel as a child, when I felt vulnerable in front of *gringos*. For this reason, it is so difficult to take off this mask that English lends me and to speak in Spanish. This is the craziness of discrimination. (The unease of this experience is recreated in the effort of writing in Spanish and not knowing where words are accented or whether the vocabulary is exact. I am painfully aware that my written Spanish reveals my assimilation in the same way as my spoken English does.)

15. Santayana writes:

[M]asks are arrested expressions and admirable echoes of feeling, at once faithful, discreet, and superlative. Living things in contact with the air must acquire a cuticle, and it is not urged against cuticles that they are not hearts; yet some philosophers seem to be angry with images for not being things, and with words for not being feelings. Words and images are like shells, not less integral parts of nature than are the substances they cover, but better addressed to the eye and more open to observation.

George Santayana, Soliloquies in England and Later Soliloquies 131–132 (1924).

Chapter 8

Who Counts?
Title VII and the Hispanic Classification

Alex M. Saragoza, Concepción R. Juarez, Abel Valenzuela, Jr., and Oscar Gonzalez

At nearly eight in the evening of July 1, 1991, few people remained in the chambers of the San Francisco Civil Service Commission when that body began its final deliberations on the definition of the term "Hispanic" for the purposes of Title VII of the Civil Rights Act. After months of intermittent discussion, several articles and editorials in the local media, and even national coverage in various magazines and newspapers, the issue was finally to come to a head. Were persons of Spanish descent covered by the Hispanic classification? The meeting was prompted by a complaint by Pete Roybal, a native of New Mexico and a veteran of the San Francisco Fire Department, who argued against the inclusion of Spaniards in the Hispanic category for the purposes of affirmative action. That night, nearly thirty years after the original passage of the legislation regarding affirmative action, in a city laced with reminders of its Spanish and Mexican past, the debate over the Hispanic classification turned bitter and deeply emotional.

Firefighters argued vehemently against inclusion of Spaniards, contending that historically Spaniards have not been among the oppressed; rather they were responsible for the destruction of the indigenous culture in Latin America. Others countered that exclusion of those of Spanish origin would be unjust and arbitrary. The controversy in San Francisco serves as a metaphor for a larger problem regarding the use of generic racial and ethnic terms in civil rights legislation. None perhaps is more difficult than the term Hispanic, given its peculiar history and the complex patterns of racism and prejudice against that group in the United States. The use of the Hispanic classification, however, is not confined to problems related to employment. Latino advocacy groups, such as the Mexican American Legal Defense and Educational Fund (MALDEF) and the National Council of La Raza, for instance, have relied on aggregated statistics to push for district

From "History and Public Policy: Title VII and the Use of the Hispanic Classification." 5 La Raza L.J. 1 (1992). Originally published in the *La Raza Law Journal*. Reprinted by permission.

elections as a means of increasing the political representation of Latinos. Thus, the uses of the Hispanic classification hold repercussions beyond affirmative action.

The politics of group identity in the 1960s framed the assumptions, including the notion of the homogeneity of Hispanics, surrounding legislation such as Title VII and the subsequent uses of the Hispanic classification. Those assumptions were in many respects mistaken or misinformed, and the flaws inherent in that legislation have surfaced in the controversy over affirmative action. In fact, the debate over the term itself fails to address a more fundamental question: how do we apply civil rights law to diverse groups of people that are aggregated under generic terms, such as Hispanic, Asian American, and arguably, Native American, and even perhaps African American?

The diversity of the groups commonly covered by the term Hispanic is complicated by a number of factors, including the particular aspects of the history of relations between the U.S. and Mexico, Puerto Rico, Cuba, and the seven distinct countries that make up Central America. Immigration from these areas has been directly affected by domestic and foreign policies of the U.S. This is not to mention the individual histories and cultures of the rest of Latin America, including the Portuguese-speaking nation of Brazil, as well as the French and British influenced islands of the Caribbean. Furthermore, the wide range of patterns of race, ethnicity, and cultural expression in Latin America, extending from the Rio Bravo (Rio Grande) to the Patagonia, defy easy generalization. More specifically, in the American Southwest a host of terms have emerged over time to describe a variety of groups currently covered by the Hispanic classification. As historian Ramón Gutiérrez puts it: "new terms were brought into the ethnic vocabulary to clearly delineate those boundaries within the Hispanic community that had developed along class, age, generation, nationality, and political lines."[1]

In short, no indelible physical characteristics, language, or cultural forms are shared by all of the people south of the U.S.-Mexico border that would invariably unify them under one ethnic or racial term. Hence, the term *Hispanic,* even in the U.S., presents several difficulties of definition. Yet, the term suggests that such commonalities exist, and that these commonalities have been the subject of similar racist or discriminatory practices in the U.S. Despite the dubiousness of this proposition, Title VII was written without regard to the problems of applying such legislation to aggregated, diverse groupings such as Hispanics. The overwhelming reference point for the civil rights act was African Americans, not Latin Americans. As a result, the courts were forced to clarify the applications of Title VII for a diverse group of people, a diversity not anticipated by the legislative language of that time.

The operable terms in the Civil Rights Act of 1964 were "race" and "color." Congress, however, failed to define these terms precisely. For the groups currently included in the term *Hispanic,* both race and color were problematic categories of definition and identification. Congressional discussion over the legislation focused on Blacks, as certain assumptions framed the use of race and color. Even for Blacks, these categories presumed manifest physical similarities that held less often than generally thought. Nevertheless, for most legislators in 1964 civil rights legislation referred primarily to Blacks, despite the amorphous use of the terms "race" and "color."[2] This ambiguity led to disputes "over whether a person is a member of a particular race . . . or indeed whether a certain classification, e.g. Hispanic, is a racial or other classification."[3] The subsequent rulings that included Hispanics under Title VII reflect the twists and turns of its application. In this regard, the courts have usually referred to an earlier legislative act for the definition of discrimination: § 1981 of the Civil Rights Act of 1866. Yet, a historical reading of § 1981 "lessens the usefulness of any comparison made of included groups under § 1981 and Title VII and returns us to the question of what the 1964 Congress . . . considered racial versus ethnic or national origin discrimination."[4] The legal history on this issue has been confounded by the question of national origin discrimination, e.g. discrimination against a Mexican because of his or her place of origin as opposed to discrimination on racial grounds.

The courts have not been clear on the issue of whether discrimination based on national origin is actionable under § 1981. "Most courts facing the question have stated that national origin discrimination itself is not covered by the statute [§ 1981]; however, where the same discrimination could be characterized as 'racial,' several courts have allowed plaintiffs to base their complaints on § 1981."[5] For example, an Oklahoma court noted that "the line between discrimination on account of race and discrimination on account of national origin may be so thin as to be indiscernible; indeed, to state the matter more succinctly, there may in some instances be overlap."[6] In *Cubas v. Rapid Am. Corp., Inc.*, the court declared that national origin discrimination "is actionable only to the extent that it is motivated by or indistinguishable from racial discrimination."[7] Nonetheless, courts "have been unable to provide a consistent definition of 'race' or 'racial discrimination' for purposes of § 1981 and, as a result, have disagreed about which nonblack minority groups are protected by the statute."[8]

A second approach has focused on the extent to which the discrimination is based on "racial animus."[9] In *Manzanares v. Safeway Stores Inc.*, the court writes:

> The measure is group to group, and plaintiff has alleged that the "group" to which he belongs—those he describes as of Mexican American descent — is to be measured against the Anglos as the standard. . . . In this holding we consider that Mexican American, Spanish American, Spanish-surname individuals, and Hispanos are equivalents, and it makes no difference whether these are terms of national origin, alienage, or whatever. It is apparent that a group so described is of such an identifiable nature that the treatment afforded its members may be measured against that afforded the Anglos.[10]

This interpretation emphasized that prejudice is "a matter of practice or attitude in the community, it is usage or image based on all the mistaken concepts of 'race.'"[11] Moreover, "If . . . a group is commonly perceived to be racially different . . . it should be protected by § 1981, regardless of its 'objective' racial composition and regardless of the motive of the discriminator."[12] According to this view, "[t]his 'common perception' approach thus adapts the statute to the reality of modern America while remaining true to the aim of its framers."[13]

But what are "identifiable nature" and "common perception?" The language of *Manzanares* reinforces the debatable assumption that Hispanics have distinguishable characteristics of one kind or another and assumes that dark-skinned Mexicans and light-skinned Chileans with a French last name are perceived equally. Furthermore, the concept of "common perception" underestimates the variability over time of such perceptions. As Ramón Gutiérrez concluded, "[f]ar from being a homogeneous group, the Hispanic population of the Southwest is complexly stratified and has a variety of historically constituted social boundaries which define it."[14] Gutiérrez emphasizes that "the process by which people define themselves and are defined by others is dynamic. Cultural identity is not a fixed and static entity; rather it ebbs and flows as history unfolds."[15] Evidence suggests the particular applicability of the *Manzanares* ruling for Mexican Americans. Yet, even here, the authors qualified their conclusion: "Of course, as with other groups generally perceived as nonwhite, individuals of Mexican descent 'pass' into the majority population."[16] And: "both the existence and virulence of discrimination have varied in different geographic areas and different times."[17]

On the other hand, for some Puerto Ricans skin color remains a key basis of discrimination, as the court found in *Felix v. Marquez.* In this case, the court noted that "color is usually mixed with or subordinated to claims of race discrimination, but considering the mixture of races and ancestral national origins in Puerto Rico, color may be the most practical claim to present."[18] But for light-skinned Puerto Ricans, claims of racial discrimination, given the reasoning in *Manzanares,* may be based on very different grounds. How then is a Puerto Rican commonly perceived?

The question remains whether the evidence marshalled in the *Felix* case extends to the expansive interpretation implied in *Manzanares.* In brief, discrimination based on skin color is central in *Felix* because of the particular history of race relations in Puerto Rico, notably the visible influence of the island's African origin population. In contrast, the African influence is less apparent in the physical characteristics of the overwhelming majority of Mexicans. The courts recognize that discrimination against Latinos may result from physical appearance, national origin, language use, surname, cultural identification, or a combination of elements. Thus, there is no common basis for discrimination against Hispanics; and we would submit there is no common perception as well.

Unity and Nationalism

The civil rights movement of the 1960s, more so perhaps than in the past, emphasized the importance of unity and common struggle in overcoming institutional racism. As many studies have shown, sharp disagreements took place within the Black civil rights movement over tactics, strategy, and ultimate goals. In this respect, the differences between Martin Luther King, Jr. and Malcolm X have become the usual example, but lack of consensus punctuated the civil rights movement throughout the 1960s and into the subsequent decade. Thus, the tendency to use the singular "movement" was a misrepresentation of actual events and processes at that time.

Nonetheless, such differences consistently met with efforts, both public and private, to lessen if not eliminate the conflicting possibilities of political differences within or among civil rights organizations. Repeatedly, it was argued that division among African Americans and other minority groups only held benefits for "white racists"; division was both a tool and an advantage of institutional racism and its supporters. The exaltation of this principle—though more often observed in the breach than in practice—led to the lumping of subgroups into monolithic communities as a politically expedient tactic.

Rhetoric portraying the African American community as singular marked the political strategy of Black civil rights advocates during the 1960s. Other ethnic and racial groups paralleled African Americans in this strategy, though with much less public notoriety. This political essentialism among African Americans quickly became widespread, due especially to the news media. For most of the American public the issue of race in this country generally implied Blacks. The "other" minority groups failed to achieve in this period the visibility or political clout, particularly in Congress, given to Blacks. This frustrated Mexican American legislators, as indicated in the remarks of Senator Montoya of New Mexico in 1972:

> We are the "invisible minority." While the black man has made the crying needs of his Ghetto children part of the nation's known history and collective conscious, we remain unseen. . . . Our efforts are fragmented. . . . And so in fragmented disorder we remain impotent; given hand-me-down programs; counted but not taken into account; seen with hindsight but not insight; asked but not listened to; a single brown face in a sea of black and white.[19]

As suggested in Montoya's comments, the strategy of Blacks to stress their group experience had been effective, pushing the senator from New Mexico to acknowledge a lack of such cohesion among "Hispanics." In sum, Mexican American legislators desired their own form of political essentialism—Hispanic versus white—with the same level of political privileges granted to Blacks.

A crucial impetus to political essentialism in the civil rights arena came from the resurgence of nationalism among Blacks, Chicanos, and other groups. Among Mexican-origin and Puerto Rican–based civil rights groups this new nationalism was often couched in cultural terms, leading to forms of cultural essentialism. These forms varied in expression and content, with everything from the vernacular (the celebration of "pachuco" talk) to traditional Mexican music and dance (the ubiquitous appearance of mariachi bands and folkloric dancers) at Chicano student-sponsored "cinco de mayo" events at innumerable college campuses by the late 1960s and into the present. Hence, the "Chicano" *movimiento* (and its corollaries among "Boricuas" [Puerto Ricans—*Eds.*] for example) sought to emphasize the commonalities among "Latino" groups as an extension of cultural essentialism and as a political ploy. As Felix Padilla has shown for Chicago, this quickly led to a new style of political activism, what he has termed "situational" Latino politics.[20] Where expedient or necessary, Mexican-American and Puerto Rican groups in Chicago forged alliances in order to increase their collective access to governmental programs, political decision-making, and publicly funded services.

On the other hand, the essentialist, nationalist discourse unleashed by the movimientos created certain tensions in this new group politics that encompassed more than one ethnic subgroup under a generic term. Padilla noted the reasons for this generic group identity:

> [T]he politicization of a situational Latino ethnic identity and consciousness entails almost a related irony and paradox. It stresses, ideologizes, and sometimes virtually recreates the distinctive and unique national-cultural identities of the groups that it mobilizes, precisely at the historical moments when these groups are being asked to take on a Latino ethnic consciousness.[21]

Thus, the nationalism of the movimiento implied an expansive notion of group identity, e.g. La Raza, that both reified particular identities ("Chicanismo" for instance), as well as a more inclusive concept embracing other Latin American origin groups (such as Puerto Ricans). Not insignificantly, the critique of the role of the United States in Latin America in the late 1960s and early 1970s added to this notion of group identity. In this view, Latin Americans were oppressed by the consequences of U.S. policy in that region, not unlike the oppression of Latinos living in this country.

Despite the anomalies and ambiguities of this new style of group politics, the benefits led to the increased use of the group identity, especially during the community action program era of the late 1960s and early 1970s. The political benefits of "lumping" the group allowed for aggregate figures to justify resources for community action groups, welfare rights organizations, and manpower training programs, among other initiatives. Distinctions due to immigration, class, national origin, length of residence in the United States or legal status were subsumed under the political expediency of generic terms. Hence, Chicano activists spoke of the Chicano community with scant attention to the importance of differentiation among people of Mexican origin in the United States. Moreover, when politically useful, Chicano advocates of civil rights legislation aggregated all Latino subgroups as one. Differences were glossed over by the rhetoric of "Brown power" and similar notions. If only implicitly, the assumptions of this strategy suggested that all the groups suffered equally and similarly from past racist practices directed at people of Latino background.

The embattled "them versus us" mentality of the civil rights movements and its attendant rhetoric produced a simplistic view of the workings of racism against Latinos in American society. The complexities of the Latino experience were lost in the political expediency of the moment, eclipsing a deeper, more accurate understanding of that experience with American racism. The gains derived from such a strategy, redoubled by the concentration of certain Latino groups in politically sensitive states, eventually compelled the use of a generic term to reflect the lumping strategy. Thus MALDEF, among other organizations, increasingly reflected the political logic of the aggregation of Latinos into one grouping. The troublesome outcomes of following such a strategy were perhaps only dimly understood at the time, as the benefits of the strategy gained momentum. For example, the redistricting and representation cases of recent years clearly demonstrate the usefulness of the aggregation strategy for opening the political process to Latino voters. In contrast, for the purposes of affirmative action, the utility of the strategy has proven to be much more problematic.

Nevertheless, any criticism or questioning of the lumping strategy has become understandably divisive in the minds of those promoting it. And in the minds of those imbued with the principles enshrined in the civil rights struggle, raising concerns over the aggregation approach only nourishes the backlash against affirmative action and civil rights in general.

A new round of issues will arise over the appropriateness of using aggregate figures to justify generic remedies, social or political. The aggregation strategy obviously "works" in areas where Latinos as a whole represent a large, powerful constituency in statistical terms, as is the case in Los Angeles. On the other hand, the divisive possibilities of the strategy are also apparent. First, as Latinos exercise their collective muscle, they will encroach on other minorities. When Latino civil rights groups pushed for district elections in Los Angeles, for example, the effort necessitated intense, and at times tense, negotiations with Black representatives. This tension had surfaced earlier in a dispute over minority hiring in which Latinos accused Blacks of being less than earnest in employing Latinos. Again in Los Angeles, the political jockeying generated by Latino political demands contributed to the electoral loss of an Asian American on the county board of supervisors.

Second, the political divisions within the Latino communities are manifest to knowledgeable observers, but with the arrival of increasing numbers of refugees and their relatives in recent years, these differences have increased. A large proportion of Nicaraguan refugees, for example, possess very conservative political views, including strong support for U.S. foreign policy in Latin America. On the other hand, many Latinos maintain more "liberal" views concerning, for instance, the role of the U.S. in Central American politics. Thus, in the representation of "Latino" political views, Nicaraguans may not necessarily identify with the perspective of other Latino elected officials.

Third, one can anticipate a growing number of Hispanic critics of affirmative action and related concepts in the future. The recent publication of Linda Chavez's *Out of the Barrio* signals a crack in the aggregation strategy. Indeed, Chavez makes telling points in the conclusion of her book on the faults of the lumping strategy. She notes, for instance, that Hispanic leaders "are willing to have everyone included in order to increase the population eligible for the [entitlement] programs."[22] In this regard, she mentions the Pete Roybal case in San Francisco as an example of the problems of this approach. She goes on to raise the issue of class difference in the application of affirmative action. Undoubtedly, as in the case of Richard Rodriguez and the English-only movement, Chavez will be used by opponents of affirmative action to discredit the concept in the same way that Shelby Steele and others have been exploited. On the other hand, Chavez acknowledges the persistence of discrimination, though "not as severe as it was [is] against blacks."[23] She suggests that current laws and legal procedures adequately protect "Hispanics" from discrimination. Yet, she fails to address the question why, after decades of these legal remedies, racist practices continue to affect Latinos. In sum, Chavez refuses to confront the nature and depth of American racism and its particular impact on people of Latin American origin. Hence, her efforts to describe the diversity among Latinos only serve to magnify questions generated by the persistence of discrimination. Recognition of the diversity of Latinos and its implications seems to have increased among Latino scholars, and even the media have begun to note the differentiation within this group. It is no longer tenable to sweep the issue under the proverbial rug. The problems generated by the reconciliation of affirmative action with the inherent diversity of the Latino population should not deter us from confronting the issue.

NOTES

1. See Ramón A. Gutiérrez, *Changing Ethnic and Class Boundaries in America's Hispanic Past,* in SOCIAL AND GENDER BOUNDARIES IN THE UNITED STATES 37, 49 (Sucheng Chan ed., 1989).

2. F. James Davis, WHO IS BLACK: ONE NATION'S DEFINITION (1991); Allen J. Matusow, THE UNRAVELING OF AMERICA: A HISTORY OF LIBERALISM IN THE 1960s (1984).

3. Stephen N. Shulman & Charles F. Abernathy, THE LAW OF EQUAL EMPLOYMENT OPPORTUNITY § 4.02[1], at 4–3 (1990).

4. *Id.* at 4–4, 4–5, n.14 (quoting Saint Francis College v. Al Khazraji, 107 S.Ct. 2022, 2026 [1987]).

5. *Comment, Developments in the Law—Section 1981,* 15 HARV. C.R.-C.L. L. REV. 29, 82–83 (1980).

6. Enriquez v. Honeywell, Inc., 431 F.Supp. 901, 904 (N.D. Okla. 1977).

7. 420 F.Supp. 633, 665 (E.D. Pa. 1976).

8. *Comment,* at 83.

9. See *Comment,* at 88 n.111 (citing Enriquez v. Honeywell, Inc., 431 F.Supp. 901, 906 [W.D. Okla. 1977]).

10. 593 F.2d 968, 970 (10th Cir. 1979).

11. *Id.* at 971.

12. *Comment,* at 89–90.

13. *Id.* at 90.

14. Gutiérrez, at 37.

15. *Id.*

16. Gary A. Greenfield & Don B. Kates, Jr., *Mexican Americans, Racial Discrimination, and the Civil Rights Act of 1866,* 63 CAL. L. REV. 662, 729 (1975).

17. *Id.*

18. 24 Empl. Prac. Dec. (CCH) 31,279 (D.D.C. 1980).

19. 118 CONG. REC. S26664 (1972).

20. Felix M. Padilla, LATINO ETHNIC CONSCIOUSNESS: THE CASE OF MEXICAN AMERICANS AND PUERTO RICANS IN CHICAGO 4–8 (1985).

21. Felix M. Padilla, *On the Nature of Latino Ethnicity,* 65 SOC. SCI. Q. 651, 662 (1984).

22. Linda Chavez, OUT OF THE BARRIO: TOWARD A NEW POLITICS OF HISPANIC ASSIMILATION 169 (1991).

23. *Id.* at 171.

Chapter 9

Race, Identity, and "Box Checking"
The Hispanic Classification in OMB Directive No. 15

Luis Angel Toro

Today's federal law of racial and ethnic classification, Office of Management and Budget (OMB) Statistical Directive No. 15, reflects the continuing view that, for the purposes of federal statistics, race is a fixed, biological trait, assigned at birth and susceptible to classification into four general types. Because these assumptions are false, and because Chicanos (and others) often self-identify as mixtures of groups that U.S. law presumes cannot mix, it is highly unlikely that anything less than a fundamental shift in the way the law conceptualizes race will result in an accurate legal definition of Latino people.

Reforming the "Hispanic" classification within the current framework will be virtually impossible. One major reason for this is that federal Indian law precludes acknowledgment of the indigenous aspect of Mexican *mestizo* identity. Recent scholarship on the legal construction of race and identity can contribute to a historically and theoretically conscious understanding of race and cultural identity that could provide a theoretical framework for a massive restructuring of Directive No. 15. This restructuring would include retirement of the "Hispanic" classification. In its place, I argue for a system that allows people to identify themselves as members of cultural groups defined not by ancestry but by recognition as a distinct group within the larger society in everyday social interaction.

The "Hispanic" classification is merely the latest legal fiction that works, intentionally or not, to prevent the Mexican-American community from overcoming the disadvantages imposed by racial subordination. The classification does not describe an authentic subcultural group within American society, nor does it help society achieve its goals. Rather, it reflects what will hopefully be the last of a series of increasingly convoluted efforts to fit the many subcultures of a multiethnic nation into a framework designed to underlie the laws of a white, expansionist, slave-holding society, convinced of its "natural" superiority, in the late eighteenth cen-

From "'A PEOPLE DISTINCT FROM OTHERS': RACE AND IDENTITY IN FEDERAL INDIAN LAW AND THE HISPANIC CLASSIFICATION IN OMB DIRECTIVE NO. 15." 26 TEX. TECH. L. REV. 1219 (1995). Originally published in the *Texas Tech Law Review*. Reprinted by permission.

tury. Considering the many changes in American society since that era, it is past time for a fundamental reconsideration of the way "race" is conceptualized in the law.

Biological Race, Directive No. 15, and the Immigrant Analogy

Directive No. 15 governs the collection of federal statistics regarding implementation of a host of civil rights and other laws. OMB has announced that it will reconsider its racial/ethnic classification scheme but has not indicated that elimination of the "Hispanic" classification is under consideration. The agency's official announcement of proposed revision noted that the data collected under the format mandated by the directive are used to enforce laws regarding voting rights and legislative redistricting, federal and private sector affirmative action programs, school desegregation, minority business development, and fair housing.

The directive defines Hispanics as the ethnic group whose "culture or origin" is Spanish, "regardless of race," and Mexican Americans are specifically described as a "Spanish cultur[al]" subgroup. The combined format declares that Hispanics are either white or Black. Because a "Black" person, under Directive No. 15, is defined as "a person having origins in any of the black racial groups of Africa," it is clear that Directive No. 15 perceives Mexican Americans as a white ethnic group. This perception is at odds with Chicano identity and the Chicano people's historical experience of racial oppression, as well as present, ongoing racial discrimination against Mexican Americans. The perception also differs from the determinations Congress made when it decided that Mexican Americans needed to be covered under laws addressing racial discrimination. The classification of Mexican Americans as white is consistent only with prior Census practice, which stopped counting "Mexicans" as a race with the 1930 Census and instructed Census takers to list Chicanos as whites when those persons were "definitely not Negro, Indian, or some other race."[1]

Directive No. 15 describes Chicano difference from the white majority as an "ethnic" rather than a racial one. In other words, it describes Chicanos as part of the "white" race, but a part that has yet to fully assimilate into the mainstream status enjoyed by members of that group. This construct, sometimes described as the "immigrant analogy," holds that minorities in American society will all progress, through hard work, down the path of assimilation taken by such white ethnic groups as the Irish, the Jews, and the Italians. Few now believe that the immigrant analogy holds true for groups such as Chicanos or immigrant communities from Asia, whose difference from majority society is defined both in racial and ethnic terms.

Directive No. 15 as a Barrier to Chicano Progress

The problems caused by the poor fit between the "Hispanic" classification and the disadvantaged minority groups it attempts to describe are numerous and well documented. First, conceptualization of the "Hispanic" classification as an "ethnic" rather than a "racial" group (the only "ethnic" group the federal government recognizes) reduces the usefulness of much federal data, along with data generated to conform to Directive No. 15. This occurs because many people who are actually members of racially subordinated minorities are labeled as "White Hispanic." This affects data concerning both "Hispanics" and African Americans. When data comparing "Whites" and "Blacks" are compiled, the presence of Mexican Americans and others misidentified as "White Hispanics" in the "White" sample will create an illusion that the disparity in income and other measures of community vitality between the majority population and the African-American community is smaller than it is, because the presence of persons in the "White" sample who do not in reality enjoy the societal benefits of "White" status will skew the results. The presence of African Americans in the "non-Hispanic" sample will, as well, although a countervailing factor is the presence in the "Hispanic" sample of persons I maintain should be deemed either white or members of other groups. This may reduce the skew, but it does not create a realistic picture of an actual cultural subgroup.

This conceptualization also ignores the racial nature of anti-Mexican subordination in the United States and the Mexican-American people's own conception of their identity. Worse, by lumping together people on both sides of what W. E. B. Du Bois called the "color line," this concept betrays forgetfulness of the reasons why our government needs to continue taking notice of a person's cultural identity. When white persons are allowed to compete with members of racially subordinated minority groups for the extremely limited resources that have been reserved for programs addressing racial discrimination, the goals of the program are defeated. This is exactly what occurs when persons for whom the description "White Hispanic" might accurately apply, along with white persons who view the Hispanic classification as a loophole through which to claim benefits meant to address the problems associated with racism, are lumped together with Chicanos in programs using the federal standards for racial and ethnic recordkeeping.

This phenomenon—"box checking"—occurs when a person who is identified in the community as being part of the white or Anglo majority claims to be a member of a racially subordinated minority group and uses that status to reap benefits meant to address the problems that group faces. Directive No. 15 makes it impossible to determine the extent of box checking in programs that follow the federal statistical system, because it lumps all people who can connect themselves to some "Spanish origin or culture" together as "Hispanics."

If extensive box checking in government programs is taking place, one would expect the beneficiaries to promote the idea of a unified Hispanic community whose contours are accurately reflected in Directive No. 15. One need look no further than the pages of *Hispanic* magazine to find exactly that sort of promotion. In its December 1993 issue, the magazine included a number of Hispanic "Bests and Worsts" and its "Top Ten Reasons to Be Hispanic."[2] The class orientation of the magazine is revealed by its advertisements for luxury items and by "Reason Number 8 to Be Hispanic": "You can order water from busboys in restaurants." After a page advertising tickets to the 1994 World Cup of soccer, the magazine goes on to its "Closet Hispanic Award," given each year to people who are not identified as members of a racialized minority group but who meet Directive No. 15's "Hispanic" definition. "Previous winners of this secret award are Vanna White, Raquel Welch, and Linda Carter, who are all Hispanic," the magazine asserts. "This year's recipients are baseball great Ted Williams (Mexican mother) and Walt Disney (born in Spain)." That neither Williams nor Disney was culturally identified as Chicano or even Latin American has no bearing on their Hispanic identity, according to the authors of this magazine. Indeed, right next to the "Closet Hispanic Award" is the "Most Ridiculous Issue," which, not surprisingly, is "Are we Hispanics, Latinos, Chicanos, Spanish, Mexican Americans, Cuban Americans, Puerto Ricans, etc., etc.? Who cares? Let's move on!"

Obviously, if box checkers are becoming successful by marketing themselves as (often quite unthreateningly white) substitutes for Chicano progress, it is in their interest to declare the substantial differences among Chicanos, Puerto Ricans, Cubans, and Spaniards "ridiculous" and something that progressive members of these communities should not address. If someone actually examined the differences among these groups, those currently benefiting from the "Hispanic" classification might lose their ability to order around busboys in restaurants; indeed, their Chicano busboy might start up a business and compete with them. One can expect that any revision of Directive No. 15 to measure more accurately the progress of Chicanos will be strongly resisted by those who wish to promote the view that being born in Spain or having a Mexican ancestor, even if one has passed out of the Chicano community, makes one Hispanic. Like the Hispanic Contractors' Association, these individuals will argue that they are part of the same community as Chicanos and have faced exactly the same racial discrimination. It is hard to believe that members of Congress who voted to establish Minority Business Enterprise (MBE) programs thought that they were creating a program for which Walt Disney would have been eligible.

Two Chicano Examples

A Mexican couple immigrates to the United States and has children. They receive a Census form in the mail and set about determining their own and their children's racial identity. Looking at the racial categories, the couple sees none that describes them. They do not view themselves as American Indians but as *mestizos*, persons of mixed European and indigenous heritage. They are not enrolled members of a recognized tribe, nor are they identified as Indians in the community in which they live. By the same token, neither are they identified as whites. In the "Hispanic origin" question, the couple sees "Mexican, Mexican American, or Chicano" specifically listed as a "Hispanic" group. They identify themselves as part of that group and as being of "Other" race on the race question.

This couple might identify their children in the same manner. Alternatively, they might believe that a "Mexican or Mexican American" is only someone who was born in Mexico. As immigrants, they may not be familiar with the term "Chicano." Since their children were born in the U.S., they answer the Hispanic origin question in the negative. Knowing that there are millions of people like their children in this country, and believing that there must be some place on the Census form for them, they think again about the race question. Obviously, their children are not white: Every day they face the avoidance behaviors and "microaggressions" exhibited by whites, designed to remind them that they are not part of that group. They do not believe that their children are part of the "Black" or "Asian/Pacific Islander" groups, so they think again about the American Indian category. Perhaps aware of the one drop rule that, at least culturally, defines as Black any person with any known African ancestor or trace of apparent African ancestry, they conclude that "community recognition" as Indian means being treated as nonwhite on the basis of apparent indigenous ancestry. Therefore, they mark their children as members of the "American Indian or Alaskan Native" race.

Now, suppose that a fourth generation Chicano is filling out a Census form. Spiritually uplifted by the cultural pride inherent in the concept of Aztlan, he identifies himself racially as "American Indian" but answers "yes" to the Hispanic origin question, marking the "Mexican, Mexican American, or Chicano" box. To the respondent, this seems like a decent reflection of his *mestizo* identity. To the Census Bureau, it is a wrong answer.

Suppose now that this same fourth generation Chicano is responding to a question under the combined race/ethnic short format permitted under Directive No. 15. Choosing between the selections, "White, Hispanic" and "American Indian" is easy. The respondent selects "American Indian" as the response, because he has never been treated as a white person in his community, because "Hispanic" seems an inaccurate description of a Chicano culture that has a strong indigenous influence, and because in physical appearance, i.e., "racially," the respondent is far closer to being a Native American than a European.

The Hispanic Classification and the OMB's Statutory Mandates

The OMB's hands would be tied if Congress had directed it to consider all Hispanics as one community in the statutes that give the agency authority to set standards for governmental data collection. Fortunately, this is not the case. In most cases, it is not possible to determine with any precision how Congress conceptualized the various communities grouped under the "Hispanic" umbrella. In others, Congress acted out of a concern that the Mexican-American community was facing racial discrimination. The "Hispanic" classification, with its embedded immigrant analogy and inclusion of persons not confronted by racial discrimination, embodies an agency rejection of congressional findings of racial discrimination against the Mexican-American community. As such, the OMB's "Hispanic" classification is probably vulnerable to challenge as an impermissible departure from statutory authority. Further, an examination of the policies behind the various statutes provides more evidence that a more specific breakdown of the groups included in the "Hispanic" classification is necessary to ensure effective implementation of the legislation.

The OMB's authority to establish racial and ethnic standards arises from a number of different sources. A 1980 statute empowers the Director of the OMB to "develop and implement Federal information policies consistent with applicable law."[3] Another section authorizes the President, acting through the Director of the OMB, to "prescribe regulations to improve the compilation, analysis, publication, and dissemination of statistical information by executive agencies."[4] It was under a predecessor of this latter provision that the Department of Commerce promulgated Directive No. 15 in 1978.

Potentially inconsistent mandates such as these demonstrate the limited utility of looking to Congress as the source of guidance on racial and ethnic classifications. Congress's inability to state what it means by terms such as "Hispanic" or "Spanish origin" has been well documented in the legislative history behind the Civil Rights Acts. When enacting Title VII of the Civil Rights Act of 1964, even Chicano representatives used multiple terms to describe the same group in a single paragraph. Nonetheless, a thorough appraisal of the legislative history leads to the conclusion that members of Congress usually meant "Mexican American and Puerto Rican" when they discussed "Hispanics" or "Spanish-speaking" people.

Congress heard extensive testimony of racial discrimination against Chicanos and Puerto Ricans when it considered the 1975 Voting Rights Amendments. During his testimony before a House subcommittee, Assistant Attorney General J. Stanley Pottinger noted that Chicanos and Puerto Ricans already received some protection under the original Voting Rights Act, because discrimination in voting against members of these groups was discrimination based on "race or color."[5] Like other testimony presented to Congress at the time, Pottinger's statements used "Spanish-surnamed" or "Spanish-speaking" as synonyms for Mexican Americans and Puerto Ricans. He specifically cautioned that a proposal by Representative Barbara Jordan of Texas was overbroad. The proposal stated that persons whose mother tongue is other than English should be covered under the Act. Pottinger felt the proposal was too broad because it included persons such as French or German speakers as protected groups. He referred to French and German Americans as "national origin" groups, in contrast to "racial minorities" such as Mexican Americans, Puerto Ricans, and Native Americans. He thought that the term "Spanish origin" was a more accurate way of describing the racial minority groups meant to be protected by the bilingual ballot requirements under consideration at the time.

No testimony documents discrimination against Spanish Americans whose experience paralleled that of other European immigrant groups. Instead, Congress examined instances of racial discrimination against Puerto Ricans and Chicanos in voting. For example, witnesses presented extensive evidence of official action designed to reduce Chicano political participation in the Chicano heartland states of California, Arizona, New Mexico, Colorado, and Texas. Further, the record is filled with statements using "Spanish-surnamed" and "Spanish-speaking" as synonyms for "Mexican American."[6]

Despite this strong evidence that Congress found Chicanos and Puerto Ricans to be racial minorities—not white ethnic groups—one exchange in the congressional hearings on the Voting Rights Act extension reveals the confusion referred to at the outset of this chapter. Chicanos are mostly *mestizo* or indigenous in origin, and the "racial" origins of Puerto Ricans include European, African, and indigenous roots.

Uncertainty existed as to whether the Supreme Court might strike down the extension of the Act to these groups if it found that they were not racial minorities. Of course, prior to the 1975 extension, cases had been successfully brought against jurisdictions in New York and Arizona for racial discrimination against members of these groups, but the Supreme Court had not ruled on the question of whether these were "racial" minorities. Congressman Herman Badillo of New York, culturally identified as Puerto Rican, was concerned that the presence of European "blood" in these groups might lead the Supreme Court to strike down a measure designed to protect them against discrimination, if that measure was passed pursuant to Congress's power under the Fifteenth Amendment, which empowers Congress to enact legislation to further racial equality.

Some Guidelines for Reform

Federal Indian law, or more accurately, the indigenous traditions that the law has addressed, provides the solution to the dilemma the OMB faces. By illustrating alternatives to bloodline as the touchstone of identity, and by recognizing "community identification," federal Indian law provides an alternate means of classifying cultural identity that does not depend on an inquiry into genealogy. The best solution to the dilemma revealed by the problems inherent in the "Hispanic" classification is for the government to *abandon the outdated racial ideology embodied in Directive No. 15 and replace it with questions designed to determine an individual's membership in a socially constructed, cultural subgroup*. These cultural subgroups, not defined by reference to a person's bloodline, would be familiar to most Americans: Chicanos or Mexican Americans, Blacks or African Americans, Korean Americans, and so on. Members of these groups recognize each other as sharing a common history and vocabulary of experience, even as they remain internally divided by class, gender, sexual orientation, and political belief—factors that Directive No. 15 does not attempt to measure.

Since the agency cannot grant formal, political recognition of the type that led the Supreme Court to permit indigenous people such as the Shawnee to escape state taxation, the OMB would inquire into social interaction to determine whether the subgroup is generally recognized in society as a "people distinct from others."[7] The agency would have to undertake a detailed survey of American culture to determine exactly how people identify themselves and how they are recognized in order to create a framework of socially recognized ethnic or cultural subgroups. The agency should give priority to group self-identification over outsider identification because outsiders may tend to lump together different groups based upon presumptions of shared characteristics of the groups. This tendency is illustrated by the way the Asian/Pacific Islander groups and the Hispanic groups are combined.

More would be gained than simply eradicating the classical scheme of racial hierarchy from U.S. law. When an individual's membership in a cultural subgroup is legally significant, the law should not be hindered by a classification scheme that misstates the person's cultural identity, nor should the collection of accurate statistics be hampered by a classification scheme that serves only to confuse and mislead those attempting to classify themselves on a government form.

Even in a regime that recognizes only the rights of individuals, minority groups need accurate definition. If the purpose of a statute is to remedy past discrimination, the different histories of various groups might justifiably lead to different types of remedies. If the purpose of a statute is to assist a racially subordinated cultural community in building its own institutions, as with the MBE programs, such a goal is subverted when members of one group are permitted to masquerade as members of another and to hijack the meager resources allotted to these programs. If the purpose is simply to monitor the health of American society, it does not help to deny divisions in society that in fact exist.

NOTES

1. See Sharon Lee, *Racial Classifications in the U.S. Census: 1890–1990*, 16 J. Ethnic & Racial Stud. 75, 78 (1993).

2. *The Best and Worst of 1993*, Hispanic, Dec. 1993, at 20.

3. 44 U.S.C. § 3504 (1988).

4. 31 U.S.C. § 1104(d) (1988).

5. *Extension of the Voting Rights Act:* Hearings before the Subcommittee on Civil and Constitutional Rights of the House Committee on the Judiciary, 94th Cong., 1st Sess. 167, 176 (1975) (statement of J. Stanley Pottinger, Assistant Attorney General, Civil Rights Division).

6. See *id.* at 262–63 (letter from J. Stanley Pottinger to Richard J. Riley, County Attorney, Cochise County, Ariz.), 265–70 (report of California Secretary of State on Compliance with California Election Code § 1611).

7. The Kansas Indians, 72 U.S. (5 Wall.) 737, 755 (1866) (quoting Worcester v. Georgia, 31 U.S. [6 Pet.] 515, 559 [1832]).

Chapter 10

Re-imagining the Latino/a Race

Angel R. Oquendo

This chapter condemns "racial" subcategories, such as "Black Hispanics" and "White Hispanics," which have been increasingly gaining currency, and ultimately suggests that such categories should be rejected. First, they project onto the Latino/a community a divisive racial dualism that, much as it may pervade U.S. society, is alien to that community. Second, they are falsely premised on the existence of an independent objective concept of race capable of meaningfully classifying individuals as "Black" or "White."

Categorizing on the basis of physical features, of course, is an accepted practice in the United States. In fact, this society has primarily used physiognomy to create the "Hispanic" category. Yet what really unites Latino/as is their unique history of oppression. Unlike other immigrant groups, the largest Latino/a groups—Mexicans and Puerto Ricans—did not come into the United States via Ellis Island; they entered through the brutal process of U.S. imperial expansion. They were militarily attacked, invaded, colonized, and annexed. This common experience has caused them to form a unified community, which now includes other people of Latin American ancestry.

Another factor that bonds the Latino/a community is their common language. Not all Latino/as in the United States speak Spanish, but they all have some connection with it. If they do not speak Spanish themselves, then it is the language of their ancestors. Because they share a language, Latino/as constitute a race in the sense proposed by Spanish philosopher Miguel de Unamuno. In fact, in categorizing Latino/as, the "Anglo" majority has emphasized this common linguistic heritage more than physical appearance. For instance, the derogatory term that cuts across the different Latino/a groups is "spik"—which emphasizes how Latino/as "speak" rather than how they look. More significantly, the anti-Latino/a movement has coalesced politically in reaction to the "English only" movement, which attacks their linguistic identity.

From RE-IMAGINING THE LATINO/A RACE." 12 HARV. BLACKLETTER L.J. 93 (1995). Originally published in the *Harvard Blackletter Law Journal*. Reprinted by permission.

A New Categorization

Soy Mexicana
soy Mexican-American
soy American of Spanish Surname (A.S.S.)
soy Latina
soy Puerto Riquena
soy Cocoanut
soy Chicana[1]

In 1978, during my last high school year in Puerto Rico, I took the SAT. Any test can be intimidating, but one that measures aptitude can make you feel insecure and challenged. These feelings were accentuated in my case because the exam was in English, and more important, was administered by an organization from the United States.

I was nervous, in part, because I was being tested by the people who kept us afloat with their massive economic support, who from afar made important decisions for us, and who generally were successful where we had failed. When they came to our land, they were well-off and they ran many of the large companies. In contrast, when we went to their land, we were poor, did the most menial jobs, and scored the lowest on intelligence tests. Therefore, the test had a greater meaning for me. It symbolized America's continuing dominion and control over Puerto Rico. I was determined to wage a battle that I could ultimately win.

Yet I was caught off guard even before the examination began. While I was filling out the personal information part, I was asked to identify myself racially. This struck me as odd for two reasons. I had never been asked such a question before, and I had never thought of myself in terms of race, even though I was aware of the concept of racial differences. I knew about the history and reality of racism, yet I did not see myself as a member of a particular race.

Fortunately, the SAT authorities were wise or benevolent enough to include "Puerto Rican" among the multiple choices and thus spared me a potentially profound existential dilemma. I had no need to check the color of my skin, feel the texture of my hair, visualize my facial features, or call to mind the physiognomy of my family and relatives. With a sense of relief, I checked the box labeled "Puerto Rican" and moved on.

At the time, I was only a kid facing an unexpected situation. Today, having now lived in the United States for over fifteen years, I have come to regard this kind of questioning as normal. In fact, until recently, I considered myself beyond astonishment with respect to issues of racial categorization. I thought that I would always find a box simply labeled "Puerto Rican," "Hispanic," "Latino," "Spanish Surnamed," or even "Other" with which I could feel comfortable.

However, racial categories have changed in the last few years. I am referring to the relatively recent tendency to subcategorize the category for Hispanics. Ever more often, surveys add to that category the following clarification "(Black and White)"—sometimes "(regardless of race)"—and qualify the White as well as the Black category with the parenthetical "(non-Hispanic)." So the list usually reads as follows:

"White (non-Hispanic)," "Black (non-Hispanic)," "Hispanic (Including White and Black Hispanics)," "Asian American," "American Indian," and "Other."

A true bureaucrat's paradise! Granted, the Hispanic category is still being made available to me. But it is more difficult for me to embrace that category with all the added attachments and qualifications. I wonder if I am being told that there is something problematic about my category? Is the message that it, unlike other categories, needs further explanation? Is it implied that after all I do belong objectively to a race but that I am being given a break as a Latino/a for some undisclosed reason? The next step will probably be to create separate classifications for Black Hispanics and White Hispanics and to force Latino/as to choose. The quandary that I narrowly escaped as a child will thus be returning with a vengeance.

The Term "Latino/a"

The term "Hispanic" has been rejected by some because of its association with Spanish colonial power. They prefer "Latino" because it lacks any such connotation and is more inclusive and descriptive. "Latino" is short for "latinoamericano." Like its English counterpart, the term refers to the people who come from the territory in the Americas colonized by Latin nations, such as Portugal, Spain, and France, whose languages are derived from Latin. People from Brazil, Mexico, and even Haiti are thus all "latinoamericanos." Individuals who are decendants of the former British or Dutch colonies are excluded.

"Iberoamericanos," in contrast, are individuals who come from American lands once occupied by Portugal and Spain, the two countries on the Iberian peninsula. Brazilians and Mexicans are iberoamericanos, but not Haitians or any of the citizens of countries once claimed by France, Britain, or the Netherlands. Finally, "hispanoamericanos" are persons from the former colonies of Spain in the "New World." The expression "Hispanic" probably derives from "hispanoamericanos."

An informal interpretation of the term "Latino" would take it to be equivalent to "hispanoamericano" or "iberoamericano." In other words, it may be used in a narrower sense to denominate only those who come from the former colonies of Spain and Portugal. In the United States, it appears to be employed in the narrowest sense to identify the children of the former Spanish possessions in the Americas.

The strict interpretation of "Latino" is more inclusive than the term "Hispanic," encompassing as it does those people who are descended from the onetime possessions of not only Spain, but also Portugal and France. However, "Latino" enthusiasts would probably exclude these people from the category because they use it to cover only people from what was once the Spanish empire in America. Therefore, in practical application, the term "Latino" is no more inclusive and descriptive than "Hispanic."

That the term "Latino" should be favored over "Hispanic" because the latter is linked to the brutal Spanish colonization of America is puzzling. "Latino," in the informal sense, is just as bound up with the Spanish colonial enterprise. The formal interpretation of Latino is associated with the similarly objectionable Portuguese and

French colonial projects, and both terms slight the rich African and Native American influence on the Latino/a community.

What I do find attractive about the expression "Latino" is, first, that it calls to mind the Latino/a struggle for empowerment in the United States. The leaders of this campaign support "Latino" because it came from the community. The Latino/a people are thus conceived of as not just acquiescing to their christening by the Anglo majority, but rather as giving themselves a name. The adoption of the term "Latino" could be regarded as part of a broader process of self-definition and self-assertion.

Second, "Latino" is a newer term that invites re-thinking and re-defining of what membership in this community is all about. This attitude of re-birth and of facing a new beginning is needed as the Latino/a community in the United States becomes larger and more diverse and strives to find itself. The third reason why "Latino" is a better term is because it is a Spanish word. It accentuates the bond between the Latino/a community and the Spanish language. Furthermore, in insisting upon being called by its Spanish name, the Latino/a community is demanding recognition and respect for its culture.

Racial Dualism

Racial subcategorization appears to be an attempt to project U.S. racial dualism onto the Latino/a community as a whole. It is possible to imagine a bureaucrat attempting to defend the move as reasonable on grounds of precision: "The categories are meant to be mutually exclusive. White Hispanics and Black Hispanics, however, are covered by two of the categories. In order to be accurate, they would have to check, in addition to the Hispanic box, either the box labeled 'White' or that labeled 'Black.' We just want to make it clear that for our purposes, they are Hispanic, even if they are additionally White or Black. We want each person to choose only one of the options."

This response is spurious. If the concern were Latino/as who might fall within two categories, it would make sense to stipulate that the rubric "Hispanic" includes people who are "racially" Asian or Indian as well as Black and White. The categories for Asian Americans and Native Americans could be adjusted accordingly to exclude Latino/as explicitly. In this way, Latino/as of Asian extraction as well as those who descend from the indigenous peoples of Latin America would know, without a doubt, which category corresponds to them.

Indeed, I think that it is no coincidence that "Indian" and "Asian" Latino/as have been left out of the picture. The decision to omit these groups reflects "racial dualism." The U.S. racial imagination posits a bifurcated racial universe, in which the Black-White divide overwhelms all other differences. This conception of race is not surprising in light of the prominence in U.S. history of the oppression of people of African ancestry by individuals of European extraction. The institutions of enslavement and discrimination have created and reinforced the perception that the opposition between these two groups is essential and universal. Racial dualism is but the other side of dualist racism.

The subcategorization of Latino/as should be rejected precisely because it projects this foreign racial dualism onto the Latino/a community. Among Mexicans, who constitute by far the majority of all Latino/as, the main physiognomic influences are not even African and European. Mexicans instead tend to descend from the indigenous peoples who populated the southern tip and southwest region of North America and the Spanish who later colonized the territory.

Furthermore, the subcategorization injects a dualism or division of the races that is alien even to those Latino/a groups, e.g., Puerto Ricans, in which the principal ethnic influences are African and European. In the words of Luis Nieves Falcón:

> Because in Puerto Rico prejudices take a subtle and personal form, there is no organized body of customs or practices against Blacks. Because social discrimination seems to operate with equal force against all lower class individuals, regardless of color, there is no sufficient basis for the emergence of racial conflicts along racial lines—though, in any case, racial lines are in fact very fluid. Puerto Ricans—white, brown, or black—have little experience with and a very limited understanding of the racial animosities that divide the North American nation and are, naturally, reluctant to take part in a struggle that is repugnant and meaningless to them.
>
> Interpreting the behavior of Puerto Ricans in the United States with respect to racial matters on the basis of their own particular racial experience, North Americans perceive that behavior as incomprehensible, ridiculous, and cowardly. It seems that they would expect White Puerto Ricans to bond on one side and Blacks on the other. Puerto Ricans are pressured to adopt one or the other racial identity, since North Americans cannot really believe that the integration achieved by Puerto Ricans—imperfect as it may be— is possible.[2]

Puerto Rican society might have been bifurcated along racial lines up to the end of the nineteenth century, when its sense of nationality was still developing. Then, José Luis González insists, the Puerto Rican "nation was so divided racially, socially, economically, and culturally, that we should instead talk of two nations." These two nations—or "ethnic groups that were true castes"—had radically different "cultural traditions" and even "Weltanschauungen."[3]

González himself notes, however, that the U.S. invasion and colonization of Puerto Rico in the twentieth century changed the society's structure in a radical way:

> The progressive dismantling of the Puerto Rican elite's culture under the impact of the transformations that the North American colonial regime brought upon the national society has had as a consequence not the North Americanization of that society but, rather, an *internal* alteration of the cultural values. The vacuum created by the dismantling of the culture of Puerto Ricans from the top has been filled certainly not by the intrusion of the North American culture but rather by the ever more palpable ascent of the culture of Puerto Ricans from the bottom.[4]

Modern Puerto Rican society, González explains, is dominated by a popular culture in which the African roots are "more important" than the European or Taíno roots and that has "an essentially Afro-Antillean character."[5] González's view was anticipated by the poet Luis Palés Matos in an interview:

The black essence lives with us physically and spiritually. Its characteristics—which have been filtered into the mulatto essence—influence in an evident way all the manifestations of our popular life. . . . I therefore know no collective feature of our people that does not show the trace of that delicious mixture from which the Antillean character derives its true tone.[6]

The African heritage is even more pervasive in the Puerto Rican community in the United States. For the Diaspora consists primarily of the impoverished sector of the Puerto Rican society, which includes even more individuals of mostly African extraction than other sectors.

Physiognomically, there are infinite gradations of color, but culturally, there is a single Afro-Antillean ethos. Thus, if a well-defined Black/White polarity ever existed among Puerto Ricans, none remains today. Even the U.S. Census Bureau realized that the realities and the perceptions of race in Puerto Rico differ from those in the United States. Lawrence Wright reports that "[b]y 1960 the United States census, which counts the population of Puerto Rico, gave up asking the race question on the island because race did not carry the same distinction there that it did on the mainland."[7] More generally, the Latino/a community is not divided along racial lines, in part due to the extent of *mestizaje* or social infusion in Latin America.

This historical background, naturally, had a decisive impact on the racial constitution and attitude of the Latino/a community. Unlike the broader U.S. society, the Latino/a community is not segregated into two "racial" groups, with different cultures, identities, and even dialects. Within this community racial consciousness and even racism endure, but of a different kind. Wright correctly observes that:

[t]he fluid Latin-American concept of race differs from the rigid United States idea of biologically determined and highly distinct human divisions. In most Latin cultures, skin color is an individual variable—not a group marker—so that within the same family one sibling might be considered white and another black.[8]

There simply are no discrete, isolated groups, such as White Latino/as or Black Latino/as. Rather, there are numerous different and overlapping shades, reflecting the individuals' heritage and to some extent correlating with their socio-economic class.

The subcategorization might, of course, find support among a minuscule minority of "mostly European" individuals among Latino/as, worried that their categorization as Hispanic might be taken to imply a renunciation of their claim to be White. The Latino/a encounter with U.S. racial dualism leads to the development of greater color consciousness. In U.S. society, possessing valid title to Whiteness requires being free from any encumbrances of Blackness. In other words, the most effective way to assert that one is White is by categorically denying any connection or kinship to Blacks: As long as one has "one drop of Black blood," one is taken to be Black. These Latino/as are probably motivated by the desire to distance themselves unequivocally from Black Latino/as. In their zeal to adopt racial dualism they forget about the *mestizaje* that is dominant in their community. They begin to think only in terms of Black or White, neglecting that the majority of Latino/as are Mexicans, whose European blood is strongly diluted not by African but by Aztec blood. Thus, their disassociation has caused them to miscategorize individuals in the tradition of racial dualism.

The Poverty of the Concept of Race

Now, what if the racial dualism bias of the subcategorization were remedied? In other words, what if the re-categorization included specifying that the category Hispanic includes all races and perhaps clarifying that the categories "White," "Black," "Asian American," "Native American," and "Other" do not include "Hispanics"? My bureaucrat could now say: "This is generally a racial classification. For policy reasons Hispanics must be treated separately, even though they do not constitute a distinct race. What we are doing is pulling Hispanics from their corresponding racial categories and artificially creating a separate category for them. The questionnaire simply reflects this reality."

The Office of Management and Budget, in its Statistical Directive 15—which regulates racial and ethnic categorization on federal forms and statistics—endorses this approach. Latino/as, like all other U.S. citizens, are taken to fall within one of the four racial groups: American Indian or Alaskan Native; Asian or Pacific Islander; Black; and White. As a separate matter, Directive 15 then divides ethnicity into "Hispanic Origin" and "Not of Hispanic Origin."

This whole approach is problematically premised on the existence of an independently meaningful concept of race that applies to all people, including Latino/as. The creation of a separate category for Latino/as is taken to be independent of their status as members of a particular race. They supposedly continue to be Black, White, or another color.

Yet, race is, at best, a highly vague category that generally classifies people in terms of the way they look. Spanish philosopher Miguel de Unamuno reports that the word "race," as used in almost every European language, comes from the Spanish or Castilean word *raza,* which means "ray" or "line." "In Castilla," Unamuno points out, "one speaks of a 'raza' of sun and each thread in a cloth is called a 'raza.'"[9] The modern term "race" apparently came to refer to a mark shared by people who are related by heritage. Not surprisingly, people with resembling physical traits, presumably due to a common genealogy, came to be seen as belonging to the same race.

To the extent that Latino/as physiognomically resemble each other and differ from other groups, they could be taken to constitute a "race." The physiognomic differences among Latino/as are probably not much greater than those among the members of other "racial" groups, such as "Whites" or "African Americans." In light of the inexorable vagueness of the concept of race, the idea of racial cohesion among Latino/as is just as plausible as the notion that Latino/as can be internally segregated by race. The concept of race is incapable of providing a meaningful basis for making significant distinctions between those who fall within and those who fall without a particular race.

The Evils of the Concept of Race

Many have repudiated the concept of race not only because of its inaccuracy but also because of the sinister purposes it has served historically. Unamuno's rejection of "racial materialism" provides a case in point. Racial materialism focuses on material or physical characteristics in defining the concept of race. Unamuno denounces "the materialist cast that is usually given to the anthropological concept of race."[10]

In a 1933 article (published on the Day of the Race, "El dia de la raza"—as Columbus Day is referred to in Spanish-speaking countries) Unamuno asserts that it is the racists who use this material concept of race and adds: "Today I feel an obligation to insist on this point, in light of the . . . barbarity, actually savagery, attained by such racism, especially in Germany."[11] He assails "the barbaric sense" given to the materialist concept of race by "the racists, those supposed Aryans of the gammadion and anti-Christian cross."[12]

If racial categories, in addition to having no intelligible substance, serve mainly as an instrument of oppression, why not just eliminate them altogether? Why not go beyond deleting subcategories, such as "Black Hispanic" and "White Hispanic," and eradicate all the general categories too: e.g., "White," "Black," "Hispanic," etc.? I would argue that these general categories should not be simply quashed, but re-anchored on the cultural or spiritual life of peoples. By reconceptualizing themselves, excluded people will be better able to recapture their identities and to struggle for social justice. Overt or crude racism, which is characterized by openly treating African Americans as inherently inferior, has been termed "old-fashioned" racism. The transition to the more subtle and covert forms of racism that prevail in modern society takes place as old-fashioned racism becomes less acceptable. The injury caused by racism cannot be segregated from the racial classification in place. In fact, racism is unjust because it only allows a person to be identified by empty racial categories. Hence, racism not only deprives people of their income; it robs people of their soul.

Transcending the Concept of Race

Just as some have argued that preserving the existing racial categories perpetuates race-consciousness, others might protest that any categorization of human beings, even along cultural lines, tends to increase divisiveness. But this may simply be the inescapable price of pursuing racial justice. Attacking racial exploitation and making amends for a long history of racial oppression requires taking the existing categories and turning them against their original purpose. The conceptual structure that singled out people in order to undermine them must now be used to empower them. If this escalates the level of conflict in the United States, so be it.

U.S. society is already ethnically divided in a profound way. This situation can only improve if people realize that what sets them apart is their cultural background and not an essence that is supposed to be mysteriously derived from their physiognomy. Difference ceases to be as threatening when it is understood on the basis of culture and history and not on the basis of empty concepts, such as material race.

The question remains whether the cultural or sociological groups should still be known as "races" or whether a new concept is called for. Inasmuch as the term "race" is so deeply associated with its "materialist" acceptation, its complete eradication appeals greatly. A better concept might be that of "ethnicities" or "ethnic groups." Despite its long "materialist" past in which it was taken to be synonymous with "race," the concept of ethnicity as used today does appear to focus on cultural rather than on physiognomic difference.

The semantic choice between "race" and "ethnicity" to refer to a particular group was once thought to have substantial consequences. Latino/as remonstrated against the Office of Management and Budget because in its Statistical Directive 15, it classified them as an ethnic group instead of a racial group. They feared that such a classification would imply that they could not participate in federal programs equally with other groups that were considered racial. For instance, many were concerned that federal courts would exclude "ethnic" groups from protection under civil rights laws aimed at racial discrimination, such as 42 U.S.C. § 1981. In 1987 the United States Supreme Court dispelled this preoccupation by holding that the Civil Rights Act of 1866, as well as the Constitution and other anti-discrimination laws, makes no distinction between "racial" and "ethnic" discrimination.

There has additionally been some concern that it would be more difficult for Latino/as, as an ethnic community, than for "racial groups" to bring class actions under Rule 23 of the Federal Rules of Civil Procedure, which require commonality, typicality, and adequate representativeness. The preoccupation became prominent in 1970 after the Supreme Court turned down an appeal from the New Mexico federal district court in *Tijerina v. Henry*. The district court dismissed a class action complaint by a group of Chicanos because their "definition of the class was 'too vague to be meaningful.'"[13]

The Supreme Court has shown in subsequent cases, however, that it does not believe that "racial" and "ethnic" class actions should be treated differently. In sum, the choice between "race" and "ethnicity" does not seem terribly important. I have a slight preference for the term "race." I feel somewhat attracted to Unamuno's call for the transformation of the material into a "spiritual" concept of race. My preference, however, is not out of deference to the adamant reluctance of ordinary and official usage to give up the term "race." I did not take into account at all a similar reluctance with respect to renouncing the term "Hispanic."

I believe it may be wise to use the word "race" for other reasons. With respect to Latino/as as well as other communities in the United States, the ordinary as well as official reflex appears to be, increasingly, to invoke the concept of ethnicity. The only exception, it seems to me, is the African American community. I think that the explanation for this is the obsession with the Black/White dichotomy. Latino/as and other groups should stand up against that obsession. They should resist the notion that what distances African Americans is qualitatively different than what separates Latino/as from the White majority. If the majority insists on declaring African Americans a distinct "racial" group, then all other "ethnic" groups should insist on being equally described. Such a stance would perhaps contribute to the de-mystification of the concept of race.

Moreover, the word "race"—or rather the Spanish equivalent *raza*—has special significance for Latino/as in the United States, particularly for Chicanos. *Raza* evokes a primeval and mythical union with the indigenous people that populated the North American expanse of Aztlan. The natives of Aztlan spread south and eventually formed the Nahuatl tribes living in Mexico as the European conquest began. The concept of race also has political connotations. "Raza" is the name taken by the organizations that initiated and have continued the struggle for political, social, and economic empowerment of the Chicano community. These groups—including the party "La Raza Unida" founded by José Ángel Gutiérrez—also encouraged Chicanos to take pride in their history and culture.

To be sure, Anthony Appiah is right when he suggests that today the term race is almost universally understood in its materialist sense.[14] But inasmuch as such usage is terribly misguided, why defer to it? Why make any effort to allow people to continue thinking in terms of the material concept of "race"—which Appiah himself regards as irremediably bankrupt? Why not take up arms against the usage, along with the underlying concept of race? Why not propose a different, more constructive use for the word "race"? People might, as a consequence, start thinking differently and realize the emptiness of their prior conceptions.

A New Latino/a Self-Understanding

Latino/as have been categorized out of the U.S. mainstream and into the dialectic of otherness. It is revealing that they are often classified along with African, Asian, and Native Americans as "non-White." Thus, the focus of the category "Hispanic" has often been physiognomy. This category has managed to survive despite its anthropological emptiness and despite the wealth of ethnological difference among individuals that fall under it. What then should be the basis of the new Latino/a self-understanding? What is the bond that unites Latino/as and gives meaning to their common existence? First, they share a unique experience of oppression and survival in the United States. Mexicans and Puerto Ricans, who constitute the largest and oldest Latino/a communities within the official borders of the United States, were attacked, invaded, colonized, annexed, and exploited by the United States.

Unlike European immigrants, Mexicans and Puerto Ricans did not just come to the United States. Rather the United States came to them. Mexicans became part of the U.S. reality as a result of U.S. expansion into the Mexican territory in the southwest region of North America. Chicanos "reached" the Anglo world in the nineteenth century as their land was taken over by the United States. The Anglos then accelerated their migration into former Mexican territory and gradually became the dominant class. The Chicano community was born as the Mexican people were gradually subjugated to minority status.

Mexican immigration in the twentieth century has been essentially directed toward those same lands that once belonged to Mexico. Mexican immigration, which parallels Anglo migration in the previous century, has strengthened the bond of the Chicano community with its Mexican roots. The new immigrants, hence, simply joined a centuries-old community, which was once one with their own. These two communities were not previously separated, but a border was established in the aftermath of the Mexican-American War. Those who arrived more recently gradually became part of the Chicano community on the basis of a shared culture and experience of subjugation.

Puerto Ricans, in turn, entered the U.S. sphere following the U.S. invasion of their country in 1898. Upon its military defeat, Spain signed the controversial Treaty of Paris, in which it transferred its colonial powers over Puerto Rico to the United States. Puerto Ricans became citizens of the United States by a unilateral act of Congress in 1917. The degree of political autonomy enjoyed by Puerto Ricans has increased throughout the years, but the United States has never given up its ultimate power over Puerto Rico.

Puerto Rican immigration to the continental United States started shortly after the military occupation but exploded after the Second World War. Puerto Ricans arrived as one of the most socially and economically impoverished groups and have retained that status. Puerto Rican immigration is not just a logical consequence but part and parcel of the United States policy of absorption of Puerto Rican land into its territory and of the Puerto Rican people into its citizenry. The United States has dominated Puerto Ricans who reside on the island, as well as those who live on the continent.

Both Chicanos and Puerto Ricans, hence, share a history of being militarily and then socially besieged. They were brought into U.S. society by war and conquest. They did not just move into U.S. territory. Instead, the confines of that territory were expanded to engulf them. Once "inside," they became an underclass, systematically perceived and treated as a conquered people.

Both Chicanos and Puerto Ricans can therefore rejoice over having managed not to be completely destroyed as a people. They have been able to survive recurrent attempts to assimilate them and to annihilate their cultural existence. Against all odds, they have been able to cultivate their Latin American roots and develop an identity that allowed them to resist the aggression. And the community that emerged has absorbed subsequent migrations of Latino/as—including Cubans, Guatemalans, Salvadorans, and Dominicans—who often share, in addition to the Latin American heritage, an experience of oppression in the United States. Just as African Americans seek to base their self-understanding on their resurrection from slavery, Latino/as should trace their identity back to their resurrection from imperialist conquest.

The Spanish language could be a second source of support for Latino/a identity. Though not spoken by all Latino/as, Spanish is a central part of their shared heritage. It is the language of their parents, grandparents, or ancestors. Through Spanish, Latino/as will be able to get close to each other and to their roots. It is therefore crucial to resurrect the Spanish language within the Latino/a community. The children should learn Spanish, not only because in many cases this helps their learning in general, but also because they will thus be able to secure a sense of identity and belonging. Spanish should also be brought to the adult population: in centers of adult education, in unions, in church organization, in prisons, in rehabilitation programs. The point is not to create a prerequisite to membership in the Latino/a community, but rather to give Latino/as an opportunity to reconnect with their past and to open up a path towards a common identity. Latino/as might thus become a spiritual race in the sense proposed by Unamuno—i.e., they might all come to speak the same language.[15]

NOTES

1. ["I am Mexican/I am Mexican-American/I am American of Spanish Surname (A.S.S.)/I am Latina/I am Puerto Rican/I am Cocoanut/I am Chicana"]. La Chrisx, *La Loca de la Raza Cósmica*, in Infinite Divisions: An Anthology of Chicana Literature 84, 88 (Tey Diana Rebolledo & Eliana S. Rivero eds., 1993).

2. Luis Nieves Falcón, Diagnóstico de Puerto Rico 275 (1972). The translation of this as well as other non-English texts in this chapter are my own.

3. José Luis González, *El país de cuatro pisos,* in El País de Cuatro Pisos y Otros Ensayos 9, 25–26, 27 (1981).

4. *Id.* at 30; see also *id.* at 34, 36.

5. *Id.* at 19; see also *id.* at 22.

6. Ángela Négron Muñoz, *Hablando con don Luis Palés Matos,* El Mundo, Nov. 13, 1932.

7. Lawrence Wright, *One Drop of Blood,* New Yorker, July 25, 1994, at 46, 52.

8. *Id.* at 52.

9. Miguel de Unamuno y Jugo, *Hispanidad,* in La Raza Vasca y el Vascuence; En Torno a la Lengua Española 264, 266 (1974).

10. Miguel de Unamuno y Jugo, *De nuevo la raza,* in La Raza Vasca y el Vascuence; En Torno a la Lengua Española 162, 164 (1974).

11. *Id.* at 162.

12. *Id.* at 163.

13. Tijerina v. Henry, 398 U.S. 922 (1970).

14. K. Anthony Appiah, *How to Succeed in Business by Really Trying,* 42 N.Y. Rev. Books 29, Jan. 12, 1995.

15. Miguel de Unamuno y Jugo, *La fiesta de la raza,* in La Raza Vasca y el Vascuence; En Torno a la Lengua Española 159 (1974).

From the Editors
Issues and Comments

Do all Americans who descend from Spanish-speaking countries have something in common? If so, what can possibly unite such a diverse group, including Cubans, Puerto Ricans, New Mexicans whose families have been here for two hundred years, migrant laborers, and Central American refugees fleeing political repression?

By what label should Americans who descend from Spanish-speaking countries identify themselves? "Latino"? "Hispanic"? Or something else? How many categories should there be, or should we abolish all categories?

Are Latinos more like blacks or like whites?

Historically, any American with a trace of recognizable black ancestry was considered black. Why is there no such "one-drop" rule for Latinos?

If you were a very light-skinned Latino who could, by parting your hair or dressing a certain way and concealing your accent, pass for white, would you do so? What would you give up, and what would you gain?

Is race—including the Latino race—biological, or is it a social construct? Note that every feature considered a marker for Latinos, such as olive skin and black hair, is also possessed by many individuals who consider themselves white. If race is a social construct, why do we construct it so?

Do you agree with some of the authors of this book that education can lead to alienation within the Latino group? If you are a Latino student, have others in your group accused you of being different? If you are a Caucasian student, do you believe you will face similar alienation from friends and family once you earn your degree?

How has Latinos' use of Spanish subjected them to discrimination? Have you ever felt threatened by another's use of a language you did not understand? Why is it important to Latinos/as to continue to speak their language?

Since the government forces its citizens to define their race, is it acceptable for courts on occasion to decide that the Latino or Chicano classification is too vague to constitute a cognizable class?

Should light-skinned Latinos be entitled to affirmative action benefits?

Suggested Readings

Arce, Carlos H., and Aida Hurtado. "Mexicans, Chicanos, Mexican Americans, or Pochos ... Que Somos? The Impact of Language and Nativity on Ethnic Labeling." *Aztlán: A Journal of Chicano Studies* 17 (1987): 103–30.

Calderón, José. "'Hispanic' and 'Latino': The Viability of Categories for Panethnic Unity." *Latin American Perspectives* 19 (Fall 1992): 37–44.

"Directive No. 15, Race and Ethnic Standards for Federal Statistics and Administrative Reporting." 43 *Federal Register* 19,260. Washington, D.C.: National Archives and Records Administration, 1978.

Ethnic Identity: Formation and Transformation among Hispanics and Other Minorities, edited by Martha E. Bernal and George P. Knight. Albany: State University of New York Press, 1993.

Giménez, Martha E. "'Latino/Hispanic'—Who Needs a Name? The Case against a Standardized Terminology." *International Journal of Health Services* 19 (1989): 557–71.

Gomez, Laura E. "The Birth of the 'Hispanic' Generation: Attitudes of Mexican-American Political Elites toward the Hispanic Label." *Latin American Perspectives* 19 (Fall 1992): 45

Griffith, Beatrice. *American Me.* Boston: Houghton Mifflin Co., 1948.

Hayes-Bautista, David. "Identifying 'Hispanic' Populations: The Influence of Research Methodology on Public Policy." *American Journal of Public Health* 70 (1980): 353

Hayes-Bautista, David, and Jorge Chapa. "Latino Terminology: Conceptual Bases for Standardized Terminology." *American Journal of Public Health* 77 (1987): 61

Keefe, Susan E., and Amado M. Padilla. *Chicano Ethnicity.* Albuquerque: University of New Mexico Press, 1987.

Klor de Alva, J. Jorge. "Telling Hispanics Apart: Latino Sociocultural Diversity." In *The Hispanic Experience in the United States: Contemporary Issues and Perspectives,* edited by Edna Acosta-Belén and Barabara R. Sjostrom, 107–36. New York: Praeger, 1988.

Lee, Sharon M. "Racial Classifications in the U.S. Census: 1890–1990." *Ethnic and Racial Studies* 16 (1993): 75

Murguia, Edward. "On Latino/Hispanic Ethnic Identity." *Latino Studies Journal* 2, no. 3 (September 1991): 8–18.

Padilla, Felix M. *Latino Ethnic Consciousness: The Case of Mexican Americans and Puerto Ricans in Chicago.* Notre Dame: University of Notre Dame Press, 1985.

Payson, Kenneth R. "Comment, Check the Box: Reconsidering Directive No. 15 and the Classification of Mixed-Race People." 84 *California Law Review* 1233 (1996).

Rodriguez, Clara E., Aida Castro, Oscar Garcia, and Analisa Torres. "Latino Racial Identity: In the Eye of the Beholder?" *Latino Studies Journal* 2, no. 3 (September 1991): 33–48.

Simon, Lisette E. "Hispanics: Not a Cognizable Ethnic Group." 63 *University of Cincinnati Law Review* 497 (1994).

Skerry, Peter. *Mexican Americans: The Ambivalent Minority*. New York: Free Press, 1993.

"Standards for the Classification of Federal Data on Race and Ethnicity: Advance Notice of Proposed Review and Possible Revision of OMB's Statistical Policy Directive No. 15." 59 *Federal Register* 29,831, 29,832. Washington, D.C.: National Archives and Records Administration, 1994.

Telles, Edward E., and Edward Murguia. "Phenotypic Discrimination and Income Differences among Mexican Americans." *Social Science Quarterly* 17 (1990): 682

Thomas, Piri. *Down These Mean Streets*. New York: Knopf, 1967.

Waters, Mary C. *Ethnic Options: Choosing Identities in America*. Berkeley: University of California Press, 1990.

Wright, Luther, Jr. "Who's Black, Who's White, and Who Cares: Reconceptualizing the United States' Definition of Race and Racial Classifications." 48 *Vanderbilt Law Review* 513 (1995).

Yankauer, Alfred. "Hispanic/Latino—What's in a Name?" *American Journal of Public Health* 77 (1987): 15.

Conquest and Immigration

How We Got (Get) Here

How did Latinos get here? The answer may be easy (conquest or immigration), but the actual routes by which the group arrived here have been accompanied by much pain. Conquest left a legacy and a mark of its own, detailed in some of the chapters that follow, while immigration presents huge challenges, including acquisition of a new language and culture and separation from friends and family. The United States has not always eased the way, either, ignoring treaty provisions and imposing impossibly high burdens on persons wishing to immigrate. The chapters in Part II explore Latinos' history of immigration and conquest, delving into such questions as the psychological effect of being a conquered people and the justice—or lack of it—in our official immigration policies. Should the United States admit essentially all comers, or are some limits defensible? And if they are defensible, what about Latin America, where the United States has been meddling, for good or ill, during much of its history? Does that history place a special obligation on this country to admit immigrants more freely than from other regions, say, Scandinavia?

Chapter 11

Latinos in the United States
Invitation and Exile

Gilbert Paul Carrasco

Throughout U.S. history periods of labor shortage have alternated with ones of labor surplus. In times of shortage, the United States has enthusiastically welcomed immigrants to fill gaps in the labor pool. More often than not, however, available employment has been characterized by harsh working conditions, enormous amounts of physical labor, and minimal remuneration. In addition to abject working conditions, immigrants have also faced discrimination and resentment.

During periods of labor surplus or economic stress, immigrants in the United States have been subjected to particular cruelty. Americans, led by various nativist organizations and movements such as the Know-Nothing Party in the 1850s or, more recently, U.S. English or California's "Save Our State" campaign, have blamed immigrants for the country's economic woes. Such xenophobic bigotry has resulted in calls for anti-immigrant legislation (including restrictions on immigration for whichever group was targeted at the time), attempts to deny public services (including elimination of bilingual education for school-aged immigrants and the American citizen children of undocumented immigrants), and, ultimately, deportation.

Mexican immigrants have usually been the subject of these seesaw trends. One reason is that Mexico and the United States share a common border. The border between the two countries stretches for two thousand miles and is marked in some places by a fence, but at most points merely by an imaginary line in the sand or by the Rio Grande River. Easy to traverse, this border facilitates immigration, both legal and illegal, as well as expulsion.

Due to their great distance from the United States, Europeans historically could not make the journey to where their labor was needed (typically the Southwestern United States) before the need was met. The only immigrants left within reach of the American Southwest were Mexicans and Asians. The Chinese and the Japanese have their own regrettable history of discrimination in the United States. The laws and policies that temporarily ended immigration from Japan and China left Mexico as

From *Latinos in the United States: Invitation and Exile* by Gilbert Paul Carrasco, in Immigrants Out! The New Nativism and the Anti-Immigrant Impulse in the United States, edited by Juan F. Perea. Copyright © 1997 by New York University. Reprinted by permission of New York University Press.

the only source to fill the labor vacuum. Mexican laborers have since become the United States' disposable labor force, brought in when needed, only to fulfill their use and be unceremoniously discarded, a trend that has been recurring for over 150 years.

From the Gold Rush to World War I

Early migration into the United States was aided by negligible border restrictions and virtually no immigration laws. The first wave of Mexican laborers was drawn to California by the Gold Rush shortly after Mexico ceded California to the United States under the terms of the Treaty of Guadalupe Hidalgo in 1848. The Gold Rush drew people from all over the world, triggering rapid population growth. Because most who flocked to California wanted to strike it rich in their own mines, unskilled manual labor was scarce and laborers were needed to work in Anglo-owned mines, railroads, and farms. The work was backbreaking, low-paying, and often dangerous, so it was difficult to find Anglos who would do it.

In addition to fulfilling labor demands, Mexicans brought with them knowledge of mining. Anglos came to California with dreams of striking it rich but had little practical experience or knowledge of how to do it. Anglos, however, soon acquired the knowledge, tools, and techniques of Latino miners.

Unfortunately for Latinos, a need for their labor and knowledge did not translate into good attitudes toward them. Popular accounts of Latinos during that period were influenced by manifest destiny, "scientific" theories of racial miscegenation, and the Mexican War. These accounts provided the Anglo miner with a negative stereotype of the Latino that led to discrimination, threats, violence, and restrictive legislation directed against Mexicans and Mexican Americans. Posters appeared in mining areas threatening violence to any "foreigners" who remained where "they had no right to be"; vigilante groups expelling Latinos from mines claimed that mineral rights and wealth in America were reserved for "Americans"; a Foreign Miners' Tax Law was imposed; and foreigners were assaulted and lynched.[1]

Anti-Latino attitudes were also fueled by greed for the much coveted gold. Latinos who labored in the fields, on the railroads, or in the mines of Anglos were not as persecuted and discriminated against as those who sought their own fortunes in the mines. Nevertheless, although nonminers were not as persecuted as miners, history records whole towns being put to the torch, rioters shooting any Mexican in sight, random murders, and other vigilante actions throughout this period.

Even while Latinos were being persecuted, their labor was needed, especially in jobs that were low-paying and labor-intensive. Such jobs included ranching, agriculture (especially for crops such as cotton and sugar beets), laying the rails that traverse the Southwest (a task made harder because most of the terrain is desert, semidesert, or mountainous), and mining (where, although their knowledge of mining techniques proved invaluable, they received lower wages for the same work their unskilled Anglo counterparts did).

The demand for Mexican labor in some labor-intensive occupations was so great that employers held Mexicans captive. One such industry was the Colorado sugar beet industry. Sugar beets require attention almost year-round and, therefore, need a semipermanent labor force. When farmers could not persuade Mexican laborers to stay year-round to perform the arduous labor, they resorted to coercion. One tactic was to refuse to make final wage payments to employees so that they were unable to leave; thus, laborers had to remain in the area until the following season to collect their pay. Essentially, farmers had a captive work force without rights of citizenship or the ability to leave.

World War I through the Great Depression

Although economic trouble marked the years 1907 and 1921, when immigrants were blamed for many of the problems, Mexican immigrants were generally welcomed into the United States until the 1930s and the Great Depression. Prior to the Depression, U.S. immigration policies were aimed mainly at keeping out Asians and southern and eastern Europeans, while allowing Mexican laborers to immigrate. For example, within a year of the enactment of the most restrictive immigration legislation in U.S. history—the Immigration Act of 1917—the first foreign labor program was initiated.

In response to pressure from agricultural employers in the Southwest, Congress included provisions in the law that allowed entry into the United States of "temporary" workers who would otherwise be inadmissible under the Act. This temporary worker—*bracero*—program was enacted for the duration of World War I and was extended until 1922, four years after the war ended. Although this program did not include the Mexican government's proposals to guarantee the contracts of immigrant workers as did later bracero agreements, it was the blueprint upon which later programs were based.

After the Depression began, Latinos found themselves unemployed and unwanted. Jobs that Latinos had been doing for years were no longer available or were performed by Anglos who were forced to resort to that type of labor. Because Latinos were historically ill-paid, many had little or no financial reserves and no choice but to go on welfare or other relief programs. Because of the Depression, Mexican workers and immigrants were no longer welcomed. In fact, they were so unpopular that many were driven from the country. For example, Latinos in Oklahoma were threatened with being burned out of their homes, in Indiana a mob forced railworkers to "give up their jobs," and in Texas signs were displayed warning Mexicans to get out of town.[2]

As the Depression lingered and county, state, and federal budgets dwindled, governments sought ways to cut welfare costs. One method used was to deny welfare benefits to Mexican laborers. This action, labeled "fair and humane" by government agents, was a move to reduce the labor surplus and at the same time to reduce welfare rolls.[3] No longer welcome in the United States, and with no way to sustain themselves, many Mexicans began a mass exodus to Mexico.

The Mexican migration was heralded by governments of various jurisdictions. They decided to expedite this process by sending lawful resident Mexican workers back to Mexico rather than carry them on the public welfare rolls; however, this decision was problematic for a variety of reasons. Legally, to expel Mexicans from the United States was as costly as keeping them afloat when their funds were depleted. Consequently, instead of using costly legal maneuvers such as public hearings and formal deportation proceedings, social workers resorted to betraying Mexicans by telling officials that they wanted to return to Mexico. This duplicitous tactic, of course, lowered the cost of expulsion considerably. It also, however, effectively deprived many of due process.

This treachery continued throughout the Depression. Tragically, some, if not most, of the repatriated Latinos were lawful permanent residents who had lived in the United States for decades, establishing homes and roots. Another result of repatriation was that many families were separated. In some instances, either one or both parents was an "alien," but children, having been born and raised in the United States, were American citizens. In some cases, the children were allowed to stay in the United States while their parents were repatriated, but in many other cases such U.S. citizens were themselves repatriated. By the end of the Depression, over 400,000 Latinos —including thousands of American citizens—were repatriated to Mexico without any formal deportation proceedings.

These repatriation programs naturally sparked protest from the Mexican government. In response, the Los Angeles Chamber of Commerce issued a statement assuring Mexican authorities that the city was in no sense unfriendly to Mexican labor. It insisted further that the repatriation policy was designed solely to help the destitute. This was supposedly the case when invalids were removed from County Hospital in Los Angeles and shipped across the border.

World War II and the Bracero Program

When the Great Depression ended at the onset of World War II, so did the labor surplus the Depression had created. Agricultural growers in the Southwest, however, began as early as 1940 to petition agencies of the United States for permission to use foreign labor to fill shortages, a precedent established during World War I. Shortly after Mexico declared war on the Axis powers on June 1, 1942, the U.S. Department of State contacted the Mexican government about the importation of labor. Mexico doubted that the labor shortage really existed and viewed the efforts of the State Department as a way of obtaining cheap labor.

Cognizant of the deportation and repatriation of Latinos during the Great Depression, the Mexican government, to protect its citizens from harsh treatment and discrimination, entered into a formal agreement with the United States. This protection was provided by a government-to-government accord signed on July 23, 1942. The Mexican Labor Program, or the Bracero Program as it is more commonly known, was first implemented on August 4, 1942, and was funded by the U.S. President's emergency fund. The program was renewed on April 26, 1943.

Under the bracero agreement, Mexico would permit its citizens to work in the United States for temporary, renewable periods under agreed-upon conditions. The conditions stipulated methods of recruitment, transportation, standards of health care, wages, housing, food, and the number of hours the braceros were allowed to work. Discrimination against braceros was prohibited. A violation of these conditions was supposed to have resulted in the suspension of braceros' availability for the violating area. Unfortunately, the terms were, for the most part, ignored by both the growers and the U.S. government; thus, migrant laborers were subjected to most oppressive working environments.

Braceros across the country were compelled to endure poor food, excessive charges for board, substandard housing, discrimination, physical mistreatment, inappropriate deductions from their wages, and exposure to pesticides and other dangerous chemicals. Although Texas was not the only state that violated the conditions of the agreement, discrimination toward braceros there was so bad that Texas lost its privilege to utilize bracero labor until after the war.

The upshot of the Bracero Program was that the U.S. government provided growers with cheap labor. Agricultural growers preferred hiring braceros to American citizens for two reasons. Growers were able to set the wages that would be paid braceros instead of basing their remuneration on the principle of supply and demand or on collective bargaining agreements. Further, braceros tended to be males who traveled alone, while Americans had their families with them, thus making it easier to provide transportation and housing for braceros.

A secondary effect of the Bracero Program was that it provided the United States with soldiers to fight the war. Although braceros were initially brought in to replace Japanese Americans who were sent to internment camps and Americans who went into the armed services or the defense industry, braceros additionally freed up many Mexican Americans for the armed services. Deferments were given to those who held defense industry jobs, few of whom were Mexican American, while workers in the agricultural industry, heavily staffed by Mexican Americans, were eligible for the draft. In short, Mexican Americans in the agricultural industry were sent off to the war while braceros were imported to replace them.

While in the armed forces, Latinos distinguished themselves as fierce and reliable soldiers. Throughout World War II, no Latino soldier was ever charged with desertion, treason, or cowardice. The bravery of Latino troops was recognized in the many medals awarded to Mexican Americans, including the Congressional Medal of Honor (the United States' highest honor), the Silver Star, the Bronze Star, and the Distinguished Service Cross. Seventeen Mexican Americans received the Congressional Medal of Honor for action in World War II and Korea. These seventeen Latino soldiers represent the highest proportion of Medal of Honor winners of any identifiable ethnic group. Because Mexican Americans seem to have gravitated to the most dangerous sections of the armed forces, they were overrepresented on military casualty lists.

Ironically, when the Mexican American soldiers returned home, they were treated no better than they had been before they left. In Texas, a funeral parlor in Three Rivers refused to bury Félix Longoria, an American soldier decorated for heroism, because he was of Mexican descent. This obviously racist action sparked a storm of controversy that ended with the intervention of then Texas Senator Lyndon B. Johnson, who secured burial for Longoria in Arlington National Cemetery. Sergeants José Mendoza López and Macario García, each awarded the Congressional Medal of Honor, were refused service in restaurants and diners because of their Mexican heritage.

Sergeant García, however, decided to challenge such discrimination against Latinos. García, after being told that he would not be served because he was a "Mexie," admonished the proprietor to serve him, declaring, "[If I am] good enough to fight your war for you, I'm good enough for you to serve a cup of coffee to." The merchant in charge of the diner refused to serve García and went so far as to attempt physically to remove García from the diner. García defended himself. The altercation ended with the arrival of the police, who sent everyone home and ordered the diner closed for the night. Later, after the incident was recounted over the national news, Sergeant García was arrested and charged with aggravated assault in an attempt by the city to save face.[4]

After the war, American soldiers returned to work, ending the labor shortage. Growers in the agricultural industry were, nonetheless, reluctant to give up bracero labor. Under the influence of agribusiness, Congress kept the program alive. The pressure they brought to bear was not enough to keep the program going on indefinitely, however, and the Bracero Program came to an end in December of 1947. Nonetheless, the use of Mexican labor did not end. For the next nine months after the end of the Bracero Program, while no agreement existed between the United States and Mexico, the number of undocumented workers in the United States increased dramatically. Both governments became concerned with the increase and pushed for renewed labor negotiations These negotiations led to a new bracero agreement in August of 1949. In addition to providing labor to the United States, the new bracero agreement stressed a reduction in the flow of undocumented workers from Mexico and the legalization of undocumented workers already in the United States.

The program resulted in 238,439 undocumented workers being recruited into the work force between 1947 and 1951. Mass legalization ended for two reasons. First, it was ineffective in stemming the tide of undocumented workers coming into the country. Most importantly, the enactment of Public Law 78 on July 12, 1951, in response to the outbreak of the Korean War, created yet another bracero program.

Under the new program, the U.S. Department of Labor was given administrative control of migration and essentially became a labor contractor. Public Law 78 conferred on the Secretary of Labor the responsibility for the certification of the need for the braceros; for authorization of their recruitment in Mexico; for transportation of the braceros to the labor camps; for guaranteeing the terms of their labor contracts; and for setting the prevailing wage. The new agreement also rectified some problems of the prior versions. The braceros were to enter contracts for periods of time ranging from six weeks to six months instead of year-long contracts. The braceros were also guaranteed work for at least 75 percent of the time for which they had contracted, as well as being paid the wages set by the Secretary of Labor.

From the Korean War to "Operation Wetback"

Public Law 78 did not stem the tide of undocumented workers. Indeed, immigration authorities started finding undocumented workers in industrial jobs, causing labor unions to proclaim undocumented traffic as destructive to their welfare. As a result of these complaints, on June 17, 1954, Herbert Brownell, Jr., the U.S. Attorney General, ordered a crackdown on illegal immigration and a massive deportation drive, "Operation Wetback."

This crackdown on illegal immigration and the ensuing process of deportation were left to the Commissioner of Immigration, Joseph P. Swing. Swing, a retired army general and reputed "professional, long-time Mexican hater," developed "Operation Wetback" along the lines of a military campaign. "Operation Wetback" was a two-fold plan that coordinated the border patrol to prevent undocumented aliens from getting into the United States while rounding up and deporting those who were already here.

"Operation Wetback" went beyond its scope, however, and Americans of Mexican descent were also deported, stirring up memories of the mass deportations of the 1930s. Many of those deported were denied the opportunity to present evidence that would have prevented their deportation. Between 1954 and 1959, "Operation Wetback" was responsible for over 3.7 million Latinos being deported. Of those, an unknown number were American citizens. In the haste to deport "illegals," only 63,500 persons were removed through formal deportation proceedings. The rest of the deportees left the United States "voluntarily."

In addition to violating the civil liberties of American citizens via questionable expulsions, "Operation Wetback" violated the human rights of the people being deported. Deportations were characterized by disrespect, rudeness, and intimidation. Reports even mentioned immigration officers "collecting fares" from persons being deported.

Ironically, the bracero program was in effect while "Operation Wetback" was being executed. Public Law 78 was extended until it finally was allowed to lapse in December of 1964. Although the bracero program was originally intended to be an emergency remedy for labor shortages during World War II, it survived the war by almost twenty years. Further, more braceros were hired in single years after the war than were hired during all of the war years combined.

Modern Labor Programs

Even after the bracero program ended, importation of Mexican labor continued under the McCarran-Walter Immigration Act of 1952. Under the Act, immigrants from Mexico were permanently admitted to the United States to ensure there would be enough laborers. To guarantee there would be a sufficient labor force, the Department of Labor lowered the admission standards for Mexican workers just days before the expiration of Public Law 78 and the Bracero Program.

Although many Mexican citizens were issued visas, or "green cards," that would allow them to live and work in the United States, most preferred to reside in Mexico. Known as commuters because they traversed the border regularly to get to work, these workers maintained the bracero lifestyle by working in the United States for days, weeks, or even months at a time, only to return to Mexico. As well as emulating bracero work patterns, these migrant workers performed similar jobs to the braceros' (i.e., low-skilled or service oriented). In 1977, approximately 1 million Mexican resident aliens lived in the United States, according to the Immigration and Naturalization Service. The actual number of commuters is unknown due to inaccurate records and varying numbers of commuters from day to day.

The McCarran-Walter Act also established a fallback Bracero Program. The "H-2 program" revived all the worst parts of its predecessors. Under the "H-2 program," the U.S. Department of Labor has power to admit foreign labor for temporary jobs if able, willing, and qualified domestic workers cannot be found at the time and place where they are needed.[5] As were workers in the Bracero Program, these migrants are totally dependent on the growers for employment. If the worker proves himself to be hard-working and faithful, he might be asked to return again the following year; if not, he can be deported without an appeal.

In 1986 the United States went through its most recent mass legalization program. The Immigration Reform and Control Act of 1986 (IRCA) gave legal status to undocumented persons who had been in the United States from January 1, 1982, to the time of application (between May 5, 1987, and May 4, 1988). Like the McCarran-Walter Act, the IRCA provided special status to migrant farmworkers. The IRCA offered legal status to special agricultural workers who could prove that they spent at least ninety "man-days" during a qualifying period doing agricultural work on specified crops. The end result of the IRCA was to legalize millions of undocumented workers and fill a labor shortage caused by the most recent immigrant expulsion, "Operation Jobs."

Obtaining Mexican labor has also been accomplished through the exportation of jobs. This phenomenon is euphemistically called the Border Industrialization Program or, as it is more familiarly known, the Maquiladora Program. The program is a system of concessions vis-à-vis Mexico that allows manufacturing and assembly plants or *maquilas* to be located in border towns in Northern Mexico and to export their products directly to the United States. Other concessions granted by Mexico have included exemptions from labor and environmental regulations.

The exemptions granted by Mexico do more than help American companies enter Mexico; they help American companies exploit Mexican labor. The *maquilas* have proven to be a financial success, but only at the expense of Mexican laborers suffering under poor working conditions, inadequate wages, deteriorating environmental conditions, and the inability to take any legal actions against their employers.

NOTES

1. Richard H. Peterson, "Anti-Mexican Nativism in California, 1848–1853: A Study of Cultural Conflict," from *Southern California Quarterly* 62 (1980), reprinted in *Historical Themes and Identity: Mestizaje and Labels* (Antoinette Sedillo López ed.; Garland Publishing, 1995), at 181–92.

2. Francisco E. Balderrama and Raymond Rodríguez, *Decade of Betrayal: Mexican Repatriation in the 1930s* (University of New Mexico Press, 1995), 99.

3. Matt S. Meier and Feliciano Rivera, *Readings on La Raza: The Twentieth Century* (Matt S. Meier and Feliciano Rivera eds.; Hill and Wang, 1974), 79.

4. Harold J. Alford, "War" from *The Proud Peoples: The Heritage and Culture of Spanish-Speaking Peoples in the U.S.*, reprinted in *Readings on La Raza* at 147–49.

5. See U.S.C. § 1101 (a)(15)(H).

Chapter 12

Greasers Go Home
Mexican Immigration, the 1920s

Rodolfo Acuña

Opposition to Mexican immigration crystallized in the 1920s. Reaction toward Mexicans intensified as their numbers became larger. In Mexico road and rail transportation was no longer disrupted by the intense fighting of the revolution. Moreover, prices in Mexico rose 300 percent faster than wages. They corresponded with a labor shortage in Colorado, Wyoming, Utah, Iowa, and Nebraska in 1920 that resulted in the heavy importation of Mexicans into those states. Industrialists imported Mexicans to work in the mills of Chicago—first as an army of reserve labor and then as strikebreakers. During the 1919–1920 and 1920–1921 seasons the Arizona Growers Association spent $325,000 recruiting and transporting Mexicans to cotton areas.

Suddenly in early 1921 the bottom fell out of the economy and a depression caused heavy unemployment. If in times of prosperity their numbers had generated hostility, in time of crisis Mexicans became the scapegoats for the failure of the U.S. economy. The corporate interests which had recruited Mexicans felt little responsibility to them and these capitalists left thousands of Mexicans throughout the country stranded and destitute. In Arizona, although transportation fees had been deducted from the pay of Mexican workers, growers did not give them return passage. *El Universal* of Mexico City on March 5, 1921, reported: "When they arrived at Phoenix a party of Mexican workers were taken to Tempe and introduced to a concentration camp that looks like a dung-heap." According to this source the men were chained and put into work parties. The situation was repeated in Kansas City, Chicago, and Colorado.

In Fort Worth, Texas, 90 percent of 12,000 Mexicans were unemployed; whites threatened to burn out Mexicans and rid the city of "cheap Mexican labor." Truckloads of Mexicans were escorted to Texas chain gangs. In Ranger, Texas, terrorists dragged a hundred Mexican men, women, and children from their tents and makeshift homes, beat them, and ordered them to clear out of town. In Chicago, employ-

Pp. 185–89 from Occupied America: A History of Chicanos, 3d ed., by Rodolfo Acuña. Reprinted by permission of Addison-Wesley Educational Publishers, Inc.

ment of Mexicans shrank by two-thirds between 1920 and 1921. Police made frequent raids and strictly enforced vagrancy laws. Conditions grew so bad that Mayor William Hall Thompson allocated funds to ship several hundred families back to the border. The *Denver Post* headlined "Denver Safety Is Menaced by 3,500 Starving Mexicans." Mexican workers from the Denver area were shipped to the border. Although these workers had been recruited to the United States, the U.S. government did little to ameliorate their sufferings. The Mexican government, in contrast, spent $2.5 million to aid stranded Mexicans.[1] Many workers would have starved if it had not been for Mexican President Alvaro Obregón.

Nativist efforts to restrict the entry of southern and eastern Europeans bore fruit with the passage of the Immigration Act of 1921. Many wanted to include Mexicans in the provisions of the act, but Congress felt that the opposition of agribusiness to their inclusion might block passage of the bill. The 1921 act was generally considered too lenient. Nativists replaced it three years later with a permanent quota act that excluded most Asians and drastically cut the flow from southern and eastern Europe, identified as "racially inferior Europe." The act started a battle between the restrictionists, who wanted to keep the country "Anglo-American" and felt too many foreigners would subvert the "American way of life," and the capitalists, who set aside prejudices for low-cost labor, remembering that the 1917 act had hurt them financially. They opposed any restrictions on the free flow of Mexicans to the United States, especially since the supply of European labor was cut.

In 1923, the commissioner of immigration turned his attention more fully to Mexicans: "It is difficult, in fact impossible, to measure the illegal influx of Mexicans crossing the border." By 1923, the economy had sufficiently recovered to entice Mexican workers to the United States in large numbers again.

This "legal" migration was accompanied by an avalanche of undocumented workers who were encouraged to avoid the head tax as well as visa charges by U.S. employers and government authorities. The new migration differed from that of earlier years, becoming more permanent. Permanency and large numbers of Mexicans alarmed nativists, who deplored the fact that the Johnson bill, which later became the Immigration Act of 1924, did not limit Mexicans. Debate over the issue of Mexican immigration was heated in both houses of Congress. The decision to exclude Mexicans from the quota was a matter of political opportunism. Albert Johnson of Washington, chairman of the House Immigration and Naturalization Committee and sponsor of the bill, bluntly stated that the committee did not restrict the Mexicans because it did not want to hinder the passage of the 1924 Immigration Act. Johnson promised that the committee would sponsor another bill to create a border patrol to enforce existing laws, and he claimed that a quota alone would not be effective. Representative John E. Raker of California seconded Johnson, and he saw no need for further legislation to restrict Mexicans. Raker felt that enforcement of existing laws would cut their numbers to a thousand annually, by ending the employers' practice of paying the head tax for them and by excluding illiterates (according to Raker, "from 75 to 90 percent of all Mexicans in Mexico are illiterate").

Nativists were not convinced. Secretary of Labor James J. Davis called for a quota for the Western Hemisphere. He was alarmed that Mexican labor had infiltrated into

U.S. industries such as iron and steel and arranged meetings with Samuel Gompers to plan a strategy to remove this "menace." Representative Martin Madden of Chicago, chairman of the House Appropriations Committee, stated, "The bill opens the doors for perhaps the worst element that comes into the United States—the Mexican *peon*. . . . [It] opens the door wide and unrestricted to the most undesirable people who come under the flag."[2] Representative John O. Box of Jacksonville, Texas, a former Cherokee county judge and ordained Methodist minister, seconded Madden and demanded a 2 percent quota for Mexicans based on the 1890 population as well as additional funds for its enforcement. Box supported an amendment to put only Mexico on a quota basis, exempting the rest of the nations in the Western Hemisphere. The Johnson bill, however, passed the House without the proposed amendment.

In the U.S. Senate, Frank B. Willis of Ohio echoed restrictionist sentiment: "Many of [them] . . . now coming in are, unfortunately, practically without education, and largely without experience in self-government, and in most cases not at all qualified for present citizenship or for assimilation into this country."[3] Senator Matthew M. Neeley of West Virginia charged: "On the basis of merit, Mexico is the last country we should grant a special favor or extend a peculiar privilege. . . . [T]he immigrants from many of the countries of Europe have more in common with us than the Mexicanos have."[4]

Antirestrictionists argued that it would be difficult to enforce such a quota, that Mexicans stayed only temporarily anyway, that they did work white men would not, and that an economic burden would result. However, the argument of Pan-Americanism proved to be the most effective. Many senators supported Pan-Americanism as a vehicle for establishing the political and economic dominance of the United States over Latin America. Senator Holm Bursum of New Mexico stated that he did not favor disrupting Pan-Americanism, that Mexico was sparsely populated anyway, and "so far as absorbing the Mexican population . . . that is the merest rot."[5]

In 1924, hostility to Mexican immigration peaked. Although border officials strictly applied the $8 head tax, plus the $10 visa fee, Mexicans still entered with and without documents. Johnson's committee, true to its promise, began hearings on the Mexican problem. Reports of the commissioner of immigration underscored that *peones* benefited from the reduction of European immigrants. In 1926, the commissioner wrote that 855,898 Mexicans entered with documents and predicted, "It is safe to say that over a million Mexicans are in the United States at the present time [including undocumented], and under present laws this number may be added to practically without limit."[6]

An open fight broke out in Congress in 1926. Restrictionists introduced two bills. The bill proposed by John Box simply sought to apply quota provisions to the whole Western Hemisphere; the other bill, sponsored by Robert L. Bacon of New York, sought to apply them only to Mexico. The Box bill emerged as the main one before the House. Western representatives opposed any attempt to restrict Mexicans. S. Parker Frieselle of California stated that he did not want California based upon a Mexican foundation: There is nothing else available to us.[7]

Representative John Nance Garner of Texas emphasized that Mexicans returned home after the picking seasons:

> All they want is a month's labor in the United States, and that is enough to support them in Mexico for six months. . . . In our country they do not cause any trouble, unless they stay there a long time and become Americanized; but they are a docile people. They can be imposed on; the sheriff can go out and make them do anything.[8]

In the end, both the restrictionists and the antirestrictionists displayed nativist and racist attitudes. The antirestrictionists wanted an open border because they needed Mexican labor. Box candidly accused opponents of his bill of attempting to attract only the "floating Mexican *peons*" for the purpose of exploiting them, charging that "they are to be imported in trainloads and delivered to farmers who have contracted to grow beets for the sugar companies." Box stated, "They are objectionable as citizens and as residents."[9] During committee hearings, Box questioned a farmer as to whether what the farmer really wanted was a subservient class of Mexican workers "who do not want to own land, who can be directed by men in the upper stratum of society." The farmer answered. "I believe that is about it." Box then asked, "Now, do you believe that is good Americanism?" The farmer replied, "I think it is necessary Americanism to preserve Americanism."[10] The quota act had drastically reduced the available labor pool and agricultural and industrial interests committed themselves to keeping the Mexican unrestricted.

In 1928, the commissioner general of immigration recommended "that natives of countries of the Western Hemisphere be brought within the quota provisions of existing law." The commissioner specifically recommended restriction of Mexicans, stating, "The unlimited flow of immigrants from the Western Hemisphere cannot be reconciled with the sharp curtailment of immigration from Europe."[11] A definite split developed between the Department of Labor, which favored putting Mexicans on a quota system, and the Department of State, which opposed it because the State Department knew that such action would seriously weaken its negotiations with Latin America concerning economic trade treaties and privileges for Anglo-American interests. Anglo-American racism was a sensitive area. Placing Mexicans on a quota would be a legal affirmation of discrimination toward all Latin Americans. State Department officials were involved in sensitive negotiations with Mexican officials, who threatened to expropriate Anglo-American oil. The State Department, representing Anglo-American foreign investors and exporters, joined southwestern industrialists to kill restrictionist measures. They attempted to sidetrack debates, and for a time congressional debate centered around enforcement of existing immigration laws. Many members of Congress were not satisfied and pushed for quantitative restrictions. Anglo-American labor supported the restrictionists, and questioned, "Do you want a mongrel population, consisting largely of Mexicans?"[12]

Growers and other industrialists joined forces with the departments of State, Agriculture, and Interior and formed a solid front to overwhelm restrictionists, heading off the passage of a bill placing Mexicans on a quota. By 1929, conditions changed, lessening Mexicans migration to the United States.

Between the turn of the century and the Great Depression, approximately one-tenth of Mexico's population shifted "north from Mexico," in one of the largest mass migrations of people in the history of the world. This movement occurred during a period of great economic and social development which saw the industrialization of the Southwest, the demise of the small farmers, a world war, recessions, and depression. Mechanization and urbanization in the Southwest required cheap labor, which became less abundant as nativist sentiment completely shut off the flow of workers from Asia and drastically limited European immigration. The reception Mexicans received was mixed. Lower- and middle-class Anglo-Americans blamed them for the disorganization of society, which was in fact caused by the restructuring of industry; in contrast, industrialists, rural and urban, saw Mexicans as necessary for building the Southwest.

Mexican workers came to the United States both because of conditions in their homeland and the increased demand for labor in northern Mexico and the United States. For the first decade of the twentieth century, Mexican labor was concentrated in the Southwest. However, World War I and the immigration acts of 1917, 1921, and 1924 drastically limited European immigration, intensifying a demand for Mexicans and Blacks in the Midwest. The flow of Mexicans followed the railroads and the expanding sugar beet industry. Stepped-up production, at the same time, forced labor agents in the Southwest to recruit Mexican labor south of the Rio Bravo even more aggressively.

Mexicans were divided into political, economic, and religious refugees. Those who came before the Mexican Revolution were protesting the dictator Porfirio Díaz and his modernization of Mexico at the expense of political liberties. Many of these refugees offered leadership to the masses of Mexicans who began to flood into the United States at the turn of the century in response to economic conditions in the United States. Perceiving the racism and exploitation of these workers, they used their newspapers to document numerous stories of injustice; they became the vanguard of labor militancy. Many refugees coming to the United States after the revolution were from the middle and upper classes. Those arriving in the 1910s were political exiles, while emigrants in the 1920s were religious refugees. Both groups, although concerned about racism, opposed any type of radical solution.

At the turn of the century, Mexicans overwhelmingly worked in rural occupations; by the 1920s, substantial numbers lived in urban centers. During this transition, the Mexicans' responses changed. Those who worked as seasonal migrants found it difficult to organize, since often the workers' community was limited to their immediate families. Uprooted from friends and associates, they were constantly on the move. Once this migration slowed, Mexicans formed temporary associations, usually *mutualistas,* to solve the most pressing problems. Frequently, Mexican merchants and the consul used these mutual aid societies as a natural vehicle for worker organization. Approaches differed according to the economic conditions in each state or region. In Texas, Mexican Americans formed LULAC (League of United Latin American Citizens), a middle-class and professional group that was committed to the Americanization of Mexicans.

On the eve of the Great Depression, the transition from Mexican to Mexican American manifested itself in the changing character of the new organizations. Mexican American *barrios* now had traceable boundaries. Moreover, the shift from temporary one-issue groups to trade unions and middle-class statewide associations was well underway. The depression would have a dramatic impact on the development of Mexican American organizations, as the nation turned away from the gold standard.

NOTES

1. Lawrence Anthony Cardoso, "Mexican Emigration to the United States, 1900–1930: An Analysis of Socio-Economic Causes" (Ph.D. dissertation, University of Connecticut, 1974), p. 97; Mark Reisler, By the Sweat of their Brow: Mexican Immigrant Labor in the United States, 1900–1940 (Westport, Conn.: Greenwood Press, 1976) pp. 39, 50–51, 53; Mark Reisler, "Passing through Our Egypt: Mexican Labor in the United States, 1900–1940" (Ph.D. dissertation, Cornell University, 1973), pp. 84–85; Paul Morgan and Vince Mayer, "The Spanish-Speaking Population of Utah: From 1900 to 1935" (Working Papers, *Toward a History of the Spanish-Speaking People of Utah*, American West Center, Mexican-American Documentation Project, University of Utah, 1973), pp. 8, 39; *El Universal* quoted in Herbert B. Peterson, *Twentieth-Century Search for Cibola's Post World War I Mexican Labor Exploitation in Arizona*, in Manuel Servin, ed., An Awakening Minority: The Mexican-American, 2nd ed. (Beverly Hills, Calif.: Glencoe Press, 1974), pp. 127–28.

2. U.S. Department of Labor, Annual Report of the Commissioner General of Immigration (Washington, D.C.: Government Printing Office, 1923), p. 16; Reisler, By the Sweat of Their Brow, pp. 55, 66–69; Job West Neal, "The Policy of the United States toward Immigration from Mexico" (Master's thesis, University of Texas at Austin, 1941), pp. 106, 107–8.

3. Quoted in Neal, p. 112.

4. Quoted in Neal, p. 113.

5. Quoted in Neal, p. 117.

6. U.S. Department of Labor, Annual Report of the Commissioner General of Immigration (Washington, D.C.: Government Printing Office, 1926), p. 10.

7. U.S. Congress, House Committee on Immigration and Naturalization, Seasonal Agricultural Laborers from Mexico: Hearing No. 69.1.7 on H.R. 6741, H.R. 7559, H.R. 9036, 69th Cong., 1st sess. (1926), p. 24.

8. U.S. Congress, Seasonal Agricultural Laborers, p. 190.

9. U.S. Congress, Seasonal Agricultural Laborers, p. 325.

10. U.S. Congress, Seasonal Agricultural Laborers, p. 112.

11. U.S. Department of Labor, Annual Report of the Commissioner General of Immigration (Washington, D.C.: Government Printing Office, 1928), p. 29.

12. Quoted in Robert J. Lipshultz, "American Attitudes toward Mexican Immigration, 1924–1952" (Master's thesis, University of Chicago, 1962), p. 61.

Chapter 13

How Much Responsibility Does the U.S. Bear for Undocumented Mexican Migration?

Gerald P. López

Conventional wisdom—informed consensus—applies classical push-pull theory to undocumented Mexican migration. The theory's success has been well-earned in view of its broad utility in explaining world mass migration over the past century. Moreover, data taken in by the informed consensus are mostly accurate. The components seem believable, particularly because their descriptive interaction brings order to what can otherwise appear to be an incomprehensible geo-political jumble. *At the same time that the theory seems to provide an objective explanation for mass migration, it implies that the destination country has a quite limited moral responsibility for the problem.*

Narrow descriptive accuracy is not, for the most part, what distinguishes the informed consensus from the following alternative explanation that sees as critical certain information the informed consensus has overlooked, disregarded or negligibly weighted. The chief distinctions are ones of interpretation.

The great weakness of the informed consensus lies in its central hypothesis that economic disparity is at the source of mass Mexican migration. This position could be translated into a causal relationship: "but for" economic disparity mass undocumented Mexican migration would not occur. This view derives from the obvious observation that economic disparity between the United States and Mexico has always played an important role in contributing to mass migration. Indeed, mass migration in modern times has rarely occurred except where economic disparity has been present.

There have been numerous instances, however, where economic disparity between nations—even adjoining nations—exists but mass migration is absent. In other words, economic disparity is necessary but not sufficient for migration. Certainly this is true of migration from Mexico to the United States. More than one expert has underscored that the same wage differential (13:1) between migrant earning in the United States and average agricultural wage rates in primary Mexican source regions has prevailed since the first decade of this century. In fact, the disparity was probably greater in earlier years. Nevertheless, mass migration from these regions was unknown until later years. Nor does economic disparity account for the pattern of Mexican migration. Primary Mexican source regions for today's undocumented migration are areas that provided labor earlier in this century. Yet the economic disparity between these source regions and the United States is no greater than that existing between numerous other regions in Mexico and this country. Economic disparity hardly accounts for the fact that the great majority of undocumented Mexicans are the strongest, most able-bodied workers who presumably could compete well in the Mexican labor market.

In contrast to conventional push-pull theory, the following hypothesis offers a more complete explanation for migration: *Where there is substantial economic disparity between two adjoining countries and the potential destination country promotes, de jure or de facto, access to its substantially superior minimal wage, that promotion encourages migrants reasonably to rely on the continuing possibility of migration, employment, and residence, until a competitive economic alternative is made available in the source country.* Substantial migration from Mexico did not begin until the United States urged and encouraged Mexican workers to fill lower echelon jobs in this country. The now discernible pattern of emigration from certain source regions coincides almost perfectly with active American promotion in those regions. The curious near-exclusivity of young males among all migrant groups is understandable when one fixes on the fact that promotional effort, particularly until recent years, sought only their services. . . .

[The author reviews over one hundred years of U.S. recruitment and solicitation of Mexican workers to show how the U.S. has induced Mexican villages to send young workers to the United States for temporary employment. After documenting how we have created this reliance by formal and informal means, he turns to the other side of the equation—*Eds.*]

The Decision-Making Calculus

It is also necessary to examine whether the decision to migrate is, as much thinking about undocumented Mexican migration assumes, an individual economic calculation. Identifying the actual decision-making unit as the household rather than the individual allows examination of the effect of migration on the household unit and the influence that unit extends on the migrant's aspirations in the United States.

Even so perceptive a commentator as Professor Wayne Cornelius has written that the migratory phenomenon can be understood by taking the rational decision making of the individual as the point of departure: "For most [Mexican migrants] the decision to go to the U.S. is an eminently rational one, in terms of differential economic returns to one's labor, as well as the high probability of finding a job in the U.S."[1] Although most evidence supports Cornelius's assertion that the decision, at least in part, is rational, it disputes his contention that the decision is an individual one. Dedicated field researchers such as Raymond Wiest and Richard Mines argue that the relevant decision-making unit is the household,[2] not the individual. Their conclusion is modern confirmation of the findings of earlier anthropological studies: the household is the appropriate unit for analysis of decisions concerning economic cooperation and production. Despite this early consensus, few studies have subsequently examined the interaction between "wage-labor migration" and the operation of the household unit. Nonetheless, the evidence accumulated by Wiest, Mines, and even Cornelius strongly supports the conclusion that the "rational individual" is not a self-contained decision-making unit, but is part of a household that makes decisions according to the demands of its living situation.

Special reasons argue for focusing on the household unit. First, the household decision-making process may differ markedly from an individual one; the difference bears heavily on the issues of aspirational evolution. For instance, it is far more persuasive to hypothesize that values undergo inevitable change sufficient to predict permanent undocumented relocation if the migrant worker is responsible for his own needs and not those of an economic unit beyond himself than if he is a member of a household unit and responsible to it. To emphasize the importance of the household unit is not to deny that some unmarried young men, and even some married men, migrate for primarily individual reasons. It is also not to deny that some migrant workers begin to operate, after awhile, according to individual needs rather than the needs of the household unit that may have initially dictated their temporary migration. These, however, are not the "normal" cases; even the evidence gathered by Cornelius confirms this fact.

Care in identifying the proper unit of economic decision making is also important if we are to determine, in Mines's terminology, the "retentive capability" of the source village.[3] That is, to understand the possibilities for dissuading undocumented migrant workers from leaving their source villages or, from another angle, to determine what must be done to encourage their remaining at home, we must understand the true decision-making process.

Finally, any culturally sensitive theory must select the appropriate decision-making unit. The simple fact is that Mexico's agricultural society, which still provides the bulk of undocumented workers, has long been characterized by close family ties and a communal struggle to survive. The typical household is perennially in danger of being unable to subsist and of disintegration. All working members of the family cooperate to insure the two essential conditions of household survival: adequate income and adequate composition to permit fulfillment of domestic functions (including child care). All members become committed to the notion of shared obligation within the household unit and to the overriding importance of subordinating individual desires to the extent necessary to perpetuate the household. Initially the older generation provides for the younger; in short time the obligation is shared. Finally, the generations' roles are reversed and with the arrival of the next generation the cycle repeats itself. Centuries of economic loyalty to one's household have transformed what was once essentially an economic decision into an entrenched cultural principle.

Adequate income has always been the most difficult of the two conditions of survival to insure. Households in agricultural Mexico traditionally pursued a variety of income-producing activities; dangerous as generalizations are, it is probably accurate to conclude that a household's most dependable means of producing more income to restore equilibrium was stepped-up agricultural production. Other means of intensifying the household effort were explored but inevitably proved unreliable.

Although intensification of agricultural production was the best means of augmenting income, it was at the same time a dangerous and limited solution because of short-term catastrophes, crude productive techniques, and shortages of cultivable land. These combined obstacles to income production often threatened to disintegrate agricultural households.

Access to a relatively superior wage structure in the United States created an opportunity to avoid household disintegration by selling male labor. For some households, particularly the landless, this new alternative may have been perceived as the only possibility for survival. From the beginning, the male head was selected by the household to migrate temporarily to the United States to earn badly needed income. In part, the male was chosen because he was the object of American promotion; the household also felt it was the role of the husband-father to make the arduous sacrifice.

In his absence, the household adjusted. Domestic functions—daily logistics and socialization of young family members—became the mother's primary responsibility. The more important adjustment, in terms of cultural acceptance of wage-labor migration, was that the contributing father retained his status as the head of the household. As long as his absences were temporary and associated with remittances, the husband-father's place was secure and unthreatened. In effect, the household adjusted to endure wage-labor migration as a necessity, but insisted that it be only temporary in nature.

The recurring nature of the temporary migrations was likely unforeseeable, and certainly undesirable from the household's point of view. Struggling to maintain equilibrium, households found themselves repeatedly sending their men to the United States far more often than would have been hoped by those who left and those who remained at home. Moreover, the process began to feed on itself, becoming, almost imperceptibly, institutionalized. Not only did experienced households begin to rely regularly and predictably on temporary migration, but new and different households began to perceive temporary wage-labor migration as the dominant emerging alternative during periods of economic crisis.

Vague promotional promises were given weight by the return of "wealthy" migrants, men able to provide monetary support out of line with their previous domestic endeavors and capable of relating tales, often exaggerated by "locker room" boastfulness. Word spread that, if a household needed income, relatively superior wages were available for the price of temporary migration to the United States. From the beginning, the persistence of household disequilibrium in the agricultural areas of Mexico and heightened awareness of the continuing availability of wage-producing labor opportunities in the United States ensured a dependable and ballooning response to the wage-labor migration market.

Since 1940, survival of the household has been further endangered by Mexico's extraordinary population growth. Population growth may be able to be matched by increases in arable land, but to date these lands have gone predominantly to Mexico's large landholders who have tended toward machine-intensive and not labor-intensive development if, in fact, they develop the land at all. As a result there is an excess of population relative to cultivable land and the number of nonagricultural employment opportunities. Thus the landless rural working class and *ejidatarios*[4] have been reduced to an almost perpetually marginal economic status and forced to turn to wage-labor migration as a means of insuring household survival.

Most researchers agree that even if the population growth were controlled, the present wage disparity between Mexico and the United States would result in mass wage-labor migration. Holding other factors constant, it appears that wage disparity determines the absolute number of undocumented migrants. The critical variable is, somewhat surprisingly, not the American but the Mexican wage. When American wages have gone up, the rate of undocumented migration remains unaffected, and when Mexican wages have decreased, migration has increased. Other studies tend to support this conclusion with data tying rates of undocumented migration to Mexican agricultural productivity, commodity prices, and farm wages.

This observation about economic conditions in Mexico, combined with the earlier description of the typical Mexican household, leads to the hypothesis that the decision to migrate for wage labor remains a function of household equilibrium. If, as a result of a decrease in Mexican wages, the household's income falls below subsistence level, the household will be sufficiently "economically motivated" to send one or more of its members to the United States to help earn income from wage labor necessary to maintain the household in Mexico.

This hypothesis is supported by the characteristics of the modern undocumented Mexican. These characteristics remain remarkably similar to those that might have been compiled in the 1880s. Although in recent years there has been an increasing number of older men, the majority of migrants are and have long been young men (between twenty-two and thirty) who are usually uneducated (less than three years). Young women seldom have migrated except with a family (an unusual occurrence) or to join a male who has already established permanent residence in the United States. A majority of undocumented migrants are married but, according to one study, fewer than 1 percent are ever accompanied by their wives. Most come from rural areas, though small towns and larger cities still contribute their share. Although an increasing number claim an urban residence, most are actually arriving in the United States at the end of a two- or three-leg migration from a rural area. While many have held temporary urban jobs, a majority continue to have substantial ties to households in a rural area. It appears that whenever the household is sufficiently motivated, it is still considered the duty of the man to migrate and the duty of the woman to assume a disproportionate share of the domestic obligation during periods of absence.

The evidence of recent years has made increasingly apparent both the extent and permanence of the reliance on employment in the United States. Professor Cornelius reports that 49 percent of those who, since 1969, migrated illegally from one long-established source village also had fathers who had previously worked in the United States, primarily in the Bracero Program. Eighty-seven percent of these same undocumented workers also had brothers or sisters who had previously migrated for wage labor. Forty-three percent of the married undocumented workers since 1969 also had one or more children who had worked in the United States. Finally, fully 62 percent of the families in Cornelius's study had members of at least two generations simultaneously going to the United States.

The likelihood that this near-permanent reliance will change anytime soon seems remote. Richard Mines's study of Las Animas, a long-time and prototypical source pueblo in the central plateau state of Zacatecas, is illustrative. An analysis of pueblo sources of disposable income revealed that, on the average, fully 60 percent of each household's income was annually derived from wages earned in the United States.

Even destination patterns for wage-labor migrants reflect the household's increasing reliance on the American wage. Professor Wiest's study of Mexican households indicates that husband-fathers working in the United States contribute a relatively high percentage of household income; these men return predictably to the household, continuing their traditional role in the domestic scheme despite their absences. In contrast, husband-fathers migrating within Mexico usually provide only a supplementary source of income, alone insufficient for household survival; these men tend to return much less predictably and to play a far reduced role in the household.

Economically inefficient and unreliable internal wage-labor migration constitutes a genuine threat to the husband-father's traditional status. Given this fact, growing reliance on wage-labor migration to the United States, as evidenced by recent destination patterns, may be seen as the household's judicious attachment to what it perceives as the best available alternative for its economic and cultural survival. Wage-labor migration, which began as a temporary means for restoring household equilibrium, has apparently become the primary source of income for the landless and *ejidatarios* in rural Mexico.

Thus, while households now rely on wage-labor migration as an economic necessity, they nonetheless view migration as a "temporary crutch." However conscious they are of their dependence, most household members still dream that something, most often the superior American wage, will enable them to permanently terminate participation in the migration cycle. Most migrant workers intend to retire to their village in Mexico when they are done with wage labor in the United States. Interestingly, one study indicates that even if offered permanent status in the United States, most Mexicans would still rather live in Mexico and temporarily migrate for wage labor.

The persistent cyclical and temporary character of undocumented migration is additional evidence that the more significant evolution is not "aspirational" but reliant in nature. Despite years of continual contact, most Mexican migrants remain uninterested in permanent relocation. Although migration has raised many migrants' economic expectations, most remain part of a household that wants nothing more than to remain together, to survive *in* Mexico.

The present predicament tests, in many ways, our capacity and will to meet the just expectations that we have generated, to admit the truth and to accept our responsibilities. What we did in the past and even now is related to what we will decide is the decent thing to do in the future. We cannot wish away past and present hypocrisy; nor should we want to if we appreciate the very nature of a political community that is even minimally just. It may be true that national boundaries and documented status can define, and indeed may once have defined, the limits of our moral obligations. But our experience with undocumented Mexican workers is fundamentally inconsistent with that comfortable and reflex-like moral posture. If we are not accountable for the present condition of undocumented Mexican workers, we are at least responsible for the commitment implicit in our long-standing relationship. If involvement and neighborhood matter, undocumented Mexican workers are part of the living and working community. They are we.

Facts cannot be ignored even by those who reject (if in fact they even consider) fundamental moral obligations. Mexican households seem to have, and certainly perceive, no short-term means of economic survival without continued access to our labor market. If, as it appears, Mexicans cannot humanely be dissuaded from coming, some form of access must be legislatively accommodated or they will simply continue to come and to work outside the boundaries of the law. The available evidence suggests that while risks and costs to present documented residents of legalized access for undocumented Mexican workers are potentially substantial, they are dwarfed by those that accompany other responses. For those who reject any moral obligation, the most compelling reason for legalizing access may well be the predictable cost of failing to do so. Selfish pragmatists may be forced to admit that legalized access encompasses, even from their perspective, the most sober, mutually advantageous and least costly short- or middle-term response to a profoundly tense and complicated dilemma.

NOTES

1. Wayne A. Cornelius, Mexican Migration to the United States: The View from Rural Sending Communities 3 (June 1976) (unpublished monograph, Center for Int'l Studies, Cambridge, Mass.).

2. Raymond Wiest, *Wage-Labor Migration and the Household in a Mexican Town*, 29 J. Anthro. R. 180, 187 (1973); Richard Mines, *The Workers of Las Animas: A Case Study of Village Migration to California*, 15 (May 1978) (unpublished research essay in Giannini Foundation of Agricultural Economics Library).

3. Mines, at 2.

4. *Ejidatarios* are those who received, under Mexico's agrarian reform program, small plots of community-owned land *(ejidos)*.

Chapter 14

Undocumented Immigrants and the National Imagination

Linda S. Bosniak

Among the many bruising battles engendered by the recent immigration wars in this country, the battle over California's Proposition 187 has touched an exceptionally deep nerve. Approved by the state's voters in 1994, this "anti–illegal alien initiative" will deny health care, education, and other public services to undocumented immigrants and require social service providers to report any service user they suspect of undocumented status. Support for Prop. 187—and now for its progeny in other states—has been wide and deep; in fact, these measures have served to mobilize reserves of mass disaffection with immigration, the likes of which have not been seen for decades. Despite the substantial popularity of such measures, however, political liberals and progressives have almost uniformly opposed them, finding them wrong-headed as a matter of policy, and offensive as well. Prop. 187 has become, for its critics, a symbol of the excesses of the current wave of anti-immigrant anxiety, and shorthand for a dangerous politics of ressentiment.

Much has been said elsewhere about the nature of the Prop. 187 enterprise, including the nature of the support it received. My concern in this chapter is, instead, with those very critics. The question I want to examine is this: What is the basis for the deeply felt antipathy toward Prop. 187 and similar restrictionist efforts among the initiative's opponents? What, precisely, do the critics understand to be wrong with Prop. 187? And how far does their aversion to such measures extend?

During the course of the "No on 187" campaign, activists set forth a variety of objections to the proposed initiative. Sometimes, the organizations that worked against it disagreed over how to articulate the arguments; their divisions were often divisions over strategy, though at times they diverged over principle as well. But in the end, the opposition's message was fairly consistent in outline, and was comprised of three principal claims.

The first was that Prop. 187 is objectionable because it is racist or xenophobic. In its most trenchant form, the racism argument charged that supporters of Prop. 187

From "Opposing Prop. 187: Undocumented Immigrants and the National Imagination." 28 Conn. L. Rev. 555 (1996). Originally published in the *Connecticut Law Review*. Reprinted by permission.

are motivated by animus against the growing population of Latinos in California, Mexicans in particular; it also charged that the initiative's "reporting requirements" will allow for a widespread campaign of racial harassment against people of color in the state. A "softer" version of the argument emphasized that ethnic minorities in the state will be affected disproportionately by the measure, since social service providers will often wrongly assume that people of color are undocumented; it further stressed that the initiative's terms will create the perception, if not the reality, of racial scapegoating, thereby fanning flames of ethnic strife in the state. Either by design or inadvertence, therefore, Prop. 187's measures will make California a less hospitable place for its minority population.

The racism critique is clearly powerful and indispensable; there is simply no way to address Prop. 187 without recognizing its deep complicity with a politics of racial anxiety in this country—and many Californians no doubt recognized as much. But despite its importance, this argument only goes so far. For as it turned out, African-Americans and Asians ended up voting for Prop. 187 in surprisingly large numbers, and the Hispanic vote in favor was substantial as well.[1] The likely reason for such broad-based minority support is that it formally targets only one relatively small segment of the immigrant population—that is, immigrants without legal immigration papers, or the undocumented. Most voters in the state, including minority voters, apparently saw the initiative less as a referendum on ethnic relations than as a response to the illegal immigration status of one specific group of newcomers and voted accordingly.

The "illegality" issue lay at the heart of the pro-187 message. Supporters promoted the initiative, in instrumental terms, as a sure-fire method of controlling undocumented immigration; the claim was that undocumented immigrants come to this country in order to obtain social benefits, so that making those benefits unavailable will deter people from coming in the first place—or will induce those who are here to go home. They also promoted the initiative as a much needed method for preventing an outlaw population from brazenly robbing Californians of their hard-earned tax-dollars. As the initiative's sponsoring organization, "Save Our State" (or S.O.S.) put it, "it's time to stop rewarding illegals for successfully breaking our laws."[2] Given the resonance of these arguments for many people in the state, opponents of Prop. 187 had to go beyond a critique of the initiative on grounds of racism to address the specific anxiety over illegal immigration promoted by the "Yes" campaign.

Opponents, therefore, set out two additional arguments against the initiative, each of which addressed the illegal immigration issue directly. First, opponents sought to refute supporters' instrumental claim that denial of social benefits to the undocumented will serve as an effective method of *immigration control*. Opponents produced data showing that undocumented immigrants come to this country not to avail themselves of public medical services and public education but to work and to join their families. According to this "no deterrence" argument, Prop. 187 won't do what it is ostensibly meant to do, which is to control unauthorized immigration.

Second, opponents of Prop. 187 made the consequentialist argument that, far from solving the state's social problems, the initiative would lead to frightening *so-*

cial pathologies for the people of California. They contended, for example, that to impose illiteracy on a class of children in the state will only undermine both the economy and the democratic fabric of society. Similarly, they pointed out, people afraid to go to the doctor will simply create the conditions for a public health catastrophe and will end up costing the state more money later on.

Each of these latter arguments against Prop. 187 was important to make because each appears to be correct as a matter of fact. Research on the causes of undocumented immigration indicates that these immigrants come to this country primarily for employment and family reunification purposes, so that denial of social benefits will poorly serve restrictionist objectives.[3]

Despite differences in style and approach among members of the opposition, however, what is striking in retrospect is the relatively narrow range of arguments that were made against Prop. 187 by opponents overall, and the corresponding absence of certain sorts of arguments almost entirely. Especially notable was the near-complete omission from the public debate of one particular opposing argument which might have seemed, in theory, an obvious one to make: that Prop. 187 should be rejected on grounds that its treatment of undocumented immigrants is *unjust*. Prop. 187 is, after all, a law that specifically targets undocumented immigrants for social exile from the most basic institutions of our society; to say that it imposes on them a comprehensive form of legal apartheid is hardly mere hyperbole. One might think that the damaging effect of these measures on their designated objects would be an excellent—and indispensable—ground for political criticism.

Yet during the debate over Prop. 187, such arguments were rarely heard—with only two consistent exceptions. First, church-based organizations often objected to the initiative on grounds that it represented an affront to the immigrants' "human dignity."[4] Second, claims that the initiative treated its designated objects unjustly were heard sometimes on behalf of undocumented children—"innocent children," as they invariably were described, who should not be made to suffer for the sins of their parents. Otherwise, what the public mainly heard—in addition to charges of racism—were empirically-based predictions that the proposed policy provisions would fail to achieve their stated goal, and arguments highlighting the deleterious effects of the law on Americans (or Californians). The former arguments, of course, are not, by their terms, concerned with matters of justice at all, and although the latter arguments address human interests by addressing the law's social consequences, their concern is the law's effect on American well-being. Even the racism argument, which is fundamentally about justice, most often characterized the problem as one in which United States citizens or lawful permanent residents of color would be either maliciously or mistakenly ensnared by the initiative's provisions. The actual referent in the justice-based race argument, in other words, was generally not the undocumented immigrants themselves but a class of nationals and perhaps lawful permanent residents of color who would be (collaterally or directly) harmed by, or in the process of, efforts to crack down on those immigrants.

The obvious question, therefore, is how we can account for the omission of the undocumented immigrant as an explicit subject of concern in most opponents' critiques of the initiative. If the initiative is meant to harm, and will in fact harm, a class of people residing and working in the state, why shouldn't the fact of this harm, both intended and actual, serve as grounds for political criticism?

In the case of many of Prop. 187's mainstream opponents, the reason for the omission is probably straightforward: they presume the moral interests of undocumented immigrants to be largely irrelevant. While these critics are concerned with the initiative's human costs, the ones they worry about are those borne by persons presumed to be members of the American national community. Undocumented immigrants—whose presence in this country, as these critics themselves often emphasized, is in violation of national law—are understood to stand outside that community; and as a result, their interests (beyond those, presumably, in being afforded a minimum of fair procedural treatment) simply don't matter.

For other opponents, however, excising the undocumented and their experience from the "No on 187" message was, I think, more troubling. These latter critics—I will call them the "progressive" critics here—at times wished to make more affirmative arguments on behalf of the undocumented, but they also recognized that an apparently pro-immigrant message would backfire given the current mood. Indeed, since the pro-187 forces had characterized the presence of undocumented immigrants as precisely the problem the initiative would serve to redress, critics considered it good strategy to deflect the debate away from the undocumented, and focus on exposing the flaws in the proponents' own reasoning and methodology. For pragmatic reasons, in other words, they narrowed their arguments.

The effort to oppose Prop. 187 raises the question of how far progressives' articulated commitment to the pursuit of social justice can be understood to extend. Despite the enormous variety of substantive and methodological concerns that characterize contemporary progressive legal and political thought, one of its consistent normative themes has been a commitment to challenging the systematic exclusion and subordination of various classes of people in our society. Progressives variously have championed breaking down boundaries against "outsiders," dismantling hierarchy and subordination, "unmasking" and criticizing the exercise of power, and attending to social "domination and oppression" as integral parts of the struggle for social justice. In so doing, they have urged greater attention to those on the losing end of such processes: to the silent, the marginalized, and those located (in one scholar's evocative phrase) "at the bottom."[5]

Undocumented immigrants would appear, at first glance, to constitute precisely the sort of class that progressives are usually most concerned about. These are people who routinely do much of our society's least desirable work—as dishwashers and janitors and sweatshop operatives and farm laborers and nannies and lawn care workers. While they formally are afforded the minimum rights of personhood under the law, they lie entirely outside the law's protections for many purposes, and they live subject to the fear of deportation at virtually all times. It would be hard to find a group of people who live further at the margins, or closer to "the bottom," than the undocumented.

As a practical matter, however, undocumented immigrants have rarely been treated as explicit subjects of progressives' concern. Outside the relatively small field of immigration law, undocumented immigrants—and noncitizens in general—have been largely absent in the work of progressive legal theorists. Indeed, in writing on exclusion and subordination, one finds little indication that the subject of alienage—or of exclusion on account of alienage—is even on the radar screen; most progressives simply seem to ignore the issue of immigration status altogether. One measure of this inattention can be found in the routine inventories of oppressed or excluded groups that progressive theorists often set out in their work. Martha Minow, for example, writes of progressives' concern in recent years with the exclusion of "women, children, disabled people and members of religious, racial and linguistic minorities," and of "other disfavored groups includ[ing] incarcerated felons, prostitutes, drug addicts, alcoholics, persons with terminal illnesses, and persons with contagious diseases."[6] When the inventories get as specific as this, the omission of noncitizens from the list is striking.

Here is the problem: Despite progressives' commitment to challenging systemic forms of subordination and marginalization, the political and legal landscape they are concerned with is most often a national landscape, and the boundaries they seek to dismantle are, most often, political and legal boundaries that exist within the already bounded community of the nation-state. Most progressive legal scholarship produced in this country devotes nearly exclusive attention to relationships among people who are already presumed to be national community members, and in this work, the nation's boundaries provide the frame for analysis. Sometimes, this frame is made explicit, as when scholars directly invoke the United States or "America" or the constitutional Republic as their community of normative concern. More often, it is entirely unspoken; that the normative world which preoccupies progressives is a national world is apparently so obvious as to require no specific assertion at all. In either case, progressives tend to possess what we might call a "national imagination,"[7] according to which political life is understood to take place in the territorial nation-state, among members of that state. But if the presumptive normative universe in the work of most progressive American scholars is the American national community, then undocumented immigrants, who are nonmembers of the American state by legal definition, present what can only be described as an awkward case.

As it turns out, progressives have assumed as given the existence of national boundaries. And this means they assume that those boundaries can legitimately be enforced against outsiders under at least some circumstances. For a community's boundaries serve to separate those on the inside from those without, and to the extent their existence is understood as an inevitable fact of life, the basis for normative critique is substantially limited.

Progressives' general presumption of the legitimacy of national borders thwarts any efforts they might make on behalf of undocumented immigrants who are already here because, simply stated, it is precisely enforcement of these borders which produces the immigrants' powerlessness here in the first place. The problem is that the sharp divide that progressive thought tends to presume between the national state's border and its interior is more fiction than reality, especially where undocumented immigrants are concerned. National border enforcement does not take place merely at the physical border, and it is not concerned merely with stopping people at the moment of territorial entry. Instead, enforcement of the border occurs wherever gov-

ernment immigration authorities have jurisdiction to enforce the immigration laws—
which in this country is virtually everywhere. And such enforcement is as concerned
with removing from the territory those people who lack legal permission to remain
as it is with preventing their entry in the first place.

This means that undocumented immigrants residing in this country are potentially
subject to government border enforcement in the form of deportation during virtually every moment of their lives. And as a consequence, they are usually reluctant to
avail themselves of any rights they do have for fear of coming to the attention of the
immigration authorities. Even if undocumented immigrants are not specifically denied access to education and health care and other social services, as Prop. 187 and
similar measures would require, and even if they are not penalized for seeking to
avail themselves of these services, the constant threat of deportation will continue to
structure their lives in this country, and will ensure their continued marginalization
and domination. To the extent that the left's acquiescence to national border enforcement allows this, any critique they may advance of Prop. 187 and other such
initiatives is ineffectual at best.

While progressives may forcefully argue, therefore, that subjecting a class of people who live and work among us to exclusion from basic human services—as Prop.
187 and its progeny do—is morally intolerable, they cannot so easily condemn efforts to keep these immigrants out in the first place, nor can they easily advocate for
an end to enforcement of the border against these immigrants altogether. In this respect, undocumented immigrants represent a terribly confounding case for progressives: for these immigrants suffer the kind of social exclusion progressives routinely
deplore, yet at the same time, their exclusion from territory and membership quite
often seems a necessary, if unfortunate, condition of political life as we have both
known and imagined it.

NOTES

1. Fifty-six percent of African-Americans voters and 57 percent of Asian-American voters
reportedly supported the proposition, as did 31 percent of the state's Hispanic voters. *After
Prop. 187: Heading North,* ECONOMIST, Nov. 19, 1994, at 29.

2. S.O.S., Save Our State, California's Illegal Immigration Control Initiative (undated promotional flyer on file with the author); Anna Cekol et al., *Backers of Anti-Illegal Immigrant
Petition Deliver Signatures,* L.A. TIMES, May 17, 1994, at A3.

3. See, e.g., Wayne A. Cornelius et al., *Introduction: The Ambivalent Quest for Immigration Control,* in CONTROLLING IMMIGRATION: A GLOBAL PERSPECTIVE 3, 37 (Wayne A. Cornelius et al.
eds., 1994).

Professor Cornelius has argued elsewhere as follows:

Having spent the past 20 years studying Mexican migrants to California, most of whom
entered illegally, I have yet to encounter a single one for whom getting access to some
tax-supported service was the principle reason for coming here.

In my own studies, as well as those of dozens of other researchers, only 2% to 5%
of would-be migrants or those interviewed on U.S. soil mentioned social services as even
a secondary or contributing factor in their decisions to migrate. In all extant studies, the
availability of higher-paying jobs and family ties with immigrants already living in this

country were the overwhelming incentives. . . . [Furthermore], [i]t is inconceivable that an immigrant family, in many cases containing at least some members who are here legally, a family that is already permanently settled in California, with at least one member of the household regularly employed, would pack up and return to a place where they have no viable economic options and no possibility of attaining anything remotely resembling even a modest U.S. standard of living. . . . If serious research is any guide, the vast majority of undocumented immigrants and their children who have been living continuously in California for five years or more will stay here, whether or not [restrictive social measures] are approved.

Wayne A. Cornelius, *Don't Vote for a Fix That Won't Work*, L.A. Times, Oct. 28, 1994, at A11.

4. *The Territorial Imperative, California Style (Editorial)*, America, Nov. 5, 1994, at 3.

5. Mari Matsuda, *Looking to the Bottom: Critical Legal Studies and Reparations*, 22 Harv. C.R.-C.L. L. Rev. 323 (1987).

6. See, e.g., Martha Minow, *Partial Justice: Law and Minorities*, in The Fate of Law 36, 36 n.20 (Austin Sarat & Thomas R. Kearns eds., 1991).

7. The phrase is Richard Rorty's. See Richard Rorty, *Unger, Castoriadis, and the Romance of a National Future*, 82 NW. U. L. Rev. 335, 343 (1988); Richard Rorty, *The Unpatriotic Academy*, N.Y. Times (op-ed), Feb. 3, 1994, at E15.

Chapter 15

Hispanic Children and Their Families

Linda Chavez

I am happy to be here this morning, in particular because I would like to talk about another side of the Hispanic story in the United States, a side that we don't hear very much about. This morning you will be treated to lot of statistics about the plight of Hispanics in the United States and much evidence of the decline in status of those Hispanics.

We tend in our concern for the poor and those who have been left behind in the economic progress of the United States to focus on Hispanics as if they were a monolithic group and as if the group were not in fact dynamic and constantly changing. I think in doing that we diminish the very real and significant progress that has taken place in the Hispanic community over the last twenty to twenty-five years, and the very real gains that ordinary Hispanic men and women are making for themselves on their own.

So I would like to talk a little bit about that this morning. I am not going to read from my prepared text, but rather just talk informally with you. Mr. Bliley has quite aptly described the various inter-ethnic divisions between the various ethnic groups that comprise the Hispanic population.

A professor from Johns Hopkins University, Professor Alejandro Portes, has referred to the idea of grouping all Hispanics together as creating a supra-ethnicity, pooling everyone as if we are all one great big Hispanic subgroup, when in fact there are very important inter-ethnic divisions. But in addition to those inter-ethnic divisions there is another division which I think explains more of what we continue to hear about the decline of Hispanics than any other single factor, and that is the very large portion of Hispanics who are in fact not native born, but are immigrants.

We tend to think of Hispanics in the United States as an indigenous, permanently disadvantaged minority group. I think a far more apt description of the Hispanic community is that of an emerging immigrant population.

Thirty-four percent of all Hispanics living in the United States as of June 1988 were, in fact, foreign born. If you include also first generation Hispanics you have

From Statement of Linda Chavez, Senior Fellow, Manhattan Institute for Policy Research, New York, N.Y. "Hispanic Children and Their Families: A Key to Our Nation's Future," Hearing before the Select Committee on Children, Youth, and Families, United States House of Representatives, 101st Congress, 1st Session, Washington, D.C., September 25, 1989, pp. 62–66.

well over a majority of the Hispanic population that was not, in fact, born in the United States, and it seems to me that when you consider that and think about that, you should harken back to the condition of other immigrant groups in the United States at other points in our history. I put forth to you the thesis that Hispanics today are much more like the immigrant Poles, Greeks, and Italians and even Jews of the early part of this century than they are like a permanently disadvantaged underclass.

I will go into a couple of examples of the ways in which this influences our statistics in a moment. But I would also note that Dr. Hinojosa referred to the fact that the growth in the Hispanic community has been at least in large part the result of higher fertility. In fact that is not true.

In the 1980 census the Mexican origin population was approximately one-quarter foreign born. Again, in June of 1988—the figures that are the most recent we have—the Mexican American population, according to the Census Bureau, was 31.4 percent foreign born. Even in this largest group the proportion of the foreign born is increasing.

Now, why does this matter? Well, rather than go into some statistical comparisons, I would like to use an analogy because I think it is one that sets out the problems of taking data and trying to use it without taking note of the very important characteristic of nativity when you are talking about the Hispanic population.

In various academic studies, we are very used to looking at comparisons between groups, between one point in time and another. For example, if we want to try and determine whether or not white Anglo students in school are doing better than Hispanic children, we might take a comparison and particularly if we had two groups that were perfectly matched otherwise, we might take a comparison group of one class of students that was Anglo and another class of students that was Hispanic.

And let's say we had thirty students in each of these classes, and we tested those students at the beginning of the year and we found out, for example, that one group, the Anglo group, scored at the median. But the next, the Hispanic group, scored, let's say 20 percent below the median.

Then in order to try and determine whether or not the Hispanic children were keeping up and making progress over that school year we would test them again at the end of the school year. Let's say that when we took the second test we found that not only had the gap not closed but in fact the gap between the scores of the Anglos and Hispanic students had widened.

We might, from that, assume that in fact Hispanics were making much slower progress than were Anglo students. And that is exactly what happens when we look at the data on earnings, for example, between non-Hispanic white males and Hispanic males, and we find that between the period 1982 and 1987, the wage gap between those groups actually grew when we compared median annual earnings.

But if we went back, and using our analogy, found out that using those two classes as comparison groups, the first class started out with thirty students and ended up with thirty students. They were basically the same students that had been in that class the entire time. But in the second class we had additional students join the class between September and June, and not only were these ten new students, but half of these students, five of them, were brand new immigrant students, and they spoke not a word of English. Would we be surprised that in fact the median scores for that second class declined precipitously between that September and June setting? I think not. I think we would know immediately that the scores of those new, non–English speaking students in fact significantly affected the median scores for the whole class, and that is exactly what I see happening in the Hispanic community.

Now, unfortunately, this thesis may have to wait until the 1990 census in order to be adequately proved because although we gather enormous mountains of statistics, we do not ask the single most important question we could ask in our census gathering data of Hispanics. And that is where were you born and when did you come to the United States if you were not in fact U.S. born.

And so our comparisons sometimes are inadequate. I cite in my prepared testimony the recent study that was put out by the Education Department called dropout rates in the United States, 1988. One of the report's most dramatic findings was that nearly 36 percent of the nation's Hispanic students or persons between the ages of sixteen and twenty-four were neither in school in October of 1988 nor were they high school graduates. Of that group nearly a third had a sixth grade education or less. These statistics were heralded in the *New York Times,* the *Los Angeles Times,* the *Washington Post,* and various of the other media as an example of the very perilous state of education for Hispanics in the United States.

And, unfortunately, when you begin to examine the data, you find two problems with it. Number one, the sample size that the department used was based on October current population surveys. The current population survey is a household survey that has approximately 60,000 households on the various months that it is taken.

Unfortunately, the size of the Hispanic population is so small on a monthly basis that every March the Census Bureau, in fact, increases or oversamples in Hispanic households in order to try and make sure that there is a sample large enough to have meaningful kinds of analysis done, but the Department of Education study did not use the March data.

It used the October data, with a very small sample size. I estimated the sample in that to be around a thousand. It may be somewhat more, somewhat less than that, and that was a very crude estimation, just based on the taking percentages of the total Hispanic population out of that 60,000 households. But worse than the sample size is the failure of the Department of Education to have anything to say about what influence the percentage of foreign born Hispanics had on their conclusions.

One of the things we know is that in 1980, the last year for which we have reliable data, of the foreign born Mexican population in the United States, 50 percent entered the United States with a sixth-grade education. And so when I look at these data and I see that a third of the Hispanic students who have supposedly dropped out have a sixth-grade education or less, automatic alarm signals go off in my head, and I assume that by and large we are talking about immigrants.

I think it is a very different issue whether or not we have a sizable population of Mexican immigrants who have come to the United States basically seeking work who have not only not dropped out of school, they have never dropped into the American educational system. That, to me, raises very different policy issues than the presence of a large indigenous population of Mexican American students who are dropping out before the sixth grade.

In addition to what I have said about the percentage of the foreign born, that large cohort of foreign born persons do, in fact, exercise a downward influence on all of the statistics related to such things as income. An estimate I did of the 1980 census data showed that if you looked at the total Hispanic data for annual earnings and took out the foreign born, you found that it would have been about 10 percent higher than with the presence of the foreign born in that grouping.

Other studies: Professor Francisco Rivera Batiz of Rutgers University released a study last year at this time showing that in fact when you compare the earnings, the hourly earnings, of native born Hispanics and compare them to the non-Hispanic white population, you find that their hourly earnings are essentially identical and that, in fact, when you compare the earnings of immigrants you find that they, too, rapidly increase with time in the United States as the immigrants learn English and as they learn important job skills that make them more eligible to compete in our labor market.

Virtually all of the studies of immigrant wages show that all immigrant groups, including Hispanic immigrants, show very, very rapid increase. Within a period of somewhere between ten and twenty years, earning gaps between native born persons and immigrants, in fact, disappear. For Mexicans, for example, the earnings between native born Mexican Americans and foreign born Mexicans disappear at about fifteen years, and after that period the foreign born actually surpass the native born in earnings. That has a lot to do with the kind of motivation and essentially human capital characteristics that immigrants bring with them.

So what that says to me is that even though the statistics on Hispanics today may not show as much progress as we would like to see, the future looks quite good for individual Hispanics. We are not going to see a change in the overall statistics for the group until there comes a point when we don't continue to have people coming in at the bottom of the economic ladder and replenishing that flow at the very bottom of the group.

So long as we look at Hispanics as one large mass of people and don't look at them as individuals who, in fact, do make individual progress up that economic ladder, we will have a somewhat distorted image. Now, having said all of this, I do want to say that things are not as rosy as I have described them for each and every group, and in fact Puerto Ricans do not seem to show the same kind of progress, and in fact there are some very, very worrying trends in the Puerto Rican community, but also increasingly in the Mexican American community with regard to the disintegration of the family.

In Puerto Rican households, about half of all Puerto Rican households are headed by females without a male present, and about half of all Puerto Rican children today are born out of wedlock. While the rates for Mexican origin persons are not as high, about a quarter of all Mexican origin children are now being born out of wedlock.

I think these are very serious issues and ones that I commend to your committee to study. Thank you.

Chapter 16

Immigration Politics, Popular Democracy, and California's Proposition 187

Kevin R. Johnson

In elegantly referring to "government of the people, by the people, and for the people," Abraham Lincoln famously tapped into the nation's enthusiasm for democracy. From the founding of this nation, however, the potential excesses of democracy also have generated considerable concern. In an attempt to avoid such excesses, the Constitution moderates popular sentiment through a representative form of government.

An odd combination of devotion to and ambivalence about democracy carries forward to this day. The debates over civic republicanism, for example, reflect differing visions about the benefits of a more democratic government. Similarly, conflicting views about trial by jury typify the sharp disagreements about democracy in action. While juries are often revered as a bastion of democracy, judges have a myriad of devices at their disposal that allow them to override perceived jury excesses. The popular initiative process, which takes a variety of forms in the various states, reflects the nation's ambivalence about democratic rule. Generally, legislative bodies, such as Congress and state legislatures, composed of elected representatives, make the law. The initiative process, as an exception to that general rule, affords voters themselves the opportunity to directly enact laws. The initiative, consistent with its Progressive era roots, often is regaled as a populist tool that may force change on a government captured by special interests. In this spirit, initiatives have furthered a number of laudable goals in some states, including eliminating the poll tax and extending the franchise to women.

On the other hand, some initiatives have been less praiseworthy. California's so-called alien land law, passed by the voters in 1920, which restricted the ability of noncitizens to own land, is a vivid historical example. What about California's recent Proposition 187? The measure would bar state and local governments in California from providing non-emergency medical care, public assistance, social services, and education to undocumented immigrants. It would further require California law enforcement, health and social service agencies, and public school officials to report

From "An Essay on Immigration Politics, Popular Democracy, and California's Proposition 187: The Political Relevance and Legal Irrelevance of Race." 70 Wash. L. Rev. 629 (1995). Originally published in the *Washington Law Review*. Reprinted by permission.

persons suspected of being undocumented to the Immigration and Naturalization Service. Perhaps due to the complexities of the initiative's provisions, debate during the heated campaign often proceeded on an abstract plane. Proponents proclaimed that passage of Proposition 187 would "send a message" to the federal government that it must address illegal immigration. Opponents, particularly ethnic activist and immigrant rights groups, countered that the initiative was nativist, racist, and motivated by antipathy toward undocumented Mexicans and, more generally, Mexican Americans.

Many factors unquestionably led to the passage of Proposition 187, including an ailing California economy, an incumbent governor searching for an issue on which to base his re-election campaign, and the growing pains of a changing multi-cultural society. The public outcry culminated in an attempt by the electorate of the state of California, at the center of the immigration firestorm, to take a stab at immigration policymaking.

One of the most vociferous, and serious, charges made by Proposition 187 opponents in the heated campaign was that, at bottom, it is racist. This often is a damning claim in our legal culture. For a variety of reasons, however, including the difficulties of proving claims of discrimination under existing constitutional doctrine, the many lawsuits challenging Proposition 187 do not squarely raise the issue. Part of the reason is that it is difficult to separate permissible from impermissible motives for supporting Proposition 187. On the one hand, an anti-undocumented, or even an anti-immigrant, law is not necessarily suspect. On the other hand, anti-people-of-color or anti-Mexican laws generally are. Some Proposition 187 supporters were motivated by impermissible factors while others were not. Some were motivated by a mix of the two. In light of the difficulties in ascertaining the motive of the electorate, a court of law in all likelihood never will address the issue that immediately jumps into the minds of many who condemn the initiative. Only in the court of history will it be decided whether Proposition 187—like the alien land laws of yesteryear—was passed for invidious reasons and thus whether it is properly classified as racist and discriminatory.

Proposition 187 as Racist?

Though more subtle in light of modern sensibilities, the Proposition 187 campaign bore some striking similarities to the campaign culminating in the passage of the alien land laws in California. The question whether the initiative might properly be classified as "racist," however, is deeply complicated. Part of its support may result from concerns with the fiscal consequences of undocumented immigration. Such a motive is not necessarily suspect. Some voters undoubtedly were fearful of a loss of control of their culture, society, and lives. Others, however, were motivated by a desire to halt the flow of Mexican immigrants to the United States and to hasten their return to Mexico. Others were unabashedly anti-Mexican, regardless of the immigration status of the persons. It also is possible that passage of Proposition 187 resulted from sheer frustration with immigration. All this said, we shall see that it is difficult to deny that the ethnicity of the stereotypical undocumented immigrant played at least some role in the passage of Proposition 187.

The Campaign for the Initiative

At the risk of understatement, California experienced a spirited, hotly contested campaign over Proposition 187. Nativist and racist as well as economic, social, and cultural themes arose in the campaign. Governor Pete Wilson, up for re-election, capitalized on public dissatisfaction with immigration by ardently supporting the initiative. Some of his campaign advertisements showed shadowy Mexicans crossing the border in mass. This was not the governor's first foray into immigration politics in the 1990s. By arguing that pregnant women unlawfully immigrate to this country to secure free medical care and to give their children U.S. citizenship, Wilson previously had attacked the provision of public assistance to the undocumented.

But seldom during the campaign were Mexicans singled out among the undocumented population. Undocumented immigrants as a group were blamed for California's fiscal and other woes, as the initiative's "Save Our State" moniker suggests. That Proposition 187 placed in jeopardy federal funding of $15 billion, an amount that dwarfed any potential savings, was virtually ignored. Other factors besides a desire to save money were at work.

Some supporters of Proposition 187 expressed hopes and aims well beyond simply fiscal ones. One of the initiative sponsors, Ron Prince, baldly asserted that "[i]llegal aliens are killing us in California. . . . Those who support illegal immigration are, in effect, anti-American."[1] Consider also one argument in the voters' pamphlet: "Proposition 187 will be the first giant stride in ultimately ending the ILLEGAL ALIEN invasion."[2] The Proposition 187 media director for southern California expressed even more disturbing concerns:

> Proposition 187 is . . . a logical step toward saving California from economic ruin. . . . By flooding the state with 2 million illegal aliens to date, and increasing that figure each of the following 10 years, Mexicans in California would number 15 million to 20 million by 2004. During those 10 years about 5 million to 8 million Californians would have emigrated to other states. If these trends continued, a Mexico-controlled California could vote to establish Spanish as the sole language of California, 10 million more English-speaking Californians could flee, and there could be a statewide vote to leave the Union and annex California to Mexico.[3]

The Views of the Drafters

The positions of the individuals who composed the committee that drafted Proposition 187 help one gain a sense of the mixed motives behind the measure. Ron Prince, whose anti-immigrant animus apparently grew out of a business dispute with a legal immigrant he later claimed was an "illegal," conjured up disturbing imagery from another era: "You are the posse and SOS is the rope."[4] Besides suggesting that Proposition 187 opponents were "anti-American," Prince linked "illegal aliens" with criminals: "[t]he . . . mindset on the part of illegal aliens, is to commit crimes. The first law they break is to be here illegally. The attitude from then on is, I don't have to obey your laws."[5]

Well before the advent of Proposition 187, Harold Ezell, Western Regional Commissioner of the Immigration and Naturalization Service (INS) in the 1980s, was infamous for comments made about "illegal aliens"—that they should be "caught, skinned and fried."[6] Ezell's statements prompted Latino activists to demand his resignation. During the debate over Proposition 187, Ezell explained that support for the measure was strong because "[t]he people are tired of watching their state run wild and become a third world country."[7]

Alan Nelson, former Commissioner of the INS, at one time was a consultant with the Federation for American Immigration Reform, which received funding from the Pioneer Fund, a group believing in racial superiority. Concerned with mass migrations from Mexico, Nelson resigned his position with the INS in the wake of conflict with the Attorney General and allegations of poor leadership and inefficiency. Richard Mountjoy, a member of the California legislature, consistently has proposed bills directed at immigrants, many of which have been bitterly opposed by immigrants' rights activists. He has little sympathy for undocumented immigrants. According to Mountjoy, undocumented mothers "come here for that birth certificate. They come here to get on the California dole."[8] "[I]f you want to stop the flow of illegal aliens to our hospitals, stop the benefits. . . . Having a child at our expense is not an emergency."[9] In Mountjoy's eyes, "[t]he people of California are subsidizing the illegal [alien] invasion to the tune of somewhere around $5 billion a year," and "[w]hen you have a flood of immigration . . . there's not long until this life boat sinks."[10]

Barbara Kiley, mayor of a city in southern California, reportedly described the children of undocumented immigrants as "those little f—kers."[11] Kiley and her husband, who is a campaign consultant, reportedly became involved in the Proposition 187 campaign as "a business consideration."[12] Mr. Kiley reportedly stated that:

> I don't mean to be inhumane, but this [undocumented] woman [seeking medical care] is a perfect example of why we need Prop. 187. . . . She has already had two children here and now she's on her third, and she doesn't even belong here. All I can say is, these people are going to have to go back home. We're paying for her care while Americans are homeless and starving in the streets.[13]

Crowing that those protesting Proposition 187 damaged their cause, Kiley stated that "[o]n TV there was nothing but Mexican flags and brown faces."[14]

Consider also the public statements of one Proposition 187 drafter, Barbara Coe. Coe's anti-immigrant crusade began after she visited a social service office where many different languages were being spoken. During that visit, Coe allegedly learned that undocumented persons were eligible for benefits for which Coe's citizen friend was not. Based on her personal experiences, Coe has contended that undocumented immigrants "are endangering, not only our financial system, but they . . . hold, not only our laws, . . . but our language, our culture, and our very history in contempt."[15]

One of her fears stems from the belief that the "militant arm of the pro-illegal activists . . . have vowed to take over first California, then the Western states and then the rest of the nation."[16]

In Coe's mind, "illegal aliens" and crime are inextricably linked:

> You get illegal alien children, Third World children, out of our schools, and you will reduce the violence. That is a fact. . . . You're not dealing with a lot of shiny face, little kiddies. . . . You're dealing with Third World cultures who come in, they shoot, they beat, they stab and they spread their drugs around in our school system. And we're paying them to do it.[17]

A "Motivating Factor": Immigrants from Mexico

Like the alien land laws, Proposition 187, though facially neutral, was directed at immigrants from a certain country. The drafters' comments make clear that the "illegal aliens" at the forefront in their minds were undocumented Mexican immigrants. Although many undocumented persons other than Mexicans settle in the United States, this never figured prominently in the debate over the initiative. Moreover, the implementation of Proposition 187 would have impacts on discrete ethnic communities. Undocumented Mexicans, Mexican-American citizens, and citizens of other minority groups viewed as foreign, such as Asian Americans, are the groups most likely to suffer the initiative's sting. Not surprisingly, Latino and Asian ethnic organizations voiced the strongest opposition in the Proposition 187 campaign. People with names such as Alan Nelson and Ron Prince, for rather obvious reasons, are unlikely to be suspected of being undocumented immigrants. Rather, those with names such as Perez and Chung will be.

Some of the anti-Mexican undertones to Proposition 187 came to fruition after the election. Some Latinos reported harassment, including racial epithets and being told to go back to Mexico. A founder of a group in Arizona seeking to place a Proposition 187–type initiative on the ballot in that state denied that it was a racial issue: "My friends have never heard a racist word out of me. I just don't like wetbacks."[18]

Proving a Discriminatory Intent

One challenge to Proposition 187 might be that, though facially neutral, it will have a discriminatory impact on immigrants and citizens of particular ethnicities and national origin groups. But the mere showing of a racially disproportionate impact alone is insufficient to establish that a facially neutral law violates the Equal Protection Clause. Rather, even for legislation adopted through initiative, the aggrieved party must establish that the law was enacted with a discriminatory intent. Such an intent can be proven through circumstantial evidence, including a "racially disproportionate effect."[19] Still, intent is difficult to prove, clearly more so than simply establishing a disparate impact on a minority group. Consequently, the intent requirement has deterred the filing of equal protection challenges to governmental action.

Intent analysis raises a variety of problems that are especially acute in evaluating lawmaking by initiative. Obviously, the larger the institution making the challenged decision, the more difficult it is to establish an invidious intent. For example, although it is difficult to determine the intent of a seven-member city council, it is even more so with respect to a 535-member legislative body, such as Congress. A variety of motives may influence a legislator's voting decision, and a legislative decision to act necessarily is a mixed bag of the intents of many different legislators. The difficulties of such an exercise are exponentially greater when the electorate of thousands, perhaps hundreds of thousands, or maybe millions, of voters made an allegedly discriminatory decision. Even if a significant portion of the electorate voted for the challenged measure for invidious reasons, it is close to impossible to establish the true intent of such a diffuse decisionmaking body.

The barriers to determining the collective intent of the electorate are heightened by the fact that invidious discrimination is not always conscious, but may operate at an unconscious level. When unconscious racism influences a voting decision, voters (or legislators, for that matter) are by definition unaware that they are acting in a discriminatory way. Perhaps in recognition of such problems, lower courts have avoided inquiry into the electorate's intent. To do so, they emphasize the sanctity of the secret ballot and have been reluctant to invalidate an initiative even if at least part of the electorate appeared to have a discriminatory purpose in voting for the law. Such an approach makes the invalidation of an initiative appear possible only if the measure is discriminatory on its face. The end result is that, in the initiative process, voters may more-or-less freely rely on invidious motives in supporting measures that have a disproportionate impact on discrete and insular minorities.

Alienage Classifications as a Proxy for National Origin Discrimination

Although racial classifications are afforded heightened constitutional scrutiny under traditional equal protection analysis, that is not always so with respect to alienage classifications. As demonstrated by the alien land laws, alienage classifications, though presumptively lawful, may veil an invidious purpose to discriminate, which would presumptively be invalid. This, however, would be very difficult to prove.

The formidable evidentiary burdens may force courts facing this type of case to attempt to achieve a result consistent with equality principles through means other than the Equal Protection Clause. For example, in *Yniguez v. Arizonans for Official English*,[20] the Court of Appeals for the Ninth Circuit invalidated on First Amendment grounds an initiative amending the Arizona constitution to compel state employees and officials to speak only English in the workplace. After finding that the initiative violated the First Amendment, the court buttressed its reasoning by emphasizing the equal protection consequences of the law: "Since language is a close and meaningful proxy for national origin, restrictions on the use of languages may mask discrimination against specific national origin groups or, more generally, conceal nativist sentiment."[21]

Like national origin and language, a link exists in the United States between national origin and immigration status. With increasing immigration from developing nations in recent years, the link has become more pronounced. A problem for the future will be determining when facially neutral laws concerning immigration and immigrants, such as reduction of benefits to lawful permanent residents, mask an invidious discrimination against certain national origin groups. Despite the recurring nature of the problem, the link between national origin and immigration status, and the analytical difficulties it creates for traditional equal protection analysis, for the most part have gone ignored.

Proposition 187 is the product of a deeply complex, perhaps unique, set of political forces in the United States. As the solid support for the measure amply demonstrates, its backing did not split along classic liberal-conservative lines. The limited political power of noncitizens made it easier for one powerful politician to use Proposition 187 and anti-immigrant/anti-immigration sentiment to build a bipartisan coalition, ensuring his re-election and the initiative's passage. The next stage in the life of Proposition 187 will be determined by the courts. Within days of the initiative's passage, immigrant advocates filed numerous lawsuits challenging the lawfulness of the initiative. The challenges in those lawsuits run the gamut from violation of the federal Constitution and statutes to claims that the initiative violates the California constitution. Curiously enough, a much-debated aspect of the passage of Proposition 187—that it is nativistic and racist—in all probability will never be decided. Such contentions will in all likelihood be lost in legalisms. Thus, although a particularly damning claim in U.S. legal culture, and one of critical importance to the affected communities, the charge will go untested and unresolved.

NOTES

1. See Patrick J. McDonnell, *Prop. 187 Turns Up Heat in U.S. Immigration Debate,* L.A. TIMES, Aug. 10, 1994, at A1.

2. Tony Miller, Acting California Secretary of State, CALIFORNIA BALLOT PAMPHLET: GENERAL ELECTION, November 8, 1994, at 54.

3. *Letter to Editor by Linda R. Hayes,* N.Y. TIMES, Oct. 15, 1994, at A18.

4. George Ramos, *Prop. 187 Debate: No Tolerance but Abundant Anger,* L.A. TIMES, Oct. 10, 1994, at B3.

5. Marc Cooper, *The War against Illegal Immigrants Heats Up,* VILLAGE VOICE, Oct. 4, 1994, at 28.

6. Olga Briseno, *Mister Migra, Harold Ezell,* SAN DIEGO UNION-TRIB., Aug. 23, 1989, at F1 (quoting Ezell).

7. Daniel B. Wood, *Ballot Vote on Illegal Immigrants Set for Fall in California,* CHRISTIAN SCI. MON., June 1, 1994, at 1.

8. *Sonya Live* (CNN television broadcast, Feb. 16, 1994).

9. Major Garrett, *Economic Plan Includes Aliens' Medical Funds,* WASH. TIMES, July 14, 1993, at A1.

10. *Sonya Live.*

11. Elizabeth Kadetsky, *Bashing Illegals in California: "Save Our State" Initiative,* NATION, Oct. 17, 1994, at 416, 418.

12. Paul Feldman, *Figures behind Prop. 187 Look at Its Creation*, L.A. TIMES, Dec. 14, 1994, at A3.

13. Sara Catania, *County Report: A Message Hits Home*, L.A. TIMES, Nov. 20, 1994, at B1.

14. Margot Hornblower, *Making and Breaking Law,* TIME, Nov. 21, 1994, at 68.

15. *Sonya Live.*

16. Carol Byrne, *Proposition 187's Uproar,* STAR TRIB., Oct. 20, 1994, at 7A.

17. Pamela J. Podger & Michael Doyle, *War of Words,* FRESNO BEE, Jan. 9, 1994, at A1.

18. Maria Puente, *States Setting Stage for Their Own Prop. 187s,* USA TODAY, Nov. 18, 1994, at 3A.

19. Crawford v. Board of Educ., 458 U.S. 527, 544 (1982).

20. 42 F.3d 1217 (9th Cir. 1994) (Reinhardt, J.), petition for reh'g en banc granted, 53 F.3d 1084 (9th Cir 1995).

21. Yniguez, 42 F.3d at 1241–42.

Chapter 17

The Racial Politics of Proposition 187

Ruben J. Garcia

In mid-1993, a group of concerned California residents were fed up with the "illegal aliens" whom they blamed for sapping the state's resources. These aliens were everywhere: crowding their children out of public schools, crowding welfare offices, and crowding the emergency rooms of hospitals. To attack these problems, these angry residents formed a political movement. They saw themselves as the last hope for California, economically battered and bleeding from tax revolts, race revolts, natural disasters, and the crash of the defense industry. Accordingly, they gave their group a bold name: "Save Our State" (SOS). Their movement placed Proposition 187—a proposal to deny undocumented immigrants the few public benefits to which they had been legally entitled—on the November 1994 California ballot. The central question of this chapter is whether Proposition 187 is an attempt to save state resources or to save the state's racial identity from becoming increasingly nonwhite.

Immigration law and politics have been historically intertwined with racial prejudice. Many of those who have called for immigration restrictions have also sought an end to the racial and cultural diversity brought by immigrants. With the end of legally sanctioned race discrimination in the 1960s, immigration rhetoric has lost some of its overt racist overtones. However, in the 1990s, many politicians and lawmakers have emphasized the difference between "legal" and "illegal" immigration. This change begs a central question: Have the racist motivations of past immigration law and policy been completely displaced by a concern for law and order? This chapter argues that immigration law and policy continue to be partially motivated by a drive for cultural and racial homogeneity.

The Bracero Programs and Operation Wetback

Agricultural employers made heavy use of Mexicans escaping economic and political persecution after the political upheaval of the Mexican Revolution of 1910.

From "CRITICAL RACE THEORY AND PROPOSITION 187: THE RACIAL POLITICS OF IMMIGRATION LAW." 17 CHICANO-LATINO L. REV. 118 (1995). Originally published in the *Chicano-Latino Law Review*. Reprinted by permission.

However, when Congress passed the Immigration Act of 1917, agricultural employers worried that the Act's literacy and head tax requirements would severely reduce their immigrant labor supply. Due to pressure from agribusiness, the government waived these requirements for Mexicans. These official actions were crucial to maintaining an exploitable, nonwhite work force of hundreds of thousands of Mexicans.

As jobs became scarce during the Great Depression, the Mexican worker population was controlled through mass deportations of persons with Spanish sounding names or Mexican features who could not produce formal papers. Over 300,000 Mexicans were deported from 1931 to 1934. Many of these persons were citizens or legal residents, but simply could not prove their status. By 1942, labor shortages and World War II had created the need for more agricultural workers. Thus, growers convinced the United States government to enter into the Bracero Program, a large-scale contract labor program with Mexico. Braceros were the perfect exploitable underclass, willing to work for low wages and in deplorable conditions.

By 1946, it became impossible to separate Mexican Americans from deportable Mexicans. Thus, in 1954, over one million people were deported under "Operation Wetback." Many United States citizens were mistakenly "repatriated" to Mexico, including individuals who looked Mexican but had never even been to that country. The program included a relentless media campaign to characterize the Operation as a national security necessity, and a tightening of the border to deter undocumented immigration.

Fictions: *The Rule of Law and Race-Neutrality*

Proponents of Proposition 187 argue that undocumented immigrants have no claim to public entitlements because of their violation of United States immigration laws. This is a "rule of law" argument—those who have entered the United States illegally in the past are worthy of punishment through the denial of public services. What does the "rule of law" argument overlook? First, the children of undocumented immigrants often come to this country at a young age with their parents and cannot be considered morally culpable for their status. Second, the focus on the crime that the immigrant commits overlooks that employers continue to violate the employer sanctions laws that Congress enacted in 1986. It also ignores that immigration law is biased in favor of wealthy, talented immigrants and those who share the dominant American political ideology. Finally, criminalization of the undocumented also belies the many contributions that they make to our economy and society.

The history of immigration policy renders suspect the characterization of the current debate over Proposition 187 as race-neutral. The "rule of law" is being used today in much the same way that "sovereignty" functioned during Chinese Exclusion—as a concept that is inconsistently applied to exclude nonwhites from American society. For example, if the rule of law is the basis for the current attacks on the undocumented, then the employers who hire undocumented immigrants should also be included in these attacks. However, while there were several border crackdowns in the weeks before the vote on Proposition 187, the INS did not stage concurrent raids on employers who hire the undocumented.

Proposition 187 was also supported by those who believed it was race-neutral. For example, Jesse Laguna, a member of the Save Our State Committee, wrote that Proposition 187 has nothing to do with race: "If Latinos are caught more often, it is because they illegally cross the border more often. Most of the Anglos I work with on . . . the 'Save Our State' Committee would feel exactly the same way if the border invaders were Canadians setting up camp in Montana and hollering for freebies."[1] This statement ignores that the Canadian border is a very porous one, and is ill-patrolled compared to the militarized United States–Mexico border. Perhaps the greatest difference between the situation of Canadians and Mexicans is that Canadians do not have to "holler for freebies" because they are accepted more readily as part of American society because of their race and not thought of as undocumented immigrants. Latinos and other nonwhites, on the other hand, are the stereotype of an "illegal alien" and thus presumed undocumented in white society. Therefore, to say that Proposition 187 is a race-neutral law ignores modern realities of discrimination in today's society, because the law will disproportionately affect people of color.

The Racialization of Crime: Fear of the Undocumented Criminal

Racial overtones also characterized the campaign to pass the initiative. In contemporary society, crime is closely associated with race, and politicians have successfully used the fear of crime to defeat opponents who were seen as too lenient on nonwhite criminals. The most famous example of this type of race-baiting was President George Bush's successful 1988 "Willie Horton" television advertisement, where he associated opponent Michael Dukakis with the parole of a Black rapist.[2] In the 1994 California elections, television commercials featured immigrants massed at the California-Mexico border as an announcer ominously spoke, "They keep coming."[3] These advertisements play into fears of crime. Since the undocumented are primarily seen as Latinos, such political advertisements only further legitimate the notion that crime is a nonwhite phenomenon and the misconception that those who do not obey immigration laws are more likely to commit other crimes once in the United States.

White Entitlement to Compliant Nonwhite Labor

Proposition 187's backers also argued that the undocumented take away benefits from citizens and permanent residents. However, these arguments are based less in fact and more on the feeling that nonwhites should not be entitled to anything not available to whites. Consider the story of Barbara Coe, one of the authors of Proposition 187:

Barbara Coe [had been caring for] a crippled World War II veteran . . . [who] suddenly had the medical coverage pulled out from under him. During a futile visit to a social services agency, she saw crowds of Asian and Spanish speakers lining up for checks that had been denied her American friend. Coe channeled her outrage into the founding of Citizens for Action Now in January 1992; a month later she established an umbrella organization of anti-illegal-immigrant groups called the California Coalition for Immigrant Reform.[4]

The assumption that Asians and Latinos seeking government services must be "illegal aliens" only fuels the belief that expression of one's culture makes others question their immigration status. The desire to keep nonwhite immigrants out of schools and health clinics while at the same time keeping them as a source of cheap labor has historic parallels to the Chinese Exclusion and Operation Wetback.

The ability to deny nonwhites full social participation can be seen as a form of white entitlement. Many whites assume that they are entitled to nonwhite labor on their terms, and able to deny these same laborers full participation in society. This attitude was exemplified by one of Proposition 187's most vocal proponents, 1994 United States Senate candidate Michael Huffington. During the campaign it was revealed that he hired an undocumented woman as a nanny in violation of the employer sanctions provisions of IRCA. Huffington refused to change his position on Proposition 187, saying that it "deals with taxing Californians for welfare, health and educational services for illegal immigrants."[5] This statement ignores that Huffington's own employee paid federal income taxes, Medicare taxes, and Social Security taxes from 1991 to 1993. Thus, even when whites know that undocumented immigrants work and pay taxes, the undocumented are still viewed as parasites on the economy.

Calls for Assimilation: Proposition 187 as a Reaction to Cultural and Racial Diversity

The calls for curbing undocumented immigration come with the rhetoric that programs and services such as bilingual education balkanize America. Many who espouse this position also support an end or a severe cutback to legal immigration as well. These groups are strong proponents of assimilationism, which would effectively eliminate any display of the immigrant's culture once in the United States. While assimilation may be good for immigrants in that it opens up economic opportunities, it is also tied to rendering nonwhites invisible to the greatest extent possible. Assimilationism confers a psychological benefit upon members of mainstream society, privileging the notion that the immigrant should aspire to American culture and deny his or her own culture. Assimilationism is also an expression of the fear of shifting demographics which will make whites the minority in some areas of the country, especially California.

Bill Ong Hing has tracked the parallels between extremist anti-undocumented attacks and assimilationist rhetoric.[6] Extremists such as former Ku Klux Klan leader

David Duke and 1992 presidential candidate Patrick Buchanan advocate for an immigration policy based on "assimilability," or whiteness. Duke has argued that undocumented immigrants are fraying the fabric of society: "We've got to begin to realize that we're a Christian society. We're part of Western Christian civilization. . . . [Because of] illegal immigration . . . [o]ur traditions are being torn away. Our values are being torn away."[7] Buchanan asked, "[I]f we had to take a million immigrants in, say, Zulus, next year or Englishmen and put them in Virginia, what group would be easier to assimilate and would cause less problems for the people of Virginia? There is nothing wrong with us sitting down and arguing that issue, that we are a European country."[8]

Many proponents of Proposition 187 also expressed concern about the increased cultural and linguistic diversity concomitant with increased immigration. Barbara Coe lamented the growing disappearance of her vision of America: "Is this America? Where do we live? What happened? How did it happen? Now we know and we're going to try to make it unhappen."[9] They admitted that Proposition 187 was less an attempt to curb illegal immigration or save state resources than a message to Washington about the severity of the immigration problem in California. However, to many of the nonwhites in California, Proposition 187 sent the message that the growing cultural diversity of California and the United States must be stopped.

Divide and Conquer: Cross-Racial Support for Proposition 187

Proponents of Proposition 187 insisted that because the measure enjoyed some support from Latinos and other nonwhites, it could not be racist. Such a view ignores the diversity of opinions in nonwhite communities. The argument that Proposition 187 is race-based has more to do with the context and history surrounding its passage than the race of the people who supported it or did not support it. This is not to say that the limited support that Proposition 187 enjoyed at the ballot box among people of color is inexplicable. For Blacks, continuing economic recession and discrimination feed resentment of immigrants perceived as taking the service jobs in their communities. The same politicians who derided Blacks as welfare dependent now use the undocumented as scapegoat. However, claims that government benefits will be readily available once the undocumented are excluded are disingenuous, because these claims come from the same politicians whose aim is to end all government welfare.

Immigration categories allow Latinos to stratify themselves around alienage/citizenship lines. Support of Proposition 187 by nonwhites may be attributable to the opportunity it gives nonwhites to ascend in society's racial hierarchy. Latino self-inclusion in the community of citizens lessens their lower status within the racial hierarchy of whites and nonwhites. Such self-identification only serves to perpetuate existing racial hierarchies, rather than challenging them as illegitimate. In this way, measures such as Proposition 187 serve to maintain white hegemony over nonwhites of all classes. Their position of dominance in the racial hierarchy is maintained through the creation of a citizen/alien hierarchy that wins over segments of the lower and middle classes.

A Tainted Lineage

Another reason for Latino support of Proposition 187 may be the way their immigrant history has been stigmatized by dominant society. With the exception of Native Americans, all Americans share an immigrant history. Yet, the immigrant history of some ethnic and racial groups is more celebrated than others. In current parlance, however, the "illegal alien" has been reified into a composite: Latinos and Latinas who surreptitiously cross the United States–Mexico border. Like most stereotypes, this one explains only part of the undocumented immigrant population. In this way, the immigrant history of more recent immigrants such as Latinos is seen as less legitimate than that of their predecessors.

Latinos' support for Proposition 187 may thus be an attempt to disassociate from the way that their immigrant history has been denigrated by anti-immigration rhetoric. Thus, for some Latinos born or naturalized in the United States, support of Proposition 187 becomes a way of identifying with dominant society. The denial of culture is not a problem solely for recent immigrants such as Latinos and Asians, but for all groups of color who seek to express their culture because anti-immigrant proposals reinforce the stereotype of the citizen as a white person. This marginalizes all who do not fit into this model, including groups such as African-Americans whose ancestors were made citizens by the Fourteenth Amendment.

The campaign to defeat Proposition 187 harms the entire Latino community. The campaign in favor of Proposition 187 suggests that there is something offensive about Latino and Latina culture. Whites continue to view Latino and Latina immigrant history as "illegal" and illegitimate, even when compared with the historical illegalities of white immigrant history. The limited Latino support for Proposition 187 may be an attempt by some Latinos to put distance between themselves and their delegitimated immigrant history. Further, it represents a sort of "passing" as white, since citizenship has been reserved for whites both historically and stereotypically. Measures such as Proposition 187 question the very basis for Latino citizenship, as evidenced in the proposals to deny citizenship to the descendants of the undocumented. Latinos and Latinas should reject the internalized hierarchies of race and citizenship status, and recognize the connection they share with the undocumented.

NOTES

1. Jesse Laguna, *Latinos Want a Tighter Border Too*, L.A. TIMES, Sept. 23, 1994, at B7.
2. Cathleen Decker, *Race Often Plays Real but Unspoken Role in Politics*, L.A. TIMES, Oct. 16, 1994, at A1.
3. *Id.*
4. Ed Leibowitz, *Master Race Theater*, L.A. WEEKLY, Oct. 14–20, 1994, at 30.

5. William Claiborne, *Huffingtons Say Employing Nanny Tested Consciences,* WASH. POST, Oct. 28, 1994, at A22.

6. Bill Ong Hing, *Beyond the Rhetoric of Assimilation and Cultural Pluralism: Addressing the Tension of Separatism and Conflict in an Immigration Driven Multiracial Society,* 81 CAL. L. REV. 863 (1993).

7. *Id.* at 872–73 (citing Robert Shogan, *Duke Will Run against Bush in Primaries,* L.A. TIMES, Dec. 5, 1991, at A1, A34).

8. *Id.* (citing Patrick Buchanan on *This Week with David Brinkley,* ABC News television broadcast, Dec. 8, 1991).

9. Leibowitz, at 32.

Chapter 18

Natives and Newcomers

Berta Esperanza Hernández-Truyol

Saturday, October 7, 1995. 7:00 P.M. Friends and I meet at an art gallery and, after looking at some of the new work, amble down the street to a local restaurant. The place is small and, as usual, crowded. We wait outside, chatting, for fifteen minutes before being seated. The owner leads us to our table, a crowded four-top arranged at a diagonal against the wall and flanked by two-tops on either side. With my computer in tow over my right shoulder and a jean jacket over my left arm, I stand at the top of the diagonal trying to figure out how I can get in to take my seat. All of a sudden, and out of the blue, I hear "Excuse me, you're in America now, you say 'excuse me,' SAVAGE, ANIMAL." It appears that a sleeve of my jacket has brushed against the Angry Diner. I have no opportunity to apologize or even to realize what has happened. Angry Diner continues to mutter unintelligibly under his breath. One of my friends, Rosa, who has been walking right behind me, upon seeing my stunned expression simply says, "Forget it, let's just sit down." By the time Meika and Mercedes, our two other friends, join us, they are rather curious—wondering what mischief I have caused. After relaying the incident to my now equally stunned friends, we move on to have our nice dinner, or try, anyway. Angry Diner, Rosa tells me later, never stopped muttering under his breath. Finally, I think peace is at hand when Angry Diner and his companion get up to leave. He moves their table towards ours so that she can negotiate a tight corner (on the other side of our table). As he passes our table, he turns around, stares at me, utters an obscenity, and shoves Meika's chair before rushing to make his final exit — this time with wait persons chasing after him. Again, we are stunned. The restaurant owner joins our table to find out what had taken place, and after hearing the whole sordid story she says, "This is America, eh? Sure it is, and he is not welcome here anymore." Her English, unlike mine, is foreign accented; her look, unlike mine, is not brown.

Imagine. It is 1996 and we are about to move into the twenty-first century. We live in a city that is known globally as The City. The City where, since the turn of the nineteenth century, Lady Liberty, the quintessential representation of freedom, has

From "NATIVES, NEWCOMERS AND NATIVISM: A HUMAN RIGHTS MODEL FOR THE TWENTY-FIRST CENTURY." 23 FORDHAM URB. L.J. 1075 (1996). Originally published in the *Fordham Urban Law Journal*. Reprinted by permission.

greeted foreign subjects. The poem gracing her impressive figure is a symbol of wel-comeness, diversity, shelter:

> Give me your tired, your poor,
> Your huddled masses yearning to breathe free,
> The wretched refuse of your teeming shore.
> Send these, the homeless, the tempest-tost to me,
> I lift my lamp beside the golden door.[1]

A Brief History of Alienage and Nativism

Historical Roots

Perhaps the heart of the problem of nativism can be explained in a New York Minute. In the play *The Melting-Pot,* a Russian Jewish "pogrom orphan" glorifies America, his new nation, thus:

> America is God's Crucible, the great Melting Pot where all the races of Europe are melt-ing and reforming! Here you stand, good folk, think I, when I see them at Ellis Island, here you stand in your fifty groups, with your fifty languages and histories, and your fifty blood hatreds and rivalries. But you won't be long like that brothers, for these are the fires of God you've come to—these are the fires of God. A fig for your feuds and vendettas! German and Frenchman, Irishman and Englishman, Jews and Russians— into the Crucible with you all! God is making the American. . . . The real American has not yet arrived. He is only in the Crucible, I tell you—he will be the fusion of all races, perhaps the coming superman.[2]

Note how the glorification of America is limited to the "races of Europe"—a rather homogeneous stock that could be put into a pot and stirred with the end re-sult looking pretty much like any of the particular individual ingredients. This recipe plainly excludes those who would not blend with, but would, rather, color the stock—Blacks, who were brought to these shores not free but chained and who had by the time of the play gained freedom in law but certainly not in fact; American In-dians, ironically the original Americans; Asians, who have experienced a history of exclusion; Latinas/os and various "others/outsiders."

Since 1820, over 61,500,000 persons, mostly immigrants, have been admitted into the United States, approximately 804,400 of them in 1994 alone. The emerging predominance of non-European sources of today's immigrants to the United States is due, in large part, to the replacement in 1965 of an immigration policy based on na-tional origins quotas by a seven-tiered preference system which favors relatives of cit-izens as well as skilled workers.

Some of the nation's newcomers are not immigrants, but rather refugees or asylees, applicants who must satisfy a different set of standards to gain entry: a "well-founded fear of persecution" if they return home. Historically, different refugee groups of a certain cause célèbre have benefited from special policy consid-erations concerning their admittance into the country. In 1960, in response to Fidel Castro's ascent to power, the United States established a refugee program specifically for Cubans. Twenty years later, President Carter created the category of "entrant" to allow admission of both Cuban and Haitian boat people arriving off the coast of Florida.

As illustrated in the Cuban-Haitian dichotomy, the often political and pragmatic nature of U.S. refugee policy continues to be the subject of much criticism from those who argue for a more liberal and moral approach based on humanitarian principles. Until the 1980s, cold-war "ideological considerations" favored those fleeing Communist or otherwise "hostile" countries, regardless of actual abuses imposed on those seeking to leave.

Socio-economic factors also play a part in the granting or denial of entry to many of those seeking refuge in this country. With the notable exception of Ethiopians and more recently Somalians, applications from Africans have been scantily approved. Also, the Cubans, Haitians, and Vietnamese who are admitted into the U.S. are disproportionately skilled, professional, and well-educated as compared to the general populace of their home countries.

Recently, in a clearly politically motivated move, this country reversed its over-thirty-year-old policy of welcoming Cubans. The United States now disallows entry to persons fleeing Cuba, going so far as to intercept Cubans fleeing the island at sea and return them to Castro's much-maligned hands. Indeed, as the income and educational levels of Cuban "boat people" have decreased, their approval and acceptance have declined steadily, particularly among their compatriots already in Florida. This change of heart simply parallels the general trend with respect to "illegal aliens": it is arguably their usually very low socio-economic status that makes their presence in this country so undesirable.

In addition to the various entrants, refugees, immigrants, and aliens in the United States, a great many non-immigrant foreigners are admitted as temporary visitors or workers, students, transient aliens, foreign government officials, and representatives of international organizations. Currently, approximately 9 percent of the United States population is foreign-born. Adding to the mix, the vast majority and increasing diversity of America's native-born populace, the final scenario resembles less and less the nostalgic melting pot image of myth and literature.

Beyond the Melting Pot captures the irony of exclusion. Although "the melting pot" is "as old as the Republic," as "the number of individuals and nations involved [in adding to the stock pot] grew, the confidence that they could be fused together waned, and so also the conviction that it would be a good thing if they were to be."[3] Paradoxically, even within the homogeneous components of the blend, "[t]here were ways of making distinctions among Welshmen and Englishmen, Yorkers and New Englanders, long before people speaking strange tongues and practicing strange religions came upon the scene."[4] It is noteworthy that even this critique fails to consider those "others/outsiders" who already were in the United States, namely the same Blacks, American Indians, Asians, and Latinas/os as well as women from all the groups who historically, and until very recently, have not even been deemed worthy of mention as a class with particularized concerns in the alienage discourse.

The first in time on our shores, the earliest natives, were the Indians. They were eventually outnumbered and overpowered by the mostly-European settlers who immigrated to the New World from such faraway places as Great Britain (England, Scotland, Wales, Ireland), Germany, Scandinavia, and French Canada—making up the homogeneous stock of oldest immigrants described by "melting pot" theorists. In fact, 95 percent of the 4.3 million immigrants that populated this country between 1840 and 1860 came from Great Britain and Germany alone.

In the 1890s, a new tide of immigrants from eastern and southern Europe, namely Italians, Slavs, Poles, Russians, Hungarians, Greeks, and Jews, broke this Nordic circle of Western and Northern Europeans. While the shifting demographics did not alone account for the rise in anti-foreign sentiment, the animus with which these newcomers were often greeted bespoke a certain degree of cultural prejudice and intolerance. As historian John Higham has noted, "[b]y western European standards, the masses of southern and eastern Europe were educationally deficient, socially backward, and bizarre in appearance."[5] The Italians, the Irish, and especially the Jews bore the brunt of early American nativism at the hands of their earlier European counterparts, who often considered their southern and eastern brothers and sisters to be members of an "inferior" and "beaten" race. The descriptions of Italians are telling:

> The Italians were often thought to be the most degraded of the newcomers. They were swarthy, more than half of them were illiterate, and almost all were victims of a standard of living lower than that of any of the other prominent nationalities. . . . Also, they soon acquired a reputation as bloodthirsty criminals.[6]

It certainly did not help the Italians (or the Irish, for that matter) to be Catholic, as even the earliest English and Irish Protestants brought with them anti-Catholic opinions and stances. For instance, the Know-Nothing Movement, a secret society formed to restrict non-Anglo Saxon immigration, gained popularity in the 1800s, and the Ku Klux Klan, another secret society formed by ex-Confederates, has since its inception been a particular nemesis of the Catholic faith and its practitioners. Despite the criticism and bashing that Catholics have received throughout American history, "the Roman Catholic Church stands out as the largest private provider of services to immigrants in the city [of New York], and in the country as well."[7]

The Irish, Protestant and Catholic alike, also experienced the mistreatment and maligning suffered by the Italians, as illustrated by the infamous "No Irish Need Apply" notations that often accompanied employment ads and help-wanted signs in New York, Boston and other cities. Jewish immigrants fared no better than their Catholic counterparts. Jewish immigrants were not allowed to vote in some states until the mid-1800s and were (and still are to some extent) privately discriminated against in schools, associations, and residential housing. During the Depression, Henry Ford of the Ford Motor Company was a leading propagator of the anti-Semitic theory of "The International Jew . . . [a] world-wide power, conspiring against all nations."[8] In the 1930s, Jews fleeing Nazism were the largest group entering America. On arrival, the Jews discovered that they had managed to escape German Nazis in order to compete against the Irish and other earlier immigrants for jobs and housing. Such competition was particularly intense in New York. Before and during World War II, the Jews were urging U.S. military intervention, while Italian and non-Jewish German immigrants hoped to avoid United States intervention and the accompanying "accusations of dual loyalty they had encountered during World War I."[9]

It was during World War I that Germans in particular became victims of nativist and nationalist fervor, expressed in the questioning of German-American (and Italian-American) loyalty. The German language and customs became increasingly suspect, with many states enacting laws to prohibit their use and with a great nativist backlash against Germans becoming evident as soon as the United States entered the war. The rejection of the "enemy within" replayed itself in World War II when thousands of Japanese were relocated from their West Coast homes to internment camps in isolated settings. The Supreme Court in *Korematsu v. United States*[10] upheld this wartime order issued by President Franklin D. Roosevelt on grounds of national security. Apparently, American nationalists, and the institutions that often succumbed to their demands, ignored or simply forgot their unwarranted maltreatment of Germans only a few decades earlier. As a noted scholar observed, "[o]ne of the saddest lessons of *Korematsu* is that we do not seem to learn much from the lessons of the past."[11]

Certainly, ethnic, religious, cultural, and economic aspects have always tainted nationalistic and nativist ideology. Undeniably, a race component figures in as well. Nowhere is this more clearly evidenced than in the experiences of those who could hardly be called "immigrants" at all, namely Blacks. During the 1700s and until the importation of slaves was outlawed in 1808, hundreds of thousands of persons were captured in Africa and involuntarily shipped to this country as slaves. However, the first Blacks arrived in America in the early 1600s as "indentured servants who could earn their way out of bondage."[12] Free Blacks, both before and after emancipation and in ways both similar to and distinct from many immigrants, encountered racism both on the streets and in the laws of America.

Although largely subordinated within American society, Blacks were not then, and are not now, exempt from nativistic/ethnocentric tendencies, as shown by the intricate and intertwined relationship between the native-born Black community and Caribbean immigrants. In the early 1900s, more than 300,000 West Indians, particularly from Jamaica and Barbados, came to the United States; half settled in New York City. Around this time, many Blacks from the South were also migrating north to places like Harlem, where they commingled and competed with persons from the Caribbean. One leading commentator has observed that "[f]requently well-educated and entrepreneurial, West Indians provided most of the city's black doctors, lawyers, and dentists, and became major landholders in the black community, evoking some resentment among native-born blacks that still exists."[13]

Puerto Ricans, whether born on the island or in the continental United States, like native-born Blacks, are also U.S. citizens. Puerto Rican migration, particularly to New York City, has added these Spanish-speaking, brown citizens to the "migration" mix and consequently, the migration/immigration and nativism discourse.

The role played by New York, and New York City in particular, as "the portal of portals,"[14] has had an extraordinary historical significance in the development of American immigration. As Elizabeth Bogen notes,

Between 1820 and 1920 two-thirds of the nation's 34 million immigrants entered through the Port of New York. Although many traveled on to other destinations, nearly half of them settled in the city. Virtually every nationality was represented. The diversity attracted more newcomers, and does so to this day. New York is still the gateway for a third of the country's immigrants, and still the American city with the most ethnically diverse population.[15]

The federal immigration station at Ellis Island was opened in 1892 and replaced Castle Garden, which had opened in 1855, as the welcoming center for the "huddled masses yearning to breathe free." Clusters of immigrants began to form ethnic neighborhoods such as "Little Italy" and "Chinatown" in the late nineteenth century. While these neighborhoods helped to preserve cultural ties and associations by keeping immigrant groups together with their own kind, they also served to fuel inter-ethnic rivalries, further exacerbating the other/outsider crisis.

Notwithstanding the millions who have been welcomed at America's door in New York City, Los Angeles, and elsewhere in the U.S., for all those who have been greeted with open arms or at least indifferent tolerance, an equal number are excluded, turned away and discriminated against privately as well as by both the state and federal governments. The most sweeping example of national nativistic policy is codified in the national origins quotas of the Johnson Act of 1924.[16] This undeniably nativist law was compelled in part by World War I, the Depression, and the Red Scare, and allotted a certain percentage of immigrant visas to groups based on their presence already in the U.S., "in an attempt to institutionalize the status quo of America's ethnic and racial mix."[17] The national origins quota system was eventually abolished and replaced, but arguably the damage had already been done.

Current Nativist Trends

Quotas, exclusions and indecent propositions like California's Proposition 187 are reminiscent of the Alien and Sedition Acts, literacy tests, and bans on foreign language which, as unconstitutional as they were, "recognized nativist exclusion as an appropriate response to fear of foreign people and foreign ideas."[18] These sentiments go far to explain much of what the legislators, politicians, and nativist organizers want to do these days, such as establish English as the official language, promote prayer in schools, and protect the American flag. It appears that, once again, we have failed to learn our lesson from the history of "cultural politics" and "Americanism."

Essentially, the argument advanced in the contemporary immigration and "illegal alien" debate is that these others/outsiders cost "us" more than "they" contribute—an ironic charge considering who built this country in the first place. The economic dimensions of nativism cannot be denied: when we need cheap labor our borders open up; when jobs are in short supply, we not only shut them closed, we want to ship the "others" home. Essentially, the overall impact that today's immigrants and aliens have on the U.S. economy in terms of employment, wages, tax contributions, social services, health and educational costs, and even housing and crime, is a complicated and multi-faceted issue that, at best, can be the subject of speculation and estimation. However, only the worst-disposed would even venture to ignore the contributions of these "outsiders" to this country, which contributions would include, in New York City for example, the many edifices, institutions, utilities, services, and atmospheres created and maintained by American immigrants and their progeny.

Whether real or imagined, the "costs" of immigration only partly explain the current rise in nativist thinking and lawmaking. The balance of the explanation lies in the changing demographics of the incoming foreign population, many, if not most with darker skin and non-Western cultural heritages, practitioners of non-Western religions and native speakers of languages other than English, some even with dramatically different alphabets. The heterogeneity of this new "stock" does not easily permit blending into the mythical melting pot.

A noted historian reports that at the turn of the century

> Nativism cut deeper than economic jealousy or social disapproval. It touched the springs of fear and hatred; it breathed a sense of crisis. Above all it expressed a militantly defensive nationalism: an aroused conviction that an intrusive element menaced the unity, and therefore the integrity and survival, of the nation itself.[19]

To be sure, the pervasiveness and insidiousness of these recent nativistic movements might well create the false impression that this is a novel idea. But, nativism is nothing new. It is as old as the republic itself and probably here to stay, even if at times it submerges beneath the surface. The plagues of America continue to be as they were—xenophobia, jingoism, nationalism, intolerance, prejudice, racism, ethnicism, sexism, homophobia, stereotyping, scapegoating, finger-pointing, race-baiting, fear-mongering, disillusionment, political discord, isolationism, and displacement, to name but a few of the sentiments expressed loudly and crudely on a daily basis over our airwaves.

As the world gets increasingly smaller and more colored, the nativists, in this age of anything but confidence and economic strength, have again lost sight of the advantages of a world community, the humanity of reaching out instead of turning away. Perhaps we are headed for critical mass—the melting pot boiling over as the fires of discontent burn out of control. To extinguish the flames we must focus not on stemming the tide of immigrants and aliens, but in changing the course of nativist thinking.

NOTES

1. Emma Lazarus, *The New Colossus,* in Emma Lazarus: Selections from Her Poetry and Prose 40 (Morris U. Schappes ed., 1944).

2. Israel Zangwill, The Melting-Pot 33–34 (1939).

3. Nathan Glazer & Daniel Patrick Moynihan, Beyond the Melting Pot 288–89 (1963).

4. *Id.* at 291.

5. John Higham, Strangers in the Land: Patterns of American Nativism 1860–1925, at 65 (2d ed. 1988).

6. *Id.* at 66.

7. Elizabeth Bogen, Immigration in New York 140 (1990).

8. Higham, at 277–86.

9. Bogen, at 20.

10. 323 U.S. 214 (1994).

11. Kenneth L. Karst, Belonging to America: Equal Citizenship and the Constitution 91 (1989).

12. Dan Lacey, The Essential Immigrant 58 (1990).

13. Bogen, at 19.

14. Elliott R. Barkan, *Portal of Portals: Speaking of the United States "As Though It Were New York"—And Vice Versa,* in Immigration to New York 218 (William Pencak et al. eds., 1991).

15. Bogen, at 11.

16. Ch. 190, 43 Stat. 153 (referred to as "The Immigration Act of 1924"; also known as the Permanent National Origins Quota Act).

17. Lacey, at 73.

18. Karst, at 86.

19. Higham, at 162.

Chapter 19

The Latino Challenge to Civil Rights and Immigration Policy in the 1990s and Beyond

Rachel F. Moran

The United States faces significant demographic changes that will shape its political destiny. As two researchers wrote recently: "Latino population growth is the future."[1] The White population is declining, the African-American population is stable, and the Latino and Asian-American populations are expanding rapidly. The Asian-American population is growing more quickly than the Latino population, but Latinos constitute a considerably larger segment of the population than Asian Americans. Consequently, Latinos are predicted to become the largest racial or ethnic minority group in America in the early part of the twenty-first century.

As the racial and ethnic diversity of the population grows, tensions have increased. Debates have raged over whether new populations, including Latinos, are assimilating to an American way of life or instead are seeking to preserve distinctive cultures and values in a pluralistic society.[2] Fears that demographic shifts will alter the balance of power among racial and ethnic groups have sparked damaging conflicts. One of the most dramatic examples of this growing discomfort was the rioting in Los Angeles that followed the acquittal of four police officers accused of beating a Black man, Rodney King. The dynamic of the violence appeared to stem not so much from Black-White hostilities as from simmering tensions among racial and ethnic groups in competition for a small piece of the American dream; conflict between African Americans and Korean-American shopkeepers seemed particularly intense. Yet, the unrest in Los Angeles was only the most recent and salient example of clashes among Whites, African Americans, Latinos, and Asian Americans in diverse, congested urban areas.[3]

In addition to these domestic conflicts regarding race and ethnicity, immigration concerns have polarized political debate. Restrictionists favor combating illegal immigration by bolstering support for the Border Patrol, creating a national identification card, and eliminating access to government benefits for the undocumented; some restrictionists also want to cut back on legal immigration. Their opponents

From "Demography and Distrust: The Latino Challenge to Civil Rights and Immigration Policy in the 1990s and Beyond." 8 La Raza L.J. (1995). Originally published in the *La Raza Law Journal*. Reprinted by permission.

favor shifting the focus to punishing employers who hire undocumented workers rather than penalizing the workers themselves; proponents of this approach typically support preserving the current level of legal immigration.[4]

Responsible leadership from academic, legal, and policymaking circles is needed to ensure that demography and distrust do not spell disaster. In particular, today's population shifts provide a critical juncture at which to explore two areas of law and policy that have been of critical importance to Latinos: civil rights and immigration. Traditional civil rights law, rooted in the experience of African Americans in the South, will require reexamination. Immigration policies that use nostalgic images of earlier immigrants from Europe as the benchmark of legitimacy also may do an injustice to recent arrivals to the United States, who must grapple with the contemporary realities of a global economy. To fairly address the rights and responsibilities of these newcomers, policymakers must confront both the international and domestic implications of American immigration policy.

The Civil Rights Model: Beyond Race

In education, shifting demographics have placed increasing strain on the use of integration as the remedy of choice for students of color. This chapter will chronicle the rise of the integration initiative and then demonstrate how Latinos have sought to alter this model of reform to fit their own needs. It will conclude that demography may be leading to distrust and dissension among various elements of the civil rights community at a time when coalition-building is likely to be essential to achieving equal educational opportunity. The push for school integration was rooted in a long-standing campaign that the National Association for the Advancement of Colored People (NAACP) began in the 1930s and 1940s. This effort directly confronted the legacy of a racial caste system in the South that mandated segregation of public facilities by law; this de jure segregation with its message of racial inferiority and subordination had been upheld in *Plessy v. Ferguson*,[5] an 1896 Supreme Court decision. The NAACP's painstaking litigation campaign culminated in the Supreme Court's declaration in *Brown v. Board of Education* that "[s]eparate educational facilities are inherently unequal"[6] when mandated by law. In part because of the need to achieve unanimity, the *Brown* opinion contained several strands of analysis, including both the need to protect racial minorities from invidious discrimination and the recognition of the central role of education in modern-day life. Some believe that *Brown* originally stood as much for the proposition that education is a fundamental right as for the proposition that race-based classifications are inherently harmful and merit close judicial review.[7]

Implementation of the *Brown* case was stymied by the need to litigate in a number of federal district courts that faced a range of local conditions. The NAACP struggled with limited resources to pursue desegregation lawsuits across the South. Even when the NAACP successfully filed suit, its efforts were hampered by the federal courts' reluctance to enter desegregation orders that would meet with decisive resistance from local citizens, school officials, and political representatives. In recognition of the dangers of exposing the federal courts to outraged reactions, the Supreme Court ordered district court judges to mandate that school systems "make a prompt and reasonable start toward full compliance" but at the same time permitted violations to be remedied "with all deliberate speed."[8]

The effort to convert *Brown* from rhetoric into reality received a significant boost when Congress passed the Civil Rights Act of 1964, which authorized federal officials to investigate school districts' compliance with *Brown* and to withhold federal funding if districts failed to comply with a negotiated agreement or court order. During the late 1960s and 1970s, these federal efforts prompted the desegregation of public schools in the South. Today, these schools are among the most racially integrated for Blacks and Whites in the United States.

As federal intervention led to significant enforcement efforts, the Supreme Court began to elaborate on the meaning of *Brown* in ways that narrowed the case's significance. In *Swann v. Charlotte-Mecklenburg Board of Education,*[9] the Court set forth the remedial implications of a finding of unlawful segregation. The Court made clear that "[t]he objective today remains to eliminate from the public schools all vestiges of state-imposed segregation."[10] In defining the scope of the district courts' equitable remedial powers, the Court noted that "judicial powers may be exercised only on the basis of a constitutional violation."[11] The Court concluded that to remedy past intentional discrimination by school officials, district courts could make limited use of racial balance in the schools "as a useful starting point in shaping a remedy to correct past constitutional violations."[12] The Court further noted that school officials had to satisfy the courts that the continued existence of a small number of one-race schools was not the product of their past or present discriminatory actions. Finally, the Court found that districts could alter attendance zones and employ busing plans that did not jeopardize children's health or impinge on the educational process.[13] After evaluating the district courts' remedial powers, the Court noted in closing:

> It does not follow that the communities served by such systems will remain demographically stable, for in a growing, mobile society, few will do so. Neither school authorities nor district courts are constitutionally required to make year-by-year adjustments of the racial composition of student bodies once the affirmative duty to desegregate has been accomplished and racial discrimination through official action is eliminated from the system. This does not mean that federal courts are without power to deal with future problems; but in the absence of a showing that either the school authorities or some other agency of the State has deliberately attempted to fix or alter demographic patterns to affect the racial composition of the schools, further intervention by a district court should not be necessary.[14]

Subsequently, African Americans sought to expand *Brown*'s scope by using it to tackle segregated school conditions in Northern and Western districts. These efforts were only partially successful. In *Keyes v. School District No. 1*, the Supreme Court indicated that school districts would be liable for segregation in the public schools only if it resulted from intentional discrimination by state officials. If the schools were segregated due to private housing patterns rather than invidious state action, the federal courts would not intervene to promote racial balance in the student population. The Court made clear that intentional discrimination could be established not just by statutes and regulations mandating public school segregation, but also by circumstantial evidence such as racially-motivated statements by school officials or racially-sensitive decisions regarding school boundaries, school closings, or school construction.[15] The Court thus indicated that where plaintiffs could amass a persuasive body of circumstantial evidence regarding state officials' racially discriminatory motives, federal judicial relief would be forthcoming.

In *Milliken v. Bradley,*[16] however, the Court demonstrated that even where such intent could be shown, the resulting relief might be extremely limited in scope. Echoing the corrective justice rationale in *Swann, Milliken* made clear that the scope of a judicial remedy would be tailored to the impact of the intentional segregative practices that had taken place.

In short, if the plaintiffs established intentional discrimination by a core urban school district, the federal courts could mandate that suburban school districts participate in desegregation efforts only if they had engaged in intentional discriminatory acts themselves or if the core district's wrongdoing had significant interdistrict effects. Because the harms associated with a core district's discriminatory assignment practices were often hard to trace, courts typically did not order suburban schools to join in a metropolitan desegregation remedy. The *Milliken* decision thus became synonymous with White flight to the suburbs, which largely defeated efforts to rectify past discrimination in urban school systems through integration.

Because the desegregation remedy was tied to remedying past discrimination, federal courts had to cease intervention once earlier wrongs had been corrected, even if serious educational inequities persisted. Increasingly in recent years, federal courts have been terminating desegregation lawsuits, even though substantial school resegregation will result. Judges have become less willing than in previous years to attribute segregated conditions in the schools to past discrimination rather than to contemporaneous private preferences and socioeconomic differences for which the schools are not responsible.

In *Dowell v. Board of Education,*[17] the Supreme Court indicated that federal district courts could bring desegregation lawsuits to a close even when schools revert to being segregated. A court-ordered desegregation plan had been implemented in Oklahoma City in 1972; five years later, the district court held that the school system had eliminated the effects of past intentional discrimination and terminated jurisdiction over the case. Afterwards, the school board adopted a Student Reassignment Plan, which would create some identifiable one-race schools. Because the federal district court found that the board's proposal was not intended to discriminate and further concluded that the reemergence of one-race schools was an outgrowth of residential patterns rather than past school board policies, the judge approved the plan. The court of appeals reversed on the ground that insofar as the plan resulted in one-race schools, it failed to preserve a system in which past segregative practices had been eliminated root and branch.

The Supreme Court overturned the court of appeals' decision because resegregation could result from voluntary, private decisionmaking, rather than from school board policies. That is, school segregation could reflect residential segregation, which in turn was a product of economics and personal preferences rather than past discrimination in the schools.[18] It was up to the district court to determine the origins of segregated school attendance patterns, and the Court remanded the case for further findings of fact. On remand, the district court held that it had properly terminated its jurisdiction.[19] The *Dowell* case signaled to federal district court judges that they could end oversight under desegregation orders if plaintiffs could not persuasively establish that there was a link between current school segregation and past discrimination.

In short, as *Brown* was implemented in subsequent decisions, the federal courts interpreted the case narrowly as establishing a desegregation remedy for intentional discriminatory acts by school officials. This approach made it difficult to address the complex web of circumstances that promote inequality. Plaintiffs often could not trace the interactive effects of various government agencies' actions; moreover, plaintiffs could not explore the interplay of private and public conduct in the perpetuation of racial inequality. The focus on corrective justice by the courts committed civil rights activists to a backward-looking perspective designed to rectify historical wrongs. This framework was not particularly suited to making prospective policy regarding race relations. In fact, the desired end state that came to be associated with *Brown* was one in which race would no longer matter in governmental decision-making. This vision of colorblindness was fundamentally an assimilationist one in which previously disadvantaged Blacks would conform to dominant White norms. Under this view, color consciousness was treated as a vestige of racism rather than the outgrowth of a healthy racial identity.[20]

Dramatic demographic shifts, particularly the explosive growth of the Latino population, have challenged the civil rights paradigm that *Brown* and its progeny exemplify. It might appear that *Brown* provides relevant solutions to pressing Latino problems. As the Latino population expands, Latino youth find themselves in highly segregated public schools. Segregation among Latino students has been steadily increasing since the 1960s; the level of Latino segregation has grown most rapidly in the West where the majority of Latinos reside. Moreover, segregation of Latino students appears to be correlated with diminished educational performance.

However, *Brown*'s approach may not work for much of the Latino student population. Latino segregation often reflects recent, rapid growth in ethnic enclaves, a development that the federal courts would likely characterize as a product of private preferences and economics. Even when Latinos are enrolled in school districts found to have engaged in wrongful segregative acts, White flight may have rendered desegregation meaningless, and lawsuits may be drawing to a close after years of judicial oversight. Just as Latinos find themselves most in need of decisive action to promote equal educational opportunity, *Brown*'s remedies seem most unavailable. Additionally, Latino activists have been cautious about certain aspects of the civil rights framework embodied by *Brown* and its progeny. In attacking the evils of discrimination against Blacks in the South, this framework has elevated race and ethnicity to a position of central importance in defining equality of opportunity. However, race and ethnicity have proven to be artificial organizing principles for Latinos because they have different racial origins and come from a range of countries. Consequently, issues related to racial and ethnic identity frequently have represented barriers to overcome, rather than sources of mutual identification and support.

Precisely because Latinos have diverse racial and ethnic origins, they often have been attuned to questions of class, rather than race or ethnicity, in formulating a reform agenda. Affluent Latinos typically have been more able than African Americans to escape segregated neighborhoods by moving to the suburbs; as a result, many Latinos believe that the most significant impediment to upward mobility is neither race nor ethnicity, but poverty.[21] In keeping with this perspective, Latino advocates have stood at the forefront of efforts to implement class-based reforms. For example, in *San Antonio Independent School District v. Rodriguez,* the Mexican American Legal Defense and Education Fund (MALDEF) attempted to elaborate on the strand of *Brown* that dealt not with racial equality but with the centrality of education in the modern State. MALDEF argued that school finance reform was constitutionally mandated because education was a fundamental right; districts therefore could not offer markedly different levels of instructional services based on the wealth of districts. In addition, MALDEF contended that class differences, just as much as racial ones, deserved strict scrutiny from the courts; thus, states could not classify districts based on their property tax bases in determining the degree of support for educational services without a compelling justification. Both arguments were unsuccessful.[22]

After its defeat in *Rodriguez,* MALDEF turned to bilingual education, emphasizing the role of language and culture as organizing principles for Latinos. Although these characteristics were treated as proxies for race and ethnicity under the traditional civil rights paradigm, this approach masked deeper differences between the Latino initiative and *Brown*'s legacy. Although some proponents of bilingual education treated it as a means of assimilating non-English-proficient and limited-English-proficient children by teaching them English, others emphasized language and culture as distinct and valued characteristics of the Latino population. While *Brown* had come to represent an assimilationist paradigm, the bilingual education push contained seeds of a pluralist conception of racial and ethnic relations.[23]

Under this vision, color consciousness was not necessarily a vestige of racism but instead could reflect a healthy racial or ethnic identity. The persistence of racial and ethnic differences did not necessarily constitute a negative outcome so long as groups were respectful and tolerant of each other's values and ways of life.[24] In the field of education, pluralist reformers have relied less on desegregation and more on multicultural curricula, bilingual education, and community control of well-financed neighborhood schools. Pluralists have demanded a prospective effort to regulate race relations and promote respect and tolerance, rather than simply a retrospective focus on doing corrective justice to eliminate racial caste.

This account of educational reform initiatives after *Brown* illustrates some of the challenges that the traditional civil rights framework confronts in the face of demographic transformations. The framework is rooted in the discrimination that African Americans suffered. As other racial and ethnic groups grow in importance throughout the nation, the bilateral model of race relations that *Brown* addressed no longer captures the richness and complexity of multilateral racial and ethnic relations. As courts withdraw from desegregation lawsuits, the *Brown* paradigm may become increasingly anachronistic for African Americans as well. Indeed, differences in the reform agendas of Latino and African-American activists may be shrinking in importance. With the decline of desegregation, both groups must turn to other strategies, including the development of new curricula responsive to diverse students' needs and school finance reform. These new initiatives often will be consistent with a forward-looking, pluralist vision of race relations, rather than a backward-looking, assimilationist conception of corrective justice. While the push for some of these changes has taken place in the courts, much will have to be directed to extrajudicial settings, such as the legislature and administrative agencies. Insofar as judicial activism is on the wane, the future of civil rights advocacy may well be determined in these more openly political channels.

Immigration Policy: A New Politics of Belonging

Just as demographic shifts challenge the limits of the civil rights framework, the increasingly global nature of the economy has heightened awareness of immigration policy and called into question long-held assumptions about the relationship between the United States and its migrant populations. Traditionally, courts have assumed that immigrants arrived to resettle permanently after formal admission to the United States. In today's global economy, however, the constant, informal flow of capital and labor across international borders means that many immigrants arrive with a tenuous and uncertain status. In particular, the fluidity of capital means that jobs can be exported to countries with cheap labor supplies. Although labor is less mobile than capital, workers too can relocate in search of employment. Itinerant laborers can do jobs that more privileged sectors of the population disdain, remaining a stratified, separate underclass. Or they may be integrated into the host country's economic, social, and political life over the long run.[25]

The United States Supreme Court's decision in *Plyler v. Doe* reflects concerns about creating a permanent underclass, particularly of undocumented immigrants, if basic services such as education are denied them. In holding that a Texas statute that denied undocumented school-age children a free public education violated the Equal Protection Clause, the Court noted that aliens, whether documented or not, were "persons" within the scope of constitutional protection because the Clause was "intended to work nothing less than an abolition of all caste-based and invidious class-based legislation."[26]

The Court's portrayal of the immigration dilemma is equally apt today, as California embarks on an effort to bar undocumented children from access to elementary and secondary education. [See chapters 14, 16, and 17, discussing Prop. 187—*Eds*.] Such rigid stratification along racial and ethnic lines raises the specter of the harms that *Plessy* perpetuated and that *Brown* and its progeny have yet to undo. In *Plyler,* the Court acknowledged that alienage was not a suspect classification and that education was not a fundamental right; therefore, strict scrutiny under the Equal

Protection Clause was inappropriate.[27] Nevertheless, the Court was concerned about a classification that burdened innocent children with a complete deprivation of education that would hamper their ability to pursue fulfilling and productive adult lives.

Applying a rational relation test with bite, the Court struck down the statutory scheme as inadequately related to the State's objectives. It found that the provision was not effective in deterring illegal immigration because the primary incentive for adults to come to the United States was jobs, not a free public education for their children. A bar on hiring undocumented persons would therefore be a far more effective deterrent than the approach the Texas legislature adopted. Moreover, the Court concluded that undocumented children could not be excluded from access to free public education to improve the educational opportunities of other students because the undocumented students were largely indistinguishable from legally resident alien children in terms of educational cost and need.[28] Finally, the Court rejected the State's argument that it could single out undocumented children for exclusion from public education because they were "less likely than other children to remain within the boundaries of the State[ ] and to put their education to productive social or political use within the State."[29] The Court found that many undocumented children were apt to stay in the United States indefinitely and even become permanent legal residents or citizens. Under these circumstances, the costs of "the creation and perpetuation of a subclass of illiterates" far outweighed any savings that would stem from denial of a free public education.[30]

The Court in *Plyler* also correctly touched on the international aspects of the immigration issue. Unlike *Brown* and related civil rights initiatives, which the courts treated as purely domestic issues, an appropriate understanding of immigration-related issues necessarily requires that the United States's treatment of newcomers be placed in a global perspective. The *Plyler* Court noted Congress's plenary power with respect to naturalization, foreign relations, and international commerce as well as its inherent power as sovereign to close its borders. The Court concluded that while classifications based on alienage were "'a routine and normally legitimate part' of the business of the Federal Government," "only rarely are such matters relevant to legislation by a State."[31] States could use classifications based on alienage to advance federal objectives and legitimate State interests, but here, Texas could not point to any clearcut federal policy advanced by its denial of a free public education to undocumented children.

The Court was deeply divided by the *Plyler* case. Four Justices dissented vigorously from the holding. The dissent argued that the majority had elevated social policy above legal analysis in reaching its decision. Although the dissent recognized that "[t]he failure of enforcement of the immigration laws over more than a decade and the inherent difficulty and expense of sealing our vast borders have combined to create a grave socioeconomic dilemma," the dissent believed that these pressing issues must be addressed by the political branches of government, not by the judiciary.

Because alienage was not a suspect classification and education was not a fundamental right, the dissent concluded that the Court was obligated to apply a rational relation test to the Texas statutory scheme. Under this standard, according to the dissent, the State's goals of preventing undue depletion of its limited resources for education and preserving the fiscal integrity of its school financing system were legitimate.

With the rise of new efforts to restrict undocumented persons' access to public benefits and services, efforts to address immigration law and policy are both timely and critical. One of the key observations in the *Plyler* case is the disjuncture between formal immigration policy and the informal realities of migrant labor flows. Although the relevance of this observation to constitutional analysis was disputed, all of the Justices seemed to agree that the failure to develop a coherent regulatory framework for immigration posed grave social dangers. To enhance the development of immigration law and policy, whether in the judicial, legislative, or executive branch or at the federal or state level, scholars and policymakers must build on the *Plyler* Court's insight by confronting the disparity between traditional images of immigration and the contemporary realities that immigrants face.

These are challenging times for lawyers, academicians, and policymakers. Traditional civil rights and immigration models will be tested by burgeoning new populations that reflect in part the growing interdependence of the world economy. To alleviate the strains on the civil rights and immigration paradigms, researchers and policymakers must work to devise creative new approaches to achieve equality of opportunity, particularly for Latinos.

NOTES

1. Jorge Chapa & Richard R. Valencia, *Latino Population Growth, Demographic Characteristics, and Educational Stagnation: An Examination of Recent Trends*, 15 Hispanic J. Behav. Sci. 165, 167 (1993).

2. Bill Ong Hing, *Beyond the Rhetoric of Assimilation and Cultural Pluralism: Addressing the Tension of Separatism and Conflict in an Immigration-Driven Multiracial Society*, 81 Calif. L. Rev. 863, 870–85 (1993).

3. *Id.* at 885–902.

4. Ronald Brownstein, *Polarization Marks Debate on Immigration Policy; Politics: One Side Would Tighten Borders, the Other Would Punish Employers; Consensus May Be Impossible*, L.A. Times, Nov. 30, 1993, at A1.

5. 163 U.S. 357 (1896).

6. 347 U.S. 483, 495 (1954).

7. See Dennis J. Hutchinson, *Unanimity and Desegregation: Decisionmaking in the Supreme Court, 1948–1958*, 68 Geo. L.J. 1, 43–44, 87 (1979).

8. Brown v. Board of Education, 349 U.S. 294, 300–301 (1955).

9. 402 U.S. 1 (1971).

10. *Id.* at 15.

11. *Id.* at 16.

12. *Id.* at 25.

13. *Id.* at 26–31.

14. *Id.* at 31–32.

15. 413 U.S. 189, at 201–203 (1973).

16. 418 U.S. 717 (1974).

17. 498 U.S. 237 (1991).

18. *Id.* at 243, 250 n.2.

19. 778 F.Supp. 1144 (W.D. Okla. 1991), motion denied, 782 F.Supp. 574 (W.D. Okla. 1992), aff'd, 8 F.3d 1501 (10th Cir. 1993).

20. *See* Gary Peller, *Race Consciousness*, 1990 Duke L.J. 758, 791–92.

21. Douglas S. Massey & Nancy A. Denton, American Apartheid: Segregation and the Making of the Underclass, 87–88, 113–14 (1993).

22. 411 U.S. 1, 18–39 (1973).

23. See Rachel F. Moran, *Bilingual Education as a Status Conflict*, 75 Calif. L. Rev . 321, 341 (1987); Rachel F. Moran, *The Politics of Discretion: Federal Intervention in Bilingual Education*, 76 Calif. L. Rev. 1249, 1252–53 (1988).

24. Hing, at 902–11; Rachel F. Moran, *Of Democracy, Devaluation, and Bilingual Education*, 26 Creighton L. Rev. 255, 303–305 (1993).

25. Kevin R. Johnson, *Los Olvidados: Images of the Immigrant, Political Power of Noncitizens, and Immigration Law Enforcement*, 1993 B.Y.U. L. Rev. 1139, 1144–47.

26. 457 U.S. 202, at 213 (1982).

27. *Id.* at 223.

28. *Id.* at 228–29.

29. *Id.* at 230.

30. *Id.*

31. *Id.* at 225.

From the Editors
Issues and Comments

Are Proposition 187 and its look-alikes racist? Or are they only legitimate measures aimed at getting control over our borders?

Is the United States experiencing a revival of hostility toward immigrants and, if so, why?

Is the United States, as a number of authors assert, at least in part responsible for the influx of immigrants from Mexico? If so, by virtue of what past actions?

Peter Brimelow's *Alien Nation* argues that any nation has the right to determine its own ethnic and cultural composition by restricting immigration. Do you agree?

Imagine that people judge you as illiterate and unintelligent because of the way you look and speak. Has this ever happened to you, perhaps because you employed "teen-talk"? If so, how did it make you feel? Why are some accents, such as upper-class English or French, deemed high status and others not?

Do you agree that Proposition 187 targets women more than men? Since it restricts social services used by the poor, is it classist as well? Is this a way to remove women and the poor from the United States, or does it really attempt to remove all illegal immigrants?

The "plenary power" doctrine allows Congress to pass racist immigration laws, such as the Chinese Exclusion Act or quotas favoring Northern Europeans, without the possibility of judicial review. Does immigration law, then, hold a mirror to U.S. racial attitudes, showing how we would treat even domestic minorities if we were not limited by the Thirteenth and Fourteenth Amendments and civil rights legislation?

Why did some minorities support Proposition 187?

Suggested Readings

Bosniak, Linda S. "Exclusion and Membership: The Dual Identity of the Undocumented Worker under United States Law." 1988 *Wisconsin Law Review 955*.

Boswell, Richard A. "Restrictions on Non-Citizens' Access to Public Benefits: Flawed Premise, Unnecessary Response." 42 *UCLA Law Review* 1475 (1995).

Brimelow, Peter. *Alien Nation: Common Sense about America's Immigration Disaster*. New York: Random House, 1995.

Butler, R. E. "Rusty." *On Creating a Hispanic America: A Nation within a Nation?* Washington, D.C.: Council for Inter-American Security, 1985.

Calavita, Kitty. *Inside the State: The Bracero Program, Immigration, and the I.N.S.* New York: Routledge, 1992.

Carens, Joseph H. "Aliens and Citizens: The Case for Open Borders." *Review of Politics* 49 (1987): 251

Chavez, Leo R. "The Power of the Imagined Community: The Settlement of Undocumented Mexicans and Central Americans in the United States." *American Anthropologist* 96 (1994): 52

———. *Shadowed Lives: Undocumented Immigrants in American Society*. 2d ed. Fort Worth: Harcourt Brace, 1998.

Clark, Juan M. *The 1980 Mariel Exodus: An Analysis and Prospect*. Washington, D.C.: Council for Inter-American Security, 1981.

Conover, Ted. *Coyotes: A Journey through the Secret World of America's Illegal Aliens*. New York: Vintage, 1987.

Davis, Marilyn. *Mexican Voices/American Dreams: An Oral History of Mexican Immigration to the United States*. New York: Henry Holt, 1990.

Dunn, Timothy J. *The Militarization of the U.S.–Mexican Border, 1978–1992: Low-Intensity Conflict Doctrine Comes Home*. Austin: CMAS Books, University of Texas, 1996.

Fan, Stephen Shie-Wei. "Immigration Law and the Promise of Critical Race Theory: Opening the Academy to the Voices of Aliens and Immigrants." 97 *Columbia Law Review* 1202 (1997).

Fiscal Impact of Undocumented Aliens: Selected Estimates for Seven States. New York: Urban Institute, 1994.

Fix, Michael, and Jeffrey S. Passel. *Immigration and Immigrants: Setting the Record Straight*. New York: Urban Institute, 1994.

Garcia, Maria Cristina. *Havana USA: Cuban Exiles and Cuban Americans in South Florida, 1959–1994*. Berkeley: University of California Press, 1996.

Golden, Renny, and Michael McConnell. *Sanctuary: The New Underground Railroad*. Maryknoll, N.Y.: Orbis Books, 1986.

Grant, Lindsey, and John H. Tanton. *Immigration and the American Conscience*. Washington, D.C.: Environmental Fund, 1982.

Griswold del Castillo, Richard. *The Treaty of Guadalupe Hidalgo: A Legacy of Conflict*. Norman: University of Oklahoma Press, 1990.

Hing, Bill Ong. "Beyond the Rhetoric of Assimilation and Cultural Pluralism: Addressing the Tension of Separatism and Conflict in an Immigration-Driven Multiracial Society." 81 *California Law Review* 863 (1993).

Hondagneu-Sotelo, Pierrette. *Gendered Transitions: Mexican Experiences of Immigration*. Berkeley: University of California Press, 1994.

Human Rights and the Mexico-U.S. Border. Philadelphia: American Friends Service Committee, Immigration Law Enforcement Project, 1990.

Johnson, Kevin R. "Civil Rights and Immigration: Challenges for the Latino Community in the Twenty-First Century." 8 *La Raza Law Journal* 42 (1995).

———. "Fear of an 'Alien Nation': Race, Immigration, and Immigrants." 7 *Stanford Law and Policy Review* 111 (1996).

———. "Free Trade and Closed Borders: NAFTA and Mexican Immigration to the United States." 27 *University of California at Davis Law Review* 937 (1994).

———. "*Los Olvidados:* Images of the Immigrant, Political Power of Noncitizens, and Immigration Law and Enforcement." 1993 *Brigham Young University Law Review* 1139 (1993).

———. "Why Alienage Jurisdiction? Historical Foundations and Modern Justifications for Federal Jurisdiction over Disputes Involving Noncitizens." 21 *Yale Journal of International Law* 1 (1996).

Lamm, Richard D., and Gary Imhoff. *The Immigration Time Bomb: The Fragmenting of America*. New York: Truman Tallet Books, E. P. Dutton, 1985.

Laughlin, Harry H. *Conquest by Immigration: A Report of the Special Committee on Immigration and Naturalization*. New York: Chamber of Commerce of the State of New York, 1939.

Lind, Michael. *The Next American Nation: The New Nationalism and the Fourth American Revolution*. New York: Free Press, 1995.

Luna, Guadalupe T. "'Agricultural Underdogs' and International Agreements: The Legal Context of Agricultural Workers within the Rural Economy." 26 *New Mexico Law Review* 9 (1996).

Neuman, Gerald L. "Aliens as Outlaws: Government Services, Proposition 187, and the Structure of Equal Protection Doctrine." 42 *UCLA Law Review* 1425 (1995).

Portes, Alejandro, and Robert L. Bach. *Latin Journey: Cuban and Mexican Immigrants in the United States*. Berkeley: University of California Press, 1985.

Schlesinger, Arthur M., Jr. *The Disuniting of America*. New York: W. W. Norton, 1992.

Schuck, Peter H. "Alien Rumination." 105 *Yale Law Journal* 1963 (1996).

Schuck, Peter H., and Rogers M. Smith. *Citizenship without Consent: Illegal Aliens in the American Polity*. New Haven: Yale University Press, 1985.

Sealing Our Borders: The Human Toll. Philadelphia: American Friends Service Committee, 1992.

Tanton, John H. *Rethinking Immigration Policy*. Washington, D.C.: Federation for American Immigration Reform, 1979.

Walzer, Michael. *Spheres of Justice: A Defense of Pluralism and Equality*. New York: Basic Books, 1983.

Nativism, Racism, and Our Social Construction as a "Problem" Group

How Once We Were Here, We Were Racialized by the Dominant Culture

Latinos, especially newcomers, have in many periods been demonized and treated in discriminatory fashion, almost as exiles in their own land. How and why has this been so? The chapters in Part III, written by leading sociologists, historians, and lawyers, examine what lies behind the hostile treatment many Latinos have received at the hands of the American government and citizenry. The term *nativism* has been coined to describe the periodic waves of anti-immigrant sentiment, coupled with white supremacy, that sweep the nation, making things difficult for Latinos and other populations perceived as foreign. We seem to be in the midst of such a period today; what does it have in common with earlier ones? The chapters that follow address these questions and explore whether nativism has an economic or racial base, and what Latinos ought to do about it.

Chapter 20

Anglo-Saxons and Mexicans

Reginald Horsman

> The Anglo-Saxon blood could never be subdued by anything that claimed Mexican origin.
>
> —James Buchanan, February 14, 1845

The decisive years in the creation of a new Anglo-Saxon political ideology were from the mid-1830s to the mid-1840s. In these years American politicians and the American population were overwhelmed by a variety of influences, both practical and theoretical, which inspired a belief that the American Anglo-Saxons were destined to dominate or penetrate the American continents and large areas of the world. Americans had faith that they would increase in such numbers that they would personally shape the destiny of other areas.

The catalyst in the overt adoption of a racial Anglo-Saxonism was the meeting of Americans and Mexicans in the Southwest, the Texas Revolution, and the war with Mexico. In confronting the Mexicans the Americans clearly formulated the idea of themselves as an Anglo-Saxon race. The use of *Anglo-Saxon* in a racial sense, somewhat rare in the political arguments of the early 1830s, increased rapidly later in the decade and became commonplace by the mid-1840s. The manner in which the Anglo-Saxon race was being isolated from other peoples was stated with clarity by Senator Benjamin Leigh of Virginia in January 1836 when opposing the abolitionist petitions. After pointing out that his fellow Congressmen had only to remember how the mobs of Cincinnati, Philadelphia, and New York had dealt with the few free Negroes in their midst to appreciate what would follow general emancipation, he candidly sketched the problem: "It is peculiar to the character of this Anglo-Saxon race of men to which we belong, that it has never been contented to live in the same country with any other distinct race, upon terms of equality; it has, invariably, when placed in that situation, proceeded to exterminate or enslave the other race in some form or other, or, failing in that, to abandon the country."[1]

The idea of the Anglo-Saxon race as a distinct, all-encompassing force was expressed with increasing frequency in the late 1830s. In February 1837 William Gilpin wrote to his father from New Orleans that while the town was still Gallic in character the "Anglo-Saxon is pushing aside the Frenchman and eating him up. The big steamers . . . are Anglo-Saxon, the huge stores and warehouses into which [goods] are piled have an Anglo-Saxon look and an Anglo-Saxon ship bears them hence. [Of] all the new part of the city, the only decent part is English."[2] When Horace Bushnell, in August 1837, delivered an oration on the principles of national greatness, he used old and familiar arguments concerning America as a land saved for events of world significance; however, he used a new precision in writing of the origin of the people for whom the New World had been preserved. "Out of all the inhabitants of the world," he said, ". . . a select stock, the Saxon, and out of this the British family, the noblest of the stock, was chosen to people our country." In contrast, the Mexican state, he said, had started with fundamental disadvantages in the character of its immigrants. If the quality of the British people was changed into that of the Mexican, "five years would make their noble island a seat of poverty and desolation." For Bushnell, God had reserved America for a special people of Saxon blood.[3]

By the 1830s the Americans were eagerly grasping at reasons for their own success and for the failure of others. Although the white Americans of Jacksonian America wanted personal success and wealth, they also wanted a clear conscience. If the United States was to remain in the minds of its people a nation divinely ordained for great deeds, then the fault for the suffering inflicted in the rise to power and prosperity had to lie elsewhere. White Americans could rest easier if the sufferings of other races could be blamed on racial weakness rather than on the whites' relentless search for wealth and power. In the 1830s and 1840s, when it became obvious that American and Mexican interests were incompatible and that the Mexicans would suffer, innate weaknesses were found in the Mexicans. Americans, it was argued, were not to be blamed for forcibly taking the northern provinces of Mexico, for Mexicans, like Indians, were unable to make proper use of the land. The Mexicans had failed because they were a mixed, inferior race with considerable Indian and some black blood. The world would benefit if a superior race shaped the future of the Southwest.

By the time of the Mexican War, America had placed the Mexicans firmly within the rapidly emerging hierarchy of superior and inferior races. While the Anglo-Saxons were depicted as the purest of the pure—the finest Caucasians—the Mexicans who stood in the way of southwestern expansion were depicted as a mongrel race, adulterated by extensive intermarriage with an inferior Indian race. Travelers delighted in depicting the Mexicans as an unimprovable breed and were particularly scathing about the inhabitants of Mexico's northern provinces. T. J. Farnham in 1840 wrote of the Californians as "an imbecile, pusillanimous, race of men, and unfit to control the destinies of that beautiful country." No one who knew "the indolent, mixed race of California," he argued, could believe they would long populate much less govern, the region. The mixed white and Indian races of California and Mexico "must fade away; while the mingling of different branches of the Caucasian family in the States" would produce a race which would expand to cover all the northern provinces of Mexico.[4]

NOTES

1. *Register of Debates,* 24th Cong., 1st sess., p. 201, Jan. 19, 1836.

2. Quoted in Thomas L. Karnes, *William Gilpin: Western Nationalist* (Austin: University of Texas Press, 1970), p. 39.

3. Horace Bushnell, An Oration, Pronounced before the Society of Phi Beta Kappa, at New Haven, on the Principles of National Greatness (August 15, 1837), pp. 5, 9, 11, 16.

4. Quoted in Robert F. Heizer and Alan M. Almquist, *The Other Californians: Prejudice and Discrimination under Spain, Mexico, and the United States to 1920* (Berkeley: University of California Press, 1971), p. 140.

Chapter 21

"Occupied" Mexico

Ronald Takaki

Mexicans viewed the conquest of their land very differently. Suddenly, they were "thrown among those who were strangers to their language, customs, laws, and habits." The border had been moved, and now thousands of Mexicans found themselves inside the United States. The treaty permitted them to remain in the United States or to move across the new southern border. If they stayed, they would be guaranteed "the enjoyment of all the rights of citizens of the United States according to the principles of the Constitution."[1]

Most remained, but they felt a peculiar alienation. "Our race, our unfortunate people will have to wander in search of hospitality in a strange land, only to be ejected later," Mexican diplomat Manuel Crescíon Rejón predicted. "Descendents of the Indians that we are, the North Americans hate us, their spokesmen depreciate us, even if they recognize the justice of our cause, and they consider us unworthy to form with them one nation and one society, they clearly manifest that their future expansion begins with the territory that they take from us and pushing aside our citizens who inhabit the land." A few years later, Pablo de la Guerra vented his frustrations before the California Senate. The "conquered" Mexicans, he complained, did not understand the new language, English, which was now "prevalent" on "their native soil." They had become *foreigners in their own land.*"[2]

What this meant for many Mexicans was political vulnerability and powerlessness. In California, for example, while Mexicans were granted suffrage, they found that democracy was essentially for Anglos only. At first, they greatly outnumbered Anglos, by about ten to one. But the discovery of gold near John Sutter's mill led to a massive migration into California; by 1849, the Anglo population had reached 100,000, compared to only 13,000 Mexicans.

Dominant in the state legislature, Anglos enacted laws aimed at Mexicans. An antivagrancy act, described as the "Greaser Act," defined vagrants as "all persons who [were] commonly known as 'Greasers' or the issue of Spanish or Indian blood . . . and who [went] armed and [were] not peaceable and quiet persons." A foreign miners' tax of $20 monthly was in practice a "Mexican Miners' Tax." The tax collectors took fees mainly from Spanish-speaking miners, including American citizens of Mexican ancestry.

Many of the miners had come from Mexico, where techniques for extracting gold had been developed. In California, they shared this knowledge with Anglo miners, introducing Spanish mining terms such as *bonanza* (rich ore) and *placer* (deposits containing gold particles). But Anglos resented the Mexicans as competitors, making no distinction between Mexicans and Mexican Americans. "The Yankee regarded every man but a native American as an interloper," observed a contemporary, "who had no right to come to California and pick up the gold of 'free and enlightened citizens.'" Anglo miners sometimes violently defended what they regarded as their "right" to the gold. In his memoir, Antonio Franco Coronel described one frightening experience: "I arrived at the Placer Seco [about March 1849] and began to work at a regular digging. . . . Presently news was circulated that it had been resolved to evict all those who were not American citizens from the placers because it was believed that the foreigners did not have the right to exploit the placers." Shortly afterward, a hundred Anglos invaded the diggings of Coronel and some other Mexicans, forcing them to flee for their lives. "All of these men raised their pistols, their Bowie knives; some had rifles, others pickaxes and shovels."[3]

Though Mexicans were a minority of the state population, they continued to constitute a sizable presence in Southern California. In Santa Barbara, for example, Mexicans represented a majority of the voters and dominated local elections. "The Americans have very little influence in the elections," complained Charles Huse in the 1850s. The Mexicans possessed a majority of the votes. When they were united, they were able to elect whomever they wished. However, Huse predicted that Anglos would have "all the power" in a few years and would not consult the Mexicans about anything. Indeed, Mexicans soon became a minority as Anglos flocked to Santa Barbara. In 1873, Mexican voters were overwhelmed at the polls. Though they elected Nicolas Covarrubias as county sheriff, they lost the positions of county assessor, clerk, treasurer, and district attorney. Politically, the Anglos were now in command. "The native population wear a wondering, bewildered look at the sudden change of affairs," a visitor noted, "yet seem resigned to their unexpected situation, while the conquerors are proud and elated with their conquest." Mexican political participation declined precipitously in Santa Barbara—to only 15 percent of registered voters in 1904 and only 3 percent in 1920.[4]

Compared to California, the political proscription of Mexicans in Texas was more direct. There, Mexicans were granted suffrage, but only in principle. A merchant in Corpus Christi reported that the practice in several counties was to withhold the franchise from Mexicans. A traveler observed that the Mexicans in San Antonio could elect a government of their own if they voted but added: "Such a step would be followed, however, by a summary revolution." In 1863, after a closely contested election, the *Fort Brown Flag* editorialized: "We are opposed to allowing an ignorant crowd of Mexicans to determine the political questions in this country, where a man is supposed to vote knowingly and thoughtfully." During the 1890s, many counties established "white primaries" to disfranchise Mexicans as well as blacks, and the legislature instituted additional measures like the poll tax to reduce Mexican political participation.

Political restrictions lessened the ability of Mexicans not only to claim their rights as citizens, but also to protect their rights as landowners. The original version of the Treaty of Guadalupe Hidalgo had contained a provision, Article X, which guaranteed protection of "all prior and pending titles to property of every description." In ratifying the treaty, however, the U.S. Senate omitted this article. Instead, American emissaries offered the Mexican government a "Statement of Protocol" to reassure Mexicans that "the American government by suppressing the Xth article . . . did not in any way intend to annul the grants of lands made by Mexico in the ceded territories." Grantees would be allowed to have their legitimate titles acknowledged in American courts.

But whether the courts would in fact confirm their land titles was another matter. In New Mexico, the state surveyor general handled conflicts over land claims until 1891, when a Court of Private Land Claims was established. Dominated by Anglo legal officials, the court confirmed the grants of only 2,051,526 acres, turning down claims for 33,439,493 acres. The court's actions led to Anglo ownership of four-fifths of the Mexican land grants.[5]

Similarly, in California, Mexican land titles were contested. Three years after the Treaty of Guadalupe Hidalgo, Congress passed a land law establishing a commission to review the validity of some twenty land grants made under Spanish rule and another five hundred by the Mexican government. The boundaries for these land grants had been drawn without surveying instruments and were loosely marked on maps indicating a notched tree, a spot "between the hills at the head of a running water," a pile of stones, and the like. Frequently, land was measured with the expression *poco más o menos,* "a little more or less." The entire Pomona Valley, for example, was described as "the place being vacant which is known by the name of [Rancho] San Jose, distant some six leagues, more or less, from the Ex-Mission of San Gabriel." U.S. land law, however, required accurate boundaries and proof of legitimate titles.

Such evidence, Mexican landholders discovered, was very difficult to provide. Unfamiliar with American law and lacking English language skills, they became prey to Anglo lawyers. If they were successfully able to prove their claim, they would often be required to pay their lawyers one-quarter of their land. Others borrowed money at high interest rates in order to pay legal fees; after they won their cases, many rancheros were forced to sell their land to pay off their debts. "The *average* length of time required to secure evidence of ownership," historian Walton Bean calculated, "was *17 years* from the time of submitting a claim to the board." Furthermore, during this time, squatters often occupied the lands, and when the rancheros finally proved their ownership, they found it difficult and sometimes impossible to remove them. In the end, whether or not they won their claims, most of the great Mexican rancheros in northern California lost their lands. . . .

The Internal Borders of Exclusion

Included as laborers, Mexicans found themselves excluded socially, kept at a distance from Anglo society. Like Caliban, they were isolated by the borders of racial segregation. Their world was one of Anglo over Mexican. Even on the large cattle ranches of Texas where Mexicans and Anglos lived together and formed loyalties and sometimes even friendships, integration did not mean equality. J. Frank Dobie, for example, described one of the workers on his family's ranch. This "old, faithful Mexican" had been employed on the ranch for over twenty years and he was "almost the best friend" Dobie had. "Many a time 'out in the pasture' I have put my lips to the same water jug that he had drunk from," he remembered fondly. But Dobie added: "At the same time neither he nor I would think of his eating at the dining table with me."[6]

Racial etiquette defined proper demeanor and behavior for Mexicans. In the presence of Anglos, they were expected to assume "a deferential body posture and respectful voice tone." They knew that public buildings were considered "Anglo territory," and that they were permitted to shop in the Anglo business section of town only on Saturdays. They could patronize Anglo cafes, but only the counter and carryout service. "A group of us Mexicans who were well dressed once went to a restaurant in Amarillo," complained Wenceslao Iglesias in the 1920s, "and they told us that if we wanted to eat we should go to the special department where it said 'For Colored People.' I told my friend that I would rather die from starvation than to humiliate myself before the Americans by eating with the Negroes." At sunset, Mexicans had to retreat to their barrios.[7]

In the morning, Mexican parents sent their children to segregated schools. "There would be a revolution in the community if the Mexicans wanted to come to the white schools," an educator said. "Sentiment is bitterly against it. It is based on racial inferiority." The wife of an Anglo ranch manager in Texas put it this way: "Let him [the Mexican] have as good an education but still let him know he is not as good as a white man. God did not intend him to be; He would have made them white if He had." For many Anglos, Mexicans also represented a threat to their daughters. "Why don't we let the Mexicans come to the white school?" an Anglo sharecropper angrily declared. "Because a damned greaser is not fit to sit side of a white girl."[8]

In the segregated schools, Mexican children were trained to become obedient workers. Like the sugar planters in Hawaii who wanted to keep the American-born generation of Japanese on the plantations, Anglo farmers in Texas wanted the schools to help reproduce the labor force. "If every [Mexican] child has a high school education," sugar beet growers asked, "who will labor?" A farmer in Texas explained: "If I wanted a man I would want one of the more ignorant ones. . . . Educated Mexicans are the hardest to handle. . . . It is all right to educate them no higher than we educate them here in these little towns. I will be frank. They would make more desirable citizens if they would stop about the seventh grade."[9]

Serving the interests of the growers, Anglo educators prepared Mexican children to take the place of their parents. "It isn't a matter of what is the best way to handle the education here to make citizens of them," a school trustee in Texas stated frankly. "It is politics." School policy was influenced by the needs of the local growers, he elaborated. "We don't need skilled or white-collared Mexicans. . . . The farmers are not interested in educating Mexicans. They know that then they can get better wages and conditions." A Texas school superintendent explained that not all school boards wanted him to enforce compulsory attendance: "When I come to a new school I always ask the board if they want the Mexicans in school. Here they told me to leave them alone. If I tried to enforce the compulsory attendance law here the board would get sore at me and maybe cause us to lose our places, so I don't say anything. If I got 150 Mexicans ready for school I would be out of a job." Another Texas superintendent explained why schools should not educate Mexican children: "You have doubtless heard that ignorance is bliss; it seems that it is so when one has to transplant onions. . . . If a man has very much sense or education either, he is not going to stick to this kind of work. So you see it is up to the white population to keep the Mexican on his knees in an onion patch."[10]

Consequently, the curriculum for Mexican students emphasized domestic science and manual training. In Los Angeles, they were taught not only manual-labor skills, but also the appropriate attitudes of hard work and disciplined behavior. "Before sending [Mexican] boys and girls out to accept positions," a Los Angeles teacher explained, "they must be taught that, technically expert though they may be, they must keep in mind that their employers carry the responsibility of the business and outline the work, and that the employees must be pliant, obedient, courteous, and willing to help the enterprise."[11]

There were educators who saw that Mexican children were capable of learning. "The Mexicans have good minds and are earnest students," a teacher stated. "The Mexican children generally are as capable intellectually as the Americans, but the Mexicans are poorer than the whites, so the comparison of their present progress in school isn't fair." Some teachers tried to give Mexican children a sense of dignity and self-respect. Ernesto Galarza recalled how his school principal "Miss Hopley and her teachers never let us forget why we were at Lincoln; for those who were alien, to become good Americans; for those who were so born, to accept the rest of us." Galarza and his fellow students discovered "the secrets of the English language" and grieved over the "tragedies of Bo-Peep." Every morning, the students stood and recited the pledge of allegiance to the flag of the United States. In his school, Americanization did not mean "scrubbing away" what made them Mexican. "No one was ever scolded or punished for speaking in his native tongue on the playground." The teachers tried to pronounce their Spanish names. "Becoming a proud American," Galarza said, "did not mean feeling ashamed of being a Mexican."[12]

Galarza's experience in school was exceptional, for Mexican children were not usually encouraged to develop self-esteem. "The Mexican children almost don't receive any education," Alonso Galvan complained to an interviewer in the 1920s. "They are taught hardly anything."[13]

NOTES

1. Rodolfo Acuña, OCCUPIED AMERICA: A HISTORY OF CHICANOS (New York, 1981), p. 199; David J. Weber (ed.), FOREIGNERS IN THEIR NATIVE LAND: HISTORICAL ROOTS OF THE MEXICAN AMERI-

CANS (Albuquerque, N.M. 1973), p. 19. The Treaty of Guadalupe Hidalgo described the newly acquired territory as places "occupied" by U.S. forces. See the terms of the treaty in Wayne Moquin (ed.), A DOCUMENTARY HISTORY OF THE MEXICAN AMERICANS (New York, 1972), pp. 182–87.

2. Acuña, OCCUPIED AMERICA, p. 20; Weber (ed.),FOREIGNERS IN THEIR NATIVE LAND, p. 176.

3. Robert F. Heizer and Alan F. Almquist, THE OTHER CALIFORNIANS: PREJUDICE AND DISCRIMINATION UNDER SPAIN, MEXICO, AND THE UNITED STATES TO 1920 (Berkeley, Calif., 1971), p. 143; Weber (ed.), FOREIGNERS IN THEIR NATIVE LAND, p. 171–73.

4. Albert Camarillo, CHICANOS IN A CHANGING SOCIETY: FROM MEXICAN PUEBLOS TO AMERICAN BARRIOS IN SANTA BARBARA AND SOUTHERN CALIFORNIA, 1848–1930 (Cambridge, Mass., 1979), p. 23, 46, 41, 187. This is an important community study that provides insights into larger patterns of Chicano experiences.

5. Mario Barrera, RACE AND CLASS IN THE SOUTHWEST: A THEORY OF RACIAL INEQUALITY (Notre Dame, Ind., 1979), pp. 26–27. This is a very useful integration of theories of race and class and the history of Chicanos.

6. David Montejano, ANGLOS AND MEXICANS IN THE MAKING OF TEXAS, 1836–1986 (Austin, Tex., 1987), p. 250.

7. Manuel Gamio, MEXICAN IMMIGRATION TO THE UNITED STATES (Chicago, 1930), p. 177.

8. Montejano, ANGLOS AND MEXICANS, pp. 226–27, 221, 194.

9. Sarah Deutsch, NO SEPARATE REFUGE: CULTURE, CLASS, AND GENDER ON AN ANGLO-HISPANIC FRONTIER IN THE AMERICAN SOUTHWEST, 1880–1940 (New York, 1987), p. 141; Rosalinda M. Gonzalez, *Chicanas and Mexican Immigrant Families, 1920–1940: Women's Subordination and Family Exploitation,* in Lois Scharf and Joan M. Jensen (eds.), DECADES OF DISCONTENT: THE WOMEN'S MOVEMENT, 1920–1940 (Westport, Conn., 1983), p. 66.

10. Montejano, ANGLOS AND MEXICANS, pp. 192–93; Paul S. Taylor, AN AMERICAN-MEXICAN FRONTIER (Chapel Hill, N.C., 1934), p. 194.

11. Montejano, ANGLOS AND MEXICANS, p. 160; Mario T. García, DESERT IMMIGRANTS: THE MEXICANS OF EL PASO, 1880–1920 (New Haven, Conn., 1981), p. 117.

12. Taylor, AMERICAN-MEXICAN FRONTIER, p. 204; Ernesto Galarza, BARRIO BOY: THE STORY OF A BOY'S ACCULTURATION (Notre Dame, Ind., 1971), p. 211.

13. Gamio, MEXICAN IMMIGRANT, pp. 222–23; García, DESERT IMMIGRANTS, p. 125.

Chapter 22

Initial Contacts
Niggers, Redskins, and Greasers

Arnoldo De León

[T]he English saw the Spanish as an embodiment of racial impurity. For hundreds of years, racial mixing or *mestizaje* had occurred in the Iberian peninsula between Spaniards and Moors. At a time when Elizabethans were becoming more and more sensitive to the significance of color—equating whiteness with purity and Christianity, and blackness with baseness and the devil—Spaniards came to be thought of as not much better than light-skinned Moors and Africans.

English immigrants to the North American colonies probably brought those ideas with them and were certainly exposed to them through anti-Catholic and anti-Spanish literature constantly arriving in the new society. Men of letters, ministers, and propagandists helped in disseminating such notions. Military clashes along the Georgia-Florida border in the eighteenth century only intensified the hatred.

As for the Mexican aborigines, the English conceived of them as degenerate creatures—un-Christian, uncivilized, and racially impure. From letters, histories, and travel narratives, English writers put together a portrait that turned the people of Mexico into a degraded humanity. The natives subscribed to heathenism, and witches and other devilish agents permeated their culture. They partook of unholy things like polygamy, sodomy, and incest and rejected Christianity outright. Furthermore, they practiced savage rituals like human sacrifice and cannibalism. Of all the Latin American inhabitants, the Mexican Indians seemed the most beastly, for though they were in many ways the most advanced of all the New World peoples, they exercised the grossest violation of civility by these practices. Stories of Aztec gods like Quetzalcoatl who were half man and half beast and accounts of exotic Aztec rites only convinced the English of the Indians' place on the fringes of humankind, with dubious claims to existence, civilization, and Christian salvation.

While such images of the Mexican natives may not have been as widespread as those held of Spaniards, they were nonetheless familiar to many colonists. In newspapers, recent histories, and re-editions of old propaganda materials, furthermore, colonists were able to read things about the origins of the Mexicans which perpetuated enriched images acquired from the mother country.

In addition to ideas that had been fashioned vicariously, there were those that arose from intimate contact with other peoples whom whites esteemed no more than the Mexican aborigines or the Spaniards. The long history of hostilities against North American Indians on the frontier and the institution of Afro-American slavery molded negative attitudes toward dark skin, "savagery," "vice," and interracial sex. The majority of those who responded to empresario calls most assuredly thought along those lines, for they came from the states west of the Appalachians and south of the Ohio River—Louisiana, Alabama, Arkansas, Tennessee, Missouri, Mississippi, Georgia, and Kentucky. A significant number were Eastern born, but had been part of the frontier movement before their transplantation into Texas. From the Southern and frontier-oriented culture they had acquired a certain repulsion for dark-skinned people and a distaste for miscegenation. Believing that the mores of their own provincial institutions should apply in the new frontier, they assumed a posture of superiority and condescension toward the natives. By conditioning, they were predisposed to react intolerantly to people they found different from themselves but similar to those they considered as enemies and as inferiors. Along with dislike for Spaniards and the Indians of Latin America, these perceptions produced a mode of thinking that set the contours of the primordial response.

And what particularly provoked this reaction? Most Tejanos were descendants of Tlascalan Indians and *mestizo* soldiers from Coahuila. Additionally, a few in Nacogdoches were the offspring of people from Louisiana and reflected that area's racial amalgam, including Indians and blacks. Throughout the province, Tejanos had intermarried among themselves and with Christianized Indian women from local missions so that the colonists continued as a mixed-blood population. Their contrast to "white" and salient kindred to "black" and "red" made Mexicans subject to treatment commensurate with the odious connotations whites attached to colors, races, and cultures dissimilar to their own.

Manifestly, Americans who immigrated to Texas confronted the native Mexicans with certain preconceptions about their character. Whites believed that the inhabitants of the province had descended from a tradition of paganism, depravity, and primitivism. Mexicans were a type of folk that Americans should avoid becoming.

The fact of the matter was that whites had little contact with Tejanos up to 1836, for most of the Mexican population was concentrated in the San Antonio and La Bahía areas, quite a distance from the Anglo colonies. But whites knew what they would find in Texas before contact confirmed their convictions. They encountered biologically decadent and inferior people because their thoughts had been shaped by the aforementioned circumstances. Thus, Mexicans lived in ways that Anglos equated with an opprobrious condition. They inhabited primitive shelters. William F. Gray, a land agent from Virginia, comparing Mexicans with the black American culture he knew, pronounced some of the Mexican homes "miserable shabby *jacales*" scarcely equal in appearance to the Afro-American houses in the suburbs of his state. Mexicans adhered to a different religion: they were completely the "slaves of Popish superstitions and despotism" and religion was understood not as an affec-

tion of the heart and soul but as one requiring personal mortification in such super-
ficialities as penances and other rituals. If Anglos and Mexicans were not inherently
different peoples, editorialized the *Texian and Emigrant's Guide* in 1835, habit, education, and religion had made them essentially so.[1]

Additionally, Texians thought that Mexicans' cultural habits clashed with American values, such as the work ethic. Mexicanos appeared a traditional, backward aggregate, an irresponsibly passive people dedicated to the present and resigned not to
probe the universe about them. An American arriving in Nacogdoches in 1833 found
the citizens there the most "lazy indolent poor Starved set of people as ever the Sun
Shined upon." He could not comprehend their lethargy by day, nor their inclination
to play the violin and dance the entire night.[2] J. C. Clopper of Ohio reasoned in 1828
that Mexicanos were "too ignorant and indolent for enterprises and too poor and
dependent were they otherwise capacitated."[3] Mexicanos habitually succumbed to
indolence and ease and indulged themselves in smoking, music, dancing, horse-rac-
ing, and other sports, noted David Woodman, a promoter for a New York and
Boston land company, while activity, industry, and frugality marched on in the new
American settlements.[4] "The vigor of the descendants of the sturdy north will never
mix with the phlegm of the indolent Mexicans," Sam Houston (the future hero of the
war for independence) argued in January 1835 in an address to the citizens of Texas,
"no matter how long we may live among them."[5] In contrast to the newcomers, Tejanos were chained by custom to complacency, and instead of committing themselves
to progress, they preferred fun and frolic. Some three years after Mexico opened
Texas to Anglo-American settlement, Anthony R. Clark complained that Spaniards
in the District of Nacogdoches, "generally of the lower sort and illitterate [*sic*],"
would rather "spend days in gambling to gain a few bits than to make a living by
honest industry."[6] William B. Dewees, who lived in San Antonio in the late 1820s,
found Bexareños totally hedonistic. "Their whole study seems to be for enjoyment.
Mirth and amusement occupy their whole time. If one is fond of balls and theatres,
he can here have an opportunity of attending one every evening. Almost every species
of dissipation is indulged in, except drinking."[7] In Goliad, the Mexicans had such a
strong predisposition for gaming that almost all the inhabitants in 1833 were gamblers and smugglers, said empresario Dr. John Charles Beales. And Alexander Mc-
Crae, touring Texas in 1835 under the auspices of the Wilmington Emigrating Society, remarked in astonishment: "I for the first time saw females betting at a public
gambling table; I do not suppose they were of respectable standing in society, from
the company they kept; but I am told that it is not all uncommon for Mexican *ladies*
to be seen gambling in public."[8]

Acting further to stimulate negative attitudes was the racial composition of Tejanos, who, in the white mind, were closely identified with other colored peoples. For
two hundred years, ideas that black men lusted for white women and notions that
slaves were of a heathen or "savage" condition had played upon Americans' fantasies; the result had been the institutional debasement of blacks because of their
race. Images of the Indian as fierce, hostile, and barbaric similarly affixed themselves
in the thoughts of white settlers, and the constant confrontation over land led more
to the reaffirmation of these images than to their dissolution. Consequently, when

whites arrived in Texas, they unconsciously transferred onto the new "colored" folk they encountered a pseudo-scientific lore acquired from generations of interaction with blacks and Indians.

Travelers, who frequently came in contact with Tejanos, plainly discerned the Mexicans' relation to the black and red peoples. At no time did Americans hold up Frenchmen, or Germans, or themselves for that matter, as a people who physically resembled Mexicans—comparison invariably was with Indians and blacks. Several factors steered discussion in that direction: Anglos were not about to elevate Mexicans to the level of European whiteness; their own sense of superiority turned Tejanos into a people lesser than themselves; and obviously, in any comparison, Mexicans were going to resemble their progenitors. Thus, whites often likened Mexicans to Africans and Native Americans. When Clopper mentioned the complexion of the Tejanos, he thought it "a shade brighter than that of the aborigines of the country."[9] On the other hand, the land agent Gray stamped Tejanos as a "swarthy looking people much resembling our mulattos, some of them nearly black." Sam Houston asked his compatriots (in the aforementioned address) if they "would bow under the yoke of these half-Indians,"[10] while abolitionist Benjamin Lundy, in Laredo in 1834, remarked that the Mexicans in the town looked like mulattoes. . . .

A related topic of much interest and elucidation was color. What whites were especially sensitive to in connection with interracial sex was that the offspring were not whites but colored people. Certainly, Tejanos did not look like Anglos, and the physical connection to Indian and black left no doubt as to whom Mexicans more closely resembled. Most observers, whether travelers or natives, noted the obvious, considering Tejanos as having bronze complexions, as being of a copper color, of being of tawny hue, or simply as having the color of Native Americans. The more opinionated among them described Tejanos as being "fully as dark as Indians."

Beyond this, fixed perceptions about Indians were transposed and cross-culturally referred. The same "olive" color whites observed in the Indians of the seaboard states, for example, they attributed to the Mexicans of Texas. Frederick Law Olmsted, reporting meticulously on the Mexicans of Central Texas during his trip to the state in the mid-fifties, met an elderly Mexican woman "strikingly Indian in feature, her hair, snow white, flowing thick over the shoulders, contrasting strongly with the olive skin." The complexion of the young *señoritas* he likewise thought "clear, and sometimes fair, usually a blushing olive."[11]

The contemptuous word *greaser* which whites used to identify Mexicans may well have applied to Indians as well, since the Indians' olive color was thought to be a result of their practice of anointing their skins with oils and greases. John C. Reid, passing through Texas as a prospective settler in the 1850s, sought to ascertain the origin of the application of the word upon finding that male Mexicans from Texas to the Pacific coast were called "greasers" and the females "greaser women." He failed to find a satisfactory explanation, learning only that it had something to do with the similarity between the Mexicans' color and that of grease. Another transient, commenting upon the vocabulary used in the El Paso region, supported this explanation: "A 'greaser' was a Mexican—originating in the filthy, greasy appearance of the natives."[12]

Then, there were those others who perceived a vestige of the Africans' coloring in Mexican *castas* as well. One traveler noted, for example, that the range of Mexicans' hues extended to African jet. Justice of the Peace Adolphus Sterne, celebrating in 1842 the rites of matrimony between a Tejano, apparently a *criollo* of the upper class, and a white woman, noticed others of the groom's compatriots in the assemblage who were apparently *mestizos*. "If their hair would be a little curly," he remarked, "they would be taken anywhere for Negroes."[13] Similarly, Benjamin F. McIntyre, a Union officer in Civil War Brownsville, conjectured that "Africa might lay some little claim" to the Mexicans' color. Actually, not too many others made such an association, at least not so explicitly. In the last analysis, however, the Tejanos' pigmentation served to stimulate similar attitudes, even if a physical resemblance between Tejano and Negro was remote. As Oscar M. Addison put it in a letter to his brother, the Brownsville Mexicans in the 1850s were of "a class inferior to common nigers [*sic*]."[14]

Then again, the unhygienic nature that white consciousness associated with the skin color of blacks was very naturally extended to Mexicanos. To whites, dark colors connoted filth and therefore Mexicans were a dirty, putrid people, existing in squalor. Thus observers made statements about Mexicans having habits "as filthy as their persons" or living in the "most shocking state of filth."[15] When a cholera epidemic plagued San Antonio in 1849, it hit the Mexican population especially hard. "If you could see the manner in which they live," one visitor commented, "you wouldn't for a moment wonder at their having the colera."

Manifestly, spin-offs from racial attitudes developed and cultivated through repeated interaction with colored peoples on the western frontier were being bestowed upon another caste in a different setting. As Olmsted reported in his notes on Texas society of the 1850s, Mexicans were regarded as "degenerate and degraded Spaniards" or, perhaps, "improved and Christianized Indians." Generally, their tastes and social instincts were like those of Africans. "There are thousands in respectable social positions [in Mexico] whose color and physiognomy would subject them, in Texas, to be sold by the sheriff as negro-estrays who cannot be allowed at large without detriment to the commonwealth," he concluded.[16]

In view of the Southern presumption that individuals with any noticeable trace of African blood were blacks and given the contempt whites had for Indian "half-breeds," it is not surprising that "niggers," "redskins," and "greasers" intimately intermingled in the Anglo-Texan mind. Moreover, whites considered racial mixing a violation of austere moralistic codes. According to Joseph Eve, U.S. chargé d'affaires to the Republic, the Texans regarded Mexicans as a race of "mongrels" composed of Spanish, Indian, and African blood. To Francis S. Latham, traveling in Texas in 1842, Mexicanos were nothing else than "the mongrel and illicit descendants of an Indian, Mexican and Spanish, pencilled with a growing feintline of the Anglo Saxon ancestry."[17] Such feelings about "mongrels" stemmed from the extensive lore American culture had developed concerning the undesirability and supposed peril of miscegenation, especially between whites and blacks. Certainly, the mixed-blood nature of Tejanos concerned Anglo Americans because of their cultural aversion to interracial passion, a subject upon which whites expressed themselves adeptly, albeit with no scientific basis. According to white beliefs, Mexicans resembled the degenerates from whom they descended. Although they inherited both the faults and the good qualities of their ancestors, unfortunately, the darker traits predominated, so that Mexicans by nature were superstitious, cowardly, treacherous, idle, avaricious, and inveterate gamblers. Miscegenation was a very serious matter which held great implications for civilization. William H. Emory, surveying the boundary between the United States and Mexico, related this idea in an incidental remark included as part of his report, finished during the Franklin Pierce administration. Attributing the decline and fall of Spanish domination in Texas and the borderlands to a "baneful" cohabitation between whites and Indians, he continued:

> Where practical amalgamation of races of different color is carried [out] to any extent, it is from the absence of the women of the cleaner race. The white makes his alliance with his darker partner for no other purpose than to satisfy a law of nature, or to acquire property, and when that is accomplished all affection ceases. Faithless to his vows, he passes from object to object with no other impulse than the gratification arising from novelty, ending at last in emasculation and disease, leaving no progeny at all; or if any, a very inferior and syphilitic race. Such are the favors extended to the white man by the lower and darker colored races, that this must always be the course of events, and the process of absorption can never work any beneficial change. One of the inevitable results of intermarriage between races of different color is infidelity. The offspring have a constant tendency to go back to one or the other of the original stock; that in a large family of children, where the parents are of a mixed race but yet of the same color, the children will be of every color, from dusky cinnamon to chalky white. This phenomenon, so easily explained without involving the fidelity of either party, nevertheless produces suspicion followed by unhappiness, and ending in open adultery.[18]

This sort of pseudoscience dictated the status of mixed-blood Tejanos in a white state.

NOTES

1. *Texian and Emigrant's Guide* (Nacogdoches), December 26, 1835, p. 4.

2. James Ernest Crisp, "Anglo-Texan Attitudes toward the Mexican, 1821–1845," Ph.D. dissertation, Yale University, 1976, p. 22.

3. J. C. Clopper, *Journal of J. C. Clopper, 1828*, Southwestern Historical Quarterly 13 (July 1909): 44–80, p. 76.

4. David Woodman, Guide to Texas Emigrants, Boston: M. Hawes, 1835, p. 35.

5. Houston to Soldiers, January 15, 1836, in The Papers of the Texas Revolution, 1835–1836, gen. ed. John H. Jenkins, 4:30.

6. Ernest W. Winkler, ed., Manuscript Letters and Documents of Early Texians, 1821–1845, Austin: Steck Co., 1937, p. 32.

7. William B. Dewees, Letters from an Early Settler of Texas, Waco: Texian Press, 1968, p. 56.

8. Joshua James and Alexander McCrae, A Journal of a Tour in Texas: With Observations, etc., by the Agents of the Wilmington Emigrating Society, Wilmington, N.C.: Printed by T. Loring, 1835, p. 15. See also Dewees, Letters from an Early Settler, p. 57, for remarks on the Mexican passion for gambling.

9. Clopper, *Journal*, pp. 71–72.

10. Houston to Soldiers, January 15, 1836, in Papers of the Texas Revolution 4:30.

11. Frederick Law Olmsted, A Journey through Texas: Or, A Saddle-Trip on the Southwestern Frontier, with a Statistical Appendix, New York: Dix, Edwards & Co., 1857; reprint, Austin: University of Texas Press, 1978, p. 161.

12. John C. Reid, Reid's Tramp: Or, A Journal of the Incidents of Ten Months' Travel . . . , Selma, Ala.: J. Hardy Co., 1858; reprint, Austin: Steck Co., 1935, p. 38; Albert D. Richardson, Beyond the Mississippi: From the Great River to the Great Ocean . . . 1857–1867, Hartford: American Publishing Co., 1867, p. 239; Lloyd Lewis, Captain Sam Grant, Boston: Little, Brown and Co., 1950, p. 142; Cecil Robinson, Mexico and the Hispanic Southwest in American Literature (revised from With the Ears of Strangers: The Mexican in American Literature), Tucson: University of Arizona Press, 1977, pp. 38–39; Américo Paredes, On "Gringo,'""Greaser," and *Other Neighborly Names*, in Singers and Storytellers, edited by Mody C. Boatright et al., Dallas: Southern Methodist University Press, 1961, pp. 285–90. Whatever the origins, the word was used commonly in reference to Mexicans.

13. Adolphus Sterne, Hurrah for Texas! The Diary of Adolphus Sterne, edited by Archie P. McDonald, Waco: Texian Press, 1969, p. 94.

14. Oscar M. Addison to His Brother, February 14, 1854, Brownsville, Texas, Addison Papers, Barker Texas History Center, University of Texas Archives, Austin.

15. John James Audubon, The Life of John James Audubon, the Naturalist, edited by Lucy Audubon, New York: G. P. Putnam's Sons, 1902, p. 410; Emanuel H. D. Domenech, Missionary Adventures in Texas and Mexico: A Personal Narrative of Six Years' Sojourn in Those Regions, London: Longman, Brown, Green, Longmans, and Roberts, 1858, p. 83. For a discussion of the psychological connection between color and dirt, see Joel Kovel, White Racism: A Psychohistory, New York: Vintage Books, 1970, pp. 81–92.

16. Olmsted, Journey through Texas, p. 454.

17. Francis S. Latham, Travels in Texas, 1842, edited by Gerald S. Pierce, Austin: Encino Press, 1971, p. 37.

18. *House Exec. Doc.* No. 135, 34th Cong., 1st Sess. (Ser. 861), 1:68–70.

Chapter 23

The Master Narrative of White Supremacy in California

Tomás Almaguer

What were the specific symbolic and material factors that contributed to the economic mobility of certain groups and the disadvantaged status of others? What were the gendered dimensions of these class-specific, racialized histories? How, for instance, were relations between men and women of different cultural groups structurally mediated by the racialization process and the imposition of a new class system? What specific role did sexuality play in the structuring and imposition of racialized class relations among Californians during this period?

The answer to these questions can be found in the way that race and the racialization process in California became the central organizing principle of group life during the state's formative period of development. Although California's ethnic populations were racialized in different ways, and the specific manifestations of racial and ethnic conflict were unique to California, at its most basic level it represented the extension of "white supremacy" into the new American Southwest. Historian George Fredrickson defines white supremacy as "the attitudes, ideologies, and politics associated with blatant forms of white or European dominance over 'non-white' populations."[1] The attempt to make race or color a basis for group position within the United States was defined initially during the colonial period when notions of "civility" and "savagery," as well as clear distinctions between "Christians" and "heathens," were used to inscribe racial difference and divide humankind into distinct categories of people. These notions provided the basis upon which European immigrants differentiated themselves from the diverse populations they encountered during their expansion into the Far West.

The cultural division of the world into different categories of humanity led white, European Americans in California to arrogantly privilege themselves as superior to non-European people of color. Although European Americans were situated unambiguously at the top of this social hierarchy, the racialized populations did not share a common structural position. Racialized relations in the state reverberated along a number of racial fault lines; they did not assume a simple binary form or erupt along one principal fault. The allocation of "group position" along these social strata was the outcome of both cultural and material considerations.

California Indians, for example, were singled out as the complete antithesis of white Californians and were summarily relegated to the very bottom of the racial hierarchy. White immigrants believed that the indigenous population was the lowest level of humankind imaginable. The California Indians wore little clothing, were perceived as horrendously ugly and dirty, ate foods "Americans" deemed unpalatable, and practiced tribal rituals and ceremonies that were anathema to European Christian practices. In short, they were cast as the extreme incarnation of all that was both uncivilized and heathen.

Other cultural groups were judged less harshly and placed between the extreme ends of the racial hierarchy. Mexicans, for instance, were perceived as much closer culturally to European-American immigrants than to their Indian counterparts. The Mexicans' mixed European ancestry, romance language, Catholic religious practices, and familiar political-economic institutions elevated them above all other cultural groups in the white man's eyes. Moreover, the continued political influence of the powerful *Californio* elite during the latter nineteenth century further attenuated more virulent expressions of anti-Mexican sentiment and allowed Mexicans to challenge Anglo-domination for a time.

Black and Asian immigrants, finally, were culturally deemed to be somewhere between the "half civilized" Mexican and "uncivilized" Indian populations. Although antiblack animosity was widespread, blacks who settled in California were at least Christian, spoke English, and had—after years of enslavement—assimilated important European cultural patterns. Most white immigrants grudgingly acknowledged this, a fact that contributed directly to blacks not becoming the major target of racist initiatives in California that they were elsewhere in the country.

Americans perceived Asian immigrants, on the other hand, to have fewer redeeming qualities and group attributes. While they too were unambiguously deemed nonwhite, these immigrants carried the extra burden of being a "peculiar" people who spoke a completely unintelligible Eastern language, had "abhorrent" culinary tastes, dressed "strangely," and practiced a form of "pagan idolatry" clearly at odds with Judeo-Christian religious traditions. In cultural terms, Chinese and Japanese immigrants, therefore, were perceived initially as more like the uncivilized and heathen Indian population than any of the other cultural minorities in the state.

In sum, European-American immigrants in nineteenth-century California inherited and routinely relied on eurocentric cultural criteria to hierarchically evaluate and racialize the various cultural groups they contended with in California. This process clearly privileged and elevated the status of white immigrants in the social structure and placed below them, in descending order, the Mexican, black, Asian, and Indian populations. . . .

The tremendous immigration of European and non-European immigrants into the state after annexation resulted in a hierarchy of group inequality in which race, not class, became the central stratifying variable. The primary racial division of Californians into white and nonwhite categories cut at right angles across the newly emergent class lines that divided capitalists, petit bourgeois commodity producers, and an increasingly segmented working class composed of free wage laborers and individuals held in precapitalist relations of production.

The imposition of a new racial order and attendant class structure in nineteenth-century California was greatly facilitated by popular ideologies that gave voice to the superordinate political and economic position of European Americans in the state. Two powerful ideas reflecting this white supremacist sentiment were fervently embraced by European-American men during the United States' westward expansion: "Manifest Destiny" and the "free labor ideology."

The United States' usurpation of Mexican territory laid the basis for rapidly transforming what would become the American Southwest along new sociocultural, political, and economic lines. This mission became the "white man's burden"—to extend their dominion over all obstacles placed in their path and to bring civilization and Christianity to the uncivilized heathens they encountered. During this period white Americans widely accepted the idea of populating all of the North American continent with a homogeneous white population. They believed it was their providential destiny to expand to the Pacific coast, bringing with them their superior political institutions, notions of progress and democracy, and their own economic system of production. Public support for extending national boundaries found fertile ground in this tumultuous period of expansion and reached its most explicit political expression in the notion of Manifest Destiny.

During the mid-nineteenth century, white supremacist practices also became intertwined inextricably with economic doctrines concerning the role of "free labor." As historian Eric Foner has shown, a free-labor ideology was widely embraced by European Americans at all class levels. White men in particular enthusiastically supported the vision of the social world this ideology promoted: an expanding capitalist society based on free wage labor. Those fervently advocating free-labor doctrines accepted the right to private property and economic individualism and fervently believed that free labor created all value. Moreover, they maintained that everyone could aspire to and achieve economic independence in a free society and that "today's laborer would be tomorrow's capitalist."[2]

The free-labor ideology associated with the Republican Party during the mid-nineteenth century helped crystallize the beliefs of European-American men about their entitlement to privileged economic mobility in the new territories. It also specifically colored the way Anglo Californians initially assessed the various minority groups they competed with for position in the state's new class structure. Free-labor adherents believed that social mobility and economic independence were only achievable in a capitalist society unthreatened by nonwhite populations and the degrading labor systems associated with them. European Americans repeatedly associated nonwhite people with various unfree labor systems that ostensibly threatened their superordinate social standing and class prerogatives in California.

Like Manifest Destiny, the underlying tenets of the free-labor ideology squarely affirmed the superior position of European-American men and helped delineate the subordinate status that people of color would occupy in the Far West.[3] As a consequence, racial lines in California quickly became linked with class divisions in unexpected and complicated ways. Outward struggles over access and group position within the class system were given concrete form and substance by the underlying racialized struggle among its chief protagonists.

The powerful impact of white supremacist notions like Manifest Destiny and the free-labor ideology had important material consequences for these contesting groups. The competition for access to valued social resources did not result, however, in purely symmetrical hierarchies based on class and race. Far from simply paralleling each other, California's new class hierarchy and racial order were mutually constitutive and intersected in complex and shifting ways that were historically contingent.

How groups were accorded access to the ownership of productive property and proletarianized within the working class was not a random selection process impervious to popular perceptions of racial differences. Who gained access to land, owned businesses, became skilled workers, and, more generally, was subjectively placed in either a "free" wage-labor market or an "unfree" labor system was fundamentally determined on the basis of race. Access to every level of the capitalist system of production introduced in nineteenth-century California was largely determined by this status. Although this capitalist economy became a highly competitive system by the late nineteenth century, it remained an institution that limited social mobility to white, European-American men.

White Californians repeatedly claimed primary access to privileged positions within the system of production and effectively thwarted attempts by the nonwhite population to compete with them on an equal footing. Nineteenth-century legislation enacted in the interest and at the behest of European Americans cemented the placement of California's nonwhite minorities in various unfree labor situations (such as slavery, indentured servitude, contracted labor, etc.) or guaranteed their exclusion altogether from certain skilled occupations and self-employment opportunities. European Americans jealously sought to protect their privileged group position in California through the use of discriminatory social closures that impeded equal access to social mobility. Racial status clearly shaped each group's life chances and served as the primary basis for determining whether one was granted access to different strata within the new class structure.

The judicial decisions that formally conferred racial status in nineteenth-century California, therefore, had important consequences for the historical trajectories of each of these groups in California. As each of these "nonwhite" groups entered into competition with European Americans at different class levels after 1850, a series of protracted conflicts erupted along a number of racial fault lines. This was registered in white opposition to black, Chinese, and Sonoran miners in the 1850s; to Chinese workers in urban industries in the 1870s and 1880s; and to Japanese small farmers at the turn of the century. Racial enmity and bitter economic struggle with white competitors punctuated minority history in California during the nineteenth century. White antipathy crystallized most intensely in the case of Native Americans, Mexicans, Chinese, and, to a lesser extent, African-American and Japanese immigrants.

There emerged during this period a strong symbolic association between different minority groups, on the one hand, and various precapitalist economic formations on the other. White antipathy toward Mexicans, Native Americans, and Chinese and Japanese immigrants was typically couched within the rubric of this "free white labor"/"unfree nonwhite labor" dichotomy: Mexicans became inimically associated with the "unproductive," semi-feudal rancho economy that European Americans rapidly undermined after statehood; Indians with a "primitive" communal mode of existence that white settlers ruthlessly eradicated through violence and forced segregation; and Asian immigrants with a "degraded" unfree labor system unfairly competing with and fettering white labor. The class specific nature of contention between these racialized groups and the European-American populations were all cast in terms of these symbolic associations.

White economic mobility and dominance in California required both the subordination of minority populations and the eradication of the precapitalist systems of production associated with them. Anglo entitlement to California's bounty could only be actualized when the symbolic and material threat these minority populations posed was effectively neutralized or overcome. . . .

Given their free-labor sentiments and their profound belief in "Manifest Destiny," European Americans migrating into the new American Southwest could have been expected to despise completely the Mexican population they encountered in California. Although these prejudices undeniably affected their initial impressions of Mexican society, white immigrants actually assigned Mexicans an intermediate location in the new society they imposed in the region. Indeed, compared to the treatment ultimately afforded other racialized groups in California, the experience of Mexicans in the nineteenth century was without parallel.

For complex reasons, Mexicans occupied a qualitatively different "group position" from that of Indians, blacks, and Asian immigrants in the new racial hierarchy. Nineteenth-century relations between Mexicans and Anglos in California were powerfully determined by the class divisions within the two populations, divisions that led to divergent historical experiences for the Mexican working class and the ranchero elite. The introduction of a new, Anglo-dominated class structure led to bitter contention between powerful Mexican rancheros and European-American capitalists for control of the most arable land in the state. The strife that developed between the old Mexican ruling class and Anglo capitalists initially overshadowed the ethnic conflict that occurred at other class levels.

Unlike black, Chinese, and Japanese immigrants, for example, Mexican workers were not initially perceived as a formidable obstacle to white working-class aspirations, primarily because of such demographic factors as the relatively small size of the Mexican population, the low percentage of adult male laborers, and their concentration away from urban economic sectors employing white laborers. By 1900, however, these class lines had been blurred, if not obliterated, as the ranchero class irretrievably surrendered its earlier privileged position. These changes, plus widespread Mexican immigration during the 1910s and 1920s, set the stage for a twentieth-century experience qualitatively different from that of the nineteenth.

Another unique feature of Anglo-Mexican relations at the time was the ability of upper-class Mexicans to resist European-American encroachment and protect themselves from the intense racial animosity and virulent discrimination that Anglos inflicted on other groups during the nineteenth century. This was principally the result of important political rights Mexicans gained at the onset of American control of California, rights based on the guarantees extended by treaty and by the U.S. Constitution and largely denied Indians, blacks, and Chinese and Japanese immigrants. For example, the Treaty of Guadalupe Hidalgo enabled Mexicans to obtain U.S. citizenship rights in 1849. Citizenship carried with it suffrage, which empowered Mexican elites to politically challenge Anglo control in areas of Mexican concentration. The citizenship rights Mexicans came to enjoy, though often circumvented, nevertheless protected them from the more onerous discriminatory legislation enacted against other racialized groups.

The claimed European descent of the Mexican ranchero elite, the so-called *gente de razon* (literally, "people of reason"), also facilitated the assimilation of segments of the upper class into European American society. The cultural distance between these Mexicans and European Americans proved less extreme than that between white immigrants and the unambiguously "nonwhite" populations. One important measure of the perceived assimilability of upper-class Mexicans was clearly evident in the degree of intermarriage between old *Californio* families and prominent Anglo immigrants. In sharp contrast, the Mexican working class was generally viewed like other racialized groups. Their degraded class status, combined with their inability to claim "pure" European ancestry, contributed to Anglo perceptions that they were unassimilable and certainly unworthy of intermarrying. Unprotected by the status European ancestry afforded the *gente de razon*, they were much more vulnerable to having their political and legal rights violated with impunity.

NOTES

1. George M. Fredrickson, WHITE SUPREMACY: A COMPARATIVE STUDY IN AMERICAN AND SOUTH AFRICAN HISTORY (New York: Oxford University Press, 1981), p. xi.

2. Eric Foner, FREE SOIL, FREE LABOR, FREE MEN: THE IDEOLOGY OF THE REPUBLICAN PARTY BEFORE THE CIVIL WAR (New York: Oxford University Press, 1970), p. 20.

3. This summary discussion of the "free-labor ideology" is primarily drawn from Foner's FREE SOIL, FREE LABOR, FREE MEN.

Chapter 24

Occupied America

Rodolfo Acuña

Central to the thesis of this monograph is my contention that the conquest of the Southwest created a colonial situation in the traditional sense—with the Mexican land and population being controlled by an imperialistic United States. Further, I contend that this colonization—with variations—is still with us today. Thus, I refer to the colony, initially, in the traditional definition of the term, and later (taking into account the variations) as an internal colony.

From the Chicano perspective, it is obvious that these two types of colonies are a reality. In discussions with non-Chicano friends, however, I have encountered considerable resistance. In fact, even colleagues sympathetic to the Chicano cause vehemently deny that Chicanos are—or have been—colonized. They admit the exploitation and discrimination, but they add that this has been the experience of most "Americans"—especially European and Asian immigrants and Black Americans. While I agree that exploitation and racism have victimized most out-groups in the United States, this does not preclude the reality of the colonial relationship between the Anglo-American privileged and the Chicano.

I feel that the parallels between the Chicanos' experience in the United States and the colonization of other Third World peoples are too similar to dismiss. Attendant to the definition of colonization are the following conditions:

1. The land of one people is invaded by people from another country, who later use military force to gain and maintain control.
2. The original inhabitants become subjects of the conquerors involuntarily.
3. The conquered have an alien culture and government imposed upon them.
4. The conquered become the victims of racism and cultural genocide and are relegated to a submerged status.
5. The conquered are rendered politically and economically powerless.
6. The conquerors feel they have a "mission" in occupying the area in question and believe that they have undeniable privileges by virtue of their conquest.

These points also apply to the relationship between Chicanos and Anglos in Mexico's northwest territory.

In the traditional historian's viewpoint, however, there are two differences that impede universal acceptance of the reality of Anglo-American colonialism in this area.

1. Geographically the land taken from Mexico bordered the United States rather than being an area distant from the "mother country."

Too many historians have accepted—subconsciously, if not conveniently—the myth that the area was always intended to be an integral part of the United States. Instead of conceptualizing the conquered territory as northern Mexico, they perceive it in terms of the "American" Southwest. Further, the stereotype of the colonialist pictures him wearing Wellington boots and carrying a swagger stick, and that stereotype is usually associated with overseas situations—certainly not in territory contiguous to an "expanding" country.

2. Historians also believe that the Southwest was won in fair and just warfare, as opposed to unjust imperialism.

The rationale has been that the land came to the United States as the result of competition, and in winning the game, the country was generous in paying for its prize. In the case of Texas, they believe Mexico attacked the "freedom-loving" Anglo-Americans. It is difficult for citizens of the United States to accept the fact that their nation has been and is imperialistic. Imperialism, to them, is an affliction of other countries.

While I acknowledge the geographical proximity of the area—and the fact that this is a modification of the strict definition of colonialism—I refute the conclusion that the Texan and Mexican-American wars were just or that Mexico provoked them. Further, I illustrate in this monograph that the conditions attendant to colonialism, listed above, accompanied the U.S. take-over of the Southwest. For these reasons, I maintain that colonialism in the traditional sense did exist in the Southwest, and that the conquerors dominated and exploited the conquered.

The colonization still exists today, but as I mentioned before, there are variations. Anglo-Americans still exploit and manipulate Mexicans and still relegate them to a submerged caste. Mexicans are still denied political and economic determination and are still the victims of racial stereotypes and racial slurs promulgated by those who feel they are superior. Thus, I contend that Mexicans in the United States are still a colonized people, but now the colonization is *internal*—it is occurring *within* the country rather than being imposed by an external power. The territories of the Southwest are states within the United States, and theoretically permanent residents of Mexican extraction are U.S. citizens. Yet the rights of citizenship are too often circumvented or denied outright.

In reality, there is little difference between the Chicano's status in the *traditional colony* of the nineteenth century and in the *internal colony* of the twentieth century. The relationship between Anglos and Chicanos remains the same—that of master-servant. The principal difference is that Mexicans in the traditional colony were indigenous to the conquered land. Now, while some are descendants of Mexicans living in the area before the conquest, large numbers are technically descendants of immigrants. After 1910, in fact, almost one-eighth of Mexico's population migrated to the United States, largely as a result of the push-and-pull of economic necessity. Southwest agribusinessmen "imported" Mexican workers to fill the need for cheap labor, and this influx signaled the beginning of even greater Anglo manipulation of Mexican settlements or *colonias.*

The original *colonias* expanded in size with the increased immigration and new settlements sprang up. They became nations within a nation, in effect, for psychologically, socially, and culturally they remained Mexican. But the *colonias* had little or no control over their political, economic, or educational destinies. In almost every case, they remained separate and unequal to Anglo-American communities. The elected representatives within the *colonias* were usually Anglo-Americans or Mexicans under their control, and they established a bureaucracy to control the political life of the Mexican settlements—for the benefit of the Anglo privileged.

Further, Anglos controlled the educational system—they administered the schools and taught in the classrooms, and designed the curriculum not to meet the needs of Chicano students but to Americanize them. The police patrolling the *colonia* lived, for the most part, outside the area. Their main purpose was to protect Anglo property. Anglos owned the business and industry in the *colonias,* and capital that could have been used to improve the economic situation within the *colonias* was taken into Anglo-American sectors, in much the same way that capital is drained from underdeveloped countries by foreign economic imperialists. In addition, the *colonias* became employment centers for industrialists, who were assured of a ready supply of cheap labor.

This pattern is one that emerged in most Chicano communities, and one that contradicts the belief in Anglo-American equality. In sum, even though the 1960 census documented that 85 percent of Chicanos are native-born U.S. citizens, most Anglo-Americans still considered them Mexicans and outsiders.

In discussing the traditional and internal colonization of the Chicano, it is not my intention to rekindle hatreds, nor to condemn all Anglo-Americans collectively for the ignominies that the Mexican in the United States has suffered. Rather, my purpose is to bring about an awareness—among both Anglo-Americans and Chicanos—of the forces that control and manipulate seven million people in this country and keep them colonized. If Chicanos can become aware of *why* they are oppressed and *how* the exploitation is perpetuated, they can work more effectively toward ending their colonization.

I realize that the initial stages of such awareness might result in intolerance among some Chicanos. However, I caution the reader that this work does not create a rationale for brown power just because it condemns the injustices of Anglo power. Extended visits in Mexico have taught me that Chicano power is no better than any other power. Those who seek power are deprived of their humanity to the point that they themselves become the oppressors. Paulo Freire has written:

> The great humanistic and historical task of the oppressed [is]: to liberate themselves and their oppressors as well. The oppressors, who oppress, exploit, and rape by virtue of

their power, cannot find in this power the strength to liberate either the oppressed or themselves. Only the power that springs from the weakness of the oppressed will be sufficiently strong to free you.[1]

It is my hope that *Occupied America* can help us perceive the social, political, and economic contradictions of the power that has enabled Anglo-American colonizers to dominate Chicanos—and that has too often made Chicanos accept and, in some instances, support the domination. Awareness will help us take action against the forces that oppress not only Chicanos but the oppressor himself.[2]

NOTES

1. Paulo Freire, *Pedagogy of the Oppressed* (New York: Herder and Herder, 1972), p. 28.
2. [In later editions, the author modifies his colonization thesis, explaining that the upsurge in Chicano activism makes this necessary. We include this selection in the belief that the thesis still retains great explanatory power, and not just historically—*Eds.*]

Chapter 25

Mexican Americans and Whiteness

George A. Martinez

During slavery, the racial divide between black and white became a line of protection from the threat of commodification: whiteness protected one against being an object of property. Even after slavery ended, it continued to be a valuable asset, carrying with it a set of assumptions, privileges, and benefits. Given this, it is hardly surprising that minorities have often sought to "pass" as white—i.e., present themselves as white persons. They did so because they thought that becoming white insured greater economic, political, and social security. Becoming white, they thought, meant gaining access to a panoply of public and private privileges, while insuring that one would avoid being the object of others' domination.

In light of the privileged status of whiteness, it is instructive to examine how legal actors—courts and others—constructed the race of Mexican Americans. In *Inland Steel Co. v. Barcelona,*[1] an Indiana appellate court addressed the question of whether Mexicans were white. The court noted that the *Encyclopedia Britannica* stated that approximately one-fifth of the inhabitants of Mexico are whites, approximately two-fifths Indians and the balance made up of mixed bloods, blacks, Japanese, and Chinese. Given this, the court held that a "Mexican" should not necessarily be found to be a white person.[2]

The Texas courts also considered the same question. In *In re Rodriguez,*[3] a Texas federal court addressed whether Mexicans were white for purposes of immigration. At that time, the federal naturalization laws required that an alien be white in order to become a citizen of the United States. The court stated that Mexicans would probably be considered non-white from an anthropological perspective,[4] but went on to note that the United States had entered into certain treaties with Mexico. Those treaties expressly allowed Mexicans to become citizens of the United States. Thus, the court held that Congress must have intended that Mexicans were white within the meaning of the naturalization laws. *In re Rodriguez* reveals how racial categories can be constructed through the political process. Through the give and take of treaty making, Mexicans became "white."

Other cases show how politics operated to turn persons of mixed blood into whites or the opposite. In immigration cases, mixed race applicants often failed to establish their whiteness. For example, in *In re Camille,*[5] the court held that the son of a white Canadian father and an Indian mother was non-white, and therefore not eligible to naturalize. Similarly, in *In re Young,*[6] the son of a German father and a Japanese mother was not a white person within the meaning of the immigration laws.[7] If these cases stand for the proposition that mixed race persons were not white, Mexicans—a mixture of Spanish and Indian—should not have counted as white. The treaties nevertheless operated to turn them into whites.

The issue of the race of Mexican Americans also arose in connection with school segregation. In *Independent School District v. Salvatierra,*[8] plaintiffs sought to enjoin segregation of Mexican Americans in the city of Del Rio, Texas. There, the court treated Mexican Americans as white, holding that Mexican Americans could not be segregated from children of "other white races, merely or solely because they are Mexicans."[9] Significantly, the court did permit segregation of Mexican Americans on the basis of linguistic difficulties and migrant farming patterns.

Mexican-American jury participation and exclusion also show how the race of Mexican Americans is constructed. For example, in *Hernandez v. State,* a Mexican American had been convicted of murder. He sought to reverse his conviction on the ground that Mexican Americans had been excluded from the grand jury and the petit jury, relying on cases holding that exclusion of blacks from jury service violated due process and equal protection. The court recognized only two classes as falling within the guarantee of the Fourteenth Amendment: the white race and the black race. It went on to hold that Mexican Americans are white for purposes of the Fourteenth Amendment. The court reasoned that to hold that the members of the various groups comprising the white race must be represented on grand and petit juries would destroy the jury system.[10] Since the juries that indicted and convicted the defendant were composed of members of his race—white persons—he had not been denied the equal protection of the laws.[11]

On review, the United States Supreme Court also imposed a group definition on Mexican Americans. The court held in *Hernandez v. Texas*[12] that "persons of Mexican descent" are a cognizable group for equal protection purposes in areas where they were subject to local discrimination—but not otherwise.[13] Defining Mexican Americans in terms of the existence of local discrimination hinders Mexican Americans in asserting their rights because not every plaintiff can afford the expense of obtaining expert testimony to prove the local prejudice.

Similarly, in *Lopez Tijerina v. Henry,*[14] the court refused to allow Mexican Americans to define themselves as a group. Plaintiffs sought to bring a class action on behalf of a class of "Mexican Americans" in order to secure equal educational opportunity in local schools. The court rejected the claim for class representation, holding that the term "Mexican American" was too vague and failed adequately to define a class within the meaning of Rule 23 of the Federal Rules of Civil Procedure, governing class actions. Since the class was not adequately defined, the court dismissed the class action complaint.

Class actions permit a lawsuit to be brought by large numbers of persons whose interests are sufficiently related so that it is more efficient to adjudicate their rights in a single action. As such, it may represent the only viable procedure for people with small claims to vindicate their rights. The *Lopez Tijerina* case, then, seems to be an example of a court refusing to allow Mexican Americans to define themselves so as to resist oppression.

Subsequently, other courts permitted Mexican Americans to sue as a class under Rule 23 by distinguishing *Tijerina* under the *Hernandez* rationale that local prejudice rendered the class sufficiently identifiable. Thus, the courts defined Mexican Americans in terms of local prejudice, a definition which, for the reasons discussed above, operated to the disadvantage of Mexican Americans in their efforts to assert their rights under Rule 23.

Federal agencies also constructed the race of Mexican Americans. The federal government has long compiled census data on persons of Mexican descent. In 1930, the Census Bureau made the first effort to identify Mexican Americans. The Bureau used the term "Mexican" to classify Mexican Americans, placing it under the rubric of "other races," which also included Indians, Blacks, and Asians. According to this definition, Mexican Americans were not considered "whites." Interestingly, the Mexican government and the United States Department of State both objected to the 1930 census definition of Mexican. Thus, in the 1950 census Mexican Americans were classified as whites. The Census Bureau experience is significant in that it presents another example of how politics have influenced the construction of race. The Office of Management and Budget (OMB) has set forth the current federal law of racial classification. In particular, Statistical Directive No. 15, which governs the collection of federal statistics regarding the implementation of a number of civil rights laws,[15] classifies Mexican Americans as white.

White identity traditionally has served as a source of privilege and protection. Since the law usually recognized Mexican Americans as white, one might have expected that social action would have reflected the Mexican American's privileged legal status as white. That, however, was not the case. Legal recognition of the Mexican American as white had only a slight impact on conduct. Far from having a privileged status, Mexican Americans faced discrimination very similar to that experienced by African Americans. Excluded from public facilities and neighborhoods and the targets of racial slurs, Mexican Americans typically lived in one section of town because they were not permitted to rent or own property anywhere except in the "Mexican Colony."[16] Segregated in public schools, Mexican Americans also faced significant discrimination in employment. Mexican Americans were earmarked for exclusive employment in the lowest brackets of employment and paid less than Anglo Americans for the same jobs.[17] Moreover, law enforcement officials have committed widespread discrimination against Mexican Americans, arresting them on pretexts and meting out harassment and penalties disproportionately severe compared to those imposed on Anglos for the same acts.[18] In all these respects, actual social behavior failed to reflect the legal norms that defined Mexican Americans as white. Although white as a matter of law, that law failed to provide Mexican Americans with a privileged status.

At one point, discrimination against Mexican Americans in Texas became so flagrant that the Mexican Ministry of Labor declared that Mexican citizens would not be allowed to go there. In 1943, Mexican Foreign Minister Ezequiel Padilla informed Texas that Mexican citizens would be allowed to go to Texas only after the wave of racial prejudice had subsided. In response, the Texas legislature, on May 6, 1943, passed a resolution that established as a matter of Texas public policy that all Caucasians were entitled to equal accommodations. Subsequently, Mexican Americans attempted to rely on the resolution and sought to claim one of the traditional benefits of whiteness—freedom from exclusion from public places. In *Terrell Wells Swimming Pool v. Rodriguez,*[19] Jacob Rodriguez sought an injunction requiring a swimming pool operator to offer equal accommodations to Mexican Americans. Plaintiff argued that he could not be excluded from the pool on the basis of his Mexican ancestry because that would violate the public policy expressed in the resolution condemning discriminatory practices against all persons of the white race. The court refused to enforce the public policy on the ground that the resolution did not have the effect of a statute. Thus, Mexican Americans could not claim one of the most significant benefits of whiteness—freedom from exclusion from public places.

The legal construction of Mexican Americans as white thus stands as an irony—thoroughly at odds with the colonial discourses that developed in the American Southwest. As happened in other regions of the world the colonizers engaged in epistemic violence—i.e., produced modes of knowing that enabled and rationalized colonial domination from the standpoint of the West.[20]

In sharp contrast to their legal construction as white, writers and other Anglo opinion-makers plainly constructed Mexican Americans as irreducibly Other. The historian David Weber writes:

> Anglo Americans found an additional element to despise in Mexicans: racial mixture. American visitors to the Mexican frontier were nearly unanimous in commenting on the dark skin of the Mexican mestizos, who, it was generally agreed, had inherited the worst qualities of Spaniards and Indians to produce a "race" still more despicable than that of either parent.[21]

Similarly, another commentator described how Anglo Americans drew a racial distinction between themselves and Mexican Americans:

> Racial myths about the Mexicans appeared as soon as Mexicans began to meet Anglo American settlers in the early nineteenth century. The differences in attitudes, temperament and behavior were supposed to be genetic. It is hard now to imagine the normal Mexican mixture of Spanish and Indian as constituting a distinct "race," but the Anglo Americans of the Southwest defined it as such.[22]

Likewise, the dean of Texas historians, Walter Prescott Webb, wrote:

> Without disparagement it may be said that there is a cruel streak in the Mexican nature, or so the history of Texas would lead one to believe. This cruelty may be a heritage from the Spanish of the Inquisition; it may and doubtless should be attributed partly to the Indian blood.[23]

Through this discourse on the Mexican American, Anglo Americans also reformulated their white selves. Anglo judges, as we have seen, did the same, ruling that Mexicans were co-whites when this suited the dominant group—and non-white when necessary to protect Anglo privilege and supremacy.

NOTES

1. 39 N.E.2d 800 (Ind. 1942).

2. *Id.* at 801.

3. 81 F. 337 (W.D. Tex. 1897).

4. *Id.* at 349.

5. 6 F. 256 (1880).

6. 198 F. 715 (1912)

7. *Id.* at 716–17. The court observed:

In the abstractions of higher mathematics, it may be plausibly said that the half of infinity is equal to the whole of infinity; but in the case of a concrete thing as the person of a human being it cannot be said that one who is half white and half brown or yellow is a white person, as commonly understood.

198 at 717.

8. 33 S.W.2d 790 (Tex. Civ. App. 1930). *Salvatierra* was the first case to decide the issue of whether segregation of Mexican Americans in public school was permissible.

9. *Id.* at 795.

10. 251 S.W.2d 531, 532, 535 (Tex. 1952).

11. *Id.* at 536. In *Sanchez v. State,* 243 S.W.2d 700 (1951), a Mexican American had been convicted of murder. He sought to challenge his conviction on the ground that his due process rights had been violated because the county had discriminated against Mexican Americans in the selection of grand jurors. The Texas court held that Mexican Americans are not a separate race, but are white people of Spanish descent. 243 S.W.2d, at 701. Thus the defendant's rights were not violated because whites were not excluded from the grand juries.

12. 347 U.S. 475 (1954).

13. *Id.* at 477–79.

14. 48 F.R.D. 274 (D.N.M. 1969).

15. Directive No. 15, *Race and Ethnic Standard for Federal Statistics and Administrative Reporting,* 43 Fed. Reg. 19,260, 19,269 (Office of Management and Budget 1978).

16. Pauline R. Kibbe, Latin Americans in Texas 123–24 (1946).

17. Carey McWilliams, North from Mexico 167, 215–16 (1948); Kibbe, at 157.

18. U.S. Commission on Civil Rights, *Mexican Americans and the Administration of Justice in the Southwest* (Summary) 2 (1970).

19. 182 S.W.2d 824 (Tex. Civ. App. 1944).

20. Ruth Frankenberg, White Women, Race Matters: The Social Construction of Whiteness 16–17 (1993). See also Robert Young, White Mythologies: Writing History and the West 127, 158, 173 (1990); Edward W. Said, Orientalism 228 (1978).

21. Foreigners in Their Native Land: Historical Roots of the Mexican Americans 59–60 (David J. Weber ed., 1973).

22. Joan W. Moore, Mexican Americans 1 (1970). See also Rodolfo Acuña, Occupied America: The Chicano's Struggle toward Liberation (1972) at 7.

23. Walter Prescott Webb, The Texas Rangers: A Century of Frontier Defense xv (1965).

Chapter 26

Race and Erasure

The Salience of Race to Latinos/as

Ian F. Haney López

On September 20, 1951, an all-White grand jury in Jackson County, Texas, indicted twenty-six-year-old Pete Hernández for the murder of another farm worker, Joe Espinosa. Gus García and John Herrera, lawyers with the League of United Latin American Citizens (LULAC), a Mexican-American civil rights organization, took up Hernández's case, hoping to use it to attack the systematic exclusion of Mexican Americans from jury service in Texas.[1] García and Herrera quickly moved to quash Hernández's indictment, arguing that people of Mexican descent were purposefully excluded from the indicting grand jury in violation of the Fourteenth Amendment's guarantee of equal protection of the laws. The lawyers pointed out, and the State of Texas stipulated, that while 15 percent of Jackson County's almost thirteen thousand residents were Mexican Americans, no such person had served on any jury commission, grand jury, or petit jury in Jackson County in the previous quarter century.[2] Despite this stipulation, the trial court denied the motion. After two days of trial and three and a half hours of deliberation, the jury convicted Hernández and sentenced him to life in prison.

On appeal, García and Herrera renewed the Fourteenth Amendment challenge. It again failed. The Texas Court of Criminal Appeals held that "in so far as the question of discrimination in the organization of juries in state courts is concerned, the equal protection clause of the Fourteenth Amendment contemplated and recognized only two classes as coming within that guarantee: the white race, comprising one class, and the Negro race, comprising the other class."[3] The Texas court held that the Fourteenth Amendment did not cover Mexican Americans in cases of jury discrimination.

With the assistance of Carlos Cadena, a law professor at St. Mary's University in San Antonio, the LULAC attorneys took the case to the United States Supreme Court. On May 3, 1954, Chief Justice Earl Warren delivered the unanimous opinion of the Court in *Hernandez v. Texas*, extending the aegis of the Fourteenth

From "RACE, ETHNICITY, AND ERASURE: THE SALIENCE OF RACE TO LATCRIT THEORY." Ian F. Haney López. Used by permission of the author. Publication in revised form forthcoming in the *California Law Review*.

Amendment to Pete Hernández and reversing his conviction. The Court did not do so, however, on the ground that Mexican Americans constitute a protected racial group. Rather, the Court held that Hernández merited Fourteenth Amendment protection because he belonged to a class, distinguishable on some basis "other than race or color," that nevertheless suffered discrimination in Jackson County, Texas.[4]

Hernandez is a central case—the first Supreme Court case to extend the protections of the Fourteenth Amendment to Latinos/as, it is among the great early triumphs in the Latino/a struggle for civil rights. *Hernandez* attains increased significance, however, because it is also the principal case in which the Supreme Court addresses the racial identity of a Latino/a group, in this instance Mexican Americans. No Supreme Court case has dealt so squarely with this question, before or since. This point is all the more striking, and *Hernandez* all the more exceptional, because at least on the surface the Court refused to consider Mexican Americans a group defined by race or color. If theorists intend, as I believe we should, to use race as a lens and language through which to assess the Latino/a experience in the United States, we must come to terms with the elision of race in *Hernandez*.

Race and Erasure

In the *United States Reports*, *Hernandez* immediately precedes another leading Fourteenth Amendment case, *Brown v. Board of Education*, having been decided just two weeks before that watershed case. Despite extending the reach of the Fourteenth Amendment by unanimous votes, the two cases differ dramatically. In *Brown*, the Court grappled with the harm done through segregation, but considered the applicability of the Equal Protection Clause to African Americans a foregone conclusion. In *Hernandez*, the reverse was true. The Court took for granted that the Equal Protection Clause would prohibit the state conduct in question, but wrestled with whether the Fourteenth Amendment protected Mexican Americans. Nevertheless, as in *Brown*, stark evidence of racism permeates *Hernandez*.

As catalogued by the Court, the evidence in the case revealed the following: First, residents of Jackson County, Texas, routinely distinguished between "white" and "Mexican" persons. Second, business and community groups largely excluded Mexican Americans from participation. Third, until just a few years earlier, children of Mexican descent were required to attend a segregated school for the first four grades, and most children of Mexican descent left school by the fifth or sixth grade. Fourth, at least one restaurant in the county seat prominently displayed a sign announcing "No Mexicans Served." Fifth, on the Jackson County courthouse grounds at the time of the underlying trial, there were two men's toilets, one unmarked, and the other marked "Colored Men" and "Hombres Aqui" ("Men Here"). Finally, with respect to jury selection itself, there was the stipulation that "for the last twenty-five years there is no record of any person with a Mexican or Latin American name having served on a jury commission, grand jury or petit jury in Jackson County," a county 15 percent Mexican American.[5]

In their brief to the Court, Hernández's lawyers placed heavy emphasis on this history of discrimination:

> While the Texas court elaborates its "two classes" theory, in Jackson County, and in other areas in Texas, persons of Mexican descent are treated as a third class—a notch above the Negroes, perhaps, but several notches below the rest of the population. They are segregated in schools, they are denied service in public places, they are discouraged from using non-Negro rest rooms. . . . They are told that they are assured of a fair trial at the hands of persons who do not want to go to school with them, who do not want to give them service in public places, who do not want to sit on juries with them, and who would prefer not to share rest room facilities with them, not even at the Jackson County court house.[6]

"The blunt truth," Hernández's lawyers insisted, "is that in Texas, persons of Mexican descent occupy a definite minority status."[7]

The Paradox of Race

Responding to the Texas court's pronouncement that regarding juries the Fourteenth Amendment contemplated only the White and Black races, the Supreme Court could have ruled that the Fourteenth Amendment protected other races as well. But it did not. Instead, while acknowledging that "[t]hroughout our history differences in race and color have defined easily identifiable groups which have at times required the aid of the courts in securing equal treatment under the laws," the Court went on to say that "from time to time *other differences* from the community norm may define other groups which need the same protection."[8] According to the Court, to prevail on his claim Hernández had to show that he was discriminated against as a member of a group marked by inchoate "other differences." Explaining this requirement, the Court suggested that "[w]hether such a group exists within a community is a question of fact,"[9] one that "may be demonstrated by showing the attitude of the community."[10] It is in its effort to assess the community attitudes toward Mexican Americans in Jackson County that the Court recited the litany of racism previously noted. Thus, the Court's finding that Hernández met the other-difference/community-attitude test rested squarely on detailed evidence of what fairly may be characterized as widespread racial discrimination.

In light of the Court's heavy reliance on the overwhelming evidence of racial discrimination presented in the case, the Court's insistence that Mexican Americans do not constitute a race seems surprising. It seems all the more startling when one recalls that at the time the Court decided *Hernandez,* national hysteria regarding Mexican immigration was running high, and also in light of evidence of possible racist antipathies toward Mexican Americans on the Supreme Court itself.[11] In part, the Court's reticence to acknowledge the cases may have stemmed from the fact that all parties characterized Mexican Americans as racially White, a consensus to which this essay will return.

In addition, however, the Court's assessment of the evidence in *Hernandez* was no doubt informed by the contemporary conception of race as an immutable natural phenomenon and a matter of biology—Black, White, Yellow, or Red, races were considered natural, physically distinct groupings of persons. Races, the Court no doubt supposed, were stable and objective, their boundaries a matter of physical fact and common knowledge, consistent the world over and across history.

Proceeding from this understanding, the Court could not help but be perplexed by the picture of Mexican-American identity presented in *Hernandez,* an identity that at every turn seemed inconstant and contradictory. Though clearly the object of severe racial prejudice in Texas, all concerned parties agreed Mexican Americans were White; though officially so, the dark skin and features of many Mexican Americans seemingly demonstrated that they were non-White; though apparently non-White, Mexican Americans could not neatly be categorized as Red, Yellow, or Black. A biological view of race positing that each person possesses an obvious, immutable, and exclusive racial identity cannot account for, or accept, these contradictions. Under a biological view of race, the force of these contradictions must on some level have served as evidence that Mexican Americans did not constitute a racial group. Thus, the Court insisted in the face of viscerally moving evidence to the contrary that the exclusion of Mexican Americans from juries in Jackson County, Texas, turned neither on race nor color.

Nevertheless, *Hernandez* is virtually unintelligible except in racial terms—in terms, that is, of racial discrimination, of segregation, of Jim Crow facilities, of social and political prejudice, of exclusion, marginalization, devaluation. The Court's evasion of race notwithstanding, the facts of *Hernandez* insist that when Pete Hernández was indicted for murder in 1951, an inferior racial identity defined Mexican Americans in Texas.

That despised identity developed in Texas over the course of more than a century of Anglo-Mexican conflict. In the early years of the nineteenth century, White settlers from the United States moving westward into what was then Spain, and after 1821, Mexico, clashed with the local people, eventually giving rise to war between Mexico and the United States in 1846. During this period, Whites in Texas and across the nation elaborated a Mexican identity in terms of innate, insuperable racial inferiority. According to historian Reginald Horsman, "By the time of the Mexican War, America had placed the Mexicans firmly within the rapidly emerging hierarchy of superior and inferior races. While the Anglo-Saxons were depicted as the purest of the pure—the finest Caucasians—the Mexicans who stood in the way of southwestern expansion were depicted as a mongrel race, adulterated by extensive intermarriage with an inferior [Native American] race."[12] These views continued, and were institutionalized, over the remainder of the last century and well into this one. According to historian Arnoldo De León "in different parts of [Texas], and deep into the 1900s, Anglos were more or less still parroting the comments of their forbears. . . . They regarded Mexicans as a colored people, discerned the Indian ancestry in them, identified them socially with blacks. In principle and in fact, Mexicans were regarded not as a nationality related to whites, but as a race apart."[13] Texas institutionalized this racial prejudice against persons of Mexican descent in the various ways catalogued by *Hernandez.* It is in the attitudes toward and the treatment of Mexican Americans, rather than in human biology, that one must locate the origins of Mexican-American racial identity.

Races do not reflect natural differentiation. Physical features, skin color, hair texture, and so on do not in and of themselves demarcate racial differences. These aspects of somatic diversity instead reflect only a myriad of subtle variations within the human species. Any biological basis to race has now been soundly repudiated. Instead, races are human inventions in which notions of transcendental, innate similarity and difference are assigned to physical features and ancestry. The assignment of racial boundaries arises in the form of social practices, and so reveals itself to be a highly contingent, historically specific process. In Texas, that process resulted in the racialization of Mexican Americans.

In this sense, ironically, the solution to the racial paradox posed in *Hernandez* lies within the "community attitudes" test advanced by the Court. The Court propounded this test as a measure of whether Mexican Americans exist as a distinct, though non-racial, group. In fact, no more accurate test could be fashioned to establish whether Mexican Americans, or any group, constitute a race. Race is not biological or fixed by nature; it is instead a question of social belief. Thus, albeit unwittingly, the *Hernandez* opinion offered a sophisticated insight into the nature of race: whether a racial group exists is always a local question to be answered in terms of community attitudes. To be sure, race is constructed through the interactions of a range of overlapping discursive communities, from local to national, ensuring that divergent and conflicting conceptions of racial identity exist within and among communities. Nevertheless, understanding race as "a question of community attitude" emphasizes that race is not biological but social. Therein lies the irony of the Court's position: avoiding a racial understanding of *Hernandez* in part due to a biological conception of race, the Court nevertheless correctly understood that the existence of Mexican Americans as a (racial) group in Jackson County turned, as race does, not on biology but on community attitudes.

Mexican American Racial Identity: White, Then and There

The biological view of race posits that group differences are deeply embedded in nature and highly determinative of group character; under this approach, racial identity is both fixed and easily known. In contrast, a social conception of race posits a virtually antithetical vision wherein both races and their associated characteristics are the products of social practices. Rather than suggesting, as a biological conception does, that racial identities are relatively homogenous and readily apparent and that race is somehow objective and indifferent to viewpoint, the social understanding of race suggests racial identities are complex creations understood and experienced in vastly dissimilar, competing, irreducibly subjective manners. Racial identity emerges as contested and fluid. The unstable nature of Mexican-American racial identity is evident in the origins of the consensus among the parties to *Hernandez* that Mexican Americans were White. This consensus illustrates the particular dynamics of Mexican-American racialization in Texas at mid-century.

When the Texas Court of Criminal Appeals heard *Hernandez,* it did so on the heels of a long line of decisions affirming the exclusion of Mexican Americans from juries. When LULAC undertook to defend Pete Hernández, it too was operating along a specific historical trajectory, participating in a continuing effort to secure Mexican-American civil rights from Texas courts. Remarkably, however, in *Hernandez* both the Texas court and the LULAC lawyers insisted that Mexican Americans were White. The court proclaimed that "Mexicans are white people," explaining that "Mexican people are not a separate race but are white people of Spanish descent."[14] The attorneys for Hernández agreed, but protested that "[w]hile legally white . . . frequently the term 'white' excludes the Mexican and is reserved for the rest of the non-Negro population."[15] How is it that the Texas courts and the LULAC lawyers both agreed Mexican Americans were White?

For LULAC, the racial identity of Mexican Americans had long been a troubling question. Founded in 1929 in Texas by members of the small Mexican-American middle class, this organization stressed both cultural pride and assimilation. These twin goals were not without their tensions, however, particularly with respect to the question of racial identity. Emphasizing the former often led LULAC to identify Mexican Americans as a distinct race. For example, LULAC's first code admonished members to "[l]ove the men of your race, take pride in your origins and keep it immaculate; respect your glorious past and help to vindicate your people"; its constitution announced, "[w]e solemnly declare once and for all to maintain a sincere and respectful reverence for our racial origin of which we are proud."[16] On the other hand, focusing on assimilation and the right to be free of widespread discrimination, LULAC often emphasized that Mexican Americans were White. "As descendants of Latins and Spaniards, Lulacers also claimed 'whiteness,'" according to historian Mario García. "Mexican Americans as 'whites' believed no substantive racial factor existed to justify racial discrimination against them."[17] To a certain extent, LULAC resolved the tension between seeking both difference and sameness by pursuing these on distinct planes: difference in terms of culture and heritage, but sameness regarding civil rights and civic participation. However, this resolution could not be maintained neatly using the notion of race as then constituted. Race inseparably conflated biology, culture, heritage, civil rights, and civic participation. In racial terms, to be Mexican and different was irreconcilable with being White and the same.

This tension notwithstanding, the decision to defend Pete Hernández constituted part of LULAC's strategy of fighting discrimination against Mexican Americans through the Texas courts. This strategy dictated as well the decision of the lawyers for Hernández to argue that Mexican Americans were White. As Mario García writes: "In [its] antisegregation efforts, LULAC rejected any attempt to segregate Mexican Americans as a nonwhite population. . . . Lulacers consistently argued that Mexicans were legally recognized members of the white race and that no legal or physical basis existed for legal discrimination."[18] For Hernández's attorneys, the decision to cast Mexican Americans as White was a tactical one, in the sense that it reflected the legal and social terrain on which they sought to gain civil rights for their community. On this terrain, being White was strategically key.

While Hernández's lawyers characterized Mexican Americans as White in order to combat discrimination and promote integration, the Texas court did not share those motives in assigning Mexican Americans the same racial identity. The Texas Court of Criminal Appeals' characterization of Mexican Americans as White in *Her-*

nandez must be viewed in light of that court's prior decisions addressing discrimination against Mexican Americans in the selection of juries. The criminal court had addressed this question on at least seven previous occasions between 1931 and its decision in *Hernandez* in 1952, consistently ruling against the Mexican-American defendant. The court had not, however, been consistent in its racial characterization of Mexican Americans.

In its initial decisions, and as late as 1948, the court construed Mexican-American challenges to jury exclusion as turning on discrimination against members of the "Mexican race." For example, *Ramirez v. State* concerned, according to the court, a challenge to "unjust discrimination against the Mexican race in Menard county,"[19] while *Carrasco v. State* raised a question of "alleged discrimination against the Mexican race on the part of the jury commission."[20] In each of these initial cases, the court denied that racial discrimination had occurred. Instead, the court concluded that the absence of Mexican Americans on local juries reflected the lack of Mexican Americans qualified under the Texas statute for jury service.

This line of reasoning proved troublesome, however. Often, the evidence adduced by the court to demonstrate the lack of qualified Mexican Americans seemed rather to demonstrate racial prejudice. In *Ramirez,* for example, decided in 1931, the court offered the testimony of several local officials as evidence regarding the lack of qualified Mexican Americans. First, the county attorney:

> Joe Flack testified that he had been county attorney for about four years and practicing law in Menard county and had resided there for more than fourteen years; that during his residence there he had not known of a person of the Mexican race . . . having been chosen as a grand juror or as a petit juror; that he knew there had been none since he had been county attorney; [and] that he did not think they were qualified to sit on the jury, as those in the county did not know English well enough and were otherwise ignorant.[21]

Next, the sheriff:

> The sheriff and tax collector of Menard county testified that . . . he did not remember that any Mexicans had ever been chosen on the grand jury list or the petit jury list since he had resided in the county; that he had never summoned a Mexican on the jury when it became his duty upon direction of the court to go out and summon jurors, and that he did not think the Mexicans of Menard county were intelligent enough or spoke English well enough or knew enough about the law to make good jurors, besides their customs and ways were different from ours, and for that reason he did not consider them well enough qualified to serve as jurors.[22]

And finally, a jury commissioner:

> Albert Nauwald testified that he was in the jury commission appointed by the district court that drew the grand jurors who indicted the appellant; that he would not select a negro to sit on the grand jury or petit jury while acting in the capacity of jury commissioner, even though the negro was as well qualified in every way to serve as a juror as any white man; that he was opposed to Mexicans serving on the jury; that he did not consider any individual Mexican's name in connection with making up the jury list; [and] that he did not consider the Mexicans in Menard county as being intelligent

enough to make good jurors, so that the jury commission just disregarded the whole Mexican list and did not consider any of them when making up their jury list.[23]

On the basis of this evidence, the appellate court concurred in the trial court's conclusion that "[t]he proof did not show that there had been discrimination against the Mexican race . . . there was no evidence that there was any Mexican in the County who possessed the statutory qualifications of a juror."[24]

The court in *Ramirez* distinguished between exclusion on the basis of racial prejudice and non-inclusion because of ignorance, insufficient intelligence, different customs and ways, and poor English. According to the court, the former was prohibited but not found in the record, while the latter was permissible and borne out by the weight of evidence. The United States Supreme Court denied certiorari without comment. Subsequently, the Texas appellate court three times more distinguished between impermissible exclusion and permissible non-inclusion in dismissing Mexican-American challenges to "racial" discrimination in jury selection. In each of these decisions, however, the evidence concerning the lack of qualified Mexican Americans seemed not to establish this lack, but rather to show in stark relief the racial discrimination complained of.

In sharp contrast to these four decisions, one by the appellate court in 1946 and two others handed down in 1951 characterized Mexican Americans as White and construed challenges concerning their exclusion from juries not in terms of race but of nationality. In these decisions, heralding the state court's approach in *Hernandez* in 1952, the court quickly rejected the defendants' claims of discrimination in jury selection on the basis of their supposed membership in the White race. For example, in *Salazar v. State*, decided in 1946, the court wrote:

> The complaint is made of discrimination against nationality, not race. The Mexican people are of the same race as the grand jurors. We see no question presented for our discussion under the Fourteenth Amendment to the Constitution of the United States and the decisions relied upon by appellant, dealing with discrimination against race.[25]

Similarly, in *Sanchez v. State*, decided in 1951, the court responded to "an exhaustive brief" on the question of discrimination against "Mexican Americans as a race" in the following terse manner: "They are not a separate race but are white people of Spanish descent, as has often been said by this court. We find no ground for discussing the question further and the complaint raised by this bill will not be sustained."[26] With these comments, the court quickly dismissed the defendants' Fourteenth Amendment challenges, dispensing not only with the question of whether there had been discrimination, but also with its previous reformulation of that same question, whether there were qualified Mexican Americans. These were questions the Texas court no longer felt compelled to answer. Instead, it relied solely on the assertion that Mexican Americans were White in order to reject contentions of impermissible discrimination in jury selection. This is the approach the court again took in *Hernandez*.

One cannot know the exact motivations behind the Texas appellate court's decision in *Hernandez* or the preceding cases to categorize Mexican Americans as White. Certainly, precedent existed for such a racial determination. For example, as early as

1897, a federal district court in Texas recognized persons of Mexican descent as "white persons" in the context of federal naturalization law, under which being White was a prerequisite for citizenship. Moreover, during the period when *Hernandez* was decided both the national government and the government of Texas moved officially to qualify Mexican Americans as White. Thus, in contrast to the 1930 census, which catalogued "Mexicans" as a distinct race, the 1940 census classified "[p]ersons of Mexican birth or ancestry who were not definitely Indian or of some other nonwhite race . . . as white."[27] Contemporaneously, Governor Stevenson of Texas reacted to a decision by the Mexican Ministry of Labor to restrict the migration of *bracero* workers to Texas "because of the number of cases of extreme, intolerable racial discrimination" by initiating a state "Good Neighbor Policy."[28] This policy formally proclaimed Mexican Americans valued state citizens and, more importantly, "members of the Caucasian race" against whom no discrimination was warranted.[29] The Texas Court of Criminal Appeals did not specifically cite these factors in its decisions characterizing Mexican Americans as White. Nevertheless, this larger trend toward according Mexican Americans White status, of which the LULAC campaign was a contributing part, may well have added to the court's growing sense between 1946 and 1952 that Mexican Americans were White persons.

It seems quite likely, however, that in addition, the desire of the court to find some basis for neatly disposing of Mexican-American claims of jury discrimination motivated it to construct Mexican Americans as White. Irrespective of the other factors that may have weighed on the court's mind, this one seems probable, especially in light of the progression of these cases. At the time the appellate court in *Hernandez* adopted a White conceptualization of Mexican Americans, the judicial rationale for rejecting claims of racial discrimination against members of that community was fast wearing thin. By 1952, persons challenging the exclusion of Mexican Americans from juries could point, as Hernández's lawyers did, to research indicating that in at least fifty Texas counties with large Mexican-American populations, no Mexican American had ever been called for jury service. They could also demonstrate convincingly that many Mexican Americans qualified for jury service, a point the state stipulated to in *Hernandez*. Finally, a full panoply of Supreme Court cases held that the Fourteenth Amendment prohibited jury discrimination of the sort apparently practiced against Mexican Americans—a roll call of cases on which, as the LULAC lawyers noted in their brief to the Court, "the State of Texas is more than proportionately represented."[30]

Against this backdrop of massive discrimination, purposeful and directed litigation, fast accumulating evidence, and clear constitutional law, the local practices of jury exclusion in Texas counties were increasingly difficult to uphold. Declaring that the Fourteenth Amendment did not protect Mexican Americans in the context of jury selection may have been the most expeditious manner by which the appellate court could immunize such local discriminatory practices. Proclaiming that Mexican Americans were White, and hence, incapable of being the victims of racial discrimination, may have been simply the means to that end. This may not have been the court's sole motivation, but it was likely the principal one.

The Salience of Race

The Supreme Court in *Hernandez* rejected a racial understanding of Mexican Americans in part because it subscribed to a conception of race as something natural and therefore stable, fixed, and immutable. Today we know race is none of these. Instead, race is always contingent on the time, place, and people involved. Racial identity turns not simply or even primarily on genetics or skin color but on the competing social meanings ascribed to ancestry and integument, and assigned as well to other aspects of identity, such as language, dress, religion, and so on. Certainly, all of these different factors contributed to the racialization of Mexican Americans in Texas in the sense of both fueling the belief in Mexican-American difference and in serving as confirmation and signifiers of that difference.

It may seem, however, that given the contingencies of race, the Court nevertheless was ultimately correct in deciding *Hernandez* on a non-racial basis. Even had the Court understood race as a social construction, one might argue, it may still have been the wiser course to decide *Hernandez* without reference to race. After all, the Court struck down the challenged discriminatory practices as it would have under a racial approach, but it managed to do so without inscribing the myth that races are real. Under this reading of the case, *Hernandez* would stand not only for the proposition that race is a social construction, but also for the proposal that, having recognized this, we dispense with the concept of race altogether.

Such a reading of *Hernandez* would not be without proponents. More than simply repudiating biological notions of race, prominent scholars such as Anthony Appiah have argued that we should abandon the idea of race itself. "The truth is that there are no races," Appiah writes, and "there is nothing in the world that can do all we ask race to do for us."[31] Good reasons argue for the call to discard all notions of race. Race comes to us out of some of the most terrible shadows of our past, only to find us in a present where race continues to justify the centering of some as privileged and empowered, and the expulsion of others as beyond the boundaries of society's care. Retaining race makes the work of racists easier, while it potentially traps antiracists in injurious myths of difference. Concluding that race is a social construction, it might make sense simply to jettison the entire scheme.

In the legal context, this is, implicitly, the drift of Christopher Ford's recent articles on efforts at racial categorization. In an article published in 1994 concerning legally recognized racial classifications, Ford warns "that there is something profoundly wrong with an 'anti-discrimination' ethic which calls forth such jurisprudential segregation and brands badges of racial identity onto the face of public life."[32] Although in that piece Ford stops short of explicitly endorsing the abandonment of legally mediated racial taxonomies, he moves closer to that position in a more recent article, where he warns that "[w]ithout at least some adjustment of principle and priority in the way we administer identity in contemporary America, we may face an increasingly bitter spiral of competitive Balkanization, the results of which are by no means likely to favor the minority groups in whose name it will all have been undertaken."[33]

If good reasons argue for repudiating all notions of race, even better ones do so with respect to Latinos/as. Latinos/as historically have not been as consistently racialized as other groups, such as Whites and African Americans. This is especially so regarding Latinos/as or Hispanics as a whole, since these categories are of recent vintage, though it is also true regarding constituent groups such as Mexican Americans or Puerto Ricans. Perhaps the arguments against thinking about groups in racial terms—that it reinforces racism, encourages subscription to false racial essences, and foments balkanization—apply with greater force to a group or groups not already primarily constructed in racial terms. Put differently, if it is true that race can be transcended most easily in the case of a heterogeneous population such as Latinos/as, the arguments for leaving race behind may be all the more difficult to reject with respect to this group. In this way, a praxis of deracination animated by a constructionist understanding of race dovetails with general calls for a non-racial conception of Latinos/as. Should we heed those calls, and eschew race? For a range of reasons, I do not believe so.

The Experience of Race

To begin with, rejecting race as a basis for conceptualizing Latino/a lives risks obscuring central facets of our experiences. Reconsider the evidence of discriminatory treatment at the root of *Hernandez*. In Jackson County, Mexican Americans were barred from local restaurants, excluded from social and business circles, relegated to inferior and segregated schooling, and subjected to the humiliation of Jim Crow facilities, including separate bathrooms in the halls of justice. Each of these aspects of social oppression substantially affected, although of course even in their totality they did not completely define, the experience of being Mexican American in Jackson County at mid-century.

To attempt to fathom the significance of such experiences, imagine being present at the moment that García called his co-counsel at trial, John Herrera, to testify about the segregated courthouse bathrooms. In picturing this episode, keep in mind that Herrera's ties to Texas stretched back at least to the original 1836 Texas Declaration of Independence, which was signed by his great, great-grandfather, Col. Francisco Ruiz, one of two Mexicans to sign that document. As excerpted from the trial court transcript, Herrera's testimony progressed like this:

> Q: During the noon recess I will ask you if you had occasion to go back there to a public privy, right in back of the courthouse square?
> A: Yes, sir.
> Q: The one designated for men?
> A: Yes, sir.
> Q: Now did you find one toilet there or more?
> A: I found two.
> Q: Did the one on the right have any lettering on it?
> A: No, sir.
> Q: Did the one on the left have any lettering on it?
> A: Yes, it did.

Q: What did it have?

A: It had the lettering "Colored Men" and right under "Colored Men" it had two Spanish words.

Q: What were those words?

A: The first word was "Hombres."

Q: What does that mean?

A: That means "Men."

Q: And the second one?

A: "Aqui," meaning "Here."

Q: Right under the words "Colored Men" was "Hombres Aqui" in Spanish, which means "Men Here"?

A: Yes, sir.[34]

Under cross-examination by the district attorney, Herrera continued:

Q: There was not a lock on this unmarked door to the privy?

A: No, sir.

Q: It was open to the public?

A: They were both open to the public, yes, sir.

Q: And didn't have on it "For Americans Only," or "For English Only," or "For Whites Only"?

A: No, sir.

Q: Did you undertake to use either one of these toilets while you were down here?

A: I did feel like it, but the feeling went away when I saw the sign.

Q: So you did not?

A: No, sir, I did not.[35]

By themselves, on paper, the words are dry, disembodied, untethered. It is hard to envision the Jackson County courtroom, difficult to sense its feel and smell; we cannot hear García pose his questions; we do not register the emotion perhaps betrayed in Herrera's voice as he testified to his own exclusion; we cannot know if the courtroom was silent, solemn and attentive, or murmurous and indifferent. But perhaps we can imagine the deep mixture of anger, frustration, and sorrow that would fill our guts and our hearts if it were we—if it were we confronted by that accusatory bathroom lettering, we called to the stand to testify about the signs of our supposed inferiority, we serving as witnesses to our undesirability in order to prove we exist.

Imagining such a moment should not be understood as giving insight into the very worst damage done by racism in this country. Nor should it be taken to suggest that everyone constructed as non-White has come up against such abuse, or has experienced it the same way. Finally, it should not be taken to imply that those denigrated in non-racial terms do not also suffer significant, sometimes far greater harms. Imagining the moment described above cannot and does not pretend to afford insight into the full dynamics of racial oppression, or to provide a solid base from which to compare other forms of disadvantage.

What it does afford, however, is a sense of the experience of racial discrimination in the United States. In this country, the sort of group oppression documented in *Hernandez*, the sort manifest on the bathroom doors of the Jackson County courthouse, has traditionally been meted out to those characterized as racially different, not to those simply different in ethnic terms. It is on the basis of race—on the basis, that is, of presumably immutable difference, rather than because of ethnicity or culture—that groups in the United States have been subject to the deepest prejudices, to exclusion and denigration across the range of social interactions, to state-sanctioned segregation and humiliation. In comparison to ethnic antagonisms, the flames of racial hatred in the United States have been stoked higher and have seared deeper. They have been fueled to such levels by beliefs stressing the innateness, not simply the cultural significance, of superior and inferior identities. To eschew the language of race is to risk losing sight of these central racial experiences.

Racial Conditions

Race should be used as a lens through which to view Latinos/as in order to focus attention on the experiences of racial oppression. However, it should also direct our attention to racial oppression's long-term effects on the day-to-day conditions encountered and endured by Latino/a communities. Consider in this vein the segregated school system noted in *Hernandez*. Jackson County's scholastic segregation of Whites and Mexican Americans typified the practices of Texas school boards: although not mandated by state law, from the turn of the century, school boards in Texas customarily separated Mexican-American and White students. In his study of the Mexican-American struggle for educational equality in Texas, Guadalupe San Miguel writes:

> School officials and board members, reflecting the specific desires of the general population, did not want Mexican students to attend school with Anglo children regardless of their social standing, economic status, language capabilities, or place of residence. . . . Wherever there were significant numbers of Mexican children in school, local officials tried to place them in facilities separate from the other white children.[36]

Though it should be obvious, it bears making explicit that racism drove this practice. A school superintendent explained it this way: "Some Mexicans are very bright, but you can't compare their brightest with the average white children. They are an inferior race."[37] According to San Miguel, many Whites "simply felt that public education would not benefit [Mexican Americans] since they were intellectually inferior to Anglos."[38] To be sure, as in Jackson County, school segregation in Texas was most pronounced in the lower grades. However, also as in that county, this fact reflects not a lack of concern with segregation at the higher grades, but rather the practice of forcing Mexican-American children out of the educational system after only a few years of school. The segregated schooling noted in *Hernandez* constitutes but one instance in a rampant practice of educational discrimination against Mexican Americans in Texas and across the southwest.

Using the language of race forces us to look to the pronounced effects on minority communities of long-standing practices of racial discrimination. These effects can be devastating in their physical concreteness, as evidenced by the dilapidated school-

house for the Mexican-American children in Jackson County's Edna Independent
School District. According to the testimony of one frustrated mother, the "Latin
American school" consisted of a decaying one-room wooden building that flooded
repeatedly during the rains, with only a wood stove for heat and outside bathroom
facilities, and with but one teacher for the four grades taught there. Such effects may
also be personal and intangible, though not for those reasons any less real, dire, or
permanent. In Jackson County, as in the rest of Texas, the Mexican-American children subject to state-sanctioned segregation no doubt suffered grave harm to their
sense of self-worth and belonging—feelings of inferiority embossed on their hearts
and minds in ways unlikely ever to be undone, in the language of Chief Justice Warren.[39]

Irrespective of their form, the conditions produced by racism profoundly degrade
the quality of life of non-White community members while also limiting their life
chances. Consider in this regard the net educational impact of school segregation on
Jackson County's Mexican-American community. In their brief to the Court, the
LULAC attorneys sought to establish that at least some Mexican Americans residing
in Jackson County possessed sufficient education to serve as jurors; the evidence they
cited from the 1950 census proved this. Of the 645 persons of Spanish surname in
that county over the age of 24, the lawyers informed the Court, "245 have completed
from 1 to 4 years of elementary schooling; 85 have completed the fifth and sixth
years; 35 have completed 7 years of elementary schooling; 15 have completed 8
years; 60 have completed from one to three years of high school; 5 have completed
4 years of high school; and 5 are college graduates."[40] Although these figures prove
that some Mexican-Americans were educationally qualified to serve as jurors, they
also demonstrate the impact of that county's systematic educational discrimination
against Mexican Americans. The figures tell us, for example, that out of the Mexican American adult population of 645 in Jackson County, only five had completed
college. Consider also two additional numbers from the census that the lawyers don't
cite: First, out of that population of 645, fully 175 had received no formal education
whatsoever; second, the median number of school years completed was a dismal 3.2
years.[41] The net educational impact of segregation on Mexican Americans in Jackson
County was nothing short of disastrous.

In Jackson County, segregated schools were just one manifestation of racial discrimination. As the evidence from that county demonstrates, the effects of long-term
racism on the conditions of minority communities are profound. Those effects warrant close attention if we hope to understand the lives of persons oppressed because
of supposed racial differences—people systematically relegated to society's bottom,
not just through the operation of individual prejudices but by institutionalized cultural, political, and juridical practices. The impact on community members, such as
widespread alienation and low levels of education, largely set the parameters of the
lives of those within the community. None but the fewest and most fortunate Mexican Americans raised in the 1950s in Jackson County, Texas, could escape the grinding poverty dictated for them by the racial prejudices of Whites there. Because these
conditions circumscribe the lives people can reasonably expect to live in this society,

racial language remains a salient vocabulary for discussing socially constituted communities, never more so than when those communities have been severely subordinated in racial terms.

NOTES

1. Gustavo C. García, *An Informal Report to the People,* in A Cotton Picker Finds Justice! The Saga of the Hernandez Case (Ruben Munguia ed., 1954).

2. Hernandez v. State, 251 S.W.2d 531, 533 (Tex. Crim. App. 1952).

3. *Id.* at 535.

4. Hernandez v. Texas, 347 U.S. 475, 477, 479–480 (1954). The Court suggested, but did not explicitly rule, that this "other basis" corresponded to ancestry or national origin. *Id.* at 479.

5. *Id.* at 481, 480.

6. Brief for Petitioner at 28–29, Hernandez v. Texas 347 U.S. 475 (No. 406).

7. *Id.* at 13.

8. *Hernandez,* 347 U.S. at 478 (emphasis added).

9. *Id.*

10. *Id.* at 479.

11. Mark Tushnet brings to light revealing comments regarding Mexican Americans made by Justice Tom Clark during a 1952 conference discussion of the segregation decisions:
> Clark, in a statement which, apart from its racism, is quite difficult to figure out, said that Texas "also has the Mexican problem" which was "more serious" because the Mexicans were "more retarded," and mentioned the problem of a "Mexican boy of 15 . . . in a class with a negro girl of 12," when "some negro girls [would] get in trouble."

Mark V. Tushnet, Making Civil Rights Law: Thurgood Marshall and the Supreme Court, 1936–1961, at 194 (1994). Tushnet adds: "These references capture the personal way the justices understood the problem they were confronting, and the unfocused quality suggests that they were attempting to reconcile themselves to the result they were about to reach." *Id.* Clark, formerly the Civil District Attorney for Texas and a Truman appointee to the Court in 1949, was replaced on the bench by Thurgood Marshall in 1967. William Lockhart et al., Constitutional Rights and Liberties: Cases, Comments, Questions 1433–35 (8 ed., 1996).

12. Reginald Horsman, Race and Manifest Destiny: The Origins of American Racial Anglo-Saxonism 210 (1981).

13. Arnoldo De León, They Called Them Greasers: Anglo Attitudes toward Mexicans in Texas 1821–1900, at 104 (1983).

14. Hernandez v. State, 251 S.W.2d 531, 535 (citing Sanchez v. State, 243 S.W.2d 700, 701 [Tex. Crim. App. 1951]).

15. Brief for Petitioner at 38, Hernandez v. Texas, 347 U.S. 475 (No. 406).

16. Mario T. García, Mexican Americans: Leadership, Ideology, and Identity, 1930–1960, at 30–31 (1989).

17. *Id.* at 43.

18. *Id.* at 48. The insistence by many in the Mexican-American community that they be considered White was also fueled by prejudice harbored against Blacks.

19. Ramirez v. State, 40 S.W.2d at 138, 139 (Tex. Crim. App. 1931).

20. Carrasco v. State, 95 S.W.2d at 433, 434 (Tex. Crim. App. 1936).

21. *Ramirez,* 40 S.W.2d at 139.

22. *Id.*

23. *Id.*

24. *Id.* at 140.

25. Salazar v. State, 193 S.W.2d 211, 212 (Tex. Crim. App. 1946).

26. Aniceto Sanchez v. State, 243 S.W.2d at 700, 701 (Tex. Crim. App. 1951).

27. United States Department of Commerce, Sixteenth Census of the United States: 1940: Characteristics of the Population 3 (1943).

28. Carey McWilliams, North from Mexico: The Spanish-Speaking People of the United States 270 (1949, Greenwood 1972).

29. *Id.* at 270–71

30. Brief for Petitioner at 29, Hernandez v. Texas, 347 U.S. 475 (No. 406).

31. Kwame Anthony Appiah, In My Father's House: Africa in the Philosophy of Culture 45 (1992).

32. Christopher A. Ford, *Administering Identity: The Determination of "Race" in Race-Conscious Law,* 82 Cal. L. Rev. 1231, 1285 (1994).

33. Christopher A. Ford, *Challenges and Dilemmas of Racial and Ethnic Identity in American and Post-Apartheid South African Affirmative Action,* 43 UCLA L. Rev. 1953, 2029 (1996).

34. Transcript of Hearing on Motion to Quash Jury Panel and Motion to Quash the Indictment, State v. Hernandez (Dist. Ct. Jackson Co., Oct. 4, 1951) (No. 2091), Record at 74–75.

35. *Id.* at 76.

36. Guadalupe San Miguel, Jr., Let Them All Take Heed: Mexican Americans and the Campaign for Educational Equality in Texas, 1910–1981, at 54–55 (1987).

37. *Id.* at 32, citing Paul S. Taylor, An American -Mexican Frontier: Nueces County, Texas (1934) (specific page attribution not given).

38. *Id.* at 51.

39. Brown v. Board of Education, 347 U.S. 483, 494 (1954).

40. Brief for Petitioner at 19, Hernandez v. Texas, 347 U.S. 475 (No. 406).

41. U.S. Bureau of the Census, U.S. Census of Population: 1950. Volume IV: Special Reports: Persons of Spanish Surname, 36–67 (1953).

Chapter 27

"The Mexican Problem"

Carey McWilliams

In the vast library of books and documents about ethnic and minority problems in the United States, one of the largest sections is devoted to "the Mexican Problem." There is a curious consistency about the documents in this section. For one thing, the singular is always used. Presumably, also, no problem existed, singular or plural, prior to 1920. *Readers' Guide* lists fifty-one articles on "the Mexican Problem" from 1920 to 1930 by comparison with nineteen articles on the same subject for the previous decade. When these articles are examined, it will be found that "the problem" apparently consists in the sum total of the voluminous statistics on Mexican delinquency, poor housing, low wages, illiteracy, and rates of disease. In other words, "the Mexican Problem" has been defined in terms of the social consequences of Mexican immigration.

It will also be found that the documents devoted to the problem have been deeply colored by the "social work" approach. With the passage of the 1924 Immigration Act, the immigrant social agencies and Americanization institutes simply had to discover a new "problem" and it was the Mexican's misfortune to appear on the scene, sombrero and all, concurrently with the impending liquidation of these agencies. As a consequence, he was promptly adopted as America's No. 1 immigrant problem. The whole apparatus of immigrant-aid social work, with its morose preoccupation with consequences rather than causes, was thereupon transferred to Mexican immigration with little realization that this immigration might not be, in all respects, identical with European immigration.

Once assembled and classified, this depressing mass of social data was consistently interpreted in terms of what it revealed about the inadequacies and the weaknesses of the Mexican character. The data "proved" that Mexicans lacked leadership, discipline, and organization; that they segregated themselves; that they were lacking in thrift and enterprise, and so forth. A mountainous collection of masters' theses "proved" conclusively that Spanish-speaking children were "retarded" because, on the basis of various so-called intelligence tests, they did not measure up to the intellectual calibre of Anglo-American students. Most of this theorizing was heavily weighted with gratuitous assumptions about Mexicans and Indians. Paradoxically, the more sympathetic the writer, the greater seems to have been the implied condescension. All in all, the conclusion is unavoidable that Mexicans have been regarded as the essence of "the Mexican Problem."

The use of this deceptive, catchall phrase has consistently beclouded the real issues by focusing attention on consequences rather than on causes. Actually the basic issues have always had to do with Anglo-Hispano relations in a particular historical setting as influenced by a specific set of cultural, economic, geographical, and social forces. Once these factors are seen in proper perspective, if only in outline form, the elusive character of "the Mexican Problem" vanishes into thin air.

Chapter 28

Citizens as "Foreigners"

Kevin R. Johnson

The "Latino-as-foreigner" phenomenon is exemplified by the treatment afforded Luis Gutiérrez, a member of Congress, in the spring of 1996. A police officer accused him of presenting false congressional credentials as he attempted to enter the nation's Capitol after attending a tribute to an all–Puerto Rican infantry unit that fought in the Korean War. One officer told Gutiérrez—who was born and raised in the United States—in the presence of his daughter and guests, that he should go back to where he came from.[1] Although embarrassed, Gutiérrez was able quickly to straighten matters out when another police officer recognized him and intervened. The police officer, after a brief suspension, was soon back at work. Unfortunately, similar incidents occur regularly to Latinos with little, if any, recourse available.

Peter Brimelow's book *Alien Nation: Common Sense about America's Immigration Disaster* illustrates how Latinos are viewed as foreign and therefore undesirable.[2] Although ostensibly concerned with immigration from Latin America, Brimelow expresses more general concern about the "Hispanic" influence in the United States and accuses the Latino leadership of creating an artificial "Hispanic identity" for illegitimate purposes, namely to reap the benefits of affirmative action. In essence, Brimelow's argument is that, because all Hispanics are "foreign" to the nation's Anglo-Saxon roots, drastic efforts should be taken to keep any more of "them" out of the country.

Persons of Latin American ancestry also are frequently charged with a related crime—failure to assimilate—that is sometimes used to rationalize their relatively low socioeconomic status in the United States. This charge continues to be made even though many Latinos are indeed assimilating into the mainstream. Note how the accusation that Latinos fail to assimilate is part of a historical pattern of blaming the outsider for deep social problems. Earlier in U.S. history, charges that persons of Chinese and Japanese ancestry failed to assimilate were employed to justify laws prohibiting Chinese immigration and interning the Japanese. Blaming immigrants of color for the hardships they suffer is similar to the once-popular claim that African-

From "Some Thoughts on the Future of Latino Legal Scholarship." Copyright © 1997 by Kevin R. Johnson. Used by permission of the author. Publication forthcoming in the *Harvard Latino Law Review*.

American poverty results from a "culture of poverty," a dubious theory championed by some social scientists in the 1970s.

By stigmatizing Latinos as "foreigners" and pressuring them to assimilate, dominant society has affected the development of Latino identity, at times in oppressive ways. In attempts to assimilate and become less foreign, some Latinos have Anglicized their Spanish surnames, declined to teach Spanish to their children, and married Anglos. Some Mexican Americans in the Southwest have gone so far as to claim they were "Spanish," thereby denying their Mexican ancestry and attempting to "pass" as white.

Because one uniting characteristic for Latinos is dominant society's view that they differ from the Anglo-Saxon ideal, time and effort would wisely be devoted by Latino scholars and activists in combating the dominant view that Latinos are "foreigners." As occurred with certain groups, such as Jewish immigrants who came from nations all over Europe, Latinos, must realize that common interests often outweigh the differences that separate national origin groups. Anti-Semitism in American culture contributed to the forging of a pan-Jewish identity. Similar pressures might well facilitate creation of a pan-Latino identity.

In combating dominant society's view that Latinos are foreigners, exploration of Latino social identity is necessary. Some common characteristics of that identity—ethnicity, the Spanish language, religious affiliation (Catholicism), and family—all differ from the Anglo-Saxon norm and contribute to the treatment of Latinos as foreigners. The dynamics of the categorization of Latinos as foreigners, and its impact in such areas as immigration, education, and law enforcement, deserves scholarly attention.

The Mistreatment of "Foreigners"

Immigration is a convenient lens through which to learn how dominant society views Latinos. Consider the anti-Mexican message of the campaign culminating in the passage of California's Proposition 187, which would deny most public benefits to undocumented persons. The Proposition 187 media director for southern California expressed blatantly anti-Mexican concerns in a letter printed by the *New York Times:*

> Proposition 187 is . . . a logical step toward saving California from economic ruin. . . .
> By flooding the state with 2 million illegal aliens to date, and increasing that figure each
> of the following 10 years, Mexicans in California would number 15 million to 20 million by 2004. During those 10 years about 5 million to 8 million Californians would
> have emigrated to other states. *If these trends continued, a Mexico-controlled California could vote to establish Spanish as the sole language of California, 10 million more
> English-speaking Californians could flee, and there could be a statewide vote to leave
> the Union and annex California to Mexico.*[3]

This statement falls squarely within the textbook definition of nativism. As history, past and recent, make clear, anti-Mexican sentiment tied to immigration is nothing new: Mexican-American citizens along with Mexican nationals were deported indiscriminately in the depths of the Great Depression.

As these events suggest, the hostility toward Mexican immigrants reveals how dominant society views Mexican Americans in the United States—as foreigners deserving of harsh treatment. Consider how the U.S. government, with popular approval, treats Mexican "foreigners." On April Fools Day 1996, a television crew videotaped the beating of a Mexican man and woman, suspected of being undocumented by law enforcement officers, after a high speed chase. Though most of the public was horrified, some argued that the victims deserved their treatment:

> I think the sheriffs were doing their job. I did M.P. work. I was accepted for the Highway Patrol but I turned it down. I can understand what they went through. Other people who are starting to file law claims, they ought to be shipped back. I know what the Mexicans do to the Americans in Mexico. They treat them like dogs. That gal that's wanting to sue. Someone ought to hit her on the head and send her back to Mexico.[4]

Contrast that episode with the Rodney King beating. When that beating is discussed, it is with reference to the unfortunate person (Rodney King) attacked by police officers. Yet, public discussion of the Mexicans' beating, for the most part, left out any mention of their names. Rather, they were portrayed as fungible, invisible, anonymous "illegal aliens" from Mexico of whom this nation has hundreds of thousands. But Alicia Sotero Vasquez and Enrique Funes Flores are human. Further demonstrating the invisibility of the victims, this incident, quite unlike the Rodney King beating, almost immediately disappeared from public consciousness. There will not be law review symposia or books analyzing the event, even though the Vasquez and Flores incident is part of a pattern of violence against undocumented Mexicans along the border.

The sensational quality of the event should not overshadow the day-to-day tragedies suffered by many Mexican immigrants in the United States. For example, within days of the videotaped beatings of Vasquez and Flores, seven Mexican citizens were killed and eighteen others injured in an automobile crash after being followed by Border Patrol agents near the U.S./Mexico border. Similarly, signs along the freeways in and about San Diego, California, include faceless shadow figures (presumably of a family), which warn drivers to watch for people running across the freeway. The signs are a response to the unfortunately common occurrence of motorists hitting undocumented persons attempting to evade the Border Patrol. Despite the human tragedy, a radio talk show host in the summer of 1996 callously stated on the air that motorists near the U.S./Mexico border should be awarded a sombrero-shaped bumper sticker for each undocumented immigrant they hit with their automobile.[5]

Immigrants from Latin American nations other than Mexico also have been subject to harsh measures. The United States took aggressive measures against Central Americans fleeing political violence in the 1980s, including detaining them while asylum applications were pending and encouraging them "voluntarily" to return to their native countries. The United States government also has indefinitely detained a number of Cuban citizens whom the Cuban government will not allow to return there. In the 1990s, the United States changed long-standing practice and refused to accept Cuban refugees fleeing harsh conditions.

Although often marginalized as "immigration" issues, these events offer a more general perspective about how Latinos are viewed by the Anglo-Saxon mainstream. Immigration is a unique area of law in which, due to the so-called "plenary power" doctrine, the courts place few legal constraints on governmental action. Landmark cases, such as the seminal Supreme Court decision upholding the exclusion of Chinese immigrants to this country in the late 1800s that permit racial and national origin discrimination, are followed to this day. Moreover, the immigration bureaucracy also enjoys considerable discretion in enforcing laws affecting the rights of non-citizens physically present in the country. Legal constraints are minimal and society is able to act as it sees fit. This allows for harsh policies directed at "illegal aliens," a loaded term often used as code for Mexican citizens.

NOTES

1. See David Jackson and Paul de la Garza, *Rep. Gutiérrez: Uncommon Target of a Too Common Slur*, CHI. TRIB., April 18, 1996, at 1. For more details, as well as Congressman Gutiérrez's reactions, see Alex Garcia, *One Day at the Capitol*, HISPANIC BUS., June 1996, at 112 (interview of Congressman Gutiérrez).

2. See Peter Brimelow, ALIEN NATION: COMMON SENSE ABOUT AMERICA'S IMMIGRATION DISASTER (1995).

3. *Letter to Editor by Linda B. Hayes*, N.Y. TIMES, Oct. 15, 1994, at sec. 1, p. 18 (emphasis added).

4. *Both Sides Speak Out on the Beatings by Deputies*, PRESS-ENTERPRISE (Riverside, California), Apr. 6, 1996, at B2.

5. *See Dan Vierra, Radio Host on Illegal Immigrants: Run 'Em Down*, SACRAMENTO BEE, Aug. 17, 1996, at B1.

From the Editors
Issues and Comments

Do you agree that the experiences of Chicanos, and perhaps Puerto Ricans, resemble colonization? If so, do the experiences of other minority groups also resemble colonization?

If racialization is not a constant but depends on local attitudes, could a Latino live a relatively racism-free life in, say, New Hampshire but not in Texas? If so, does he or she cease to be a Latino while living in New Hampshire since *Latino* means a person of Latin-American descent who is racialized by the dominant culture?

Are all immigrant groups racialized and constructed as inferior when they first arrive here? The Irish and Jews were first regarded as nonwhite, then joined the white group over time. Will this also happen to Latinos? To blacks?

Why did courts at various times and for various purposes classify Mexican Americans as white or nonwhite?

Was the intense racialization of Latinos in this country's early years a function of labor need, the need to justify conquest, or something else? Why were early immigrants from, say, Norway, not treated in similar fashion to that described in some of the selections?

How would you feel if you were deported by mistake, with no chance to explain that you belong here, to a country that your grandparents happened to be from? Imagine that the government decided to return all the Bosnian refugees, and your ancestors were from that country. What if you were deported simply because you showed a resemblance, physically and in your family name, to other Bosnians? Would you think it was your fault for not having documentation with you? Do you think the American citizens who were deported to Mexico in past indiscriminate roundups felt similarly? Why did international agreements and treaties, such as that of Guadalupe Hildalgo, not stop these abuses?

Why is anti-Latino sentiment increasing in virulence most sharply in California rather than somewhere else?

Should a Latino who is tried for a crime be entitled to a jury with Latinos on it? Or are Latinos essentially white so that an all-white jury that was otherwise acceptable would be fair?

Suppose that the environment changes radically so that all the white people are sickly, have trouble expressing themselves, and die early in life. Latinos and blacks move into leadership positions and take control of industry. Would whites change their names to Rodriguez and Ramirez and try to "pass" for Latino or black?

202

Suggested Readings

Nativism and Racism

Acuña, Rodolfo F. *Anything but Mexican: Chicanos in Contemporary Los Angeles.* London: Verso, 1996.

———. *A Community under Siege: A Chronicle of Chicanos East of the Los Angeles River 1945–1975.* Los Angeles: Chicano Studies Research Center, University of California at Los Angeles, 1984.

American Committee for the Protection of the Foreign Born. *Our Badge of Infamy: A Petition to the United Nations on the Treatment of the Mexican Immigrant.* N.p., 1959. Reprinted in *The Mexican American and the Law,* edited by Carlos Cortes. New York: Arno Press, 1974.

Balderrama, Francisco E., and Raymond Rodriguez. *Decade of Betrayal: Mexican Repatriation in the 1930s.* Albuquerque: University of New Mexico Press, 1995.

Barrera, Mario. *Race and Class in the Southwest: A Theory of Racial Inequality.* Notre Dame: University of Notre Dame Press, 1979.

Bennett, David H. *The Party of Fear: From Nativist Movements to the New Right in American History.* Chapel Hill: University of North Carolina Press, 1988.

Blauner, Robert. *Racial Oppression in America.* New York: Harper & Row, 1972.

Carleton, Don E. *Red Scare! Right Wing Hysteria, Fifties Fanaticism, and Their Legacy in Texas.* Austin: Texas Monthly Press, 1985.

Clopper, J. C. "Journal of J. C. Clopper, 1828." *Southwestern Historical Quarterly* 13 (July 1909): 44–80.

A Cotton Picker Finds Justice! The Saga of the Hernandez Case, edited by Ruben Munguia. N.p., 1954.

Dana, Richard Henry. *Two Years before the Mast.* Boston: Houghton Mifflin, 1911.

Daniel, Cletus E. *Bitter Harvest: A History of California Farm Workers, 1870–1941.* Ithaca, N.Y.: Cornell University Press, 1981.

Farnham, Thomas Jefferson. *Life, Adventures, and Travel in California.* New York: Nafis & Cornish, 1847.

Foreigners in Their Native Land: Historical Roots of the Mexican Americans, edited by David J. Weber. Albuquerque: University of New Mexico Press, 1973.

Galarza, Ernesto. *Farmworkers and Agribusiness in California, 1947–1977.* Notre Dame: University of Notre Dame Press, 1977.

———. *Merchants of Labor: The Mexican Bracero Story, an Account of the Managed Migration of Mexican Farm Workers in California, 1942–1960.* Charlotte, N.C.: McNally & Loften, 1964.

Gamio, Manuel. *The Life Story of the Mexican Immigrant: Autobiographical Documents.* Chicago: University of Chicago Press, 1931. Reprint, New York: Dover Publications, 1971.

————. *Mexican Immigration to the United States: A Study of Human Migration and Adjustment,* Chicago: University of Chicago Press, 1930. Reprint, New York: Dover Publications, 1971.

Garcia, Juan Ramon. *Operation Wetback: The Mass Deportation of Mexican Undocumented Workers in 1954.* Westport, Conn.: Greenwood Press, 1980.

Garcia, Mario T. *Desert Immigrants: The Mexicans of El Paso, 1880–1920.* New Haven: Yale University Press, 1981.

Gomez, David F. *Somos Chicanos: Strangers in Our Own Land.* Boston: Beacon Press, 1973.

Heizer, Robert F., and Alan J. Almquist. *The Other Californians: Prejudice and Discrimination under Spain, Mexico, and the United States to 1920.* Berkeley: University of California Press, 1971.

Higham, John. *Strangers in the Land: Patterns of American Nativism 1860–1925.* 2d ed. New Brunswick, N.J.: Rutgers University Press, 1988.

Hoffman, Abraham. *Unwanted Mexican Americans in the Great Depression: Repatriation Pressures, 1929–1939.* Tucson: University of Arizona Press, 1974.

Immigrants Out! The New Nativism and the Anti-Immigrant Impulse in the United States, edited by Juan F. Perea. New York: New York University Press, 1996.

Larson, Jane E. "Free Markets Deep in the Heart of Texas." 84 *Georgetown Law Journal* 179 (1995).

Latham, Francis S. *Travels in Texas,* 1842. Edited by Gerald S. Pierce. Austin, Tex.: Encino Press, 1971.

McWilliams, Carey. *Factories in the Fields: The Story of Migratory Farm Labor in California.* Boston: Little, Brown, 1939.

————. *Southern California: An Island on the Land.* Santa Barbara, Calif.: Peregrine Smith, 1946.

Menchaca, Martha. *The Mexican Outsiders: A Community History of Marginalization and Discrimination in California.* Austin: University of Texas Press, 1995.

Mirande, Alfredo. *Gringo Justice.* Notre Dame: University of Notre Dame Press, 1987.

Montejano, David. *Anglos and Mexicans in the Making of Texas, 1836–1986.* Austin: University of Texas Press, 1987.

Morgan, Patricia. *Shame of a Nation: A Documented Story of Police-State Terror against Mexican Americans in the U.S.A.* Los Angeles: Los Angeles Committee for the Protection of the Foreign Born, 1954.

Olmstead, Frederick Law. *A Journey through Texas: Or, A Saddle-Trip on the Southwestern Frontier, with a Statistical Abstract.* New York: Dix, Edwards & Co., 1857. Reprint, Austin: University of Texas Press, 1978.

Parédes, Americo. *"With His Pistol in His Hand": A Border Ballad and Its Hero.* Austin: University of Texas Press, 1958.

Peterson, Richard H. "Anti-Mexican Nativism in California, 1848–1853: A Study in Cultural Conflict." *Southern California Quarterly* 62 (Winter 1980): 309–28.

Reid, John C. *Reid's Tramp: Or, A Journal of the Incidents of Ten Months' Travel . . .* Selma, Ala.: J. Hardy Co., 1858. Reprint, Austin, Tex.: Steck Co., 1935.

Reisler, Mark. *By the Sweat of Their Brow: Mexican Immigrant Labor in the United States, 1900–1940.* Westport, Conn.: Greenwood Press, 1976.

Rodriguez, Clara E. *Puerto Ricans: Born in the U.S.A.* Boston: Unwin Hyman, 1989.

Romo, Ricardo. *East Los Angeles: History of a Barrio.* Austin: University of Texas Press, 1983.

———. "Responses to Mexican Immigration 1910–1930." *Aztlán: International Journal of Chicano Studies Research* 6 (1975): 173

Rosenbaum, Robert J. Mexicano Resistance in the Southwest: "The Sacred Right of Self-Preservation." Austin: University of Texas Press, 1981.

Ruiz, Vicki L. "By the Day or Week: Mexicana Domestic Workers in El Paso." In *"To Toil the Livelong Day": America's Women at Work, 1780–1980,* edited by Carol Groneman and Mary Beth Norton, 269. Ithaca, N.Y.: Cornell University Press, 1987.

Samora, Julian, Joe Bernal, and Albert Pena. *Gunpowder Justice: A Reassessment of the Texas Rangers.* Notre Dame: University of Notre Dame, 1979.

Samora, Julian, with Jorge A. Bustamente, and Gilbert Cardenas. *Los Mojados: The Wetback Story.* Notre Dame: University of Notre Dame Press, 1971.

Seguin, Juan N. *Personal Memoirs of John N. Seguin: From the Year 1834 to the Retreat of General Woll from the City of San Antonio.* San Antonio, Tex.: Printed at the Ledger Book and Job Office, 1858.

Shirley, Dame. *The Shirley Letters from the California Mines, 1851–1852.* New York: A.A. Knopf, 1949.

Sterne, Adolphus. *Hurrah for Texas! The Diary of Adolphus Sterne.* Edited by Archie P. McDonald. Waco, Tex.: Texian Press, 1969.

U.S. Commission on Civil Rights. *Mexican American Education Study: Ethnic Isolation of Mexican Americans in the Public Schools of the Southwest.* Washington, D.C.: Government Printing Office, 1971.

U.S. Commission on Civil Rights. *Mexican Americans and the Administration of Justice in the Southwest.* Washington, D.C.: Government Printing Office, 1970.

Webb, Walter Prescott. *The Texas Rangers: A Century of Frontier Defense.* 2d ed. Austin: University of Texas Press, 1965.

Young, Robert. *White Mythologies: Writing History and the West.* New York: Routledge, 1990.

The Social Construction of Race

Appiah, K. Anthony. "Are We Ethnic? The Theory and Practice of American Pluralism." *Black American Literature Forum* 20 (1986): 209

———. "The Conservation of 'Race.'" *Black American Literature Forum* 23 (1989): 37

———. "The Uncompleted Argument: Du Bois and the Illusion of Race." In *"Race," Writing, and Difference,* edited by Henry Louis Gates, Jr. Chicago: University of Chicago Press, 1986.

Cavalli-Sforza, Luigi L. "The Genetics of Human Populations." *Scientific American* 231 (September 1974): 80

Cavalli-Sforza, Luigi L., Paolo Menozzi, and Alberto Piazza. *The History and Geography of Human Genes.* Princeton: Princeton University Press, 1994.

Ford, Christopher A. "Administering Identity: The Determination of 'Race' in Race-Conscious Law." 82 *California Law Review* 1231 (1994).

Gates, Henry Louis, Jr. "Talkin' That Talk." In *"Race," Writing, and Difference,* edited by Henry Louis Gates, Jr. Chicago: University of Chicago Press, 1986.

Gossett, Thomas F. *Race: The History of an Idea in America.* Dallas: Southern Methodist University Press, 1975.

Gotanda, Neil. "A Critique of 'Our Constitution Is Color-blind.'" 44 *Stanford Law Review* 1 (1991).

Kevles, Daniel J. *In the Name of Eugenics: Genetics and the Uses of Human Heredity*. New York: Knopf, 1985.

Lee, Jayne Chong-Soon. "Navigating the Topology of Race." 46 *Stanford Law Review* 747 (1994).

Lewontin, Richard C. "The Apportionment of Human Diversity." *Evolutionary Biology* 6 (1972): 381

Nei, Masatoshi, and Arun K. Roychoudhury. "Genetic Relationship and Evolution of Human Races." *Evolutionary Biology* 14 (1982): 1

Omi, Michael, and Howard Winant. *Racial Formation in the United States: From the 1960s to the 1990s*. 2d ed. New York: Routledge, 1994.

Ringer, Benjamin B., and Elinor R. Lawless. *Race-Ethnicity and Society*. New York: Routledge, 1989.

San Juan, Epifanio Jr. *Racial Formations/Critical Transformations: Articulations of Power in Ethnic and Racial Studies in the United States*. Atlantic Highlands, N.J.: Humanities Press, 1992.

Part IV

Racial Construction and Demonization in Mass Culture

Media Treatment and Stereotypes

If, as most scholars believe, race is a social construct (as opposed to a biological reality), the content of that construct in the case of Latinos is often dominantly negative, especially in mass culture, where the media depict Latinos as lazy, criminal, dirty, happy-go-lucky, and uninterested in assuming the role of informed citizenship. Many of the images coined in connection with Latinos seem similar in function to the Sambo, mammy, coon, and uncle one sees in black history, but with some notable differences. How do these images form and proliferate? And what can one do, within First Amendment limitations, to combat them?

Chapter 29

Racial Depiction in American Law and Culture

Richard Delgado and Jean Stefancic

Outsider groups argue that free speech law inadequately protects them against certain types of harm. We believe that conventional First Amendment doctrine is most helpful in connection with small, clearly bounded disputes. Free speech and debate can help resolve controversies over whether a school disciplinary or local zoning policy is adequate, over whether a new sales tax is likely to increase or decrease net revenues, whether one candidate for political office is a better choice than another. Speech is less able, however, to deal with systemic social ills, such as racism, that are widespread and deeply woven into the fabric of society. Free speech, in short, is least helpful where we need it most.

Consider racial depiction, for example. Several museums have featured displays of racial memorabilia from the past. One exhibit recently toured the United States. Filmmaker Marlon Riggs produced an award-winning one-hour documentary, *Ethnic Notions*, with a similar focus. Each of these collections depicts a shocking parade of Sambos, mammies, coons, uncles—bestial or happy-go-lucky, watermelon-eating—African Americans. They show advertising logos and household commodities in the shape of blacks with grotesquely exaggerated facial features. They include minstrel shows and film clips depicting blacks as so incompetent, shuffling, and dim-witted that it is hard to see how they survived to adulthood. Other images depict primitive, terrifying, larger-than-life black men in threatening garb and postures, often with apparent designs on white women.

Seeing these haunting images today, one is tempted to ask: "How could their authors—cartoonists, writers, film-makers, and graphic designers—individuals, certainly of higher than average education, create such appalling images? And why did no one protest?"

Mexican Americans

Images of Mexican Americans fall into three or four well-delineated stereotypes—the greaser; the conniving, treacherous bandido; the happy-go-lucky shiftless lover of

From "Images of the Outsider in American Law and Culture: Can Free Expression Remedy Systemic Social Ills?" 77 Cornell L. R. 1258 (1992). Originally published in the *Cornell Law Review*. Reprinted by permission.

song, food, and dance; and the tragic, silent, tall, dark, and handsome "Spanish" type of romantic fiction—which change according to society's needs. As with blacks, Asians, and Indians, most Americans have relatively few interpersonal contacts with Mexican Americans; therefore, these images become the individual's only reality. When such a person meets an actual Mexican American, he or she tends to place the other in one of the ready-made categories. Stereotyping thus denies members of both groups the opportunity to interact with each other on anything like a complex, nuanced human level.

During and just after the conquest, when the U.S. was seizing and then settling large tracts of Mexican territory in the Southwest, "Western" or "conquest" fiction depicted Anglos bravely displacing shifty, brutal, and treacherous Mexicans. After the war ended and control of the Southwest passed to American hands, a subtle shift occurred. Anglos living and settling in the new regions were portrayed as Protestant, independent, thrifty, industrious, mechanically resourceful, and interested in progress; Mexicans, as traditional, sedate, lacking in mechanical resourcefulness and ambition. Writers both on and off the scene created the same images of indolent, pious Mexicans—ignoring the two centuries of enterprising farmers and ranchers who withstood or negotiated with Apaches and Comanches and built a sturdy society with irrigation, land tenure, and mining codes.

In the late conquest period, depiction of this group bifurcated. Majority-race writers created two images of the Mexican: the "good" (loyal) Mexican peon or sidekick, and the "bad" fighter/greaser Mexican who did not know his place. The first was faithful and domestic; the second, treacherous and evil. As with other groups, the second ("bad") image had sexual overtones: the greaser coveted Anglo women and would seduce or rape them if given the opportunity. Children's books of this time, like the best-selling Buffalo Bill series, were full of Mexican stereotypes used to reinforce moral messages to the young: They are like this, we like that.

The first thirty years of this century saw heavy Mexican immigration of mainly poor workers. The first Bracero programs—official, temporary importation of field hands—appeared. With increasing numbers, white-only signs and segregated housing and schools appeared, aimed now at Mexicans in addition to blacks. With the increased risk of interaction and intermarriage, novels and newspaper writing reinforced the notion of these immigrants' baseness, simplicity, and inability to assimilate.

The movies of this period depicted Latins as buffoons, sluts, or connivers; even some of the titles were disparaging: for example, *The Greaser's Gauntlet*. Films featured brown-skinned desperadoes stealing horses or gold, lusting after pure Anglo women, shooting noble Saxon heroes in the back, or acting the part of hapless buffoons. Animated cartoons and short subjects, still shown on television, featured tequila-drinking Mexicans, bullfighters, Speedy Gonzalez and Slowpoke Rodriguez, and clowns—as well as Castilian caballeras, light-skinned, upper class, wearing elaborate dresses and carrying castanets.

World War II brought the need for factory and agricultural workers and a new flood of immigrants. Images softened to include "normal," or even noble, Mexicans, like the general of Marlon Brando's *Viva Zapata*. Perhaps realizing it had overstepped, America diminished the virulence of its anti-Mexican imagery. Yet the Western genre, with Mexican villains and bandits, continues; and the immigrant speaking gibberish still makes an appearance. Even the most favorable novel and film of the post-war period, *The Milagro Beanfield War,* ends in stereotypes.

A few Anglo writers found their own culture alienating or sick and sought relief in a more serene Southwest culture. As with the Harlem Renaissance, these creative artists tended to be more generous to Mexicans, but nevertheless retained the Anglo hero as the central figure or Samaritan who uplifts the Mexican from his or her traditional ignorance.

How Could They? Lessons from the History of Racial Depiction

The depiction of ethnic groups of color is littered with negative images, although the content of those images changes over time. In some periods, society needed to suppress a group, as with blacks during Reconstruction. Society coined an image to suit that purpose—that of primitive, powerful, larger-than-life blacks, terrifying and barely under control. At other times, for example during slavery, society needed reassurance that blacks were docile, cheerful, and content with their lot. Images of sullen, rebellious blacks dissatisfied with their condition would have made white society uneasy. Accordingly, images of simple, happy blacks, content to do the master's work, were disseminated.

In every era, ethnic imagery comes bearing an enormous amount of social weight. Nevertheless, we sense that we are in control—that things need not be that way. We believe we can use speech, jiujitsu fashion, on behalf of oppressed peoples. We believe that speech can serve as a tool of destabilization. It is virtually a prime tenet of liberal jurisprudence that by talk, dialog, exhortation, and so on, we present each other with passionate, appealing messages that will counter the evil ones of racism and sexism, and thereby advance society to greater levels of fairness and humanity.

Consider, for example, the current debate about campus speech codes. In response to a rising tide of racist incidents, many campuses have enacted, or are considering enacting, student conduct codes that forbid certain types of face-to-face insult. These codes invariably draw fire from free-speech absolutists and many campus administrators on the ground that they would interfere with free speech. Campuses, they argue, ought to be "bastions of free speech." Racism and prejudice are matters of "ignorance and fear," for which the appropriate remedy is more speech. Suppression merely drives racism underground, where it will fester and emerge in even more hateful forms. Speech is the best corrective for error; regulation risks the spectre of censorship and state control. Efforts to regulate pornography, Klan marches, and other types of race-baiting often meet similar responses.

But modernist and postmodern insights about language and the social construction of reality show that reliance on countervailing speech that will, in theory, wrestle with bad or vicious speech is often misplaced. This is so for two interrelated reasons: First, the account rests on simplistic and erroneous notions of narrativity and change, and second, on a misunderstanding of the relation between the subject, or self, and new narratives.

The First Reason—Time Warp: Why We (Can) Only Condemn the Old Narrative

The racism of other times and places does stand out, does strike us as glaringly and appallingly wrong. But this happens only decades or centuries later; we acquiesce in today's version with little realization that it is wrong, that a later generation will ask "How could they?" about us. We only condemn the racism of another place (South Africa) or time. But that of our own place and time strikes us, if at all, as unexceptionable, trivial, or well within literary license. Every form of creative work (we tell ourselves) relies on stock characters. What's so wrong with a novel that employs a black who . . . , or a Mexican who . . . ? Besides, the argument goes, those groups are disproportionately employed as domestics, are responsible for a high proportion of our crime, are they not? And some actually talk this way; why, just last week, I overheard . . .

This time-warp aspect of racism makes speech an ineffective tool to counter it. Racism is woven into the warp and woof of the way we see and organize the world—it is one of the many preconceptions we bring to experience and use to construct and make sense of our social world. Racism forms part of the dominant narrative, the group of received understandings and basic principles that form the baseline from which we reason. How could these be in question? Recent scholarship shows that the dominant narrative changes very slowly and resists alteration. We interpret new stories in light of the old. Ones that deviate too markedly from our pre-existing stock are dismissed as extreme, coercive, political, and wrong. The only stories about race we are prepared to condemn, then, are the old ones giving voice to the racism of an earlier age, ones that society has already begun to reject. We can condemn Justice Brown for writing as he did in *Plessy v. Ferguson,* but not university administrators who refuse remedies for campus racism, failing to notice the remarkable parallels between the two.

The Second Reason: Our Narratives, Our Selves

Racial change is slow, then, because the story of race is part of the dominant narrative we use to interpret experience. The narrative teaches that race matters, that people are different, with the differences lying always in a predictable direction. It holds that certain cultures, unfortunately, have less ambition than others, that the majority group is largely innocent of racial wrongdoing, that the current distribution of comfort and well-being is roughly what merit and fairness dictate. Within that general framework, only certain matters are open for discussion: How different? In what ways? With how many exceptions? And what measures are due to deal with this unfortunate situation and at what cost to whites? This is so because the narrative leaves only certain things intelligible; other arguments and texts would seem alien.

A second and related insight from modern scholarship focuses not on the role of narratives in confining change to manageable proportions, but on the relationship between our selves and those narratives. The reigning First Amendment metaphor—the marketplace of ideas—implies a separation between subjects who do the choosing and the ideas or messages that vie for their attention. Subjects are "in here," the messages "out there." The pre-existing subjects choose the idea that seems most valid and true—somewhat in the manner of a diner deciding what to eat at a buffet.

But scholars are beginning to realize that this mechanistic view of an autonomous subject choosing among separate, external ideas is simplistic. In an important sense, we are our current stock of narratives, and they us. We subscribe to a stock of explanatory scripts, plots, narratives, and understandings that enable us to make sense of—to construct—our social world. Because we live in that world, it begins to shape and determine us, who we are, what we see, how we select, reject, interpret, and order subsequent reality.

These observations imply that our ability to escape the confines of our own preconceptions is quite limited. The contrary belief—that through speech and remonstrance alone we can endlessly reform ourselves and each other—we call the *empathic fallacy*. It and its companion, the pathetic fallacy, are both based on hubris, the belief that we can be more than we are. The empathic fallacy holds that through speech and remonstrance we can surmount our limitations of time, place, and culture, can transcend our own situatedness. But our examination of the cultural record, as well as postmodern understandings of language and personhood, both point to the same conclusion: The notion of ideas competing with each other, with truth and goodness emerging victorious from the competition, has proven seriously deficient when applied to evils, like racism, that are deeply inscribed in the culture. We have constructed the social world so that racism seems normal, part of the status quo, in need of little correction. It is not until much later that what we believed begins to seem incredibly, monstrously wrong. How could we have believed that?

Racism is not a mistake, not a matter of episodic, irrational behavior carried out by vicious-willed individuals, not a throwback to a long-gone era. It is ritual assertion of supremacy, like animals sneering and posturing to maintain their places in the hierarchy of the colony. It is performed largely unconsciously, just as the animals' behavior is. Racism seems right, customary, and inoffensive to those engaged in it, while also bringing them psychic and pecuniary advantages.

What Then, Should Be Done? If Not Speech, What?

So, what can be done? One possibility we must take seriously is that nothing can be done—that race-based subjugation is so deeply embedded in our society, so useful for the powerful, that nothing can dislodge it. However, we offer four suggestions for a program of racial reform. We do this while underscoring the limitations of our own prescriptions, including the near-impossibility of getting a society to take seriously something whose urgency it seems constitutionally unable to appreciate. First, society should act decisively in cases of racism that we do see, treating them as proxies for the ones we know remain unseen. Second, past mistreatment will generally prove a more reliable basis for remedial action (such as affirmative action or reparations) than future- or present-oriented considerations; the racism of the past is the only kind that we recognize and condemn. Third, whenever possible we should employ and empower minority speakers of color and expose ourselves to their messages. Their reality, while not infallible and certainly not the only one, is the one we must heed if we wish to avoid history's judgment. It is likely to be the one society will adopt in thirty years.

Scholars should approach with skepticism the writings of those neoconservatives, including some of color, who make a practice of telling society that racism is ended. Finally, we should deepen suspicion of remedies for deep-seated social evils that rely on speech and exhortation. The First Amendment is an instrument of variable efficacy, more useful in some settings than others. Overextending it provokes the anger of oppressed groups and casts doubt on speech's value in settings where it is, in fact, useful. With deeply inscribed cultural practices that most can neither see as evil nor mobilize to reform, we should forthrightly institute changes in the structure of society that will enable persons of color—particularly the young—to avoid the worst assaults of racism. As with the controversy over campus racism, we should not let a spurious motto that speech be "everywhere free" stand in the way of outlawing speech that is demonstrably harmful, that is compounding the problem.

Because of the way the dominant narrative works, we should prepare for the near-certainty that these suggestions will be criticized as unprincipled, unfair to "innocent whites," wrong. Understanding how the dialectic works, and how the scripts and counterscripts work their dismal paralysis, may, perhaps, inspire us to continue even though the path is long and the night dark.

Chapter 30

Bordertown

From Assimilation Narrative to Social "Problem"

Charles Ramírez Berg

Not only is *Bordertown* an excellent illustration of the way the assimilation narrative overlaps with the Chicano social melodrama, it is also a paradigmatic example of the entire class of Chicano social problem films. Here, Robin Wood's delineation of the horror genre's normality-Monster conflict as symbolic of the tension between the Dominant and the Other will prove useful. Wood gives the formula for the basic horror film as "normality threatened by the Monster."[1] Similarly, the basic formula for the minority social melodrama is the mainstream threatened by the margin. Indeed, the "problem" of the ethnic/racial problem films is the perceived threat the margin's very existence poses to the dominant. The dilemma ethnic/racial Others raise for the American mainstream is how to combine two essentially incompatible ideas: the dominant's desire to preserve and protect its identity as a superior, racially pure in-group by exclusionary practices, and the implementation of the democratic ideal that guarantees freedom, equality, and opportunity for all American citizens.

Bordertown follows the standard rags-to-riches-to-rags assimilation narrative. Johnny Ramírez, a tough kid from East Los Angeles, matures into a responsible adult and acquires ambition and dedication when, as the judge who delivers his law school's commencement address puts it, "he realized his opportunities and duties as an American citizen." Johnny dreams of being on the Supreme Court, but his first court appearance reveals him to be a miserable lawyer. He loses an easy case to rich socialite Dale Elwell (Margaret Lindsay), who is defended by an upper-crust lawyer friend. When he is called a "shyster" by the defense attorney, Johnny throws him to the ground, a violent outburst that has him disbarred.

Rejecting the entreaties of the parish padre to content himself with humble work in the Mexican Quarter, Johnny leaves Mamá and the barrio to obtain what he now understands to be the only things that matter in America: power and money. "A guy's entitled to anything he can grab," he tells his uncomprehending mother just before he goes, "I found that out. And I'm for grabbing from now on." Before long he is managing a casino for a bumbling but well-meaning Anglo proprietor, Charlie Roark (Eugene Pallette), in a Mexican bordertown. Though he rebuffs Charlie's wife's (Bette Davis) amorous advances, she falls so deeply in love with him that she secretly murders her husband to free herself for Johnny. When he still shows no interest in her, Marie frames him for Charlie's murder, jeopardizing his ongoing courtship of Dale. Marie's crack-up on the witness stand (in one of the most memorable scenes of Davis's career) frees Johnny to return to Dale. But alone on a deserted highway one night, she rejects his proposal. "Marriage isn't for us," she tells him. "You belong to a different tribe, Savage." Pulling free from his grasp, she accidentally runs into a passing car and is killed.

Johnny sells the casino, uses the money to endow a law school in the barrio and returns, in his words, "back where I belong . . . with my own people."

Let me now single out the narrative and ideological features of Bordertown that are common to the Chicano social problem films that followed. Among them are:

Stereotypical Inversion. Hollywood films that try to boost ethnics often begin by denigrating Anglos (think, for example, what a band of oafish louts the Anglos in *Dances with Wolves* are). *Bordertown* is no exception, peopled as it is by frustrated, oversexed blondes (Marie); flighty, materialistic socialites (Dale and her "fast" crowd of idle rich thrill-seekers); harsh and inflexible authority figures who operate from a strict brown-and-white moral code that justifies their intolerance of others ("If you knew any law," the judge tells Johnny after his fight in the courtroom, "you'd still be mentally unfit to practice."); crude simpletons (like Johnny's boss, Charlie Roark); and gangsters (the group that eventually buys the casino from Johnny). Naturally the Chicano protagonist makes the sound ethical choice when he recoils from such a thoroughly venal Anglo universe and retires to the moral haven of the *barrio*.

This pattern is the basis for the conflict in the Anglo-centered social problem narratives—the stories about an Anglo protagonist fighting for social justice. In these films the white hero mediates between an oppressed Chicano and a monolithically hostile Anglo citizenry: Leslie Benedict (Elizabeth Taylor) versus the intolerant Texans in *Giant*; the idealistic law professor (Glenn Ford) pitted against a politically ambitious lawyer and an angry mob in *Trial*; and the cynical-but-courageous newspaper editor (Macdonald Carey) opposed to the racist townsfolk in *The Lawless*. And in a couple of Chicano-centered films (those with a Mexican-American protagonist) the stereotypical inversion is even more pointed. Except for a sympathetic sheriff, the Anglos in *My Man and I* are a band of chiselling low-lifes, and those in *A Medal for Benny* a community of hypocrites.

The Undiminished Stereotyping of Other Marginal Groups. In Hollywood films dealing with a particular ethnic or racial group, the three key elements are the Anglo mainstream, the minority group, and the relationship between them. Busily building that specific ethnic group up and knocking the Anglo down, these films generally partake in a strange kind of Other tunnelvision, losing sight in the process of their insensitive stereotyping of any but the focused-upon ethnic or racial group. (An extreme recent example is the positive portrayal of the Sioux in *Dances with Wolves* existing alongside the film's vicious, cardboard depiction of the Pawnees.) In *Bordertown*, though Marie's Chinese servant appears in only a handful of scenes, he is the stereotypical hopping, misarticulating (substituting *l*'s for *r*'s) Chinese presence. Marie herself is a variation on the stereotypical "easy" blond. Another example: Johnny may be a bad lawyer, but he is a lot better than his Mexican defense attorney. Johnny has to prompt him to move for a dismissal of charges after Marie's breakdown on the witness stand.

This practice in effect maps Others' relation to the mainstream. In *Bordertown*, for instance, Mexican Americans are marginal, Mexican nationals more so, and Chinese Americans even more so. Interestingly, both *Giant* and *My Man and I* place their poor white characters—Jett Rink (James Dean) in *Giant* and Mr. and Mrs. Ames (Wendell Corey and Claire Trevor) in *My Man and I*—further from the center than Mexican Americans.

The Male Chicano Protagonist. Hollywood follows the path of least resistance in constructing its heroes. In the rare instance of a film hero being an ethnic character, Hollywood is careful to make him as palatable to mainstream audiences as possible. This is done mainly in three ways: (1) by making the protagonist male, (2) by casting Anglos in ethnic and racial roles (Douglas Fairbanks in *The Mark of Zorro* [1920] and Tyrone Power in the 1940 remake), and (3) by giving the Other protagonist upper class status (Zorro is a member of the landed gentry; his rebellion is in essence the struggle of New World elites to wrest California from Spanish aristocrats). It should not be surprising, therefore, that only one of the protagonists of these social problem films (Esperanza in the progressive *Salt of the Earth*) is female. Since in Hollywood films an ethnic woman can only be an overprotective matriarch, the "other woman," or a harlot, this practice automatically relegates Chicanas to stereotypical roles.

The Overprotective Mamá. The naive, good-natured, long-suffering mother, like Johnny's, is the norm in these films, and the typical way ethnic mothers are portrayed in Hollywood movies in general, from *The Jazz Singer* to *I Remember Mama* (1948), from *Scarface* (1932) to *The Godfather* (1972). In the assimilation narrative, the mother figure serves as the font of genuine ethnic values and is the protagonist's (and the narrative's) cultural conscience. When the hero listens to the voice of "his people" he is listening to his mother. (In *A Medal for Benny*, the one case where this is reversed and the father is present but the mother is absent, Benny's simple, ineffectual father simply takes the mother's place as the resigned but authentic voice of goodness.) The Chicano protagonist's coming home to *mamá* in the end (having failed to establish a relationship with any other women) confirms her castrating power. From the patriarchal point of view, she makes him a weak hero with an unresolved Oedipal complex incapable of straying far from her apron strings.

Usually she stunts his growth by her smothering solicitude. But Johnny Monterez's mother in *Right Cross* reveals a darker, racially biased side to this (s)mothering. "There's no gringo alive," she tells her son's friend, Rick, "who don't think he's better than ten *mexicanos.*" Later, behind Rick's back, she indicates her distrust of him and all gringos. "That Rick," she tells Johnny, "born a gringo, die a gringo." The Mexican mother can't win in these films. Passive, obsequious ones raise weak Chicano males, active ones teach him to hate Anglos.

The Absent Father. Anglo families are complete and ideal, ethnic families fragmented and dysfunctional. The father's absence, from *Bordertown* to *La Bamba,* is seldom explained. Once again, from the male-dominant point of view, the lack of an organizing paternal sensibility makes for an abnormal, structurally unstable family unit, subtly establishing the psycho-social reasons why ethnics are different from—and inferior to—the mainstream.

From the patriarchal perspective, the missing father is indicative of abnormal Oedipal development. Never able to identify fully with the father, the Chicano male cannot symbolically become like him, nor can he take his productive, "masculine," place in society. This interrupted transition from pleasure principle to reality principle, from the familial order to the social one, helps explain his antisocial behavior: Johnny Ramírez's sudden flash of violence in *Bordertown,* Johnny Monterez's short temper and Anglo paranoia in *Right Cross,* Angel's "murder" of the white girl in *Trial.* Instead of repressing his desire for his mother, the Chicano protagonist's mother love exists right on the surface. No wonder he is plagued by unfulfilled sexual and social relations and returns to her. Due to his arrested psychological development, the realm of (mainstream) language and culture are forever closed to him. From the phallocentric standpoint, he is relegated to "the half-light of the imaginary"[2] along with his mother.

This defective development results in two kinds of fatherless protagonists in Chicano social problem films: (1) the psychologically flawed ones, like Johnny Ramírez, who can't succeed no matter how hard they try; and (2) the "salvageable" ones, less severe cases like Johnny Monterez in *Right Cross* and Chuchu Ramírez in *My Man and I,* who, evidently to compensate for the absence of the father, find an Anglo father surrogate to help them make the transition into the mainstream. For Johnny Monterez, it is his Anglo friend, Rick (Dick Powell), a happy-go-lucky sports writer ("Help me!" Johnny pleads with Rick at one point). For Chuchu Ramírez it is none other than the President of the United States: wherever he goes, he carries a cherished letter from the chief executive with him that specifies Chuchu's place in American society. "The measure of your new country's greatness," the letter reads, "lies in its guarantee of justice and equality for all, and it counts on you to do your part to further that principle." For Chuchu, being a good American means being a patriotic "son"; his unquestioned ideological allegiance confers manhood.

Not coincidentally, the three Chicano male characters who are most well adjusted—Angel Obregón (Sal Mineo) in *Giant,* Tommy Cantanios (Lalo Rios) in *The Ring,* and Ramón Quintero (Juan Chacón) in *Salt of the Earth*—live in well-functioning (nonstereotypically portrayed) households. These films' break with Hollywood conventions (and the corresponding ideological baggage that goes with them) is indicative of the ways they operate to expose gaps in the dominant ideology rather than paper over them.

The Absent Chicana. Except for the protagonist's mother, Chicanas do not exist, and certainly not as someone our Chicano hero would be romantically interested in. The implied message: Chicanas are so inferior to Anglo women they may be omitted from consideration altogether. Here the progressivity of the exceptions only proves the rigidity of the rule. The most notable is Rosaura Revueltas's Esperanza in the independently-produced *Salt of the Earth.* Sonny Garcia (Gail Russell) in *The Lawless* is an independent woman committed to helping her people, but her character deteriorates as she takes on the narrative function of guide/love interest for the Anglo editor.

Besides *Salt of the Earth*, only two films depict an all-Chicano romance. To its credit, the entire narrative in *A Medal for Benny* is propelled by Joe's (Arturo De Cordova) attempts to capture Lolita's (Dorothy Lamour) heart. But the film's conclusion frames their union in dominant terms: Joe is most worthy of Lolita's attention when he becomes a proper American and joins the army to fight the "Japs" in the war. In contrast, for Tommy and his girl (Rita Moreno) in *The Ring*, the system is the problem, not the solution. They overcome numerous obstacles and gain a more mature relationship *despite* the system, not because of it. Finally, there is the interesting case of Juana (Elsa Cárdenas) in *Giant*, who marries into the Benedict family and becomes the only Chicana character in all these movies whose romantic involvement with an Anglo man goes unimpeded. (Johnny's sister has an Anglo boyfriend in *Right Cross,* but Johnny strongly disapproves of the relationship, and its outcome remains unclear at film's end.)

The Alluring but Flawed Gringa. In light of the above, the protagonist's only option for romantic involvement is with an Anglo woman. But given the pattern of stereotypical inversion and Hollywood's trepidation about portraying interracial love stories, she is bestowed with severe emotional and psychological problems (Dale Elwell is a materialistic snob and a bigot and Marie's sexual starvation drives her to lust and murder). As a result, the romance is sabotaged from the onset. Thus by the use of an insidiously contorted self-preserving logic, Anglo patriarchy maintains its genetic "purity" in part by negatively stereotyping Anglo women as childish miscreants. Thus Chuchu's fascination with the troubled Marie (Shelley Winters) in *My Man and I* is both inexplicable (what could she possibly have to offer him?) and ideologically nonthreatening (as a marginal bar fly, her mingling with and marrying a Mexican is of little consequence to the dominant).

The other impediment to cross-cultural romances is the male ethnic character's considerable psychological defects, already alluded to. In *Trial,* the most reactionary of the Chicano social melodramas, Angel Chavez (Rafael Campos) is convicted of killing a white girl. Though the movie never proves that he is guilty of homicide, the prosecution's case (and, ultimately, the movie's) is that he tried to rape her and she died of a weak heart. This reiterates the powerful patriarchal fear of Other male's violation of white womanhood. The male Other (re)presents two kinds of threats, (1) biological (his tainting of the dominant gene pool) and, (2) sexual (always framed as his inevitable defilement of white women, never as his presenting the Anglo male with romantic competition for the Anglo woman). With a psychologically defective Chicano male, the impossibility of legitimate sexual union is rationalized and the dual threat safely contained. As these convoluted narrative-ideological dynamics disclose, the real violation to white women comes not from the male Other but from patriarchy's degradation of them.

The Reductive Definition of Success. Even given that in the American system the range of opportunities available to its minority members has been severely restricted throughout history, the options presented to the Chicano protagonist—succeed and die (morally or actually) or fail and live (in squalor though in moral equanimity)—are simplified in the extreme. This sort of absolutism is standard given Hollywood's wish-fulfillment narratives that define success—the quest to become the boxing champ of the world, or a Supreme Court justice—as an all-or-nothing proposition. Posed in such totalizing terms, however, the number of "successes" the American system allows in the movies is minuscule (one per protagonist per film) and these films reveal that both in and out of the movies achieving success is all but impossible for most people.

Hollywood has been expounding, explaining and defending the exclusionistic logic of this fable for decades, selling audiences the illusion of success even as they swallow the bitter pill of (preferred, safe) failure. Nevertheless, Anglo audiences can at least obtain pleasure from their identification with the Anglo hero's success. Mexican-American audiences, on the other hand, must learn to identify with the Anglo hero in order to enjoy "the freedom of action and control over the diegetic world that identification with a [white] hero provides."[3] To the extent that such marginal viewer identification works, it justifies, celebrates and naturalizes the WASP norm, and becomes a means of Other viewers approaching the mainstream and internalizing its values. But spectators from the margin are divided subjects, and at some point they must realize that they are different from the Anglo hero, producing alienation and estrangement in them, and serving to exacerbate their marginality.

And Hollywood's providing Mexican-American protagonists in the Chicano-centered social problem films (save for *Salt of the Earth*) does not really improve the situation. A principal reason is that the heroes in these movies do not enjoy the sort of unbridled success available to Anglo protagonists. They get a greatly scaled-down version of Anglo success or they get failure. Johnny Ramírez cashes in and returns to East L.A. ("To do what?" we may well wonder as the film ends.) In *Right Cross*, Johnny Monterez injures his right hand swinging at his Anglo "friend." This ends his fighting career, but domesticates him (somehow ridding him of his bad temper, his inferiority complex, and his "paranoia" about the WASP system). In the conclusion of *My Man and I*, Chuchu is freed from jail and wins the heart of his beloved: a troubled, alcoholic blond. Giving up his dream of boxing as a career, Tommy in *The Ring* burns his cape and gloves in an oil drum in his backyard. With Lucy's help, he learns to be satisfied with life in the *barrio*. In the Hollywood cinema, Anglo protagonists succeed by succeeding; in the Chicano social problem films, Mexican-American protagonists succeed by failing.

Finally, again except for *Salt of the Earth,* this either/or-ism denies Chicano characters the possibility of redefining success in less grandiose—and more personal and local—terms. Working in their neighborhoods or otherwise contributing to the incremental betterment of their people is seldom a "successful" option. Sonny Garcia's local activism in *The Lawless* is an important exception. But by and large no Chicano characters redefine success in the positive, personal, and regional way that the protagonist in *Pinky* (1949, dir. Elia Kazan) does when she decides to stay in her home town and teach Black students at a nearby nursing school. Since there is no middle ground, no possibility for regional success, there is no mistaking the fact that from the dominant's point of view (given Hollywood cinema's definition of success), the Chicano's return to the *barrio* represents a Big Failure.

When an Anglo hero, from Will Kane (Gary Cooper) in *High Noon* to Deckard (Harrison Ford) in *Blade Runner,* turns his back on the system and retreats from it, it signifies the ultimate heroism—the rugged individual rejecting a contemptible system. But when a Chicano makes the same rejection, he doesn't ride into the sunset with Grace Kelly or discover a new Eden with Sean Young, he returns to the *barrio,* often alone. The Chicano couldn't make it in the big time, not so much rejecting the system as rejected by it. Clearly, WASP heroes have what it takes to succeed and have the added luxury of electing to accept or deny the system that allowed them that success. Other heroes have only what it takes to fail.

Given the constraints of the ideological patterns just described, it is obvious that the deck is stacked in significant ways against Chicanos in these films. Add to this the strictures of the Hollywood formula, which demands that an accessible hero find a happy resolution to the conflicts animated by the narrative, and we can appreciate why many of these social problem films deprecate the group they mean to celebrate. That *any* Hollywood film would ever attempt to tackle the Chicano "problem" is in a way amazing. That a few (*The Lawless, Giant,* and *The Ring* within the studio system; *Salt of the Earth* outside it) treated Chicanos humanely and contributed meaningfully to the discourse on American prejudice is astounding.

To be sure, much more work remains to be done with these films. Individual close readings are needed to investigate more fully the Anglo-centered films (Good Samaritan narratives, more interested in their WASP heroes' redemption than in the fate of the Chicano characters) and the Chicano-centered ones (variations cut from the *Bordertown* template or about how Chicanos need to become "naturalized" to enter the mainstream).

And it's time for a full-blown appreciation of *Giant,* one of the most enlightened of all of Hollywood's wide-screen epics. Its female protagonist allows it to question some of the key principles of the dominant ideology: patriarchy, the imperialistic bent of America's westward expansion ("We really stole Texas, didn't we?" Leslie tells Bick [Rock Hudson] the day after she meets him. "I mean away from Mexico."), racism, the class system and the social construction of manhood. Most impressively, it argues that the betterment of *Tejanos* will come not by simply adjusting an existing system, but by intermarriage and the raising of Anglo consciousness. Dramati-

cally, Leslie's aiding the impoverished Mexican-American ranch workers is important but ideologically it is secondary to the fact that Bick's son married Juanna, that
Bick now has a *mestizo* grandson, and that (even if it's only at a familial level) Bick
rejected racism. *Giant* is a fascinating anomaly—a long, sprawling, big-budget movie
made in the regressive 1950s that follows through on its liberal program *and* was a
critical and box office success.

NOTES

1. Robin Wood, "The American Nightmare: Horror in the 70s" and "Normality and
Monsters: The Films of Larry Cohen and George Romero," Chapters 5 and 6 in *Hollywood
from Vietnam to Reagan* (New York: Columbia University Press, 1986).
2. Laura Mulvey, "Visual Pleasure and Narrative Cinema," in Gerald Mast and Marshall
Cohen, eds., *Film Theory and Criticism* (New York: Oxford University Press, 1985), p. 804.
3. Laura Mulvey, "Afterthoughts on 'Visual Pleasure and Narrative Cinema' inspired by
Duel in the Sun," in Constance Penley, ed. *Feminism and Film Theory* (New York: Routledge,
1988), p. 70.

Chapter 31

The Border According to Hollywood
The Three Caballeros, Pancho, and the Latin Señoritas

David R. Maciel

North American border cinema updated a much overdone tradition—comedy at the expense of Mexican-origin characters. Reminiscent of the television series *The Cisco Kid and Pancho, Zorro,* and *Sergeant Garcia,* three tasteless contemporary film comedies are *Losing It, Viva Max,* and *The Three Amigos.* All three share a Mexican border setting and all attempt to secure laughs by directing ridicule at the Mexican border residents.

Losing It

Losing It follows four young Anglo teenagers who head to Tijuana for fun, excitement, and in search of a *bordello* for the obvious reason that the movie title indicates. With the exception of one of the young men (played by Tom Cruise), the rest of the boys are the worst of the ugly Americans abroad and of North American youth characterizations. Tijuana, Mexicanos, and the border setting are the victims as stereotypes of the worst kind abound. *Los Angeles Times* film critic Kevin Thomas observed:

> Never mind that the kids eventually get their comeuppance, because the film spends most of its time smirking and sneering at every conceivable stereotype of Mexican border-town. . . . If sleazy atmosphere were everything, *Losing It* would have it made, for production designer Robb Wilson King . . . has spared no pains in convincingly passing off Calexico as Tijuana, making it appear as the most garish Sodom and Gomorrah imaginable.[1]

The general view of Tijuana conveyed in *Losing It* is similar to the appearance of the border in films at the turn of the century, in films from the "greaser" cycle, or in the 1934 movie *Bordertown.* Tijuana is portrayed as a dirty, sleazy, criminal, and despicable area. Not a single positive trait of Tijuana is evident in the film.

Viva Max

Viva Max, or how the Mexicans reclaimed the Alamo, is neither good comedy nor good satire. The silly plot portrays Peter Ustinov as a Mexican general who, in dire need of a deed of valor to regain the respect of his men, decides to invade the United States and recapture the Alamo. The slap-stick episodes of the taking of the Alamo and the Texas National Guard attempting to re-capture it are more dumb than humorous. It could be argued that *Viva Max* is really a satire of Texas mythology and stereotypes. Many scenes and types in the film point in this direction. Up to a point, the Texas parody might have been the purpose of the movie. However, the Mexicans do not escape the usual portrayal by Hollywood. And of course, Mexican-origin actors are nowhere to be seen. The Mexican characters are all played by Anglos or actors of other ethnic groups such as Peter Ustinov.

The main character, the Mexican general, and the rest of his men are cast within the classic Hollywood stereotype of the Mexicans—slow, dumb, lazy, and cowardly. What began as an interesting idea with potential resulted in a superficial, negative, and demeaning film of a classic border historical theme.

The Three Amigos

Bad comedy and gross stereotyping reached new heights even for Hollywood in *The Three Amigos.* Chevy Chase, Steve Martin, and Martin Short play three silent-film stars who made their fame as *Magnificent Seven* types. They call themselves The Three Amigos. One of their films is viewed by the townsfolk of a small Mexican village who are being terrorized by El Guapo and his ruffians. The bandits in the film are reminiscent of the endless Mexican *bandidos* who appeared in hundreds of westerns. As in *The Magnificent Seven,* the townspeople send for The Three Amigos to help rid them of El Guapo. Mistakenly the heroes believe they are sought for a performance or special show. Upon their arrival in town they realize that it is not make-believe. When El Guapo learns of their presence and almost has them killed, they abandon the village but quickly repent and ultimately defeat the villains, save the pueblo, and ride off into the sunset saying that wherever justice is needed, they will be there.

What begins with much promise as a parody of traditional westerns quickly deteriorates into fierce clashes, degrading stereotypes, and a disturbing portrayal of Mexican characters, women, and the border. The accent of the comedy in *The Three Amigos* is again humor at the expense of the Mexican-origin characters. They are either poor, helpless, defenseless, passive individuals who need to be saved by the clever, brave, strong Anglos, or they are no match against "The Three Amigos."

It is no surprise that the Dirección General de Cinematografía in Mexico has barred all of these films. One will never see these border comedies or crime movies shown commercially in Mexico. For once, a justification could be made for censorship on the basis of quality or offensiveness to the nationality, character, and culture of a country.

Exemplary Border Comedy: Born in East L.A.

The one laudable Hollywood border comedy is *Born in East L.A.* Combining parody and social satire, director and star Cheech Marín takes direct aim at various U.S. and Mexican institutions, character types, and perceptions. In the movie Rudy Robles (Guadalupe Rudolfo Robles), played by Marín, is a third-generation Chicano who accidentally gets caught in an INS raid. Because he has no way to prove his U.S. citizenship, he is deported to Tijuana. Unable to speak Spanish, Rudy finds himself experiencing the tribulations of Mexican immigrants. After a series of mishaps while trying to recross into the United States, he begins to creatively adapt to the border circumstance. In Tijuana, Rudy comes into contact with two secondary characters, the coyote and hustler Jimmy (Daniel Stern), who befriends him, and the love interest (played by Kamala López). There is much humor and fun in various scenes, satirizing border-Chicano and -Anglo societal traditions. The film closes with hundreds of undocumented Latinos overrunning the Border Patrol agents, crossing into the United States with the Neil Diamond song "Coming to America" in the background.

Born in East L.A. won first prize at the Havana International Film Festival in 1987. As in the case of other contemporary Chicano films, it does represent a first. It is a major commercial Hollywood border film starred in, written by, and directed by a Chicano artist.

NOTES

1. *Los Angeles Times,* April 8, 1983, VI:4.

Chapter 32

Born in East L.A.
An Exercise in Cultural Schizophrenia

Alicia Gaspar de Alba

The bridges that stretch across the U.S.-Mexico border simultaneously separate and join two nations. Conceptually, the different languages that bridge Chicano/a subjectivity perform the same functions: they separate and join two cultural realities across the landscape shared by both—a geographical, political, and personal space known as the border. The border epitomizes the contradictions and conflicts of a binational, tricultural, and multilingual identity; the border incorporates both difference and *differánce* because Chicano/a identity is always in the process of defining itself in contrast to "the other side," and that process is/has been always historically specific.

The overriding question of Chicano/a subjectivity is not, primarily, "Who am I?" (that one comes later) but "*What* am I?" The "what" in the question refers to nationality. Given the relational and oppositional nature of Chicano/a citizenship in an Anglo-dominated country, "What am I?" is further complicated by the mirror-image projected from without: "What do they think/say I am?"

Cheech Marín's *Born in East L.A.* (Universal Studios, 1987) is a low-budget Hollywood production which criticizes the racist notions of "nativism" and American citizenship that the Border Patrol enforces. The film satirizes the racist assumption that Chicanos/as are not "real" Americans and need to carry their documentation to prove their identity/citizenship. Marín is both the subject and the object of *Born in East L.A.* As the object, he is described in the promotional copy on the video box as the "illegal alien" who gets "accidentally deported" and tries time upon unsuccessful time to "sneak back into the United States," only to realize that he was not "born to run . . . from the immigration service." As the subject, Marín is the Chicano filmmaker using the issue of citizenship and the cinematic device of mistaken identity as metaphors for a state of cognitive disorientation, a psychological effect of colonization that I call *cultural schizophrenia*. The perception of this state is fundamental to

From *The Alter-Native Grain: Theorizing Chicano/a Popular Culture* by Alicia Gaspar de Alba, in Culture and Difference: Critical Perspectives on the Bicultural Experience in the United States, edited by Antonia Darder. Copyright © 1995 by Antonia Darder. Reproduced with permission of Greenwood Publishing Group, Inc., Westport, Conn.

the evolution of Chicano/a consciousness. Culture, as defined by *Webster's* and as it applies to my use of the term cultural schizophrenia, means "the customary beliefs, social forms, and material traits of a racial, religious, or social group." Apart from its clinical definition of mental disorder, schizophrenia signifies "the presence of mutually contradictory or antagonistic parts or qualities." Integrating these denotations, cultural schizophrenia is the presence of mutually contradictory or antagonistic beliefs, social forms, and material traits in any group whose racial, religious, or social components are a hybrid (or *mestizaje*) of two or more fundamentally opposite cultures.

Because this hybridity, in the case of all "New World" peoples, is a product of conquest, we can deduce that cultural schizophrenia is a psychological effect of colonization. The colonized mentality is first and foremost a split identity, part conquered, part conqueror, "both tyrant and slave," "the victor, and the vanquished," as Corky González (1972) says in his epic poem *I Am Joaquín* (pp. 18, 40).

Moreover, the history of colonization is directly linked to racism, which in colonial New Spain, as Tomás Rivera (1992) reminds us, was reinforced and normalized by a semiotic apparatus:

> The colonial mind was preoccupied with color. When a child born to a couple was darker than the parents, he/she was called a *salto atrás*, a jump backwards, but if the child was lighter, he/she was considered a *salto adelante,* a jump forward; and if the child was the same color as the parents, a *tente en el aire,* suspended (p. 410).

I argue that the awareness of cultural schizophrenia is fundamental to the evolution of Chicano/a consciousness because that awareness leads to identity crisis, to rupture between the outwardly-defined persona (or the colonized mind) and the inwardly-identified self. In this moment of differentiation, Chicano/a consciousness becomes aware of itself as not only separate from, but more importantly resistant to, the hegemonic constructs of race and class. Marín's tragicomic film enacts these constructs as the politics of assimilation and immigration.

Although the protagonist of the film, Rudy Robles (self-represented by Cheech), is a third-generation native of Los Angeles, he is being "sent back where he came from." Ironically, where he came from is where he is being deported from. But who is *he?* "Let's start with your name," says the INS official. "Rudy Robles," he says, sure of himself at first, but then he admits that this is not his "real name." "My whole name is Guadalupe Rudolfo Robles." Two names, two identities. Which is the real one? To the INS official who finds Rudy's "real name" in his computer records, Rudy is a 57-year-old "illegal alien" who has been caught and deported nine times. Rudy denies the imposed identity by pointing out his differences: "I'm not 57," and "I'm no illegal." But despite his fluent English (i.e., his East L.A. slang), without the proper documentation to "prove" his citizenship, Rudy is identified as the "Other" Guadalupe Rudolfo Robles, and "returned" to Mexico, where he is told he belongs. Rudy's "I'm an American citizen, you idiots!" serves as the central paradox of the film. He may think of himself as a citizen of the United States, but it is what the idiots think he is that determines his fate. As Rudy's case demonstrates, Chicano/a identity is, ultimately, a border identity: neither side wants you and you can't go home.

If neither citizen nor alien, what is a Chicano/a? Ultimately, this question leads to *concientización,* an epiphany of political consciousness—not for the mainstream audience, who may find Rudy's "desperate attempts to sneak back into the States" hilarious,[1] but for the Chicano/a audience for whom issues of citizenship, borders, and identity are historically problematic, having plagued Chicano/a subjectivity for a century and a half. As Coco Fusco (1990) says in "The Latino 'Boom' in Hollywood," *Born in East L.A.* epitomizes the way "geographical frontiers have been internalized, creating a sense of fragmented identity" (p. 54). Awareness of the apparatuses that produce this fragmentation is a form of resistance both to the forces of assimilation and to the self-denigration and inferiority complex that infect the "colonized mind."

Ethnographic Criticism and the Native I/Eye

Another approach to an analysis of resistance is to monitor the audience reception to the text, as in ethnographic criticism. Reception theory, Tania Modleski (1991) explains in *Feminism without Women,* has at its base the premise that audiences generate a plurality of responses to any given text. Unlike the Frankfurt School of criticism, ethnographic critics argue that there is not merely one response, or one meaning, or one effect to be gleaned from a text. The radio, for example, was read by Frankfurt critic Theodor Adorno as a text that produces passivity and subservience in the audience. By creating a "false consciousness" in the consumer of mass culture, a demand for products and entertainment that are ultimately forms of oppression, mass culture manipulates the audience into complacent acceptance of the status quo.

Informed by their Marxist underpinnings, the Frankfurt critics see mass culture only as the modern opiate of the people. Ethnographic critics, on the other hand, taking their cue from the poststructuralists and the Birmingham School of cultural studies, believe that mass culture elicits multiple responses from its audiences that range from submission to resistance. One way to probe that multiplicity, then, is to monitor audience reception in the way that Janice Radway did for her study on romance novels and their impact on midwestern housewives—by traveling to the site to observe, survey, and interview the participants and letting them speak for themselves. A danger that Modleski (1991) sees to the ethnographic criticism approach is that "by focusing on the audience member's response to texts, the critic might wind up re-subscribing to an apolitical view of the individual as sole producer of meanings and unwittingly endorsing a pluralist, anything-goes kind of criticism" (p. 37).

NOTES

1. From the promotional copy on the video box.

REFERENCES

Fusco, C. 1990. "The Latino 'Boom' in Hollywood." *Centro Bulletin*, 2(8) (Spring).

González, R. "Corky." 1972. *I am Joaquín/Yo soy Joaquín: An epic poem*. New York: Bantam.

Modleski, T. 1991. *Feminism without women: Culture and criticism in a "postfeminist" age*. New York: Routledge.

Rivera, T. 1992. "Richard Rodriguez's Hunger of Memory as Humanistic Antithesis," in J. Olivares (ed.), *Tomás Rivera: The Complete Works*. Houston: Arte Publico Press.

Chapter 33

Lone Star and the Faces of Despair in INS Raids

Elvia R. Arriola

John Sayles's recent film *Lone Star* is a good example of popular culture which educates viewers about a complex social and political history by simply relating the life of a town and its people. Very briefly, the film situates a murder mystery in a south Texas U.S.-Mexico border town after a member of the nearby military base out on a desert excursion finds a skeleton, a Mason ring, and a sheriff's badge. A follow-up investigation produces a bullet and identifies the victim as a male who had died at least thirty-five years prior, about the time Rio County's much-hated Sheriff Wade had disappeared without a trace. Described by old-timers as an arrogant racist and iron-fisted bully, Wade had ruled this territory bordering on the Rio Grande with ruthless exercises of the southern white male privilege he enjoyed. Flashback stories reveal everything from beatings of people who threatened his authoritarian enforcement of the racially segregated patterns of 1950s America in south Texas to brutal murders of "coyotes,"[1] who had defied Wade's payoff system for being allowed to transport undocumented Mexicans across the border. Wade had killed or at least physically or financially hurt many of those who had questioned his run of law enforcement in Rio County.

I was struck by the ease with which *Lone Star*'s characters, events, and situations embodied so many concepts critical to the discourse on identity politics, power, and oppression. It also provides an excellent point of departure for exploring the ways in which social borders are created, internalized, and used by others and ourselves to shape and reshape our identities. *Lone Star*'s characters and their stories can be used to explore how relations between individuals seemingly of the same culture, race/ethnic group, etc., come to exist nearly "worlds apart" as their experiences, marked by factors like age, class, education, and personal history illustrate the tension, conflict, and transformation that arise from either accepting or rejecting the value system of a "borderlands." The history in *Lone Star* centers on the meaning a town and its people give to the U.S.-Mexico border and to border crossings. At the same time, the film's fluid use of flashbacks breaks down the border between

From "LatCrit Theory, International Human Rights, Popular Culture, and the Faces of Despair in INS Raids." 28 U. Miami Inter-Am. L. Rev. 245 (1997). Originally published in the *University of Miami Inter-American Law Review*. Reprinted by permission.

the past and the present. In the fictional Rio County, several characters' stories illustrate the shifting attitudes of various social groups and individuals for whom the U.S.-Mexico border means having an identity and sense of community with the better "us" (whites), while maintenance of the border prevents being overtaken by the lesser "them" (Mexicans and African Americans). The changing methods of policing the U.S.-Mexico border are portrayed through flashback stories of the 1950s when local and state officials were the primary enforcers of the international boundaries, as contrasted with today, where the U.S. side of this boundary is policed by the federal government through the Immigration and Naturalization Service (INS) Border Patrol.

Certain relationships in *Lone Star* serve as metaphors for the ways in which an individual self-constructs borders as a way to shape an identity or role in a community or a relationship. This is best illustrated by the conflict-filled relationship between two female characters, a mother and a daughter. Each represents first and second generation Mexican-American women whose identities have been critically shaped by the value system of the borderlands, a not uncommon situation for millions of Mexican, Latinas/os, and Chicanas/os living in the Southwest today. The story of the elder Mercedes Cruz, who is frequently at odds with the views of her daughter Pilar, involves not only a secret crossing of the Rio Grande as an illegal "wetback," but also the loss of a young husband to an untimely and violent death at the hands of the hated Sheriff Wade. Mr. Cruz had served as a "coyote" for Mexicans desiring to cross the border illegally to work in the United States, but he had also underestimated the depth of Wade's powerful rage against those who defied the payoff system for his "protection." The border cost Mercedes Cruz her husband.

Meanwhile, a past secret affair with Wade's possible killer, an Anglo, has produced a complex mystery by which Mercedes comes into some money that enables her to open a restaurant. She gives birth to a daughter who grows up not knowing she is half Anglo and half Mexican, who thinks her father was the unjustly murdered Mr. Cruz, and who does not understand that it was her mother's fear of incest and not racism which destroyed her first love to an Anglo boyfriend. These secrets underlie the tense emotional and intergenerational borders which have arisen between Mercedes and her daughter, Pilar, because each has a different view of the role of the border crossings in their lives. Mrs. Cruz has buried the memories of her life of poverty in Mexico and her river crossing as if the events occurred in another life;[2] yet she allows her daughter to nurture the belief that her father was a martyr. That story has undoubtedly played a role in the shaping of Pilar's identity as a "Tejana" citizen who questions the borderlands' hypocritical value system. Pilar decries her mother's denial of her heritage and her mother's harsh treatment of recent Mexican immigrants while manager of the town's largest restaurant staffed by Mexican workers. Pilar is a politicized Tejana who views her duties as a high school teacher as requiring her to teach a multicultural history of the United States through which the complex intersection of racism and classism in the Southwest are exposed.

Age, culture, class, education, and power intersect in a tense scene between the two women, which dramatizes how each sees her "Latina identity" differently from the other. The daughter's conflict with her once-*mojada*[3] mother shows when she questions her mother's tyrannical management of the workers in her large and prosperous Mexican restaurant. Pilar also disapproves of her mother's distrust of her workers and her demand to them that they "speak English only." The mother/daughter tensions illustrate how differently they have experienced and internalized or rejected the dominant value system. In another scene, the daughter is seen arguing with defensive colleagues over the role of multiculturalism in the curriculum. Meanwhile, her own mother has identified with the oppressor's values and has come to believe in the paradigm of "us/them" based on race, class, language, nationality, and residence status as the shaper of people's identities and their moral worth. Mrs. Cruz's identity critically depends on internalized oppression. She denies her own ties to the life of poverty her workers have left behind, by not only demanding that they speak "English only," but also by summoning the Border Patrol on the *mojados* she often sees running from the river and across her backyard to safety. Mercedes' actions reinforce her acquired identity as the good "American citizen," and that of the *mojados* as the bad and illegal "aliens." It is a scene that illustrates how deeply some immigrants internalize the values and meaning given to physical borders by a dominant culture and region like that of Texas and the southwestern United States, especially where the transition leads to personal success accompanied by gratitude and loyalty to the new sovereign power.

Mrs. Cruz's own river crossing long ago and her acquired identity as a wealthy *Americana* clash in another scene where, instead of summoning the Border Patrol, she provides shelter to a *mojado* she recognizes as one of her valued employees and his intended wife. Seeing the young woman injured and helpless, Mrs. Cruz crosses her self-constructed border—a border which separates her identity as a U.S. nationalized citizen and vigilante from her identity as a compassionate Mexican woman who is unable to barricade her own feelings of compassion and, as a result, ends up providing the immigrants with shelter and aid.

Lone Star's examination of the lives of blacks, whites, and browns in Rio County reminded me of, and also reshaped my understanding of, the paradigm of white supremacy over black and brown. Again I understand how white supremacy is capable of nurturing intergroup conflict and hostilities between members of "the oppressed." I saw how the hypocrisy of immigration law enforcement, which has focused so heavily on one border, the Southwest, has managed to escape criticism for its racist nature and has continued to exist because fear, economic need, and greed allow the system to thrive. The stories of killings, loves lost, and dehumanization in Rio County were all centered on the somewhat peaceful yet tense coexistence of African Americans, Mexicans, and whites—a coexistence which depended upon the values of greed, racism, white male supremacy, fear, deceit, denial, and struggles for power and control.

I had these formative ideas in mind one day when I opened up the *Austin-American Statesman* daily newspaper and read on the front page about the latest INS raid in Austin which affected about four or five construction companies and nine hundred workers.[4] My musings on LatCrit theory, border crossings, and the usefulness of stories in popular culture to explore the intersection of law and social justice forced me to look at the newspaper article about the INS raid with a fresh and most offended view. I would like to suggest that one goal of LatCrit theory, then, is to humanize the law and policy through more detailed stories, designed to expose the need for more humane treatment of those Latinas/os known as Chicanas/os, Mexicans, and Mexican Americans whose lives, especially in the Southwest, have been blighted by the INS practice known as the workplace raid.

INS raids, when assessed by way of the standard newspaper article with its skimpy details about who, when, and what happened, tells the American voter that Mexicans, at least in Texas, are taking jobs away from good American workers. Accounts of INS raids encourage readers to believe that, even if it is illegitimate to target such workers solely on the basis of their skin color or their accented English, no sanctions will be imposed on the offending federal agents. Furthermore, it may appear legal from these published accounts to enforce the law, not on employers, but rather to focus on the workers. In fact, rarely does an account of a typical INS raid reveal the names of the employers who have been caught violating the Immigration Reform and Control Act's prohibition against hiring a worker without proof of citizenship or legal residence. Nor does any published account ever explore the impact of a raid on the lives of the people caught without legal papers or of the failure of the INS to come up with nondiscriminatory methods of enforcement. Because there is so little focus on the employers, there is nothing said about the value of educating them on how to spot illegal documents or forcing them to produce proof that they are not engaging in rehires of illegal workers. Of course, never does an account of an INS raid consider the possibility that the INS's approach to apprehending workers, with its heavy focus on the Mexican population and on people with brown skin, smacks of blatant human rights abuses when the consequences of getting caught are to send a worker off to be detained and deported without due process or time to contact the family he or she is leaving behind. Nothing in contemporary accounts of INS raids ever suggests that there might be a need to put more of a burden on the employer rather than the worker. In fact, enforcement fines on employers have been substantially relaxed in recent years.

I wonder how a different kind of account of an INS raid would change our views of this nation's compliance with basic human rights if one humanized the same stories of recent INS raids and of the design and enforcement of INS policy. The typical studies on INS raids offer at best cold, impersonal data which only report the numbers. A newspaper article, which typically is full of facts and stories, is totally lacking in that kind of information when it comes to write-ups on an INS raid. One has to wonder who is discouraging the newspapers from carrying out their usual task of providing the names of employers who are recidivists in the area of noncompliance with INS regulations. What one gets instead are the propagandist versions of INS raids. For example, one newspaper account reports that in Texas over the last three to four months, over 5,000 workers have been arrested and detained by the INS; however, we are provided with no information that would help us learn about the industry that tends to employ undocumented workers. Over 98 percent of immigrants arrested were Mexican. In Austin, they were 100 percent Mexican, and they included Mexican and American legal residents.

Humanizing law and policy can connect the data to reality and the numbers deported to the people and their experiences of pain, humiliation, fear of "la migra," abandonment of children, economic and health needs, and discrimination. Thus, for example, I want to get at the underlying experiences which define the term "deportation" in a common INS raid. It is no longer enough for me to know of the numbers deported; rather, I want to know: who they deported, where they lived and worked, who employed them, how many times have they been deported and later returned to the same employer, how they got back, whom they are leaving behind, how long they have resided in this country, how they were spotted, whether the INS was contacted by the employer's competitors, whether they were treated well, and whether distinctions were made on the job site based on skin color and language. Answers to these tell me that the term "deportation" has a life behind it—the life of a worker, a husband, a father, a mother, a child, a community, and so on. It means being kicked out of the place you are currently calling home. It means no way of making arrangements for children whose parents won't be coming home that night. It means no right to pick up some belongings or to go home to pick up valid identification. It means no right to pick up medication if suddenly you are being put on a bus or a train back to Mexico. It means even being charged for that bus or the train that is now going to take you thousands of miles away from your home.

To return to *Lone Star,* consider a truly horrific scene featuring the killing of Mr. Cruz, who has been caught driving a truckload of Mexican men across the border into Rio County. One should not believe that the rules Cruz defied, of getting protection for such transports in return for a bribe, are a thing of the past. While it is a brutal picture of the costs of a system which depends on the enforcement of "borders," it also communicates an important reality—that of the high personal risks presented in making these continual crossings. An Austin paper recently reported the story of a truck which was found abandoned on a Texas highway in the middle of the summer. Twelve men were found dead, suffocated in a locked truck which had been abandoned by their driver, who most likely feared being caught by the Border Patrol.[5] Stories like this demonstrate the need to expose the hypocrisy, the injustice, and the fundamental wrongness of the largely exclusive focus on Mexicans and brown people as the source of the United States' immigration problems.

I will end with a short story based on my own first-hand experience with the impact of an INS raid. I was educated in Mexico for what would have been my high school years. For two years, I lived in a boarding school which opened its doors to approximately 350 day students. By my third year, the school closed its residency program, and I had to live temporarily in the home of a second cousin in Guadalajara, whom I stayed with for a total of five months. I soon learned that my second cousin's husband was living in California and that he sent money back to the family once a month. I think he worked in a meat packing plant. This was a very small house. There were three adults, three teenagers, and six small children sharing three rooms, a courtyard, and a water closet.

One day, my cousin's husband appeared on the front doorstep without prior notice. He had been caught in an INS raid and deported with nothing on him other than the clothing on his back and a few dollars. I was only fifteen years old at the time, so I was very naïve about the violence connected to INS raids and deportation methods.

My family certainly had contact in the United States with many people who had crossed the border illegally; we sometimes hired the friends of friends who needed jobs doing anything, which in our home was domestic service. But now I was on the other side of the border. I heard Señor Bolaños describe in painful detail the experience of being treated, in his words, "no better than cattle." He and hundreds of men had endured bad food, little water, and a long three-day train ride to the Mexican interior, which for him was at least close to home. Many people were actually sent thousands of miles away from their original hometowns. They had no money and no ability to contact their families; overall he described it as a very frightening event.

The financial impact was felt in my cousin's household for several months, because Señor Bolaños returned to California as soon as he could, but was unable to get his old job back. They became dependent on the money that my family was sending to temporarily board me there, which was about fifty dollars a month. We ate beans and tortillas for a very long time. I got sick. My cousins got sick. I felt the malnutrition even through the next term. I eventually moved out and went to live in a boarding house and convent. I never forgot the feelings of anger and frustration upon learning about my second cousin's plight. When my vacation came up, I told my dad all about it. I excitedly described what I had learned about the Bolaños family's plight. As I spoke, my father looked at me with what appeared to be both resignation and sadness, as he responded, "mija,[6] that's just the way it is. These things go on all the time. You just never hear about it."

NOTES

1. The term *coyote* is shared by the Spanish and English languages to identify night-prowling desert canines. Thus, the term applies to men and women who assist groups of Mexican nationals across the southern U.S.-Mexico border, usually at night through the desert, at often exploitive prices. For colorful descriptions by selected interviewees in an oral history project, of repeated and successful efforts to cross the California-Mexico border on foot, see Marilyn P. Davis, Mexican Voices/American Dreams: An Oral History of Mexican Immigration to the United States (1990).

2. The idea of swimming to a new life by crossing the river evokes the fundamentalist Christian image of rebirth by way of full-bodied baptisms in lakes, ponds, or ritualistic pools.

3. In Spanish, *mojada* is the equivalent of the American derogatory label *wetback*, long used in Southwestern jargon to stereotype Mexicans, whether legal or illegal, who have crossed into the U.S. territories by swimming the Rio Grande in unpatrolled regions of the nineteen-hundred-mile U.S.-Mexico border.

4. Enedelia J. Obregon, *In 2 Days, INS Arrests 900 Illegal Workers*, Austin-Am. Statesman, Aug. 21, 1996, at A1.

5. See Karen Fleshman, *Public Forum: Illegal Immigrants Part of Our Society,* Austin-Am. Statesman, May 31, 1996, at A11. The American Friends Service Committee has also recently released a study called "Migrant Deaths at the Texas-Mexico Border, 1985–1994," which details the number, causes, and characteristics of the deaths of undocumented migrants who die while trying to cross the U.S.-Mexico border. See *Migrant Deaths at the Texas-Mexico Border, 1985–1994,* AFSC Newsletter (Am. Friends Serv. Comm., Texas-Arkansas-Oklahoma Headquarters, Austin, Tex.) Apr. 1996, at 6 (on file with author).

6. *Mija* is a shortened version of "mi hija," which affectionately translates into "my daughter."

Chapter 34

Big Time Players

Gerald P. López

So, what's new? For the umpteenth time, we Latinos haven't made it onto some list of nationally prominent folks—in this case, onto "The *Newsweek* 100" of cultural elite. Big deal. Besides, the whole thing was only a send up, wasn't it? My own impression was that the cover story was either a silly puff piece designed to break up the monotony of the fall campaigns or a clever bit of satire designed to tweak the noses of both Dan Quayle and all those who would be furious not to be mentioned among his mortal enemies. So forget about it. Right?

Well, shrugging off our absence from such lists apparently isn't quite so simple or easy for many Latinos in this country. The day after reading *Newsweek*'s cover story I must have overheard dozens of comments about "The *Newsweek* 100." In San Francisco, where I live, Latinos in a local Mission District *taqueria* championed their own personal favorites. Edward James Olmos. Gloria Estefan. Ruben Blades. Christina. Raul Julia. And at Stanford, where I teach, suggestions were sometimes more obscure but no less heartfelt. Sandra Cisneros. Oscar Hijuelos. Gloria Anzaldúa. Culture Clash.

Having no Latinos on "The *Newsweek* 100" might not get under our skin were it not so utterly familiar—so obviously a part of a larger story. We Latinos are regularly treated as if we aren't "players" on the national cultural scene, ironically, by many of the same potentates, gatekeepers, and dealmakers who made the *Newsweek* list. Check out the latest books promoted by the big houses, the latest movie releases issued by the big studios, the latest Broadway/off Broadway/off-off Broadway productions, and every fall's new television schedule. Am I missing something or in 1992 aren't we pretty much as invisible as ever? We're all to conclude, I suppose, that there are almost no stories we tell, almost no stories to be told about us, and almost no roles we competently fill.

But our absence from the nation's consciousness isn't limited to "simple" matters of pop culture. When Los Angeles exploded after the Simi Valley jury's acquittal of officers Powell, Wind, Koon, and Briseno, it took most people weeks before they re-

From Newsweek, October 8, 1992. Originally published in *Newsweek*. Used by permission of the author.

237

alized Latinos were everywhere entangled as burned-out merchants, unemployed workers, injured bystanders, eager looters, and, yes, as common residents in the neighborhoods of South Central and Pico Union. You see, Latinos simply didn't fit the stock story lines about race and urban problems. Apparently, it had been some time since most folks had taken a careful look not just at Los Angeles but at Chicago, New York, Dallas, and even Washington, D.C. In fact, it remains true that when people think about the goings on in this country—in making up lists of the cultural elite or analyzing urban unrest—they most often don't even seem to see twenty-five or so million Latinos anywhere in sight.

In this regard, the presidential candidates are hardly exceptions. Although the nine states with the highest concentrations of Latinos account for 202 of the total 538 electoral votes in this country (three-fourths of the 270 votes needed to win), the political campaigns in those states look basically identical to the bus and train rides the candidates have taken everywhere else. Whatever the outcome of the November elections, even Latinos can read the writing on the wall. The candidates apparently believe we influence presidential politics about as much as *Newsweek* thinks we influence popular culture.

Of course, in some sense, all of them—the presidential candidates, *Newsweek* and everyone else with any clout—are justified in overlooking Latinos. If they're only interested in other big-time players, then perhaps we still don't cut it. We certainly don't produce major sitcoms, we don't run the National Endowment for the Humanities, we don't own the country's largest chain of bookstores, and we don't publish one of the nation's largest newspapers. And, though we do talk, write, sing, act, direct, sculpt, design, and paint, only a very small handful of us have become anything like household names, much less heavily influential, on the national scene. It's also true we don't have a large stable of easily identified spokespersons ready, willing and able to offer a pithy quote or a talking-head interview to journalists working under deadline pressure searching a Latino perspective. And, even if our voting numbers are on the rise, we may still "give away" our votes all too predictably to hold national candidates strongly accountable to our needs and aspirations.

But this justification seems a little too facile. Why we haven't yet hit the big time on the cultural scene may have much more to do with how doors get opened than with our lack of talent, interest or discipline. Why we may not serve as ready-made experts on a range of national issues may have more to do with how networks operate than with our lack of expertise or insight. Why we may not historically have voted in effective blocs may have more to do with how, in various ways, our votes have been diluted than with our own "innate" or "cultural" indifference to electoral politics. In any event, it seems profoundly disingenuous for presidential candidates, *Newsweek,* and everybody else with sizable clout to deny that it is within their power to make at least some Latinos influential right before our very eyes. Think only of how the New Right and the media marketed Linda Chavez as an expert on pretty much everything.

It's not at all obvious what Latinos should do about being so out of the loop. One understandable impulse is to continue to push for a certain level of representation in matters of cultural and political significance. We might correct for blindspots in the national consciousness by insisting that *Newsweek* reserve at least a few slots for us on its list ("at least include us on the 'Keep An Eye On' list of 10 runner-ups"), that media at least nominally mention Latinos when talking about race relations and urban problems ("it's not—and never has been—just a black/white thing"), and that the campaigns at least nod in our direction in their strategies and speeches ("Republicans can trot out their Linda Chavez again, Democrats their Henry Cisneros, and Ross Perot whomever he comes up with"). Such measures may well slowly change national consciousness. Change habits and minds will follow, goes this familiar thinking.

But let's face it. Much as some have tried, this approach has so far hardly paid big dividends. Latinos have not been able to strongly influence, much less ourselves become a central part of, the national powers-that-be, the national intelligentsia, and the national media. Just as importantly Latinos have not been able to sway the American mass culture on issues of central importance to us. (Weren't the 80s supposed to be the decade of the Latino?) Even if we finally succeeded in making certain elite lists, being on people's minds, and being taken into account in national campaigns, it will hardly prove a panacea for most of us. Just ask those African Americans who share so many inner cities with millions of Latinos whether the political conspicuousness of Jesse Jackson or the cultural prominence of Spike Lee has done much lately to get them something other than dead-end jobs, abysmal education, and a lot of flak for being "pathological."

Don't misunderstand. I'm not against our making elite lists, being on people's minds, and being taken into account in national campaigns. But making "The *Newsweek* 100" is hardly worth spending our time scrambling around, too often at the edges and near the bottom, squeezing ourselves into categories and programs often formulated with other groups in mind. The fact is over 5 million of us—fully one-fourth of us—live in poverty, over 42 percent of our young adults dropped out of high school in 1990, and the great majority of us disproportionately face threatening environmental dangers. What we Latinos need is not so much popular recognition as effective ways of working together—and with others wherever possible—to fundamentally change the entirely unacceptable situation we still find ourselves in. And for that we now must look—as many of us always have—not to the powers-that-be but to our own considerable collective ingenuity.

Chapter 35

Still Looking for America
Beyond the Latino National Political Survey

Luis Fraga, Herman Gallegos, Gerald P. López, Mary Louise Pratt, Renato Rosaldo, José Saldivar, Ramon Saldivar, and Guadalupe Valdés

On December 14, 1992, at a press conference held in Washington, D.C., the authors of the first ever Latino National Political Survey (LNPS) made public their findings. With the help of a public relations firm, these scholars packaged their conclusions and comments in a manner shrewdly calculated to capture national publicity. They wanted to focus attention, possibly for the first time, on the nation's 25 million inhabitants of "Spanish" descent (to use the national census term). And, unashamedly, they wanted to market their ambitious survey of 2,817 Latinos—face to face interviews, often more than 90 minutes long, with 1,546 Mexicans, 589 Puerto Ricans, and 682 Cubans in 40 metropolitan areas, funded by the Ford, Rockefeller, Spencer, and Tinker Foundations—permitting Latinos "to speak for themselves" to the rest of the country.

The "press kit" hit the jackpot. The next morning, December 15, 1992, newspaper readers across the United States, from Los Angeles to New York and places in between, could hardly miss front-page stories about Latinos. "Poll Finds Hispanics Desire to Assimilate" said the *New York Times*. "Hispanics Feeling at Home" declared *USA Today*. "Hispanic Views Defy Predictions" announced the *Dallas Morning News*. "Surprising Diversity Discovered in Latinos" remarked the *San Diego Union Tribune*, and "Study Debunks Stereotypes of Hispanics' Beliefs" trumpeted the *Kansas City Star*. Latinos and the story told about them by the LNPS had hit the big time, if only for several days.

In the months since its release, the LNPS has already had a palpable effect on national political debate, though perhaps not in the way intended. Take immigration policy. Survey data showed significant Latino majorities agreed with the statement "there is too much immigration." And, to make certain no one missed the point, the

From STILL LOOKING FOR AMERICA: BEYOND THE LATINO NATIONAL POLITICAL SURVEY. Prepared by the Stanford Center for Chicano Research, Public Outreach Project, Stanford University, September 1993. Used by permission.

survey's authors and the media both stressed this finding, often characterizing it as something of a dramatic revelation. As a result, the LNPS instantly became a handy citation for anyone wishing to document Latino support for newly proposed federal and state anti-immigration policies aimed transparently at Latinos—for a proposal, backed by President Clinton, to increase the powers and numbers of border agents, for a proposal to charge fees at the border, for a proposal to deny undocumented residents access to public medical care and schools, and even for a proposal to amend the Constitution to deny citizenship to U.S.-born children of undocumented residents.

The trouble with this "Latinos favor anti-immigration proposals" story is that there is no evidence to support it—at least not in the LNPS or anywhere else. It is one thing to support the statement "there is too much immigration," quite another to back the constitutional obliteration of citizenship by birth. Indeed, answers to other questions in the LNPS might even be interpreted to suggest the "Latinos favor these anti-immigration proposals" story has it exactly backwards. (The survey's results reveal Latinos are quite divided on whether citizens should be hired over non-citizens, and few of the thousands of people interviewed by the LNPS's authors named immigration as the most important national problem.) In any event, the current immigration debate, whatever its outcome, suggests both the potential influence of the LNPS and the potential for the distortion of its results. The LNPS has already achieved a notable prominence in the agenda-setting world of politics, law, and business, perhaps even beyond the expectations of its authors.

Latino Politics: The Next Phase

In the last several years, Latino efforts to elect Latino candidates have begun to pay off. Voting rights lawsuits, voter registration crusades, community education programs, and get-out-the-vote campaigns have together put more Latino candidates on the ballot and in office. According to the National Association of Latino Elected and Appointed Officials, the numbers of Latinos elected nationally rose from 3,063 in 1984 to 5,170 in 1993. In those states with significant Latino populations (Arizona, California, Florida, New Mexico, New York, and Texas), the number of Latino elected officials increased from a total of 1,185 in 1973, to an estimated 3,321 in 1989. These successes, in turn, have helped boost the prospects of finding Latinos in a wide range of appointed positions—from highly visible Cabinet posts to low level agency jobs, from state judgeships to county planning commissions.

Only fools and knaves treat these achievements as anything but modest and long overdue gains. In no area of the country can Latinos be described as adequately represented by and in the political institutions that govern them. Certainly, the percentages of Latino elected officials still do not approach the percentages of Latino inhabitants in the population at large. For that matter, gains in representation have by no means insured changes in the course of governance, at least not if you pay any attention to the many problems in Latino communities for which political institutions still seem unwilling to respond. Over one-fourth of the Latino population lives below the poverty line; in 1990, nearly 75 percent of Latino students had been placed in "non-academic" tracks in school; nearly 50 percent of all Latinos had less than high school education, while college enrollments dropped. Latino perspectives on American politics seem to comprehend these mixed results. If the LNPS data are at all indicative, Latinos seem to appreciate the enhanced possibilities for both full incorporation in the body politic and the evolution of political institutions fully representative of and responsive to all the governed population. At the same time, they seem judiciously insistent on the continued need for the legal, political, economic, and cultural mechanisms that, finally, seem to have begun counteracting a history of marginalization and prejudice. In the LNPS terms, Latinos may "love" and "feel pride in" the United States, but they trust government officials "to do what is right" only some of the time.

This self-respecting skepticism entails, we believe, a new challenge for Latinos, though not the one "discovered" by the LNPS. The authors and the interpreters of the survey insisted Latinos (especially Latino leaders and organizations) must confront the embarrassing reality that there doesn't appear to be a Latino community—and hence no coherent constituency and no intelligible demand for redress of past and current grievances. In pressing this view, they would appear to have measured Latino life experiences by the standards of a rigidly homogeneous model of community, one that seems ill-suited to understanding groups of people they themselves describe as diverse. And, to suit their own arguments, they contradicted and exaggerated their data, missing the many points of similarities and affinities that most would imagine harmonious with many lucid images of community.

In their rush to shame established Latino leaders and "politically correct" scholars, the authors and the interpreters of the LNPS overlooked evidence of a different sort of challenge confronting Latinos, one that those surveyed may well understand as already having materialized. Insofar as the processes of democratization continue to move forward, a dilemma begins unmistakably to emerge: As Latinos achieve political representation, they must correspondingly shift the basis upon which they make demands for social justice. At a minimum, they can no longer ground their views singularly or perhaps even principally on having been unjustly excluded. Instead, they confront a world where their political successes impel them to transform the very idea of a political vision that will hold together as the millennium approaches.

The dilemma may well be daunting but it is not without precedent. In other countries, and for other groups in the United States, similar challenges have been confronted over the years. African Americans face this predicament, though they themselves seem of many minds about whether they even must acknowledge the quandary, much less whether they regard themselves as having managed it successfully. For that matter, we read the LNPS as confirming that many Latinos seem perhaps already to be trying to come to grips with exactly how their successes influence the ways in which they have historically marshalled their energies and articulated their positions. Those surveyed seem to be telling us that we may already be in the next phase of Latino politics in the United States, so it seems important both to heed their message and to wonder provisionally how the transformation might be negotiated.

Certainly some dynamics of the evolution seem traceable. Everywhere from Washington, D.C., to small towns, forces hostile to change seem to be telling Latinos "through elections and appointments, you've made it into the room, so now sit down and shut up." This demand, in turn, produces a fair amount of consternation and pessimism among Latinos. They do not want to deny their new successes, but they certainly never imagined victory meant nothing more than becoming part of business as usual. They end up spending a fair amount of time and energy trying to fashion inventive answers to more or less the same question: How can you avoid being entirely co-opted without invoking images and employing rhetoric far more suitable to days when there wasn't a Latino face to be found in nearly any decision-making body?

To some degree, Latinos may simply find themselves in the process of taming their own exaggerated expectations of what it would mean finally to integrate political life. Not too many years ago it was still easy to believe that being represented was nearly tantamount to tending a group's needs. Perhaps in retrospect such views seem hopelessly innocent and romantic, but they did seem roughly to explain for Latinos why for so many years "Anglo America" seemed so relatively well served by the business of politics. In any event, today everyone seems uncommonly savvy. They realize representation means winning a seat at the table, a voice in negotiations over policy, a chance to advance the interests of the represented, and the opportunity to persuade others to join in their support. And they appreciate the reality that "minority representatives" still remain minorities, often lacking the numbers to win majority votes and the resources with which to address the very concerns that prompted the need for representation in the first place.

If this lesson in *realpolitik* has not always been good news, it certainly puts a fine point on the nature of American politics. Once upon a time Latinos, like other oppressed groups, might well have been inclined to say "we want no part of coalitions." They assumed a stable solidarity within their own group and often projected a monolithic unity. The world is no longer quite so simple, and we doubt it ever was. Nowadays it is painfully evident that Latinos can't function productively as part of their own national origin group much less as part of a wildly more diversified body politic unless they are willing to do some serious coalition work. And if the coalition work doesn't feel risky a fair amount of the time, then either they are not working very hard at it or they are not part of any coalition with a chance of reaching precisely those social arrangements and ideas that have for so long kept groups like Latinos out of the action.

Just as Latinos are beginning to accept the inescapability of coalition work, they seem simultaneously to understand their capacity to act—through their leaders and on their own—not simply as an "interest group" but as an influence in determining "mainstream" United States. Despite the tendency on the part of the designers and interpreters of the LNPS to read Latino values in relation to "core American values," the last several years reveal how much, if anything, the very structure of the mainstream and the very nature of American core values are very much up for grabs— whether we're talking about women's rights, education, ecology, sexual liberty, religion, taxation, or the responsibilities of government to those within its geographical boundaries. In any case, many Latinos seem to grasp that the entirety of political life in the United States is no less a matter of coalition and persuasion than life within their own national origin groups.

In order to shape mainstream views, Latinos need to take themselves seriously enough to offer their own comprehensive vision of what this democracy should look like—not just about a set of high profile "minority" issues, but about life for everyone who calls this country home. This is a tall order, we realize. Broadening America's vision of itself ultimately means getting many powerful groups to abandon the (often unconscious) assumption that their sensibilities speak to everyone's needs and aspirations. At the same time, a willingness to chart a course for all people in the United States means getting Latinos to abandon the (often unconscious) assumption that politics can never be anything but a battle of raw self-interest.

Of course, Latinos have had considerable experience in fashioning coalitions. At local levels and in international circles, they have helped piece together compacts ranging across economic, social, cultural, legal, and political domains—including trade, labor, criminal, health, and religious issues. From hard experience, they have begun to appreciate not only that coalition politics often require compromise but that coalitions, at least at their best, are something more than paranoid federations of segregated enclaves.

At the same time, Latinos have played bigger roles in shaping substantive visionary statements than they typically get credit for. In taking stands on Supreme Court nominations and legislative proposals, they have begun to develop their own distinctive views of constitutions and legal jurisprudence. In pushing for employee stock options and worker cooperatives, they have moved to democratize markets, demanding that standards of equality and participation be extended to economic life and not just a narrow sphere of government. And in refusing to abandon their language and traditions, they have staked a claim to a culturally pluralist society that deliberately structures institutions so that all communities and social classes share prestige and respect.

For all this experience, Latinos certainly have not been encouraged to take the lead in building visions of America's democratic future. To some degree, perhaps they have brought this upon themselves. At least to the extent they have continued to regard their "interest group" politics as both entirely consuming and inconsistent with a more comprehensive agenda for the national community, they may well have failed to seize opportunities for taking the lead on behalf of the entire nation. But more frequently their attempts to articulate larger visions of the United States have fallen on deaf ears. Too many non-Latinos seem unwilling to imagine Latinos as creators of the mainstream—as national leaders, as originators of popular culture. And too many non-Latinos continue to box Latinos into the very same narrow brand of "identity politics" they condemn.

If indeed we find ourselves in the next phase of Latino politics in the United States, it is testimony to what Latinos have come to understand over the years. Never expecting to be invited to play a major role in this democracy, Latinos nevertheless have taken it upon themselves to make the most of their situation. While they astutely have been unwilling to abandon their embrace of "interest group" thinking, they have also not deluded themselves into believing there is anything like a safe, "separatist" retreat from messy coalition work. And while they have wisely refused to acquiesce in demands to think and behave *exactly* like everybody else in the United States, they have also been eager to declare openly their affinities with non-Latinos, their loyalties to their country, and their willingness to pitch in and lead.

Along with the authors of the LNPS, we believe Latinos express views that cannot easily be squared with either familiar world ideologies or conventional American party politics. They seem to be approaching their lives and their country from constructively iconoclastic angles—angles that reflect perhaps more a response to their conditions than a choice of fashionable philosophy. Unlike the authors and other interpreters of the LNPS, however, we believe that trying to apprehend evolving Latino attitudes through stereotypes or counter-stereotypes is precisely to miss what may well be most original about their situation and their positions. In light of the ambitions that seem to have informed the authors and funders of the LNPS, it would be a sad injustice to neglect what makes Latinos so distinctively American.

From the Editors
Issues and Comments

Have you ever heard someone speak the term *greaser* or *spic* and how did that make you feel? Did you object?

The chapters in Part IV have introduced you to a number of media stereotypes—the carefree lover of song and dance; the bandito; the lazy, shiftless Mexican who loves to take siestas in the shade of a cactus; the tall, dark, handsome type; the suave, diplomatic Latino; the glamorous señorita with castanets; and others. Are these stereotypes:

- 100 percent false, or do they perhaps have a grain of truth?
- Functional, as two of the authors suggest, serving different purposes for mainstream society at different times?
- Harmless, perhaps even necessary, when used as literary devices, because every story or novel requires stock characters?

Should Latino (or black) films portray that community warts and all, showing drugs, crime, and gangs, or should they highlight the positive aspects of the community?

Why can't minorities who object to their characterization in the media just "speak back" to these stereotypes, using freedom of expression in their favor?

Is the system of freedom of expression covertly racist if it tolerates demeaning pictures and stereotypes of minority groups, when a successful reply to such images requires a microphone, TV air time, or expensive ads?

Do Latino or black filmmakers stereotype whites?

Suppose you are interviewing for a position with a small company located in an area of the country with a very small minority population. The position requires a considerable amount of technical knowledge. You have a strong Latino/a heritage, but you are light-skinned and often mistaken for Caucasian. While waiting to be interviewed, you strike up a conversation with a fellow applicant who is a Mexican American with a dark complexion. You discover that your fellow applicant holds a degree, with honors, from an acclaimed technical school as well as having several years' experience in the field in which you are applying. During your interview, you discover that you are extremely underqualified for the position, having no technical degree and very little experience. The interviewer is candid with you about the qualifications of your fellow applicant, but expresses ethnic concerns. Not knowing your

Latino/a heritage, the interviewer tells you that according to popular perceptions, Latinos/as are shiftless, lazy people and can't or shouldn't be trusted with responsibility. The interviewer, while impressed with the other applicant, fears that the firm's clients won't want to deal with him and that he won't fit in with the other workers. Even though the other applicant is more qualified, you are offered the position. Would you accept the job?

If a journalist or survey organization issues a "feel good" report on the Latino condition that emphasizes progress and a rosy future, is that damaging?

Suggested Readings

Berg, Charles Ramírez. "Images and Counterimages of the Hispanic in Hollywood." *To-nantzin* 6 (November 1988): 12–13.

———. "Immigrants, Aliens, and Extraterrestrials: Science Fiction's Alien 'Other' as (among Other Things) New Hispanic Imagery." *CineAction!* 18 (Fall 1989): 3–17.

———. "Stereotyping in Films in General and of Hispanics in Particular." *Howard Journal of Communications* 2 (Summer 1990): 286–300.

Chicana (W)rites on Word and Film, edited by María Herrera-Sobek and Helena María Vira-montes. Berkeley: Third Woman Press, 1995.

Chicano Cinema: Research, Review, and Resources, edited by Gary D. Keller. Binghamton, N.Y.: Bilingual Review/Bilingual Press, 1985.

Delpar, Helen. "Mexico, the MPPDA, and Derogatory Films, 1922–1926." *Journal of Popular Film and Television* 12 (Spring 1984): 34–41.

Fregoso, Rosa Linda. *"Born in East L.A. and the Politics of Representation."* Cultural Studies 4 (October 1990): 264–80.

Fusco, Coco. "The Latino 'Boom' in American Film." *Centro Bulletin* 2 (1990): 48

Galería de la Raza. *Cactus Hearts/Barbed Wire Dreams: Media, Myths, and Mexicans,* art exhibition curated by Yolanda Lopez (1988).

Garcia, Juan R. "Hollywood and the West: Mexican Images in American Films." In *Old Southwest/New Southwest: Essays on a Region and Its Literature,* edited by Judy Nolte Lensink, 75. Tuscon: Tuscon Public Library (distributed by University of Arizona Press), 1987.

Hart, James D. *American Images of Spanish California.* Berkeley: Friends of the Bancroft Library, University of California, 1960.

Herrera-Sobek, María. *The Bracero Experience: Elitelore versus Folklore.* Los Angeles: UCLA Latin American Center Publications, University of California, 1979.

Images of Mexico in the United States, edited by John H. Coatsworth and Carlos Rico. San Diego: Center for U.S.-Mexican Studies, University of California, San Diego, 1989.

Johannsen, Albert. *The House of Beadle and Adams and Its Dime and Nickel Novels: The Story of a Vanished Literature.* 3 vols. Norman: University of Oklahoma Press, 1950–1962.

Lacy, James M. "New Mexican Women in Early American Writings." *New Mexico History Review* 34 (1959): 1

Lamb, Blaine P. "The Convenient Villain: The Early Cinema Views the Mexican-American." *Journal of the West* 14 (1975): 75

Langum, David J. "Californios and the Image of Indolence." *Western Historical Quarterly* 9 (April 1978): 181–96.

Maciel, David R. "The Celluloid Frontier: The U.S.-Mexico Border in Contemporary Cinema, 1970–1988." *Renato Rosaldo Lecture Series Monograph* 5 (1989): 1–34.

Noriega, Chon A. "Citizen Chicano: The Trials and Titillations of Ethnicity in the American Cinema, 1935–1962." *Social Research: An International Quarterly of the Social Sciences* 58 (Summer 1991): 413–38.

Paredes, Americo. "On 'Gringo,' 'Greaser,' and Other Neighborly Names." In *Singers and Storytellers*, edited by Mody C. Boatright et al. Dallas: Southern Methodist University Press, 1961.

Paredes, Raymund A. "The Mexican Image in American Travel Literature, 1813–1869." *New Mexico Historical Review* 52 (January 1977): 5–29.

———. "The Origin of Anti-Mexican Sentiment in the United States." *New Scholar* 6 (1977): 130–65.

Perez, Richie. "From Assimilation to Annihilation: Puerto Rican Images in U.S. Films." *Centro Bulletin* 2 (1990): 8

Pettit, Arthur G. *Images of the Mexican American in Fiction and Film.* College Station: Texas A & M University Press, 1980.

Robinson, Cecil. *Mexico and the Hispanic Southwest in American Literature.* Revised from *With the Ears of Strangers: The Mexican in American Literature.* Tucson: University of Arizona Press, 1977.

Roeder, George H., Jr. *Mexicans in the Movies: The Image of Mexicans in American Films, 1894–1947.* Unpublished manuscript, University of Wisconsin, 1971.

Saragoza, Alex M. "Mexican Cinema in the United States, 1940–1952." In *History, Culture, and Society: Chicano Studies in the 1980s,* issued by National Association of Chicano Studies. Ypsilanti, Mich.: Bilingual Press/Editorial Bilingue, 1983.

Torres, Luis R. "The Chicano Image in Film." *Caminos* 3 (November 1982): 8.

———. "Distortions in Celluloid: Hispanics and Film." *Agenda: A Journal of Hispanic Issues* 11 (May–June 1981): 37–40.

———. "Hollywood and the Homeboys: The Studios Discover Barrio Gangs." *Nuestro* 3 (April 1979): 27–30.

Trevino, Jesus Salvador. "Latino Portrayals in Film and Television." *Jump Cut* 30 (March 1985): 14–16.

———. "Latinos and Public Broadcasting: The 2% Factor." *Jump Cut* 28 (1983): 65.

Trulio, Beverly. "Anglo-American Attitudes toward New Mexican Women." *Journal of the West* 12 (1973): 229

Valle, Victor, and Rodolfo D. Torres. "The Idea of Mestizaje and the 'Race' Problematic: Racialized Media Discourse in a Post-Fordist Landscape." In *Culture and Difference: Critical Perspectives on the Bicultural Experience in the United States,* edited by Antonia Darder, 139–53. New York: Bergin & Garvey, 1995.

Weber, David J. "Here Rests Juan Espinoza: Toward a Clearer Look at the Image of the 'Indolent' Californios." *Western Historical Quarterly* 1 (January 1979): 61–68.

———. "Stereotyping of Mexico's Far Northern Frontier." In *An Awakened Minority: The Mexican American,* edited by Manuel P. Servin, 18–24. 2d ed. Beverly Hills, Calif.: Glencoe Press, 1974.

Williams, Linda. "Type and Stereotype : Chicano Images in Film." *Frontiers* 5 (Summer 1980): 14–17.

Woll, Allen L. "Bandits and Lovers: Hispanic Images in American Film." In *The Kaleidoscopic Lens: How Hollywood Views Ethnic Groups,* edited by Randall M. Miller. Englewood, N.J.: Jerome S. Ozer, 1980.

————. *The Latin Image in American Film.* Los Angeles: UCLA Latin American Center Publications, [1977] 1980.

Woll, Allen L., and Randall M. Miller. "Hispanic Americans." In *Ethnic and Racial Images in American Film and Television: Historical Essays and Bibliography,* edited by Allen L. Woll and Randall M. Miller. New York: Garland Publishing, 1987.

Part V

Counterstories

We Begin to Talk Back and "Name Our Own Reality"

The press, cartoonists, speakers, and filmmakers may have drawn derogatory images of Latino buffoons, shoot-you-in-the-back desperadoes, and Latin lovers with nothing to do but sing songs and strum the guitar, but Latino artists and writers have not stood still for such treatment. Instead, they have composed counterstories, narratives, *corridos* (ballads), and *cuentos* (stories) of their own to challenge and displace the pernicious images society created for their people. Even lawyers and legal scholars have begun composing such stories and questioning the dominant narrative or understanding on which the law of race rests. Part V examines how this process has been taking place.

Chapter 36

My Grandfather's Stories and Immigration Law

Michael A. Olivas

The funny thing about stories is that everyone has one. My grandfather had them, with plenty to spare. When I was very young, he would regale me with stories, usually about politics, baseball, and honor. These were his themes, the subject matter he carved out for himself and his grandchildren. As the oldest grandson and his first godchild, I held a special place of responsibility and affection. In Mexican families, this patrimony handed to young boys is one remnant of older times that is fading, like the use of Spanish in the home, posadas at Christmas, or the deference accorded all elders.

Sabino Olivas's world featured three verities, ones that he adhered to his entire life: political and personal loyalties are paramount; children should work hard and respect their elders; and people should conduct their lives with honor. Of course, each of these themes had a canon of stories designed, like parables, to illustrate the larger theme, and, like the Bible, to be interlocking, cross referenced, and synoptic. That is, they could be embellished in the retelling, but they had to conform to the general themes of loyalty, hard work, and honor.

Several examples will illustrate the overarching theoretical construction of my grandfather's world view, and show how, for him, everything was connected, and profound. Like other folklorists and storytellers, he employed mythic heroes or imbued people he knew with heroic dimensions. This is an important part of capturing the imagination of young children, for the mythopoeic technique overemphasizes characteristics and allows listeners to fill in the gaps by actively inviting them to rewrite the story and remember it in their own terms. As a result, as my family grew (I am the oldest of ten), I would hear these taproot stories retold both by my grandfather to the other kids, and by my brothers and sisters to others. The core of the story would be intact, transformed by the teller's accumulated sense of the story line and its application.

One of the earliest stories was about New Mexico's United States Senator Bronson Cutting, and his death in a plane crash after attempting to help Northern New

From *The Chronicles*, My Grandfather's Stories, and Immigration Law: The Slave Traders' Chronicle as Racial History." 34 St. Louis U. L.J. 425 (1990). Originally published in the *Saint Louis University Law Journal*. Reprinted by permission.

Mexico Hispanics regain land snatched from them by greedy developers. Growing up near Tierra Amarilla, New Mexico, as he did, my grandfather was heir to a long-standing oral tradition of defining one's status by land ownership. To this day, land ownership in Northern New Mexico is a tangle of aboriginal Indian rights, Spanish land grants, Anglo and Mexican greed, treaties, and developer domination. Most outsiders (that is, anyone south of Santa Fe) know this issue only by having seen *The Milagro Beanfield War*, the Robert Redford movie based on John Nichols's book. But my grandfather's story was that sinister forces had somehow tampered with Senator Cutting's plane because he was a man of the people, aligned against wealthy interests. Senator Cutting, I was led to believe as I anchored the story with my own points of reference, was more like Jimmy Stewart in *Mr. Smith Goes to Washington* than like the Claude Rains character, who would lie to get his own greedy way.

Of course, as I grew older, I learned that the true story was not exactly as my grandfather had told it. Land ownership in New Mexico is complicated; the Senator had his faults; and my grandfather ran afoul of Cutting's political enemy, Senator Dennis Chavez. But the story still held its sway over me.

His other favorite story, which included a strong admonition to me, was about how he and other Hispanics had been treated in Texas on their way to World War I. A trainload of soldiers from Arizona and northern New Mexico, predominantly of Mexican origin (both New Mexico and Arizona had only recently become states), were going by train to camp in Ft. Hays, Kansas. Their train stopped in a town near Amarillo, Texas, and all the men poured out of the train to eat at a restaurant, one that catered to train travelers. But only to some. A sign prominently greeted them: "No colored or Mexicans allowed," and word spread among them that this admissions policy was taken seriously.

My grandfather, who until this time had never been outside the Territory or the State of New Mexico (after 1912), was not used to this kind of indignity. After all, he was from a state where Hispanics and Indians constituted a majority of the population, especially in the North, and it was his first face-to-face encounter with racism, Texas style. Shamefacedly, the New Mexicans ate the food that Anglo soldiers bought and brought to the train, but he never forgot the humiliation and anger he felt that day. Sixty-five years later, when he told me this story, he remembered clearly how most of the men died in France or elsewhere in Europe, defending a country that never fully accorded them their rights.

The longer, fuller version, replete with wonderful details of how at training camp they had ridden sawhorses with saddles, always ended with the anthem, "Ten cuidado con los Tejanos, porque son todos desgraciados y no tienen verguenza" (Be careful with Texans because they are all sons-of-bitches and have no shame). To be a *sin verguenza*—shameless, or without honor—was my grandfather's cruelest condemnation, reserved for faithless husbands, reprobates, lying grandchildren, and Anglo Texans.

These stories always had a moral to them, with implications for grandchildren. Thus, I was admonished to vote Democrat (because of FDR and the Catholic JFK), to support the National League (because the Brooklyn Dodgers had first hired Black players and because the relocated Los Angeles Dodgers had a farm team in Albuquerque), and to honor my elders (for example, by using the more formal *usted* instead of the informal *tú*).

All of this is by way of explaining why I am predisposed to tell stories, and accordingly, to listen to them. Not only were stories profoundly important in my own ethnic heritage, but they were nurtured in the Catholic schools I attended and in the seminary, where I studied for eight years to become a Catholic priest (I left before ordination). Even in my graduate work in American literature, I wrote my first book on John Updike, one of the premier observers and storytellers of our time. The scene in *The Centaur*, where Updike's father's classroom becomes a braying, bleating, barking menagerie, remains one of my favorites in all of literature.

My objection, if that is the proper word, to the *Chronicle of the Space Traders* [In which a force of extraterrestrials offers to trade three treasures in return for all American blacks; the United States quickly votes to accept the trade—*Eds.*] is not that it is too fantastic or unlikely to occur, but rather the opposite: This scenario has occurred, and occurred more than once in our nation's history. Therefore, it is unintentionally ahistorical. Not only have Blacks been enslaved, as the *Chronicle* sorrowfully notes, but other racial groups have been conquered and removed, imported for their labor and not allowed to participate in the society they built, or expelled when their labor was no longer considered necessary.

Consider the immigration history and political economy of three groups whose United States history predates Bell's: Cherokee removal and the Trail of Tears; Chinese laborers and the Chinese Exclusion Laws; and Mexicans in the Bracero Program and Operation Wetback. [The author's treatment of the first two groups is not included—*Eds.*] These three racial groups share different histories of conquest, exploitation, and legal disadvantage; but even a brief summary of their treatment in United States law shows commonalties of racial animus, legal infirmity, and majority domination of legal institutions guised as "political questions." I could have also chosen the national origins or labor histories of other Indian tribes, the Filipinos, the Native Hawaiians, the Japanese, the Guamese, the Puerto Ricans, or the Vietnamese; in other words, the distinct racial groups whose conquest, colonization, enslavement, or immigration histories mark them as candidates for the Space Traders' evil exchange.

Mexicans, the Bracero Program, and Operation Wetback

Nineteenth century Mexican and Mexican American labor history in the United States is one of agricultural labor. In the Southwestern and Western United States, Mexicans picked half of the cotton and nearly 75 percent of the fruits and vegetables by the 1920s. By 1930, half of the sugar beet workers were Mexican, and 80 percent of the farmhands in Southern California were Mexican. As fields became increasingly mechanized, it was Anglo workers who rode the machines, consigning Mexicans to stoop-labor and hand cultivation. One observer noted: "The consensus of opinion of ranchers large and small . . . is that only the small minority of Mexicans are fitted for these types of labor [i.e., mechanized agricultural jobs] at the present time."[1]

Most crucial to the agricultural growers was the need for a reserve labor pool of workers who could be imported for their work, displaced when not needed, and kept in subordinate status so they could not afford to organize collectively or protest their conditions. Mexicans filled this bill perfectly, especially in the early twentieth century Southwest, where Mexican poverty and the Revolution forced rural Mexicans to come to the United States for work. This migration was facilitated by United States growers' agents, who recruited widely in Mexican villages, by the building of railroads (by Mexicans, not Chinese) from the interior of Mexico to El Paso, and by labor shortages in the United States during World War I.

Another means of controlling the spigot of Mexican farm workers was the use of immigration laws. Early labor restrictions through federal immigration law (and state law, as in California) had been aimed at Chinese workers. When agricultural interests pressured Congress to allow Mexican temporary workers during 1917–1921, the head tax (then set at $8.00), literacy requirements, public charge provisions, and Alien Contract Labor Law provisions were waived. By 1929, with a surplus of "native" United States workers facing the Depression, the supply of Mexicans was turned off by reimposing the immigration requirements.

While United States nativists were pointing to the evils and inferiority of Southern European immigrants, Mexicans were characterized as a docile, exploitable, deportable labor force. As one commentator noted:

> Mexican laborers, by accepting these undesirable tasks, enabled [Southwestern] agriculture and industry to flourish, thereby creating effective opportunities for [white] American workers in the higher job levels. . . . The representatives of [United States] economic interests showed the basic reason for their support of Mexican immigration[;] employers of the Southwest favored unlimited Mexican immigration because it provided them with a source of cheap labor which would be exploited to the fullest possible extent.[2]

To effectuate control over the Southern border, the Border Patrol was created in 1924, while the Department of Labor and the Immigration Bureau began a procedure in 1925 to regulate Mexican immigration by restricting the flow to workers already employed or promised positions.

During the Depression, two means were used to control Mexican workers: mass deportations and repatriations. Los Angeles was targeted for massive deportations for persons with Spanish-sounding names or Mexican features who could not produce formal papers, and over 80,000 Mexicans were deported from 1929 to 1935. Many of the these persons had the legal right to be in the country, or had been born citizens but simply could not prove their status; of course, many of these workers had been eagerly sought for perishable crops. In addition, over one-half million Mexicans were also "voluntarily" repatriated, by choosing to go to Mexico rather than remain in the United States, possibly subject to formal deportation.

By 1940, the cycle had turned: labor shortages and World War II had created the need for more agricultural workers, and growers convinced the United States government to enter into a large scale contract-labor program, the Bracero Program. Originally begun in 1942 under an Executive Order, the program brokered laborers under contracts between the United States and Mexico. Between 1942 and 1951, over one-half million "braceros" were hired under the program. Public funds were used to seek and register workers in Mexico who, after their labor had been performed, were returned to Mexico until the crops were ready to be picked again. This program was cynically employed to create a reserve pool of temporary laborers who had few rights and no vesting of equities.

By 1946, the circulation of bracero labor, both in its certification and its deportation mechanism, had become hopelessly confused. It became impossible to separate Mexican Americans from deportable Mexicans. Many United States citizens were mistakenly "repatriated" to Mexico, including men with Mexican features who had never been to Mexico. To correct these errors, a system of "drying out wetbacks" was instituted, what Ernesto Galarza termed a "dehydration" or "desiccation" process.[3] This modest legalization process gave some Mexican braceros an opportunity to regularize their immigration status and remain in the United States while they worked as braceros.

In 1950, under these various mechanisms, 20,000 new braceros were certified, 97,000 agricultural workers were dehydrated, and 480,000 old braceros were deported back to Mexico. In 1954, over one million braceros were deported under the terms of "Operation Wetback," a "Special Mobile Force" of the Border Patrol. The program included massive roundups and deportations, factory and field raids, a relentless media campaign designed to characterize the mop-up operation as a national security necessity, and a tightening up of the border to deter undocumented immigration.

The Bracero Program, dehydration, and Operation Wetback all presaged immigration programs of the 1980s. During this time, the INS began "Operation Jobs," a massive early 1980s workplace-raid program of deportations; a legalization program under the Immigration Reform and Control Act of 1986, an amnesty as a political tradeoff for employer sanctions; and a re-enacted Bracero-style program of H2A-workers, a labor contracting provision of temporary work visas for needed agricultural workers.

In two of his books based on folktales from Tierra Amarilla, New Mexico, the writer Sabine Ulibarri has re-created the Hispano-Indian world of rural, northern New Mexico. In *Cuentos de Tierra Amarilla* (*Tales From Tierra Amarilla*),[4] he collects a variety of wonderful tales, rooted in this isolated town that time has not changed, even today. My grandfather enjoyed this book, which I read to him in his final years, 1981 and 1982. But his favorite (and mine) was Ulibarri's masterwork, *Mi Abuela Fumaba Puros* (*My Grandmother Smoked Puros* [Cigars]),[5] in which an old woman lights cigars in her house to remind her of her dead husband.

My grandfather loved this story, not only because it was by his more famous *tocayo*, but because it was at once outlandish ("mujeres en Nuevo Mexico no fumaban puros" that is, women in New Mexico did not smoke cigars) and yet very real. Smells were very real to him, evocative of earlier events and *cuentos*, the way that tea and madeleines unlocked Proust's prodigious memory. Biscochitos evoked holidays, and empanadas Christmas. Had he outlived my grandmother, he would have had mementos in the house, perhaps prune pies or apricot jam.

My grandfather's world, with the exception of his World War I sortie in Texas and abroad, was small but not narrow. He lived by a code of behavior, one he passed to his more fortunate children (only one of whom still lives in New Mexico) and grandchildren (most of whom no longer live in New Mexico). But for me, no longer in New Mexico, reading Derrick Bell's *Chronicle* is like talking to my grandfather or reading Sabine Ulibarri; the stories are at once outlandish, yet very real. I also believe, with Richard Delgado, "Stories, parables, chronicles, and narratives are powerful means for destroying mindset—the bundle of presuppositions, received wisdoms, and shared understandings against a background of which legal and political discourse takes place."[6]

Folklore and corridos have always held a powerful place in Mexican society. Fiction has always held a powerful place in the human experience, and the *Chronicles* will inform racial jurisprudence and civil rights scholarship in the United States in ways not yet evident. Critical minority renderings of United States racial history, immigration practices, and labor economy can have equally compelling results, however, recounting what actually happened in all the sordid details. If Derrick Bell's work forces us to engage these unsavory practices, he will have performed great service—he will have caused us to examine our grandfathers' stories and lives. . . .

As a deterrent to Central American refugees and as "bait" to attract their families already in the United States, the INS began in the 1980s to incarcerate undocumented adults and unaccompanied minors in border camps. One, near Brownsville, Texas, was once used as a United States Department of Agriculture pesticide storage facility. The INS has defied court orders to improve conditions in the camps, and by 1990, hundreds of alien children were being held without health, educational, or legal services. Haitian boat persons were being interdicted at sea, given "hearings" on the boats, and repatriated to Haiti; by 1990, only six of 20,000 interdicted Haitians had been granted asylum. The INS had begun a media campaign to justify its extraordinary practices on land and on sea. The cycle of United States immigration history continued, and all was ready for the Space Traders.

NOTES

1. P. Taylor, MEXICAN LABOR IN THE UNITED STATES IMPERIAL VALLEY 42 (1928).

2. Robert A. Divine, AMERICAN IMMIGRATION POLICY, 1924–1952 at 58–59 (1957).

3. Ernesto Galarza, MERCHANTS OF LABOR: THE MEXICAN BRACERO STORY 63–64 (1964).

4. Sabine Ulibarri, CUENTOS DE TIERRA AMARILLA (1971). Sabine Ulibarri, also a native of Tierra Amarilla, told me he had known of my grandfather because the town was small and because their names were so similar. My grandfather, who never met Ulibarri (who was twenty years younger), called him his *tocayo* (namesake).

5. Sabine Ulibarri, MI ABUELA FUMABA PUROS (1977).

6. Richard Delgado, *Storytelling for Oppositionists and Others: A Plea for Narrative*, 87 MICH. L. REV. 2411, 2413 (1989).

Chapter 37

Storytelling for Oppositionists and Others

Richard Delgado

Everyone has been writing stories these days. And I don't just mean writing about stories or narrative theory, important as those are. I mean actual stories, as in "once-upon-a-time" type stories. Derrick Bell has been writing "Chronicles"; others have been writing dialogues, stories, and metastories. Many others have been daring to become more personal in their writing, to inject narrative, perspective, and feeling—how it was for me—into their otherwise scholarly, footnoted articles and, in the case of the truly brave, into their teaching.

Many, but by no means all, who have been telling legal stories are members of what could be loosely described as outgroups, groups whose marginality defines the boundaries of the mainstream, whose voice and perspective—whose consciousness—has been suppressed, devalued, and abnormalized. The attraction of stories for these groups should come as no surprise. For stories create their own bonds, represent cohesion, shared understanding, and meanings. The cohesiveness that stories bring is part of the strength of the outgroup. An outgroup creates its own stories, which circulate within the group as a kind of counter-reality.

The dominant group creates its own stories, as well. The stories or narratives told by the ingroup remind it of its identity in relation to outgroups, and provide it with a form of shared reality in which its own superior position is seen as natural.

The stories of outgroups aim to subvert that ingroup reality. In civil rights, for example, many in the majority hold that any inequality between whites and nonwhites is due either to cultural lag, or inadequate enforcement of currently existing beneficial laws—both of which are easily correctable. For many minority persons, the principal instrument of their subordination is neither of these. Rather, it is the prevailing mindset by means of which members of the dominant group justify the world as it is, that is, with whites on top and browns and blacks at the bottom.

Stories, parables, chronicles, and narratives are powerful means for destroying mindset—the bundle of presuppositions, received wisdoms, and shared understandings against a background of which legal and political discourse takes place. These

From "Storytelling for Oppositionists and Others: A Plea for Narrative." 87 Mich. L. Rev. 2411 (1989). Originally published in the *Michigan Law Review*. Reprinted by permission.

matters are rarely focused on. They are like eyeglasses we have worn a long time. They are nearly invisible; we use them to scan and interpret the world and only rarely examine them for themselves. Ideology—the received wisdom—makes current social arrangements seem fair and natural. Those in power sleep well at night—their conduct does not seem to them like oppression.

The cure is storytelling (or as I shall sometimes call it, counterstorytelling). As Derrick Bell, Bruno Bettelheim, and others show, stories can shatter complacency and challenge the status quo. Stories told by underdogs are frequently ironic or satiric; a root word for "humor" is *humus*—bringing low, down to earth. Along with the tradition of storytelling in black culture, there exists the Spanish tradition of the picaresque novel or story, which tells of humble folk piquing the pompous or powerful and bringing them down to more human levels.

Most who write about storytelling focus on its community-building functions: stories build consensus, a common culture of shared understandings, and deeper, more vital ethics. Counterstories, which challenge the received wisdom, do that as well. They can open new windows into reality, showing us that there are possibilities for life other than the ones we live. They enrich imagination and teach that by combining elements from the story and current reality, we may construct a new world richer than either alone. Counterstories can quicken and engage conscience. Their graphic quality can stir imagination in ways in which more conventional discourse cannot.

But stories and counterstories can serve an equally important destructive function. They can show that what we believe is ridiculous, self-serving, or cruel. They can show us the way out of the trap of unjustified exclusion. They can help us understand when it is time to reallocate power. They are the other half—the destructive half—of the creative dialectic. Stories and counterstories, to be effective, must be or must appear to be noncoercive. They invite the reader to suspend judgment, listen for their point or message, and then decide what measure of truth they contain. They are insinuative, not frontal; they offer a respite from the linear, coercive discourse that characterizes much legal writing.

Storytelling and Counterstorytelling

The same object, as everyone knows, can be described in many ways. A rectangular red object on my living room floor may be a nuisance if I stub my toe on it in the dark, a doorstop if I use it for that purpose, further evidence of my lackadaisical housekeeping to my visiting mother, a toy to my young daughter, or simply a brick left over from my patio restoration project. No single true or all-encompassing description exists. The same holds true of events, especially ones that are racially charged. Often, we will not be able to ascertain the single best description or interpretation of what we have seen. We participate in creating what we see in the very act of describing it.

How can there be such divergent stories? Why do they not combine? Is it simply that members of the dominant group see the same glass as half full, minorities as half empty? I believe more is at work; stories war with each other. They contend for, tug at, our minds. To see how the dialectic of competition and rejection works—to see the reality-creating potential of stories and the normative implications of adopting one story rather than another—consider the following series of accounts, each describing the same event.

A Standard Event and a Stock Story That Explains It

The following series of stories revolves around the same event: A black(or Latino, or Asian, or Indian) lawyer interviews for a teaching position at a major law school (school X) and is rejected. Any other race-tinged event could have served equally well for purposes of illustration. This particular event was chosen because it occurs on familiar ground—many readers of this chapter are past or present members of a university community who have heard about or participated in events like the one described.

The Stock Story

Setting: A professor and student are talking in the professor's office. Both are white. The professor, Blas Vernier, is tenured, in midcareer, and well regarded by his colleagues and students. The student, Judith Rogers, is a member of the student advisory appointments committee.

Rogers: Professor Vernier, what happened with the minority candidate, John Henry? I heard he was voted down at the faculty meeting yesterday. The students on my committee liked him a lot.

Vernier: It was a difficult decision, Judith. We discussed him for over two hours. I can't tell you the final vote, of course, but it wasn't particularly close. Even some of my colleagues who were initially for his appointment voted against him when the full record came out.

Rogers: But we have no minority professors at all, except for Professor Chen, who is untenured, and Professor Tompkins, who teaches Trial Practice on loan from the district attorney's office once a year.

Vernier: Don't forget Mary Foster, the Assistant Dean.

Rogers: But she doesn't teach, just handles admissions and the placement office.

Vernier: And does those things very well. But back to John Henry. I understand your disappointment. Henry was a strong candidate, one of the stronger blacks we've interviewed recently. But ultimately he didn't measure up. We didn't think he wanted to teach for the right reasons. He was vague and diffuse about his research interests. All he could say was that he wanted to write about equality and civil rights, but so far as we could tell, he had nothing new to say about those areas. What's more, we had some problems with his teaching interests. He wanted to teach peripheral courses, in areas where we already have enough people. And we had the sense that he wouldn't be really rigorous in those areas, either.

Rogers: But we need courses in employment discrimination and civil rights. And he's had a long career with the NAACP Legal Defense Fund and really seemed to know his stuff.

Vernier: It's true we could stand to add a course or two of that nature, although as you know our main needs are in Commercial Law and Corporations, and Henry doesn't teach either. But I think our need is not as acute as you say. Many of the topics you're interested in are covered in the second half of the Constitutional Law course taught by Professor White, who has a national reputation for his work in civil liberties and freedom of speech.

Rogers: But Henry could have taught those topics from a black perspective. And he would have been a wonderful role model for our minority students.

Vernier: Those things are true, and we gave them considerable weight. But when it came right down to it, we felt we couldn't take that great a risk. Henry wasn't on the law review at school, as you are, Judith, and has never written a line in a legal journal. Some of us doubted he ever would. And then, what would happen five years from now when he came up for tenure? It wouldn't be fair to place him in an environment like this. He'd just have to pick up his career and start over if he didn't produce.

Rogers: With all due respect, Professor, that's paternalistic. I think Henry should have been given the chance. He might have surprised us.

Vernier: So I thought, too, until I heard my colleagues' discussion, which I'm afraid, given the demands of confidentiality, I can't share with you. Just let me say that we examined his case long and hard and I am convinced, fairly. The decision, while painful, was correct.

Rogers: So another year is going to go by without a minority candidate or professor?

Vernier: These things take time. I was on the appointments committee last year, chaired it in fact. And I can tell you we would love nothing better than to find a qualified black. Every year, we call the Supreme Court to check on current clerks, telephone our colleagues at other leading law schools, and place ads in black newspapers and journals. But the pool is so small. And the few good ones have many opportunities. We can't pay nearly as much as private practice, you know. [Rogers, who would like to be a legal services attorney, but is attracted to the higher salaries of corporate practice, nods glumly.] It may be that we'll have to wait another few years, until the current crop of black and minority law students graduates and gets some experience. We have some excellent prospects, including some members of your very class. I'm sure you know Patricia Maldonado, who is an articles editor on your own journal.

Rogers: [Thinks: I've heard that one before, but says] Well, thanks, Professor. I know the students will be disappointed. But maybe when the committee considers visiting professors later in the season it will be able to find a professor of color who meets its standards and fits our needs.

Vernier: We'll try our best. Although you should know that some of us believe that merely shuffling the few minorities in teaching from one school to another does nothing to expand the pool. And once they get here, it's hard to say no if they express a desire to stay on.

Rogers: [Thinks: That's a lot like tenure. How ironic; there are certain of your colleagues we would love to get rid of, too. But says] Well, thanks, Professor. I've got to get to class. I still wish the vote had come out otherwise. Our student committee is preparing a list of minority candidates that we would like to see considered. Maybe you'll find one or more of them worthy of teaching here.

Vernier: Judith, believe me, there is nothing that would please me more.

In the above dialogue, Professor Vernier's account represents the stock story—the one the institution collectively forms and tells about itself. This story picks and chooses from among the available facts to present a picture of what happened: an account that justifies the world as it is. It emphasizes the school's benevolent motivation ("look how hard we're trying") and good faith. It stresses stability and the avoidance of risks. It measures the candidate of color through the prism of preexisting, well-agreed-upon criteria of conventional scholarship and teaching. Given those standards, it purports to be scrupulously meritocratic and fair; Henry would have been hired had he measured up. No one raises the possibility that the merit criteria employed in judging Henry are themselves debatable, chosen—not inevitable. No one, least of all Vernier, calls attention to the way in which merit functions to conceal the contingent connection between institutional power and the things rated.

The discussion gives little consideration of the possibility that Henry's presence on the faculty might have altered the institution's character, helped introduce a different prism and different criteria for selecting future candidates. The account is highly procedural—it emphasizes that Henry got a full, careful hearing—rather than substantive: a black was rejected. It emphasizes certain "facts" without examining their truth—namely, that the pool is very small, that good minority candidates have many choices, and that the appropriate view is the long view; haste makes waste.

The dominant fact about this first story, however, is its seeming neutrality. It scrupulously avoids issues of blame or responsibility. Race played no part in the candidate's rejection; indeed the school leaned over backwards to accommodate him. A white candidate with similar credentials would not have made it as far as Henry did. The story comforts and soothes. And Vernier's sincerity makes him an effective apologist for his system.

Vernier's story is also deeply coercive, although the coercion is disguised. Judith was aware of it but chose not to confront it directly; Vernier holds all the cards. He pressures her to go along with the institution's story by threatening her prospects at the same time that he flatters her achievements. A victim herself, she is invited to take on and share the consciousness of her oppressor. She does not accept Vernier's story, but he does slip a few doubts through cracks in her armor. The professor's story shows how forceful and repeated storytelling can perpetuate a particular view of reality. Naturally, the stock story is not the only one that can be told. By emphasizing other events and giving them slightly different interpretations, a quite different picture can be made to emerge.

[Following two other stories—the one told by the disappointed candidate himself, and the one told by the judge in his order dismissing John Henry's legal complaint—the author continues as follows—*Eds.*]

Al-Hammar X's Counter Story

None of the above stories attempts to unseat the prevailing institutional story. Henry's account comes closest; it highlights different facts and interprets those it does share with the standard account differently. His formal complaint also challenges the school's account, but it must fit itself under existing law, which it failed to do.

A few days after word of Henry's rejection reached the student body, Noel Al-Hammar X, leader of the radical Third World Coalition, delivered a speech at noon on the steps of the law school patio. The audience consisted of most of the black and brown students at the law school, several dozen white students, and a few faculty members. Chen was absent, having a class to prepare for. The Assistant Dean was present, uneasily taking mental notes in case the Dean asked her later on what she heard.

Al-Hammar's speech was scathing, denunciatory, and at times downright rude. He spoke several words that the campus newspaper reporter wondered if his paper would print. He impugned the good faith of the faculty, accused them of institutional if not garden-variety racism, and pointed out in great detail the long history of the faculty as an all-white club. He said that the law school was bent on hiring only white males, "ladies" only if they were well-behaved clones of white males, and would never hire a professor of color unless forced to do so by student pressure or the courts. He exhorted his fellow students not to rest until the law faculty took steps to address its own ethnocentricity and racism. He urged boycotting or disrupting classes, writing letters to the state legislature, withholding alumni contributions, setting up a "shadow" appointments committee, and several other measures that made the Assistant Dean wince.

Al-Hammar's talk received a great deal of attention, particularly from the faculty who were not there to hear it. Several versions of his story circulated among the faculty offices and corridors ("Did you hear what he said?"). Many of the stories-about-the-story were wildly exaggerated. Nevertheless, Al-Hammar's story is an authentic counterstory. It directly challenges—both in its words and tone—the corporate story the law school carefully worked out to explain Henry's non-appointment. It rejects many of the institution's premises, including we-try-so-hard, the-pool-is-so-small, and even mocks the school's meritocratic self-concept. "They say Henry is mediocre, has a pedestrian mind. Well, they ain't sat in none of my classes and listened to themselves. Mediocrity they got. They're experts on mediocrity." Al-Hammar denounced the faculty's excuse making, saying there were dozens of qualified black candidates, if not hundreds. "There isn't that big a pool of Chancellors, or quarterbacks," he said. "But when they need one, they find one, don't they?"

Al-Hammar also deviates stylistically, as a storyteller, from the others, including John Henry. He rebels against the "reasonable discourse" of law. He is angry, and anger is out of bounds in legal discourse, even as a response to discrimination. Judith and John Henry were unsuccessful in getting others to listen. So was Al-Hammar, but for a different reason. His counterstory overwhelmed the audience. More than just a narrative, it was a call to action, a call to join him in destroying the current story. But his audience was not ready to act. Too many of his listeners felt challenged or coerced; their defenses went up. The campus newspaper the next day published a garbled version, saying that he had urged the law faculty to relax its standards in order to provide minority students with role models. This prompted three letters to the ed-

itor asking how an unqualified black professor could be a good role model for anyone, black or white.

Moreover, the audience Al-Hammar intended to affect, namely the faculty, was
even more unmoved by his counterstory. It attacked them too frontally. They were
quick to dismiss him as an extremist, a demagogue, a hothead—someone to be taken
seriously only for the damage he might do should he attract a body of followers.
Consequently, for the next week the faculty spent much time in one-on-one conversations with "responsible" student leaders, including Judith Rogers.

By the end of the week, a consensus story had formed about Al-Hammar's story.
That story-about-a-story held that Al-Hammar had gone too far, that there was more
to the situation than Al-Hammar knew or was prepared to admit. Moreover, Al-
Hammar was portrayed not as someone who had reached out, in pain, for sympathy
and friendship. Rather, he was depicted as a "bad actor," someone with a "chip on
his shoulder," someone no responsible member of the law school community should
trade stories with. Nonetheless, a few progressive students and faculty members believed Al-Hammar had done the institution a favor by raising the issues and demanding that they be addressed. They were a distinct minority.

The Anonymous Leaflet Counter Story

About a month after Al-Hammar spoke, the law faculty formed a special committee
for minority hiring. The committee contained practically every young liberal on the
faculty, two of its three female professors, and the Assistant Dean. The Dean announced the committee's formation in a memorandum sent to the law school's ethnic student associations, the student government, and the alumni newsletter, which
gave it front-page coverage. It was also posted on bulletin boards around the law
school.

The memo spoke about the committee and its mission in serious, measured
phrases—"social need," "national search," "renewed effort," "balancing the various
considerations," "identifying members of a future pool from which we might draw."
Shortly after the memo was distributed, an anonymous four-page leaflet appeared in
the student lounge, on the same bulletin boards on which the Dean's memo had been
posted, and in various mailboxes of faculty members and law school organizations.
Its author, whether student or faculty member, was never identified.

The leaflet was entitled, "Another Committee, Aren't We Wonderful?" It began
with a caricature of the Dean's memo, mocking its measured language and high-
flown tone. Then, beginning in the middle of the page the memo told, in conversa-
tional terms, the following story:

"And so, friends and neighbors [the leaflet continued], how is it that the good law
schools go about looking for new faculty members? Here is how it works. The appointments committee starts out the year with a model new faculty member in mind.
This mythic creature went to a leading law school, graduated first or second in his or
her class, clerked for the Supreme Court, and wrote the leading note in the law review on some topic dealing with the federal courts. This individual is brilliant, per-

sonable, humane, and has just the right amount of practice experience with the right firm.

"Schools begin with this paragon in mind and energetically beat the bushes, beginning in September, in search of him or her. At this stage, they believe themselves genuinely and sincerely colorblind. If they find such a mythic figure who is black or Hispanic or gay or lesbian, they will hire this person in a flash. They will of course do the same if the person is white.

"By February, however, the school has not hired many mythic figures. Some that they interviewed turned them down. Now, it's late in the year and they have to get someone to teach Trusts and Estates. Although there are none left on their list who are Supreme Court clerks, etc., they can easily find several who are a notch or two below that—who went to good schools, but not Harvard, or who went to Harvard, yet were not first or second in their classes. Still, they know, with a degree verging on certainty, that this person is smart and can do the job. They know this from personal acquaintance with this individual, or they hear it from someone they know and trust. Joe says Bill is really smart, a good lawyer, and will be terrific in the classroom.

"So they hire this person because, although he or she is not a mythic figure, functionally equivalent guarantees—namely first- or second-hand experience—assure them that this person will be a good teacher and scholar. And so it generally turns out—the new professor does just fine.

"Persons hired in this fashion are almost always white, male, and straight. The reason: We rarely know blacks, Hispanics, women, and gays. Moreover, when we hire the white male, the known but less-than-mythic quantity, late in February, it does not seem to us like we are making an exception. Yet we are. We are employing a form of affirmative action—bending the stated rules so as to hire the person we want.

"The upshot is that whites have two chances of being hired—by meeting the formal criteria we start out with in September—that is, by being mythic figures—and also by meeting the second, informal, modified criteria we apply later to friends and acquaintances when we are in a pinch. Minorities have just one chance of being hired—the first.

"To be sure, once every decade or so a law school, imbued with crusading zeal, will bend the rules and hire a minority with credentials just short of Superman or Superwoman. And, when it does so, *it will feel like an exception*. The school will congratulate itself—it has lifted up one of the downtrodden. And, it will remind the new professor repeatedly how lucky he or she is to be here in this wonderful place. It will also make sure, through subtle or not-so-subtle means, that the students know so, too."

But (the leaflet continued), there is a coda.

"If, later, the minority professor hired this way unexpectedly succeeds, this will produce consternation among his or her colleagues. For, things were not intended to go that way. When he or she came aboard, the minority professor lacked those standard indicia of merit—Supreme Court clerkship, high LSAT score, prep school background—that the majority-race professors had and believe essential to scholarly success.

"Yet the minority professor is succeeding all the same—publishing in good law reviews, receiving invitations to serve on important commissions, winning popularity with students. This is infuriating. Many majority-race professors are persons of relatively slender achievements—you can look up their publishing record any time you have five minutes. Their principal achievements lie in the distant past, when aided by their parents' upper class background, they did well in high school and college, and got the requisite test scores on standardized tests which test exactly the accumulated cultural capital they acquired so easily and naturally at home. Shortly after that, their careers started to stagnate. They publish an article every five years or so, often in a minor law review, after gallingly having it turned down by the very review they served on as editor twenty years ago.

"So, their claim to fame lies in their early exploits, the badges they acquired up to about the age of twenty-five, at which point the edge they acquired from Mummy and Daddy began to lose effect. Now, along comes the hungry minority professor, imbued with a fierce desire to get ahead, a good intellect, and a willingness to work 70 hours a week if necessary to make up for lost time. The minority person lacks the merit badges awarded early in life, the white professor's main source of security. So, the minority's colleagues don't like it and use perfectly predictable ways to transfer the costs of their discomfort to the misbehaving minority.

"So that, my friends, is why minority professors

(i) have a hard time getting hired; and,
(ii) have a hard time if they are hired.

"When you and I are running the world, we won't replicate this unfair system, will we? Of course not—unless, of course, it changes us in the process."

This second counterstory attacks the faculty less frontally in some respects—for example, it does not focus on the fate of any particular minority candidate, such as Henry, but attacks a general mindset. It employs several devices, including narrative and careful observation—the latter to build credibility (the reader says, "That's right"), the former to beguile the reader and get him or her to suspend judgment (everyone loves a story). The last part of the story is painful; it strikes close to home. Yet the way for its acceptance has been paved by the earlier parts, which paint a plausible picture of events, so that the final part demands consideration. It generalizes and exaggerates—many majority-race professors are not persons of slender achievement. But such broad strokes are part of the narrator's art. The realistically drawn first part of the story, despite shading off into caricature at the end, forces readers to focus on the flaws in the good face the dean attempted to put on events. And, despite its somewhat accusatory thrust, the story, as was mentioned, debunks only a mindset, not a person. Unlike Al-Hammar X's story, it does not call the chair of the appointments committee, a much-loved senior professor, a racist. (But did Al-Hammar's story, confrontational as it was, pave the way for the generally positive reception accorded the anonymous account?)

The story invites the reader to alienate herself or himself from the events described, to enter into the mental set of the teller, whose view is different from the reader's own. The oppositional nature of the story, the manner in which it challenges and rebuffs the stock story, thus causes him or her to oscillate between poles. It is insinuative: At times, the reader is seduced by the story and its logical coherence—it is a plausible counter-view of what happened; it has a degree of explanatory power.

Yet the story places the majority-race reader on the defensive. He or she alternately leaves the storyteller's perspective to return to his or her own, saying, "That's outrageous, I'm being accused of. . . ." The reader thus moves back and forth between two worlds, the storyteller's, which the reader occupies vicariously to the extent the story is well-told and rings true, and his or her own, which he or she returns to and reevaluates in light of the story's message. Can my world still stand? What parts of it remain valid? What parts of the story seem true? How can I reconcile the two worlds, and will the resulting world be a better one than the one with which I began?

Why Outgroups Should Tell Stories and Why Others Should Listen

Subordinated groups have always told stories. Black slaves told, in song, letters, and verse, about their own pain and oppression. They described the terrible wrongs they had experienced at the hands of whites, and mocked (behind whites' backs) the veneer of gentility whites purchased at the cost of the slaves' suffering. Mexican Americans in the Southwest composed *corridos* (ballads) and stories, passed on from generation to generation, of abuse at the hands of gringo justice, the Texas Rangers, and ruthless lawyers and developers who cheated them out of their lands. Native American literature, both oral and written, deals with all these themes as well. Feminist consciousness-raising consists, in part, of the sharing of stories, of tales from personal experience, on the basis of which the group constructs a shared reality about women's status vis-à-vis men.

This proliferation of counterstories is not an accident or coincidence. Oppressed groups have known instinctively that stories are an essential tool to their own survival and liberation. Members of out-groups can use stories in two basic ways: first, as means of psychic self-preservation; and, second, as means of lessening their own subordination. These two means correspond to the two perspectives from which a story can be viewed—that of the teller, and that of the listener. The storyteller gains psychically, the listener morally and epistemologically.

The member of an outgroup gains, first, psychic self-preservation. A principal cause of the demoralization of marginalized groups is self-condemnation. They internalize the images that society thrusts on them—they believe that their lowly position is their own fault. The therapy is to tell stories. By becoming acquainted with the facts of their own historic oppression—with the violence, murder, deceit, co-optation, and connivance that have caused their desperate estate—members of outgroups gain healing. The story need not lead to a violent act; Frantz Fanon was wrong in writing that it is only through exacting blood from the oppressor that colonized people gain liberation.[1] Rather, the story need only lead to a realization of how one came to be oppressed and subjugated. Then, one can stop perpetrating (mental) violence on oneself.

So, stories—stories about oppression, about victimization, about one's own brutalization—far from deepening the despair of the oppressed, lead to healing, liberation, mental health.[2] They also promote group solidarity. Storytelling emboldens the hearer, who may have had the same thoughts and experiences the storyteller describes, but hesitated to give them voice. Having heard another express them, he or she realizes, I am not alone.

Yet, stories help oppressed groups in a second way—through their effect on the oppressor. Most oppression, as was mentioned earlier, does not seem like oppression to those perpetrating it. It is rationalized, causing few pangs of conscience. The dominant group justifies its privileged position by means of stories, stock explanations that construct reality in ways favorable to it. The stories are drastically at odds with the way most people of color would describe their condition. Artfully designed parables, chronicles, allegories, and pungent tales can jar the comfortable dominant complacency that is the principal anchor dragging down any incentive for reform. They can destroy—but the destruction they produce must be voluntary, a type of willing death. Because this is a white-dominated society in which the majority race controls the reins of power, racial reform must include them. Their complacency—born of comforting stories—is a major stumbling block to racial progress. Counterstories can attack that complacency.

What is more, they can do so in ways that promise at least the possibility of success. Most civil rights strategies confront the obstacle of otherness. The dominant group, noticing that a particular effort is waged on behalf of blacks or Latinos, increases its resistance. Stories at times can overcome that otherness, hold that instinctive resistance in abeyance. Stories are the oldest, most primordial meeting ground in human experience. Their allure will often provide the most effective means of overcoming otherness, of forming a new collectivity based on the shared story.

Members of outgroups should tell stories. Why should members of ingroups listen to them? They should listen to stories, of all sorts, in order to enrich their own reality. Reality is not fixed, not a given. Rather, we construct it through conversations, through our lives together. Racial and class-based isolation prevents the hearing of diverse stories and counterstories. It diminishes the conversation through which we create reality, construct our communal lives. Deliberately exposing oneself to counterstories can avoid that impoverishment, heighten "suspicion," and enable the listener and the teller to build a world richer than either could make alone. On another occasion, the listener will be the teller, sharing a secret, a piece of information, or an angle of vision that will enrich the former teller; and so on dialectically, in a rich tapestry of conversation, of stories. It is through this process that we can overcome ethnocentrism and the unthinking conviction that our way of seeing the world is the only one—that the way things are is inevitable, natural, just, and best—when it is, for some, full of pain, exclusion, and both petty and major tyranny.

Listening to stories makes the adjustment to further stories easier; one acquires the ability to see the world through others' eyes. It can lead the way to new environments. A willing listener is generally "welcomed with open arms." Listening to the stories of outgroups can avoid intellectual apartheid. Shared words can banish sameness, stiffness, and monochromaticity and reduce the felt terror of otherness when hearing new voices for the first time. If we would deepen and humanize ourselves, we must seek out storytellers different from ourselves and afford them the audience they deserve. The benefit will be reciprocal.[3]

NOTES

1. Frantz Fanon, THE WRETCHED OF THE EARTH (1968).
2. See Derrick A. Bell, Jr., AND WE ARE NOT SAVED 215–21 (1987).
3. Al-Hammar X graduated in the top 15 percent of his class, enrolled in a famous LL.M. program, and plans to become a law professor; Judith Rogers continued to be friendly with Professor Vernier, and actually succeeded in making him more receptive to minority candidates; John Henry was hired at Howard, where he had a long and illustrious career; the students at school X formed a committee to press for more minority and women professors. They did all the things Al-Hammar X suggested except disrupt classes. Two years later, the school hired two black women and a Hispanic male, maintaining, however, that this was not the result of student pressure but rather its own long-term recruiting.

Chapter 38

Lay Lawyering

Gerald P. López

Lawyering means problem-solving, which in turn entails perceiving that the world we would like varies from the world as it is and trying to move in the desired direction. Solving human problems sometimes requires changing the physical world or overcoming ourselves, but it also can entail trying to persuade others to act in ways that will change the world into something closer to what we desire. All of us so act when we solve problems; lawyers do no more. We can see lawyers' problem-solving simply as an instance of human problem-solving. To understand lawyering, therefore, we must examine the activity characterized here as "lay lawyering"—the things one person does when he helps another solve a problem.

Human beings think about social interaction in story form. We see and understand the world through "stock stories."[1] These stories help us interpret the everyday world with limited information and help us make choices about asserting our own needs and responding to other people. These stock stories embody our deepest human, social, and political values. At the same time, they help us carry out the routine activities of life without constantly having to analyze or question what we are doing. When we face choices in life, stock stories help us understand and decide; they also may disguise and distort. To solve a problem through persuasion of another, we therefore must understand and manipulate the stock stories the other person uses in order to tell a plausible and compelling story—one that moves that person to grant the remedy we want.

To understand how and why we use storytelling to solve problems, we must look to our daily living—to concrete, mundane moments of problem-solving. Capturing in thought what we are and what we do in these moments is our conception of lay lawyering. What are our stories? What do they imply? What remedial cultures emerge to resolve conflicting stories about the same situation? How does a lay lawyer go about his work? What does his work say about us and the order we have created?

In most cultures we know, people talk about the meaning of the stories they tell and live by—both as speculative matter and in ceremonies where one is seeking a remedy from another. Talking about what a story means inevitably creates room for rival interpretations; debate extends beyond what the facts are to what the facts as found mean. Just as rival stories argue to an audience with remedy-giving power that "this is the circumstance that should lead you to grant the remedy sought," rival interpretations argue that "this is the meaning that you should give to the finding of facts and that should lead you to a particular conclusion." And just as a storyteller will play up, downplay, or hide particular features in telling a story that he hopes makes sense, so too will the storyteller emphasize, de-emphasize, or obscure certain factual features in asserting that a particular meaning should be given to facts as found. In trying to convince an audience to adopt a particular meaning and arrive at a particular conclusion, both forms of persuasion rely upon and try to exploit what we know about likeness judgments and the way we interpret. In other words, debate over what the finding of facts means and debate over what the finding of facts is share an internal structure that echoes and is allegiant to the way we capture and make meaning.

As much as the two forms of persuasion share, they are often conceived of and treated quite differently in the remedy-seeking ceremonies of many cultures. What the facts are is thought to be a matter of demonstration, not persuasion. The historical reconstruction that makes up much of storytelling is considered more trustworthy if it simply presents the facts without any instrumental or predetermined direction. We can find the true and real world, says the convention, and we simply should report it in the story. Despite both occasional reminders that this convention embraces a cognitive impossibility and open acknowledgments that it is often at odds with the instrumental nature of remedy-seeking stories, most cultures abide by and even exalt the pretense that what happened can be found and reported without bias. In contrast, what facts as found mean is a matter openly to be debated, often in the most explicitly self-serving fashion. While perhaps a storyteller optimally would like to tell a story that seems to demonstrate a single, self-evident and inescapable meaning, he customarily is allowed and encouraged to persuade an audience of the appropriateness of a particular (and not coincidentally self-interested) interpretation. What is—what was "demonstrated" to be in and through the story—must be assigned a meaning, and it is usually thought to be to the advantage of all concerned to allow self-interested advocacy to that end.

While debate over what the facts mean (argument) is encouraged to be more explicitly persuasive than debate over what the facts are (storytelling), argument as an act of persuasion is constrained in most cultures in a way that storytelling is not. Argument is, by and large, allowed to appeal primarily to values that are already conventionally acceptable. Most cultures allow people in remedy-seeking ceremonies to talk in explicit terms about only certain features of the stories they tell and live by. What is permissible varies from ceremony to ceremony within a culture and changes as a culture's conventions and values evolve over time. But at any point in time and in any of a culture's ceremonies, an instrumental storyteller generally may draw out and underscore in explicit terms only those meanings that the culture has in the past determined can be debated and relied upon openly. If in remedy-seeking ceremonies making meaning through likeness judgments is by its nature a process tied to tradition, argument is by custom generally that process's most conservative act of persuasion.

By contrast, stories by their very nature can appeal to what is, by convention, still taboo in a culture. Because facts themselves capture and reflect values, what cannot be argued explicitly can be sneaked into a story. Indeed, the genius of storytelling as an act of persuasion is that it buries argument in the facts. Stories can thereby circumvent the existing constraints on the meaning that can be given to the facts as found. Put differently, relevance is for story a much looser standard than it is for argument. If argument tames a story by underscoring conventionally acceptable meanings, stories may be said simultaneously to turn loose and make available meanings as yet formally "illegitimate" to proffer and defend explicitly. However formally taboo, these meanings are not in fact insignificant to understanding and explaining previous conclusions drawn by audiences in similar circumstances and to persuading the immediate audience of a meaning that will lead to the remedy sought. What a story means is what an audience "holds" that it means in the circumstance, and it may be the story (with all its potential meanings) or the argument that best explains the holding.

The dichotomy between story and argument should not be cast too boldly. At times and in particular cultural ceremonies, story and argument merge. "This is what happened" may be nearly the equivalent of "This is the meaning." And, in all ceremonies, people often argue in explicit propositional terms about which competing story makes most sense in the circumstance (for example, "What you think happened can't be true . . ."), just as argument about what the facts as found mean is often cast in conditional narrative forms ("Imagine the following variation of the facts . . . "). That story and argument can at times be nearly equivalent acts of persuasion in remedy-seeking ceremonies and that both are often employed in the process of determining both what the facts are and what the facts mean does not detract, however, from the customarily drawn distinction in function. If the ostensible purpose of instrumental storytelling is to "demonstrate" to the audience that this is what happened, the purpose of argument over possible and proffered interpretations is to persuade the audience that this is what the happening means in the circumstance. And if compared to argument, story can seek to persuade only with considerable circumspection, it can also do so with greater license about what meaning should be given to the facts as found.

While storytelling and argument together provide a complementary means for participating in an audience's meaning-making process, our deployment of these two forms of persuasion sounds very much like hypocrisy. And it may be. What one claims are the facts in and through a story is never an unbiased report of the world; what one explicitly argues the facts mean is not always all that (or actually what) one intends the audience to understand as the real meaning. Yet in some ways hypocrisy is necessary to civilized life. In describing civilization as the result of sublimating our basic drives, perhaps Freud underestimated the affirmative need for order, stability, shared meaning, and convention. Even if all we consider true or real is a fabrication, we have to believe that some story reports the world as it is in order to take the next step. And even if stories do more arguing than we openly admit and appeal to values that we deny—at least insofar as we do not allow explicit arguments to invoke them—it may be that these conventions are necessary to accommodate our individual and collective needs. Through argument we affirm conventionally acceptable and often aspirational values, and we establish broad social norms that operate over time. We often wish to endorse values that we cannot live up to because we think they are necessary as ideals for a civilized society. To live communally, we all need to know what is legitimate behavior.

At the same time, we perceive the need to make room for communities within communities, for exceptional responsibilities and needs, and for the evolution of conventionally acceptable values. Perhaps we also sense the need to hear and to remind ourselves that, whatever our aspirations, we have continuing human wants and fears and angers. Through stories we acknowledge human variety and weakness. If arguments speak to and about the rational person, stories speak to and about the whole (emotional, irrational, mystical, needing, loving, hating, and rational) person. We use both stories and arguments as we do because we need them. If our conventional deployment of story and argument in remedy-seeking ceremonies is often beguiling, that may be necessary if a civilized culture is to make room for our need to idealize and to be. In short, we pretend because we must.

And at some level we recognize our pretense. There is widespread evidence of a general appreciation for the distinct yet complementary functions of story and argument. In day-to-day living, many of us seem able to recognize that how and in what form one argues about what the facts are often diverges from how and in what form one argues about what the facts mean. We know that typically we must at least appear simply to be reporting the world while at the same time we are free to argue about what it all means. Many also seem to sense that the facts themselves and not some explicitly stated argument will argue best about what meaning to give to the facts as found. We may be trying to remind ourselves of these conventions when we repeat in quite different circumstances aphorisms like "less is more" and "better left unsaid."

The distinction between story and argument defines, in part, our response to certain literary genres. Greek tragedy, for example, characteristically pits the acceptable and legitimate meanings of life (those that can be talked about and debated explicitly) against those that are still taboo and illegitimate (those that by contemporary convention can be talked about and debated only through the story line). Both professional and lay storytellers play off what they know or sense to be conventionally acceptable and taboo, both in substance and in form. In turn, audiences often respond as they are expected to respond because they are aware that the storyteller is playing with the hypocrisy that, through convention, governs meaning-making in a complex civilization.

[For the author's analysis of stories about immigration, see chapters 13 and 46—*Eds.*]

NOTES

1. The knowledge structures I have labeled "stock stories" have been variously described as "scripts," "schemas," "frames," and "nuclear scenes." I make no effort to distinguish between various usages. The substantial literature about thinking in story form ranges across disciplines.

Chapter 39

Masks and Resistance

Margaret E. Montoya

For stigmatized groups, such as persons of color, the poor, women, gays, and lesbians, assuming a mask is comparable to being "on stage"—the experience of being acutely aware of one's words, affect, tone of voice, movements, and gestures because they seem out of sync with what one is feeling and thinking. At unexpected moments, we fear that we will be discovered to be someone or something other than who or what we pretend to be. Lurking just behind our carefully constructed disguises and lodged within us is the child whom no one would have mistaken for being anything other than what she was. Her masking was yet imperfect, still in rehearsal, and at times unnecessary.

For Outsiders, being masked in the legal profession has psychological as well as ideological consequences. Not only do we perceive ourselves as being "on stage," but the experience of class-jumping—being born poor but later living on the privileged side of the economic divide as an adult—can also induce schizoid feelings. As first-year law students don their three-piece suits, they make manifest the class ascendancy implicit in legal education. Most Latinas/os in the legal profession now occupy an economic niche considerably higher than that of our parents, our relatives, and frequently our students. Our speech, clothes, cars, homes, and lifestyle emphasize this difference.

The masks we choose can impede our legal representation and advocacy by driving a wedge between self, *familia,* and community. As our economic security increases, we escape the choicelessness and lack of control over vital decisions that oppress communities of color. To remain connected to the community requires one to be Janus-faced, able to present one face to the larger society and another among ourselves. Janus-faced not in the conventional meaning of being deceitful, but in the sense of having two faces simultaneously. One face is the adult one that allows us to make our way through the labyrinth of the dominant culture. The other, the face of the child, is one of difference, free of artifice. This image with its dichotomized char-

From "MASCARAS, TRENZAS, Y GREÑAS: UN/MASKING THE SELF WHILE UN/BRAIDING LATINA STORIES AND LEGAL DISCOURSE." 17 HARV. WOMEN'S L.J. 185 (1994); 15 CHICANO-LATINO L. REV. 1 (1994). Originally published in the *Harvard Women's Law Journal* and the *Chicano-Latino Law Review.* Reprinted by permission.

acter fails to capture the multiplicity, fluidity, and interchangeability of faces, masks, and identities upon which we rely.

Throughout history, masking and unmasking have been used to explore the inner self—the person hiding behind the public face. These themes can be found in works produced by Euro-American males included in the traditional academic canon. Shakespeare's "All the world's a stage/And all the men and women merely players"[1] illustrates this idea. Figuring out how to present oneself in public has elements of a theatrical performance for everyone.

Latinoamericano writers also have employed mask metaphors. Octavio Paz's analysis of the Mexican psyche pertains specifically to the experience of the Mexican immigrant:

> The Mexican, whether young or old, *criollo* or *mestizo,* general or laborer or lawyer, seems to me to be a person who shuts himself away to protect himself: his face is a mask and so is his smile. In his harsh solitude, which is both barbed and courteous, everything serves him as a defense: silence and words, politeness and disdain, irony and resignation. . . . He builds a wall of indifference and remoteness between reality and himself, a wall that is no less impenetrable for being invisible. The Mexican is always remote, from the world and from other people. And also from himself.[2]

Blaming the Mexican for his remoteness, Paz shows little understanding of the mask as a strategy for resisting external subordinating forces. He concludes by urging humanity to tear off the mask, to eschew the disguise so that the naked self can find transcendence in the company of others locked in their own feelings of solitude.

The genre of contemporary Latin American poetry called public poetry eschews this concept of universality, reaching instead for solidarity and community through "a celebratory return to 'ordinary' discourse and 'ordinary' experience."[3]

The legal profession provides ample opportunity for role-playing, drama, storytelling, and posturing. Researchers have studied the use of masks and other theatrical devices among practicing lawyers and in the law school environment. Mask imagery has been used repeatedly to describe different aspects of legal education, lawyering, and law-making. Some law students are undoubtedly attracted to the profession by the opportunity to disguise themselves and have no desire or need to look for their hidden selves. Some, however, may resent the role-playing they know to be necessary to succeed in their studies and in their relations with professors and peers. Understanding how and why we mask ourselves can help provide opportunities for students to explore their public and private personalities and to give expression to their feelings.

> *Esto es el exilio*
> *Este tenerme que inventar un nombre,*
> *una figura,*
> *una voz nueva.*
> *Este tener que andar diciendo de donde soy*
> *que hago aquí.*
> *Esto es el exilio*
> *esta soledad clavándose en mi carne. . . .*

> This is exile
> this having to invent a name for myself,
> a face, a new voice.
> This having to go around saying
> where I'm from
> what I'm doing here.
> This is exile
> this solitude biting into my flesh. . . .[4]

My memories from law school begin with the first case I ever read in Criminal Law. I was assigned to seat number one in a room that held some 175 students. The case was entitled the *People of the State of California v. Josefina Chavez.*[5] It was the only case in which I remember encountering a Latina, and she was the defendant in a manslaughter prosecution. The facts, as I think back and before I have searched out the casebook, involved a young woman giving birth one night over the toilet in her mother's home without waking her child, brothers, sisters, or mother. The baby dropped into the toilet. Josefina cut the umbilical cord with a razor blade. She recovered the body of the baby, wrapped it in newspaper and hid it under the bathtub. She ran away, but later she turned herself in to her probation officer.

The legal issue was whether the baby had been born alive, for purposes of the California manslaughter statute, and was therefore subject to being killed. The class wrestled with what it meant to be alive in legal terms. Had the lungs filled with air? Had the heart pumped blood? For two days I sat mute, transfixed while the professor and the students debated the issue. Finally, on the third day, I timidly raised my hand. I heard myself blurt out: What about the other facts? What about her youth, her poverty, her fear over the pregnancy, her delivery in silence? I spoke for perhaps two minutes, and when I finished, my voice was high-pitched and anxious.

An African American student in the back of the room punctuated my comments with "Hear! Hear!" Later other students thanked me for speaking up and in other ways showed their support. I sat there after class had ended, in seat number one on day number three, wondering why it had been so hard to speak. Only later would I begin to wonder whether I would ever develop the mental acuity, the logical clarity to be able to sort out the legally relevant facts from what others deemed sociological factoids. Why did the facts relating to the girl-woman's reality go unvoiced? Why were her life, anguish, and fears rendered irrelevant? The Law demanded that I disembody Josefina, her behavior and her guilt, that I silence her reality which screamed in my head.

Perhaps my memory has played tricks with me. I decide to look for the casebook and reread the *Chavez* case. I am surprised, after years of thinking about the case, to learn that her name was Josephine and not Josefina. My memory distorted her name, exaggerating her ethnicity, her differences. The facts in the opinion are even more tragic than I remembered:

> The defendant was an unmarried woman about 21 years of age. She had previously had an illegitimate child, and at about 12:30 A.M. on March 31, 1946, she gave birth to the child here in question. She lived with her mother and sisters in a small house having two bedrooms, with a bathroom off the kitchen porch. On this night the mother slept in the

back bedroom, and the defendant occupied the front bedroom with her two sisters. She had attempted to conceal the fact of her pregnancy from her family by wearing a girdle and loose sweaters. . . .

After going to bed on the evening of March 30, she had several attacks of what she called "cramps." . . . She made a third trip [to the bathroom] about 12:30 A.M., the other members of her family being asleep. She left the doors open and no lights were turned on. As she was sitting on the toilet she "felt a little pressure on the lower bones. Then I knew the baby was going to be born." . . . She knew from her previous experience that the placenta had to be removed and so, after the baby was in the toilet "a little while," she expelled the placenta by putting pressure on her stomach. She did not notice whether the baby's head was under water, because the afterbirth fell over its head. It took two to three minutes for the placenta to come out. She then turned on the light and found a napkin and pinned it on herself. She then removed the baby from the toilet, picking it up by the feet, and cut the cord with a razor blade. She testified that the baby was limp and made no cry; that she thought it was dead; and that she made no attempt to tie the cord as she thought there was no use. She then laid the baby on the floor and proceeded to take further care of herself and clean up the room. The baby remained on the floor about fifteen minutes, after which she wrapped it in a newspaper and placed it under the bath tub to conceal it from her mother. She then returned to bed and the next day went about as usual, going to a carnival that evening. On the next day, April 1, her mother discovered the body of the infant under the bath tub.[6]

The legal issue in the case is also somewhat different from what I recall. The question presented is not only whether the baby was born alive for purposes of the California manslaughter statute, but also whether the statute required that the baby be entirely separate from its mother with the umbilical cord cut before being considered a person. The court concurred with the jury's finding that a baby in the process of being born but with the capability of living an independent life is a human being within the meaning of the homicide statutes. The appellate court affirmed the judgment of the lower court, concluding that a criminal act had been committed because of the mother's "complete failure . . . to use any of the care towards th[e] infant which was necessary for its welfare and which was naturally required of her."[7]

The appellate opinion focused on the legal personhood of the dead baby, but questions of criminal intent, mens rea, and diminished capacity thread through the case. Contextualization of the facts through the use of gender-linked and cultural information would inform our understanding of the latter legal issues. Contextual information should have been relevant to determining the criminality of her behavior. Josephine Chavez's behavior seems to have been motivated as much by complex cultural norms and values as by criminal intent.

A discussion raising questions about the gender-, class-, and ethnicity-based interpretations in the opinion, however, would have run counter to traditional legal discourse. Interjecting information about the material realities and cultural context of a poor Latina woman's life introduces taboo information into the classroom. Such information would transgress the prevalent ideological discourse. The puritanical and elitist protocol governing the classroom, especially during the 1970s, supported the notion that one's right to a seat in the law school classroom could be brought into question if one were to admit knowing about the details of pregnancies and self-abortions, or the hidden motivations of a *pachuca* (or a *chola,* a "homegirl" in today's Latino gang parlance). By overtly linking oneself to the life experiences of poor women, especially *pachucas,* one would emphasize one's differences from those who seemed to have been admitted to law school by right.

Information about the cultural context of Josephine Chavez's life would also transgress the linguistic discourse within the classroom. One would find it useful, and perhaps necessary, to use Spanish words and concepts to describe accurately and to contextualize Josephine Chavez's experience. In the 1970s, however, Spanish was still the language of Speedy Gonzales, José Jimenez, and other racist parodies. To this day, I have dozens of questions about this episode in Josephine Chavez's life. I yearn to read an appellate opinion which reflects a sensitivity to her story, told in her own words. What did it take to conceal her pregnancy from her *familia?* With whom did she share her secret? How could she have given birth with "the doors open and no lights . . . turned on?"[8] How did she do so without waking the others who were asleep? How did she brace herself as she delivered the baby into the toilet? Did she shake as she cut the umbilical cord? I long to hear Josephine Chavez's story told in what I will call Mothertalk and Latina-Daughtertalk. Mothertalk is about the blood and mess of menstruation, about the every month-ness of periods or about the fear in the pit of the stomach and the ache in the heart when there is no period. Mothertalk is about the blood and mess of pregnancy, about placentas, umbilical cords, and stitches. Mothertalk is about sex and its effects. Mothertalk helps make sense of our questions: How does one give birth in darkness and in silence? How does one clean oneself after giving birth? How does one heal oneself? Where does one hide from oneself after seeing one's dead baby in a toilet?

Latina-Daughtertalk is about feelings reflecting the deeply ingrained cultural values of Latino families: in this context, feelings of *verguenza de sexualidad* ("sexual shame"). Sexual experience comes enshrouded in sexual shame; have sex and you risk being known as *sin verguenza,* shameless. Another Latina-Daughtertalk value is *respeto a la mama y respeto a la familia.* Familias are not nuclear nor limited by blood ties; they are extended, often including foster siblings and *comadres y compadres, madrinas y padrinos* (godmothers, godfathers, and other religion-linked relatives). Josephine Chavez's need to hide her pregnancy (with her head-to-toe mask) can be explained by a concern about the legal consequences as well as by the *verguenza* within and of her familia that would accompany the discovery of the pregnancy, a pregnancy that was at once proof and reproof of her sexuality. Josephine's unwanted pregnancy would likely have been interpreted within her community and her familia and by her mother as a lack of *respeto.*

I sense that students still feel vulnerable when they reveal explicitly gendered or class-based knowledge, such as information about illicit sexuality and its effects, or personal knowledge about the lives of the poor and the subordinated. The legal academy even today affords little opportunity to use Spanish words or concepts. Students respond to their feelings of vulnerability by remaining silent about these taboo areas of knowledge.

The silence had profound consequences for me and presumably for others who identified with Josephine Chavez because she was Latina, or because she was female, or because she was poor. For me, the silence invalidated my experience. I reexperienced the longing I felt that day in Criminal Law many times. At the bottom of that longing was a desire to be recognized, a need to feel some reciprocity. As I engaged in His/Their reality, I needed to feel Him/Them engage in mine.

Embedded in Josephine Chavez's unfortunate experience are various lessons about criminal law specifically and about the law and its effects more generally. The opinion's characteristic avoidance of context and obfuscation of important class- and gender-based assumptions is equally important to the ideological socialization and doctrinal development of law students. Maintaining a silence about Chavez's ethnic and socio-economic context lends credence to the prevailing perception that there is only one relevant reality.

As a child I had painstakingly learned my bicultural act: how to be a public American while retaining what I valued as Mexican in the most private parts of my soul. My childhood mask involved my outward self: how I looked, how I sounded. By college, my mask included more subtle aspects of my personality and intellect: a polysyllabic vocabulary, years of tested academic achievement, and a nascent political philosophy wrapped up in the ideology of being Chicana. Law school, however, challenged the effectiveness of my mask and jeopardized its coherence. My mask seemed brittle and permeable. At other times, it seemed solid and opaque. My cache of cultural, linguistic and gender-linked disguises seemed inadequate; the private me was threatened with unwanted exposure. The private me was suffocating. The private me was leaking out.

I recall that my Criminal Law professor supported my comments, even though his own Socratic dialogue had neither invited such remarks nor presented Josephine Chavez as a complex person worthy of our attention. I remember that he later invited me and a small number of students for a social gathering at his home. I sensed that the invitation was a significant gesture of inclusion, that he viewed me as belonging in the same way the other students belonged and in a way that I never felt. Over time, I figured out that my interpretations of the facts in legal opinions were at odds with the prevailing discourse in the classroom, regardless of the subject matter. Much of the discussion assumed that we all shared common life experiences. I remember sitting in the last row and being called on in tax class, questioned about a case involving the liability of a father for a gift of detached and negotiable bond coupons to his son. It was clear that I was befuddled by the facts of the case. Looking at his notes on the table, the professor asked with annoyance whether I had ever seen a bond. My voice quivering, I answered that I had not. His head shot up in surprise. He focused on who I was; I waited, unmasked. He became visibly flustered as he carefully described the bond with its tear-off coupons to me. Finally, he tossed me an easy question, and I choked out the answer. [For additional discussion of the case of Josephine Chavez, see chapter 82—*Eds*.]

This was one instance of feeling publicly unmasked. In this case, it was class-based ignorance which caused my mask(s) to slip. Other students may also have lacked knowledge about bonds. Maybe other students, especially those from families with little money and certainly no trust funds, stocks or bonds, also would have felt unmasked by the questioning. But I felt isolated and different because I could be exposed in so many ways: through class, ethnicity, race, gender, and the subtleties of language, dress, make-up, voice, and accent.

For multiple and overlapping reasons I felt excluded from the experiences of others, experiences that provided them with knowledge that better equipped them, indeed privileged them, in the study of The Law, especially within the upper class domain that is Harvard. Not knowing about bonds linked the complexities of class-jumping with the fearful certainty that, in the eyes of some, and most painfully in my own/my mother's eyes, I would be seen as *grenuda*: dirty, ugly, dumb and uncombed. [See chapter 7 for further discussion of Montoya's famous hair metaphor—*Eds.*]

It was not possible for me to guard against the unexpected visibility—or, paradoxically, the invisibility—caused by class, gender, or ethnic differences that lurked in the materials we studied. Such issues were, after all, pervasive, and I was keenly sensitive to them. Sitting in the cavernous classrooms at Harvard under the stern gaze of patrician jurists was an emotionally wrenching experience. I remember the day one of the students was called on to explain *Erie v. Tompkins*. His identification of the salient facts, his articulation of the major and minor issues, and his synopsis of the Court's reasoning were so precise and concise that it left a hush in the room. He had already achieved and was able to model for the rest of us the objectivity, clarity, and mental acuity that we/I aspired to.

The respect shown for this type of analysis was qualitatively different from that shown for contextual or cultural analysis. Such occurrences in the classroom were memorable because they were defining: rational objectivity trumped emotional subjectivity. What They had to say trumped what I wanted to say but didn't. I have no memory of ever speaking out again to explain facts from my perspective as I had done that one day in Criminal Law. There was to be only one Latina in any of my cases, only one Josephine. While I was at Harvard, my voice was not heard again in the classroom examining, exploring, or explaining the life situations of either defendants or victims. Silence accommodated the ideological uniformity, but also revealed the inauthenticity implicit in discursive assimilation.

I had arrived at Harvard feeling different. I understood difference to be ineluctably linked with, and limited to, race, class, and gender. The kernel of that feeling I first associated with Josephine Chavez, that scrim of silence, remains within me. It is still my experience that issues of race, ethnicity, gender, or class are invisible to most of my white and/or male colleagues. Issues of sexual orientation, able-bodiedness, and sometimes class privilege can be invisible to me. My truths require that I say unconventional things in unconventional ways.[9]

Speaking out assumes prerogative. Speaking out is an exercise of privilege. Speaking out takes practice.

Silence ensures invisibility. Silence provides protection. Silence masks.

NOTES

1. William Shakespeare, *As You Like It*, act 2, scene 7.
2. Octavio Paz, THE LABYRINTH OF SOLITUDE 29 (1961).

3. Mike Gonzalez and David Treece, THE GATHERING OF VOICES: THE TWENTIETH-CENTURY POETRY OF LATIN AMERICA xiv–xv (1992).

4. *Id.* at 345 (quoting Giaconda Belli, Gonzalez & Treece, trans.).

5. People v. Josephine Chavez, 176 P.2d 92 (CAL. APP. 1947).

6. *Id.* at 92–93.

7. *Id.* at 96.

8. *Id.* at 92.

9. Jerome M. Culp, Jr., *You Can Take Them to Water but You Can't Make Them Drink: Black Legal Scholarship and White Legal Scholars,* 4 U. ILL. L. REV. 1021 (1992). Culp illustrates the way in which Professor Patricia Williams challenges how we come to understand what is law:

> So *The Alchemy of Race and Rights* has transformed madness into knowledge and knowledge into a different way of looking at law, and that is what legal scholarship must be about—but seldom is. If white scholars are to understand some of what black scholars and people are saying, they must begin to appreciate stories that are unconventional. Only in the madness of the unconventional is it possible for truth to be found—at least a truth that includes the lives and experiences of black people.
> *Id.* at 1040–41.

Chapter 40

Mexican Americans as a Legally Cognizable Class

Richard Delgado and Vicky Palacios

Long inured to their status as "the forgotten minority,"[1] few Chicanos find it surprising that, even after a decade of intensive civil rights activity on behalf of Blacks, the status of Chicanos as a legally cognizable minority is still in doubt. Indeed, the law's failure strikes a familiar chord; almost every Chicano has experienced at some point in his life having the following reasoning applied against him: (1) Our firm (agency, school district) regards Chicanos as white; (2) we do not discriminate against whites; and (3) therefore, we do not discriminate against Chicanos. This argument rests, of course, on the premise that Chicanos are indistinguishable from members of the majority culture and race and are simply not a minority group for purpose of remedial action.

What is surprising is that in certain areas of civil rights litigation this same argument, albeit in a somewhat more sophisticated form, receives judicial approval. This chapter examines two of these areas: the status of Chicanos under equal protection doctrine and their status under Rule 23 governing class actions [as defined by the Federal Rules of Civil Procedure—*Eds.*].

Inability of Chicanos to avail themselves of "class" status severely limits the effectiveness of attempts to redress grievances through litigation. Class actions enable a single plaintiff or group of plaintiffs to sue on behalf of an entire class. This procedural device possesses the substantial advantages of economy and res judicata effect as well as considerable political and psychological impact. By the same token, access to equal protection coverage enables a plaintiff to give his complaint constitutional dimensions and thus, in certain circumstances, to secure a stricter standard of judicial review.

Are Chicanos a legally-definable class? Among the characteristics common to many Chicanos are: Spanish language as the mother tongue; Mexican ancestry; Spanish surname; a distinct culture and history; a genetic heritage that results in certain recurring physical traits; economic, educational, and political exclusion from the mainstream of American life; perception by Anglos, including many government

From "Mexican Americans as a Legally Cognizable Class under Rule 23 and the Equal Protection Clause." 50 Notre Dame Lawyer 393 (1975), Copyright © by *Notre Dame Law Review,* University of Notre Dame. Originally published in the *Notre Dame Law Review.* Reprinted by permission.

agencies, as a minority; and perception by Chicanos themselves as a non-Anglo group.

The almost mystical significance given the Spanish language as the carrier of Chicano culture has been commented upon by a number of ethnologists and other social scientists. A Chicano university professor has written:

> In the beginning was the Word, and the Word was made Flesh. It was so in the beginning, and it is so today. The language, the Word, carries within it the history, the culture, the traditions, the very life of [our] people. . . . We cannot even conceive of a people without a language, or a language without a people. The two are one and the same. To know one is to know the other.[2]

The refusal of Mexican Americans to surrender their native tongue has at times meant the forfeiture of substantial benefits. In schools, for example, bilingualism has often been suppressed, and, if not suppressed, rarely recognized as an asset. Some states require the ability to speak English as a condition of voting or holding political office. Others require that court proceedings and legal notices be in English. Chicano persistence in retaining the use of Spanish in the face of such pressures testifies to the likelihood that Spanish usage is, and will continue to be, a partial—but highly reliable—index of membership in the Chicano class.

Another characteristic held in common by Chicanos is their ancestry. The precise characterization of this ancestry, however, has been the subject of controversy. In a study on Mexican-American education, the United States Commission on Civil Rights, which used the terms "Mexican American" and "Chicano" interchangeably, declared:

> [T]he term Mexican American refers to persons who were born in Mexico and now reside in the United States or whose parents or more remote ancestors immigrated to the United States from Mexico. It also refers to persons who trace their lineage to Hispanic or Indo-Hispanic forebears who resided within Spanish or Mexican territory that is now part of the Southwestern United States.[3]

This definition suffers from overinclusiveness, since an individual of pure Scandinavian descent who was at one time a Mexican citizen but later immigrated to the United States would qualify as a Chicano. A more accurate definition of Chicanos in terms of ancestry would be "any individual residing in the United States who traces his lineage to Indo-Hispanic or Hispanic ancestors who are living or once lived in Mexico or the Southwestern United States." Such a definition excludes Mexican citizens still living in Mexico but includes those Mexican citizens who are registered aliens. The definition would also include descendants of the colonial Spaniards with little or no Indian blood who, like the Mexican alien, identify with the culture and social goals of the Mexican American. At the same time, the requirement that Hispanic forebears come from the Southwest excludes those of Spanish descent who settled on the East Coast of the United States, since they have generally been assimilated into the dominant society and rarely identify with the culture of the Mexican American.

An additional feature shared by many Chicanos is Spanish surname. The cultural fusion of the native Meso-Americans and the Spanish was such that at one time virtually all residents of the American Southwest carried Spanish surnames. But today not all Chicanos bear Spanish surnames, nor are all persons bearing Spanish surnames Chicano. Because of the practice of women taking the husband's surname, those Chicanas who have married Anglos no longer bear Spanish names. Similarly, the Spanish surname of a Chicano husband is carried by his Anglo wife, who may have little attachment to the Chicano culture. This blurring effect obviously increases as generations pass. It is nonetheless true that most Chicanos still bear Spanish surnames. This is due to the tendency of Chicanos, like most ethnic minorities, to limit social interaction to members of their own group. This ethnic closure results in a high incidence of ethnic intramarriage.

The most important of the ties which bind Chicanos is their culture. Culture has been termed the very essence of an individual's social identity. Marcos de Leon, a California educator, has characterized the function of the Chicano culture in the life of the individual member as "all encompassing." It comprises the group's ideas, habits, values, and institutions; it is the force that gives the group cohesion and direction. It supplies the system of beliefs that enables the group to establish social and political structures. Aesthetics also plays a part since culture includes the group's preferences with regard to the graphic and plastic arts, folklore, music, drama, and dance.

Culture, of course, manifests itself differently from community to community and even from individual to individual. Particularly in view of the geographic dispersion of Chicanos, it would be a mistake to assume that the existence of a common culture results in individuals who are carbon copies of each other. Nevertheless, the United States Commission on Civil Rights has found that "Mexican Americans share common traits, common values, and a common heritage which may be identified as components of a general Mexican American cultural pattern."[4] This cultural pattern, the Commission concludes, "sets them apart as a distinct and recognizable group."[5] The unwillingness of the dominant society to recognize the rich culture of the Mexican American creates a tension in the lives of many Chicanos, who see themselves as forced to choose between retaining the traditions of their people and gaining the educational and economic benefits of participation in the dominant society. Most have chosen to keep their culture. However, they have had to do so at the price of being stereotyped as backward, inferior, or, at best, quaint.

An additional feature that binds Chicanos is their physical appearance. Anthropologists Ginsberg and Laughlin have written about ethnic populations and the effect of their isolation or mixture on their genetic pools. Regardless of what other implications may follow from the existence of a distinct gene pool, it is at least clear that many Chicanos share a phenotype of physical characteristics. This commonality in phenotype bolsters the identifiability of the Chicano class. In writing of the history of the Chicano in this country, one author tells of the halt brought to the migration of Mexican laborers into this country by Depression unemployment. To alleviate the pressures created by unemployment, the Government simply deported Mexican laborers by the carload. Their legal rights ignored, thousands fell victim to a dragnet established and enforced by federal, state, and local agencies. Even Chicanos who were United States citizens were summarily deported. Merely looking

"Mexican" sufficed. "Visual identification or stereotype" was the criterion generally employed.

For centuries, Anglos have associated a combination of brown skin and certain other physical traits with people of Mexican ancestry. *Recopilación de Leyes de los Reinos de las Indias,* a 1680 compilation of nearly 200 years of law dealing with the Indians of Meso-America, expressly recognized the existence of a new "race," the mestizo of the Americas.[6] In more modern times, the United States Commission on Civil Rights has also noted the similarities in the appearance of Chicanos: "Many Mexican Americans exhibit physical characteristics of the indigenous Indian population that set them apart from typical Anglos. In fact, some Anglos have always regarded Mexican Americans as a separate racial group."[7]

In the popular mind, Mexicans have long appeared "different" from whites. One study of community attitudes toward Chicanos in Chicago in the 1940s cites a number of examples illustrating these perceptions. One resident of an Italian neighborhood, for example, was quoted as saying, "I don't want my kids to associate with the Mexicans. God made people white and black, and he meant there to be a difference."[8]

Though many of the references to the Chicano's brown color have in the past been negative, Chicanos have turned this derogatory reference into a source of pride and self-awareness, much the same way Negroes have done with the word "black." While this turnabout has done much to improve the Chicano's self-image and sensitize the Anglo to the feeling of pride Chicanos have about themselves, there remain those who equate dark skin with inferiority. So long as this negative attitude persists, physical characteristics will continue to be another source of commonality among Chicano people.

Economic and political disenfranchisement is another aspect of life shared by Chicanos. Chicanos consistently suffer from underparticipation and over-participation in various social institutions. In public education, for example, Chicanos have one of the highest dropout rates of any ethnic group. Data compiled by the United States Commission on Civil Rights show that, if present trends continue, by the year 2000 only one-half of the Chicano school population will graduate from high school.

The reasons for this educational gap are not hard to find: poverty, language handicap, migrancy, and cultural insensitivity on the part of teachers and school administrators. Even when an individual Chicano manages to escape or surmount the effect of these factors and obtains a baccalaureate or graduate degree his efforts are typically not rewarded to the same extent as the Anglo's. Because of demands within his group as well as constraints imposed by discriminatory attitudes in the larger society, success-oriented Chicanos have limited opportunities to take advantage of educational and occupational opportunities. Other studies show that minorities who attain a high level of education and enter the professions are likely to find their opinions are not as highly valued by their colleagues as are opinions of members of the dominant culture.

Mexican Americans have also endured exclusion from the American mainstream in the employment area. In the Southwest, Chicanos have an overall unemployment rate about double that of whites. Chicanos are markedly underrepresented in the more prestigious and high-paying professions and in many of the trades. That unemployment in the Chicano sector is not merely a lingering residue of bygone discrimination is shown by the disproportionately high unemployment rate among Chicano teenagers.

Regional data indicate that the poverty many Chicanos suffer is severe enough to affect their health and longevity. One Chicano community reported an infant mortality rate five to six times the national rate for white infants. In many southwestern communities, Chicanos fall victim in disproportionate numbers to diseases associated with low socioeconomic conditions.

In certain areas, however, the Chicano can claim the dubious distinction of overparticipation in American institutions. One such area is the courts and penal institutions; another, the military service. Chicano adults, in common with Blacks, form a disproportionate share of the nation's prison population, and serve longer sentences for comparable crimes. Reports of police brutality are much more frequent in barrio and ghetto neighborhoods. Chicano juveniles, like Chicano adults, fare poorly at the hands of the justice system. One New Mexico counselor testified before the Commission on Civil Rights that minor violations such as curfew offenses, stealing cantaloupes, and the like, were frequently overlooked in the case of Anglo children. When the violator was a Chicano youth, however, formal charges were frequently pressed and became part of the juvenile's official record.

Another area of Chicano overrepresentation is the military service. The Mexican-American male has been an active participant in the military; the casualty rate for Chicanos in the Vietnam war was over 50 percent higher than their proportion to the total population. This figure prompted Chicano observers to note that where government agencies have exercised diligence and sincerity in their search for minorities they have been met with success. Unlike jury commissioners and private employers, draft boards have had little difficulty finding "qualified" people. In Nueces County alone, over 75 percent of the men killed in Vietnam bore Mexican-American names.

In politics, despite a few isolated successes, the Chicano community as a whole remains largely voiceless. Most Mexican Americans are native born and they comprise the second largest minority in the nation. Yet political participation by Chicanos remains low and there are still relatively few elected officials from the Chicano sector. Among the reasons for this phenomenon are attempts by some to discourage Mexican-American voting. Chicanos in some areas have experienced such discouragement by means ranging from outright intimidation to laws which endeavor to make registration difficult.

A related indicator of class separateness is community attitudes that emphasize the ways in which a group's members are unlike members of the dominant society. Chicanos, like other minority groups, can recount a wide variety of personal experiences in which they have been the targets of prejudice. A California school principal told the Civil Rights Commission that he always seated the Chicano students behind the Anglo students at graduation ceremonies because he felt it made for a "better looking stage." A California teacher explained that she asked an Anglo boy to lead a row of Chicano youngsters to an activity because his father was a rancher and the boy needed to get used to giving orders to Mexicans. Another educator reported that she calls on Anglo children to assist Chicano children who hesitate in recitation because the "American" pupil is more likely to give a correct response and because it is good educational practice to draw out "American" children and give them a feeling of importance by having them help the "Mexicans."

The mass media have also contributed to the formation of negative stereotypes of the Chicano people. Tomás Martinez has analyzed the way in which advertisers promote racism by portraying stereotypes such as the "Frito Bandito." Television and newspaper commercials presenting "typical Mexican villages" or Mexican outlaws reinforce the belief that Mexicans are lazy, unambitious persons in need of underarm deodorant. Such commercials, Martinez suggests, are not harmless jokes or portrayals of cartoon characters. They are caricatures, whose function is to reaffirm symbolically the inferior social status of Mexicans and Mexican Americans in the eyes of the American public. In so doing, the advertisements suggest to the audience that such comical, lazy, and unkempt people want what Anglos have by virtue of their superior culture. The advertisements encourage the viewer to purchase the product because it is the duty of a member of the superior culture.[9]

The final index of the Chicano's separateness is the perception he has of himself and his people. Much of what the Chicano feels about himself can be learned from the terms he chooses to identify his cultural group. One such term which has come into use is *la Raza*. Although literally translated "the race," the phrase more properly connotes the cultural and historical ties which unite Spanish-speaking people. An early forerunner of this designation was "la Raza Cosmica," a phrase coined by the nineteenth-century philosopher Jose Vasconcelos, who believed that Mexicans would form the cosmic, ideal people because of their particular blood mixture. This theory is said to have been the Mexican response to Anglo-Nordic historians who considered the Mexicans inferior half-breeds. Meier and Rivera write of the term *la Raza* that it connotes "not racial but ethnic solidarity, and a sense of common destiny."[10] Another commentator states: "La Raza has become more than a slogan: it has become a way of life for a people who seek to fully realize their personal and group identity; and obtain equality of rights and treatment as citizens of the United States."[11] It is this sense of a common destiny which illustrates the feeling of community in the use of *la Raza*.

More and more Mexican Americans are choosing to refer to themselves as "Chicano." The word itself is said to be a shortened version of "Mexicano," pronounced perhaps at one time by the Mexican Indians as "Meh-chee-cano." This term has undergone a number of changes in meaning. Originally it was derogatory, and many older Mexican Americans still consider it pejorative and refuse to use it. Later it came into popular use among the more militant Chicanos and to some it still connotes militancy. More recently, however, "Chicano" has been used by Mexican Americans as a symbol of awareness and pride in their ethnic identity. In *Chicano Manifesto* Armando Rendon writes:

> I am a Chicano. What that means to me may be entirely different from what meaning the word has for you. To be Chicano is to find out something about one's self which has lain dormant, subverted, and nearly destroyed.[12]

Although Chicano problems are not new, Mexican-American self-awareness, so long unvoiced, is perhaps best expressed by activists in the Chicano movement. Rendon characterizes the revolt as "primarily an internal conversion," involving an expansion of the individual's personality, background, and future as the individual Chicano perceives that all Chicanos have traveled the same paths, suffered the same indignities, and undergone the same deprivation. He then realizes that while some may have adjusted and survived better than others by adopting the Anglo's ways, all are bound by "a common birthplace; a common history, learned from books or by word of mouth; and a common culture much deeper than the shallow Anglo reservoir."[13] This growing realization increases the Chicano's sense of identity and unity with other Chicanos and strengthens his desire to work for the enhancement of equal opportunity for his people in every phase of American life.

Chicanos have a word to express the kinship they feel—*carnalismo*. The closest literal translation would be "brotherhood," but *carnalismo* expresses much more. Of *pachuco*[14] origin, *carnalismo* carries with it the unique frame of reference the Chicano's history has given him.

Taken together, the class characteristics discussed thus far demonstrate that the Chicano falls outside the mainstream of American life for many purposes. He is not in any sense an "average" American. His heritage and ancestry, his present welfare and future goals are at variance with those of the dominant society. It is these variances that make the Chicano a separate and identifiable class.

NOTES

1. See, e.g., United States Commission on Civil Rights, Stranger in One's Land (1970); Cruz Reynoso, et al., *La Raza, the Law, and the Law Schools*, 1970 U. Toledo L. Rev. 809, 815–16 (1970).

2. Armando B. Rendon, Chicano Manifesto 29–30 (1971).

3. United States Commission on Civil Rights, Mexican American Education Study, Report 1: Ethnic Isolation of Mexican Americans in the Public Schools of the Southwest 7 n.1 (1971).

4. U.S. Commission on Civil Rights, Mexican American Education Study, Report 3: The Excluded Student 30 (1972).

5. *Id.*

6. Rendon, at 67.

7. The Excluded Student, at 11.

8. Rendon, at 24.

9. Tomás M. Martinez, *Advertising and Racism: The Case of the Mexican American,* in Voices: Readings from *El Grito* 48, edited by Octavio Romano-V, 1971.

10. Matt S. Meier and Feliciano Rivera, The Chicanos: A History of Mexican American Americans xix (1972).

11. United States Commission on Civil Rights, The Mexican American 69 (1968).

12. Rendon, at 319.

13. *Id.* at 113.

14. David F. Gomez, Somos Chicanos—Strangers in Our Land xii (1973).

Chapter 41

American Apocalypse

Richard Delgado

The waiter arrived with our plates. "That looks good," I said, scrutinizing my vegetables. Then Kowalsky leaned forward in his chair. "As you know, I'm an equal opportunity critic. I do have a theory, although I'd like the two of you to agree not to represent it as anything more than that. I don't want to seem too hard on some of my fellow conservatives."

Both Rodrigo and I nodded. "We'll take it in that spirit," I promised.

Kowalsky's Theory: The Upcoming Race War

Assured of our promises, Kowalsky began: "Have you ever wondered why my fellow conservatives seem bent on eliminating affirmative action? I mean, not simply cutting it back but eliminating it root and branch?"

Rodrigo and I looked at each other. "I assume out of principle," I said with a shrug.

"And to cater to their constituencies," Rodrigo added.

"I'm not so sure," Kowalsky replied. "Especially as to the latter. Many corporations that initially opposed affirmative action now support it. They find it's not so bad for business. The new workers fit right in, and the firm gains credibility in new sectors of the population. As for the principled reasons, we all know what arguments conservative theorists give for opposing it. I subscribe to some of them, as you know, although in my opinion they call for restructuring, not eliminating the program."

Rodrigo interjected: "So if it's not because of corporate pressure or killer reasons of principle, why do conservatives want to put an end to affirmative action?"

"I was thinking about this recently. In a way, affirmative action is the perfect issue for my side. It never goes away. It reliably delivers votes. And it enables people like me to point out how unprincipled you liberals are and how we are morally superior. It's easy to attack it in a thirty-second sound bite. But defending it takes forty-five

From "Rodrigo's Fourteenth Chronicle: American Apocalypse." 32 Harv. C.R.–C.L. L. Rev. 275 (1997). Originally published in the *Harvard Civil Rights–Civil Liberties Law Review*. Reprinted by permission.

minutes, while the public's eyes glaze over. It has been the perfect vote getter year after year. Yet, my fellow conservatives at think tanks, leadership institutes, and other elite circles across the land are trying to get rid of it decisively and forever. Initiatives in California and elsewhere, bills in Congress."

"And those three recent Supreme Court decisions," Rodrigo interjected.

"Right," Kowalsky replied. "Making it harder for states to redraw voting districts to increase minority representation, making it easier for school districts to end desegregation plans, and applying the higher, constitutional standard of compelling state interest to federal affirmative action programs—not to mention the Fifth Circuit decision in *Hopwood*, which bars any consideration of race in higher education admissions. All these give evidence of the same thing: the political right is prepared to destroy affirmative action once and for all."

"And you think this is more than just muscle flexing?" I asked. I was curious where the young conservative wunderkind was going.

"I do," Kowalsky continued. "Otherwise the right would opt for a series of gradual cutbacks, and not sweeping measures like California's Civil Rights Initiative. Affirmative action enables my side to argue that we are the defenders of the just and the true. It reliably inflames working class and ethnic whites, who are led to believe that blacks are getting away with something."

"Even though the levels of school drop-outs, unemployment, suicide, poverty and infant mortality for minority communities are the highest in the country and approaching those of the Third World," Rodrigo added.

"And your people still lag in undergraduate and graduate enrollment," Kowalsky went on, "as well as in middle and upper management jobs and virtually every circle that matters—except sports and entertainment. As I said, it's a perfect issue. It enables people like me to rally the troops and depict liberals as the source of unhappiness and job insecurity for blue collar whites like my family."

"And I suppose you have a theory for why your co-religionists are doing this?" I coaxed.

"I think they are gearing up for a race war," Kowalsky said quietly. "It's not a conspiracy, exactly. Rather, it's the product of a general sense that it's time to pick a fight. Caucasians will cease being a majority in this country about midway through the next century. At that point, political and voting power should logically shift to groups of color: African Americans, Asians, and Latinos. White opinionmakers don't want this to happen. So, they're gearing up for a fight. It's one of the oldest tricks in the world: provoke your enemy until he responds, then slap him down decisively. You get to impose your regime and sleep well at night too because you can maintain that it was all his fault."

"So, right-wingers are trying to increase minority misery to the point where we react, to the point where violence breaks out?" I asked incredulously.

"Yes, like the sixties. Only this time, it will be different. The rebellion will be put down just as before. But this time, instead of enacting sympathetic measures, like the Civil Rights Act of 1964, to ameliorate poverty and redress racial injustice, society will put in place repressive acts increasing police surveillance, criminalizing sedition, and establishing martial law. We will then sail into the next century secure. White political and economic power will be assured by a host of new laws and executive orders resembling those of South Africa under the apartheid regime. The new redistricting decision is just the first of many such rulings that will prevent blacks and Latinos from ever obtaining political power. And gatherings, organizing, and street marches will be ruthlessly suppressed. The U.S. will have a system of apartheid, in effect, with whites wielding power over a large but increasingly powerless black and brown population of laborers and domestics."

"And the idea is to provoke this confrontation before it is too late?" Rodrigo leaned forward, his expression serious.

"Yes, it would need to be done fairly soon, before power passes peacefully," Kowalsky replied. "That's why you see everything we were talking about earlier: welfare cutbacks calculated to increase misery in communities of color, voting rights retrenchment, and withdrawal of scholarships that enable future leaders of color to get a college education. We also see attacks on 'big government,' which is seen as an employer and defender of minorities, denials that the recent wave of black church burning means anything, and most of all, the elimination of affirmative action."

"I thought you didn't like big government," Rodrigo interjected.

"I don't," Kowalsky replied. "But good and bad reasons argue against it. Some of my friends on the right oppose it because they see the federal government as having a black face. That's despicable and wrong."

We were silent for a moment. Then Rodrigo said, "I used to think all we had to do was wait, that demography would produce a peaceful change of power sooner or later. You've given me pause."

"A great convulsion, in which whites decisively put down a black and brown insurrection, would be exactly what's needed," Kowalsky said. "And one doesn't need conspiracy theories to understand the host of anti-minority and anti-poor measures that are coming into play right now. Whites have simply decided enough is enough: it's time to take a stand. If millions across the country, as well as conservative elites at dozens of think tanks and institutes, have the same sense—that it's our turn—it produces the same result: everyone agrees tacitly that something must be done. And so the product is a coordinated campaign. It may already have started in California, our most ethnically diverse state."

"Laz," I burst out. "I used to think leftists were paranoid, always afraid the government was spying on their meetings, compiling dossiers on them, and so on. Of course, some of that turned out to be true. But this idea of yours goes further than anything I've heard. For one thing, our legal system and Constitution would never stand for it. We have the Bill of Rights, the Fourteenth Amendment."

"All of which can be overridden by a compelling state interest, as you well know, Professor," Laz replied levelly. "Do you have any doubt the current Supreme Court would find one if civil unrest broke out in every major city across the nation?"

"*Korematsu* could serve as a precedent," Rodrigo pointed out. "The Court could hold that emergency measures like curfews, surveillance, wiretaps, sweeps, and even preventive detention of leaders of color are justified. We baited the Indians at Wounded Knee until they responded. Then we wiped them out. Unfortunately, more historical precedent supports Laz's grim scenario than any of us would like."

"Our Latino friends could cite the zoot suit riots in the 1940s, when America went through a wave of anti-immigrant, nativist sentiment," Laz added. "Roving gangs of Anglo sailors started the riots. When Latinos responded, we threw them into jail, charging them with breaching the peace and provoking civil disorder. Congress instituted Operation Wetback, in which tens of thousands of Mexican Americans, many of them legal immigrants or even citizens, were rounded up and deported to Mexico."

"For the first time, a religious theory is being put forward for white supremacy," Rodrigo interjected. "It combines with the pseudoscientific one espoused by books like *The Bell Curve* to produce a mentality among whites that they are entitled to remain on top no matter what the population statistics show. Consider all the interest in our own Civil War, for example. PBS recently pioneered a series on the subject. New books are coming out, including some excellent ones by Shelby Foote. Why else such a revival of interest if people were not starting to think, at least on an unconscious level, that a new war is coming up?"

"Recent books about the civil rights revolution do the same thing," Rodrigo replied. "Jack Greenberg's otherwise fine book, for example, emphasizes the role of whites in charting the course of the desegregation campaign. 'Look how much whites have sacrificed for blacks,' these books seem to say. This way of presenting history legitimizes white anger now. Blacks are depicted as ingrates who don't appreciate all that good white liberals have done for them. This enables them, as well as the Democratic Party, to look the other way, or even join in the opposition to minority gains. During the period just before the Civil War broke out, the South drafted local boys and armed them. That's how they got an army. The near future could witness much the same thing."

Kowalsky added, "We are seeing the beginnings of that now in the militia movement. Private groups are buying high-tech weapons, training in the woods, developing their own ideology and leadership structure. They keep in touch by e-mail, newsletters, and conventions. They interpret every move by the civil rights community as an attack on them and their values. That's the advantage of an ideology that demonizes the other side. If you decide at the outset that X is an enemy, you begin to interpret X's every action as justifying your visiting violence on him. That's the lesson of Chief Sitting Bull and Wounded Knee. It's also that of the Japanese internment cases, which held, based on the slenderest evidence, that the mere existence of Japanese citizens living peaceably on the West Coast threatened national security. You try your best to provoke the other side into responding. When they don't, you simply declare that milder and milder actions on their part are provocations. Eventually their mere existence is an outrage that cannot be ignored, as with the Japanese."

"That may have been true historically," I conceded. "But do you really think it could happen today? Your theory, Laz, may be a useful interpretive approach to understanding what is going on—all the goading and stiffening of the spine. Many whites are uneasy and spoiling for a fight. As a psychological hypothesis to explain all the muscle-flexing and general ugliness, what you say makes much sense. Threatened people do often look to pick a fight, to re-establish who's boss. But surely you can't think we are preparing literally for a race war, can you?"

"Only time will tell," Laz replied. "Consider what happened in the Ruby Ridge standoff in Idaho. Federal officials provoked the family until they reacted, and then they shot Randy Weaver's wife. Of course, in that case the shoe was on the other foot. But conservatives learned their lesson all too well. As your Huey Newton once said, 'It's not paranoia if they really are out to get you.' Hate crimes are increasing, as are incidents of campus racism and hate speech. Every major city reports Rodney King type incidents in which white police beat men of color to death. African-American columnist Carl Rowan recently described how white racism operates inside many political departments, including the elite federal Alcohol, Tobacco, and Firearms agency, which recently held a 'Good Ol' Boys Roundup' in the Tennessee mountains, featuring T-shirts with Dr. Martin Luther King's face behind a target and O. J. Simpson in a noose.[1] Another showed white cops arresting a black, sprawled across a police car, under the heading 'Boys on the Hood.' A lawsuit featured evidence that ATF agents frequently used the word 'nigger' and placed Ku Klux Klan cards and other paraphernalia prominently in the offices of black agents.[2] Recent stories even suggest that the CIA may have played a role in starting the crack epidemic that has devastated black neighborhoods. I'm afraid that my theory may literally come true, at a broad national level. You mentioned earlier, Professor, that our institutions, the law and the police, might serve as a bulwark against white supremacist repression. I'm afraid they may prove to be among the most enthusiastic supporters."

Rodrigo interjected: "To summarize your point then, Laz, it's not just wild-eyed patriots and supremacists who are talking about holding the line, preserving America as a white society, and resisting the changes that would otherwise set in when the numbers of browns and blacks exceed those of whites. The cruder elements are arming, while conservative churches are preaching a return to early values with thinly veiled references to race. Thus, they are laying the theological basis for a race war. Conservatives across the board are taunting blacks and liberals, calling us balkanizers, tribalists, and barbarians. They are dismantling affirmative action and ethnic studies departments, while cutting programs of critical importance to the inner city poor. It does look like a coordinated effort to prod blacks, to provoke us into lashing back so that society can respond with armed force."

"Don't forget that legal and constitutional change will accompany the armed suppression," Laz added. "Constitutional amendments and new laws will assure that there cannot be a second uprising, ever. We may have already seen the beginning of this in bills authorizing new prisons and expanding the number of new police officers, reviving the death penalty, and providing mandatory sentences for crimes associated with the underclass of color. I hate crime, as you know, and think these measures are not a bad idea. But they're aimed just at blacks, something any self-respecting conservative should detest. English-only laws and ruthless immigration measures make things hard for Latinos and Asians. Congress is even considering abolishing citizenship for the children of undocumented immigrants. The thinly veiled purpose of the amendment is to keep America white."

After a pause, Laz continued: "You see, I said I was an equal opportunity critic. I support much of what my fellow conservatives say and do, but not this. I felt an obligation to tell the two of you. I still believe in neutral principles, in rewarding hard work and treating all persons with similar respect. Everyone deserves the right to be treated as an individual and to have his or her fundamental humanity respected. But I'm alarmed at some of the steps my fellow conservatives are taking. There are better ways to return America to its individualist roots than to goad already suffering populations, until recently mired in segregation and Jim Crow laws, into what will prove to be a bloody and decisive defeat."

All three of us sat silently for a moment in the now nearly deserted restaurant. Then I asked a question that had been on my mind for some time: "And what about Latinos, Laz? If you don't mind my saying so, you've been speaking in generalizations so far. I may agree with your basic premise that something frightening is in store and that this is the reason for all the pushing and shoving and goading going on right now. But you have been speaking in terms of 'people of color,' 'minorities,' and 'the poor community' as though they were all one. Somehow, I feel that Latinos are different. Don't you?"

In Which Laz Refines His Thesis and Rodrigo Explains the Role Latinos May Play in the Conservative Backlash to Come

"I'm not sure," Laz replied. "I haven't known many Latinos, except for Rodrigo, who I gather is half one. I grew up in an eastern city in a tenement district full of Poles and Croatians. Rodrigo, what do you think?"

Rodrigo smiled. "The Professor asks a good question. It reminds us we must always guard against the danger of essentialism and assuming that all minorities are the same. I'm part Latin, as you know, so ever since I returned here I've been following the fortunes of Chicanos, Puerto Ricans, Central Americans, and other Latino groups. Their relationship to the broader civil rights struggle, and to blacks, is complex."

"It certainly is," I agreed. "Sometimes Latinos and blacks are at each other's throats. Other times they work together to challenge oppressive measures that threaten them both, such as the backlash against affirmative action. How do you think all this bears on the racial troubles Laz thinks elite groups are trying to stir up?"

Rodrigo glanced at his friend. "I asked Laz the other day where he stood on the right-wing positions on immigration, bilingual teaching, and English-only. He said he disagreed vehemently with his fellow conservatives on immigration—you know his family immigrated from an East European country with little money—and did not feel strongly on the other two. He said it's certainly in the interest of new immigrants to learn English as quickly as possible, but he didn't think forcing them to do so made sense. Instead we should be offering them help to do something most of them are highly motivated to do anyway. And he disagreed vehemently with California governor Pete Wilson's suggestion during the Proposition 187 campaign that all Californians be required to carry identity cards and to produce them on official demand, particularly when they are seeking a job, entering school, or requesting non-emergency health care. I'm not putting words in your mouth, Laz, I hope?"

"Rodrigo's got it right," Laz said. "I'm certainly not an expert on Latinos, but there is something peculiar about the conservative position regarding them. It's similar to the one they are taking with respect to blacks—increasing their misery, hounding them, taking away things they hold dear. But there's also a different note, a sort of background noise emanating from right wing think tanks and leadership groups. It's an interference almost, and it's different. Latinos in some respects remind me of the 'coloreds' in South Africa. Not a very exalted position, I concede, but let me throw the idea out for discussion."

We were silent for a moment, absorbing what Laz had said.

"It's a devastating metaphor," I said. "My heart sank when you said it. As you know, in the old South African regime, the 'coloreds'—Indian and Chinese immigrants and other non-black national origin groups—served as overseers and clerks in the oppressive regime of apartheid. They were treated a little better than blacks but not afforded the full status of whites. Do you think this is what's in store for our Latino friends in the bleak racial future you foresee?"

"It could be," Rodrigo said. "For one thing, it would account for the recent phenomenon of right-wing Chicanos and Latinos we're seeing."

"I assume you mean people like Linda Chavez, Richard Rodriguez, and Kevin Tebedo."

"Them and many others," Rodrigo replied. "It would explain why certain issues are coming to the forefront right now, why it seems that Latinos are going to be next on the hot seat. We're next because our high birth rate and the relative ease of illegal immigration mean that our numbers will begin to exceed those of blacks by early in the next century. If the political right can split Latinos off from blacks, this will be a big coup. Otherwise, the combined numbers of people of color would soon make a formidable force."

"Please don't take this the wrong way, Rodrigo," I said. "I know you identify with your Latin roots. But why would society have anything to fear from Latinos? By and large your people have been a quiet, hardworking, peaceable group. Chicano activism, for example, has taken mainly the form of an occasional high school walkout or a gathering of farm workers standing outside supermarkets urging shoppers not to buy grapes. Hardly at the level of the Black Panthers, Louis Farrakhan, and urban riots—things that strike fear at the heart of white power elites."

"It's true, Professor," Rodrigo conceded. "We've not seen the same level of militancy you've seen with blacks. But the potential is always there. Latinos have become increasingly restless and willing to fight back. There are more Latino leaders, professors, and lawyers—intellectuals who could lead an upsurge of activism in concert with blacks. In our own field, Professor, a new organization, the 'Lat-Crits,' has recently sprung up, applying the powerful insights of Critical Race Theory to the situation and problems of Latinos. They are analyzing structures such as the black-white binary, the civil polity model of immigration law, and the legal bases for challenging English-only and English preference rules. They are urging solidarity and even nationalism within and among the various Latino communities. If a race war comes and Latinos stand shoulder to shoulder with blacks, the whole thing could take longer and be bloodier than if only blacks and a few sympathizers had to be put down. If Latinos can be cowed into submission or better yet, bought off beforehand, so much the better for whites."

"That all seems plausible. But do you really think that conservatives are reacting merely to the potential for Latino resistance?"

"Well, there could be another reason. Have you read about the conservative fixation, bordering on obsession, with Latin America?"

I must have looked blank, for Rodrigo continued: "In the mid-1980s a number of young conservatives did tours of duty in Latin America. Many of them came away convinced that the region had a frightening potential for social unrest."

"Funniest thing," I said ironically. "Many of those countries are controlled by vicious military regimes in concert with a few immensely wealthy families. The gap between the wealthy and the poor is even greater than it is here."

"Some conservatives warned that unrest and disruption could break out in that region, causing hordes of brown-skinned refugees to pour across our borders. They feared that socialist regimes like Cuba might emerge throughout that region and that local Chicanos and Central Americans might join forces with their south-of-the-border compatriots, opening a sort of second front here. In his Witan memo, John Tanton also warned of our rapid breeding rate. 'Perhaps this is the first time,' he queries, 'in which those with their pants up are going to get caught by those with their pants down?'"[3]

"Distasteful," Laz said with a grimace. "No wonder he was drummed out of certain mainline conservative organizations."

"Others, however, welcomed him back," Rodrigo pointed out. "It could be this fear of Latin America that drives part of the current crackdown on an otherwise peaceful group."

"The carrot and the stick," I said. "Another old strategy."

"Exactly," Rodrigo said. "English-only laws and referenda like California's Proposition 187 tell Latinos that they must not make trouble, that their role is to blend in as soon as possible."

"To assimilate, in other words," I said.

"Right. To learn English, live in white neighborhoods, join the consumerist culture. And, in contrast to blacks, assimilation is an option with many Latinos. Compared to blacks, we have a high rate of intermarriage. And many of us look white."

"Or at least not black," I said.

"Something in between. The idea is to coerce Latinos to go the one way and not the other, to identify with the white overlords and not the black resistance. Many of us are that way already; we try to be suave and ingratiating, like Ricardo Montalban."

"Now I see the parallel Laz was drawing to the class system in South Africa. The idea is to punish Latinos for not fitting in and reward them when they go along with the dominant group. They then can be allowed to hold certain jobs and serve as buffers between the white overlords and the black underclass."

"Do you suppose this accounts for the many conservatives in prominent positions who are adopting Hispanic children?" Rodrigo asked.

"It could," I replied. "They may be modeling, consciously or not, assimilationist behavior. They are saying, if you behave, I'll take you in. They would never adopt a black kid. But they desperately don't want Latinos opening a second front right now, at least not until they've taken care of business with the blacks."

"Tension is running high right now between Latinos and blacks," Rodrigo mused. "A recent colloquy in a national magazine featured leading Latino theorist Jorge Klor de Alva discussing black-brown tensions with African American studies professor Cornel West.[4] Could it be that on some level the two groups realize the roles elite groups have in mind for them?"

"Maybe that's what Laz called 'background noise,'" I ventured, "something that goes on just outside consciousness, an unstated realization of trouble brewing ahead."

Later, my mind kept returning to my lunchtime conversation and my companions' interpretations of a wide spectrum of events, actors, organizations, and writers on the right. What role would Latinos, the other major group of color, play in the years ahead? Would they opt for the demeaning status of functionaries and white wanna-bes that Rodrigo had warned might be in store for them? I sincerely hoped not: a people with a great tradition deserved better. Perhaps the cultural distaste for the *pocho*[5] and the ingrained pride and attachment many Latinos feel for their culture would protect against the fate that Rodrigo had warned against. I recalled how even liberal social workers attempted to create Mexicans as a "problem" group requiring help after the United States closed its doors to immigrants, threatening unemployment in the Americanization industry. The number of master's theses proliferated, and social workers began specializing in this new problem group in an effort to teach them American ways of speaking, cooking, and dressing, when they had perfectly good recipes and family structure of their own. Then, Latinos had resisted pressures to acculturate. Would they do so again?

NOTES

1. See Carl Rowan, *Law Enforcement Needs to Clean Up Its Act,* DENV. POST, July 18, 1995, at B7; *Senate Panel to Investigate ATF Picnic,* WASH. POST, July 15, 1995, at A13.

2. Id.

3. Jean Stefancic and Richard Delgado, NO MERCY: HOW CONSERVATIVE THINK TANKS AND FOUNDATIONS CHANGED AMERICA'S SOCIAL AGENDA 11 (1996).

4. See *Our Next Race Question: The Uneasiness between Blacks and Latinos,* HARPERS, Apr. 1996, at 55.

5. *Pocho* is a slang term for an individual of Mexican extraction who does not speak Spanish and has lost touch with his or her roots.

From the Editors
Issues and Comments

What stories do you have to tell? Do you have trouble getting people to believe the true accounts you give of what happens to you?

In what ways do you use stories to persuade?

If you are not Latino, how do your stories differ from the ones you would tell if you were?

If you are a member of an outsider group, such as Mexican American or Puerto Rican, what stories does the group tell about itself that let you know you are a member?

In what ways do Montoya's, Rodrigo's, Laz's, and Olivas's stories surprise you or cause you to disagree? Which do you identify with and why?

If you are a member of an outsider group, do you think you will reach more people if you tell counterstories or wear the "mask" of the dominant group—that is, use the forms of storytelling that people are used to hearing?

Do you prefer to hear stories that are familiar—that use plots, events, characters, and themes like those you meet every day? Or do you prefer stories that are unfamiliar or unusual?

Do counterstories take a very long time to register and be accepted? If so, why?

Do you agree with Derrick Bell's space-traders allegory? Does Michael Olivas prove that something similar happened to Latinos at several points in their history?

Have you ever had the impression that members of a different racial group simply could not hear a certain kind of story? If so, which stories and which groups?

Do you agree with Laz that antiminority forces would like to provoke a violent reaction, which can then be put down with force?

Suggested Readings

Baron, Jane B. "Resistance to Stories." 67 *Southern California Law Review* 255 (1994).

Bracamonte, José A. "Foreword: Minority Critiques of the Critical Legal Studies Movement." 22 *Harvard Civil Rights–Civil Liberties Law Review* 297 (1987).

———. "The National Labor Relations Act and Undocumented Workers: The De-Alienation of American Labor." 21 *San Diego Law Review* 29 (1983).

Colloquium: "LatCrit Theory: Naming and Launching a New Discourse of Critical Legal Scholarship." 2 *Harvard Latino Law Review* 1 (1997).

Delgado, Richard. "Brewer's Plea: Critical Thoughts on Common Cause." 44 *Vanderbilt Law Review* 1 (1991).

———. "The Ethereal Scholar: Does Critical Legal Studies Have What Minorities Want?" 22 *Harvard Civil Rights–Civil Liberties Law Review* 301 (1987).

———. "The Imperial Scholar: Reflections on a Review of Civil Rights Literature." 132 *University of Pennsylvania Law Review* 561 (1984).

———. "The Imperial Scholar Revisited: How to Marginalize Outsider Writing, Ten Years Later." 140 *University of Pennsylvania Law Review* 1349 (1992).

———. "When a Story Is Just a Story: Does Voice Really Matter?" 76 *Virginia Law Review* 95 (1990).

———. "Words That Wound: A Tort Action for Racial Insults, Epithets, and Name-Calling." 17 *Harvard Civil Rights–Civil Liberties Law Review* 133 (1982).

Espinoza, Leslie G. "Masks and Other Disguises: Exposing Legal Academia." 103 *Harvard Law Review* 1878 (1990).

Farber, Daniel A., and Suzanna Sherry. "Telling Stories out of School: An Essay on Legal Narratives." 45 *Stanford Law Review* 807 (1993).

Gonzalez, Rodolfo "Corky." *I Am Joaquin. Yo Soy Joaquin.* Toronto: Bantam Books, 1972.

Greenfield, Gary A., and Don B. Kates, Jr. "Mexican Americans, Racial Discrimination, and the Civil Rights Act of 1866." 63 *California Law Review* 662 (1975).

Kennedy, Randall L. "Racial Critiques of Legal Academia." 102 *Harvard Law Review* 1745 (1989).

Moran, Rachel F. "Bilingual Education as a Status Conflict." 75 *California Law Review* 321 (1987).

Rangel, Jorge C., and Carlos M. Alcala. "Project Report: De Jure Segregation of Chicanos in Texas Schools." 7 *Harvard Civil Rights–Civil Liberties Law Review* 307 (1972).

Rendon, Armando B. *Chicano Manifesto.* New York: Collier Books, 1972.

Romero, Leo, Richard Delgado, and Cruz Reynoso. "The Legal Education of Chicano Students: A Study in Mutual Accommodation and Cultural Conflict." 5 *New Mexico Law Review* 177 (1975).

Salinas, Guadalupe. "Mexican-Americans and the Desegregation of Schools in the Southwest." 8 *Houston Law Review* 929 (1971).

San Miguel, Guadalupe. *"Let All of Them Take Heed": Mexican Americans and the Campaign for Educational Equality in Texas, 1910–1981.* Austin: University of Texas Press, 1987.

Rebellious Lawyering and Resistance Strategies

We Fight Back

Latinos have not always passively accepted their fates described in Parts IV and V. Lawyers, scholars, artists, and citizen activists have fought back, demanding fair, nonracist treatment at the hands of the authorities and of fellow citizens. The chapters in Part VI describe some of those strategies and the lives of some notable rebels, including lawyers who broke the law "on principle."

Chapter 42

The Idea of a Constitution in the Chicano Tradition

Gerald P. López

I have lived and worked in various cities and on both coasts. But in some ways (and perhaps even against my will) L.A. is still home—the place where I was born and raised, and the place where my mother, sister, brother, and most of my extended family still live. What I now think about the world around me, not surprisingly, first came to life in the Chicano part of this city, East L.A. In my early East L.A. days, religion meant Catholic, fantasy meant cruising in your own car, glamour meant an ethnicized variation in some Hollywood theme, and fish meant Friday. No less important for a sports-crazy boy, baseball meant Koufax, and basketball meant Baylor and West and, yes, wanting desperately to beat the Celtics for the world championship. I've grown some since those days and changed my mind some too about these and other dimensions of life—except of course about the moral importance of beating the Celtics. But for me, as for you, it remains true that we cannot separate who we are from what we try to understand.

Two memories frame what a constitution meant for me in the tradition of East L.A. life. In one, I am four years old and in a car with my father and mother, canvassing the streets of East L.A., posting flyers on telephone poles. The flyers, in Spanish and English, urge everyone to vote for our candidate in an upcoming election. Like most Chicanos then and now, my parents were Democrats; the candidate was a Republican, the only one I was ever to see my family support. Even at four having to tell the world that "our candidate is a Republican" felt oxymoronic. But with his extraordinary directness, my father explained this switch in allegiance: he told me simply that the candidate would fight—fight both for what Chicanos were and for what we wanted.

In the other memory, I am with my family and thousands of other Chicanos in a park in East L.A. Fireworks, music, speeches, *gritos,* costumes, food and drink abound. Somehow these rituals, in all their ornamental and hyperbolic detail, expressed for me even at nine the collective pride I had come to anticipate and to savor on these patriotic occasions. After all, we were celebrating Cinco de Mayo in the

From "The Idea of a Constitution in the Chicano Tradition." 37 J. Legal Educ. 162 (1987). Originally published in the *Journal of Legal Education.* Reprinted by permission.

park that day, and in remembering Mexico's small military victory over the French at Puebla, we were observing a moment that had come to signify something spiritually constitutive in the history of our people. My mom and dad even took time off from work—the highest tribute.

These memories obliquely yet accurately portray the idea of a constitution, not only in my early East L.A. days but, I think, in the Chicano tradition of living in this country. My father's reason, his *constitutional* reason, for backing a Republican candidate echoed a more general understanding in our community. Constitutions result from fighting. They establish social arrangements that express both in their original detail and in their ongoing adjustments what fighting continues to be about—not just in elections but in day-to-day living.

If ever you doubt this fighting, take a look through my eyes at the wear and tear on people like my relatives and friends here in East L.A., the homely heroes we Chicanos celebrate in our stories, ballads, and murals. Some of these people have been here for generations, anchored in our habits and ideas, learning from and teaching their grandparents and parents, their children and grandchildren what it means to be self-reliant as a people. Others only recently have arrived, undocumented and "unwanted," except of course to bus our tables, stitch together our clothes, harvest our food, clean our bathrooms, and care for our children. Old-timers and newcomers alike survive only to the extent that they quickly learn to temper the daily fighting with considerable self-irony. Laughter helps counter the fury, desperation, and resignation induced by so many events and so many people. As a largely poor and subordinated people, Chicanos have inevitably struggled against the faults and limits of existing arrangements and thinking, faults and limits reluctantly engraved in constitutions. In this important sense, Chicano tradition in this country—our relationship to work, love, laughter, and to other people—necessarily unites self-realization and transformation.

Yet as important as transforming these arrangements was and is in the Chicano tradition, the Constitution itself had no particularly privileged place in our life in East L.A. or, for that matter, in the Chicano tradition generally. We did celebrate the Fourth of July as well as Cinco de Mayo; the celebrations were not in any crude sense rival observances. But the Cinco somehow expressed who we were, whereas the Fourth and its symbolic siblings, the flag and the Constitution, somehow all heralded the tradition of those with whom we regularly fought. Indeed, the language of the Constitution, particularly then and even now, does not readily afford an explanation for what seem to be the daily realities in Chicano life. To that extent our experience and the Constitution daily marginalize one another, sometimes threaten entirely to abandon each other.

In order literally to survive (to live *in* our history and *through* our practices), we Chicanos in East L.A. and elsewhere nurtured a separate tradition, parallel to the "grand tradition" of constitutional life in this country. For years most of us lived this non-converging tradition, as did our ancestors, only vaguely aware of the resistance it offered to what others would have us become. Over the past three decades, however, living this tradition has itself become a deliberate strategy in our efforts to define, *constitutionally*, what one can most importantly do with one's life. We now acutely appreciate that our tradition, like every other, necessarily represents one argument in the national and historical debate about the meaning of "American destiny."

In Chicano tradition the idea of a constitution differs at its roots from what a constitution means to most people, particularly the fortunate. In the grand tradition most believe that through a constitution we can lift our public life above the fallen and compromised realm of factional politics. Like all faiths, this idea of a constitution embraces rival interpretive dogmas. Living within the grand tradition are strict textualists and loose supplementers, proponents and opponents of judicial activism, those who believe in the structural rebellion expressed through this nation's two reconstructions and those who are skeptical of it. But all engaged in this ideological debate remain within the grand tradition insofar as they share the belief that, at our best and as a people, we can, through a constitution, somehow transcend conflict and heal by rising above our nature.

For all that may be honorable in this grand idea of a constitution, it contradicts Chicano experience in this country. Constitutions have been prominent in our life not for their healing but primarily for the injuries they have permitted and inflicted—in the workplace, on the streets, in the home, and in the minds and hearts of many a struggling and bewildered Chicano. And, if anything, factional politics become more prominent when the stakes get higher, as they frequently do whenever a constitution enters any political conversation. In our experience, constitutional interpretations and constitutional decisions reflect the provisional containment of fighting, not its transcendence. As Chicanos see it, through a constitution we in this country publicly announce that "for the moment, there's no battle here," not always confident the words will create, much less reflect, the reality.

Whatever world Madison presupposed in condemning factions as corruptions of a unified, public-spirited citizenry, today's national community aspires to a simple unity by regularly requiring non-converging traditions like our own to betray themselves. Chicanos know well the not-so-subliminal refrain: Vacate your history, your culture, your relationship to work, love, and others, and join with us as one in America's constitutional tradition. We even hear again these days, not always indirectly, that to be fully public-spirited we would have to change the very way we talk. Most Chicanos, after all, express their experience of the constitution in terms other than doctrinal, and often even in terms other than popular newsspeak or civics-babble. In this sense, we participate in the traditional national faith only inarticulately, through accounts that many find uneducated and confused and treat as somehow not quite part of constitutional discourse. In the eyes of the grand tradition, Chicano accounts of constitutional experiences and ideas somehow lack the "larger-than-life" quality, the "more-all-embracing-than-factional" spirit that distinguishes constitutional talk worth having—in scholarly journals, in the Supreme Court, and in New England town meetings.

Yet that very same talk others find constitutionally inarticulate ironically confirms, if only partially, why living in their own non-converging tradition offers Chicanos more than just a comforting familiarity. For those of us in the Chicano tradition, reminding ourselves through our daily language that we are not somehow "larger than life" through a constitution can be emancipating. We fight about a life constitutionally worth leading, and we know it. We fight with you and among ourselves, in our kitchens and in the fields, and in the formal constitutional battles we are increasingly entering. Chicanos live a dramatic, and often heated, conversation about things that matter, mundane and monumental. Our tradition embodies the continuity of our conflicts, and draws on their wisdom even as we continue to move against things as they are. At our best, we express in our practices an idea of a constitution at once far more aggressively skeptical and far more romantic than the grand tradition accommodates: we refuse to accept that you need believe in transcendence or else give up entirely.

Of course, we are not always at our best. We can and have been corrupted both by the desire to make our struggle disappear and by the promise that "Americanizing" ourselves will make us feel more a part of this country. We recognize that both the desire and the promise are retreats: life holds more than leaving behind your poor past, becoming successful "on your own," expressing yourself freely, and secretly yearning for a utopian world, free of conflict and power. Yet recognizing these venerable retreats does not always mean avoiding them. They live in each of us, as in each of you, offering themselves as "honorable" and "practical" alternatives to a life fully lived in our own tradition. If, as a people, Chicanos manage generally not to acquiesce in these retreats, that always fragile achievement may express more a response than a choice—a response to our identity that meets an obligation to which our history, our day-to-day lives, and our aspirations call us.

Returning to the streets of this city reminds me that, over the years, Chicanos have made alliances and even some occasional friendships, most notably with people living in other non-converging traditions—Asians, feminists, Blacks, Native Americans, other Latinos, and certain members of both the intellectual community and the white working class. Still other moments on these very same streets convince me that, in some ways, each of us continues to find the other's nostalgia faintly ridiculous. You think our spiritual attachment to Cinco de Mayo quaint and quixotic; we think your attachment to the idea of a constitution in the grand tradition self-deluding. The truces we live by, in this city and in this country, apparently can't always disguise or alter residual sentiment.

I do not pretend that the idea of a constitution in Chicano tradition is radically discontinuous with all elements of the grand tradition. Our tradition certainly shares with classical republican thought the somewhat blurry image of a self constituted through others and through its relation to work, and of people making a living while simultaneously battling in public life. But unlike the grand tradition, Chicano tradition fights hard not to accept as settled the present arrangement of institutions and ideas. To acquiesce in what people now live and think would be to abandon the very spirit in us that rebels against all that has degraded our ancestors and contemporaries, and all that works even now, in newly emerging forms, to subordinate our descendants.

We won't celebrate the constitution's bicentennial in the grand tradition, and we'll be better for it.

Chapter 43

Early Chicano Activism
Zoot Suits, Sleepy Lagoon, and the Road to Delano

Rodolfo Acuña

World War II and the Chicano

Raúl Morin, in *Among the Valiant,* has documented the Chicanos' contribution to the war effort. Morin expressed the sense of betrayal that many Chicano soldiers experienced because of the racism at home. Morin wrote that 25 percent of the U.S. military personnel on the infamous Bataan "Death March" were Mexican Americans and that, in World War II, Mexicans earned more medals of honor than any other ethnic or racial group.

When the war began, about 2.69 million Chicanos lived in the United States, approximately one-third of whom were of draft age. According to Dr. Robin R. Scott, between 375,000 and 500,000 Chicanos served in the armed forces. In Los Angeles Mexicans comprised one-tenth of the population and one-fifth of the casualties.[1]

Throughout the war Mexicans were treated as second-class citizens. For example, Sergeant Macario Garcia, from Sugarland, Texas, a recipient of the Congressional Medal of Honor, could not buy a cup of coffee in a restaurant in Richmond, California. "An Anglo-American chased him out with a baseball bat." The Garcia incident was not isolated.

The "Sleepy Lagoon" case (1942) and the zoot-suit riots (1943) insulted Mexicans throughout the United States. The events in Los Angeles generated sympathy and solidarity from as far away as Chicago. Angelenos as well as other North Americans had been conditioned for these events by the mass deportations of the 1930s. The war-like propaganda conducted during the repatriation reinforced in the minds of many Anglos the stereotype that Mexican Americans were aliens. The events of 1942 proved the extent of Anglo racism. Euroamericans herded Japanese Americans into internment camps. When the Japanese left, Mexicans became the most natural scapegoats.

Pp. 253–59, 324–27 from Occupied America: A History of Chicanos, 3rd ed., by Rodolfo Acuña. Copyright © 1988 by Rodolfo Acuña. Reprinted by permission of Addison-Wesley Educational Publishers, Inc.

During the war, Los Angeles became a magnet for the rapid migration of all races to the area. The mass influx overtaxed the infrastructure's ability to serve the expanding population. The Mexican *barrios,* already overcrowded, were the most affected, as the city's economic growth drew many Mexicans from other regions. Whites took higher paying defense jobs, while Mexicans assumed their place in heavy industry.

Mexicans occupied the oldest housing stock; segregation was common; and many recreational facilities excluded Mexican Americans. For instance, they could not use swimming pools in East Los Angeles and in other Southland communities. Often Mexicans and Blacks could only swim on Wednesday—the day the county drained the water. In movie houses in places like San Fernando, Mexicans sat in the balcony.

In this environment, a minority of Chicano youth between the ages of thirteen and seventeen belonged to *barrio* clubs that carried the name of their neighborhoods— White Fence, Alpine Street, El Hoyo, Happy Valley. The fad among gang members, or *pachucos* as they were called, was to tattoo the left hand, between the thumb and index finger, with a small cross with three dots or dashes above it. Many *pachucos,* when they dressed up, wore the so-called zoot suit, popular among low-income youths at that time. Pachucos spoke *Spanish,* but also used *Chuco* among their companions. Chuco was the *barrio* language, a mixture of Spanish, English, old Spanish, and words adapted by the border Mexicans. Many experts indicate that the language originated around El Paso among Chicanos, who brought it to Los Angeles in the 1930s.

Although similar gangs existed among Anglo youth, Angelenos with little sense of history called gangs a Mexican problem, forgetting that the Euroamerican urban experience caused the gang phenomenon. The *Los Angeles Times,* not known for its analytic content, reinforced this stereotype and influenced the public with stories about "Mexican" hoodlums.

The "Sleepy Lagoon" case was the most notorious example of racism toward Chicanos in this era. The name came from a popular melody played by band leader Harry James. Unable to go to the public pool, Chicanos romanticized a gravel pit they frequently used for recreational purposes. On the evening of August 1, 1942, members of the 38th Street Club were jumped by another gang. When they returned with their home boys, the rival gang was not there. Later they witnessed a party in progress at the Williams Ranch nearby. They crashed the party and a fight followed.

The next morning José Díaz, an invited guest at the party, was found dead on a dirt road near the house. Díaz had no wounds and could have been killed by a hit-and-run driver, but authorities suspected that some members of the 38th Street Club had beaten him, and the police immediately jailed the entire gang. Newspapers sensationalized the story. Police flagrantly violated the rights of the accused and authorities charged twenty-two of the 38th Street boys with criminal conspiracy. "According to the prosecution, every defendant, even if he had nothing whatsoever to do with the killing of Díaz, was chargeable with the death of Díaz, which according to the prosecution, occurred during the fight at the Williams Ranch."[2]

The press portrayed the Sleepy Lagoon defendants as Mexican hoodlums. A special committee of the grand jury, shortly after the death of José Díaz, accepted a report by Lt. Ed Duran Ayres, head of the Foreign Relations Bureau of the Los Angeles Sheriff's Department, which justified the gross violation of human rights suffered by the defendants. Although the report admitted that discrimination against Chicanos in employment, education, schooling, recreation, and labor unions was common, it concluded that Chicanos were inherently criminal and violent. Ayres stated that Chicanos were Indians, that Indians were Orientals, and that Orientals had an utter disregard for life. Therefore, because Chicanos had this inborn characteristic, they too were violent. The report further alleged that Chicanos were cruel, for they descended from the Aztecs who supposedly sacrificed 30,000 victims a day! Ayres wrote that Indians considered leniency a sign of weakness, pointing to the Mexican government's treatment of the Indians, which he maintained was quick and severe. He urged that all gang members be imprisoned and that all Chicano youths over the age of eighteen be given the option of working or enlisting in the armed forces. Chicanos, according to Ayres, could not change their spots; they had an innate desire to use a knife and let blood, and this inborn cruelty was aggravated by liquor and jealousy. The Ayres report, which represented official law enforcement views, goes a long way in explaining the events around Sleepy Lagoon.

The Honorable Charles W. Fricke permitted numerous irregularities in the courtroom during the trial. The defendants were not allowed to cut their hair or change their clothes for the duration of the proceedings. The prosecution failed to prove that the 38th Street Club was a gang, that any criminal agreement or conspiracy existed, or that the accused had killed Díaz. In fact, witnesses testified that considerable drinking had occurred at the party before the 38th Street people arrived. If the theory of conspiracy to commit a crime had been strictly pressed, logically the defendants would have received equal verdicts. However, on January 12, 1943, the court passed sentences ranging from assault to first-degree murder.

The Sleepy Lagoon Defense Committee had been organized to protect the defendants' rights. It was chaired by Carey McWilliams, a noted journalist and lawyer. McWilliams and other members were harassed and red-baited by the press and by government agencies. The California Committee on Un-American Activities, headed by State Senator Jack Tenney, investigated the committee charging that it was a Communist-front organization and that Carey McWilliams, had "Communist leanings" because he opposed segregation and favored miscegenation. Authorities, including the FBI, conducted heavy surveillance of the committee and support groups such as El Congreso de los Pueblos de Habla Español (the Spanish-Speaking Congress). The FBI viewed it as a Communist front, stating that it "opposed all types of discrimination against Mexicans."[3]

On October 4, 1944, the Second District Court of Appeals reversed the lower court in a unanimous decision stating that Judge Fricke had conducted a biased trial, that he had violated the constitutional rights of the defendants, and that no evidence existed that linked the Chicanos with the death of José Díaz.

After the Sleepy Lagoon arrests Los Angeles police and the sheriff's departments set up roadblocks and indiscriminately arrested large numbers of Chicanos on countless charges, most popular being suspicion of burglary. These arrests naturally made headlines, inflaming the public to the point that the Office of War Information became concerned over the media's sensationalism as well as its racism.

The tension did not end there. Large numbers of servicemen on furlough or on short-duration passes visited Los Angeles. Numerous training centers were located in the vicinity, and the glitter of Hollywood and its famous canteen attracted hordes of GIs. Sailors on shore leave from ships docked in San Pedro and San Diego went to Los Angeles looking for a good time. Most were young and anxious to prove their manhood. A visible "foe" was the "alien" Chicano, dressed in the outlandish zoot suit that everyone ridiculed. The sailors also looked for Mexican girls to pick up, associating the Chicanas with the prostitutes in Tijuana. The sailors behaved boisterously and rudely to the women in the Mexican community.

In the spring of 1943 several small altercations erupted in Los Angeles. In April marines and sailors in Oakland invaded the Chicano *barrio* and Black ghetto, assaulted the people, and "depantsed" zoot-suiters. On May 8 a fight between sailors and Chicanos, many of whom belonged to the Alpine, broke out at the Aragon Ballroom in Venice, California, when some high school students told the sailors that *pachucos* had stabbed a sailor. Joined by other servicemen, sailors indiscriminately attacked Mexican youths. The battle cry was; "Let's get 'em! Let's get the chili-eating bastards!" Twenty-five hundred spectators watched the assault on innocent Chicano youths; the police did virtually nothing to restrain the servicemen, arresting instead the victims, charging them with disturbing the peace. Although Judge Arthur Guerin dismissed the charges for want of sufficient evidence, he warned the youths "that their antics might get them into serious difficulties unless they changed their attitudes." The press continued to sensationalize the theme of "zoot-suit equals hoodlum."[4]

The "sailors riots" began on June 3, 1943. Allegedly, a group of sailors had been attacked by Chicanos when they attempted to pick up some Chicanas. The details are vague; the police supposedly did not attempt to get the Chicano side of the story, but instead took the sailors' report at face value. Fourteen off-duty police officers, led by a detective lieutenant, went looking for the "criminals." They found nothing, but made certain that the press covered the story.

That same night, sailors went on a rampage; they broke into the Carmen Theater, tore zoot-suits off Chicanos, and beat the youths. Police again arrested the victims. Word spread that *pachucos* were fair game and that they could be attacked without fear of arrest.

Sailors returned the next evening with some two hundred allies. In twenty hired cabs they cruised Whittier Boulevard, in the heart of the East Los Angeles *barrio*, jumping out of the cars to gang up on neighborhood youths. Police and sheriffs maintained that they could not establish contact with the sailors. They finally did arrest nine sailors, but released them immediately without filing charges. The press portrayed the sailors as heroes. Articles and headlines were designed to inflame racial hatred.

Sailors, encouraged by the press and "responsible" elements of Los Angeles, gathered on the night of June 5 and marched four abreast down the streets, warning Chicanos to shed their zoot suits or they would take them off for them. On that night and the next, servicemen broke into bars and other establishments and beat up Chicanos. Police continued to abet the lawlessness, arriving only after damage had been done and the servicemen had left. Even though sailors destroyed private property, law enforcement officials still refused to do their duty. When the Chicano community attempted to defend itself, police arrested them.

Events climaxed on the evening of June 7, when thousands of soldiers, sailors, and civilians surged down Main Street and Broadway in search of *pachucos*. The mob crashed into bars and broke the legs off stools, using them as clubs. The press reported five hundred "zoot suiters" ready for battle. By this time Filipinos and Blacks also became targets. Chicanos had their clothes ripped off, and the youths were left bleeding in the streets. The mob surged into movie theaters, where they turned on the lights, marched down the aisles, and pulled zoot-suit-clad youngsters out of their seats. Seventeen-year-old Enrico Herrera, after he was beaten and arrested, spent three hours at a police station, where he was found by his mother, still naked and bleeding. A twelve-year-old boy's jaw was broken. Police arrested over six hundred Chicano youths without cause and labeled the arrests "preventive" action. Angelenos cheered on the servicemen and their civilian allies.

Panic gripped the Chicano community. At the height of the turmoil servicemen pulled a Black off a streetcar and gouged out his eye with a knife. Military authorities, realizing that the Los Angeles law enforcement agencies would not curtail the brutality, intervened and declared downtown Los Angeles off limits for military personnel. Classified naval documents prove that the navy believed it had a mutiny on its hands. Documents leave no doubt that military shore patrols quelled the riot, accomplishing what the Los Angeles police could or would not do.

For the next few days police ordered mass arrests, even raiding a Catholic welfare center to arrest some of its occupants. The press and city officials provoked the mob. An editorial by Manchester Boddy on June 9 in the *Los Angeles Daily News* (supposedly the city's liberal newspaper) stated:

> The time for temporizing is past. . . . The time has come to serve notice that the City of Los Angeles will no longer be terrorized by a relatively small handful of morons parading as zoot-suit hoodlums. To delay action now means to court disaster later on.[5]

Boddy's statement taken alone would not mean much; it could be considered to be just one man's opinion. But consider that before the naval invasion of East Los Angeles, the following headlines had appeared in the *Times:*

November 2, 1942: "Ten Seized in Drive on Zoot-Suit Gangsters"

February 23, 1943: "One Slain and Another Knifed in 'Zoot' Fracas"

March 7, 1943: "Magistrate 'Unfrocks' Pair of Zoot-Suiters"

May 25, 1943: "Four Zoot-Suit Gangs Beat Up Their Victims"

June 1, 1943: "Attacks by Orange County Zoot-Suiters Injure Five"

During the assault servicemen were encouraged by headlines in the *Los Angeles Daily News,* such as "Zoot Suit Chiefs Girding for War on Navy," and in the *Los*

Angeles Times, such as "Zoot Suiters Learn Lesson in Fight with Servicemen." Three other major newspapers ran similar headlines that generated an atmosphere of zoot-suit violence. The radio also contributed to the hysteria.

Rear Admiral D. W. Bagley, commanding officer of the naval district, took the public position that the sailors acted in "self-defense against the rowdy element." Privately Bagley directed his commanders to order their men to stop the raids and then conducted a low profile cover-up. Sailors were, however, not the only vandals. Army personnel often outnumbered sailors. According to Commander Fogg, on June 8, 1943, hundreds of servicemen were "prowling downtown Los Angeles mostly on foot—disorderly—apparently on the prowl for Mexicans." By June 11, 1943, in a restricted memo, the navy and army recognized that the rioting resulted from "mob action. It is obvious that many soldiers are not aware of the serious nature of riot charges, which could carry the death sentence or a long prison term."

On June 16 the *Los Angeles Times* ran a story from Mexico City, headlined "Mexican Government Expects Damages for Zoot Suit Riot Victims." The article stated that "the Mexican government took a mildly firm stand on the rights of its nationals, emphasizing its conviction that American justice would grant 'innocent victims' their proper retribution." Federal authorities expressed concern, and Mayor Fletcher Bowron assured Washington, D.C., that there was no racism involved. Soon afterward Bowron told the Los Angeles police to stop using "cream-puff techniques on the Mexican youths." At the same time he ordered the formation of a committee to "study the problem." City officials and the Los Angeles press became exceedingly touchy about charges of racism. When Eleanor Roosevelt commented in her column that the riots had been caused by "longstanding discrimination against the Mexicans in the Southwest," on June 18 the *Los Angeles Times* reacted with the headline "Mrs. Roosevelt Blindly Stirs Race Discord." The article denied that racial discrimination had been a factor in the riots and charged that Mrs. Roosevelt's statement resembled propaganda used by the communists, stating that servicemen had looked for "costumes and not races." The article said that Angelenos were proud of their missions and of Olvera Street, "a bit of old Mexico," and concluded "We like Mexicans and think they like us."

Governor Earl Warren formed a committee to investigate the riots. Participating on the committee were Attorney General Robert W. Kenny; Catholic bishop Joseph T. McGucken, who served as chair; Walter A. Gordon, Berkeley attorney; Leo Carrillo, screen actor; and Karl Holton, director of the California Youth Authority.

The committee's report recommended punishment of all persons responsible for the riots—military and civilian alike. It took a left-handed slap at the press, recommending that newspapers minimize the use of names and photos of juveniles. Moreover, it called for better-educated and trained police officers to work with Spanish-speaking youth.

Little was done to implement the recommendations of the report, and most of the same conditions exist today in Los Angeles city and county. "The kid gloves are off!" approach of Sheriff Eugene Biscailuz has, if anything, hardened since the 1940s.

During World War II, police authorities sought to strengthen social control of the *barrios* and spied extensively on the Mexican community. Most available data on this phenomenon can be obtained through the federal Freedom of Information Act. Little is known about domestic spying at the local or state levels, since these government units are not required to provide copies of their reports to individuals or organizations.

Dr. José Ángel Gutiérrez has done pioneer research in this area. Through the Freedom of Information Act, he received documents proving that the FBI spied even on patriotic groups such as LULAC (League of United Latin American Citizens) and later the G.I. Forum. In 1941, the FBI's Denver Office reported on the LULAC chapter of Antonio, Colorado. Its officers included a county judge and a town marshal. The FBI also investigated respected leaders such as George I. Sanchez and Alonso Perales, reporting that the Mexican community distrusted Sanchez because he had converted to reformed Methodism.

In May 1946, the FBI infiltrated a Los Angeles meeting of LULAC. An informant asserted that participants had a long history of communist activity but made no effort to document the statement. Early in the 1950s, the FBI again investigated LULAC because it demanded racial integration. In Pecos, Texas, the FBI spied on the local LULAC council because a member wanted to be on the Selective Service Board. . . .

The Road to Delano: Creating a Moment

By the mid-1960s, Chicano militancy concerned growers and other employers. The purpose of immigration policy was to control not only Mexicans but Chicanos. After 1965, this policy became more restrictive, designed to regulate both the flow of workers and the wages paid. Essential to this strategy was the criminalization of Mexican labor, which devalued and degraded the work performed by Mexicans and Chicanos. Criminalization intensified the division of labor and resulted in Chicanos, to avoid discrimination, pecking down on the undocumented worker; it also justified increased use of police power against all Mexicans, whether documented or undocumented.

The first step in the criminalization process was the passage of restrictive legislation that directly affected the documented immigration of Mexicans. Liberals such as Senator Edward Kennedy sponsored legislation in 1965 designed to correct the past injustice of excluding Asians from legal entry. Nativists took the opportunity to broaden the legislation and, for the first time, placed Latin America and Canada on a quota system. The law specified that 170,000 immigrants annually could enter from the Eastern Hemisphere and 120,000 from the Western. Up to this time Mexico had been the principal source of Latin American immigration; the new law put a cap of 40,000 from any one nation. Unfortunately, few Chicanos or progressive organizations protested the law. And it was not until the 1970s that its full impact was felt; at that time it became a popular cause for progressives.

Many Chicanos have incorrectly labeled the second half of the 1960s as the birth of the Chicano movement. Mexicans in the United States have responded to injustice and oppression since the U.S. wars of aggression that took Texas and the Southwest from Mexico. Middle-class organizations generally spoke for the community, since its members had the education, money, and stability to maintain more or less permanent associations. Established Anglo power brokers also recognized these organizations.

By the mid-1960s, traditional groups such as LULAC and the G.I. Forum, along with recently formed political groups such as Mexican American Political Association (MAPA) and Political Association of Spanish-Speaking Organizations (PASSO), were challenged. For better or worse, the established Mexican-American associations had served as agents of social control, setting the norm for conduct. The rise of cultural nationalism challenged the acceptance of assimilation as a goal. Sectors of youth, women, and more militant activists were skeptical of traditional methods of struggle and advocated direct action. They also questioned the legitimacy of established leaders.

For the most part, LULAC and Forum leaders at first rejected "street politics"—marches, walkouts, confrontations, civil disobedience, and so on. Over the years their ties with the system tightened. At the same time, the civil rights, antinuclear, and anti-Vietnam movements, along with community action programs, legitimated an ideology of confrontation, creating a new awareness among Chicanos that resulted in a demand for self-determination by *los de abajo* (the underdogs) and youth. Also important was that sectors of the North American left, as well as government agencies, no longer dealt with established groups exclusively but recognized more militant Chicanos organizations. This, for a time, broke the monopoly of the Mexican-American middle class. Moreover, rank-and-file members of LULAC and the Forum grew closer to the new Chicano agenda.

César Chávez and the United Farm Workers

César Chávez gave the Chicano movement a national leader. In all probability Chávez was the only Mexican American to be so recognized by the mainstream civil rights and antiwar movements. Chávez and his farm workers were also supported by the center Mexican-American organizations along with the left.

On September 8, 1965, the Filipinos in the Agricultural Workers Organizing Committee (AWOC) struck the grape growers of the Delano area in the San Joaquin Valley. Filipino workers had been encouraged by a victory in the spring of 1965 in the Coachella Valley, where the U.S. Labor Department announced that *braceros* would be paid $1.40 an hour. The domestic pickers received 20¢ to 30¢ an hour less. Joined by Mexicans, the Filipinos walked out, and ten days later they received a guarantee of equivalent pay with *braceros*. When the Filipinos requested the same guarantee in the San Joaquin Valley, growers refused, and led by Larry Itlong, they voted to strike. The strike demands were simple: $1.40 an hour or 25¢ a box. The Di Giorgio Corporation became the major target. The rank and file of the National Farm Workers Association (NFWA) voted on September 16 to join the Filipinos. The termination at the end of 1964 of Public Law 78 significantly strengthened the union's position.

Chávez emerged as the central figure in the strike. Born in Yuma, Arizona, in 1927, he spent his childhood as a migrant worker. His father had belonged to farm labor unions and Chávez himself had been a member of the National Farm Labor Union. In the 1940s he moved to San José, California, where he married Helen Favila. In San José Chávez met Father Donald McDonnell, who tutored him in *Rerum Novarum,* Pope Leo XIII's encyclical which supported labor unions and social justice. Through Father McDonnell Chávez met Fred Ross of the Community Service Organization (CSO). He became an organizer for the CSO and learned grass-roots strategies. Chávez rose to the position of general director of the national CSO, but in 1962 he resigned, moving to Delano, where he began to organize his union. Chávez went door to door visiting farm workers. Delano was chosen because of its substantial all-year farm-worker population; in 1968, 32 percent of the 7,000 harvest workers lived and worked in the Delano area year round.

Chávez concentrated his efforts on the Mexican field hands, for he knew the importance of nationalism in solidifying an organization. He carefully selected a loyal cadre of proven organizers, such as Dolores Huerta and Gil Padilla, whom he had met in the CSO. By the middle of 1964 the NFWA was self-supporting.

A year later the NFWA had some 1,700 members. Volunteers, fresh from civil rights activities in the South, joined the NFWA at Delano. Protestant groups, inspired by the civil rights movement, championed the cause of the workers. A minority of Catholic priests, influenced by Vatican II, joined Chávez. Anglo-American labor belatedly jumped on the bandwagon. In Chávez's favor was the growing number of Chicano workers living in the United States. Over 80 percent lived in cities, and many belonged to unions. Many, in fact, belonged to big labor such as the United Auto Workers (UAW).

The times allowed Chávez to make his movement a crusade. The stabilization of a large part of the Mexican-American workforce made the forging of an organization possible. And, finally, the end of the *bracero* program took a lethal weapon from the growers.

The most effective strategy was the boycott. Supporters were urged not to buy Schenley products or Di Giorgio grapes. The first breakthrough came when the Schenley Corporation signed a contract in 1966. The Teamsters unexpectedly refused to cross picket lines in San Francisco. Rumors of a bartenders' boycott reached seventy-five-year-old Lewis Solon Rosenstiel, Schenley's president, who decided that a settlement was advisable. Soon afterward Gallo, Christian Brothers, Paul Masson, Almaden, Franzia Brothers, and Novitiate signed contracts.

The next opponent was the Di Giorgio Corporation, one of the largest grape growers in the central valley. In April 1966, Robert Di Giorgio unexpectedly announced he would allow his workers at Sierra Vista to vote on whether they wanted a union and who would represent them. Di Giorgio did not act in good faith and his agents set out to intimidate the workers.

With the support of Di Giorgio the Teamsters opposed the farm workers and bid to represent the workers. Di Giorgio, without consulting the NFWA, set the date for the election. The NFWA urged its followers not to vote, since it did not have time to campaign or to participate in establishing the ground rules. It needed enough time to return eligible voters to the Delano area. Out of 732 eligible voters only 385 voted; 281 voters specified that they wanted the Teamsters as their union agent. The NFWA immediately branded the election as fraudulent and pressured Governor Edmund G. Brown, Sr., a friend of Di Giorgio, to investigate the election. Brown needed the Chicano vote as well as that of the liberals who were committed to the farm workers. The governor's investigator recommended a new election, and the date was set for August 30, 1966.

That summer an intense campaign took place between the Teamsters and the NFWA. A state senate committee investigated charges of communist infiltration of the NFWA; the committee found nothing to substantiate charges. As the election neared, Chávez became more somber. He had to keep the eligible voters in Delano, and he had the responsibility of feeding them and their families as well as the army of strikers and volunteers. The Di Giorgio campaign drained the union's financial resources. Some weeks before the strike vote, Chávez reluctantly merged the NFWA and AWOC into the United Farm Workers Organizing Committee (UFWOC).

Teamsters red-baited the UFWOC and circulated free copies of Gary Allen's John Birch Society pamphlet. The UFWOC passed out excerpts from *The Enemy Within,* in which Robert Kennedy indicted James Hoffa and the Teamsters in scathing terms; association with the Kennedy name helped. Finally the vote was taken. The UFWOC won the election, 573 votes to the Teamsters' 425. Field workers voted 530 to 331 in favor of the UFWOC. Soon afterward the Di Giorgio Corporation and the UFWOC signed a contract.

Other growers proved to be more difficult. In 1967 the Giumarra Vineyards Corporation, the largest producer of table grapes in the United States, was targeted. When Giumarra used other companies' labels to circumvent the boycott, in violation of the Food and Drug Administration rules, the union boycotted all California table grapes. Boycott activities spread into Canada and Europe. Grape sales decreased significantly. Some of the slack was taken up by the U.S. Defense Department. In 1966 U.S. troops in Vietnam were shipped 468,000 pounds of grapes; in 1967, 555,000 pounds; in 1968, 2 million pounds; and by 1969, more than 4 million pounds. Later the U.S. Defense Department spent taxpayers' money to buy large quantities of lettuce when the union boycotted this product. In the summer of 1970 the strike approached its fifth year. In June 1970 a group of Coachella Valley growers agreed to sign contracts, as did a majority of growers. Victories in the San Joaquin Valley followed.

After this victory the union turned to the lettuce fields of the Salinas Valley, where growers were among the most powerful in the state. During July 1970 the Growers-Shippers Association and twenty-nine of the largest growers in the valley entered into negotiations with the Teamsters. Agreements signed with the truckers' union in Salinas were worse than sweetheart contracts: they provided no job security, no seniority rights, no hiring hall, and no protection against pesticides.

Many growers, like the Bud Antle Company (a partner of Dow Chemical), had dealt with the Teamsters since the 1950s. In 1961, in return for a $1 million loan, Antle signed a contract with the truckers. By August 1970 many workers refused to abide by the Teamster contracts and 5,000 walked off the lettuce fields. The growers launched a campaign of violence. Jerry Cohen, a farm-worker lawyer, was beaten unconscious. On December 4, 1970, Judge Gordon Campbell of Monterey County jailed Chávez for refusing to obey an injunction and held him without bail. This arbitrary action gave the boycott needed publicity. Dignitaries visited Chávez in jail; he was released on Christmas Eve.

By the spring of 1971 Chávez and the Teamsters signed an agreement that gave the UFWOC sole jurisdiction in the lettuce fields and that allowed George Meany, president of the AFL, and Teamsters president Frank Fitzsimmons to arbitrate the situation. Throughout the summer and into the fall, however, growers refused to disqualify Teamster contracts and gradually the situation became stalemated.

The fight with the Teamsters hurt the UFWOC since it turned its attention from servicing contracts. Chávez refused help from the AFL for professional administrators, believing that farm workers had to learn from their own mistakes. According to *Fresno Bee* reporter Ron Taylor, although Chávez was a patient teacher, he did not delegate authority and involved himself with too much detail. Farm workers had never had the opportunity to govern themselves and Chávez had to build "ranch committees" from the bottom up. This took time and the corporate ranchers who ran agribusiness had little tolerance for democracy.

NOTES

1. Raúl Morin, Among the Valiant (Alhambra, Calif.: Border, 1966), p. 16.

2. Ismael Dieppa, "The Zoot-Suit Riots Revisited: The Role of Private Philanthropy in Youth Problems of Mexican-Americans" (DSW dissertation, University of Southern California, 1973), p. 14; See Carey McWilliams Papers at the Special Collections Library at the University of California at Los Angeles.

3. Robin Fitzgerald Scott, *The Mexican-American in the Los Angeles Area, 1920–1950: From Acquiescence to Activity* (Ph.D. dissertation, University of Southern California, 1971), pp. 223, 225.

4. Dieppa, p. 15, emphasizes the sex motive, stating that there were five servicemen to every girl.

5. FBI report, January 14, 1944. The *Eastside Journal,* June 9, 1943, wrote an editorial defending the zoot-suiters; it pointed out that 112 had been hospitalized, 150 hurt, and 12 treated in the hospitals.

Chapter 44

"Breaking the Law" on Principle

Michael A. Olivas

Professor Martha Minow's article, "Breaking the Law: Lawyers and Clients in Struggles for Social Change,"[1] identifies three risks inherent in the lawyer-client relationship that occur when the client breaks the law to pursue social, political, or legal change: a risk of nonrepresentation, where no accomplished lawyer will take the case; a risk of terminated representation, when ethical requirements may jeopardize an unpopular client's defense; and a risk of truncated representation, where the lawyer's choice of tactics may undermine the very premise of the client's grievance.

Consider the first risk. When unpopular clients break the law, they may face a difficult time in securing representation. If the client is wealthy, however, he or she will be able to secure counsel, however reprehensible or unpopular the crime. Minow does not argue the ethical or constitutional reasons for representation of politically-motivated offenders; rather her concern is that for the system to work requires saboteurs to challenge legal complacency, which in turn necessitates lawyers willing to commit themselves.

There can be no doubt that in the United States, this willingness to test the legal barriers is essential to change. Having excellent counsel certainly increases the likelihood of effecting change through litigation, and makes the change more substantial and precedential. This proposition is illustrated in the classic example Minow employs, that of Martin Luther King, Jr., held in jail in Birmingham, Alabama. This particular incident is certainly one of the central events in United States civil rights history. Reverend King's incarceration had great moral and symbolic significance for his political agenda of overturning racial apartheid, and played out on national television, demonstrating how unjust public laws were for blacks. This and similar incidents led to a series of changes in civil rights laws.

In the second scenario, principled would-be law-breakers divulge to their attorney that they intend to break a law. Do lawyers have a "Tarasoff" duty to warn (or withdraw)?[2] Minow poses the question in an example she cites, where a client that would

From "'Breaking the Law' on Principle: An Essay on Lawyers' Dilemmas, Unpopular Causes, and Legal Regimes." 52 U. Pitt. L. Rev. 815 (1991). Originally published in the *University of Pittsburgh Law Review*. Reprinted by permission.

import and distribute RU-486, the "abortion pill" available in Europe, could well violate Food and Drug Administration (FDA) regulations and be held in criminal contempt. Her analysis concludes that the Model Code allows the company's attorneys the discretion to serve their client without disclosing the intended lawbreaking. If consulted before the client violates the law, the lawyer may advise the client on the likely or probable consequences of their proposed actions. In so doing, however, Minow warns, legal representation itself risks furthering a fraudulent scheme or ongoing crime.

Minow's third risk is a variation of T. S. Eliot's *Murder in the Cathedral,* doing what may be the right thing for the wrong reasons.[3] This is a paradox of compelling stature, where a client's principles may preclude a defense that could minimize the very real personal harm that the client's conviction would cause. Recent rulings by the Fourth Circuit in Rule 11 proceedings pose just such a dilemma for William Kunstler's attorneys.[4] The famous civil rights litigator filed a suit against prosecutors and public officials in North Carolina, alleging harassment of Native Americans during a criminal investigation. He and his co-counsel held a press conference to draw public attention to the alleged harassment. The prosecutors sought sanctions alleging that Kunstler had filed the suit "for publicity, to embarrass state and county officials, to use as leverage in criminal proceedings, to obtain discovery for use in criminal proceedings, and to intimidate those involved in the prosecution of [the Indian activists]."[5] Kunstler vowed, "I'm not going to pay any fine. I'm going to rot in jail if that's what I have to do to dramatize this thing."[6] The same court also recently upheld Rule 11 sanctions against Julius Chambers, Director of the NAACP Legal Defense Fund (LDF), for charges stemming from an employment discrimination case brought by the LDF against the U.S. Army. The court reduced the $85,000 fine but upheld the sanctions, holding that the attorneys had not met their "responsibility to explore the factual bases for the clients' suits . . . instead charging forward with the litigation in disregard of its manifest lack of merit."[7]

At bottom is Minow's contention that each of these three types of dilemma poses "genuine dangers," particularly if our system is not supple enough to consider principled claims or to accommodate pluralistic approaches to the law. She urges an expanded role for "legal process" courses so that students learn "the historic traditions of lawyers defending people who break the law for political reasons."[8] Consider three further examples:

Case 1: The Case of Unaccompanied Refugee Children: Legal Clinics and the Risk of Cooptation

Thousands of unaccompanied children who have felt the violence in their Central American countries are being detained in refugee camps in the United States, most in shameful conditions without access to basic necessities of education, health care, or legal services. Because immigration procedures, including deportation, are considered civil rather than criminal proceedings, little process is due these alien children under the Constitution. Immigration law requires extraordinary legal advice, yet the

Immigration and Naturalization Service (INS) has actively discouraged its detained aliens from getting it. Children are particularly vulnerable in the asylum process; nonetheless, at present, no statutory or common law right guarantees appointed counsel or guardians for children trapped in the immigration labyrinth.

In early 1989, to stem the tide of Central American refugees and asylum seekers, the INS decided to detain these aliens in border facilities and tent-shelters. Earlier, many asylum seekers had been processed quickly in mass adjudications, often conceding their deportability and being sent back to their home country. Under this policy, unaccompanied children awaiting a decision were released to family members, church groups, or other community assistance organizations. The children were unaccompanied either because they had fled their country without adults, they were sent ahead by family members who had hoped to shield them from harm, or they had become separated from adults during flight. The INS policy of detaining children and adults has led to an expansion of detention facilities in rural areas. INS figures for 1990–1991 show over 3,600 aliens in Texas detention facilities, and 2,500 alien children in California. Predictably, the facilities are ramshackle: one site in Texas has been sardonically dubbed "El Corralon" (The Corral), while another is a former Department of Agriculture pesticide storage facility. A 1991 study of the children in these facilities revealed that virtually all suffered from advanced and untreated cases of post-traumatic shock syndrome. These children have virtually no access to health care or personal counseling, even though many have been severely traumatized by the war in their country, by the arduous and dangerous trip North, and by their incarceration here. The children are provided no educational services, even though every child in Texas is required to enroll in school during the school year. The centers have no libraries, teacher aides, or organized instruction. Like the adults, the detained alien children have little access to attorneys, telephones, or other legal means to prepare their cases.

Because the INS couches its actions in national defense terms ("securing our borders" and "intercepting drug trafficking"), little community outrage has been heard over these actions. The Red Cross has been coopted into operating one of the facilities, garbing the center with legitimacy, while community newspapers have been lulled into believing that the policy is humanitarian. Further, INS officials counted on the remoteness of the camps, the economic incentive to the poor communities, and the distance from legal services to keep their practices from undergoing public scrutiny.

The practice of detaining alien minors has advanced two ulterior motives. First, to discourage other refugees from migrating to the United States.[9] Second, authorities hoped to "bait" undocumented families into revealing themselves to authorities. As a result of these practices, family members in the United States, even those with permission to be in the country, have found it intimidating or impossible to locate their children. In *Flores v. Meese*[10] and *Perez-Funez v. INS*,[11] many of these INS practices concerning children came to light. In these cases, the courts found that the INS had acted to deprive unaccompanied alien minors of their rights to full hearings and due process. In another case, the judge found "a persistent pattern and practice of misconduct," use of "intimidation, threats, and misrepresentation," and evidence of "a widespread and pervasive practice akin to a policy" concerning pressure on Salvadorans to concede their rights.[12]

As a result of the remote locations of the facilities, INS policies on transfer, availability of legal resources, and poor response by organized bars, legal assistance to unaccompanied children is virtually non-existent. For example, even though Laredo, Texas, is hundreds of miles away from San Antonio (the tenth largest city in the United States), over 80 percent of the San Antonio region immigration caseload is in Laredo. To make matters worse, no immigration judge lives in or is appointed on a regular basis in Laredo. Therefore, all hearings are consolidated into alternating weeks when a judge does ride the circuit. This irregular schedule precludes attorneys (most of whom live in San Antonio) from arranging their schedules to synchronize with those of the judges. A visiting federal judge found that aliens were not even provided adequate lists of legal services. For example, the list (in English) included names and numbers of lawyers who did not handle immigration cases, and failed to include a free legal assistance program. He characterized this and other practices as "bad faith."[13] An ABA inspection team issued a report noting that legal services to detained aliens were "grossly inadequate."[14] Even when courts have been persuaded that detained aliens have been deprived of basic legal information on their rights, and have ordered changes designed to increase information and services, the INS has "not diligently respected [injunctions and temporary restraining orders], nor were agents disciplined for failing to adhere to terms."[15]

Most troubling has been the INS practice of transferring aliens as a means of depriving them of counsel.[16] Because the policy of establishing rural detention centers virtually assures that the refugees and asylum seekers will not have access to counsel, transfer to one of them is tantamount to a deprivation of counsel. In a troubling decision, a United States district court upheld the practice, noting INS's discretionary authority to make custodial decisions. In several instances, transfers have even been made after counsel was retained or as a blatant attempt to deny counsel. The policies and practices of INS have ensured that legal services for detainees have been minimal or nonexistent.

The United States has been extraordinarily generous in extending refugee assistance to victims fleeing communism, and to victims of wars raging in countries that have been United States allies. However, actions carried out by client states or by clandestine United States operations have a different history. Central American children, trapped between wars in their home countries and an immigration system in the United States that accords them no reasonable treatment, deserve special attention and protection. To do less is to continue a shameless, selfish, shortsighted policy.

Under these circumstances, what role may law schools play in ameliorating such a devastating situation? In Minow's terms, "law schools should pay greater attention to the social and economic conditions that might inspire [such] clients."[17] Once the aliens are detained on this side of the border, however, clients' coerced concessions of deportability do not always leave much play-in-the-joints for fancy lawyering or maneuvering within the system. This very lack of options has resulted in Minow's first dilemma, that of the children, many of whom have meritorious asylum claims, not being able to obtain counsel in time to render significant assistance. This may be traced in part to a virtual absence of immigration law being taught by American law schools. The Association of American Law Schools' 1990 data show approximately fifty full-time law teachers who teach in this field. It is likely that not all of the courses in immigration law would include substantial material on refugees, refugee rights, or unaccompanied children. Further, only a handful of refugee legal activists teach law on a full-time basis, and even fewer write the articles so critical to consciousness-raising and legal reform. In addition, clinical legal education is only partially suited to remedy such a legal system breakdown as these children experience.

However, at my own law school, we pooled our resources and agreed to try to provide clinical legal assistance. We decided to offer a between-semester clinical credit refugee project, with concentrated instruction in Houston, and a supervised field experience. We arranged for seven students to spend sixty hours in a week on a pro bono bar project in the Valley. Another fourteen students worked in Houston, trying to secure bond redetermination hearings and doing country research necessary for ongoing asylum cases. We sponsored conferences and coordinated course coverage so that more students could train as immigration lawyers. Were we successful? It is hard to say. Student enthusiasm ran high, yet at two o'clock in the morning I could not help but wonder if we are simply legitimizing INS in its pernicious practices, and I recall the faces of the children who fled war only to wind up at El Corralon.

Case 2: The Boycott of Israeli Military Courts by Israeli and Palestinian Lawyers

As complicated as the conditions in Central America have been in contributing to the shameful United States policy of interning unaccompanied children, they pale in comparison with the historical complexity and instability of the Middle East. One recent legal development presents the dilemma posed by Professor Minow, when persons who break the law for political reasons may not find representation. The case of the Israeli Defense Forces (IDF), the Intifada, and Palestinian defendants in Israeli military courts actually poses a corollary dilemma to that faced by lawyers for unaccompanied Central American children: what are a lawyer's obligations when faced with mass prosecutions and inadequate resources, under circumstances in which the political reasons for the conflict are seemingly intractable? At several times since 1989, Arab and Israeli lawyers who defend Palestinians in Israeli military courts have organized boycotts and withheld their legal services to draw attention to the unsatisfactory conditions of detainment—conditions so dreadful that human rights organizations around the world have severely criticized them.

The lawyers, after many attempts to bring problems to the attention of IDF officials, Israeli Bar officers, and court administration, decided they had no choice but to strike. Their first work stoppage was for a month, beginning January 3, 1989, during which time they met with Israeli authorities to express their dissatisfaction. On February 2, they announced a month-long continuation of the strike, as their demands had not been met. Still dissatisfied, they returned to the courts on March 12. By July 1989, conditions for the lawyers and their clients had deteriorated to the extent that they felt compelled to call another strike, which lasted from July 20 to August 20, 1989.

Their demands identified a variety of conditions that made it impossible for the lawyers to represent clients in military courts. First, many of the lawyers had themselves been arrested, detained, and physically attacked by IDF soldiers. In addition, they raised concerns about their clients and their clients' conditions: arrest and detention procedures, their access to clients held in detention, extensions of detention, opportunities for bail, extended periods of pretrial detention, trial delays, and sentencing policies. The arrest and detention policies are secret, and all Israeli soldiers or police officers are authorized to make warrantless arrests. Offenses can range from stone-throwing, to unauthorized meetings, to nonpayment of taxes, to more serious charges. Such suspects need not be brought before a judge for eighteen days; six months of detention can be ordered unless charges have been filed; there are no deadlines for the state to try a case. Arrestees have no clear right to counsel, and withholding access to an attorney is at the discretion of the military investigator, "if he is of the opinion that this is necessary for reasons of local security or if the good of the investigation demands it."[18] Not surprisingly, Palestinians charged with crimes are nearly always compromised in their defense. As a prominent Israeli military prosecutor in the Gaza put it,

> Every person who is accused is found guilty. Sometimes on the basis of criteria which no Israeli court of law would accept. In 99 percent of the cases the accused comes to court with a signed confession of guilt. That's suspicious. What's more, it's disturbing. And I say this as a former prosecutor.[19]

Moreover, even basic necessities essential to the representation of clients were absent. For example, no photocopying machines or telephones are available in the Ramallah court, one of the largest of the West Bank facilities; most of the courts have no facilities to meet privately with clients or family members. Even in those settings where a limited right to counsel exists, such as detention extension hearings, the lawyers discovered that their clients were denied their rights. They charged:

> The hearing to extend the detention is often held in the prison or the prison camp itself with as many as one hundred to one hundred fifty or more hearings held in the same prison camp in a single day. All this occurs without granting the detainee the opportunity to speak and without the presence of his attorney, or after a lengthy and almost useless struggle by the attorney in order to attempt to be present at the time of the detention. At times, this extension of detention occurs in the absence of the detainee himself. In rare cases, we have found detainees for whom no arrest order exists at all.[20]

Virtually no detainees are able to secure release on bail, and because bail is nigh-impossible to secure, they face extended detention until their case happens to come to trial. There is no provision for a bail hearing before a judge. Many detainees, particularly those charged with rock throwing or for illegally participating in a demonstration, had a disincentive to wait for trial and allege their innocence when the wait was longer than their sentence would be.

Under these circumstances, the lawyers felt that they had no choice but to strike and draw attention to this unacceptable situation. It is far from clear what alternatives they had, or what effect their work stoppage had on their working conditions. As all the reports note, some conditions improved slightly as a result of the publicity, but the underlying political causes remained unresolved.

How would United States professional norms and disciplinary codes treat such a work stoppage, undertaken in response to such clearly unlawful state behavior? It would be difficult to imagine a more apt United States analogy than the case of unaccompanied refugee children. If lawyers refused to participate in that process (out of principle rather than apathy, the current state), however, the children's fates would likely be as sealed as they are at present. Moreover, if a refusal to participate would sabotage the process, there would be a swift deployment of contempt citations or Rule 11 sanctions, and likely disciplinary action taken against the lawyers.

Withholding legal representation is rare, and, as in a recent New York City instance, usually concerns personnel issues, working conditions, or wages, rather than systemic principles. How would attorneys fare in our system, if they struck over principle as in the case of unaccompanied refugee children? In Texas, as in many jurisdictions, they would likely not fare well, and would arguably run afoul of several disciplinary rules.

Such an attorney would first need to keep the client informed, consistent with Martha Minow's concern that lawyers not undermine their clients' interest. The lawyer would need to discuss all options with her client and the client must understand the possible consequences of the lawyer's strike and agree to them.

After conferring with her client, and securing a clear agreement to a strike, an attorney might be cited under Texas Rules 3.02 and 3.04, "Minimizing the Burdens and Delays of Litigation" and "Fairness in Adjudicatory Proceedings." These Texas Rules have ABA Model Rule counterparts (3.2 and 3.4),[21] and are designed to reduce dilatory tactics and unreasonable courtroom behavior. Rule 3.02 states, "In the course of litigation, a lawyer shall not take a position that unreasonably increases the costs or other burdens of the case or that unreasonably delays resolution of the matter";[22] Rule 3.04 requires that a Texas lawyer not "engage in conduct intended to disrupt the proceedings" or "knowingly disobey, or advise the client to disobey, an allegation under the standing rules of or a ruling by a tribunal except for an open refusal based either on an assertion that no valid obligation exists or on the client's willingness to accept any sanctions arising from such disobedience."[23]

According to the recorder for the Texas Rules revision, the rules largely recodified previous Texas Code provisions for production of evidence and other Texas rules of evidence, procedure, and courtesy. Sanctions brought under the previous provisions were for abject disrespect, frequent expressions of sarcasm or accusatory behavior, openly critical remarks, and the like. While Texas Code 3.04(d) commentary refers to "repeated violations" and complementary provisions cite "habitually violat[ing] an established rule,"[24] the commentators also note that "a knowing violation of other rules or even of one order of a tribunal respecting such matters should subject a lawyer to discipline under paragraph (d)."[25] Under these provisions, attorneys should know that even their respectful and nonaccusatory declination to participate in the legal process through a strike, grounded in principle, insulated by their client's full knowledge and permission, drawing attention toward systemic unfairness, could trigger these Code provisions. Further findings of contempt are not reviewable by appeal or writs of error. Thus, striking lawyers held in contempt would likely find themselves incarcerated, with their only avenue of appeal a habeas corpus proceeding. Their clients, even though liable on the face of the Code, would likely be allowed time to secure new counsel, as judges would hold that they did not fully appreciate the consequences of their lawyers' withholding counsel. If this scenario occurred, the clients' principles of noncompliance would be undermined, while the real injury would fall on the lawyer's head.

Case 3: "Oscar Z. Acosta, Chicano Lawyer"

In the early 1970s, two novels appeared that were widely read and admired, *The Autobiography of a Brown Buffalo* and *The Revolt of the Cockroach People* by Oscar Zeta Acosta, a lawyer in real life. Acosta became a counter-cultural hero, whose character later figured prominently in Hunter S. Thompson's popular "Fear and Loathing" series, where he became the wild Samoan attorney, Dr. Gonzo. Acosta's two novels have been widely studied by literary scholars, particularly emphasizing his search for identity as a Mexican American, and the bawdy, picaresque depiction of his life in the late 1960s, when Chicano political consciousness was awakened on campuses.

In *Brown Buffalo,* he flees from his Legal Aid position and drives across the country and Mexico to find himself and discover his role in life. After a harrowing series of drug- and alcohol-related incidents, he returns to California, determined to become "Zeta, the world-famous Chicano lawyer who helped to start the last revolution."[26] In *Revolt,* Acosta blends historical and political events into his narrative, having decided to become someone of importance:

> I will change my name. I will learn Spanish. I will write the greatest books ever written.
> I will become the best criminal lawyer in the history of the world. I will save the world.
> I will show the world what is what and who the fuck is who. Me in particular.[27]

He then sets out on a variety of escapades, deftly meeting and incorporating figures from the times. He runs for Los Angeles County Sheriff; he defends Chicanos charged with political crimes; he testifies before the Los Angeles school board after a student walkout; he sues to get at the truth of a murdered reporter. These events and people become transmogrified into Acosta's tales in prose reeking of anger and a sense of the absurd. Acosta takes on a pseudonym, Buffalo Z. Brown, for its Mexican cultural antecedents and for the wistful significance of the American buffalo, doomed to extinction. As one scholar put it:

> The masks and use of fictionalization in ethnic autobiography are important keys to understand the intent and purpose of the autobiographer, for they help him to evaluate not only himself but also his race. In this particular case, *Brown Buffalo* represents the Chicano's confusion at the start of the Chicano Movement, while *Cockroach People* tells

us where he is heading as a result of this Movement. The reader travels with Acosta in his search for an identity because he can relate so strongly with the human emotions the narrator experiences, while at the same time he learns and arrives at an understanding of the history and ideology of the Chicano Movement.[28]

Although ostensibly fiction, Acosta's work, in several instances, draws from the author's real-life experience as a lawyer, as in the poignant portrait of the demoralizing work of a poverty lawyer, and in his handling of political cases, woven into *The Revolt of the Cockroach People*. One of these, *Castro v. Superior Court of Los Angeles County*,[29] actually broke new ground and fits Martha Minow's classification of cases that need to be undertaken for their monkey-wrenching value. In his fictional treatment of the case, all hell is breaking out in East Los Angeles, home to a half-million Mexican Americans. This parallels history. On March 3, 1968, many high school students began a series of walkouts, and by the time the strike was over, a week later, the "blowouts" had given many young Chicano students their first taste of politics:

> Overnight, student activism reached levels of intensity never before witnessed. A few Mexican American student activists had participated in civil rights marches, anti–Vietnam War protests, and had walked the picket lines for the farmworker movement. But the high school strike of 1968 was the first time students of Mexican descent had marched en masse in their own demonstration against racism and for educational change. It was also the first time that they had played direct leadership roles in organizing a mass protest.[30]

Several leaders of the strike and ten students were indicted by a grand jury in June 1968 and became known locally as the "LA Thirteen." This entire episode is recounted by Acosta in *Revolt*. Acosta and his co-counsel, in real life, attacked the indictments of the "LA Thirteen" on first amendment grounds, charging that the indictments were politically motivated, that the state educational code provisions under which they had been indicted were overbroad, and that both felony and misdemeanor counts should be dropped. The court of appeals agreed on all points, save the last, and preserved the misdemeanor counts. These misdemeanor counts had already been dismissed during collateral charges brought in municipal court, and the appeals court remanded for fact-finding on whether the District Attorney could press for further prosecution on the misdemeanors. When the charges were not refiled, victory for the "LA Thirteen" was complete.

In *Castro*, Acosta had also challenged the racial composition of the grand jury, but with the decision in the writ proceeding, this issue was set aside. In another, similar case, however, Acosta advanced the argument that because it was a politically-motivated prosecution, the appeals court should quash the grand jury indictments on the grounds that the juror selection process was racist in its virtual exclusion of Mexican Americans.[31] Acosta's data, for example, showed that in 1968, when 12.4 percent of Los Angeles County was Hispanic, only 3 grand jurors out of 171 serving that year were Hispanic, or 1.8 percent. This ratio of 6.9 available jurors to 1 juror called exceeded southern black grand juror ratios found discriminatory by the United States Supreme Court in earlier cases.

Los Angeles presented an additional feature in seating its grand juries, as each superior court judge was allowed to nominate two jurors. In 1969, 7 Hispanics had been nominated by 5 judges to the 189 positions. From 1959 to 1969, 25 of 1690 (2.8 percent) grand jurors in Los Angeles county courts were Hispanic. Acosta decided to subpoena the judges to find out why they had nominated so few Hispanics to their grand juries.

The trial court ruled against Acosta, finding that ten "Spanish-surnamed" persons had been nominated, of which a majority were Mexican American. "Therefore, it cannot be said that Mexican-Americans or persons with Spanish surnames were excluded from the 1969 grand jury."[32] Acosta, however, wanted to depose the superior court judges, including the then-presiding judge, about their nominations, which, he argued, were too few for the percentage of Latinos in the Los Angeles population at large. Acosta argued that, "as applied to a county containing over one-half million Spanish-surnamed persons, the peoples' 'explanations' of chronic tokenism in grand jury representation are inadequate, if not racist."[33]

The state had asserted that the low level of education explained why so few Latino jurors had been chosen. Acosta offered counter evidence, drawing from United States Census data and other cases that a sixth-grade education was the minimum education necessary to be called for grand jury duty. As the appeals court noted, Acosta intended to show that, with very few exceptions, the judges of the respondent court were by reason of birth, education, residence, wealth, social and professional associations, and similar factors not acquainted with the qualifications of eligible potential grand jurors of petitioners' class and that they did not make an adequate effort to overcome this alleged deficiency.[34] The appeals court, having found for Acosta on this point, granted the writ.

This was Acosta's last major case before he disappeared off the coast of Mexico in May 1974. In December 1986, he was declared legally dead. In 1989, his son arranged to have his two novels reissued, so that a new generation of readers could appreciate Acosta's lawyering skills. Acosta fit neatly within Minow's typology of lawyers who, through their representation of unpopular clients and causes, force the system to confront its political underpinnings. The Chicanos who became Acosta's clients felt that they had pursued peaceful solutions to improve community conditions. When they exercised their first amendment rights, the full force of the Los Angeles police power, including the political aspirant District Attorney, was directed at them. Acosta's defense tactics, challenging the racial composition of the grand jury process and the racial bona fides of the judges in the appointment process, led to acquittals of the defendants in both trials on all the major charges. His combination of acute political instincts and deft lawyering did not compromise his clients' interests, and largely vindicated them.

NOTES

1. Martha Minow, *Breaking the Law: Lawyers and Clients in Struggles for Social Change,* 52 U. Pitt. L. Rev. 723 (1991).

2. Tarasoff v. Regents of Univ. of Cal., 17 Cal. 3d 425, 131 Cal. Rptr. 14, 551 P.2d 334 (1976) (therapist had duty to warn identifiable potential victim of potential harm threatened by patient).

3. In *Murder in the Cathedral* the Archbishop is killed, but his ostensibly heroic action is undermined by his hubris, as he sought martyrdom.

4. *In re* Kunstler, 914 F.2d 505 (4th Cir. 1990).

5. *Id.* at 520.

6. *Don J. DeBenedictis, Rule 11 Snags Lawyers*, A.B.A. J., January 1991, at 17.

7. Blue v. United States Dep't. of the Army, 914 F.2d 525, 550 (4th Cir. 1990).

8. Minow, at 750.

9. Press release from Department of Justice, February 23, 1989, reprinted in CENTRAL AMERICAN ASYLUM-SEEKERS: HEARING BEFORE SUBCOMMITTEE ON IMMIGRATION, REFUGEES, AND INTERNATIONAL LAW OF THE HOUSE COMMITTEE ON THE JUDICIARY, 101st Cong., 1st Sess. 51 (1990) (Statement of Alan Nelson, Commissioner, INS) (INS enforcement plan "sends the message loud and clear to those thousands motivated only by economic betterment for themselves who use the asylum application to circumvent the process of awaiting for immigrant status in their home countries"). Economic hardship is not a criterion for refugee or asylum status.

10. Flores v. Meese, 681 F.Supp. 665 (C.D. Cal. 1988) (routine strip searches of detained alien juveniles violated juveniles' fourth amendment rights). This was overturned in 1990, 913 F.2d 1315 (9th Cir. 1990), but because the Ninth Circuit decided to rehear it en banc, the opinion was withdrawn.

11. 619 F.Supp. 656 (C.D. Cal. 1985).

12. Orantes-Hernandez v. Meese, 685 F.Supp. 1488, at 1504, 1505 (C.D. Cal. 1988).

13. *Id.* at 1498.

14. ABA COORDINATING COMMITTEE ON IMMIGRATION LAW, LIVES ON THE LINE: SEEKING ASYLUM IN SOUTH TEXAS 19 (1989).

15. Orantes-Hernandez, 685 F.Supp. 1495.

16. *Id.* at 1509.

17. Minow, at 749.

18. IDF Order No. 1220, 78(c) 1–2, reprinted in LAWYERS COMMITTEE FOR HUMAN RIGHTS, BACKGROUND MEMORANDUM: BOYCOTT OF THE MILITARY COURTS BY WEST BANK AND ISRAELI LAWYERS, app. A (1989) [hereinafter LCHR, 1989].

19. *Id.*

20. January 1, 1989, Press Release, reprinted in LCHR, 1989, at app. B, No. 6.

21. *Robert P. Schuwerk & John F. Sutton, Jr., A Guide to the Texas Disciplinary Rules of Professional Conduct*, 27 HOUS. L. REV. 1, 237, 269–70 (1990) [hereinafter *Guide*].

22. TEX. GOV'T CODE ANN. § 9 (Vernon Supp. 1991) (Tex. State Bar Rule 3.02).

23. *Id.*, Tex. State Bar Rule 3.04(c)(5), (d).

24. *Guide*, at 289. See also TEX. GOV'T CODE ANN. § 9 (Vernon Supp. 1991) (Tex. State Bar Rule 3.04(c)(1)).

25. *Id.* at 289.

26. Oscar Acosta, THE AUTOBIOGRAPHY OF A BROWN BUFFALO 199 (1972).

27. Oscar Acosta, THE REVOLT OF THE COCKROACH PEOPLE 31 (1973).

28. Kimberly Kowalczyk, Oscar Zeta Acosta: The Brown Buffalo and His Search for Identity, 16 AMERICAS REV. 198, 206 (Fall-Winter 1988).

29. Castro v. Superior Court, 9 Cal. App. 3d 675, 88 Cal. Rptr. 500 (1970).

30. Carlos Munoz, Jr., YOUTH, IDENTITY, POWER: THE CHICANO MOVEMENT 65 (1989). Carlos Munoz, Jr., who knew Acosta and appears in REVOLT as one of the East LA Thirteen, is a pro-

fessor of ethnic studies at the University of California, Berkeley. I am grateful to him for his assistance during discussions in March 1991.

31. Montez v. Superior Court, 10 Cal. App. 3d 343, 88 Cal. Rptr. 736 (1970). Acosta had raised this issue in Castro, but the judges decided the case without reaching the merits of this argument. The record, however, was well developed, and the transcript for this motion to quash in Castro filled more than a thousand pages. Castro v. Superior Court, 9 Cal. App. 3d 675, 680, 88 Cal. Rptr. 500, 504, 6 (1970).

32. *Id.* at 347 n.6, 88 Cal. Rptr. at 738 n.6.

33. Petitioners' Reply Brief at 4, Montez v. Superior Court, 10 Cal. App. 3d 343, 88 Cal. Rptr. 736 (1970) (Civ. No. 36021).

34. Montez, 88 Cal. Rptr. at 740.

Chapter 45

Life in the Trenches

Oscar *"Zeta" Acosta*

. . . That really affected my whole thing with the result that, when I got out of the service, I attempted suicide. Naturally, I chickened out like everybody else, but I ended up in psychiatry. I started school at San Francisco State and I started writing. I was majoring in creative writing and mathematics and I dug both of them. I had one more semester to go to get my degree in math but, by that time, I was halfway through a novel, so I dropped out to finish that and then intended to go back. I never did because by that time it was 1960, the Kennedy campaign and I got involved in that. I hadn't had a political thought up until then. I decided I didn't want to be either a mathematician or a professional writer after that involvement, but I did finish the novel and submitted it to three publishers, all of whom almost accepted it. They all said that I was great, earthy, poetic, the most brilliant unpublished writer in the world, but I was writing about Chicanos at that time—it was a Romeo and Juliet story of Okies and Chicanos in the valley—and that subject wasn't acceptable. So I decided I would write because that is what I am, a writer, but that I didn't want to have to write or to be a professional writer.

Since I was interested in politics and Chicanos, I decided to go to law school then work with Chávez and the farmworkers and be a union organizer. So I did it and got involved in the black civil rights movement for the next four years in San Francisco, but it wasn't really me. I told people that it wasn't just black and white, that there were Chicanos, too, and they laughed at me so I told them to go fuck themselves and they split. I graduated from San Francisco Law School, a night law school, in 1965. I was working at the *San Francisco Examiner* all of this time through college and law school as a copy boy, along with all of the political activity. When I got out, I took the bar exam and flunked it. It was the first time I had flunked an exam in my life and it was the third major trauma, so I ended up back with the psychiatrist. I studied for the bar again and passed it a couple of months later.

I became a legal aid lawyer in Oakland in a half-black, half-Chicano section. I hated it with a passion. I'd wake up in the morning and throw up. All we'd do was sit and listen to complaints. There were so many problems and we didn't do anything. We didn't have a direction, skills or tools.

After a year, I became totally depressed. I couldn't do anything, so I said fuck it to everything and I told the psychiatrist to shove it and to stick the pills up his ass. I said I'd been with him on and off for ten years and that I was still as fucked up as when I began, just taking ten times as many pills. I took off and ended up in Aspen.

I met some people who were pretty nice to me, including Hunter S. Thompson, the writer, and I started dropping acid and staying stoned most of the time and doing all kinds of odd jobs—construction work and washing dishes—and, within about three months my head was clear. I felt like I knew who I was, what I was and what I was supposed to do. I stayed there for about six months and then I was on my way to Guatemala to smuggle guns to the revolutionaries down there and to write about them. I got stopped in Juárez and thrown in jail. When I got out I called my brother who suggested that I go to Los Angeles. Well, I hated it. Being from up north, I was subjected to this old prejudice between Northern and Southern California, which was ridiculous. I asked my brother why I should go there and about a newspaper called *La Raza*. That was in January 1968. I arrived here in LA in February, intending to stay for a few months, write an article about it and then get out.

Then the high school walkouts occurred and I agreed to take a few misdemeanor cases. Two months later, thirteen of the organizers of the walkouts were busted on sixteen counts of conspiracy which could have resulted in forty-five years in prison for each of them. I agreed to take the case. It was my first major case, my first criminal case and here I am three years later. I haven't been able to get away and I don't think I ever will leave. This is it for me because I've gone through intensive changes in myself and my consciousness has developed about Chicanismo, La Raza, revolution and what we're going to do, so it looks like I'm here to stay. It seems to me that at some point in your life you have to make a stand, and I've decided that I might as well be here as anywhere else. This, East Los Angeles, is the capital of Aztlán, because there are more of us here than anywhere else.

To understand where I am you have to understand how the Chicano Movement has developed. In 1967 and 1968 young Chicano students, both in high school and college, began to identify as Mexican Americans. The first issue was what to call themselves. They began to organize coffee-houses and clubs but were mainly interested in the educational system. So, in March 1968, they had massive high school walkouts from four of the Mexican-American high schools in East Los Angeles. The result was numerous busts and that is when I became involved. Those walkouts were the first major activity by Chicanos as Chicanos in the history of this country. There had been labor groups and political-type groups, but there had never been any group organized to organize and politicize the community as Chicanos on broad-based issues. There are two million Chicanos here in Southern California. I think we're the largest ethnic minority in the Southwest—certainly here in Los Angeles we are. Statistically, we're the lowest in education, with an eighth-grade education being the median, and we're the lowest in housing and jobs. We have the problems here in Los Angeles and the Southwest that the blacks have throughout the country.

But the history of the Southwest is totally different from the history of the rest of the country, which is something that most people don't understand, and they don't understand that this historical relationship is what causes the attitudes that exist here today. They tend to see us as immigrants, which is absolutely wrong. We were here before the white man got here. The American government took our country away from us in 1848, when the government of Mexico sold us out. They sold not only the land, but they basically sold us as slaves in the sense that our labor and our land was being expropriated. The governments never gave us a choice about whether or not to be American citizens. One night we were Mexican and the next day we were American. This historical relationship is the most important part of the present day relationships, but it's totally ignored or unknown or rejected by the Anglo society.

In 1968, when we started making a movement toward attaining better education and schools, we wanted the literature to reflect our heritage and our culture. We started meeting with school boards and the city council and we began to know the enemy. At that point I think that most of us believed we could integrate into the society and get a piece of the action, since nobody denied that we had problems. But now, three years later, there have been few changes. Now there are two assemblymen in the California legislature, one Congressman, and one member of the school board who are Chicanos, and that is it for a class that constitutes 13 percent of the population.

In 1968, our first problem was that of identity. As time went on we no longer questioned that. We had chosen a name—Chicano—whether we had Spanish or Indian blood, and we knew that we existed alone. That is, we relate to Mexico, but in a nostalgic way. We know that when the going gets rough, the Mexican government ain't going to do shit for us. And we know that no other aspect of the broad movement is going to do shit for us. They'll pay lip service, they'll condescend to us, but basically they're just as paternalistic to us as the white racist pigs. For example, I've spoken at numerous rallies for the Panthers, for Angela Davis, and every time I get the same bullshit treatment. I'm the last on the program with five minutes to speak and we get no offers of any real unity or working together.

I think that the Black Movement has been co-opted. Three years ago I used to know a lot of heavy blacks. They're just not around anymore. I'm talking about the Black Panthers. They're just rhetoric; they're just sucking in that money. They talk heavy as hell, but when it comes down to what they're fighting for I don't think even they know what they're fighting for because they're integrating into the society that they despise as fast as that society allows them to. I made this decision during Corky's trial.

Corky González is head of the Crusade for Justice, which is based in Denver. He is also a poet, a street-fighter, a theorist and an organizer, and he is recognized by a lot of Chicanos as the boss, the leader. Chávez is like a grandfather to the Movement. We respect him and love him and would help him anytime he asked, but we don't feel that his progress, his ideology, is Chicano enough. César used the white liberal population quite a bit and, more than anything, this offends the average Chicano. It is bad because they take jobs that Chicanos should be taking and using them is the easy way out. There were probably more competent white militants three years ago than there were available Chicanos, but we feel that he should have trained his own people more as we do now.

Corky was on trial on a weapons charge arising out of the August 29, 1970, police riot here, where three people, including Rubén Salazar, were killed by the police. Corky had been trying to get away from the violence with his two children when the police busted him for a traffic violation, suspicion of robbery, and a concealed weapons charge. He was on a truck with a lot of people and we never denied that somebody on it had a loaded pistol, but it wasn't Corky. He wouldn't dare carry a goddamn gun around with him. He's a leader. He doesn't have to carry a gun for the same goddamn reason that Nixon doesn't have to. But we didn't stress that point at the trial for fear of alarming the jury and perhaps inflaming the press and cops. Why should we give them an excuse to shoot at Corky like they did at Rubén when they thought that he was a leader?

What I did stress in picking the jury was whether they would be prejudiced if Huey Newton testified for Corky. See, Huey had called and said he wanted to talk to me. I asked him if he'd come down and be a character witness for Corky. I thought it would be a great show of unity. Everybody said he would. Then, after I'd announced it all over town and picked a jury by hammering at that question, he wouldn't come or talk to me on the phone, so I have nothing more to do with the Black Movement. I'm talking about the professional revolutionaries, not the people.

I think in the past year or so the Chicano movement has begun to solidify. After the August 29th thing, there was the National Chicano Moratorium "non-violent march for justice" on January 31, 1971. It was against police brutality and repression and was non-violent until the end when fighting broke out and the cops swarmed out of the police station with everything, including twelve-gauge shotguns firing buckshot balls straight into the crowd. After two hours, one person was dead, thirty seriously injured, and there was about a half-million dollars' worth of damage, including seventy-eight burned police cars.

Things have gotten heavier since then and Chicano consciousness is spreading. Everybody in "El Barrio" is a Brown Beret. It's a concept, an idea. M.E.CH.A (Movimiento Estudiantil Chicano de Aztlán): the Chicano-student movement is also growing. Aztlán is the land we're sitting on now. The land where my forefathers lived hundreds of years ago before they migrated to the valley of Mexico. The Aztecs referred to the entire Southwest as Aztlán. Now the Chicano movement has no need for anyone else's ideas but our own. We have a way of life that we've learned from childhood. The concept of *la familia,* the respect for elders is not Sunday-school bullshit with us. It's part of our culture. A Chicano can no more disrespect his mother than he can himself. Which means he can, but at great cost to himself. The concept of community—of La Raza—isn't a political term to us as I feel it is to black and white radicals. The term brother is a social term to us, one we learn before we learn about politics.

We don't kid ourselves anymore. We know we're headed for a head-on collision with the rest of society. We're absolutely convinced of it and we're not being paranoid or nothing. We know that the main thing we want now is not better education or better jobs or better housing, because we know that they are not possible to achieve. It is not possible as the result of the history of human nature and the animal instinct against the races integrating in the liberal sense of the word.

You can't be a class or a nation without land. Without it, it doesn't have any meaning. It's that simple. So we are beginning to see that what we're talking about is getting land and having our own government. Period. It is that clear-cut. As to what land, that is still in the future. We have to develop the consciousness of land as the principal issue, just as three years ago we had to develop the consciousness of identity as the principal issue.

The black man came here as a slave. He is not of this land. He is so removed from his ancestry that he has nothing but the white society to identify with. We have history. We have culture. We had a land. We do feel solidarity with the American Indians because we are Indians. We have a total unification in ideology but no unification organizationally. I look upon them as my blood brothers. It is the Indian aspect of our ancestry that gives meaning to the term "La Raza." We are La Raza. Of course there is Spanish and European blood in us, but we don't always talk about it because it is not something that we are proud of. For me, my native ancestry is crucial. This consciousness is beginning to develop now, symbolized in the word *tierra*. We want our land back and this is what we are going to be fighting for.

I don't think you're going to see too much more of demonstrations against education or things of that sort. I think that has petered itself out. A lot of kids have gotten into OEO projects and school projects as a result of the movement, so they've been in college for a few years now and they are as hip to what's being taught in the colleges as the white radicals have been for some years now. They think it is a waste of time, that it takes away what little you have of your identity.

A perfect example is the National La Raza Law Students Association, here in Los Angeles, which I am pretty much associated with. The very first day they started school here on some OEO project I went in and spoke and told them, "Half of you will never be lawyers. Those of you that do are going to become so only because of your race. You got into these programs because you're Chicano. So you owe something to your Raza. Yet, I predict that in three years I'm going to be fighting 50 percent of you guys. You're going to be my enemies." They laughed. But it is a fact. This past year I've been working on these major cases of importance to Chicanos not only organizationally but legally, and often I've been unable to get the assistance of the Chicano law students. My prophecy to them has come true, except I was wrong in one respect. It is not 50 percent I'm fighting. It is about 75 percent. This is why I'm no longer pushing for more school programs, more handouts, more welfare. I think that will destroy the movement. They are attempting with those to do the same things they did to blacks.

For example, with the law students when I was doing this judges' thing in 1971, they didn't want to be associated with it because they were afraid that it might affect their future, their careers. That judges' thing was my third challenge to the Grand Jury system here. I was defending the "Biltmore Six," six young Chicanos who were busted for allegedly trying to burn down the Biltmore Hotel one night in 1970, when Reagan was delivering a speech. They were indicted by a Grand Jury and I contended that all Grand Juries are racist since all grand jurors have to be recommended by Superior Court judges and that the whole thing reeks of "subconscious, institutional racism." I was trying to get the indictments squashed on that basis.

To prove my contention I subpoenaed all 109 Superior Court judges in Los Angeles and examined them all under oath about their racism. After almost a year of work on this, the judge on that case, Arthur Alarcón, who is Mexican American, rejected the motion. The way it looks now, I think we're just about finished with that whole legal game.

I'm the only Chicano lawyer here. By that I mean the only one that has taken a militant posture, to my knowledge, in the whole country. When I got here I decided that if I was going to become anything legal I couldn't use the profession as it was. Lawyers are basically peddlers of flesh. They live off of other people's misery. Well, I couldn't do that. I made a decision that I would never charge a client a penny. As a matter of fact, I end up supporting some of my clients. I get money by begging, borrowing, and stealing. Sometimes I get a grant from some foundation like Ford. For a while I was under a Reggie program, although all I was doing was political, criminal work and they knew it. I don't even have an office. I'm in court practically every day.

I relate to the court system first as a Chicano and only seldom as a lawyer in the traditional sense. I have no respect for the courts and I make it clear to them from the minute I walk in that I have no respect for the system. That I'm against it and would destroy it in one second if I had the physical power to do it. The one thing I've learned to do is use criminal defense work as an organizing tool. That is my specialty. I organize in the courtroom. I take no case unless it is or can become a Chicano Movement case. I turn it into a platform to espouse the Chicano point of view so that that affects the judge, the jury, the spectators. We organize each case, set up defense committees, student groups, and use the traditional methods of organizing.

I think one thing I haven't mentioned enough yet, which is a very pertinent thing, is what drugs have done for me personally. I think psychedelic drugs have been important to the development of my consciousness. I don't think I'd have gotten to where I am without the use of these drugs. They've put me into a level of awareness where I can see myself and see what I'm really doing. Most of the big ideas I've gotten for my lawyer work have usually come when I am stoned. Like the Grand Jury challenge was the result of an acid experience. A lot of the tactics I employ I get the ideas for when I am stoned, which is not to say that I wouldn't get them if I wasn't stoned. A lot of my creativity has sprung from my use of these psychedelic drugs. And this doesn't just apply to me. When I got here to LA three years ago, I only knew one other guy who was taking acid. Guys were shooting heroin and they'd say to me "You dope addict. Are you crazy?" Now, just about all of my friends have tried or are taking acid. I think the acid experience is part and parcel of the radical Chicano Movement.

I don't have much contact with many of the other radical lawyers here. I think a lot of them are still finding themselves. Consequently, they'll often chicken out of something at the last minute. I think it's chickenshit, reactionary, and that they're the enemies of the people. I like them; they're nice guys, but it's too late for these personal things. Too many of them aren't doing the work that has to be done.

Now some of the Chicano law students are thinking of organizing a collective, but I've disagreed because I think it is looking to the future as any other lawyer would do. They are thinking in terms of money to make, cases to take. They're thinking of business. For me, to think of the future is inconsistent with my thinking of the present. It is only the present that is important. I think you develop yourself much more if you don't think of those things, if you think only of the job: defending Chicanos and organizing around the case.

Chapter 46

The Work We Know So Little About

Gerald P. López

I met someone not long ago who too many of us regrettably have come to regard as unremarkable, someone who might well find herself, along any number of fronts, working with a lawyer in a fight for social change. I'll call her María Elena. She lives with her two children in San Francisco's Mission District where she works as a housekeeper. She works as a mother too. And as a tutor of sorts. And as a seamstress. And as a cook. And as a support for those other women—those other Irish-American women, African-American women, Chinese-American women, and most especially those other Latinas—with whom she finds herself in contact. She works in much the same way as many other low-income women of color I've known over the years—women who surrounded me while I was growing up in East L.A., women who helped out in certain fights I participated in while practicing in San Diego, women who largely sustain various formal and informal grassroots efforts that a number of our law students now work with in those communities of working poor that line the east side of Highway 101 on the peninsula, from San Francisco through San Jose.

How María Elena and her children make it from day to day tells us all a great deal about where we live, whom we live with, and even about how peoples' actual experiences measure up to the "American dream"—a contrast that nowadays tends to get obscured and even denied around an election year. Indeed, our own lives are tied inescapably to the María Elenas in our communities. These women are important parts of our economy, indispensable parts of certain of our worklives, and even intimate parts of some of our households. In a very palpable way, María Elena's struggles implicate us. More perhaps than we acknowledge and more perhaps than feels comfortable, she and we help construct one another's identities. We're entangled.

Historically, you'd think that how the María Elenas of our communities make it from day to day should have played an obvious and central role in training those whose vocation is to serve as lawyers in the fight for social change. After all, the lives in which these lawyers intervene often differ considerably from their own—in terms of class, gender, race, ethnicity, and sexual orientation. Without laboring to understand these lives and their own entanglements with them, how else can lawyers begin to appreciate how their professional knowledge and skills may be perceived and deployed by those with whom they strive to ally themselves? How else can they begin to speculate about how their intervention may affect their clients' everyday relationships with employers, landlords, spouses, and the state? And how else can they begin to study whether proposed strategies actually have a chance of penetrating the social and economic situations they'd like to help change?

But, as my niece might say, "Get a clue!" Whatever else law schools may be, they have not characteristically been where future lawyers go to learn about how the poor and working poor live. Or about how the elderly cope. Or how the disabled struggle. Or about how gays and lesbians build their lives in worlds that deny them the basic integrity of identity. Or about how single women of color raise their children in the midst of underfinanced schools, inadequate social support, and limited job opportunities. Indeed, in many ways both current and past lawyers fighting for social change and all with whom they collaborate (both clients and other social activists) have had to face trying to learn how largely to overcome rather than to take advantage of law school experience. What's ultimately extraordinary, I think, is that these relationships work at all and that we can even sometimes fully realize an allied fight for social change.

If you think this overstates all that together confronts the María Elenas of our communities and those lawyers with whom they work, take a brief glimpse through my eyes at María Elena's life and what it seems to say about any future relationship she might have with even the best lawyers. Thirty-one years old, she first set foot in this country a little over eight years ago. She came from Mexico with her husband, their two-year-old son, their three-month-old daughter, and no immigration documents. Not unlike thousands upon thousands of others, the family worked its way from San Diego, through Los Angeles, to Gilroy—picking flowers, mowing lawns, and harvesting fruit—surviving on the many day laborers' jobs that pervade the secondary labor market in this state and living in situations the rest of us would recoil from. Nearly two years later, they finally landed in the Mission District, expecting to reunite with some cousins and gain some stability. Instead, they found only confusing tales from various sources about how their *primos* had been deported after an INS factory raid in the East Bay.

More by force of habit than anything else, María Elena found herself trying to make do—hustling a place to live and her first job as a housekeeper. But the frustrations and indignities of undocumented life already had begun to take their toll on her husband. He couldn't find stable work; he couldn't support his family; he couldn't adjust to the sort of shadowy existence they seemed compelled to endure. Somewhere along the line, María Elena can't quite remember when, he just sort of withdrew from it all. From her, from the children, from trying. He wasn't violent or drunken. He just shrank into himself and didn't do much at all for months. And then one day when María Elena and the kids returned from grocery shopping, he was gone.

That was some four years ago and (it doesn't take much talking to María Elena to realize) many lonely, confused, hurt, angry, scared, and even guilty tears ago. It was also some 1,300-plus housekeeping days ago. For María Elena has come to realize the hard way that housekeeping for her and for so many other women of color no longer serves as the first and worst of jobs in a work career in the United States—as, for example, it once did in the late nineteenth century and still to some degree does for women from Western Europe. It's not that María Elena hasn't tried to find a job that pays better, that offers benefits and job security. She'd be interested, for example, in pursuing a recently publicized opening for some low-level industrial job, except that other Latinas have told her about the employer's so-called fetal protection policy—one that either endangers the health of future children or forces women to get sterilized. And she episodically searches for openings as a custodian and as an electronics assembler—jobs which most of us think of as being on the bottom rung of the job ladder, but which in most regards would be a step up for her and other housekeepers. She's found these jobs very hard to come by, however, except for the occasional openings on night shifts which her obligations to her kids just won't permit her to take.

Though she may be stuck in her job as a housekeeper, there's something unresolved and edgy about María Elena's daily existence. Things are always moving for her and her kids. Getting off to school and work. Coordinating the kids' return with a neighbor's afternoon schedule. Timing her own return with enough space to care for their needs and anxieties, particularly about school. Dealing with their illnesses while still honoring her housekeeping obligations. Often she drags her kids places others would not, and sometimes she leaves them alone when those of us who can afford the luxury of help would never consider it. She never has enough money to buy everything they see around them, but she tries to make sure they get what they need. When times get bad, they cut back. All in all, she seems to be a master of planned improvisation—about food, shelter, and medical care. You can feel her will and drive, and you can easily imagine her children's best efforts to help out. You can also sense, however, the interconnectedness of a range of difficult conditions any one of which might drive most of us to feeling that things had gotten out of control.

As if life weren't eventful enough, last year proved particularly epochal for María Elena and the kids. She decided to try to legalize their status in the United States through the provisions of the Immigration Reform and Control Act—the so-called amnesty program. It wasn't so much that the decision demanded that she resolve complex feelings about national allegiance; instead, it seemed to require that she make their lives vulnerable to law, to lawyers, and to government bureaucracy. For diffuse reasons, María Elena has come to regard law and lawyers as more dangerous than helpful. And time and again she has experienced governmental bureaucracies as inscrutable, senseless, and unchangeable. Even many of the lawyers and social service providers who advertised their willingness to help with legalization seemed, so far as she could tell, gouging, disorganized, or both.

So, in her effort to retain some control over the situation, María Elena cautiously took advantage of a self-help program designed and delivered by a service organization which a number of her neighbors and local church groups had recommended as trustworthy and able. She found the program direct, accessible, and patient. In her words, "They kinda knew what we had to hear—you know, what we were going through, what we needed to do. From step one on." In this sense, she was lucky. For while some 70 percent of applicants both in the Bay Area and nationally undertook to complete their legalization applications on their own, most did not have the advantage of any effective outreach efforts, much less programs that spoke directly to their needs.

Still, María Elena experienced the message she heard about the law's demands as profoundly threatening and disorienting. After all, being told she now had to prove that she and her children had been in this country continuously for the last five years ran against everything she had trained herself to do while here. Like virtually every other undocumented worker, she had become expert at not leaving a paper trail. And she had found many people willing to accommodate her efforts to achieve a certain invisibility. Every one of her previous employers, for example, paid her in cash for her work—though perhaps not so much to protect her and her children, as to protect themselves, since they rarely paid minimum wage and never paid into social security for her housekeeping. Now, through some perverse irony, she was being told that she'd better hope that she hadn't been too good at covering her tracks.

Some rewarding moments have marked María Elena's effort to qualify for legalization. She seems, for example, now to take considerable pride in her own ingenuity—an ingenuity that managed to uncover the shardlike pieces of evidence of her family's continuing presence here. But the experience has not been without its considerable anxieties, and not just because María Elena profoundly mistrusts the INS. One former employer (a family of married doctors whose house and children María Elena cared for over a fifteen-month period) mistakenly feared that documenting María Elena's employment would expose them to criminal liability both for having employed an undocumented worker and for having not paid minimum wage or contributed to social security. While the couple somewhat grudgingly wrote a short note on their personal stationery to help María Elena meet the application deadline, they refused a subsequent INS request—a quite standard one—for a notarized statement. So María Elena found herself again trying to talk the couple into helping—doing her best to explain the law, to avoid inadvertently antagonizing them, and to help them work through the embarrassment they seemed to fear in making a notarized admission.

The simple fact is that instability will remain the law of life for María Elena and her kids—at least for some time. Even if she convinces this couple to cooperate, she's a long way from knowing she's going to get her green card—the key to insuring her continued future employment and her family's existence here in the United States. Initially, she must await INS approval of her current application for a temporary permit—with all that implies about the notorious vagaries of INS discretion. Then, if all goes well, she must still negotiate her way through phase two of the legalization procedure—the so-called ESL/Civics requirement, which demands demonstrated knowledge of English, U.S. history, and government. Yet until quite recently no one knew for sure what phase two actually would require of her and other applicants. Certainly, INS hadn't helped to dispel the confusion, since it kept changing (sometimes radically changing) its incomplete proposed regulations—even after some people were supposed to begin applying on November 7, 1988. And, for the longest time, lawyers, community service organizations, and educators couldn't possibly walk people through the maze with any confidence, since they couldn't predict—and probably shouldn't have been predicting—what the INS would finally decide to sanction.

So, like so many other people in her position, María Elena does her best to sort her way through the confusion. She's tried to reconcile the cautious advice of certain church and service organizations with the glitzy radio ads promoting private programs that guarantee green cards—all the time remembering to keep her ear to the ground for the ever-evolving rumors that make their way around the Mission. She heard somewhere that certain courses at community colleges and high schools have been or will be certified by the INS as meeting the ESL/Civics requirements. But she's found a number of schools increasingly cautious about promising anything, others suspiciously willing to promise too much, and most courses with waiting lists backed up seemingly forever. Meanwhile, to bring matters full circle, she's begun to sense that the employers she now works for would very much like her to get all this taken care of—so that they can know whether they can depend on her or have to hire another housekeeper.

For all her problems, María Elena just can't see herself seeking a lawyer's help, even at places with so positive a reputation as, say, the Immigrant Legal Resource Center, the Employment Law Center, or California Rural Legal Assistance. "Being on the short end and being on the bottom is an everyday event in my life," she says, half-smiling. "What can a lawyer do about that?" That doesn't make it all right, she admits. But she says she's learned to live with it—to deal with it in her own ways. In any event, lawyers and law all seem to conjure up for her big, complicated fights— fights that, as she sees it, would pit her against a social superior, her word against that of a more respected someone else, her lack of written records against the seemingly infinite amount of paper employers seem able to come up with when they must. Because she retains her sense of order by focusing on keeping her family's head above water, lawyers and law most often seem irrelevant to and even inconsistent with her day-to-day struggles.

Were María Elena alone in these sentiments, lawyers might have little cause for concern. But you may be surprised to learn that María Elena is scarcely unique in her views about lawyers and law—though, to be sure, some of her problems may well be peculiarly the product of her immigration status. In fact, we are beginning to discover that many other low-income women of color—Asian Americans, Native Americans, Latinas, Blacks—apparently feel much the same way as María Elena, even if they were born here and even when their families have been in this country for generations. Much else may well divide these women — after all, political and social subordination is not a homogeneous or monolithic experience. Still, their actions seem to confirm María Elena's impulses and their words seem to echo María Elena's own.

The little thus far uncovered about whether and how people translate perceived injuries into legal claims seems to confirm what apparently the María Elenas in our communities have been trying to tell us for quite some time, each in her own way. *Low-income women of color seldom go to lawyers, and they institute lawsuits a good deal less frequently than anybody else.* More particularly, they convert their experiences of oppression into claims of discrimination far less often than they (and everybody else) press any other legal claim. Indeed, most learn never even to call oppressive treatment an injury; if they do, many simply "lump it" rather than personally pressing it against the other party, much less pressing a formal claim through a lawyer. For all the popular (and I might add exaggerated) descriptions bemoaning how litigious we've all become, nearly all careful observers concede that low-income women of color seek legal remedies far too infrequently, especially when discriminated against at work. Partly as a result, they still seem to endure regularly the injustice and the indignities that those in high office insist just don't exist much in this enlightened era—at least not in their circles, where everyone seems to be doing just fine.

Most of us presume that this state of affairs bespeaks the unfortunate failure of these women constructively to use lawyers and law—an inability to serve their own needs. You know the litany as well as I do—it almost rolls off the tongue. Lack of information and knowledge about their rights. Limited resources for using legal channels. Limited understanding of the legal culture. And if you're sitting there thinking that this litany still retains real explanatory bite, you're right. The anticipation of rejections by unresponsive agencies, the cost and unavailability of lawyers, the technical obstacles to pursuing causes of action all serve in advance as background assumptions deterring low-income women of color from pressing formal claims. But if you listen carefully to people like María Elena, you begin to realize that they're saying something else is also going on—something that both they themselves and the lawyers with whom they work often find even more difficult to overcome.

Apparently, in order to use law (particularly antidiscrimination law) and lawyers, many low-income women of color must overcome fear, guilt, and a heightened sense of destruction. In their eyes, such a decision often amounts to nothing less intimidating than taking on conventional power with relatively little likelihood of success. It also means assuming an adversarial posture toward the very people and institutions that, in some perverse ways, you've come to regard as connected to you, at least insofar as they employ you when others will not (put aside at what wage, under what conditions, and with what benefits). And it seems inevitably to entail making your life entirely vulnerable to the law—with its powers to unravel the little you've got going for yourself and your family. In effect, turning to law and lawyers seems to signify a formal insurrection of sorts—an insurrection that, at least for these low-income women of color, foreshadows discomfiting experiences and negative consequences.

Instead of using law and lawyers, most low-income women of color often deal with oppressive circumstances through their own stock of informal strategies. Sometimes they tend to minimize or reinterpret obvious discrimination. María Elena, for example, tells me she often chalks up bad treatment to personal likes or dislikes or denies that it could really be about her. At the same time, these women also employ certain more proactive devices in an effort to alter the situations in which they work. For example, the loose network of housekeepers of which María Elena is a part (including both formal work cooperatives and informal support groups), seems to be trying to transform their relationship with employers from master/servant to customer/skilled service provider, all in the somewhat vague but hardly irrational hope that current wages, conditions, and benefits will improve along the way.

Yet for the most part, these low-income women of color have fewer illusions about these strategies than you might first presume. They know that you can't explain away all discriminatory treatment and that you can't alter every oppressive situation through informal devices. And they even seem to sense that while they may perceive their own less formal approach to their problems as self-sustaining, it often turns out to be self-defeating. After all, they know better than the rest of us that too many of them still get paid too little, for too many hours of work, in terrible conditions, with absolutely no health benefits or care for their children, and with little current hope of much job mobility over the course of their lifetimes.

Still, you shouldn't facilely condemn the sense of skepticism many low-income women of color feel about the intervention of lawyers and law, particularly if you appreciate (as no doubt you do) that lawyers and law can hardly ensure them the help they need. These women simply find themselves drawn to those informal strategies more within their control and less threatening than subjecting the little they have to the invasive experience and uncertain outcomes of the legal culture. Their collective past has taught them that seeking a legal remedy for their problems will not likely improve their position, and may well fracture their fragilely constructed lives. If low-income women of color and the very best lawyers at places like the Immigrant Legal Resource Center and the East Palo Alto Community Law Project would seem to offer one another special possibilities, they simultaneously present reciprocally enigmatic challenges. Each potentially threatens the very aspirations that hooking up with the other is meant in part to fulfill.

Somehow in the midst of all this, the María Elenas of our communities and at least the very best lawyers with whom they work still manage more than occasionally to make contact, to get things done, and even to find credible self-affirmation in the collective effort. In some instances, no doubt, they join together out of desperation. If you need or want to help badly enough, you can often figure out ways to hook up and make the relationship work. That is nothing to scoff at. It may well suggest how most things get done in this world, and it certainly says something about the human spirit under pressure.

At its best, this joint effort at fighting political and social subordination can be a story of magnificent mutual adaptation. At those times, both the María Elenas of our communities and those lawyers with whom they work face the enigma of their relationship head on. Both try to be sensitive to, without uncritically acquiescing in, their respective needs and concerns. Both depend on the other to make some sense of how their overlapping knowledge and skills might inform a plausible plan of action. Both try to connect their particular struggle to other particular struggles and to particular visions of the state and the political economy. And both inevitably challenge the other as together they put a part of themselves on the line. In short, when things go well they seem capable of favorably redefining over time the very terms that otherwise circumscribe their capacity to take advantage of one another's will to fight.

Still, you should realize that legal education's historical disregard of practice with the politically and socially subordinated survives in all of us, even as some of us continue to try to break with this past. All of us (practitioners, teachers, students, other lay and professional activists) have learned, to one degree or another, not even really to notice inspired and imaginative work in fights against subordination, much less to study how it happens, how it might be taught, and what it might mean for us all. It's not simply that I think we have screwed-up views about lawyering for social change. More critically, we don't even treat it, because we don't even see it, as remarkably complex and enigmatic work—with multiple and even elusive dimensions, presenting massive conceptual and empirical challenges, and cultural and interpersonal dynamics more daunting and even more self-defining than we are accustomed to handling. Just as we have come to regard María Elena as too unremarkable to pay much attention to, so too have we come to understand working with her as like anything else in law, except (to be truthful) a lot more lightweight, formulaic, and intellectually vapid.

At the heart of the matter, we simply must come to realize that we all make those communities we call our own. That the problems of the María Elenas of this world are our problems, the future of María Elena's children is our future, and that the failure to share what clout we do exercise is ultimately our own failure, and a tragic and even dangerous one at that. We have a rare chance over the next several years to bring to life the systematic study of the work we know so little about, work that in many ways tells us precisely what we need most to know about ourselves—those sorts of things we'd often rather not hear, much less change. If we're big enough as people and honest enough as an institution, then in the near future María Elena and those others with whom she lives and labors might even come to recognize themselves as mattering—as systematically mattering—to the training we provide and the practice of law we help inspire.

Chapter 47

Revolutionary Art and Artists

Margaret E. Montoya

Much recent work by Chicano/a artists introduces counterhegemonic narratives, challenging, rejecting, and displacing the purportedly objective interpretations embedded in such concepts as meritocracy, consent, and individualized rights. Carl Gutiérrez-Jones, for example, argues that the stereotypic and racist constructions and representations of Chicanos-as-criminals provide justifications for the surveillance and policing practices of the state while simultaneously engendering a self-disciplining of Chicano/a desire, conscience, and imagination. His *Rethinking the Borderlands* is laced with the Gramsci-Foucauldian views that the disciplining forces of the state function most effectively when articulating with the consent of the subordinated community, a consent that emerges from the manipulations of legal rhetoric. Gutiérrez-Jones shows how this dynamic can be destabilized through the discursive and representational techniques of Chicano/a artists.

The borderlands metaphor in Gutiérrez-Jones's title defines the spheres of cultural conflict where the Chicano/a artist "unable to affect directly the panoptic institutions of the Anglo society relies on the uncanny ability of panoptic structures to be turned back on the internalized desires engendered by those who control the strategies of the institutions."[1] Both Chicanos and Chicanas resist being constructed through Anglo narratives as dependent, criminally inclined, and marginal among the producers of cultural and literary and, by extension, academic capital. Gutiérrez-Jones's objectives are not limited to this reframing of dominant sociolegal narratives through Chicano/a interpretation. The most provocative part of the book identifies the borderlands as sites of patriarchal contestation between Chicanos and Chicanas. Chicanas, lesbians and straights, struggle against being constructed through Chicano narratives as rape-shamed, un-voiced, and effaced.

Once having drawn the Chicana into the borderlands of his critique, Gutiérrez-Jones pauses to interrogate the propriety of his intervention as a "non-Chicana" into discussions about the "Chicana's own cultural self-exploration, self-definition, and self-invention."[2] Raising appropriate concerns about displacing Chicana discussions

From "Book Review—Carl Gutiérrez-Jones, Rethinking the Borderlands: Between Chicano Culture and Legal Discourse (Berkeley: University of California Press, 1995)." 5 (3) Soc. Legal Stud. 435 (1996). Originally published in *Social and Legal Studies*. Reprinted by permission of Sage Publications, Ltd.

and acknowledging the policing and panoptic functions of the critic, he eschews notions of consent, hegemonically embedded as they are with coercion and illusion. Gutiérrez-Jones instead proposes that the translation practices used by María Helena Viramontes in her story "Cariboo Café" (from *The Moths and Other Stories*, 1985) offer a mechanism for the non-Chicana to enter into an oblique dialogue with Chicana narratives:

> Resisting the monological authority of the law, the story presents multiple distinct voices, which are significantly *not* resolved into a judgmental closure by either an omniscient narrator or a reflective character. The problem of reading the events recounted and the desires expressed is thus placed in a frame which recognizes differing criteria calling out for translation, a frame whose thematic lack of a "key" is supported by a structure which is oriented toward process, not product.[3]

Such practices, he tantalizingly suggests, are available for other cross-cultural and cross-disciplinary readings.

Employing a different, although related, multivoiced technique, Gutiérrez-Jones reads the "homosocial" texts of Edward James Olmos's *American Me* and Oscar Zeta Acosta's *Revolt of the Cockroach People* against the academic texts of historian Deena González and Patricia Preciado Martín's story "The Ruins" (in *Days of Plenty, Days of Want*, 1988). He characterizes Mexicana and Chicana mourning practices found in González's study of nineteenth-century wills and testaments and other more recent fictive narratives about loss as a "pursuit of a socially and politically situated grieving" and a "means of contestation" against U.S. hegemony through the reverse manipulation of legal rhetoric.[4]

Rethinking the Borderlands is also a complex dialogue between two voices that re/enacts Chicano/a linguistic history: the voice (heard in Gutiérrez-Jones's elegant expository prose) that speaks a polysyllabic and unaccented English signaling our arrival and legitimacy in the academy and the larger society, y *la voz de resistencia* [heard in the narratives] that invokes the syntactically unorthodox English that we use to create our polylingual stories and to invent our hybrid identities.

NOTES

1. Carl Gutiérrez-Jones, Rethinking the Borderlands: Between Chicano Culture and Legal Discourse 88 (1995).
2. *Id.* at 118.
3. *Id.* at 121.
4. *Id.* at 153.

From the Editors
Issues and Comments

Do you think that direct action by Latinos—such as high school walkouts and grape boycotts—has been more, or less, successful than similar actions employed by blacks?

Do you agree with Gerald López that the U.S. Constitution means little to the Chicano community and can only come to acquire meaning through struggle and fighting?

Should people of color consistently confront racism and unthinking prejudice and remarks every time they meet them, or would this be exhausting and unfair?

Should radical lawyers, as Michael Olivas puts it, sometimes break the law on principle? Is this any different from similar illegality on the part of the KKK or white supremacist groups?

Oscar "Zeta" Acosta envisions "a head-on collision with the rest of society" in store for Chicanos as an unavoidable consequence of developing Chicano consciousness and the demands of justice. Is he referring to a purely institutional collision or an actual uprising? Were Martin Luther King, Jr., and Mohandas Gandhi revolutionaries, even though they both espoused nonviolence? What about Acosta? Do you feel that his "collision" has already taken place? Or is it waiting to happen?

Do you think Acosta's espousal of drug use as "part and parcel of the radical Chicano Movement" helps or hurts the movement?

Suppose you are counsel to a group of disgusted radicals insistent on working for racial justice but impatient with the slow pace of progress. Peaceful means of protest, such as boycotts and sit-ins, have brought about little change. The group is now considering introducing a secret virus into every computer in the United States that will disable it for one month. Although the virus is meant to be a nuisance rather than to cause permanent harm, their action will in fact violate federal law. As legal counsel, what do you advise the group? Would you warn them about the possible consequences of their proposed course of conduct? Turn them in? Resign as their lawyer?

Should lawyers for minority communities live in those communities and send their children to community schools? What if a technically able and deeply committed Anglo lawyer prefers not to? If you were his or her supervising attorney at a storefront law firm serving the community, would you insist that he or she move into the community or resign?

Can resistance be carried out through art?

Suggested Readings

Acosta, Oscar "Zeta." *The Autobiography of a Brown Buffalo*. 2d ed. New York: Vintage, 1989.

———. *The Revolt of the Cockroach People*. 2d ed. New York, Vintage, 1989.

———. *The Uncollected Works*, edited by Ilan Stavans. Houston: Arte Publico Press, 1996.

Allsup, Carl. *The American G.I. Forum: Origins and Evolution*. University of Texas Center for Mexican American Studies Monograph no. 6. Austin: University of Texas Press, 1982.

American G.I. Forum of Texas and Texas State Federation of Labor. *What Price Wetbacks?* Austin: G.I. Forum of Texas, 1954. Reprinted in *Mexican Migration to the United States,* edited by Carlos Cortes. New York: Arno Press, 1976.

Chavez, Cesar. "The California Farm Workers' Struggle." *Black Scholar* 7 (June 1976): 16–19.

Colloquium: "Representing Latina/o Communities: Critical Race Theory and Practice." 9 *La Raza Law Journal* 1 (1996).

García, Ignacio M. *United We Win: The Rise and Fall of La Raza Unida Party*. Tucson: Mexican American Studies and Research Center, University of Arizona, 1989.

Garza, Edward D. *LULAC: The League of United Latin American Citizens*. San Francisco: R and E Research Associates, 1972.

Gómez-Quiñones, Juan. *Mexican Students por La Raza: The Chicano Student Movement in Southern California, 1967–1977*. Santa Barbara, Calif.: Editorial La Causa,1978.

Gonzalez, Rodolfo "Corky." "Chicano Nationalism: The Key to Unity for La Raza." In *A Documentary History of the Mexican Americans,* edited by Wayne Moquin, 488–93. New York: Bantam Books, 1972.

Greenfield, Alice. *The Sleepy Lagoon Case: A Pageant of Prejudice*. Los Angeles: Citizen's Committee for the Defense of the Mexican-American Youth, 1942.

Hammerback, John C., Richard J. Jensen, and José Ángel Gutiérrez. *A War of Words: Chicano Protest in the 1960s and 1970s*. Westport, Conn.: Greenwood Press, 1985.

Huerta, Dolores. "Dolores Huerta Talks: About Republicans, Cesar, Her Children and Her Home Town." *Regeneración* 2 (1975): 20–24.

Jenkins, J. Craig. *The Politics of Insurgency: The Farm Worker Movement in the 1960s*. New York: Columbia University Press, 1985.

Levy, Jacques. *Cesar Chavez: An Autobiography of La Causa*. New York: W. W. Norton, 1975.

López, Gerald P. *Rebellious Lawyering: One Chicano's Vision of Progressive Law Practice*. Boulder, Colo.: Westview Press, 1992.

———. "Reconceiving Civil Rights Practice: Seven Weeks in the Life of a Rebellious Collaboration." 77 *Georgetown Law Journal* 1603 (1989).

———. "Training Future Lawyers to Work with the Politically and Socially Subordinated: Anti-Generic Legal Education." 91 *West Virginia Law Review* 305 (1989).

Marin, Christine. *A Spokesman of the Mexican American Movement: Rodolfo "Corky" Gonzalez and the Fight for Chicano Liberation, 1966–1972.* San Francisco: R & E Research Associates, 1977.

Marquez, Benjamin. *LULAC: The Evolution of a Mexican American Political Organization.* Austin: University of Texas Press, 1993.

Martínez, Elizabeth. "Histories of 'the Sixties': A Certain Absence of Color." *Social Justice* 16 (Winter 1989): 175–84.

Matthiessen, Peter. *Sal Si Puedes: Cesar Chavez and the New American Revolution.* New York: Random House, 1969.

Mazon, Mauricio. *The Zoot-Suit Riots: The Psychology of Symbolic Annihilation.* Austin: University of Texas Press, 1984.

Muñoz, Carlos, Jr. *Youth, Identity, Power: The Chicano Movement.* London: Verso, 1989.

Muñoz, Carlos, Jr., and Mario Barrera. "La Raza Unida Party and the Chicano Student Movement in California." *Social Science Journal* 19 (April 1982): 101–20.

Nabakov, Peter. *Tijerina and the Courthouse Raid.* Albuquerque: University of New Mexico Press, 1969.

Romo, Ricardo. "Southern California and the Origins of Latino Civil-Rights Activism." *Western Legal History* 3 (1990): 379

Rosales, Francisco Arturo. *Chicano! The History of the Mexican American Civil Rights Movement.* Houston: Arte Publico Press, 1996.

Sleepy Lagoon Defense Committee. *The Sleepy Lagoon Case.* Los Angeles: The Committee, 1944.

Stavans, Ilan. *Bandido: Oscar "Zeta" Acosta and the Chicano Experience.* New York: HarperCollins, 1995.

Symposium: "Latinos and the Law: Twenty Years of Legal Advocacy and Lessons for Advancement." 14 *Chicano-Latino Law Review* 1 (1994).

Taylor, Ronald B. *Chavez and the Farm Workers.* Boston: Beacon Press, 1975.

U.S. Commission on Civil Rights. *Mexican Americans and the Administration of Justice in the Southwest.* Washington, D.D.: Government Printing Office, 1970.

Valdez, Luis. *Zoot Suit and Other Plays.* Houston: Arte Publico Press, 1992.

Revisionist Law

Does the Legal System Work for Us?

In addition to writing counterstories and parables like those the reader met in Part VI, Latino advocates have been challenging racist or unresponsive legal structures through more conventional scholarship and analysis. Part VII introduces the reader to some of the best of this literature. Some authors challenge the current stingy approach to affirmative action and the social neglect of the poverty that blights many Latino families' lives. Others call attention to the Indian ("Indio") tradition within much of Latino culture, and also to the pernicious consequences of the "black/white binary," according to which almost everyone thinks of race in terms of black and white. We include, as well, excerpts of law review articles criticizing the legal system for indeterminacy and for allowing hurtful legal rules and doctrines to grow up regarding issues dear to the Latino community, such as language rights.

Chapter 48

The Mexican-American Litigation Experience: 1930–1980

George A. Martinez

Perhaps surprisingly, some commentators have argued that minority scholars often have been excluded from the debate regarding key issues of race or civil rights law. Arguably, any such exclusion caused the literature dealing with race and American law to be distorted and seriously incomplete. In response, critical race scholars have begun to explore civil rights issues. Nonetheless, to date, no one has undertaken a critical examination of the Mexican-American litigation experience in light of contemporary jurisprudential and critical scholarship. This chapter seeks to help fill that void.

In particular, the chapter explores a jurisprudential point: legal indeterminacy in the context of Mexican-American civil rights litigation. Traditional legal theory has recognized that legal doctrine is sometimes indeterminate in that it does not always dictate results. For example, H. L. A. Hart writes that "[i]n every legal system a large and important field is left open for the exercise of discretion by courts and other officials in rendering initially vague standards determinate, in resolving the uncertainties of statutes, or in developing and qualifying rules only broadly communicated by authoritative precedents."[1] More recently, pragmatists, critical legal scholars, and others have argued that law is indeterminate in the sense that legal materials— statutes and court decisions—often permit a judge to justify multiple outcomes to lawsuits.

In light of this open texture, legal theorists have argued that judicial decisions are often not logically compelled but instead the result of conscious or unconscious discretionary policy choices. Accordingly, one of my goals is to demonstrate that courts' decisions either for or against Mexican Americans were often not inevitable or compelled. In so doing, policy choices of the courts are revealed and brought to the surface. Exposing the exercise of judicial discretion and the lack of inevitability in civil rights cases is important for two reasons. At one level, it helps reveal the extent to

From "Legal Indeterminacy, Judicial Discretion and the Mexican-American Litigation Experience: 1930–1980." 27 U.C. Davis L. Rev. 555 (1994). Originally published in the *University of California at Davis Law Review*. Copyright © 1994 by the Regents of the University of California. Reprinted by permission.

which the courts have helped or failed to help establish the rights of Mexican Americans. At another, exposing false necessity in judicial decision-making by explaining how the decision might have gone another way—i.e., offering a counterstory—is important because it may help break down barriers to racial reform. Drawing on critical race theory, legal pragmatism, and the philosophy of science, I argue that providing judges with counterstories or alternative perspectives on civil rights issues is one way to help them overcome the "unthinking conviction that [their] way of seeing the world is the only one—that the way things are is inevitable, natural, just, and best."[2] By acknowledging their limited perspective, judges can avoid serious moral error and promote justice in civil rights cases.

[The author comprehensively reviews dozens of cases dealing with public swimming pools, school desegregation, land grants, and bilingual education, concluding as follows—*Eds.*]

The cases indicate that a number of courts generally exercised their discretion by taking a position against Mexican Americans on key issues. For example, in the effort to desegregate public accommodations, the courts ruled against Mexican Americans where they might have done otherwise. Likewise, the judiciary chose to reject Mexican-American efforts to reclaim land. Similarly, with respect to the effort to desegregate the public schools, most courts exercised their discretion to permit the segregation of Mexican Americans for "benign" reasons—e.g., linguistic difficulties—or because the segregation was "merely" de facto. Finally, with respect to bilingual education, courts generally exercised discretion to limit access to bilingual and bicultural education.

Exposing the exercise of judicial discretion is vitally important because it helps reveal the extent to which the courts have helped, or failed to help, establish the rights of Mexican Americans. In this regard, the inescapable conclusion is that courts could have done significantly more to vindicate justice on behalf of this group.

Critical race scholars have argued that civil rights gains are cyclical and tend to be cut back. This chapter provides new support for that argument. The cases reveal that the rights of Mexican Americans were often cut back through the use of judicial discretion. For example, in the area of school desegregation, the early cases held that Mexican Americans could not be segregated solely on the basis of race. That right, however, was immediately limited because most courts allowed the segregation of Mexican Americans for "benign" reasons, and school boards often justified segregation on that basis. Similarly, after the Supreme Court decision in *Brown v. Board of Education,* most courts narrowly interpreted Brown to bar only de jure segregation. Thus, the Court's refusal to bar de facto segregation limited the rights of Mexican Americans. Finally, in the area of bilingual education, the courts construed earlier cases so as to limit the right to bilingual education.

Important as these conclusions are, they nevertheless hold out the hope of racial reform. Exposing the lack of inevitability in civil rights decision-making may help break down barriers to racial reform. Critical race scholars have argued that a significant barrier to racial reform is the majoritarian mindset. Richard Delgado has described this mind set as "the bundle of presuppositions, received wisdom, and shared understandings against a background of which legal [decision-making] takes place."[3]

The view that judicial decision-making is highly influenced by the perspective and preconceptions of the judge, and that the perspective of the dominant group may present a barrier to racial reform, finds substantial support in the recent revival of pragmatism in legal philosophy. Pragmatists treat "thinking as contextual and situated."[4] Thinking is "always embodied in practices—habits and patterns of perceiving and conceiving."[5] Thus, pragmatists have recognized that one cannot view the world except through one's preconceptions. Applying this notion to legal decision-making, they have emphasized the importance of context and perspective to the act of judging. Significantly, pragmatists also have recognized that the dominant perspective can stand in the way of racial reform. Both critical race scholars and pragmatists offer a similar explanation for how this happens. The general idea is that the dominant perspective or mind set makes current social and legal arrangements seem fair and natural. Bringing this mind set to the bench, judges may commit moral error in civil rights cases because narrow habits of perceiving lead them to believe that the way things are is inevitable or just.

One way to help judges break down mind set, broaden their perspectives, and promote justice in civil rights cases, is to provide counterstories—i.e., explain how decisions were not inevitable. Through this process judges can "overcome ethnocentrism and the unthinking conviction that [their] way of seeing the world is the only one—that the way things are is inevitable, natural, just, and best" and thereby avoid moral error when deciding any civil rights case.[6] Similarly, pragmatists have stressed that justice may be advanced only if judges try to grasp the world from perspectives that run counter to the dominant one. As Martha Minow has explained, the effort to take the perspective of another may help us see that our perspective is limited and that the status quo is not inevitable or fair.[7] To break down narrow habits of perceiving that stand in the way of racial reform, lawyers and activists must stand ready to offer alternative perspectives or counterstories that explain how decisions were not inevitable.

Some commentators have questioned whether counterstories can transform the consciousness of the dominant group. Contrary to those commentators, however, the idea that generating alternative visions of reality can advance racial reform finds important support in the philosophy of science and contemporary philosophy of law. In this regard, it is helpful to consider Thomas Kuhn's classic account of scientific change. Kuhn argued that during periods of normal science, perception is dependent on conventional "paradigms." According to Kuhn, a scientific revolution occurs when there is a transition from one paradigm to another. Paradigm changes cause scientists to see the world differently. At times of scientific revolution, then, scientists experience shifts of perception—the scientists' perception of their environment must be reeducated. According to Kuhn, the transition between competing paradigms is a conversion experience that cannot be forced by logic.[8]

Applying these notions to judicial decision-making, one leading pragmatist and philosopher of law, Judge Richard Posner, argues that major changes in law often result from a similar conversion process.[9] Such conversion results from a perceptual shift where one comes to see the world differently. According to Judge Posner, this process explains the major shifts that have occurred in law, including the expansion and recognition of civil rights. Thus, the key turning points in American law simply reflect changing outlooks. Judges and lawyers began to look at legal doctrine in a new way. Providing judges with alternative perspectives or counterstories may help stimulate a paradigm shift in the area of race.

Beyond this, exposing the exercise of discretion through counterstories is one way to help insure that the Mexican-American experience is reflected in legal discourse. In this regard, feminists have argued that women's experience has not been recognized by the law. To solve the problem of women's exclusion from legal discourse, Robin West has suggested that women must flood the legal market with their own stories.[10] In this way, legal discourse is forced to consider the perspective of women. For similar reasons, critical race scholars have emphasized the importance of telling the silenced stories and unrecorded perspectives of outsider groups. Thus, offering counterstories is one way to help insure that legal discourse takes accounts of the Mexican-American experience.

Finally, exposing the lack of inevitability in judicial decision-making may also promote a renewed sense of community. Recently, legal scholars have emphasized the importance of promoting communitarian values. Pragmatism suggests that exposing the lack of inevitability in judicial decision-making may foster a sense of community. As one of the leaders in the revival of American pragmatism, Richard Rorty, has explained, when the contingent character of human projects is recognized, "[o]ur identification with our community—our society, our political tradition, our intellectual heritage—is heightened."[11] This occurs "when we see this community as ours rather than nature's, shaped rather than found, one among many which men have made."[12] Similarly, once the contingent character of judicial decision-making is fully recognized, it may generate a renewed sense of community—the community may be viewed as ours rather than nature's. With luck and effort, one day Mexicans and other outsiders will take their rightful place as full members of that community.

NOTES

1. H. L. A. Hart, The Concept of Law 132 (1961).
2. Richard Delgado, *Storytelling for Oppositionists and Others: A Plea for Narrative*, 87 Mich. L. Rev. 2411, 2439 (1989).
3. *Id.*, at 2413.
4. Thomas C. Grey, *Holmes and Legal Pragmatism*, 41 Stan. L. Rev. 787, 798 (1989).
5. *Id.*
6. Delgado, at 2439.
7. Martha Minow, *Foreword: Justice Engendered*, 101 Harv. L. Rev. 60 (1987).
8. See Thomas S. Kuhn, The Structure of Scientific Revolutions 150–51 (2d ed. 1970).
9. Richard A. Posner, The Problems of Jurisprudence 459 (1990).
10. Robin West, *Jurisprudence and Gender*, 55 U. Chi L. Rev. 1, 65 (1988).
11. Richard Rorty, Consequences of Pragmatism 166 (1982).
12. *Id.*

Chapter 49

The Black/White Binary Paradigm of Race

Juan F. Perea

This chapter is about how we are taught to think about race. I believe that most such thinking is structured by a paradigm that is widely held but rarely recognized for what it is and does. It is crucial, therefore, to identify and describe this paradigm and to demonstrate how it binds and organizes racial discourse, limiting both the scope and the range of legitimate viewpoints in racial discourse.

The Power of Paradigms

Thomas Kuhn, in *The Structure of Scientific Revolutions,*[1] describes the properties of paradigms and their power in structuring scientific research and knowledge. While Kuhn writes in connection with scientific knowledge, many of his insights are useful in understanding paradigms and their effects more generally. A paradigm is a shared set of understandings or premises which permits the definition, elaboration, and solution of a set of problems defined within the paradigm. It is an accepted model or pattern that, "like an accepted judicial decision in the common law[,] . . . is an object for further articulation and specification under new or more stringent conditions."[2]

Thus, a paradigm is the set of shared understandings that permits us to distinguish which facts matter in the solution of a problem and which facts don't. As Kuhn writes,

> In the absence of a paradigm or some candidate for paradigm, all of the facts that could possibly pertain to the development of a given science are likely to seem equally relevant. As a result, early fact-gathering is a far more nearly random activity than the one that subsequent scientific development makes familiar.[3]

Paradigms thus define relevancy. In so doing, they control fact-gathering and investigation. Data-gathering efforts and research are focused on understanding the facts and circumstances that the relevant paradigm has taught us are important.

Paradigms are crucial in the development of science and knowledge because, by setting boundaries within which problems can be understood, they permit detailed inquiry into these problems. In Kuhn's words, a "paradigm forces scientists to investigate some part of nature in a detail and depth that would otherwise be unimaginable."[4] Indeed, it is this depth of research that eventually yields anomalies and discontinuities and, ultimately, the necessity to develop new paradigms. However, as a paradigm becomes the widely accepted way of thinking and of producing knowledge on a subject, it tends to exclude or ignore alternative facts or theories that do not fit the expectations produced by the paradigm.

Kuhn uses the concept of "normal science" to describe the elaboration and further articulation of the paradigm, and the solution of problems that are perceivable because of the paradigm. Scientists and researchers spend almost all of their time engaged in normal science, conducting their research under the rules prescribed by the paradigm and attempting to solve problems cognizable and derivable from the paradigm. However, normal science "often suppresses fundamental novelties because they are necessarily subversive of its basic commitments."[5] As Kuhn describes, normal science "seems an attempt to force nature into the performed and relatively inflexible box that the paradigm supplies. No part of the aim of normal science is to call forth new sorts of phenomena; indeed those that will not fit the box are often not seen at all."[6] As normal research progresses in depth and detail within a paradigm, unexpected discoveries come to light, yielding anomalies that are not adequately explained by the current paradigm. In time, scientists are forced to abandon the old paradigm and replace it with some new understanding that explains better the observed anomalies.

Literature and textbooks play an important role in producing and reproducing paradigms. Kuhn identifies textbooks and popularizations, conveying scientific knowledge in a language more accessible to the general public, as authoritative sources of established paradigms. Textbooks and literature derived from them intend to communicate the particular paradigm or set of paradigms that constitute the current tradition of a science. Although Kuhn suggests that science is more vulnerable to textbook distortions of history than other disciplines because of the assumed objectivity of scientific inquiry,[7] I believe his insights regarding paradigms, "normal science," and textbooks are extremely useful in explaining the persistent focus of race scholarship on Blacks and Whites, and the resulting omission of Latinos/as, Asian Americans, Native Americans, and other racialized groups from such scholarship. If science as a discipline is more vulnerable to textbook distortions of history, I believe this is only a matter of degree, because law, through its reliance on precedent, is also highly dependent on paradigms. Kuhn recognized as much when he used judicial precedent, and subsequent decisions based on precedent, as an example of paradigm elaboration.[8] Although Kuhn felt that the extent to which the social sciences had developed paradigms was an open question,[9] race scholarship both inside and outside of law is dominated by a binary paradigm of race.

Describing the Binary Paradigm of Race

Paradigms of race shape our understanding and definition of racial problems. The most pervasive and powerful paradigm of race in the United States is the Black/White binary. I define this paradigm as the conception that race in America consists, either exclusively or primarily, of only two constituent racial groups, the Black and the White. Many scholars of race reproduce this paradigm when they write and act as though only the Black and the White races matter for purposes of discussing race and social policy. The current fashion of mentioning "other people of color," without careful attention to their voices, their histories, and their real presence, is merely a reassertion of the Black/White paradigm. If one conceives of race as primarily of concern only to Blacks and Whites, and understands "other people of color" only through some unclear analogy to the "real" races, this just restates the binary paradigm with a slight concession to demographics.

In addition, the paradigm dictates that all other racial identities and groups in the United States are best understood through the Black/White binary paradigm. Only a few writers even recognize that they use a Black/White paradigm as the frame of reference through which to understand all racial relations. Most writers simply assume the importance and correctness of the paradigm, and leave the reader grasping for whatever significance descriptions of the Black/White relationship have for other people of color. As I shall discuss, because the Black/White binary paradigm is so widely accepted, other racialized groups like Latinos/as, Asian Americans, and Native Americans are often marginalized or ignored altogether. As Kuhn wrote, "those that will not fit the box are often not seen at all."[10]

Andrew Hacker and Two Nations

Andrew Hacker's famous book, *Two Nations: Black and White, Separate, Hostile, Unequal,* provides an excellent example.[11] Its title, proclaiming two nations, Black and White, boldly professes the Black/White binary paradigm. Although Hacker recognizes explicitly that a full perspective on race in America requires inclusion of Latinos/as and Asians, this recognition is, in the context of the entire book, insignificant and underdeveloped. His almost exclusive focus on Blacks and Whites is clearly intentional: "*Two Nations* will adhere to its title by giving central attention to black and white Americans."[12]

Hacker's justification is that "[i]n many respects, other groups find themselves sitting as spectators, while the two prominent players try to work out how or whether they can co-exist with one another."[13] This justifies marginalization with marginalization. What Hacker and so many other writers on race fail, or decline, to understand is that, by focusing only on Blacks and Whites, they both produce and replicate the belief that only "two prominent players," Black and White, count in debates about race. Other non-White groups, rendered invisible by these writers, can thus be characterized as passive, voluntary spectators.

Hacker describes in detail only conditions experienced by White or Black Americans. He first characterizes the White nature of the nation and its culture:

America is inherently a "white" country: in character, in structure, in culture. Needless to say, black Americans create lives of their own. Yet, as a people, they face boundaries and constrictions set by the white majority. America's version of *apartheid,* while lacking overt legal sanction, comes closest to the system even now being reformed in the land of its invention.[14]

Of course, Latinos/as, Asian Americans, Native Americans, Gypsies, and all non-White Americans face "boundaries and constrictions set by the white majority," but the vision Hacker advances counts only Blacks as significantly disadvantaged by White racism.

Similarly, Hacker describes Blackness as uniquely functional for Whites:

As James Baldwin has pointed out, white people need the presence of black people as a reminder of what providence has spared them from becoming. . . . In the eyes of white Americans, being black encapsulates your identity. No other racial or national origin is seen as having so pervasive a personality or character.[15]

According to Hacker, then, Blackness serves a crucial function in enabling Whites to define themselves as privileged and superior, and racial attributes of other minorities do not serve this function.

Hacker's chapter titles largely tell the story of the binary paradigm. Chapter 2, on "Race and Racism," discusses only White and Black perceptions of each other. Chapter 3, "Being Black in America," is followed by a chapter on "White Responses." Hacker's omission of non-Black minority groups in his discussion of specific topics similarly suggests these groups' experiences do not exist. Chapter 9, on segregated schooling, describes only the experience of segregation of Blacks, making no reference to the extensive history of segregation in education suffered by Latinos/as. Chapter 10 asks, "What's Best for Black Children?" with no commensurate concern for other children. Similarly, Chapter 11, on crime, discusses only perceptions of Black criminality and their interpretation. In discussing police brutality, Hacker describes only White police brutality against Blacks. One finds not a single word about the similar police brutality suffered by Latino/a people at the hands of White police officers. Nor are there any words in these chapters describing the experiences of Native Americans or Asian Americans.

The greatest danger in Hacker's vision is the implication that non-White groups other than Blacks are not really subject to racism. Hacker seems to adopt the deservedly criticized ethnicity theory, which posits that non-White immigrant ethnics are essentially Whites-in-waiting who will be permitted to assimilate and become White. This is illustrated best in Chapter 8, "On Education: Ethnicity and Achievement," which offers the book's only significant discussion of non-White groups other than Blacks. Asians are described in "model minority" terms, because of high standardized test scores (on a group basis). Latinos/as are portrayed both as below standard, because of low test scores, and as aspiring immigrants. Describing Asian Americans, Latinos/as and other immigrant groups, Hacker writes:

Members of all these "intermediate groups" have been allowed to put a visible distance between themselves and black Americans. Put most simply, none of the presumptions of inferiority associated with Africa and slavery are imposed on these other ethnicities.[16]

While a full rebuttal of this quotation must wait for another time, its inaccuracy can be quickly demonstrated. Consider, for instance, the observations of historian David Weber, who described early Anglo perceptions of Mexican people: "American visitors to the Mexican frontier were nearly unanimous in commenting on the dark skin of Mexican mestizos who, it was generally agreed, had inherited the worst qualities of Spaniards and Indians to produce a 'race' still more despicable than that of either parent."[17] Rufus B. Sage expressed the common view of Mexicans in 1846:

> There are no people on the continent of America, whether civilized or uncivilized, with one or two exceptions, more miserable in condition or despicable in morals than the mongrel race inhabiting New Mexico. . . . To manage them successfully, they must needs be held in continual restraint, and kept in their place by force, if necessary—else they will become haughty and insolent. As servants, they are excellent, when properly trained, but are worse than useless if left to themselves.[18]

More briefly, the common perception of Mexican Americans was that "[t]hey are an inferior race, that is all."[19]

Incredibly, and without any supporting evidence, Hacker writes that "[m]ost Central and South Americans can claim a strong European heritage, which eases their absorption into the 'white' middle class."[20] He continues, "[w]hile immigrants from Colombia and Cyprus may have to work their way up the social ladder, they are still allowed as valid a claim to being 'white' as persons of Puritan or Pilgrim stock."[21] Hacker's comments are simply incredible. While some Latinos/as may look White and may act Anglo (the phenomenon of passing for White is not limited to Blacks), Hacker's statement is certainly false for millions of Latinos/as. Current anti-immigrant initiatives targeted at Latinos/as and Asians, such as California's Proposition 187 and similar federal legislation targeting legal and illegal immigrants, California's Proposition 209, and the unprecedented proposal to deny birthright citizenship to the U.S.-born children of undocumented persons, debunk any notion that the presence of Latino/a or Asian people will be accepted or tolerated easily by the White majority.

Cornel West and the Black/White Binary Paradigm

Cornel West is one of the most well known and well regarded philosophers and commentators on race in the nation. While West writes with much more insight than Hacker, his recent book, *Race Matters,* is also limited by and reproduces the Black/White binary paradigm of race.[22] A collection of essays West wrote on race and race relations, its principal subject is the relationship of Blackness to Whiteness and the exploration of avenues to alter the unsatisfactory state of that relationship. And while this focus is of course worthy of his attention, he overlooks and ignores relevant subject matter that lies outside the paradigm. West describes the binary nature of our public discourse about race:

> We confine discussions about race in America to the "problems" black people pose for whites rather than consider what this way of viewing black people reveals about us as

> a nation. . . . Both [liberals and conservatives] fail to see that the presence and predica-
> ments of black people are neither additions to nor defections from American life, but
> rather *constitutive elements of that life.*[23]

This statement is accurate, and I would only fault West for not recognizing that exactly the same statement is true of Latinos/as, Asians, and Native Americans as well as Blacks: we are all constitutive of American life and identity to a degree that has not been fully recognized, and which is in fact actively resisted.

West's near-exclusive focus on Blacks and Whites, and thus his reproduction of the Black/White binary paradigm, is apparent throughout the book. Chapter 2, entitled "The Pitfalls of Racial Reasoning," presents a powerful critique of racial reasoning within the Black community that immobilized Black leaders, who were generally unable to criticize Clarence Thomas when he was appointed to the Supreme Court. West's binary conception of the nation emerges when he describes the "deep cultural conservatism in white and black America. In white America, cultural conservatism takes the form of a chronic racism, sexism, and homophobia. . . . In black America, cultural conservatism takes the form of a [*sic*] inchoate xenophobia (e.g., against whites, Jews, and Asians), systemic sexism, and homophobia."[24] Like Hacker's conception of "two nations," West sees binary Americas, one White, one Black. In addition, West's reference to Black xenophobia, directed at Whites, Jews, and Asians, sets the stage for his later description of Black distrust of Latinos/as as well.

West also describes the binary paradigm from a Black point of view, referring to the "black bourgeois preoccupation with white peer approval and black nationalist obsession with white racism."[25] Blacks, in their way, are as preoccupied with Whites as Whites are with Blacks.

In his chapter "Malcolm X and Black Rage," West describes Malcolm X's fear of cultural hybridity, the blurring of racial boundaries that occurs because of racial mixture. Malcolm X saw such hybridity, exemplified by mulattos, as "symbols of weakness and confusion."[26] West's commentary on Malcolm X's views gives us another statement of the binary paradigm: "The very idea of not 'fitting in' the U.S. discourse of positively valued whiteness and negatively debased blackness meant one was subject to exclusion and marginalization by whites and blacks."[27] Although the context of this quotation is about Black/White mulattos, West's observation is crucial to an understanding of why Latinos/as, neither White nor Black, are perpetually excluded and marginalized. The reified binary structure of discourse on race leaves no room for people of color who do not fit the rigid Black and White boxes supplied by the paradigm. Furthermore most Latinos/as are mixed-race mestizos or mulattos, therefore embodying the kind of racial mixture that Malcolm X and, I would argue, society generally tend to reject. West's observation about mixed-race people who do not fit within traditional U.S. discourse about race applies in full measure to Latinos/as.

When West writes about the struggle for Black civil rights in shaping the future of equality in America, he recognizes the need for Blacks to repudiate anti-Semitism and other racisms in order to sustain the moral position garnered through the struggle for civil rights. However, he makes ambivalent comments about the possibilities for coalition with other groups:

[A] prophetic framework encourages a coalition strategy that solicits genuine solidarity with those deeply committed to antiracist struggle. . . . [B]lack suspicions of whites, Latinos, Jews, and Asians runs deep for historical reasons. Yet there are slight though significant antiracist traditions among whites, Asians, and especially Latinos, Jews and indigenous people that must not be cast aside. Such coalitions are important precisely because they not only enhance the plight of black people but also because they enrich the quality of life in America.[28]

This paragraph warrants probing. Given America's history of racism, Black suspicions of every group may seem well-founded. For example, with respect to Latinos/as, during the nineteenth century as during the present, identification with Anglos by upper-class Mexicans meant becoming more racist and disparaging toward lower-class and darker-skinned Mexicans and Blacks. However, West's characterization of Latino/a, Asian, and Native American resistance to Anglo domination and racism as "slight though significant"[29] seems belittling, ill-informed, and marginalizing of Latino/a, Asian, and indigenous people. This comment can be understood as the kind of "inchoate xenophobia" West himself finds in the Black community.

Another possible reason for this distrust of Latinos/as may stem from a widespread sense that Blacks are being displaced by immigrant Latinos/as. Toni Morrison writes specifically about this distrust. In her essay "On the Backs of Blacks," Morrison describes the hatred of Blacks as the defining, final, necessary step in the Americanization of immigrants. "It is the act of racial contempt [banishing a competing black shoe-shiner] that transforms this charming Greek into an entitled white."[30] Morrison sees Blacks as persistently victimized by Americanizing processes, always forced to "the lowest level of the racial hierarchy."[31] The struggles of immigrants, according to Morrison,

> are persistently framed as struggles between recent arrivals and blacks. In race talk the move into mainstream America always means buying into the notion of American blacks as the real aliens. Whatever the ethnicity or nationality of the immigrant, his nemesis is understood to be African American.[32]

Morrison is right that American "Whiteness" is often achieved through distancing from Blacks. Latinos/as participate in the paradigm, by engaging in racism against Blacks or darker-skinned members of Latino/a communities. Current events, however, belie Morrison's notion of American blacks as "the real aliens." Mexican and other Latino/a and Asian aliens have become targets of state and federal legislation denying them medical and educational resources. The legal attack on entitlement programs and affirmative action programs is an attack on Blacks, Latinos/as, and Asians.

In Cornel West's writing, we see the influence of the Black/White binary paradigm from the point of view of a leading Black writer on race. His view shares points in common with Andrew Hacker. Both agree on the concepts of White and Black Americas (the "two nations"), and both focus exclusive attention on the relationship between Blacks and Whites, although they describe the nature of this relationship in very different terms. Both writers seem indifferent toward the history and conditions experienced by other non-White, non-Black groups, while Hacker considers, unrealistically, all non-Blacks as aspiring immigrants on the path to assimilation with Whites. West, like Morrison, views non-Black groups with great suspicion. Morrison, in particular, seems to accept Hacker's view that all non-Blacks are (or will be) the enemies of Blacks as they Americanize and assimilate.

Taken together, these views pose serious problems for Latinos/as. Viewing Latinos/as as aspiring immigrants is, in most cases, a deeply flawed view, for two reasons. First, Mexican Americans and Puerto Ricans, like all U.S.-born Latinos/as, are not immigrants. Mexicans occupied the Southwest long before the United States ever found them. Second, this utopian view of immigrant assimilation takes no account of the systemic racism that afflicts Mexican Americans and Puerto Ricans. The utopian view serves White writers like Hacker because they can perpetuate the view that the United States has only a single race problem—the traditional binary problem of the White relationship with Blacks—rather than a more complex set of racisms that, if recognized, would demonstrate that racism is much more systemic and pervasive than is usually admitted.

One can thus discern how the binary paradigm interferes with liberation and equality. If Latinos/as and Asian Americans are presumed to be White by both White and Black writers (a presumption not borne out in the lived experience of most Latinos/as and Asians), then our claims to justice will not be heard or acknowledged. Our claims can be ignored by Whites, since we are not Black and therefore are not subject to real racism. And our claims can be ignored by Blacks, since we are presumed to be, not Black, but becoming White, and therefore not subject to real racism. Latinos/as do not fit the boxes supplied by the paradigm. . . .

[The author goes on to show how the same Black/White paradigmatic thinking operates in law and legal casebooks, then continues as follows—*Eds.*]

My review of important literature on race establishes the existence of the Black/White binary paradigm and its structuring of writing on race. The "normal science" of race scholarship specifies inquiry into the relationship between Blacks and Whites as the exclusive aspect of race relations that needs to be explored and elaborated. As a result, much relevant legal history and information concerning Latinos/as and other racialized groups end up omitted from books on race and constitutional law.

The omission of this history is extraordinarily damaging to Mexican Americans and other Latinos/as. When this history is omitted, students get no understanding that Mexican Americans have long struggled for equality. The absence of Latinos/as from histories of racism and the struggle against it enables people to maintain existing stereotypes of Mexican Americans. These stereotypes are perpetuated even by America's leading thinkers on race. Paradigmatic descriptions and study of White racism against Blacks, with only cursory mention of "other people of color," marginalizes all people of color by grouping them, without particularity, as somehow analogous to Blacks. "Other people of color" are deemed to exist only as unexplained analogies to Blacks. Uncritical readers are encouraged to continue assuming the paradigmatic importance of the Black/White relationship, while ignoring the experiences of other Americans who also are subject to racism in profound ways.

It is time to ask hard questions of our leading writers on race. It is also time to demand answers to these questions about inclusion, exclusion, and racial presence that go beyond perfunctory references to "other people of color." In the midst of profound demographic changes, it is time to question whether the Black/White binary paradigm of race fits our highly variegated current and future population. Our "normal science" of writing on race, at odds with both history and demographic reality, needs reworking.

NOTES

1. Thomas S. Kuhn, THE STRUCTURE OF SCIENTIFIC REVOLUTIONS (2d ed. 1970).

2. *Id.* at 23.

3. *Id.* at 15.

4. *Id.* at 24.

5. *Id.* at 5.

6. *Id.* at 24.

7. See, e.g., *id.* at 138.

8. See *id.* at 23.

9. See *id.* at 15.

10. *Id.* at 24; see also Juan F. Perea, *Los Olvidados: On the Making of Invisible People* 70 N.Y.U. L. REV. 965 (1995); Anne Sutherland, GYPSIES: THE HIDDEN AMERICANS (1986).

11. Andrew Hacker, TWO NATIONS: BLACK AND WHITE, SEPARATE, HOSTILE, UNEQUAL (1992).

12. *Id.* at xii.

13. *Id.*

14. *Id.* at 4.

15. *Id.* at 30, 32.

16. *Id.* at 16.

17. David J. Weber. FOREIGNERS IN THEIR NATIVE LAND: HISTORICAL ROOTS OF THE MEXICAN AMERICANS 59 (1973).

18. *Id.* at 72, 74 (quoting 2 RUFUS B. SAGE: HIS LETTERS AND PAPERS, 1836–1847 [LeRoy R. and Ann W. Hafen eds., 1956]).

19. This was the justification offered by Texas school officials for segregating Mexican Americans in 1929. See Jorge C. Rangel & Carlos M. Alcala, *Project Report: De Jure Segregation of Chicanos in Texas Schools,* 7 HARV. C.R.-C.L. LAW REV. 307, 307 (quoting Paul Schuster Taylor, AN AMERICAN MEXICAN FRONTIER 219 [1934]).

20. Hacker, at 10.

21. *Id.* at 12.

22. Cornel West, RACE MATTERS (1993).

23. *Id.* at 2–3.

24. *Id.* at 27.

25. *Id.* at 66.

26. *Id.* It is interesting to note the similarity between Malcolm X's sense that mixed-race people introduced "confusion" into the otherwise clear structures of Black and White, and Andrew Hacker's sense that Hispanics introduce "incoherence" into the otherwise "clear" vision of Black and White races that Hacker describes in such depth. These observations suggest one reason for the continued adherence to a Black/White paradigm despite its inadequacy: the paradigm does simplify and makes racial problems more readily understood than if we began to grapple with them in their full complexity.

27. *Id.*

28. *Id.* at 28–29.

29. *Id.* at 28.

30. Toni Morrison, *On the Backs of Blacks*, in ARGUING IMMIGRATION 97 (Nicolaus Mills ed., 1994).

31. *Id.*

32. *Id.* at 98.

Chapter 50

The Black/White Binary
How Does It Work?

Richard Delgado

Rodrigo began, "I just got back from a two-day conference hosted by the Latino law students of a major school. It drew an impressive cast, with speakers like Rodolfo Acuña and Carlos Muñoz, as well as the usual complement of law professors. After hours, some of us were talking about the role of Latinos in American politics. We wondered why our relatively large group has had so little impact on national civil rights policy, especially in areas like immigration reform, bilingual education, poverty, and English-only. On all these fronts, we've been relatively ineffectual, compared to blacks. Some thought it had to do with exo-marriage and assimilation, and the way the Latino community lacks cohesion, being made up of so many different national-origin groups. But I think it's something different, namely, the black/white binary."

"What's that?" I asked.

"It's an idea that's just now emerging as a means of understanding American civil rights law and the place of nonblack groups in it," Rodrigo replied. "The idea is that the structure of antidiscrimination law is dichotomous. It assumes you are either black or white. If you're neither, you have trouble making claims or even having them understood in racial terms at all."

"I think I follow you," I replied. "But could you fill it out a little more? Assuming that our system does incorporate such a dichotomy, how does that render nonblack minority groups one-down, as opposed to, say, one-up, compared to blacks?"

"That's the next step," Rodrigo replied. "At the conference, no one had worked that out yet. But it's an important question. America's racial future looks increasingly mixed up. Latinos will overtake blacks as the most numerous minority early next century. The Asian population, too, is increasing rapidly. Multiracial people are demanding their own voice and census category. A simplistic paradigm of racial relations, based on an either-or, A-or-B model, won't work much longer. I've been trying to figure out why this is so."

From "RODRIGO'S FIFTEENTH CHRONICLE: RACIAL MIXTURE, LATINO-CRITICAL SCHOLARSHIP, AND THE BLACK-WHITE BINARY." 75 TEX. L. REV. 1181 (1997). Originally published in the *Texas Law Review*. Reprinted by permission.

"And do you have any inkling?" I asked.

"You remember, Professor, how Critical Legal Studies early on developed the notion of the fundamental contradiction?"

"Of course," I replied. "At the time a breathtaking breakthrough, it explains many of the strains and tensions running through our system of law and politics. It led to powerful critiques of the public-private distinction, judicial indeterminacy, and rights. Were the Latinos at your conference working on something similar?"

"I think we were," Rodrigo replied. "But without knowing it. And it's that very same black/white binary. People are just starting to talk about it. You may have seen an article or two. If one's paradigm identifies only one group as deserving of protection, everyone else is likely to suffer. Not only that, even members of one's own group are apt to think of themselves as black or white. It's quite a disabling instrument. We may have to blast the dichotomy—embrace the full multifariousness of life—if we're ever going to get anywhere."

"Didn't I read somewhere that early litigators arguing on behalf of Chicanos and other Latino groups embraced something called the 'other white' strategy?" I asked.

"They did," Rodrigo replied. "It's the logical extension of the kind of thinking that the black/white binary predisposes you to. The only way to get relief is to maintain that your client, a Mexican American or Puerto Rican, is white and thus should not be the object of social discrimination."

"Not exactly empowering," I commented wryly. "But I believe you were going to tell me of some other ways the binary does its pernicious work."

"In addition to the way just mentioned—namely that it fetters our own minds," Rodrigo said, "preventing us from articulating, or even imagining, how our victimization is a serious, group-based form of oppression."

"You must do so, and in the most complete fashion possible," I said. "If the binary is to serve as Latinos' fundamental contradiction, you have to spell out exactly how this structure of thought renders our people one-down. Otherwise, it's simply an observation, a descriptive statement no more useful than 'many Latinos speak Spanish,' or 'many have ancestors from Latin America or the Caribbean.'"

"I agree," Rodrigo replied. "Without such an explanation, the insight kind of runs out of gas."

"So, what are your ideas on how the black/white paradigm injures Latinos and other nonwhite groups?"

The Black/White Paradigm and the Social Reproduction of Inequality—Doctrine's Role

"As you know, Professor, the mainstay of American civil rights law is the Equal Protection Clause. Rooted in Reconstruction-era activism and aimed at the wholly laudable purpose of redressing slavery, that clause nevertheless produces and reproduces inequality for my people."

"The Equal Protection Clause?" I replied, raising my eyebrows. "That crown jewel in our jurisprudence, centerpiece of justice, and source of civil rights breakthroughs like *Brown v. Board of Education*? It's this that you think subordinates and injures Latinos? That's paradoxical, to put it mildly. I think I need to hear more."

"Let me try," Rodrigo replied calmly. "An analogy occurred to me on the plane. Consider a different constitutional principle, namely, protection of the right of property. How does that function in a society like ours?"

"I suppose you're going to say that it benefits the haves, while disadvantaging or leaving as they are the have-nots, thus increasing the gap between the propertied and those who have less of that commodity."

"Exactly," Rodrigo replied. "And the same is true of other constitutional principles. The Free Speech Clause increases the influence of those who are articulate and can afford microphones, TV air time, and so on. In the same way, the Equal Protection Clause produces a social good, namely equality, for those falling under its coverage—blacks and whites. These it genuinely helps—at least on occasion. But it leaves everyone else unprotected. The gap between blacks and other groups of color grows, all other things being equal."

"It sounds strange when you first explain it," I said. "The idea of the Equal Protection Clause producing inequality. But you may have a point. As with those other clauses, the black/white paradigm could marginalize Latinos because of the way the clause and the other Civil War amendments were aimed at redressing injustices to blacks, principally slavery."

"I've thought of two other doctrinal sources of inequality," Rodrigo added. "Would you like to hear them?"

"Of course," I said. "I assume they also have to do with the black/white paradigm?"

"They do. The first is the very notion of civil rights. In American law, this means rights bestowed by the civil polity. But Latinos—many of them, at any rate—are not members of that polity. Rather, they want to immigrate here. In this respect they stand on a different footing from blacks. I'm sure you know, Professor, that the plenary power doctrine in immigration law means that someone desiring to immigrate to the U.S. has no power, enforceable in court, to compel equal treatment. U.S. immigration law can be as racist and discriminatory as Congress wants."

"Immigrants have due process rights, rights to a hearing, that sort of thing," I pointed out.

"But only once they're here," Rodrigo replied. "Not to get here in the first place. Since virtually all present-day Hispanics and Latinos, like Asians, come from somewhere else, this limitation affects them drastically. Yet it is inherent in our liberal notion of civil rights and implicit in the black/white binary. Blacks, and even Indians, were here originally or from very early days. Once society decided to count them as citizens, their thoughts and preferences began to figure into the political equation. Even if they were often out-voted and oppressed, their voices at least counted. A Mexican peasant desiring to immigrate in search of a better life, or a Guatemalan village activist fearful that the government wants to kill him, or a Chinese boat person does not count. They can come here only at sufferance, only if Congress decides to let them in.”

“For example, through a Bracero program, a student visa, or some other category benefiting the U.S., such as that for investors,” I added. “What’s your second doctrinal source of inequality?”

“It’s related to the one I just mentioned,” Rodrigo said. “I’m sure you’ve heard, Professor, of the self-definition theory of nationhood?”

“In immigration law, you mean?” I asked. Rodrigo nodded. “I have. Going back to an article and a book co-authored by Peter Schuck, the argument holds that nations have the inherent right to decide how to define themselves.[1] Otherwise, according to Schuck, any group could force a nation like ours to undergo radical transformation merely by moving here. This no group has the right to do. Tapping neorepublican principles, the argument has proved influential in the immigration debate by supplying an ostensibly neutral principle for limiting immigration. And I suppose you think there’s something wrong with it?”

“I do,” Rodrigo replied. “The current contours of the U.S. citizenry are shaped by past immigration policies, which were overtly racist. Recently, those policies have been eased somewhat, but only a little. Thus, to ask a body of citizens like ours what sort of person they would like to let in is to invite the answer: as non-threatening and as much like us as possible. And probably in small numbers, too. If we were a more diverse society, that would not be so bad. But the way things stand, the principle of national self-determination that Schuck and others tout merely reproduces more of the same.”

“So, Rodrigo, you think you have found the DNA, so to speak, that reproduces inequality for Chicanos and Hispanics. A triple dynamic, inherent in Equal Protection doctrine and contractarian politics, that excludes and injures your people.”

“Yes, but more than mere doctrine holds us back. If it were just that, we could make gains by working outside the legal arena, by mobilizing and educating, for example. Something happened at the conference that I think you’ll find interesting. It illustrates a third way binary thinking injures Latinos. Would you like to hear?”

The Out-of-Mind Phenomenon

I nodded vigorously. “I love conference dynamics. Something zany happens at almost every one. I’d love to hear.”

“It’s not all that earthshaking,” Rodrigo replied. “But I think it captures something. The conference, as I mentioned, featured a star-studded cast. Attendance was fairly good, even though the event was held in the law school, near the edge of campus. The curious thing is that only one law professor from the huge faculty of the host school showed up. The dean, who had been scheduled to introduce the keynote speaker, begged off at the last minute, pleading important business, and sent the associate dean instead. He didn’t even stay to hear the address itself.”

“Maybe they were just busy,” I said a little lamely, trying to excuse my colleagues at that other school, several of whom I knew personally.

"I'm sure that's true," Rodrigo conceded. "But suppose the eminent panel of conferees had been black, consisting of Derrick Bell, Cornel West, John Hope Franklin, Leon Higginbotham, and others of that stature. In fact, the Latino speakers were just as stellar in terms of reputation and standing in their fields."

"Are you saying that attendance would have been better?" I asked.

"I'm not sure it would have been better," Rodrigo replied. "But I suspect the law faculty would have put in at least token appearances. They would have gushed over the speakers, shaken their hands warmly, and told them how glad they were that they were here, how much the students needed them, and so on. They would have shown solidarity and engaged in at least a few minutes of chit-chat before, of course, taking off for their offices and their next manuscripts."

"I hope you're not saying their failure to show up was a deliberate affront?" I asked.

"More likely just a matter of priorities. On any given day, dozens of major events take place at a large university. The professors probably saw the conference as just one of many possible demands on their time, like that reception for the married students or that lecture on Proust being held across campus. No conspiracy or conscious boycott operated, but the result was the same: they didn't show up. If we'd been blacks, they would have. It's as simple as that."

"I know that faculty pretty well," I said. "What you recount is surprising. They're all liberals and deep-dyed supporters of civil rights."

"I wouldn't doubt it," Rodrigo replied. "The faculty know, on some level, that Latinos have terrible troubles and need help. But the classic, the essential racial group is blacks. If you're a liberal law professor, you donate time to the NAACP Legal Defense Fund. When someone mentions 'civil rights,' you immediately think black."

"And so Latinos are simply out of mind because of the black/white binary," I added.

"We're not part of the mindset or discourse. People don't think of us in connection with civil rights struggles. Another mechanism is geographical. Many Latinos, Chicanos for example, don't live in the cities. They're farmworkers or field hands. But when you think of civil rights, you immediately think of city problems—like gangs, urban blight, segregated run-down schools, and unemployment—that afflict mainly blacks."

"Puerto Ricans are by-and-large an urban group," I pointed out.

"True, and some urban programs do include them. But many Latinos are not included, especially in the West and Southwest. They fall almost entirely outside traditional civil rights consciousness, even though their struggles with pesticides, insecticides, field sanitation, and education for their kids are just as serious as those of inner-city dwellers."

"I'm beginning to see the force of the black/white paradigm," I interjected. "It looks like it really does disadvantage our people."

"And I hope you'll help me figure out more ways that it does. We've touched on three."

"I'm game. Do you have others in mind?"

Practical Consequences of the Black/White Paradigm

"I think the paradigm not only has doctrinal and conceptual consequences, limiting the way we think of race and racism, but it also has highly concrete real-world ones as well."

"Do you have an example?"

"Let's say you're an employer or state bureaucrat. You are distributing assets—things of value, like benefits, contracts, or jobs. You can give a job, say, to one of two equally qualified candidates. One's a black, the other a Hispanic. You probably give it to the black. The black can sue you. He or she has all those civil rights statutes written with him or her in mind. To be sure, courts have held that Hispanics may also sue for discrimination. But the employer may not know that. And the Equal Protection Clause does not protect brown litigants as unconditionally and amply as it does blacks. The binary makes the black the prototypical civil rights plaintiff. When people read of Latinos suing for school or job discrimination, they are always a little surprised."

"Latinos ought to publicize this fact," I said.

"That's the problem. We have fewer leaders who could do so. Affirmative action produced a generation of college-trained black leaders and professionals beginning about thirty years ago. Today, these people are mayors of cities and members of Congress. That body boasts a long-standing Black Caucus, but only a much smaller and more recently formed Hispanic one. Also, the entire federal bench includes fewer than thirty Latino judges today. It contains many more black ones, even though the two groups' numbers are almost the same in the general population. And the reason is simple: affirmative action started earlier with blacks. Even today, the average employer thinks of affirmative action in black, not Puerto Rican, Laotian, or Chicano terms. A Laotian or Chicano law teaching candidate shows up, and even liberal law faculty have to remind themselves, 'Oh, yes, they qualify for affirmative action, too.'"

"That's a problem of mindset and conception," I said. "The way society thinks of a group—or fails to think about it—influences the way it behaves toward them. If you're out of mind because everyone is thinking in dichotomous terms, how successful will you be in having your needs noticed and addressed? Listeners may even decide you're at fault for your own predicament, a whiner when you call attention to the way no one attended your conference," I warned my young protégé.

Symbol, Myth, and the Role of the Black/White Binary

"I'll be careful," Rodrigo agreed. "But it's interesting to notice why it's necessary. I think the black/white binary conveys to everyone that there's just one group worth worrying about. People conveniently forget that the early settlers exterminated 95 percent of the Indian population, or that many Puerto Rican, Chicano, and Indochinese families are just as poor and desperate as black ones. But only the one group, blacks, has moral standing to demand attention and solicitude. Those others don't. And to make absolutely sure they don't, we deploy appropriate myths and images.

Asians are the model minority—smart, quiet, sure to rise in a generation or two; Mexicans are happy-go-lucky cartoon characters or shady actors who sneak across the border, earn some money, and then send it to their families back home. No one today could get away with speaking of blacks in comparably disparaging terms, at least in public. But as recently as the 1960s the national Frito-Lay Corporation used the logo of a sleeping Mexican bandito, hat pulled over his eyes, dozing under a cactus. And the imagery deployed by the political right in the English-only and immigration reform campaigns is nearly as vicious: Latinos come across as criminals, welfare loafers, and drug dealers. If we were part of the civil rights paradigm, no one would dare do this, at least so openly."

"And you think the black/white paradigm is the reason?" I asked.

"Not alone," Rodrigo replied. "But it supplies the conditions that allow it to happen. If one's prevailing cultural image is not that of a noble warrior, like Martin Luther King, but of someone who takes siestas or steals jobs from deserving Americans, why would anyone want to help you?"

"In some ways, those images of Latinos are even more devastating than the ones society has disseminated about blacks, overtly until very recently, and covertly today. They justify society not only in ignoring your misery but in making war against you."

"I'm sure you've heard of the militarized border that is just beginning," Rodrigo interjected.

"I have, and of the imagery that is being deployed by the political right to justify it—the 'waves of immigrants,' the 'horde of welfare recipients,' the 'tide' of brown-skinned welfare mothers just waiting to have babies here so they can gain citizenship, the unassimilability of Latino people and their dubious loyalty."

"Even though Latino servicemen and women have given their lives and won medals for heroism far out of proportion to their numbers and exceeding those of every other racial group," Rodrigo interjected. "And consider the issue of language. If an immigrant French couple speak French to each other or English with a French accent, that's considered a sign of high status and culture. A Mexican worker speaks Spanish and he or she is considered stupid or disloyal."

Later, I kept coming back to this and other conversations Rodrigo and I had had recently about the role of nonblack groups in America's future. Would a country which I had served for more than forty years as a professor and civil rights advocate adjust peaceably to a century in which whites will begin to be outnumbered by blacks and browns? And would those two groups be able to work together toward mutual goals—or would the current factionalism and distrust continue into the future, with the various minority groups competing for crumbs while majoritarian rule continued unabated?

NOTES

1. See Peter H. Schuck and Rogers M. Smith, Citizenship without Consent: Illegal Aliens in the American Polity 121, 9–41, 116–40 (1985); Peter H. Schuck, *The Transformation of Immigration Law,* 84 Colum. L. Rev. 1, 1, 4–5, 49–65, 85–90 (1984).

Chapter 51

The Intersection of Immigration Status, Ethnicity, Gender, and Class

Kevin R. Johnson

Give me your tired, your poor . . .[1]

Everything is mucho good.
Soon we own the neighborhood.
We have a hobby—it's called breeding.
Welfare pay for baby feeding.[2]

The INS estimated that, as of October 1992, approximately 3.4 million undocumented persons resided in the United States, a figure much lower than many had previously estimated. Despite the stereotype, only about 39 percent (1.3 million) of the total were from Mexico. Nationals of Canada (97,000) and Poland (91,000) ranked fourth and fifth in the number of their citizens who are undocumented in the United States. Approximately 43 percent (1.4 million) of the undocumented population resided in California, the state in which anti-immigrant backlash was perhaps the strongest in the early 1990s. Six states, New York (449,000), Texas (357,000), Florida (322,000), Illinois (176,000), New Jersey (116,000), and Arizona (57,000), along with California, accounted for an estimated 86 percent of the total undocumented population in the country.

Contrary to the popular stereotype that all undocumented persons surreptitiously entered the country, the INS estimated that roughly one-half of the undocumented persons in the United States were visa overstays—visitors lawfully admitted for a temporary period, such as tourists, business travelers, and students—who failed to depart as required by the terms of their visas. The INS saw the obvious, yet crucial, inference to be drawn from this piece of data: "This significant part of the population has generally been overlooked in discussions of U.S. policy options for reducing unauthorized immigration."[3]

The magnitude of visa overstays as a source of the undocumented population suggests that a focus on border enforcement operations, such as ones in the 1990s in El Paso, Texas (Operation Blockade, later renamed Operation Hold the Line in response to public criticism), and San Diego, California (Operation Gatekeeper), even if completely effective, will not address half the problem. Border enforcement strategies, as exemplified by these two operations, are almost exclusively aimed at the southern border with Mexico and designed to halt persons from entering without inspection. The INS has recognized that the majority of those who enter without inspection are from Mexico, while many of the rest are natives of Central America. The failure to address the visa overstay component of the undocumented population is evidence that the actual desire of restrictionists is not to reduce all components of the undocumented population, but instead to reduce the number of undocumented Mexicans in the United States.

The focus on illegal immigration from Mexico is one way in which the ethnicity of immigrants appears to have influenced immigration enforcement policies. The changing demographics of immigration undoubtedly have contributed to the anti-immigration backlash. Before 1965, discriminatory national origin quotas favored northwestern European immigrants at the expense of immigrants from nations in other parts of the world. Since Congress lifted the quotas in 1965, lawful immigrants have come increasingly from developing nations. For example, of the total immigrants admitted in fiscal year 1993, the four leading feeder nations were Mexico, China, the Philippines, and Vietnam. The same pattern appears to hold true for undocumented immigrants. According to the INS, at least fifteen of the top twenty source countries of the undocumented population in fiscal year 1993 were developing nations populated primarily by people of color.

The illegal alien stereotype fails to incorporate women, despite the obvious fact that women immigrate, both lawfully and unlawfully, to the United States. Indeed, for fiscal year 1983 through 1993, about one-half of the immigrants admitted to the United States for permanent residence were women. Naturalization rates in recent years appear to have been slightly higher for women than for men. Women, as well as men, flee persecution in their native lands and seek asylum in the United States. Women and families, many of whom are needy of, but ineligible for, health and other benefits, have increased as a proportion of the undocumented Mexican population. Undocumented women who migrate to the United States tend to remain longer in the country than men, thus indicating that women may comprise a greater proportion of the undocumented population than simple migration patterns might otherwise suggest. At the same time, undocumented women may be even more vulnerable to exploitation in the labor market than undocumented men. The law, however, generally offers no special protections for undocumented women.

Others have analyzed gender bias in various provisions of the immigration laws. For example, consider the Immigration Marriage Fraud Amendments of 1986 (IMFA),[4] which were designed to crack down on sham marriages contracted between citizens and noncitizens for the purpose of allowing noncitizens to immigrate to the United States. IMFA required that a spouse of a citizen or lawful permanent resident seeking to immigrate to the United States be afforded conditional lawful permanent resident status for two years, after which both husband and wife had to petition for permanent status for the immigrant. "[U]nder these circumstances, many immigrant women were reluctant to leave even the most abusive of partners for fear of being deported. When faced with the choice between protection from their batterers and protection against deportation, many immigrant women chose the latter."[5] Attempting to ameliorate that harsh impact, Congress in the Immigration Act of 1990 allowed for a waiver of the law's requirements for hardship caused by domestic violence. Nonetheless, some criticized the waiver provisions as too onerous for many abused immigrant women, and Congress further relaxed the requirements in 1994. Thus, it took two acts of Congress, and eight years, to remedy the harsh, yet apparently unconsidered, impact on women.

IMFA spoke in gender-neutral terms but had gender-specific impacts. Similarly, the political debate over the reduction of public assistance to immigrants generally fails to weigh the disproportionate impact of such measures on immigrant women. This is so even though women undoubtedly use certain benefits more than men, prenatal care being the clearest example. The unavailability of education for undocumented children also would have a disproportionate impact on women, who often are in charge of child care, either as single parents or by default in two-parent households. The same is true for other public benefits, such as general assistance, and social services, including battered women's shelters.

One might contend that, because the stereotype of the woman immigrant is more favorable than its male counterpart, undocumented women are better off than men in the political marketplace. The undocumented male is feared as a criminal while the undocumented woman is seen as a responsible child-care provider or housecleaner (with whom many in some localities have almost daily contact). This assertion contains a grain of truth. Similarly, there probably is more concern with criminal minority males than with minority welfare mothers. The political process intentionally imposes sanctions, which in some ways have been increasingly harsh in recent years, on the criminals. With respect to welfare, however, the gender impacts often are obscured, if not ignored. Although Congress may willfully seek to punish criminal aliens in ways that have a disproportionate impact on immigrant men, it often wholly ignores the gender impacts on women, as illustrated by IMFA.

The same is true with respect to the gender impact of public assistance restrictions on the undocumented. While some men are affected by the criminal alien provisions of the immigration laws (i.e., those convicted of certain crimes), poor undocumented women, whether guilty of a crime or not, as a group are adversely affected by benefit restrictions. That the impact of the laws on immigrant women as a group are ignored more often than not demonstrates the power of the "quadruple whammy." [Class, gender, ethnicity, and citizenship—*Eds.*] Immigrant women often are blindsided in the process without any consideration of their interests.

Because public assistance programs are designed for the poor, eligibility restrictions necessarily will fall heavily on poor immigrants. For the most part, only the poor among the undocumented, by no means the entire group, will be adversely affected. For example, visa overstays, many of whom come to this country on student, business, and tourist visas, who have resources at their disposal will not be affected.

The class consequences of restrictions on the availability of public benefits to immigrants, however, are largely ignored.

One's first reaction might be that the quadruple whammy is insurmountable in the political process. But, the overlapping interests of communities concerned with immigrant access to public benefits create opportunities as well as problems. Namely, a potential cross-over of interests may permit the building of coalitions between many diverse communities. Specifically, immigrant rights, welfare rights, and women's rights groups, as well as ethnic activist groups, have common interests at some level in ensuring the availability of public benefits to immigrants. Efforts to resist reduction of the minimal public benefits afforded immigrants appeal to each of these diverse constituencies.

Diverse coalitions at various times have wrought positive change in the immigration laws. The political efforts of women and immigrant groups resulted in congressional relaxation of the more onerous requirements of the immigration marriage fraud laws. The increasing recognition of gender-based persecution for purposes of asylum also resulted, in part, from the efforts of both women's and refugee groups. In a similar vein, lesbian and gay organizations allied with immigrant rights groups in successfully convincing Congress to repeal a provision of the immigration laws that, as interpreted, allowed the exclusion of homosexuals from admission into the country. Related efforts have resulted in the granting of asylum to lesbians and gay men fearing persecution in their native countries.

Of course, cleavages between poor minority citizens and immigrants loom large. A well-publicized instance of interethnic conflict is that between Koreans and African Americans in South Central Los Angeles. Even if exaggerated by media reports, such conflict must be addressed. Needless to say, commonalities of interest will need to be identified before alliances can be built. Though the formidable impediments to broad-based alliances may be impossible to overcome, this does not mean that they are unworthy of exploration. Social change efforts have demonstrated that litigation alone cannot achieve the desired ends. Consequently, novel political strategies must be considered. Even if one concludes that the impediments to coalition-building cannot be overcome, recognition of the impact of multiple marginalization on immigration law and policy is important in itself. Lawmakers and policymakers should consider the multiple impacts of immigration policy decisions on various communities. The ethnic, class, and gender impacts of immigration-related policies, including public benefits and services, should no longer be ignored.

NOTES

1. Emma Lazarus, *The New Colossus,* in Emma Lazarus: Selections from Her Poetry and Prose 40, 41 (Morris U. Schappes ed., 1944) (poem written for Bartholdi Pedestal Fund in 1883, now inscribed on a plaque on the Statue of Liberty).

2. Robert Reinhold, *A Welcome for Immigrants Turns to Resentment,* N.Y. Times, Aug. 25, 1993, at A1, A12 (quoting portion of parody of Mexican immigrants circulated in California State Assembly).

3. Robert Warren, Immigration and Naturalization Service, Estimates of the Unauthorized Immigrant Population Residing in the United States, by Country of Origin and State of Residence: October 1992, at 16–17 (1994) (unpublished paper on file with author).

4. Pub. L. No. 99-639, 100 Stat. 3537 (codified as amended in scattered sections of 8 U.S.C.).

5. Kimberlè Crenshaw, in *Mapping the Margins: Intersectionality, Identity, Politics, and Violence against Women of Color,* 43 Stan. L. Rev. 1241, 1247 (1991).

Chapter 52

Bringing International Human Rights Home

Berta Esperanza Hernández-Truyol

What if we were to globalize our domestic legal practice by integrating international human rights norms into human/civil rights jurisprudence? A wealth of human rights laws awaits us to which we have denied ourselves access in the past and of which we could make greater and better use in the future. To be sure, the current political-social climate favors isolationism, while, for its part, Congress has loudly articulated a misdirected "stay within the lines" (i.e., borders) policy which is not likely to comport with this perspective. Nonetheless, the benefits to be reaped from the incorporation of accepted human rights principles into our domestic rights discourse merit careful attention.

The aim of this "bridge-building" proposal is to provide a blueprint for co-existence in this diverse world. Although many bridges remain to be built, we must concentrate on joining philosophical and international forces to build one grand structure—a bridge that can transport all individuals regardless of sex, race, national or social origin, class, religion, sexuality, color, or political beliefs comfortably into the twenty-first century.

My personal experience is not unlike that of many Latinas/os. Born in Cuba, I grew up in Puerto Rico. The environment in which I lived my formative years has made a dramatic difference in my life and how I see the world. If you contemplate a global melange you might have a glimpse of the diversity with which I lived every day of my life until I went to college in the States. We were big and small, brown-eyed and blue-eyed, blondes and brunettes, but one significant factor we shared was that we were all de Borinquen. Sure, we were a diverse peoples, but we were all united—we were all *boricua*. Little did I know that being *boricua* makes you somehow "diferente"—an outsider—in the U.S. Being "diferente," however, does not and should not mean we cannot be unified; indeed we all were as *boricua*.

I would like to suggest we build a bridge that will address the alleged "great racial divide" that exists in this country. In order to have the solid bridge I envision, the divide needs to be exposed and healed. For one, the racial divide must be recognized

From "Building Bridges: Bringing International Human Rights Home." 9 La Raza L.J. 69 (1996). Originally published in *La Raza Law Journal*. Reprinted by permission.

as having a lot more than two color components. Everything appears to be based upon a black/white dichotomy, or what the media portray as a black/white divide, which, by its nature, excludes entire segments of this country's population. Yet being American is much more than being black or white or brown. Recognition of the multidimensionality of all peoples should be acknowledged as a way to describe, though not define, the citizens and residents of the United States. Certainly for Latinas/os and Asians to be excluded defies credibility. On the other hand, collapsing them into the black/white dichotomy would deny their separate identities and silence their possibly different voices, thus revealing the imperfection of a binary classification scheme.

Much more than race defines each and every one of us as unique individuals. For example, we are male and female; gay and lesbian and non-gay and non-lesbian; we enjoy different levels of education; we span a broad range of social and economic classifications and of mental and physical abilities; we speak many tongues; and we are Catholic, Protestant, Santera/o, Buddhist, Muslim, Hindu, and Jew. Thus, in looking at the world and in building bridges to traverse it, we have to look at the people, not some singular characteristic that can be isolated and manipulated to effect a myth of insurmountable racial or ethnic or sex-based or sexuality-based or religious-based divisions.

This multidimensional perspective leads to a further part of the bridge: the segment connecting our domestic practice to international law. International human rights law is U.S. law and some of the rights protected by international human rights law when incorporated into our jurisprudence can develop, expand, and transform our domestic concept of civil rights.

The Relevant International Human Rights Norms

International human rights norms are, without doubt, legally enforceable rights, not merely aspirational statements of moral goals. To be sure, acknowledgement of the existence of legally enforceable human rights limits the power of governments, i.e., the obligation of States to respect inalienable human rights is a limitation on States' sovereignty—supposedly a "supreme, absolute power [of an] independent State to govern."[1] Thus, recognition of legally enforceable international human rights makes States accountable to individuals and to other States for any violation of recognized rights, even those of a State's own citizens. This, of course, is the lesson learned by the international community of nations from the Trials at Nuremberg, a tragedy in world history that effectively placed the protections of individuals at the heart of international law.

U.S. domestic law itself recognizes the existence of international law. For example, the Constitution gives Congress the power to "define and punish . . . [o]ffenses against the Law of Nations." Moreover, it defines the relationship between international law and domestic law by designating treaties as "the supreme law of the land." In addition, case law recognizes that customary international law—law that emerges from practices of States that is deemed to be obligatory—is U.S. law. Thus, adopted treaties or recognized customary principles are binding domestic law.

What about the concept of reservations—unilateral statements by States that can limit their international obligations—in human rights treaties? Although the notion of reservations is accepted in international law, the Vienna Convention on the Law of Treaties prohibits reservations that are "incompatible with the object and purpose of the treaty."[2] Moreover, reservations designed to excuse parties from commitments made with respect to non-derogable rights will fail and the reserving State will remain bound. In all events, a reservation designed to enable a State to suspend a non-derogable fundamental right will most likely be deemed incompatible with the object and purpose of the treaty. Consequently, prohibitions against racial discrimination and genocide, and perhaps even sex discrimination, laws will be invalid.

Binding international human rights norms provide significant protections beyond our "domestic" civil rights laws. For example, the International Covenant on Civil and Political Rights (ICCPR) and the Universal Declaration of Human Rights protect individuals from discrimination on the basis of race, color, sex, language, religion, political or other opinion, national or social origin, property, birth or other status. Other protected rights are privacy, education, health, life, and association.

While the international legal system affords many opportunities to expand the reach of domestic protections of individual rights, it is not perfect. One weakness of the system is the immense gap between women's legal and their real world/life status. Significantly, both the United Nations and the U.S. Department of State, neither a bastion of gender equality, have recognized that women's true position around the world is one of inequality. With these considerations in mind, consider the possible impact of an international human rights analysis on some specific matters of concern to communities of color.

The U.S. is the only industrial state that still imposes the death penalty, not without causing legal professionals, including Supreme Court Justices, much alarm. A jarring example surfaced recently when Supreme Court Justice Blackmun, a Nixon appointee who is not to be mistaken for a liberal in criminal cases, stepped down with the public pronouncement that, after years of voting to sustain capital sentences, he had concluded that the death penalty is unconstitutional. Just prior to stepping down, Justice Blackmun, in his dissent in *Callins v. Collins,*[3] recognized the disparate application of the death penalty:

> Twenty years have passed since this Court declared that the death penalty must be imposed fairly, and with reasonable consistency, or not at all, and, despite the effort of the states and courts to devise legal formulas and procedural rules to meet this daunting challenge, the death penalty remains fraught with arbitrariness, discrimination, caprice, and mistake.[4]

Blackmun's words are chilling in light of these facts: Between 1973 and 1992, a total of 4,704 convicted murderers were sentenced to death, but only 188 of them, or 4 percent, were executed; 1,815 of those death row prisoners, or 39 percent, succeeded in having their death sentences lifted by judicial review or executive clemency;

451 of those sentenced to die—nearly 10 percent—had their underlying convictions overturned on appeal.[5]

One U.S. death penalty case, *Stanford v. Kentucky*,[6] upholds imposition of the death penalty on a minor. The U.S. finds itself in notable company: only six other countries worldwide are known to have executed juveniles in the last decade—Barbados (which has since raised the age to eighteen), Iran, Iraq, Nigeria, Pakistan, and Bangladesh. In contrast to U.S. law, Article 6.5 of the ICCPR prohibits the imposition of the death penalty on juveniles and on pregnant women. When President Carter first submitted the ICCPR to Congress for its constitutionally mandated advice and consent, his transmittal included a blanket reservation against Article 6.5. Effectively, the reservation as submitted by President Carter provided that the U.S. retained its sovereign right to execute persons under eighteen as well as pregnant women.

However, when President Bush resubmitted the ICCPR to Congress in 1991, the reservation against the prohibition of imposition of the death penalty applied only to the execution of minors, not pregnant women. This U.S. acceptance of the ICCPR's prohibition against the imposition of the death penalty on pregnant women raises an intriguing question about the relationship of the international norm to U.S. domestic law. Has the U.S., by ratifying this human rights treaty, constitutionally prohibited the imposition of the death penalty on pregnant women? It seems that the answer is yes: the United States, by treaty, has agreed to limit its sovereign right to impose the death penalty in certain cases. This creates an interesting constitutional analytical construct because that prohibition would not be based upon Eighth Amendment jurisprudence—the basis for the U.S. death penalty jurisprudence. Rather, the prohibition would be constitutionally mandated by the Supremacy Clause.

Although the withdrawal of the reservation with respect to pregnant women was more likely than not the result of the Reagan/Bush Administrations' "choice" politics, the rationale is of no moment. The significance of the action lies in the prohibition of a domestic remedy by virtue of the application of international treaty law, the supreme law of the land. This is concrete evidence of the possible domestic impact of international human rights norms: the expansion, development and transformation of U.S. rights jurisprudence.

Next, consider the way various international human rights provisions afford grounds upon which to challenge the legality of Proposition 187 and its clone legislation. By agreeing to be bound to the non-discrimination provisions of ICCPR, every State party "undertakes to respect and to ensure to all individuals within its territory and subject to its jurisdiction the rights recognized in the present Covenant without distinction of any kind, such as race, colour, sex, language, religion, political or other opinion, national or social origin, property, birth or other status."[7] Thus, ICCPR alone provides six bases of protection on equality grounds with four—language, social origin, birth or "other status"—not being part of the U.S. Equal Protection safety net. Further, the ICCPR protects against "arbitrary or unlawful interference with . . . privacy, family, home or correspondence, [and] unlawful attacks on . . . honour and reputation,"[8] and provides that "[e]very child shall have, without any discrimination as to race, colour, sex, language, religion, national or social origin, property or birth, the right to such measures of protection as are required by his status as a minor, on the part of his family, society, and the State."[9] Moreover, additional provisions protect the rights to life, health, education, right to receive and impart information, and of association.

With these norms in mind, it is instructive to review Proposition 187. Its purpose is clearly articulated in its findings and declaration that the people of California have suffered and are suffering personal injury, damages, and economic hardship because of the presence of "illegal aliens" in the state. Certainly, the choice of language itself is deeply troubling. Its design is to identify a discrete group: immigrants, real people, whose criminality is simply their entry into the territorial jurisdiction of the U.S. without proper documentation. In fact, these people, who more often than not come to work to be able to support and provide for their families—an exemplary showing of family values—fill low-skilled, low-cost jobs that U.S. citizens will not accept.

The Proposition's very definition of who is eligible to receive the social benefits addressed by the law—public education, health care, welfare benefits, or social services—is disheartening, if not perverted. Certainly, two of the three eligibility classifications—those stating that U.S. citizens and aliens lawfully admitted as permanent residents are eligible to receive the specific benefits addressed—are plainly acceptable. The third category, however, is troubling. It provides for the grant of benefits to an alien lawfully admitted for a temporary period of time without regard to that alien's status at the time benefits are sought. By focusing on time of entry rather than when the application for benefits is made, such provision may be discriminatory. For example, Proposition 187 does not limit eligibility to receive benefits based upon a person's illegal presence in the jurisdiction. Rather, the provision simply bases eligibility on a person's legal entry. In this regard, consider that over 50 percent of illegal foreigners in this country are persons who overstay their visa, i.e., who enter legally but whose continued presence is illegal, or those who are from visa waiver States who only need a round trip ticket to enter the jurisdiction, but then do not return and thus also may be illegally present. Significantly, the demographics of those who overstay—Western and Eastern Europeans and other non-Latina/o Whites—are such that they might not be identified as "diferente" and thus not given the dubious label "illegal aliens."

To be sure, the ICCPR's non-discrimination framework, and even our own narrower laws, suggest a grave equal protection problem. If indeed the concern is for the scarcity of economic resources, should we not be concerned about illegal presence as well as entry? In this regard it is noteworthy that all the enhanced enforcement efforts currently afoot are aimed at border crossings, as evidenced by border patrol increases, whereas enforcement efforts to curb the other forms of illegal presence are virtually non-existent.

Myriad human rights problems also inhere in the investigatory techniques set out in Proposition 187. The law requires untrained administrative personnel, such as teachers and welfare or hospital intake clerks, to report persons whom they suspect are illegal aliens. Human rights issues arise, among other places, in the information or data such administrators must use to establish their "suspicion": the person's appearance, complexion, hair color and texture, and manner of dress—thinly veiled substitutes for national or social origin, color, race, and ethnicity—all classifications protected under the ICCPR. A separate basis for suspicion can be a person's manner of talking, such as speaking "foreign-accented" or "broken" English, or speaking Spanish—all matters falling within the ICCPR's language protection.

The proposition's refusal to provide primary and secondary education violates not only the right to schooling, but the right of association and the right to impart and receive information. The persons whose rights are hindered are not only the children (and parents of the children) being denied access to schools, but also those children (and parents of those children) who are allowed to stay in school but whose instruction is going forward without the presence or participation of those excluded. Similarly, the denial of medical services effects a denial not only of the right to health but also of other protected rights. For example, if one considers maternal and infant health issues, Proposition 187 interferes with women's right to equality on the basis of sex. The related concerns of maternal and infant mortality effect a possible denial of the protected right to life both of the mothers who die while pregnant, in childbirth or thereafter from complications and of the infants who die in childbirth or during infancy because of the denial of services.

These examples of the intersection of domestic and international human rights norms serve to underscore the thesis of this essay: a wealth of international human rights norms can develop, expand, and transform our domestic rights jurisprudence. By bringing such norms home and using them diligently in our courts, we can bring their protection a little closer to reality. At the very least we can engage in discourse that will facilitate our bridge-building to a better place in the new century.

NOTES

1. BLACK'S LAW DICTIONARY 1396 (6th ed. 1990).
2. *Vienna Convention on the Law of Treaties,* U.N. DOC. A/CONF. 39/27, art. 19 (1969).
3. Callins v. Collins, 114 S.Ct. 1127, 1128–38 (1994) (Blackmun, J., dissenting).
4. *Id.* at 1130.
5. David O. Stewart, *Dealing with Death,* 80 Nov. A.B.A J. 50, 50 (1994).
6. 492 U.S. 361 (1989).
7. *International Covenant on Civil and Political Rights,* Dec. 19, 1949, art. 2, 999 U.N.T.S. 171.
8. *Id.* art. 17.
9. *Id.* art. 24.

Chapter 53

Chicano Indianism

Martha Menchaca

In this chapter I describe forms of racial repression experienced by people of Mexican origin living under the legal system of the United States. I also document cases in which people of Mexican descent were compelled to argue that they should be treated as Caucasians in order to gain the legal rights of full citizens. Focusing on citizenship and racial legislation from 1848 to 1947, I argue that the U.S. legal system accorded privilege to whites and, conversely, legitimated the inferior treatment of racial minorities. Because Mexican-origin people were of mestizo descent (Spanish and Indian ancestry), they were placed in an ambiguous legal position. Their Indian ancestry linked them to people of color, subjecting them to heightened racial discrimination, while their Spanish ancestry linked them to whites, protecting them from the full impact of the racial laws of the period.

My fundamental aim is not to argue that Mexican-origin people are unaware of their indigenous past or that they have no indigenous historical consciousness. Rather, it is to show that they are among the dark-skinned people who historically have been discriminated against by this country's legal system. In embarking on this exploratory venture, I found it necessary to examine documents in which information about the racial repression of Mexican-origin people could be obtained. As primary sources, I consulted federal and state supreme court records and nineteenth-century citizenship legislation. These legal discourses illustrate more than a century of arguments used to justify racial discrimination in the United States.

U.S. Violation of the Treaty of Guadalupe Hidalgo

Through annexation, conquest, and purchase, the United States acquired Mexico's northern frontier between 1845 and 1854 (Weber 1982). The four border states of California, Arizona, New Mexico, and Texas contained numerous small and large settlements of Mexican residents. Mexico also lost parts of its northern frontier that

From *Chicano Indianism: A Historical Account of Racial Repression in the United States* by Martha Menchaca. Reprinted by permission of the American Anthropological Association from AMERICAN ETHNOLOGIST 20:3, August 1993. Not for further reproduction.

today include Nevada, Utah, parts of Colorado, and small sections of Oklahoma, Kansas, and Wyoming; these areas contained no Mexican settlements and remained under the control of indigenous peoples. At the termination of the Mexican-American War, the American states had the power to determine citizenship eligibility requirements, a power given to them by the Constitution of the United States (U.S. Const. art. IV, sec. 2, cited in Hyman and Wiecek 1982:517–531). As a consequence, the states were able to bar American Indians and all other racial minority groups from obtaining full citizenship privileges (Feagin 1989). The states proposed that only "free whites" (for example, whites who were not indentured servants or criminals) had all the desirable characteristics to receive such privileges (Hull 1985:11, 12; Kansas 1941:79, 80, 85; Konvitz 1946:318). Because most political privileges could be acquired only by a citizen, individuals who did not qualify for citizenship received limited civil rights.

When the United States acquired Mexico's northern frontier, the mestizo ancestry of the conquered Mexicans placed them in an ambiguous social and legal position (Tate 1969). In the U.S. government bureaucracy, it became unclear whether Mexicans were to be accorded the citizenship rights of white citizens or were to be treated as Indian inhabitants. Most government officials argued that Mexicans of predominantly Indian descent should be extended the same legal status as the detribalized American Indians (*People v. De La Guerra* 1870; *United States v. Joseph* 1876; *United States v. Lucero* 1869; *United States v. Santistevan* 1874). Mexicans, on the other hand, argued that under the Treaty of Guadalupe Hidalgo and international laws, the U.S. government agreed to extend all Mexican citizens—regardless of their race—the political rights enjoyed by white citizens. These rights were accorded to them on the basis of the international principle guaranteeing inhabitants of ceded territories the nationality of the successor state unless other provisions are made in the treaty of peace (Kansas 1941).

The Treaty of Guadalupe Hidalgo was exchanged and ratified in Queretaro, Mexico, on May 30, 1848, officially ending the Mexican-American War. It stipulated the political rights of the inhabitants of the ceded territory (including the Indians), set the U.S.-Mexico border, and brought several binational agreements on economic relations to closure. However, Anglo-American legislators violated the treaty and refused to extend Mexicans full political rights. The legislators were able to disenfranchise many Mexicans by arguing that such people were of Indian descent and therefore could not claim the political privileges of white citizens.

Conflicting Racial Laws in the Conquered Territories

In 1848, with the end of the Mexican-American War, the United States politically disenfranchised all Indians of the Southwest by rescinding Mexico's racial laws in the newly conquered territories. Since 1812, Mexico had given Indians the right to claim citizenship and full political rights (Knight 1990; Morner 1967; *United States v. Lucero* 1869; Weber 1982). Mexico also no longer practiced a legally based racial caste system. Thus, new racial restriction policies instituted in the conquered territories came to threaten the civil rights of the Mexicans because under U.S. Laws, Indians and "half-breeds" were not considered citizens (Kansas 1941; Naturalization Act of 1790, ch. 3, sec. 1; see In re *Camille* 1880).

The eradication of Mexico's racial caste system had begun in the late 1700s when the Spanish crown resolved that generations of miscegenation had thoroughly blurred racial distinctions (Knight 1990; Morner 1967). In 1812, the legal basis of the racial ranking order was finally abolished. The racial caste system, which for two centuries had distinguished individuals on the basis of race, became nonfunctional for political and social purposes. Its gradual breakdown resulted from the growth of the mestizo population and the political power obtained by upper-class mestizos. By the turn of the nineteenth century, the mestizos had become the majority and were heavily represented in the upper classes.

Before the breakdown of the racial caste system, Mexico's population had been divided among Spaniards, *castas,* and Indians (Lafaye 1974; Morner 1967; Vigil 1984). Distinguishing the population on the basis of parental origin had been an adequate legal method of according economic privilege and social prestige to the Spaniards. The Spaniards included both *peninsulares,* individuals who had been born in Spain and were of full European descent, and *criollos,* who were also of full European descent but had been born in the New World. As miscegenation increased among the Spanish elite, the criollo category eventually came to be redefined. The castas were mestizos and other persons of mixed blood. The Indian category included only people of full indigenous descent.

Of the various racial groups, the Spaniards enjoyed the highest social prestige and were accorded the most extensive legal and economic privileges. The legal system did not make distinctions between peninsulares and criollos. Nevertheless, the Spanish crown instituted policies requiring that high-level positions in the government and the Catholic church be assigned to peninsulares (Haring 1963), on the rationale that only peninsulares were fervently loyal to the Spanish crown. Exceptions were made when a new colony was established in the Americas and when a peninsular was unwilling to accept the appointment. It was required, however, that a criollo taking such an appointment be a son of peninsulares. Peninsulares were appointed to positions such as viceroy, governor, captain-general, archbishop, and bishop, whereas criollos were appointed to less prestigious positions, such as royal exchequer (treasurer, comptroller) and judge, and, after 1618, to mid-level administrative positions in the church (as priests or directors of schools).

The social and economic mobility of the rest of the population was seriously limited by the legal statuses ascribed to their ancestral groups. In theory, Indians were economically more privileged than mestizos because they held title to large parcels of communal land protected by the Spanish crown and the Catholic church (Haring 1963; Morner 1967). However, regardless of their landed property, the Indians were accorded little social prestige in Mexican society and were legally confined to subservient social and economic roles regulated by the Spanish elite. Most Indians were placed in *encomiendas* and *repartimientos* (Indian communities where land and labor were controlled by Spanish missionaries or government officials), Indian pueblos, or haciendas and were held in a perpetual state of tutelage. The mestizos enjoyed a higher social prestige than the Indians but were considered inferior to the Spaniards. They were also often ostracized by the Indians and the Spaniards, and they did not enjoy certain legal privileges accorded to those groups. For example, most mestizos were barred by royal decree from obtaining high- and mid-level positions in the royal and ecclesiastical governments (Haring 1963; Morner 1967). Moreover, the Spanish crown did not reserve land for the mestizos as it did for the Indians. For the most part, the only economic recourse most mestizos had was to enter the labor market or migrate toward Mexico's northern and southern frontiers. Each migrant who was the head of a household was awarded 150 acres and exempted from taxation for a period of approximately ten years (León-Portilla 1972; Rubel 1966; Weber 1982). After 1680, mestizos were occasionally allowed to become parish priests in Mexico's frontier settlements or in sparsely populated areas.

By the late 1700s, the rigid racial order had relaxed owing to changes in the interracial sexual and cohabitation practices of the Spanish elite (Bonifaz de Novello 1975; Morner 1967). It had become common for upper-class Spanish males to take mestizo or Indian women as concubines and afterward legitimate their offspring. In such cases the racial status of the child became criollo and not mestizos. These criollos had the racial status of Spaniards but were not accorded the corresponding legal privileges. They were barred from positions reserved for the Spaniards of full European descent, and they suffered certain sanctions for marrying peninsular women. By the early 1800s, large numbers of criollos, mestizos, and Indians were becoming increasingly defiant of bounded social roles and were trespassing their borders with deliberate speed. Criollos attempted to pass for peninsulares in order to obtain more social privileges. Indians often passed for mestizos in order to obtain wage labor in the urban centers, mestizos passed for Indians as a means of acquiring the land titles of the Indians (Bonifaz de Novello 1975; Morner 1967), and mestizos who had amassed great fortunes tried to improve their social standing by passing for criollos. The blurring of the racial distinctions made it difficult for the Spanish crown to enforce the laws and the prescribed social norms, in particular because the majority of the population was indistinguishably mestizos.

The final blow to the racial order came about through the political defection of the masses. By the early 1800s, movements to liberate Mexico from Spanish colonial rule had erupted throughout the country, and as a consequence the Spanish crown attempted to avert revolutionary action by instituting the 1812 Spanish Constitution of Cadiz. The new constitution legally abolished the casta system and the racial laws. Theoretically, the constitution conferred on Spaniards, mestizos, and Indians the same political rights regardless of racial origin. The laws of Cadiz, however, were unable to avert the national independence movements. In 1821, the masses won the Mexican War for Independence and instituted a provisional constitution (the Plan de Iguala) reaffirming the racial philosophy of the Constitution of Cadiz. After the War of Independence, race could no longer be legally used to prevent Indians and mestizos from exercising citizenship rights. For example, it became common for mestizos and full-blooded Indians to be elected to the presidency. All subsequent Mexican constitutions ratified the spirit and language of the Constitution of Cadiz.

In northern Mexico, the frontier experienced the same legislative changes as the interior. Indians were considered Mexican citizens and were accorded full political rights. In New Mexico, southern Arizona, and California the acculturated Indians and the secularized mission Indians actively exercised those rights (Spicer 1962; Weber 1982). In New Mexico numerous Pueblo Indians were elected to town and county political offices, and in California acculturated American Indians often held high-ranking posts in the military (Heizer and Almquist 1971; *United States v. Ritchie* 1854; *United States v. Vallejo* 1861). Of course the new laws had limited effects on the majority of the American Indians, because Mexico held title to territories inhabited by unconquered indigenous populations. The majority of the Shoshone, Navajo, Apache, and Comanche Indians had not been conquered by the Mexican state. And the new legislation did not eradicate the Mexican elites' attitudes of racial and economic superiority toward the American Indians and mestizos.

When Mexico ceded its northern territory to the United States, then, it had already abolished all racial restrictions on citizenship. The Indians had theoretically been incorporated as Mexican citizens. In practice, of course, this legislation had not abolished racial prejudice and discrimination in Mexico, and the Indians continued to be stigmatized as uneducated people. However, the mestizo racial category had taken on a new social meaning. Because most of the population was mestizo, being mestizo had become a source of pride rather than a stigma. The European race continued to hold high social prestige in Mexico, but the masses no longer considered it the only prestigious racial group (Knight 1990; Vigil 1984). In the legal domain, race could no longer be used as a civil rights barrier.

The racial policies of the United States, however, were less liberal than Mexico's. The United States at that time conferred full citizenship rights on "free whites" only. Thus, the states' constitutional right to deny Indians U.S. citizenship introduced the ideological and legal foundation for limiting the Mexican people's political rights. Moreover, government officials often used the Mexicans' indigenous heritage to undermine the civil rights language of the Treaty of Guadalupe Hidalgo. Article VIII of the treaty stated that the United States agreed to extend U.S. citizenship to all Mexican citizens, regardless of ancestry, who remained in the ceded territories. If individuals did not want U.S. citizenship, they had to so indicate within one year; otherwise they would become citizens automatically (cited in Tate 1969). Under Article IX the United States further agreed that Mexicans who chose to become U.S. citizens would have all the attendant rights. Article IX stipulated that "Mexicans who, in the territories aforesaid, shall not preserve the character of citizens of the Mexican Republic . . . shall be incorporated into the Union of the United States, and be admitted at the proper time . . . to the enjoyment of all the rights of citizens of the United States" (cited in Tate 1969:20).

Regardless of the treaty, however, the U.S. government refused to ratify the racial equality laws of Mexico. When the annexed southwestern territories joined the Union, their state constitutions did not extend to American Indians the political rights guaranteed by the Treaty of Guadalupe Hidalgo and the Mexican constitution. And soon after the enactment of the treaty, controversy arose over the citizenship status of the Mexicans. The exclusionary Indian citizenship laws, endorsed by the southwestern legislators, became the legal basis for limiting the political rights of the Mexicans. Government representatives commonly argued that the language of the treaty and the U.S. Constitution was unclear as to whether Mexicans of Indian descent should be treated as American Indians or should be extended the privileges of whites (Surace 1982; *United States v. Joseph* 1876; *United States v. Lucero* 1869; *United States v. Ritchie* 1854; *United States v. Santistevan* 1874).

Ironically, the political privileges that the Spanish and Mexican governments had previously given people in the Southwest were abolished by the U.S. racial laws. The Mexican mestizos and Indians entered a new racial caste-like order in which their civil rights were limited. Given the nature of the U.S. racial system and its laws, the conquered Mexican population learned that it was politically expedient to assert their Spanish ancestry; otherwise they were susceptible to being treated as American Indians (Padilla 1979). At the same time, as this historical blueprint suggests, it became politically expedient for American Indians to pass for Mexican mestizos if they wished to escape the full impact of the discriminatory Indian legislation (Forbes 1973). Let us now examine how the political disenfranchisement of the Indians affected the Mexican population.

The Denial of Citizenship for American and Mexican Indians

After ratification of the Treaty of Guadalupe Hidalgo, government representatives of the annexed region began to pass new racial-restriction citizenship laws (Cal. Const. 1849, art. II, sec. 1; New Mexico Organic Law [Act] of 1850, sec. 6, cited in First Legislative Assembly 1851:20; Organic Act of Arizona 1863, revised 1864, ch. 24, sec. 6, cited in Hoyt 1877:226; Tex. Const. 1845, art. III, sec. 1). Most American Indians were prohibited from obtaining citizenship, and the anti-Indian legislation adversely affected the Mexicans of partial or full Indian descent. Unless a Mexican was predominantly white, he or she was subject to racial harassment (Forbes 1973; Tate 1969). Those classified as Mexican Indians were not entitled to exercise full political rights or even basic civil rights: they were not allowed to vote, practice law, marry Anglo-American women, or run for political offices such as district judge (Konvitz 1946; Murphy 1970). They were also subject to severe human rights infringements, such as being placed in debt peonage and being forced to live on reservations.

After the annexation of Mexico's northern frontier, the southwestern territories and states enacted ruthless, discriminatory Indian legislation. The Anglo-American legislators were able to enforce the laws with the help of the U.S. military and the Anglo-American settlers. It became common policy to place American Indians on reservations, drive them out of the southwest, or exterminate them. . . .

I have described some of the racial repression experienced by people of Mexican origin in the United States, intending not to document all forms of racial discrimination but rather to examine how the legal system was used to deny Mexican-origin people their political rights. As part of my analysis, I have also examined the circumstances that strongly influenced some Mexican-origin people to assert their Caucasian ancestry in court in order to obtain their full rights of citizenship.

Court and legislative records from 1848 to 1947, I argue, reveal that the skin color of Mexican-origin people strongly influenced whether they were to be treated by the legal system as white or as non-white. During the nineteenth century, Mexican-origin individuals who were predominantly of Indian descent were subject to heightened racial discrimination. They were, for example, not allowed to become naturalized citizens if they were immigrants, to vote in the states of California and Arizona, to practice law in the state of Arizona, or to be exempted from segregationist legislation. The segregationist laws continued to affect darker-skinned Mexicans into the mid-twentieth century. Furthermore, nineteenth- and early-twentieth-century legal records indicate that although New Mexican state officials attempted to confer full citizenship privileges on "Mexicanized American Indians," the federal government rescinded their actions. In the legal domain, the federal government failed to acknowledge the existence of people who practiced both Mexican and American Indian traditions; these individuals experienced greater racial discrimination than the rest of the Mexican population. The legal records also indicate that *under the law* Mexican-origin people of predominantly Caucasian ancestry were ostensibly allowed to exercise the full political rights of citizens. However, the question of whether they could actually exercise those political rights is beyond the scope of this article. In the state of Texas, for example, local governments found alternative legal methods of discriminating against Mexicans who were identified as white. In the *Independent School District v. Salvatierra* court case, it was determined that "white Mexican students" could be legally segregated if they did not speak English.

I also argue that the Treaty of Guadalupe Hidalgo played three major roles in protecting the Mexican-origin population. In 1898, as a result of the treaty, the Naturalization Act of 1790 became inapplicable to Mexican immigrants (Kansas 1941); unlike other racial minorities, Mexican immigrants were exempted from the act and allowed to apply for naturalization. In the nineteenth century, the treaty also served to protect the political rights of some Mexicans, albeit only those of predominantly Caucasian ancestry; in the states of California and Arizona, "white Mexican males" were given the right of suffrage because the state legislators concluded that the treaty gave certain types of Mexicans full political rights. And in the twentieth century, the treaty was used to help dismantle de jure school segregation for the Mexican-origin students of the Southwest. In *Mendez v. Westminster* (1946, 1947) McCormick ruled that the treaty and the Fourteenth Amendment prohibited the unequal treatment of the Mexican population (Wollenberg 1974). *Mendez* was used in subsequent school desegregation cases and became the legal foundation for ending the era of de jure school segregation.

In sum, the record reveals a history of racial repression and discrimination against members of the Mexican-origin community in the United States. Government officials used the people's indigenous ancestry to deny them equal citizenship rights and to keep them in a politically subordinate position. Indianism was used to construct an image of Mexican-origin people as inferior and therefore deserving of separate and unequal treatment. With respect to future scholarship on the racial history of the Chicano people, I trust that this exploration has demonstrated the value of using legislative and judicial records as evidence that this American minority group has experienced severe racial discrimination in the United States.

REFERENCES

Bonifaz de Novello, Maria Eugenia. 1975. *La Mujer Mexicana: Analysis Historico.* Mexico City: Impresa Mexicana.

Feagin, Joe. 1989. *Racial and Ethnic Relations.* Englewood Cliffs, N.J.: Prentice Hall.

Forbes, Jack D. 1973. *Aztecas del Norte: The Chicanos of Aztlan.* Greenwich, Conn.: Fawcett Publications.

Haring, Clarence H. 1963. *The Spanish Empire in America.* New York: Harbinger.

Heizer, Robert, and Alan F. Almquist. 1971. *The Other Californians: Prejudice and Discrimination under Spain, Mexico, and the United States.* Berkeley: University of California Press.

Hoyt, John P., comp. 1877. *The Compiled Laws of the Territory of Arizona.* Detroit: Richmond, Backus and Co.

Hull, Elizabeth. 1985. *Without Justice for All: The Constitutional Rights of Aliens.* Westport, Conn.: Greenwood Press.

Hyman, Harold M., and William M. Wiecek. 1982. *Equal Justice under the Law: Constitutional Development, 1835–1875.* New York: Harper and Row.

Kansas, Sidney. 1941. *U.S. Immigration: Exclusion and Deportation, and Citizenship of the United States of America.* 2d edition. Albany, N.Y.: M. Bender.

Knight, Allen. 1990. "Racism, Revolution, and Indigenismo: Mexico, 1910–1940." In *The Idea of Race in Latin America, 1870–1940,* ed. R. Graham. Pp. 71–113. Austin: University of Texas Press.

Konvitz, Milton R. 1946. *The Alien and the Asiatic in American Law.* Ithaca, N.Y.: Cornell University Press.

Lafaye, Jacques. 1974. *Quetzalcoatl and Guadalupe.* Chicago: University of Chicago Press.

León-Portilla, Miguel. 1972. "The Norteño Variety of Mexican Culture: An Ethnohistorical Approach." In *Plural Society in the Southwest,* ed. E. Spicer and R. Thompson. Pp. 77–101. New York: Weatherhead Foundation.

Morner, Magnus. 1967. *Race Mixture in the History of Latin America.* Boston: Little, Brown and Co.

Murphy, James. 1970. *Laws, Courts, and Lawyers: Through the Years in Arizona.* Tucson: University of Arizona Press.

Padilla, Fernando. 1979. "Early Chicano Legal Recognition, 1846–1897." *Journal of Popular Culture* 13:564–74.

Rubel, Arthur. 1966. *Across the Tracks: Mexican Americans in a Texas City.* Austin: University of Texas Press.

Spicer, Edward. 1962. *Cycles of Conquest: The Impact of Spain, Mexico and the United States on the Indians of the Southwest, 1533–1960.* Tucson: University of Arizona Press.

Surace, Samuel. 1982. "Achievement, Discrimination, and Mexican Americans." *Comparative Studies in Society and History* 24:315–39.

Tate, Bill. 1969. *The Guadalupe Hidalgo Treaty of Peace 1848 and the Gadsden Treaty with Mexico 1853*. Truchas, N.M.: Tate Gallery and Rio Grande Sun Press.

Vigil, Diego. 1984. *From Indians to Chicanos*. Prospect Heights, Ill: Waveland Press.

Weber, David. 1982. *The Mexican Frontier, 1821–1846: The American Southwest under Mexico*. Albuquerque: University of New Mexico Press.

Wollenberg, Charles. 1974. "*Mendez v. Westminster:* Race, Nationality and Segregation in California Schools." *California Historical Society Quarterly* 53:317–332.

Chapter 54

Rodrigo's Chronicle

Richard Delgado

"Excuse me, Professor, I'm Rodrigo Crenshaw. I believe we have an appointment."

Startled, I put down the book I was reading and glanced quickly first at my visitor, then at my desk calendar. The tall, rangy man standing in my doorway was of indeterminate age—somewhere between twenty and forty—and, for that matter, ethnicity. His tightly curled hair and olive complexion suggested that he might be African American. But he could also be Latino, perhaps Mexican, Puerto Rican, or any one of the many Central American nationalities that have been applying in larger numbers to my law school in recent years.

"Come in," I said. "I think I remember a message from you, but I seem not to have entered it into my appointment book. Please excuse all this confusion," I added, pointing to the pile of papers and boxes that had littered my office floor since my recent move. I wondered: Was he an undergraduate seeking admission? A faculty candidate of color like the many who seek my advice about entering academia? I searched my memory without success.

"Please sit down," I said. "What can I do for you?"

"I'm Geneva Crenshaw's brother. I want to talk to you about the LSAT, as well as the procedure for obtaining an appointment as a law professor at an American university."

As though sensing my surprise, my visitor explained: "Shortly after Geneva's accident, I moved to Italy with my father, Lorenzo, who was in the Army. After he retired, we remained in Italy, where he worked as a civilian at the same base where he had been serving. I finished high school at the base, then attended an Italian university, earning my law degree last June. I've applied for the LL.M. program at a number of U.S. law schools, including your own. I want to talk to you about the LSAT, which all the schools want me to take, and which, believe it or not, I've never taken. I'd also like to discuss my chances of landing a teaching position after I earn the degree."

From "Rodrigo's Chronicle." 101 Yale L.J. 1357 (1992). Originally published in the *Yale Law Journal*. Reprinted by permission of the Yale Law Journal Company and Fred B. Rothman & Company.

I reflected a moment, then said: "Your situation is somewhat unusual. But I'll do my best. I didn't know Geneva had a brother."

"We're only half-siblings," he explained, "and separated by nearly twenty years. But I've kept in touch as best I could, and I'm grateful to you for bringing her message to the attention of your friends. She has a rather acerbic manner, as you know. But she respects you and your work enormously."

"Your sister is a remarkable woman," I said. "I have learned at least as much from her as she from me. You said you are going to be taking the LSAT. What are your concerns about that?"

"The usual," he replied, "including that I don't see why I should have to take it at all. I graduated fourth in my class at a law school even older than yours. I should think it would be obvious to anyone that I can read a case or make a legal argument. But I'm more than a little worried about the cultural bias people tell me the test contains. I'm proficient in English, as you can tell. But I've been away from the United States for nearly ten years; I'm afraid some of the questions may assume information I lack simply because I've taken half my schooling outside the culture."

"I've made the same argument myself in the case of minorities in the United States," I said. "But it goes nowhere. They say the test is not biased because it predicts law school grades, which always seemed like a non sequitur to me. I didn't realize that we required the test for foreign law graduates." I paused, then added, "Maybe they think it provides a check against grades, which might vary from one system to another."

"Yet in each system," Rodrigo countered levelly, "those grades reflect, in most cases, broader and more pervasive forms of cultural power, including the backgrounds and advantages of those who earn them. They also correspond to the law firm jobs and prestigious government positions the students will hold after they graduate. Identifying the LSAT as a predictor of grades, or even of later job performance, tells us only that this narrow test will identify people who thrive in particular types of environments—the ones, of course, that rely on the test to do a certain type of screening."

Not bad, I thought—I hoped he would come to my law school. But instead I asked: "So, what are you going to do? If you skip the test, you can kiss your LL.M goodbye."

"I know, I know," he said, "if I have to take the test, I will. I bought one of those practice books. I'm sure I'll do OK—although I can't help thinking the whole thing is a waste of time."

"I agree—on both scores," I added. . . .

[Rodrigo and the Professor discuss the law school hiring market, then continue as follows—*Eds.*]

"As I mentioned, my program of studies at Bologna centered on the history of Western culture. I'm mainly interested in the rise of Northern European thought and its contribution to our current predicament. During my early work I had hoped to extend my analysis to law and legal thought."

"I think I know what you will say about legal thought and scholarship. Tell me more about the big picture—how you see Northern European thought."

"I've been studying its rise in the late Middle Ages and decline beginning a few decades ago. I'm interested in what causes cultures to evolve, then go into eclipse. American society, even more than its European counterparts, is in the early stages of dissolution and crisis. It's like a wave that is just starting to crest. As you know, waves travel unimpeded across thousands of miles of ocean. When they approach the shore, they rise up for a short time, then crest and lose their energy. Western culture, particularly in this country, is approaching that stage. Which explains, in part, why I am back." . . .

Rodrigo went on: "I'm sure all the things I'm going to say have occurred to you. Northern Europeans have been on top for a relatively short period—a mere wink in the eye of history. And during that time they have accomplished little—except causing a significant number of deaths and the disruption of a number of more peaceful cultures, which they conquered, enslaved, exterminated, or relocated on their way to empire. Their principal advantages were linear thought, which lent itself to the development and production of weapons and other industrial technologies, and a kind of messianic self-image according to which they were justified in dominating other nations and groups. But now, as you can see"—Rodrigo gestured in the direction of the window and the murky air outside—"Saxon-Teuton culture has arrived at a terminus, demonstrating its own absurdity."

"I'm not sure I follow you. Linear thought, as you call it, has surely conferred many benefits." (Hmm, I thought of countless examples. Just that morning I had read about a new medical breakthrough developed at an American research university. Only two weeks ago I had my car rebuilt by a mechanic who [I hope] was well versed in linear thought. The day before I had baked a batch of brownies following a ten-step recipe.) "And is it really on its last legs? Aside from smoggy air, Western culture looks firmly in control to me."

"So does a wave, even when it's cresting—and you know what happens shortly thereafter. Turn on your computer, Professor," Rodrigo said, pointing at my new terminal. "Let me show you a few things."

For the next ten minutes, Rodrigo led me on a tour of articles and books on the West's economic and political condition. His fingers fairly danced over the keys of my computer. Accessing data bases I didn't even know existed, he showed me treatises on the theory of cultural cyclicity; articles and editorials from *The Economist*, *Corriere della Sera*, the *Wall Street Journal*, and other leading newspapers, all on our declining economic position; material from the *Statistical Abstract* and other sources on our increasing crime rate, rapidly dwindling fossil fuels, loss of markets, and switch from a production- to a service-based economy with high unemployment, an increasingly restless underclass, and increasing rates of drug addition, suicide, and infant mortality. It was a sobering display of technical virtuosity. I had the feeling he had done this before and wondered how he had come by this proficiency while in Italy.

Rodrigo finally turned off the computer and looked at me inquiringly. "A bibliography alone will not persuade me," I said. "But let's suppose for the sake of argument that you have made a prima facie case, at least with respect to our economic problems and to issues concerning race and the underclass. I suppose you have a theory on how we got into this predicament?"

"I do," Rodrigo said with that combination of brashness and modesty that I find so charming in the young. "As I mentioned a moment ago, it has to do with linear thought—the hallmark of the West. When developed, it conferred a great initial advantage. Because of it, the culture was able to spawn, early on, classical physics, which, with the aid of a few borrowings here and there, like gunpowder from the Chinese, quickly enabled it to develop impressive armies. And, because it was basically a ruthless, restless culture, it quickly dominated others that lay in its path. It eradicated ones that resisted, enslaved others, and removed the Indians, all in the name of progress. It opened up and mined new territories—here and elsewhere—as soon as they became available and extracted all the available mineral wealth so rapidly that fossil fuels and other mineral goods are now running out, as you and your colleagues have pointed out."

"But you are indicting just one civilization. Haven't all groups acted similarly? Non-linear societies are accomplishing at least as much environmental destruction as Western societies are capable of. And what about Genghis Khan, Columbus, the cruelties of the Chinese dynasties? The Turkish genocide of the Armenians, the war machine that was ancient Rome?"

"True. But at least these other groups limited their own imperial impulses at some point."

"Hah! With a little help from their friends," I retorted.

"Anyway," continued Rodrigo, "these groups produced valuable art, music, or literature along the way. Northern Europeans have produced next to nothing—little sculpture, art, or music worth listening to, and only a modest amount of truly great literature. And the few accomplishments they can cite with pride can be traced to the Egyptians, an African culture."

"Rodrigo, you greatly underestimate the dominant culture. Some of them may be derivative and warlike, as you say. Others are not; they are creative and humane. And even the ones you impeach have a kind of dogged ingenuity for which you do not give them credit. They have the staying and adaptive powers to remain on top. For example, when linear physics reached a dead end, as you pointed out, they developed relativity physics. When formalism expired, at least some of them developed Critical Legal Studies, reaching back and drawing on existing strands of thought such as psychoanalysis, phenomenology, Marxism, and philosophy of science."

"Good point," admitted Rodrigo a little grudgingly, "although I've already pointed out the contributions of Gramsci, a Mediterranean. Fanon and your Critical Race Theory friends are Black or brown. And Freud and Einstein are, of course, Jews. Consider, as well, Cervantes, Verdi, Michelangelo, Duke Ellington, the current crop of Black writers—non-Saxons all."

"But Northern Europeans, at least in the case of the two Jewish giants," I interrupted.

"True, people move," he countered.

"Don't be flip," I responded. "Since when are the Spanish and Italians exempt from criticism for 'Western' foibles? What about the exploitive capacity of the colonizing conquistadors? Wasn't the rise of commercial city-states in Renaissance Italy a central foundation for subsequent European cultural imperialism? Most ideas of Eurocentric superiority date to the Renaissance and draw on its rationalist, humanist intellectual, and artistic traditions."

"We've had our lapses," Rodrigo conceded. "But theirs are far worse and more systematic." Rodrigo was again eyeing my computer.

Wondering what else he had in mind, I continued: "What about Rembrandt, Mozart, Shakespeare, Milton? And American popular culture—is it not the envy of the rest of the world? What's more, even if some of our Saxon brothers and sisters are doggedly linear, or, as you put it, exploitive of nature and warlike—surely you cannot believe that their behavior is biologically based—that there is something genetic that prevents them from doing anything except invent and manufacture weapons?" Rodrigo's earnest and shrewd retelling of history had intrigued me, although, to be honest, I was alarmed. Was he an Italian Louis Farrakhan?

"The Saxons do all that, plus dig up the earth to extract minerals that are sent to factories that darken the skies, until everything runs out and we find ourselves in the situation where we are now." Then, after a pause: "Why do you so strongly resist a biological explanation, Professor? Their own scientists are happy to conjure up and apply them to us. But from one point of view, it is they whose exploits—or rather lack of them—need explaining."

"I'd love to hear your evidence."

"Let me begin this way. Do you remember that famous photo of the finish of the hundred-meter dash at the World Games this past summer? It showed six magnificent athletes straining to break the tape. The first two finished under the world record. All were Black."

"I do remember."

"Black athletes dominated most of the events, the shorter ones at any rate. People of color are simply faster and quicker than our white brothers and sisters. Even the marathon has come to be dominated by people of color. And, to anticipate your question, yes I do believe the same holds true in the mental realm. In the ghetto they play 'the dozens'—a game that requires throwaway speed. The dominant group has nothing similar. And take your field, law. Saxons developed the hundred-page linear, densely footnoted, impeccably crafted article—saying, in most cases, very little. They also brought us the LSAT, which tests the same boring, linear capacities they developed over time and that now exclude the very voices they need for salvation. Yet you, Matsuda, Lawrence, Torres, Peller, and others toss off articles with ridiculous ease—critical thought comes easy for you, hard for them. I can't, of course, prove your friends are genetically inferior; it may be their mindset or culture. But they act like lemmings. They go on building factories until the natural resources run out, thermonuclear weapons when their absurdity is realized and everyone knows they cannot be used, hundred-page law review articles that rehash cases when everyone knows that vein of thought has run dry—and they fail even to sense their own danger. You say they are adaptive. I doubt it."

"Rodrigo," I burst in. "You seriously misread the times. Your ideas on cultural superiority and inferiority will obviously generate resistance, as you yourself concede. Wait till you see how they respond to your hundred-yard dash example; you're sure to find yourself labeled as racist. Maybe we both are—half the time I agree with you. But even the other things you say about the West's predicament and its need for an infusion of new thought—things I strongly agree with—will fall on deaf ears. All the movement is the other way. This is a time of retrenchment. The country is listening to the conservatives, not to people like you and me."

"I know," said Rodrigo. "I've been reading about that retrenchment. We do get the *New York Times* in Italy, even if it comes a few days late."

"And so you must know about conservative writers like Allan Bloom, Thomas Sowell, Glenn Loury, Roger Kimball, Shelby Steele, E. D. Hirsch, and Dinesh D'Souza and the tremendous reception they have been receiving, both in popular circles and in the academy?"

"Yes. I read D'Souza on the flight over, in fact. Like the others, he has a number of insightful things to say. But he's seriously wrong—and hardly represents the wave of the future, as you fear."

"They certainly represent the present," I grumbled. "I can't remember a period—except perhaps the late 1950s—when I have seen such resistance to racial reform. The public seems tired of minorities, and the current Administration is no different. The backlash is apparent in the university setting as well: African-American studies departments are underfunded and the exclusionary Eurocentric curriculum is making a comeback."

"But it's ordinary, natural—and will pass," Rodrigo responded. "In troubled times, a people turns to the past, to its own more glorious period. That's why these neoconservative writers are popular—they preach that the culture need not change direction to survive, but only do the things it did before, harder and more energetically."

"What our psychologist friends call 'perseveration,'" I said.

"Exactly. In my studies, I found that most beleaguered people do this, plus search for a scapegoat—a group they can depict as the source of all their troubles."

"An old story," I agreed ruefully. "D'Souza, for example, places most of the blame for colleges' troubles at the doorstep of those demanding minorities who, along with a few deluded white sympathizers, have been broadening the curriculum, instituting Third World courses, hiring minority professors, and recruiting 'unqualified' students of color—all at the expense of academic rigor and standards. He says the barbarians—meaning us—are running the place and urges university administrators to hold the line against what he sees as bullying and a new form of racism."

"Have you ever thought it curious," Rodrigo mused, "how some whites can see themselves as victimized by us—a pristine example of the sort of post-modern move they profess to hate. I suppose if one has been in power a long time, any change seems threatening, offensive, unprincipled, and wrong. But reality eventually intervenes. Western culture's predicament runs very deep—every indicator shows it. And, there are straws in the wind, harbingers of hopeful change."

"Rodrigo, I'll say this for you—you've proposed a novel approach to affirmative action. Until now, we've struggled with finding a moral basis for sustaining what looked like breaches of the merit principle, like hiring a less qualified over a more qualified person for racial reasons. But you're saying that white people should welcome nonwhites into their fold as rapidly as possible out of simple self-interest—that is, if they want their society to survive. This is something that they are not accustomed to hearing, to put it mildly. Do you have any support for this assertion?"

"Turn on your computer again, Professor. This won't take but a minute."

I obliged him, and was treated to a second lightning display of technological wizardry as Rodrigo showed me books on Asian business organization, Eastern mysticism, Japanese schooling, ancient Egyptian origins of modern astronomy and physics, and even on the debt our Founding Fathers owed the Iroquois for the political ideas that shaped our Constitution. He showed me articles on the Japanese computer and automobile industries, the seemingly more successful approach that African and Latino societies have taken to family organization and the treatment of their own aged and destitute, and even the roots of popular American music in Black composers and groups.

"It's only a beginning," Rodrigo said, switching off my computer. "I want to make this my life's work. Do you think anyone will listen to me?"

"It's hard to say. I don't know if the times are right. Most Americans believe that their economic problems are just temporary and that they have the best, fairest political system in the world—conveniently forgetting a chapter or two of their own history. But never mind that. Let me ask you instead a personal question: If things are really as bad as you say, why are you, who have a choice, thinking of returning? Shouldn't you remain safely in Italy while your native culture self-destructs? When a wave crests, then hits the beach, it creates an immediate commotion. There's a lot of foam, a loud noise, a great expenditure of energy, and sometimes an undertow. I should think someone like you would be at some risk here—particularly if you go around speaking as candidly as you have to me today—notwithstanding our much-vaunted system of free expression."

"I'm back for family reasons. Geneva and my other half-brothers and sisters are here. And since my father died, I have no other relatives in Italy. Your decreasing quality of life and high white-collar crime rate gave me pause. And I could be quite comfortable in Italy, now that I've got my military service out of the way. I suppose I thought, as well, that with a little more training I could do something to ease the pain of my native country as it goes through a difficult transition."

"You mean helping America adjust to its new multiracial character, plus its own shrinking share of world markets?" I asked.

"That and more," Rodrigo answered quietly. "The dominant group will need help. All of us will."

"What if they don't see it that way?" I pressed. "Has a dominant group ever given up power gracefully? Has it ever abandoned the modes of thought, military organization, and extractive industries that brought it to power without a struggle? And if so, how are we—I mean those who believe like you—going to conduct such a campaign? I'm afraid they have all the power. You may think truth and history are on your side. But what if they don't go along?"

"They will," Rodrigo replied with conviction, "as soon as they recognize their own dilemma. The early Visigoths destroyed themselves by warring. We can help the current dominant culture avoid a similar fate. We may even have some friends and allies in the majority group—ones who believe as we do. Maybe we can bill our offerings as 'hybrid vigor'—something they already endorse."

"And, once again—what if they refuse? Paradigms change slowly. What if your transformation requires a hundred years?"

"In that case, we can simply use sabotage and what you call terrorism to speed things up. The more advanced, the more technologically complex a society becomes, the more vulnerable it is to disruption. Imagine what a few strategic and nonviolent taps on telephone switching stations around the country could do—or a few computer viruses, for that matter. Disruption is economically efficient for the subordinated group. In Italy, the government tried for a time to exclude leftist organizations. A few kidnappings and commando raids, and they were ready for serious negotiation. Something like that could happen here—or do you think I'm wrong, Professor?"

"Rodrigo, I have many doubts about all the things you have said—and particularly this one. If you repeat even half of what you have told me today to your colleagues or students, you will find yourself out of academia on your ear—and probably disbarred to boot."

"I had no idea those were the rules of discourse. On the Continent we discuss these things openly—especially since recent events in Eastern Europe showed that rapid reform is, in fact, possible. Your society certainly perpetrated plenty of terrorism on Blacks, Chicanos, and Indians. Nevertheless, if one cannot discuss these things in—how do you put it?—polite company—I'll keep them to myself and for my close friends. I don't want to be seen as having an attitude problem."

Our conversation soon concluded. I had to prepare for a faculty colloquium I was to give at my new school that afternoon, and Rodrigo quickly excused himself, saying he had to get ready for the LSAT—"that dinosaur relic of an outmoded system of thought"—that coming Saturday. But I couldn't shake his image. Here was a man who spoke what he saw. I feared for him.

Chapter 55

Choosing the Future

Ian F. Haney López

To many, it may seem that race is fate, in the sense that one is born into a race, and that there is little if anything to be done about it. Yet, taking seriously the notion that race is a social construction means accepting the idea that race in the United States, and one's own racial identity in particular, are partially products of the choices we make as a society and as individuals. "If race lives on today," Barbara Fields points out, "it does not live on because we have inherited it from our forbears of the seventeenth century or eighteenth or nineteenth, but because we continue to create it today."[1] A race, once established in popular thought, does not take on a life of its own, independent from the surge of social forces. Instead, we continue to revitalize race at every moment, as a society, and, more pertinent to this discussion, as individuals. "Simone de Beauvoir wrote that one is not born a woman," Henry Louis Gates, Jr., has noted, adding "no, and one is not born a Negro."[2] Neither is one born White. Rather, one becomes White by virtue of the social context in which one finds oneself, to be sure, but also by virtue of the choices one makes. It is in this ability to choose, an admittedly constrained ability but one nonetheless always present, that Whites as individuals and as a community possess the power to dismantle Whiteness.

In order to see this, it may be helpful to use the terms chance, context, and choice to disaggregate the functioning of race in our daily lives.[3] Chance refers to features and ancestry, context to the contemporary social setting, and choice to quotidian decisions. In the workings of race, chance, context, and choice overlap and are inseverable. Nevertheless, these terms allow an analysis of race that focuses on the extent to which race is, and is not, a matter of volition.

Chance and context together largely define races. Chance encompasses features and ancestry in that we have no control over who our parents are or what we look like. Because of the importance of morphology and ancestry, chance may seem to occupy almost the entire geography of race. Certainly, for those who subscribe to biological notions of race, chance seems to account for virtually everything: One is born some race and not another, and therefore fated to a particular racial identity, with no human intervention possible. However, because race is socially constructed, the role of chance is actually minimal. In largest part, racial identity is not directly a function of features and ancestry, but rather of the context-specific meanings that attach to these elements of identity. Context is the social setting in which races are recognized, constructed, and contested; it is here that race gains its life. Within a social context, racial systems of meaning, although inconstant and unstable, are paramount in establishing the social significance of certain features, such as skin color, and of particular ancestries, for instance European. Context superimposed on chance largely defines racial identity in the United States.

Chance and context, however, are not racially determinative. Choice composes a crucial third ingredient in the construction of racial identities. Features and ancestry gain their racial significance through the manner in which they are read by social actors. Yet people exercise conscious choices with regard to their features and ancestry in order to alter the readability of their identity. In this respect, consider the popularity of hair straightening, blue contact lenses, and even facial surgery.[4] Or note that in 1990 alone $44 million was spent on chemical treatments to literally lighten and whiten skin through the painful and dangerous application of bleach.[5] In our highly racialized society, few people leave their looks to chance; we instead constantly seek to remake them in obeisance to the power of racial aesthetics. So too with ancestry. Ancestry seems to be a biological concept, yet it is instead largely a social one. If an individual drew a family tree back over a few hundred years, assuming that he or she was descended from each ancestor in only one way, it would have nearly a million branches at the top.[6] Identifying one's ancestry, then, involves a large degree of choice, where this choice turns at least partially on the social significance of one line of descent versus another. At the same time, decisions regarding mates, which can be understood as the prospective creation of lines of descent, are also heavily influenced by the racial status of the respective persons involved. Because the significance of ancestry and the status of prospective mates vary in racial terms, decisions in these areas become decisions about racial identity. Features and ancestry may seem to be securely in the province of chance, and their significance a function simply of context, but in fact race is also partially a matter of the choices people make.

Racial choices occur both on mundane and on epic levels. Perhaps the most graphic illustration of choice in the construction of racial identities comes in the context of "passing." The ability of some individuals to change race at will powerfully indicates the chosen nature of race. The majority of racial decisions, however, are of a much more mundane nature. Because race in our society infuses almost all aspects of life, many daily decisions take on racial meanings. For example, seemingly inconsequential acts like listening to country and western music or moving to the suburbs constitute means of racial (dis-)affiliation. So too do a myriad of other actions taken every day by every person, almost always without conscious regard for the racial significance of their choices. It is here, in deciding what to eat, how to dress, whom to befriend, and where to vacation, rather than in the dramatic decision to leap races, that most racial choices are rendered. These common acts are not racial choices in the sense that they are taken with a conscious awareness of their racial implications, or in the sense that these quotidian decisions by themselves can establish or change a person's racial identity. Racial choices must always be made from within specific contexts, where the context materially and ideologically circumscribes the range of available choices and also delimits the significance of the act. Nevertheless, these are racial choices, if sometimes only in their overtone or subtext, because they resonate in the complex of meanings associated with race. Given the thorough suffusion of race throughout society, in the daily dance of life we constantly make racially meaningful decisions.[7]

Drawing upon this conception of choice, the challenge for Whites committed to dismantling Whiteness can be broken down into three steps. First, Whites must overcome the omnipresent effects of transparency and of the naturalization of race in order to recognize the many racial aspects of their identity, paying particular attention to the daily acts that draw upon and in turn confirm their Whiteness. Second, they must recognize and accept the personal and social consequences of breaking out of a White identity. Third, they must embark on a daily process of choosing against Whiteness. For those who decide to dismantle Whiteness, these steps pose considerable difficulties. They must ask themselves to what extent their identity is a function of their race, how this racial self is constituted in daily life, and what choices they might make to escape the circular definition of the self implied in the unconscious acceptance of a racialized identity. Then they must make those choices. All of this will be supremely difficult and, unless many Whites undertake similar efforts, will probably also do little to dismantle Whiteness. Yet there is at least the promise of personal reconstruction, and there is also the optimism that springs not from the likelihood of eventual success but from the decision to resist.[8] Moreover, the possibility exists that ultimately Whiteness as now constituted might be ended. If the racial systems of meaning that tie Whites and non-Whites together into hierarchies of social worth are to be brought down, it will only be through choice and struggle.

Of course, it is not clear what sort of racial future would emerge if Whiteness is eventually dismantled. Perhaps the deconstruction of Whiteness would lead to a truly colorblind society by resulting in the collapse of all notions of race, thereby producing a future in which personal identities are no longer constructed in racial terms and the term "race" has no meaning. In such a universe, human variability would no longer be measured by reference to races, and every current manner of distinguishing people—for example, gender and class—would be radically transformed by the absence of a racial referent. Indeed, perhaps the complete elimination of Whiteness and races generally would work an even more profound change on our society. Howard Winant, a leading proponent of the social constructionist theory of race, offers an extreme evaluation of the implications of a totally raceless future:

> The five-hundred year domination of the globe by Europe and its inheritors is the historical context in which racial concepts of difference have attained their present status as fundamental concepts of human identity and inequality. To imagine the end of race is thus to contemplate the liquidation of Western civilization.[9]

However, it might be that deconstructing Whiteness does not portend the liquidation of civilization, or even the end of racial ideas. Perhaps without White supremacy race would continue to be socially relevant as a popular synonym for ethnicity or culture, simply another word in a vocabulary that recognizes and respects human diversity, with no one supposing that race constitutes a transhistorical identity. Winant, in a less apocalyptic moment, pictures a bright future in which race does not stand in for inequality:

> [W]e may have to give up our familiar ways of thinking about race once more. If so, there may also be some occasion for delight. For it may be possible to glimpse yet another view of race, in which the concept operates neither as signifier of comprehensive identity nor of fundamental difference, both of which are patently absurd, but rather as a marker of the infinity of variations we humans hold as a common heritage and hope for the future.[10]

Whatever the racial future, one thing is certain. The tightly wrought nature of Whiteness and non-Whiteness insures that such scenarios are very far off. In the meantime, we must begin the difficult process of fathoming the construction of Whiteness, in order better to choose against it.

NOTES

1. Barbara Fields, *Slavery, Race and Ideology in the United States of America*, 181 NEW LEFT REVIEW 95, 117 (1990).

2. Henry Louis Gates, Jr., LOOSE CANONS: NOTES ON THE CULTURE WARS 34 (1992).

3. These terms are developed more fully in Ian Haney López, *The Social Construction of Race: Some Observations on Illusion, Fabrication, and Choice*, 29 HARV. CIVIL RIGHTS–CIVIL LIBERTIES L. REV. 1, 39–53 (1994). [Reprinted in part as Chapter 3 in this volume].

4. See Kathy Russell, Midge Wilson, and Ronald Hall, THE COLOR COMPLEX: THE POLITICS OF SKIN COLOR AMONG AFRICAN AMERICANS (1992).

5. *Id.* at 51.

6. Anthony Appiah, *The Uncompleted Argument: Du Bois and the Illusion of Race*, in "RACE," WRITING AND DIFFERENCE 21, 26 (Henry Louis Gates ed., 1985).

7. Renato Rosaldo, *Others of Invention: Ethnicity and Its Discontents*, VILLAGE VOICE, Feb.13, 1990, at 27.

8. See Derrick Bell, CONFRONTING AUTHORITY: REFLECTIONS OF AN ARDENT PROTESTER (1994).

9. Howard Winant, RACIAL CONDITIONS: POLITICS, THEORY, COMPARISONS xiii (1994).

10. *Id.* at 21.

Chapter 56

The Well-Defended Academic Identity

Gerald P. López

My nineteen years of experiences and conversations in and around law schools have made plain that nearly all people of color deeply understand, from the very moment they enter legal academic life, that color—race and ethnicity—is dangerously two-sided. It's okay to *be* Black or Latino or Asian American or Native American. In fact, it's more than okay. Law schools think it's part of your job to be a "minority" in dealing with students, in serving on a range of law school and university committees and in making an appearance at alumni functions. I've heard white faculty complain bitterly when colleagues of color don't fill these roles willingly and capably. "We might as well have hired a white guy," is a surprisingly common and rather unselfconscious refrain.

If it's okay and even mandatory in certain law school settings to be Black or Latino or Asian American or Native American, people of color have always known that, at the same time, they run a great risk in being perceived as anything more than a "status quo plus" addition to a faculty. Even when no one explicitly identifies this risk, it characteristically filters the experiences of people of color, reflecting I think a hard-earned "sixth sense" about the world. One way or another, the message about *not* presenting yourself as beyond status quo plus comes through loud and clear. "Don't be hung up on who you are in mixed company." "Don't make folks around you too uncomfortable." "Use your race and ethnicity 'judiciously.'" "Be understated." You realize you're being told, in effect, to exorcise what's politically volatile about being of color in the United States or on a law school faculty—in casual conversations, in serious arguments, in classrooms, and in print. Otherwise, the message goes, you invite the full range of what one colleague of mine graphically describes as "primitive" responses in him and in noteworthy numbers of your other white colleagues. You invite, among other responses, dismissals describing you as "insecure," "preoccupied," and even "paranoid"; you invite snickers at what will be described as your obvious attempts "to parlay color into advancement"; you invite charges of "privileging essentialist claims in intellectually unsophisticated ways."

As much as Latinos, Asian Americans, Native Americans, and African Americans understand in their bones that color has always been dangerously two-sided in legal academic life, each of us has probably spent time trying to deny what we know. After all, we have been heard to say to one another with great pride that from the beginning there have been people of color who have refused to be nothing more than status quo plus in their academic life. Think only of famous figures like W. E. B. Du Bois and considerably less famous, though no less rebellious, figures like Americo Paredes, Carlos Bulosan, James Youngblood Henderson. And, after all, we constantly remind ourselves that each day some person of color, and probably each person of color on some days, violates cultural taboos in conversation, argument, classroom, and print.

Try as we might, however, we simply can't rid ourselves of what we know about the dangerous two-sidedness of who we are. Even if we managed to forget what Du Bois and Paredes and Bulosan and Henderson have themselves told us about the price they paid in resisting suppression, and even if we managed to forget the many bloodied colleagues of color who either punish themselves for giving in on too many days or who exhaust themselves in taking on *all* that surrounds them *all* of the time, we still would have to entirely deny what we ourselves live every single day in order to rid ourselves of the dangerous two-sidedness of who we are. And for most of us, thank goodness, that's more denial—more self-annihilation—than we can endure.

There are signs, I realize, that suggest that perhaps I've overstated both the dangerousness and the two-sidedness of color. In the past ten years or so, for example, people of color on law school faculties have begun in some modestly significant numbers to take the chance of being regularly perceived as considerably more than just being judiciously Black, Latino, Asian American, Native American—not just in what we say in conversations and serious arguments, but in what we do in the classroom and increasingly in print. In trying to draw on, share, and develop distinctive bodies of knowledge, we would seem to be giving the lie to, or at least ending the reign of, the status-quo-plus vision of race and ethnicity in law school culture. Yet, it is precisely this relatively recent "coming out" of modestly significant numbers of people of color, coupled with the response I believe it has generated in a diverse range of legal academics, that convinces me, again and again and again, of the insidiously dangerous two-sidedness of color in legal academics.

The more in recent years people of color write, think, and teach in ethnically authentic ways, the more I sense a palpable unrest at my own and other schools. The more formidable we people of color perceive our challenge to a range of favored ideas (of the right, the center, *and* the left), the more I hear an uncommonly ungenerous opposition to our work and to our judgments of it. Mind you, the opposition is not just critical, by which I mean appreciative, skeptical, in thoughtful disagreement; that sort of response is not only to be expected but encouraged. Instead, the opposition is, for me, perplexingly dismissive—of the work, of our judgments of it and, for that matter, of the judgments of those white legal academics who find the work an important contribution to legal thought.

The rhetoric of this opposition runs the range of familiar tropes, reflecting, as it does, the diversity of legal thought. In more or less public conversations, you will hear someone say something like, "Misses some doctrinal subtleties and, anyway, I disagree with the call she makes on . . ." Another will ask, "Where's the law?" Another still will observe, "If you can't measure it, how are we to know what to make of these claims?" Yet another will argue something like "An overly material idea of oppression, and a regrettable misread of her own experience." The rhetoric of more or less private conversations differs, too, again tracking the diversity of familiar mainstream legal thought. You will hear one say something like, "This work is self-indulgent." Or "This work ends up being all about suffering, and like most law and humanities enterprises, has nothing programmatic to recommend it." Another will lament that "this work ends up unfortunately confirming that what oppression basically teaches you is how to be oppressed." Another still will blurt out that "an appeal to the authentic voice of . . . the African woman or whatever other form of relatively primitive consciousness you can dredge up is just [not] a very productive way to go at this time."

However diverse the tropes in these public and private conversations, the opposition converges around a basic consensus: At bottom, they insist they simply don't learn from this self-consciously of-color work. In their minds, nothing in the experiences of people of color seems to being paying off; nothing translates into serviceable ideas for legal thought. There just doesn't seem to be any promise in it. Perhaps more to the point, they no longer see any reason to recruit and retain for their own faculty those people of color who seem inclined to try to make a contribution through this way of thinking, teaching and writing. That they or anyone else once thought differently seems now, in retrospect, obviously misguided—a regrettably romanticized view of what people of color could ever have been expected to offer, draw on, share, and develop. Their position seems roughly the parliamentary equivalent of saying about a whole group of faculty candidates of color "Are we ready to vote?" Or, worse still, "Do we even need to vote?"

When we hear virtually *any* variation on these claims, even if tired and overworked, we feel frightened and we pause. And, you should realize, we pause more than momentarily and more than occasionally. We pause to reconsider what we are doing in our conversations, our arguments, our classrooms, and in our scholarship. We pause because for good reason we remain peculiarly at work on who and what we are in this world. We pause because we really do feel the pressing need to get our "story straight" and our "act together." After all, we're not just talking about producing scholarship as part of the job we happen to have, we're talking about trying to contribute to an evolving view about ourselves and those around us with which we might today and tomorrow fight off the social and political subordination we still see in the world and in our own sense of individual and collective self.

Still I must say that, after all the pausing I've done over these last several years, after all my reconsideration of the promise and the quality of this self-consciously of-color work, I just don't buy the oppositions' basic claim. If, as they insist, they're just not learning from what we're thinking, teaching, and writing, then how do you readily explain what I've witnessed on both coasts, in elite and non-elite schools, in private and state universities? Over the last nineteen years, conversations, arguments, classrooms, and scholarship have *all* changed in ways that reflect, at least in significant respects, the self-consciously of-color ideas we've introduced. Don't get me wrong. Perhaps they don't reveal our influence as much as they reveal the influence of feminist thought. And they haven't changed in content or in method anywhere near as much as most people of color would like, myself particularly included. But the contrast between nineteen years ago and now, ten years ago and now, and even five years ago and now would seem undeniable and, for me at least, renders implausible the opposition's basic claim.

For remember, in this relatively brief period of time, a quite small group of legal academics of color have helped shape how many think about a range of issues and activities central to legal and social life. Concepts already much worked over, such as equality, have been nonetheless surprisingly and unsettlingly reexamined; ideas largely tacit, like those ostensibly justifying current and proposed immigration law and policy, have been made explicit, forcefully taken on, and reconceived; histories like those of the internment have been excavated, shared, and effectively acted upon; basic political and doctrinal "truths" like the First Amendment's relationship to racist speech have been provocatively challenged; strategies much pursued but seldom studied, such as civil rights litigation, have been recast in terms of both their pragmatic and constitutive dimensions; relationships like those between the United States and tribal sovereignties have been surfaced and explored in what can only be described as a national embarrassment of detail; practices like those of both teachers in law schools and lawyers claiming to fight for social change have been treated as central to legal training, have been critiqued and even reinvisioned.

Those legal academics who claim nowadays not to learn from self-consciously of-color work don't so much straightforwardly deny these and other related changes as they try smoothly and minimally (which is to say, indiscernibly) to adapt to them. In doing so, they draw daily on a range of what have become for me increasingly familiar adaptive maneuvers. They've learned casually to weave into conversations of-color words and notions or, better still, over time, their own equivalents. They've learned urbanely to integrate into their arguments previously unmentioned of-color concepts and literature or, better still, over time, their own equivalents. They've learned to prepare themselves cooly to note and respond to previously unstudied yet tenaciously hard-to-avoid of-color observations made in their classrooms. Perhaps most tellingly, they've learned "naturally" to revise what they claim always to have known, considered, said, and meant in their own written work in order to account in some way for those of-color views that gain undeniable prominence. Locked together in their opposition to self-consciously of-color work, these legal academics have created for themselves, more than a little, a world of revision—sometimes imperceptible, frequently impossible to evaluate, revision.

And, as you revise and revise, you simultaneously find yourself insisting there's nothing you're learning from almost *any* of this self-consciously of-color work— never quite knowing whether and at what point you've lost sight of the paradox and irony expressed in your own stance. "This work," you keep saying to yourself, and soon begin believing and saying to others, "tells you only what you already knew or already rejected in some other form." And pretty soon you're wondering out loud why your faculty needs anyone or certainly anyone *else*—of color or not—who plans to spend significant chunks of time doing this sort of thinking, teaching, and writing. And, along with other colleagues perhaps quite different from yourself but nonetheless of much the same mind about this of-color heterodoxy, you ultimately find yourself trying not only to dismiss this self-consciously of-color work, but trying to render it inconsequential, absent from your world. You try to rid yourself of the presence of colleagues who say what you don't want to hear or deal with.

Of course it's not that easy. Certain of your colleagues, who don't themselves do this sort of work, find it nonetheless significant, if no less flawed than other genres of thought. Certain other of your colleagues, working in or parallel to this law and humanities tradition, debate you and yours in committee and faculty meetings. Certain of your students, despite your best efforts, persist in grounding their views in, or making arguments uncomfortably similar to, those subversive ideas you'd like very much to escape. And some tenured and even untenured faculty of color, if not at your own school then certainly in one way or another too close by, seem inclined now more than ever to keep doing this beyond-status-quo-plus work. Their persistence reflects, you realize, not so much any sort of familiarly praised bravery but more that they seem just not to care much any longer about the by now customary primitive reprisals. Still, you aim to deliver your message to potential entering and lateral hires: Stay away from this self-consciously of-color work or your chances of coming and staying here aren't much to speak of.

From the Editors
Issues and Comments

What is gained by recognizing how law is discretionary or the product of the dominant paradigm(s)? What does history tell us about the way law has been used to create and justify the existing social order and the repression of outsider groups?

If law is indeterminate and highly discretionary, should Latinos and other minorities rely on it as a tool for social advancement?

Is it only possible to recognize paradigms when they start to break down, and is this beginning to happen with the black/white paradigm?

How can one change a paradigm or the way the legal system treats a given issue or group, such as women or Latinos? Do breakthroughs come only when white elites' self-interest dictates it? Can storytelling or counterstorytelling help blast a paradigm?

Do dominant practices and perspectives ever become dysfunctional, even for the dominant group, as Rodrigo argues? If so, can outsiders help introduce new ones?

Do private choices and law construct whiteness, as Ian Haney López argues? Do they construct Mexican Americans to suit the interests of the majority, now as white, now as nonwhite, as George Martinez argues?

If you were director of litigation for the newly formed Latino Defense Fund (an umbrella organization) and you wanted to challenge the black/white binary, what kind of case would you pick for your challenge?

The date is 150 years in the future. Latinos are the largest group in the United States, slightly larger than whites and considerably larger than Asians and blacks. What legal, political, and social changes do you foresee?

Suggested Readings

Carrasco, Enrique R. "Collective Recognition as a Communitarian Device: Or, Of Course We Want to Be Role Models!" 9 *La Raza Law Journal* 81 (1996).

Colloquium: "International Law, Human Rights, and LatCrit Theory." 28 *University of Miami Inter-American Law Review* 177 (1997).

Davis, Adrienne D. "Identity Notes Part One: Playing in the Light." 45 *American University Law Review* 695 (1996).

Delgado, Richard. "Affirmative Action as a Majoritarian Device: Or, Do You Really Want to Be a Role Model?" 89 *Michigan Law Review* 1222 (1991).

———. "Campus Antiracism Rules: Constitutional Narratives in Collision." 85 *Northwestern University Law Review* 343 (1991).

———. *The Coming Race War? And Other Apocalyptic Tales after Affirmative Action and Welfare.* New York: New York University Press, 1996.

———. "Left-Right Parallels in Recent Writing about Race." 91 *Columbia Law Review* 1547 (1991).

———. "Minority Law Professors' Lives: The Bell-Delgado Survey." 24 *Harvard Civil Rights–Civil Liberties Law Review* 349 (1989).

———. "Recasting the American Race Problem." 79 *California Law Review* 1389 (1991).

———. *The Rodrigo Chronicles: Conversations about America and Race.* New York: New York University Press, 1995.

Delgado, Richard, and Jean Stefancic. "Norms and Narratives: Can Judges Avoid Serious Moral Error?" 69 *Texas Law Review* 1929 (1991).

Durkee, Ellen. "Special Problems of Custody for Unaccompanied Refugee Children in the United States." In *Michigan Yearbook of International Legal Studies* 203 (1982).

Espinoza, Leslie G. "The LSAT: Narrative and Bias." 1 *American University Journal of Gender and Law* 121 (1993).

Grillo, Trina. "The Mediation Alternative: Process Dangers for Women." 100 *Yale Law Journal* 1545 (1991).

Hacker, Andrew. *Two Nations: Black and White, Separate, Hostile, Unequal.* New York: Scribner's, 1992.

Haney López, Ian F. "Community Ties, Race, and Faculty Hiring: The Case for Professors Who Don't Think White." *Reconstruction* 1, no. 3 (1991): 46.

Harris, Angela. "Foreword: The Jurisprudence of Reconstruction." 82 *California Law Review* 741 (1994).

Hernández-Truyol, Berta Esperanza. "Women's Rights as Human Rights—Rules, Realities and the Role of Culture: A Formula for Reform." 21 *Brooklyn Journal of International Law* 605 (1996).

Johnson, Kevin R. "Racial Restrictions on Naturalization: The Recurring Intersection of Race and Gender in Immigration and Citizenship Law." 11 *Berkeley Women's Law Journal* 142 (1996).

Martinez, John. "Trivializing Diversity: The Problem of Overinclusion in Affirmative Action Programs." 12 *Harvard BlackLetter Law Journal* 49 (1995).

Moran, Rachel F. "Unrepresented." *Representations* 55 (1996): 139.

Olivas, Michael A. "The Education of Latino Lawyers: An Essay on Crop Cultivation." 14 *Chicano-Latino Law Review* 117 (1994).

———. "Legal Norms in Law School Admissions: An Essay on Parallel Universes." 42 *Journal of Legal Education* 103 (1992).

———. "Unaccompanied Refugee Children: Detention, Due Process, and Disgrace." 1 *Stanford Law and Policy Review* 159 (1990).

Ontiveros, Maria L. "To Help Those Most in Need: Undocumented Workers' Rights and Remedies under Title VII." 20 *N.Y.U. Review of Law and Social Change* 607 (1993–94).

Perea, Juan F. "Ethnicity and Prejudice: Reevaluating 'National Origin' Discrimination Under Title VII." 35 *William and Mary Law Review* 805 (1994).

———. "Ethnicity and the Constitution: Beyond the Black White Binary Constitution." 36 *William and Mary Law Review* 571 (1995).

Piatt, Bill. "Born as Second Class Citizens in the U.S.A.: Children of Undocumented Parents." 63 *Notre Dame Law Review* 35 (1988).

Ramirez, Deborah A. "The Mixed Jury and the Ancient Custom of Trial by Jury *De Medietate Linguae*: A History and a Proposal for Change." 74 *Boston University Law Review* 777 (1994).

Ressler, Everett, Neil Boothby, and Daniel Steinbock. *Unaccompanied Children: Care and Protection in Wars, Natural Disasters, and Refugee Movements.* New York: Oxford University Press, 1988.

Roithmayr, Daria. "Deconstructing the Distinction between Bias and Merit." 85 *California Law Review* (forthcoming 1997).

Romany, Celina. "Women as *Aliens:* A Feminist Critique of the Public/Private Distinction in International Human Rights Law." 6 *Harvard Human Rights Journal* 87 (1993).

Symposium: "Latinos and the Law: Twenty Years of Legal Advocacy and Lessons for Advancement." 14 *Chicano-Latino Law Review* 1 (1994).

Tamayo, William R. "When the 'Coloreds' Are Neither Black nor Citizens: The United States Civil Rights Movement and Global Migration." 2 *Asian Law Journal* 7 (1995).

Torres, Gerald. "Critical Race Theory: The Decline of the Universalist Ideal and the Hope of Plural Justice—Some Observations and Questions of an Emerging Phenomenon." 75 *Minnesota Law Review* 993 (1991).

———. "Local Knowledge, Local Color: Critical Legal Studies and the Law of Race Relations." 25 *San Diego Law Review* 1043 (1988).

Villarreal, Carlos. "Culture in Lawmaking: A Chicano Perspective." 24 *University of California at Davis Law Review* 1193 (1991).

———. "Limits on Lawmaking: A Chicano Perspective." 10 *St. Louis University Public Law Review* 65 (1991).

Williams, Robert A., Jr. "Taking Rights Aggressively: The Perils and Promise of Critical Legal Theory for Peoples of Color." 5 *Law and Inequality Journal* 103 (1987).

Part VIII

Assimilationism

Maybe Our Best Strategy Is Just to Duck?

One option, at least for light-skinned Latinos, is to try to assimilate—to fit into society at large, not make waves, adopt prevailing manners and inflections, and even try to "pass for white" by changing one's name and concealing one's heritage. Even darker-skinned Latinos may sometimes insist they are Spanish or Portuguese. How viable is this strategy, what costs does it impose on one who deploys it, and what are the ethical consequences of turning one's back, as it were, on one's community? Can one embrace two cultures, assimilating to the majority culture at the workplace, say, but lapsing into one's own at home or while with one's family and friends—or does this produce a kind of dangerous schizophrenia? Is depoliticizing identity questions, when possible, a good idea so as to reduce social tensions? Will Latinos' troubles inevitably disappear as the group follows the path of earlier immigrant groups and enters the American mainstream? Is hanging onto Latino identity, especially if this means a conservative, traditional, anti-intellectual one, a positive disservice? The essays in Part VIII address these and other issues.

Chapter 57

A Scholarship Boy

Richard Rodriguez

I stand in the ghetto classroom—"the guest speaker"—attempting to lecture on the mystery of the sounds of our words to rows of diffident students. "Don't you hear it? Listen! The music of our words. '*Sumer is i-cumen in. . . .*' And songs on the car radio. We need Aretha Franklin's voice to fill plain words with music—her life." In the face of their empty stares, I try to create an enthusiasm. But the girls in the back row turn to watch some boy passing outside. There are flutters of smiles, waves. And someone's mouth elongates heavy, silent words through the barrier of glass. Silent words—the lips straining to shape each voiceless syllable: "*Meet meee late errr.*" By the door, the instructor smiles at me, apparently hoping that I will be able to spark some enthusiasm in the class. But only one student seems to be listening. A girl, maybe fourteen. In this gray room her eyes shine with ambition. She keeps nodding and nodding at all that I say; she even takes notes. And each time I ask a question, she jerks up and down in her desk like a marionette, while her hand waves over the bowed heads of her classmates. It is myself (as a boy) I see as she faces me now (a man in my thirties).

The boy who first entered a classroom barely able to speak English, twenty years later concluded his studies in the stately quiet of the reading room in the British Museum. Thus with one sentence I can summarize my academic career. It will be harder to summarize what sort of life connects the boy to the man.

With every award, each graduation from one level of education to the next, people I'd meet would congratulate me. Their refrain always the same: "Your parents must be very proud." Sometimes then they'd ask me how I managed it—my "success."

(How?) After a while, I had several quick answers to give in reply. I'd admit, for one thing, that I went to an excellent grammar school. (My earliest teachers, the nuns, made my success their ambition.) And my brother and both my sisters were very good students. (They often brought home the shiny school trophies I came to want.) And my mother and father always encouraged me. (At every graduation they were behind the stunning flash of the camera when I turned to look at the crowd.)

As important as these factors were, however, they account inadequately for my academic advance. Nor do they suggest what an odd success I managed. For although I was a very good student, I was also a very bad student. I was a "scholarship boy," a certain kind of scholarship boy. Always successful, I was always unconfident. Exhilarated by my progress. Sad. I became the prized student—anxious and eager to learn. Too eager, too anxious—an imitative and unoriginal pupil. My brother and two sisters enjoyed the advantages I did, and they grew to be as successful as I, but none of them ever seemed so anxious about their schooling. A second-grade student, I was the one who came home and corrected the "simple" grammatical mistakes of our parents. ("Two negatives make a positive.") Proudly I announced—to my family's startled silence—that a teacher had said I was losing all trace of a Spanish accent. I was oddly annoyed when I was unable to get parental help with a homework assignment. The night my father tried to help me with an arithmetic exercise, he kept reading the instructions, each time more deliberately, until I pried the textbook out of his hands, saying, "I'll try to figure it out some more by myself."

When I reached the third grade, I outgrew such behavior. I became more tactful, careful to keep separate the two very different worlds of my day. But then, with ever-increasing intensity, I devoted myself to my studies. I became bookish, puzzling to all my family. Ambition set me apart. When my brother saw me struggling home with stacks of library books, he would laugh, shouting: "Hey, Four Eyes!" My father opened a closet one day and was startled to find me inside, reading a novel. My mother would find me reading when I was supposed to be asleep or helping around the house or playing outside. In a voice angry or worried or just curious, she'd ask: "What do you see in your books?" It became the family's joke. When I was called and wouldn't reply, someone would say I must be hiding under my bed with a book.

(How did I manage my success?)

What I am about to say to you has taken me more than twenty years to admit: *A primary reason for my success in the classroom was that I couldn't forget that schooling was changing me and separating me from the life I enjoyed before becoming a student.* That simple realization! For years I never spoke to anyone about it. Never mentioned a thing to my family or my teachers or classmates. From a very early age, I understood enough, just enough about my classroom experiences to keep what I knew repressed, hidden beneath layers of embarrassment. Not until my last months as a graduate student, nearly thirty years old, was it possible for me to think much about the reasons for my academic success. Only then. At the end of my schooling, I needed to determine how far I had moved from my past. The adult finally confronted, and now must publicly say, what the child shuddered from knowing and could never admit to himself or to those many faces that smiled at his every success. ("Your parents must be very proud. . . .")

Chapter 58

LULAC and the Assimilationist Perspective

David G. Gutiérrez

Despite the fact that few Mexicans were formally deported [during the Depression—
Eds.], repatriation for most individuals and families was a traumatic, disorienting,
and sorrowful course undertaken under extreme duress. Many of the repatriates believed that Mexicans had been unfairly blamed for events over which they had no
control. Despised and vilified after spending ten, fifteen, or even twenty or more productive years as hard-working, though isolated, members of the American working
class, Mexican immigrant workers seemed to bear the brunt of Americans' resentment about the economic catastrophe. A famous *corrido* of the period underscores
the sense of injustice and ingratitude many Mexicans clearly felt. "Los Deportados"
lamented,

Los güeros son muy malores [*sic*]	The Anglos are very bad fellows
se valen de la ocasión	They take advantage
Y a todos los mexicanos	And to all the Mexicans
nos tratan sin compasión	They treat us without pity
Hoy traen la gran polvareda	Today they bring great disturbance
y sin consideración	And without consideration
Mujeres, niños, y ancianos	Women, children, and old ones
nos llevan a la frontera,	They take us to the border,
nos echan de esta nación	They eject us from this country
Adiós paisanos queridos	Goodbye dear countrymen
Ya nos van a deportar	They are going to deport us
Pero no somos bandidos	But we are not bandits
Venimos a camellar.	We came to toil.[1]

As "Los Deportados" expressed so poignantly, the political climate symbolized by
the repatriation campaigns placed intense political and social pressures on the ethnic
Mexican population of the United States, which continued even after hundreds of

thousands of Mexican nationals and their children had returned to Mexico. The scapegoating that occurred at this time rekindled Americans' disdain for working-class Mexicans, and as always, their disdain was directed at Mexican Americans as well as the newer immigrants. For Americans of Mexican descent this situation was like the rubbing of salt in old wounds. Torn between their cultural ties, their nationality, and their awareness that American citizenship did not necessarily protect them from such excesses, Mexican Americans faced some tough decisions as to what their attitudes toward the repatriation campaigns ought to be. As in previous periods of increasing social stress, in the late 1920s and 1930s opinion among Mexican Americans (and the Mexican nationals who remained in the United States) on the complex issues intertwined with the repatriation crisis remained deeply ambivalent. Between the late 1920s and the mid-1930s, however, opinion and debate on these questions began to harden and polarize.

In the winter of 1921 an article by former Texas Congressman James L. Slayden appeared in an issue of the *Annals of the American Academy of Political and Social Science* that was devoted to Mexican immigration. A long-time observer of Mexican immigration trends in his state, Slayden proved to be one of the few Americans active in public life who was perceptive enough to recognize the deep impact mass Mexican immigration was having on the existing Mexican American population. From Slayden's point of view Mexican immigrants represented a threat to the existing Texas Mexican population not so much because immigrants competed with Mexican Americans for jobs and housing as because Anglo Texans generally refused to acknowledge any meaningful distinctions between Mexican Americans and Mexican immigrants. Whether one was a citizen of the United States made no difference: to white Texans a Mexican was a Mexican, and that was the end of it. As Slayden put it, "In Texas, the word 'Mexican' is used to indicate the race, not a citizen or subject of the country. There are probably 250,000 Mexicans in Texas who were born in the state but they are [defined as] 'Mexicans' just as all blacks are negroes though they may have five generations of American ancestors."[2]

While Slayden was making his observations about the peculiarities of racial classification in Texas, some Mexican Americans in that state were themselves pondering the implications of their ambiguous status in American society. As migration from Mexico continued into the 1920s they began to chafe at the thought that Americans were equating them with immigrants who, in many cases, had just recently entered the United States from the interior of Mexico. Although most of these native-born Texas Mexicans harbored no ill will toward their immigrant neighbors, worsening economic conditions and the intensification of anti-Mexican sentiment among Anglo Americans caused many of them to wonder whether the new immigrants were undermining their already tenuous position in Texas society. Having lived in the United States their entire lives, and in many cases having served the United States as members of the armed forces in World War I, increasing numbers of Texas Mexicans began to take exception to Anglo Americans' nonchalant dismissal of them as mere Mexicans. They gradually concluded that the only way to stop this indiscriminate lumping of American citizens with newly arrived Mexican immigrants was to take a stand against continuing large-scale immigration from Mexico. This was a painful decision, but from their point of view prudence dictated that Americans of Mexican descent had to be concerned with the immediate well-being and future health of Mexicans already in the United States. Mexico would simply have to take care of its own.

Although similar sentiments had been heard in Mexican American communities since the 1850s, these attitudes took on new salience with the establishment of a different type of Mexican American organization in Texas in the years immediately after World War I. Having returned from service in the armed forces, many Mexican Americans were no longer content to accept treatment as second-class citizens. Consequently, in the early 1920s Mexican American community leaders in several Texas cities established a number of new civic organizations designed to protect and advance the interests of their people. The three largest of these new groups were El Orden Hijos de América (The Order of the Sons of America), El Orden Caballeros de America (The Order of the Knights of America), and the League of Latin American Citizens. Such groups were formed by lower-middle-class members of the Texas Mexican community, and their leaders were typically attorneys, restaurateurs, teachers, printers, and small entrepreneurs serving the Spanish-speaking community. By 1927 these groups had established an extensive network of chapters throughout the state of Texas. The Sons of America, for example, had councils in Somerset, San Antonio, Pearsall, and Corpus Christi. The Knights of America were active primarily in the San Antonio area, and the League of Latin American Citizens had established chapters in the south Texas towns of Harlingen, Brownsville, Laredo, Gulf, Penitas, McAllen, La Grulla, and Encino.

As their names indicated, these new organizations espoused a political perspective that departed significantly from the philosophies of older Mexican American voluntary associations, such as the *mutualistas* and honorific societies. Unlike earlier groups, which had based their organizations on the principle of mutual cooperation between Mexican immigrants and Americans of Mexican descent, from their inception the new organizations pointedly excluded non-American citizens from membership.

To these organizations, Mexican Americans were American citizens and thus should make every effort to assimilate into the American social and cultural mainstream. Although most were generally proud of their ethnic heritage, they believed that Mexican Americans had focused too much on maintaining their ethnicity and culture in the United States and, in the process, had hindered their progress as participating members of American society. Thus, while members of these new organizations continued to profess respect for Mexico and for their Mexican cultural heritage, they insisted that the best way to advance in American society was to convince other Americans that they too were loyal, upstanding American citizens. In keeping with these beliefs the new Mexican American organizations carefully cultivated what they considered to be an appropriate American public image by conducting their proceedings in English, by prominently displaying the American flag in their ceremonies, stationery, and official iconography, by singing such songs as "America" at their gatherings, and by opening their meetings with a recitation of the "George Washington Prayer."

The political agendas of the Sons of America, the Knights of America, and the League of Latin American Citizens all reflected these basic premises. For example, the by-laws of the Sons of America articulated the political assumptions and general plan of action by asserting, "As workers in support of the ideal that citizens of the United States of America of Mexican or Spanish extraction, whether native or naturalized, [we] have a broad field of opportunity to protect and promote their interests as such; [and are committed] to elevate their moral, social and intellectual conditions; [and] to educate them . . . in the proper extension of their political rights."[3] Members hoped to implement these principles by organizing voter registration and poll-tax campaigns, by mounting battles against the segregation of Mexican Americans in public facilities, and by insisting on more adequate representation of Mexican Americans on Texas juries.

Such ideas quickly gained currency after some of the Texas-based groups were consolidated into a new, larger organization just before the Great Depression. After a preliminary series of meetings in 1927 and 1928 in which the terms of consolidation of the various organizations were negotiated, the League of United Latin American Citizens (LULAC) was officially founded at a meeting in Corpus Christi on February 17, 1929. The original delegates met again at Corpus Christi in May of that year to codify the objectives agreed to in principle at the founding convention. Drafting a constitution and a formal statement of principles they called "The LULAC Code," Texans Manuel C. Gonzales, Alonso S. Perales, Benjamin Garza, J. T. Canales, Luis Wilmot, and others agreed to a series of objectives that came to define the organization's basic philosophy and political program for the next sixty years. Foremost among these objectives was a pledge to promote and develop among LULAC members what they called the "best and purest" form of Americanism. They also resolved to teach their children English and to inculcate in them a sense of their rights and responsibilities as American citizens, and they promised to fight discrimination against Mexican Americans wherever they encountered it.

In many ways the new organization exemplified the integrationist strains of thought that had slowly evolved among some Mexican Americans over the previous years. LULAC's founders believed that Mexican Americans had for too long been denied the full enjoyment of their rights as American citizens and that it was now time to change the situation. Both LULAC's constitution and the LULAC Code emphasized that the best way to rectify the appalling conditions facing Mexican Americans was to organize as American citizens; thus LULAC's founders rejected outright the notion that they were merely Mexicans who happened to reside in the United States. Although LULAC members insisted that their organization did not represent a political club, most of the group's goals were clearly political in nature. Thus even though LULAC's by-laws specifically prohibited direct involvement in partisan elections, the group's leaders encouraged members to participate in politics and use their "vote and influence" to support "men who show by their deeds, respect and consideration for our people."[4] They remained extremely sensitive to the anti-Mexican sentiment that was building up in Texas and other parts of the Southwest during the first years of the depression, however, and so from the outset were careful to disavow the use of political tactics that might be interpreted as radical. Despite such caution, they asserted their strong commitment to "destroy any attempt to create racial prejudices against [Mexican Americans], and any infamous stigma which may be cast upon them [by] demand[ing] for them the respect and prerogatives which the Constitution grants us all."[5]

LULAC leaders consciously chose to emphasize the American side of their social identity as the primary basis for organization. Consequently, in pursuit of much-needed reforms they developed a political program designed to activate a sense of Americanism among their constituents. Considering themselves part of a progressive and enlightened leadership elite, LULAC's leaders set out to implement general goals and a political strategy that were similar in form and content to those advocated early in the century by W. E. B. Du Bois and the National Association for the Advancement of Colored People: for "an educated elite" "to provide the masses with appropriate goals and lift them to civilization."[6] LULAC's political activities varied from chapter to chapter according to local political circumstances, but in general the organization adopted a three-pronged plan of attack in the 1930s and 1940s that strongly emphasized desegregated public education for Mexican American children; encouraged Mexican American citizens to register, pay their poll taxes, and vote; and supported aggressive local legal campaigns to combat discrimination against Mexican Americans in public facilities and on juries.

Although the depression constrained LULAC's organizing and proselytizing efforts, the organization proved remarkably successful in expanding its membership base after 1929. Utilizing "Flying Squadrons" of organizers who traveled to distant communities in cars or chartered buses, LULAC grew throughout the 1930s in Texas, and by the outbreak of World War II the organization had established viable chapters in New Mexico, Arizona, California, and Kansas. By the early 1940s LULAC claimed at least eighty dues-paying chapters nationwide, making it the largest and best-established Mexican American civil rights organization in the United States.

LULAC also proved remarkably successful in achieving many of its stated political goals. Indeed, despite the generally hostile political environment facing Mexican Americans during this era, LULAC scored a number of significant legal victories in Texas, and the organization assisted Mexican Americans in other states in mounting effective challenges against local discriminatory practices. From 1929 through World War II LULAC organized successful voter registration and poll-tax drives, actively supported political candidates sympathetic to Mexican Americans, and aggressively attacked discriminatory laws and practices in communities throughout Texas and the Southwest. More important over the long run, LULAC also achieved a number of notable legal victories in the area of public education. Following a strategy in which it focused its energies on legal challenges to discriminatory practices in one community at a time, LULAC began to chip away at the structure of the de jure segregation of Mexican American students. For example, in the organization's first legal challenge in 1930, LULAC lawyers brought suit against the Del Rio, Texas, School District for discriminating against Mexican American students. LULAC ultimately lost most of the major points contested in *Independent School District v. Salvatierra*, but the case was only the opening salvo in what proved to be a long legal struggle in which LULAC and other groups successfully argued that discrimination violated the equal-protection and due-process clauses of the Fourteenth Amendment to the U.S. Constitution. Similar LULAC efforts in the 1940s and 1950s built on this important precedent and helped Mexican Americans and other minority groups attack the separate-but-equal doctrine that was ultimately overturned in the famous *Brown v. Board of Education* case in 1954.[7]

NOTES

1. For this, and for similar examples of *corridos* of the depression era, see Nellie Foster, "The Corrido: A Mexican Culture Trait Persisting in Southern California" (M.A. thesis, University of Southern California, 1939).

2. James L. Slayden, *Some Observations on the Mexican Immigrant*, ANNALS OF THE AMERICAN ACADEMY OF POLITICAL AND SOCIAL SCIENCE 93 (January 1921): 125.

3. Preamble, "Constitución y Leyes de la Orden Hijos de América," 1927, Box 1, Folder 3, O. Douglas Weeks Papers, LULAC Archives, Benson Latin American Library, University of Texas Austin.

4. O. Douglas Weeks, *The League of United Latin American Citizens: A Texas Mexican Civic Organization,* SOUTHWESTERN POLITICAL AND SOCIAL SCIENCE QUARTERLY 10 (December 1928): 257–78.

5. LULAC Constitution, Box 1, Folder 7, Weeks Papers.

6. August Meier, NEGRO THOUGHT IN AMERICA, 1880–1915: RACIAL IDEOLOGIES IN THE AGE OF BOOKER T. WASHINGTON (Ann Arbor: University of Michigan Press, 1963), 192. Although there is little evidence that Du Bois's ideas directly influenced LULAC's leadership, the similarities between LULAC's evolving political ideas and those of the NAACP during this period are striking.

7. For descriptions of LULAC's general political and legal efforts during this period, see Mario T. García, MEXICAN AMERICANS: LEADERSHIP, IDEOLOGY, AND IDENTITY, 1930–1960 (New Haven, Conn.: Yale University Press, 1989), 40–41, 46–53; and Richard A. García, RISE OF THE MEXICAN AMERICAN MIDDLE CLASS: SAN ANTONIO, 1929–1941 (College Station: Texas A&M University Press, 1991), 282–99.

Chapter 59

Melting Pot or Ring of Fire?

Kevin R. Johnson

In the spring of 1996, I was sitting in a bar close to the Pacific Coast Highway in Manhattan Beach, California, an upper-middle-class, predominantly white suburb of Los Angeles. Funeral services for my father's uncle, my great-uncle (known as "Brown-eyes" or "Brownie" to distinguish him from his blue-eyed twin), had just finished. I had an hour to burn with my father and stepbrother while I waited for my return flight to Sacramento. Thoughts about my uncle streamed through my mind. He thoroughly enjoyed life. He was always upbeat. But he worried. A life of economic insecurity for him and his family no doubt contributed to the worries. Over the coming days, I wondered how it must have been when he became the first Anglo in his family to marry a Mexican-American woman, Rosie. They had grown up together in a working-class neighborhood near downtown Los Angeles where Mexican Americans and Anglos lived side-by-side. They spent fifty years there before moving to the desert in retirement.

While my mind wandered, a tall Anglo fellow sitting on the barstool next to us rambled to anyone who would listen about a recent visit to Texas. Then came what, in retrospect, was inevitable—a joke, which went something like this: "How do you make sure nobody steals the stereo speakers in your car?" Without waiting for a response, he eagerly offered the punch line: "You put a sign on them saying '*no habla español.*'" Nobody laughed. I wondered why I had to hear this kind of stuff. Why couldn't I grieve with a beer and not have to deal with issues of race that cut to the core of my identity? I wished that, as for many Anglos, my identity could be "transparent," a non-issue in my daily life. The joke made me think of the many Spanish-speakers that I knew and my inability to identify any who stole stereo speakers. This story, in addition to showing that words may hurt and marginalize, demonstrates the limits of assimilation for Latinos.

In recent years, Latinos with high media profiles, such as Linda Chavez and Richard Rodriguez, have unabashedly embraced assimilation for Latinos. In her book *Out of the Barrio*, Chavez explores a "new theory" of assimilation that argues that Latinos, like previous waves of white "ethnic" immigrants, should assimilate, and in fact are doing so. Yet, separate and unequal Latino enclaves in many cities suggest that assimilation is far from complete. Economic disparities show no signs of dissipating. The anti-immigrant backlash, which is in no small part an attack on all persons (immigrants and citizens) of Mexican ancestry in the United States, including persons who trace their ancestry in this country for centuries, is a testament to the limits of assimilation.

On a human level, the experiences of my mother, a most ardent assimilationist, demonstrate the problems faced by Latinas seeking to assimilate. Nor am I, a Harvard-educated law professor, immune to them. Indeed, my experience in the Manhattan Beach bar suggests the contrary.

Latino assimilation implicates issues central to race, ethnicity, and nationhood. A growing body of literature analyzes generally the voluntary adoption of a racial identity. My experiences exemplify how, because race is a social construction, there is some choice in deciding to be a Latino. For the most part, I was never forced to present myself as Mexican American. Although it may be difficult for some Latinos to "pass" as white due to phenotype, surname, or language skills, I could, if I chose. I might have ignored my background and hoped that nobody would remember, find out, or care. In some circumstances, I could shed my ethnicity and blend in. At other times (for example, with people who knew of my background), this was not possible. To do so, I would have had to deny a family history that was central to my identity during my formative years. Exemplifying the volitional nature of racial identity, my brother, with blond hair and blue eyes, exercised his right to choose in a different way. He never identified as Mexican American.

My wife, Virginia Salazar, is from a traditional Mexican-American family in La Puente, California, east of East Los Angeles, with dark brown hair, brown eyes, and a light complexion. Those in her mother's family generally have fair complexions and light brown hair; those in her father's family generally have dark skin and dark brown hair bordering on black. Although both her parents speak Spanish, she was not taught the language at home. To our surprise, our first two children, Teresa and Tomás, have blond hair and blue eyes and fair complexions. They were embraced by the family proudly, with occasional reference to their being *hueros*, or "white ones." Such references hint at the value of whiteness in U.S. society. Our third child, Maria Elena, looks more like us, with olive-colored skin and brown eyes. Some have referred to her as our "Mexican" baby or *la morena* (the dark one).

The phenotypic diversity among a family of five Mexican Americans under one roof should make it clear that the Mexican-American community is far from one-dimensional. If Mexican Americans are a diverse group, Latinos are even more so. Mixtures of race, national origin, immigration status, class, culture, education, political outlook, and many other characteristics abound.

One aspect of Latino diversity is the large number of those of mixed Latino/Anglo backgrounds. While poignant books by Greg Williams[1] and Judy Scales-Trent[2] have documented the experiences of persons with one black and one white parent, the discussion of mixed race people has not focused on Latinos of mixed parentage. This is true despite the high rates of intermarriage between Latinos and Anglos and the many mixed Latino/Anglo people in the United States. As the Latino population in the United States increases, one can expect the number of intermarriages and children of mixed race to increase as well.

Some of my experiences exemplify the difficulties of forcing people into hard-and-fast categories, which law and society inevitably attempt to do. Mixed race people regularly face this difficulty. For example, in the United States census, what demographic box should a person check who does not fit neatly into any of the enumerated racial or ethnic categories? Or consider admission to educational programs and employment. None of the recognized categories fully nor accurately describes a mixed race/ethnicity person. One hates to be in the unsavory position of denying one's background. At the same time, one fears being accused of claiming to be a minority simply to obtain a "special" preference.

Ultimately, the assimilation experiences of Latinos tell us much about race, ethnicity, and nationhood in the United States. Mexican Americans in the Southwest, and Latinos throughout the country, have been defined as a race of people different from and inferior to whites. Latinos are viewed as foreign to the nation's Anglo-Saxon core. Difficulties of assimilation for Latinos persist in part because of their definition as the other. My mother's story reflects these difficulties. Moreover, it serves as a metaphor for the assimilation of Mexican Americans in the Southwest. My experiences reflect the amorphousness of the concepts of race and ethnicity, the difficulties resulting from racial uncertainty, and the complexities of a multiracial experience in a time of identity politics.

The Myth of Spain and Assimilation through Denial

Despite their Mexican roots, my mother and grandmother were ardently assimilationist in outlook. Marrying Anglo men was part of the assimilationist strategy. Another aspect of the plan was for my mother and grandmother to claim that they were not of *Mexican,* but *Spanish,* ancestry.

Always the storyteller, one of my grandmother's favorite stories concerned her mixed Spanish-French background, with particular emphasis on the Spanish. This theme, in fact, found its way into many of her stories. My mother also emphasized her "Spanish" ancestry. My grandmother, with her indigenous phenotype, and my mother, with her olive-colored skin, seemed no different from the other Mexican Americans in the San Gabriel Valley. My great grandmother, who never mentioned her Spanish ancestry in my presence, was a Mexican citizen who lived in Mexico during my younger years. All of our relatives in the Imperial Valley, only a few miles from the U. S./Mexico border, were Mexican American. My mother's magical Spanish ancestry was thus very much an exaggeration.

This claim of Spanish heritage is not at all uncommon. Many Latinos understand at least implicitly that being classified as Mexican is disfavored in the United States, and it was especially disfavored in the Southwest before development of the civil rights consciousness of the 1960s. The phenomenon of Latinos attempting to "pass" as Spanish, and therefore as white, is a variation of the "passing" of other minorities as white. To many Anglos, being "Spanish" is more European, and therefore more acceptable, than being of Latin American ancestry. My mother and grandmother knew the southern Californian world in which they lived and the racial hierarchy that existed, even if they recognized it in simplified terms (i.e., that many people did not like Mexicans and that they had better convince them they were not Mexicans).

This Spanish mythology was part of my mother's assimilationist leanings. To this day, rather than pronounce her maiden name (Gallardo) in proper Spanish, which requires a special "ll" sound similar to "y," she says it as it would be said in English, as in the word "fallen." Consequently, the word "lard" and all of the images that it connotes stick out right in the middle.

In no small part because of her assimilationist approach, my mother consciously avoided teaching her children Spanish. She spoke Spanish, though she lost some of it over the years. Like many in her generation, Spanish was considered an educational impediment. The theory was that we needed to master English (which would not be possible if we learned Spanish) so that we could succeed in school, a view held to this day by some Latinos. In my mother's generation, it was not uncommon to suffer punishment for speaking any language other than English in the public schools. When I was growing up, my mother and grandmother spoke Spanish only when they wanted to have a private conversation in our presence. My mother would become irritable, rare for her, when my brother and I teased her for speaking "Mexican." "It is *Spanish*," she would emphasize. "There is no *Mexican* language."

While my mother and grandmother lived in a state of denial, the Anglo men in the family often emphasized their Mexican-ness, though in dramatically different ways. When my grandmother talked about her Spanish background, my step-grandfather would sarcastically respond: "Get off it. You're a Mexican like the rest of them." Weakly saying that he did not know anything and laughing uncomfortably, my grandmother would appear wounded. Similar exchanges occurred regularly. In a much more constructive way, my father would emphasize the positiveness of my mother's Mexican background to me. He told me in my younger years that the mixture of his "Swedish" (an exaggeration) and my mother's Mexican bloodlines was good.

My mother's and grandmother's assimilationism also meant adoption of the dominant society's racial attitudes. From an early age, my grandmother reminded me never to bring home an African-American girlfriend. She jokingly would say things to me like "don't bring home anyone who wants pork chops." Though she said this with a laugh, I understood her seriousness. Although my mother would never say such things, I sensed her agreement. My mother and grandmother also considered immigrants from Mexico as lessers, referring to them (jokingly, of course) as "wetbacks" or "Julios." These distinctions between themselves and Mexican immigrants were part of their denial of their Mexican ancestry and efforts to "pass" as Spanish.

NOTES

1. Gregory Howard Williams, Life on the Color Line (1995).
2. Judy Scales-Trent, Notes of a White Black Woman: Race, Color, Community (1995).

Chapter 60

Out of the Barrio

Linda Chavez

"We cannot assimilate—and we won't!" The words reverberate through the hall as the crowd of mostly Mexican American students clap their hands wildly. The man shouting from the podium is Arnold Torres, former executive director of the League of United Latin American Citizens, the oldest Hispanic civil rights organization in the United States. The scene is a familiar one, though the setting is new. Torres and I are debating the future of Hispanics before an audience at Stanford University. The young men and women in the audience wear blue jeans and T-shirts, proclaiming their loyalties to rock groups and social causes with equal enthusiasm. In a few years most of this youthful radicalism will be bridled by mortgage payments on suburban homes. But for now these students want no part of the Anglo establishment.

Torres's words strike me as odd. Surely he can't be talking about these kids, or about himself or me or any one of the other Mexican Americans onstage: a Pulitzer Prize–winning journalist, a tenured professor, and an assistant to the governor of California. In fact, Torres's purpose is not so much to suggest that Hispanics are incapable of entering the mainstream as to exhort them to remain outside—separate and distinct from the majority culture. It is a view widely shared by Hispanic leaders, though rarely expressed so boldly.

Today more than twenty-one million Hispanics are living in the United States, and the Hispanic population is increasing five times as fast as the rest of the population. Some demographers predict that in less than a hundred years Hispanics will account for nearly one-third of the nation's people. If Torres's view prevails, and Hispanics either cannot or will not assimilate, it will represent a dramatic shift in the history of American ethnic groups and could alter the fate of Hispanics and the country. It would mean that for the first time a major ethnic immigrant group, guided by its leaders, had eschewed the path of assimilation. Every previous group—Germans, Irish, Italians, Greeks, Jews, Poles—struggled to be accepted fully into the social, political, and economic mainstream, sometimes against the opposition of a hostile majority. They learned the language, acquired education and skills, and adapted their own customs and traditions to fit into an American context. Assimilation proved an effective model for members of these ethnic groups, who now rank among the most successful Americans, as measured by earnings and education. But a quarter of a century ago another model emerged and challenged assimilation as a guide to the behavior of ethnic groups. This model originated in the civil rights movement of the 1960s.

The Civil Rights Model

By midcentury it was clear that blacks had not been assimilated into American society as other groups had. Immigrants—even those from southern and eastern Europe, whose appearance, culture, and language set them apart from previous groups that had settled in the United States—had gradually been accepted into the social and economic mainstream. But blacks had been kept outside it for generations. They remained a separate, distinct, and obviously disadvantaged group. It was clear that a more aggressive policy would have to be pursued if blacks were ever to become full and equal participants in the society. The Civil Rights Act of 1964 was a far-reaching attempt to change the behavior of private individuals, as well as of government bodies. It prohibited discrimination in public accommodations, in employment, and in any programs that received federal funds. Along with laws that prohibited discrimination in voting and education, the act guaranteed that each person should be considered on his or her own merits, without imposing limits or conferring privileges on the basis of race.

Like the assimilation process, civil rights laws promised to blur distinctions between people—at least the invidious ones based on prejudice. Such laws could lift barriers that had prevented blacks and others who suffered discrimination from competing, but they could not, overnight, erase the effects of decades of discrimination. Even if the 1964 Civil Rights Act had immediately eradicated racial discrimination—which of course it did not—it would still have taken a generation or more for blacks to "catch up" in education, earnings, and other measures of social and economic well-being. And there were no guarantees that blacks, or any other group, would succeed as a group; the only guarantee was that individuals would have the right to try to succeed by the same rules that applied to all persons. But rising expectations and impatience drove the civil rights movement to a radical transformation in the 1960s and 1970s.

When equal opportunity did not immediately produce equal results, civil rights leaders shifted away from arguing for a neutral, color-blind process. They insisted instead that the process produce equal outcomes for all groups, which could happen only if society became even more color conscious. Equal opportunity gave way to affirmative action. It was no longer sufficient for employers to guarantee an impartial selection process in hiring or promoting individuals. Federally mandated affirmative action programs, for example, forced employers who received government contracts to set goals for hiring a certain percentage of minorities and women. Race, gender, and national origin once again became important factors in hiring, firing, and promoting employees. The principles of affirmative action were extended to education and even to voting, when blacks (and, later, Hispanics) became entitled to vote in election districts in which they made up the majority of voters.

Hispanics and the New Entitlements

The changes brought about by the civil rights movement had a profound effect on Hispanics. Unlike blacks, who had been a part of the national consciousness for well over a century, Hispanics were virtually unknown to most Americans and ignored by policy makers and politicians, at least at the national level. In 1960 there were only about seven million Hispanics in the United States, 4 percent of the population. Most of these were either Mexican Americans who had lived in the Southwest for generations, many of whom were poor and uneducated, or Puerto Ricans who had migrated from the island to the Northeast after World War II and were faring poorly, especially in New York. In the decade after 1960, one million Cuban refugees fleeing Fidel Castro's Communist revolution in their homeland added to the Hispanic population, settling mostly in southern Florida. These groups were diverse, sharing no history or agenda. Within three decades, however, Hispanics became an important and powerful interest group, whose leaders argued that Hispanics could succeed only by mimicking the strategy of the black civil rights movement.

In the mid-1960s money from the War on Poverty began to pour into minority communities for self-help programs in education and housing. Schools, universities, and employers began devising special programs aimed at the recruiting of minorities. Foundations, too, were creating projects and forming organizations to help minorities develop their economic and political potential. So long as Hispanics remained a separate and disadvantaged group, they were entitled to affirmative action programs, compensatory education, government set-asides, and myriad other programs. Previous immigrants had been eager to become "American," to learn the language, to fit in. But the entitlements of the civil rights era encouraged Hispanics to maintain their language and culture, their separate identity, in return for the rewards of being members of an officially recognized minority group. Assimilation gave way to affirmative action.

The effect of this change was twofold: it strengthened Hispanic ethnic identity, since entitlement was based on membership in an officially designated minority group; and it placed a premium on disadvantaged status. Hispanic leaders developed a vested interest in showing that Hispanics were, as the head of one Hispanic organization described it, "the poorest of the poor, the most segregated minority in schools, the lowest paid group in America and the least-educated minority in this nation."[1] Such descriptions justified Hispanics' entitlement to affirmative action programs, but they also created a perverse standard of success. To succeed at the affirmative action game, Hispanics had to establish their failure in other areas. The point of this game was for Hispanics to show that they were making less social and economic progress than other groups and therefore deserved greater assistance. Hispanic leaders, ignoring tangible evidence to the contrary, complained as Representative Edward Roybal (D.-Calif.) did: "we are no better off today than we were in 1949."[2] Others invoked the specter of "a permanent Hispanic underclass," as if to ensure no end to Hispanic entitlement.

Real Progress

Despite the general pessimism of Hispanic leaders, the evidence suggests that Hispanics are making real progress today. What's more, if ever the analogy between blacks and Hispanics was a fair one, it no longer is. Most native born Hispanics have leaped over blacks in achievement, and those Hispanics who are most disadvantaged are, by and large, recent immigrants. Still, Hispanic leaders insist that all Hispanics, even new immigrants, should be entitled to affirmative action programs and other ethnic entitlements that are the legacy of the civil rights movement. What these leaders fail to acknowledge is that Hispanics are succeeding as most other groups before them did, by acquiring the education and skills to advance in this society. Even newcomers, who start off on the bottom rungs of the economic ladder, climb quickly. Within one or two generations living in the United States, the great majority of Hispanics are integrated into the social and economic mainstream.

The story of Hispanic progress and achievement is largely untold. Hispanics are still regarded and treated as a permanently disadvantaged minority. Their leaders seem more intent on vying with blacks for permanent victim status than on seeking recognition for genuine progress by Hispanics over the last three decades. [My] purpose is to tell the story of that progress: But it is also to warn that attempts to keep Hispanics outside the mainstream of this society—speaking their own language, living in protected enclaves, entitled to privileges based on disadvantage—could derail that progress. Ultimately, individual Hispanics will choose whether they wish to become part of the larger society or remain separate from it, but public policy can and does influence that choice.

NOTES

1. Raul Yzaguirre, speech at the Leadership Conference on Civil Rights Fortieth Annual Conference Dinner, May 8, 1990.

2. NALEO Education Fund, "First National Conference on Latino Children in Poverty" (Washington, D.C.: NALEO, 1987), 4.

Chapter 61

Masks and Acculturation

Margaret E. Montoya

[The author invites the reader to consider how culture and stories interweave in the lives of outsiders, now combining to create masks, now to "create new options for expression, personal identity, cultural authenticity and pedagogical innovation." She then continues as follows:]

> I put on my masks, my
> costumes and posed for each
> occasion. I conducted myself
> well, I think, but
> an emptiness
> grew
> that no thing
> could fill. I think
> I hungered for myself.[1]

One of the earliest memories from my school years is of my mother braiding my hair, making my *trenzas*. In 1955, I was seven years old and in second grade at the Immaculate Conception School in Las Vegas, New Mexico. Our family home with its outdoor toilet was on an unpaved street, one house from the railroad track. I remember falling asleep to the subterranean rumble of the trains.

Nineteen fifty-five was an extremely important year in my development, in my understanding of myself in relation to Anglo society. I remember 1955 as the year I began to think about myself in relation to my classmates and their families. I began to feel different and to adjust my behavior accordingly.

My sister, brother, and I dressed in front of the space heater in the bedroom we shared. Catholic school girls wore uniforms. We wore blue jumpers and white blouses. I remember my mother braiding my hair and my sister's. I can still feel the part she would draw with the point of the comb. She would begin at the top of my head, pressing down as she drew the comb down to the nape of my neck. "Don't move," she'd say as she held the two hanks of hair, checking to make sure that the

From "Mascaras, Trenzas, y Greñas: Un/Masking the Self while Un/Braiding Latina Stories and Legal Discourse." 17 Harv. Women's L.J. 185 (1994); 15 Chicano-Latino L. Rev. 1 (1994). Originally published in the *Harvard Women's Law Journal* and the *Chicano-Latino Law Review*. Reprinted by permission.

part was straight. Only then would she begin, braiding as tightly as our squirming would allow, so the braids could withstand our running, jumping, and hanging from the monkey bars at recess. "I don't want you to look *grenudas*," my mother would say. ["I don't want you to look uncombed."]

Hearing my mother use both English and Spanish gave emphasis to what she was saying. She used Spanish to talk about what was really important: her feelings, her doubts, her worries. She also talked to us in Spanish about gringos, Mexicanos, and the relations between them. Her stories were sometimes about being treated outrageously by gringos, her anger controlled and her bitterness implicit. She also told stories about Anglos she admired—those who were egalitarian, smart, well-spoken, and well-mannered.

Sometimes Spanish was spoken so as not to be understood by Them. Usually, though, Spanish and English were woven together. *Grenuda* was one of many words encoded with familial and cultural meaning. My mother used the word to admonish us, but she wasn't warning us about name-calling: *grenuda* was not an epithet that our schoolmates were likely to use. Instead, I heard my mother saying something that went beyond well-groomed hair and being judged by our appearance—she could offer strategies for passing that scrutiny. She used the Spanish word, partly because there is no precise English equivalent, but also because she was interpreting the world for us.

The real message of *grenudas* was conveyed through the use of the Spanish word—it was unspoken and subtextual. She was teaching us that our world was divided, that They-Who-Don't-Speak-Spanish would see us as different, would judge us, would find us lacking. Her lessons about combing, washing and doing homework frequently relayed a deeper message: be prepared, because you will be judged by your skin color, your names, your accents. They will see you as ugly, lazy, dumb, and dirty.

As I put on my uniform and my mother braided my hair, I changed; I became my public self. My *trenzas* announced that I was clean and well-cared-for at home. My *trenzas* and school uniform blurred the differences between my family's economic and cultural circumstances and those of the more economically comfortable Anglo students. I welcomed the braids and uniform as a disguise which concealed my minimal wardrobe and the relative poverty in which my family lived.

As we walked to school, away from home, away from the unpaved streets, away from the "Spanish" to the "Anglo" part of town, I felt both drawn to and repelled by my strange surroundings. I wondered what Anglos were like in their big houses. What did they eat? How did they furnish their homes? How did they pass the time? Did my English sound like theirs? Surely their closets were filled with dresses, sweaters, and shoes, *apenas estrenados*.[2]

I remember being called on one afternoon in second grade to describe what we had eaten for lunch. Rather than admit to eating *caldito* (soup) *y tortillas*, partly because I had no English words for those foods, I regaled the class with a story about what I assumed an "American" family would eat at lunch: pork chops, mashed potatoes, green salad, sliced bread, and apple pie. The nun reported to my mother that I had lied. Afraid of being mocked, I unsuccessfully masked the truth, and consequently revealed more about myself than I concealed.

In those days before the ecumenical reforms, Catholicism still professed great concern about sinning. Although elementary school children were too young to commit most sins, lying was a real spiritual danger. Paradoxically, we were surrounded by Truth disguised in myriad ways. Religious language was oblique and filled with multiple meanings: Virgin Mother, Risen Son, bread that was the Body and wine that was the Blood. Our teachers, the nuns, were completely hidden—women without surnames, families, friends, or homes of their own. They embodied the collapsing of the private into the public. Their black and white habits hid their breasts, waists, legs, hair color, and hair texture.

Our school was well integrated with "Spanish" students because it was located in a town with a predominantly Latino population. The culture of the school, however, was overwhelmingly Anglo and middle class. The use of Spanish was frowned upon and occasionally punished. Any trace of an accent when speaking English would be pointed out and sarcastically mocked. This mocking persisted even though, and maybe because, some of the nuns were also "Spanish."

I remember being assigned to tutor another second-grader in reading. He wore denim overalls, had his hair shaved for some medical procedure and spoke mostly Spanish. I think of him now, and perhaps thought of him then, as being exposed— exposed by not being able to read, exposed by not having a uniform, exposed by not having hair, exposed by not knowing English. From my perspective as a child, it all seemed connected somehow—Spanish-ness, sickness, poverty, and ignorance.

By the age of seven, I was keenly aware that I lived in a society that had little room for those who were poor, brown, or female. I was all three. I moved between dualized worlds: private/public, Catholic/secular, poverty/privilege, Latina/Anglo. My *trenzas* and school uniform were a cultural disguise. They were also a precursor for the more elaborate mask I would later develop.

Presenting an acceptable face, speaking without a Spanish accent, hiding what we really felt—masking our inner selves—were defenses against racism passed on to us by our parents to help us get along in school and in society. We learned that it was safer to be inscrutable. We absorbed the necessity of constructing and maintaining a disguise in public. We struggled to be seen as Mexican but also wanted acceptance as Americans at a time when the mental image conjured up by that word included only Anglos.

Mine is the first generation of Latinas to be represented in virtually every college and university and in anything approaching significant numbers. But, for the most part, we find ourselves isolated. Rarely has another Latina gone before us. Rarely do we find another Latina whom we can watch to try and figure out all the little questions about subtextual meaning, about how dress or speech or makeup are interpreted in this particular environment.

My participation in the Chicano student movement in college fundamentally changed me. My adoption of the ethnic label as a primary identifier gave me an ideological mask that serves to this day. This transformation of my public persona was psychically liberating. This nascent liberation was, however, reactive and inchoate. Even as I struggled to redefine myself, I was locked in a reluctant embrace with those whose definitions of me I was trying to shrug off.

When I arrived as a student at Harvard Law School, I dressed so as to proclaim my politics. During my first day of orientation, I wore a Mexican peasant blouse and cutoff jeans on which I had embroidered the Chicano symbol of the *aguila* (a stylized eagle) on one seat pocket and the woman symbol on the other. The *aguila* reminded me of the red and black flags of the United Farm Worker rallies; it reminded me that I had links to a particular community. I was never to finish the fill-in stitches in the woman symbol. My symbols, like my struggles, were ambiguous.

The separation of the two symbols reminds me today that my participation in the Chicano movement had been limited by my gender, while in the women's movement it had been limited by my ethnicity. I drew power from both movements—I identified with both—but I knew that I was at the margin of each one.

As time went on, my clothes lost their political distinctiveness. My clothes signified my ambivalence: perhaps if I dressed like a lawyer, eventually I would acquire more conventional ideas and ideals and fit in with my peers. Or perhaps if I dressed like a lawyer, I could harbor for some future use the disruptive and, at times, unwelcome thoughts that entered my head. My clothing would become protective coloration. Chameleon-like, I would dress to fade into the ideological, political, and cultural background rather than proclaim my differences.

Academic success traditionally has required that one exhibit the linguistic and cognitive characteristics of the dominant culture. Until challenged by recent empirical research by Chicano social scientists, retention of traditional Mexican-American culture was believed to impede successful adjustment within mainstream American society. This "damaging-culture" model provided a rationale for advocating the complete assimilation of Latinos into the mainstream culture.

The wide-spread acceptance of assimilationist thought fueled social and familial pressure on Latinos to abandon traditional values and lifestyles in order to achieve educational and economic upward mobility. Acculturation into the dominant culture is a concomitant of education. Virtually all Latino students with a college-level education appear to be highly assimilated into Anglo culture.

To support their academic progress, Latinos have encouraged their children to speak English well and have tolerated other aspects of acculturation, such as changes in friends, clothes, and recreational preferences. Students learn to adopt masks of the dominant culture which avoid the negative values ascribed to traditional Latina/o culture. Latina/o history is replete with stories about those who changed their names, lost the Spanish language and with it any trace of a Spanish accent, or deliberately married out of the culture. In short, some did whatever was necessary to be seen as not different by the majority.

Some Latinos, like other Outsiders, move away from their ethnic communities and want nothing to do with those they left behind. Many others, however, see education as the only ladder for themselves and for their community. Academic success does not come without costs, however. Latinas/os who pursue higher education often end up feeling doubly estranged because of the socialization process: estranged not only from their ancestral roots but from the dominant culture as well.

Feeling masked because of ethnic and racial differences is directly linked to the process of cultural assimilation, and to the pervasive Latina/o resistance against assimilation; against being seen as *agringada,* of becoming a *gringa,* of being taken for something one never wanted to become. Assimilation has become yet another mask for the Latina/o to hide behind. I have a clay mask made by Mexican artisans that captures this idea but from a different perspective. The outermost mask is a white skeleton face wearing a grimace. The second layer shows a face with an aquiline nose and a goatee suggesting the face of the Spaniard, the colonizer of indigenous Mexico. This second mask parts to show the face of a pensive Aztec. This clay sculpture suggests the indigenous Indian preserved behind the false masks, the death mask, the conquistador mask. In other words, the sculpture represents all of us who have been colonized and acculturated—who have succeeded in withholding a precious part of our past behind our constructed public personas.

Belonging to a higher economic class than that of one's family or community and affecting the mannerisms, clothing styles, or speech patterns that typify the privileged classes can strain familial and ethnic bonds. Families, even those who have supported the education and advancement of their children, can end up feeling estranged from them and resentful of the cultural costs of their academic and economic success. Accusations of *vendida,* "selling-out," forgetting the ethnic community, and abandoning the family can accompany academic success.

Even when family or friends do not recriminate, internal doubts plague the student about what one has given up in order to achieve academic success. Concerns about ethnic identity and personal authenticity are imbedded within the question "Who am I really?" We have been told, "You don't seem Latina," or have been asked, "How Latina are you?" Such comments, when made by Anglos, imply that we have risen above our group. We are special, better, acceptable. When made by Latinos, however, the question carries an innuendo of cultural betrayal and the threat of cultural excommunication.

The public environment in which we live our professional lives can be profoundly different from the homes we came from. The details of our lives bear little resemblance to the culture in which we once were immersed. We feel ourselves moving between different worlds, putting on one face and taking off another.

There are times when the strands of our lives resist being woven into a neat braid. Recently I happened upon an autobiography, *Always Running: La Vida Loca, Gang Days in L.A.,* written by Luis J. Rodriguez. I found the book while on a trip to Cambridge as an elected director of the Harvard Alumni Association. I had attended a long day of meetings in the rarefied seclusion of the Harvard Faculty Club, where I always feel like a spectator rather than a participant. The building evokes the "clubiness" of its name: dark wood paneling, well worn rugs, rooms called libraries. I can never seem to dress well enough or choose words, accents, or voices carefully enough to feel that I belong there. Occasionally, I can give voice to my experience—to one Latina's experience.

After one such day, I wandered into a bookstore in Harvard Square. I leafed through the Rodriguez book. Suddenly, I focused on my cousin's name, Rodolfo "Sonny" Gomez, listed among those to whom the book was dedicated. Rodriguez didn't state it explicitly, but it was, presumably, a list of his homeboys and homegirls who didn't survive *la vida loca*. I knew that but for the grace of God . . . Sonny could have had my fate and I, his.

Standing in the bookstore, my eyes filled with tears. We both stood with a foot in two worlds. I remembered Sonny; he drove a yellow MG convertible, introduced me to the music of Bob Dylan, talked about Karl Marx and Chicanismo.

My multiple identities do not usually clash as violently as they did at that particular moment. Those moments set me apart from the privileged majority, the experience of being yanked back unpredictably into powerlessness. Throughout the last decade, Latinos and others have challenged the efficacy of the assimilationist model, pointing out the heterogeneity of orientations and experiences among Latinos. They have demonstrated that "integration with one's ancestral culture is conducive to success and adjustment in American society."[3] Sociocultural adjustment is now understood as a multifaceted process that depends upon complex variables rather than a unilevel process whereby the customs of one culture are merely substituted for those of another.

Latinos have long exhibited bicultural behavior and values, but until recently no discourse or body of literature established the validity of such cultural integration. Contemporary Latina/o poetry and fiction exhibit this bilingual and bicultural character. Latina/o public discourse increasingly mirrors private speech.

As Latinas/os begin to construct our varied identities, we can still feel caught between the traditional understanding of what "real Latinas/os" are like and the strategies we invoke to respond to novel situations. Resolution of these issues need not be an isolating, individualistic, or secretive process, alienating us from our families or our communities. Despite important historical, ethnic, and linguistic differences, stories of assimilation told from the various perspectives of subordinated groups have strains of similarities. In addition to the personal and collective pain that we experience because of societal pressures to assimilate, Latinas/os face the disquietude of being masked for some of the same reasons as other Outsiders.

Being masked may be a universal condition in that all of us control how we present ourselves to others. But a fundamental difference marks feeling masked because one is a member of one or more oppressed groups within the society. When members of the dominant culture mask themselves to control the impressions they make, such behavior is not inherently self-loathing. But when we attempt to mask immutable characteristics of skin color, eye shape, or hair texture because they historically have been loathsome to the dominant culture, then the masks of acculturation can be experienced as self-hate. Moreover, unmasking for members of the dominant culture does not spark the fear or depth of humiliation that it does for the subordinated, for whom the unmasking is often involuntary and unexpected.

For Outsiders, unmasking is a holistic experience: I do not have separate masks for my female-ness and Latina-ness. The construction of my public persona includes all that I am. My public face is an adjustment to the present and a response to the past. Any unmasking resonates through the pathways of my memory. For Outsiders, the necessity of unmasking has been historical. Strategies are passed on from one generation to another to accommodate, to resist, to subvert oppressive forces. Involuntary unmasking is painful, it evokes echoes of past hurts, hurts one has suffered, and hurts one has heard stories about.

Outsiders are also faced with the gnawing suspicion that the public identities available to them are limited to those reflecting the values, norms, and behavior of the dominant ideology. Through my cultural disguise, I sought to mirror the behavior of those who mattered more than I. As a child, I altered or denied my language, my clothes, my foods. My *trenzas* helped me to fit in, to get by, to move up. As an adult, I still alter or deny my self/selves, both consciously and unconsciously.

A significant aspect of subordination is the persistence with which we mimic the styles, preferences, and mannerisms of those who dominate us, even when we have become aware of the mimicry. Lost to the Outsider are those identities that would have developed but for our real and perceived needs to camouflage ourselves in the masks of the Master. Lost to all are the variety of choices, the multiplicity of identities that would be available if we were not trapped by the dynamics of subordination, of privilege.

NOTES

1. Alma Villanueva, *Mother, May I?* in Contemporary Chicana Poetry 303, 324 (Marta Ester Sanchez ed., 1985).

2. *Apenas estrenados* is a Spanish concept that has no English equivalent. *Estrenar* connotes wearing something for the first time and conveys the special privilege that attaches to the first wearing. We had few opportunities to *estrenar* new clothes.

3. Raymond Buriel, *Integration with Traditional Mexican-American Culture and Sociocultural Adjustment,* in Chicano Psychology 95, at 97 (Joe L. Martinez, Jr., and Richard H. Mendoza eds., 2d ed. 1984).

Chapter 62

Straddling Separate Worlds

Ruben Navarrette, Jr.

It was in my sophomore year that I finally realized the development of a siege mentality among some minority students.

I witnessed, and to some degree facilitated, the subconscious dividing of the Harvard community in two camps. *Us* and *them.* We were advocates—progressive Chicano students who "knew who they were," embraced their culture, and were ready to uphold their sacred responsibility to *la comunidad* and sympathetic white liberal faculty who tried to ease our alienation. We were "down with brown." They were detractors—conservative politicians appealing for the votes of those who felt reversely discriminated against, professors frightened by classroom populations that were changing colors, newspaper columnists talking about merit who had forgotten that their first break in journalism had come from an influential uncle, and fellow Chicanos seeking acceptance by denouncing affirmative action benefits that they had already accepted. We considered Them to be all those who had never wanted Us to attend schools like Harvard in the first place and now wanted to limit our numbers or encumber our experience. We wanted to destroy a status quo that had systematically disenfranchised our parents and our parents' parents. They wanted to maintain that status quo and pined away for the good ol' days when one could go one's whole life and never encounter a Mexican as an equal. Mexican-Americans at Harvard . . . imagine!

If Us and Them were at war, then paranoia defined the battlefield. Those who were not friends were automatically enemies. Trust was a precious commodity, distributed sparingly. I was still convinced that there were inflexible standards for what constituted a Real Mexican. Instinctively, unscrupulously, I applied those standards to other Mexican-Americans on campus, including those in RAZA, in a kind of ethnic litmus test to assess authenticity. I remember that, in my mind, authenticity implied loyalty. A foolish assumption of youth: Those *most* like you will not betray you.

What eventually ensued on our campus and, I would learn, on other college campuses around the country, was a messy game of ethnic "Truth or Consequences."

The exercise was conceived in difference. There were differences among the one hundred twenty-five Mexican-American undergraduates at Harvard just as there are differences among the twenty million Mexican-Americans in the United States. Some students were from mixed marriages; some were not. Some were from upper middle-class families; some were not. Some had worked in the fields as children; some had not. Some spoke Spanish; some did not.

The exercise thrived in difference. The rules of the game were simple. The contestants might be two Harvard Chicanos, similar yet different. The difference is noted. It might be a difference in skin color, Spanish-speaking ability, religion, even political affiliation. At first glance, it appears unlikely that both people can be authentic. The difference dictates that one must be a real Mexican, the other a fraud. The objective of the game becomes for the contestants to each assert his or her own legitimacy by attacking the ethnic credibility of their opponent. *More ethnic than thou.* The weapons are whispers. A pointed finger. A giggle. A condescending remark from one to another.

"Oh, with your background, I don't think you'd understand my point . . ."

Owing to rigid, traditional—some might say stereotypical— conceptions of Mexican culture, *authentic* meant dark-skinned, Spanish-speaking, Catholic, lower-class, and loyal to family. So a young Mexican-American man with light skin and an Irish surname, or a young Chicana who votes Republican and whose mother is a college professor might both start off at a disadvantage. I remember a beautiful girl with a Mexican-American mother and a white father who, as a freshman, was told by a senior in RAZA that she might have difficulty being accepted, trusted by the group because of her mixed lineage. This, of course, after he slept with her. Sex, I learned early, is the oldest weapon of all.

Finally, the game ended in a cynical pool of hurt feelings and lost friendships. The winners, having savaged their opponent with slander, accusation, and innuendo, stood victorious; reward took the form of that elusive Harvard carrot, acceptance and respect. A reward, if not from the institution itself, at least from fellow Mexican-Americans there.

Chapter 63

Neither Here nor There

Earl Shorris

When the theory of the melting pot still operated in the United States, artists said, in a flat-footed way, I am an American writer or painter or composer. They did not want to be Italian-American or Irish-American or Jewish-American, for the hyphen, that lonely segment of the great line of human society, separated them from the rest of the Americans; it cast them back into the inhospitable world from which they had so recently escaped.

Even so, some of the writers who came in the great waves of immigration of the late nineteenth and early twentieth centuries wrote of the old country, for memory was all they knew, and if it was good writing, like that of Isaac Bashevis Singer, the literature of some universal country located in Poland or Germany or Italy, their work was widely read first by their fellow immigrants and later translated into other languages. For the most part, however, the literature of the European immigrants was neither about Europe nor America; it was about becoming American. The accompanying music went beyond being American, it was downright chauvinistic: George M. Cohan was not an Irish-American dandy, he was a "Yankee Doodle dandy, . . . born on the Fourth of July."

The wish for assimilation overwhelmed the connection to the old world; the artists of those generations had either to paint, write, dance, and make music for an audience bent upon assimilation or be content to keep their work within a narrowing world. The purpose of the famous "Bintel Brief," a column in the *Jewish Daily Forward*, was to help the immigrant population of the Lower East Side of New York understand their new country and become a part of it. Detailed news of an immigrant's homeland was not likely to be found in the *Forward*. The paper was true to its name; it did not look back.

Black writers, known then as Negroes, but not hyphenated, dealt with their problems as Americans, grievously wronged Americans, but Americans nevertheless. The genius of Richard Wright, Ralph Ellison, and James Baldwin grew out of their *American* anger, not their African ancestry. Alex Haley, a black writer, did finally produce a book about his African heritage, but it was not art; *Roots* had the labored grace of good intentions.

During the 1950s, when the drive for assimilation was at its peak, the "happens to be" artists appeared: "I am an American writer who happens to be black" or "I am an American violinist who happens to be Jewish." In other words, ethnicity was an accident; one was American by choice, and in a time dominated by a vague conception of the existential burden of freedom, choice was all that mattered. Twenty years later, it was too late for white artists to be anything but Americans. It was time for black artists to take their turn at struggling with the hyphen, but black culture was so woven into the general American culture that separating out antecedents was impossible; the language of American music and literature could not be described as black or white. And Wright, Baldwin, and Ellison knew little, if anything, about African literature and certainly could not read, write, or even speak an African language. Racism—not the hyphen of language, story, or song—separated blacks from other American artists.

For one group of American artists, however, the hyphen had a different meaning; Latinos could not abandon the old country or its culture, for they were too close to home. Martí did not write about American issues while he lived in New York; he wrote about Cuba. Nor did Hostos or Ricardo Flores Magón concern himself with life in the States. They were sojourners; they all expected to go back. Others came to the United States as transporters, people who never left their home. The first Latin-American poet to win a Nobel Prize was a teacher who lived on Long Island, New York, but Gabriela Mistral did not write American poetry; her work belonged to Chile.

Contemporary Latino artists have been to the old country, even if the old country is Miami rather than La Habana. Many, perhaps most, have lost their fluency in Spanish, but few have lost their grandmothers. And even if they had, the constant flow of newcomers from Latin America and the contact between native born U.S. citizens and newcomers make it all but impossible for Latino artists to avoid the hyphen; they are a discrete segment in the long line of culture. They live in a situation which removes the power of choice from their artistic lives, no matter how much they wish it were otherwise. The memoirist Richard Rodriguez argues, in finely crafted English prose, that he is a happens-to-be, but he isn't, he cannot be. To change his situation he would have to be able to "pass" for Anglo; only then would he have the option of inviting the problems of inauthenticity upon himself.

The real issue for Latino artists, the one that can be chosen, involves artistic antecedents. When Yreina Cervantez stands on a scaffold under a freeway in Los Angeles painting a mural of chicano history, she is perfectly aware of her antecedents among the Mexican muralists; she welcomes them; they are her muses. David Hayes-Bautista, who oversees the Chicano Studies Library at UCLA, includes all of Mexican and Spanish literature in the category; he is a collector of antecedents, a man with a view of chicano culture so generously inclusive it verges on universality, which would be logical nonsense (a set cannot be a member of itself). Latino musicians and composers stand gladly on the shoulders of the giants of the old country, although both Latin jazz and conjunto music have a mixed and very complicated ancestry.

The connection of Latino art to its old-country roots would seem incontestable, as the critic Luis Leal, among others, has said, but Héctor Calderón, reviewing Leal's book on Aztlán, claimed that Latino literature has no past, only a future. In support of his argument he quoted the critic and author of a book of interviews with chicano writers, Juan Bruce-Novoa, who says that these writers could not be influenced by Mexican literature, since most of them have not read the work of Mexican writers.[1] Bruce-Novoa wishes to make of chicano literature a new version of the *Jewish Daily Forward;* he wants it to be a literature that does not look back, an immigrant literature, not a literature of sojourners or, worse, transporters. He is the radical intellectual cousin of Richard Rodriguez, a happens-to-be on the most profound level.

There is also something tragic about Bruce-Novoa's position, for in his desire to paint chicanos free of Mexican influence, he perforce paints them ignorant, primitive, or at the very least innocent, much as critics of an earlier period wanted to find Nelson Algren a genuine American primitive and were dismayed to discover he was a well-educated, extremely widely read man who had spent years in the company of Simone de Beauvoir.

Calderón and Bruce-Novoa may be correct about some chicano artists, a few natural writers or born painters, but in the main chicanos and other Latinos in the arts now hold advanced academic degrees in art, music, literature, or creative writing. To suggest that Mexican literature does not influence chicano artists because they have not read it no longer agrees with reality. Elba Sánchez, who writes deliciously sensual, rhythmic poems, teaches literature to Spanish-language students at the University of California at Santa Cruz. Barbara Carrasco holds an M.F.A. from UCLA. Ruben Blades and Martin Espada are attorneys. Sandra Cisneros attended the Iowa Writers' Workshop. The painters César Martínez and Arturo Rodríguez are familiar not only with Mexican, Cuban, and Spanish painting; they are both deeply interested in Latin-American and world literature. The novelist and journalist Ron Arias has a passionate interest in Juan Rulfo; he and I have spent hours discussing the work of the great Mexican novelist. Chicano writers not only know the work of the Mexicans, they also know some of the writers personally, well enough to admire and like Carlos Fuentes and to detest Octavio Paz.

It is too late for Bruce-Novoa's thesis; the development of Latino culture within U.S. culture has proceeded in two directions at once—it has become sophisticated in both English and Spanish; the painters know Siqueiros, Goya, and Warhol; the writers have studied Hemingway, Faulkner, Fuentes, Paz, Rulfo, Poniatowska, García Márquez, the streets and the movies; the musicians know polkas, paso dobles, merengues, cumbias, salsa, and the blues. It is too late for Latino art to choose one direction or the other; unlike earlier immigrant cultures, it is destined to have a long, ironic life in both the old country and the new, to be a culture neither here nor there—not pocho, meaning the degradation of two cultures, but Latino.

NOTES

1. It is difficult to understand how Bruce-Novoa arrived at his theory, given that the single most important and influential chicano writer, Tomás Rivera, had a Ph.D. in Spanish literature from the University of Oklahoma, a center of Mexican studies.

Chapter 64

Harvard Homeboy

Ruben Navarrette, Jr.

"I'm a homeboy now. At Harvard, I didn't fit."
—José Luis Razo (Harvard Class of 1989)

A writer friend warned me that this case brings no easy answers. No "obvious conclusions" can be drawn by the story of José Luis Razo, the former Harvard student who was convicted of armed robbery in Orange County two months ago. "The whole thing seems problematic," my friend cautioned. "My hunch is that the kid's shoulders can't stand much metaphor. Forget it." Still, I fear there is much that remains unsaid. So I say it.

The day after the Harvard Class of 1989 received the golden passports that would open any door of their choosing, Joe Razo, who would have been among them, was instead in a courtroom in Santa Ana facing a possible fifteen years in prison.

So came to an end the drama, two years after it was first played out in the national media, of the Latino honors student from La Habra who, a jury decided, held up at least six stores and fast-food restaurants during school breaks over the course of eighteen months.

If one seeks tragedy—dishonor, if you will—the drama will not disappoint. The wasted future of a bright young man imprisoned in a correctional system that leaves those it punishes scarred and beaten, seldom corrected. The pain of a family that sacrificed much of their own lives to enhance his. The white alumni offended by his abuse of Ivy League benevolence—"See what happens when. . . ."

People following the story can only guess at the "why" of Razo's turning from the educational fast track to armed robbery. Psychologists offer simplistic theories about self-destructive "sun children"—bright minority students who excel beyond expectation and then turn away from the guiding light of success to burn out like a shooting star. In New York, a writer draws what seems an insightful comparison between the Razo case and that of Eddie Perry, a black honors student from Exeter, bound for

From L.A. Times, August 5, 1989, Metro Pt. 2, p. 8. Originally published in the *Los Angeles Times*. Reprinted by permission of the author.

Stanford on a scholarship, who was killed as he was mugging an undercover police-man near Harlem. Razo himself says he felt "alienated" in Cambridge. Harvard, in characteristic fashion, disclaims responsibility. "An isolated case," Harvard says. Ah. . . .

Four years ago, Joe and I entered Harvard as two of thirty-five or so Mexican Americans in the Class of '89. Some of those students were from wealthy families and private schools in the Southwest; others were from poor, Spanish-speaking fam-ilies. Some wanted to take their Harvard degree "back to the community"; others in-tended to take it only as far as Wall Street. In Harvard's eyes, we were similar; in fact, we had our differences.

Unfortunately, at Harvard as in the world in general, what makes people dif-ferent is not always respected. Insecurity as to whether you really "belong" in a foreign environment can breed intolerance toward others. At its extreme, it be-comes a kind of contest to "fit in"—a contest that seems to have only one kind of winner.

At Harvard, Joe and I were friends. Yes, I think that's fair to say. Sometimes we argued politics or talked football over a few beers; we felt comfortable with one an-other, I think. It was our school that my friend never felt comfortable with. He seemed to pass through a stage that many scared and alienated young people in elite schools go through—wearing his ethnicity like a badge. Or was it more like a shield? I remember him in the costume of an East L.A. "homeboy"—the khaki pants, the Pendleton shirt, the bandanna around his head. I remember his tattoos and his home-sickness for La Habra. I remember seeing him with a black eye and learning that he had been in a fistfight with a couple of local "townies" because of a racist remark they made. Young working-class whites sometimes resent the presence of Chicanos on an elite hometown campus that remains largely closed to them. It's ironic that Joe felt shut out from the campus, too.

Harvard Chicano. Twenty years in existence and the term still seems an enigma, a paradox that doesn't lend itself to a neat definition. Two concepts, once as distinct as oil and water, now are joined in the name of educational progress. Who are the people who bear the weight of that label? A policy-maker's "model minority," one whose excellence will make affirmative action easier. A "teacher's pet" always wav-ing her arm with the right answer. A high school counselor's "overachiever" needing little guidance. Most of all, a tearful parent's pride and joy, proof that with hard work anything is possible.

Since the central character in this tragic play is a personification of this paradox, one is tempted to romanticize his experience. A respected Chicano studies professor who knows neither Joe nor Harvard speculates that "Ivy League racism made Razo miserable at Harvard; he committed those crimes to get out." I've heard others say that Joe's story is really one of a scared young man who wanted off the fast-moving treadmill that a well-meaning society had placed him on. Maybe. But gaps appear in the drama that aren't filled by even the most sweeping of "obvious conclusions." Within the context of life at Harvard, Razo's rebellious appearance was not unusual. Many freshmen adopt a costume, a mannerism, a way of presenting themselves to others. In the Commune on the Charles, the extraordinary is ordinary. But not every student who sports torn Levi's, or a serape, around Harvard Yard commits armed robbery during summer vacation. There must be more.

At his trial, mention was made of Razo's dabbling in drugs. Seeking shelter from his somewhat charmed life, he entered the hallucinogenic world of PCP. For him, this world promised acceptance. It is, after all, a world already inhabited by hundreds of thousands of young Latinos like him, or unlike him—those that he had always been told he didn't have to be like.

With the emergence of drugs into the drama, many people lost interest. Razo was no longer a "good victim."

It is tempting to take the complex human experience that began to unfold during Razo's trial and reduce it to a more manageable drug story, but the critical onlooker presses for more.

Some of us know, and few will admit, that Joe Razo experienced a kind of double alienation while at Harvard. Confused and alone, he instinctively sought refuge in the one corner of that foreign world that appeared familiar.

The Mexican-American students' association at Harvard is called Raza; its professed goal for twenty years has been to provide a support system for students who, on their application, checked the box marked "Mexican American/Chicano." Raza works with the admissions office to ensure active recruitment of Latino high school students, and the organization's rhetoric promises that it will make every effort to provide emotional support when they arrive in Cambridge. In short, Raza is supposed to help create a nurturing environment in which Latinos can adjust to life at Harvard without necessarily surrendering their cultural identity at the front gate.

Yet those who know these types of student organizations also know that sometimes they become as intolerant of individual differences as they accuse the campus community at large of being. Ethnic organizations do sometimes develop an image deemed "proper" for their group and exclude those who appear to contradict that image.

To those members of Raza eagerly awaiting their admittance to the world of BMWs and designer suits, Razo and his East L.A. look represented that sort of contradiction. He was an embarrassment to some, a reminder of how close they still were to the world they'd left behind. He was dressed like the kid whose fate, we had been told, we could escape if we studied hard. So we did. And when, through all our effort, we arrived safely in the ivy-covered world of cashmere and Kennedys, there he was—staring us in the face and forcing us to deal with the painful realization that we had not progressed nearly as far as we thought we had. He made us feel uncomfortable, then guilty for feeling uncomfortable.

I remember my last conversation with Joe, before finals in our sophomore year—the boyish expression on his face as he described his eagerness to go home. He asked if I had time for lunch; I frowned and said no, some errand in the Square. He understood. None of us ever had time for Joe.

A few weeks later I was in California, clerking for the state attorney-general's office. My father called and asked if I'd read the morning paper. "A guy from Harvard was arrested," he said. "Did you know him?" Yes, I did.

As I punch out the painful impressions of that time, my father looks over my shoulder and seems intrigued by the element of betrayal. "This happened at Harvard?" he asks. "Are you saying that the higher we climb, the less united we become?" Maybe that is what I am saying. Or maybe this is personal. Maybe this is just guilt, another confession by another Latino at Harvard. Maybe.

Maybe I just want people to think about what happens when a young man walks a tightrope between two very different worlds. Each has a claim on him. Harvard homeboy. Between the worlds that those two words represent is, perhaps, a barrier that should not be crossed.

From the Editors
Issues and Comments

Is it common to want to appear normal—to fit in—in whatever group we find our-selves? If so, what is wrong with the assimilationist impulse? Can it not be an ad-vantage to be light-skinned enough, and speak English well enough, to "pass"?

Do we all use masks to hide something we feel others will not approve of? Or, if you are a member of a minority group, do you think that with so many who are al-ready alike (namely, white), it is equally common to want to accentuate our differ-ences, to provide some distinguishing feature that separates us from the herd?

Is assimilation in the sense of conscious effort to appear Anglo or "Spanish" con-temptible, a refusal to stand with the underdog, and a form of near-treason?

Why do you think being able to speak a second language, through learning or for-eign travel or residence, is greatly valued in the professional world, and yet one who speaks that language from birth finds this ability devalued?

Suppose you are of indeterminate ethnicity. By parting your hair one way and adopting a certain way of dress and posture, you can appear Latino; another way, Anglo. Which would you choose, and why?

If you are a member of a minority group, how do you feel when a close friend says, "I don't think of you as a . . ."?

Do you think LULAC would have made as much progress in their fight for rights if they had included noncitizens? Do you agree with their tactics? What rights do you think noncitizens should enjoy?

Do you think people who discriminate against a certain Latino would stop if the Latino could present a birth certificate conclusively proving that he or she is Span-ish?

Can *anti*-assimilationist pressures—such as pressures within Latino organizations to be radical—be just as suffocating as those emanating from mainstream society to embrace the dominant culture?

Can Harvard (or any other elite organization) drive a Latino crazy?

What's wrong with being a "scholarship boy/girl"? Are you one?

"Harvard Homeboy" made a public spectacle of José Luiz Razo and provided am-munition for critics of affirmative action. Was it irresponsible journalism—or did it raise legitimate issues? Note that many white youths have run-ins with the police—why is Razo's case any different?

452

Suggested Readings

Barrera, Mario. *Beyond Aztlán: Ethnic Autonomy in Comparative Perspective*. New York: Praeger, 1988.

Chicanas/Chicanos at the Crossroads: Social, Economic, and Political Change, edited by David R. Maciel and Isidro D. Ortiz. Tucson: University of Arizona Press, 1996.

de la Garza, Rodolfo O. *Chicano Elite Perceptions of the Undocumented Worker: An Empirical Analysis*. Working Papers in U.S.-Mexican Studies, no. 31. La Jolla: Center for U.S.-Mexican Studies, University of California, San Diego, 1981.

De Leon, Arnoldo. *Ethnicity in the Sunbelt: A History of Mexican Americans in Houston*. Houston: University of Houston Press, 1989.

Ethnicity: Theory and Experience, edited by Nathan Glazer and Daniel Moynihan. Cambridge, Mass.: Harvard University Press, 1975.

Fernandez, Carlos A. "La Raza and the Melting Pot: A Comparative Look at Multiethnicity." In *Racially Mixed People in America*, edited by Maria P. P. Root, 126. Newbury Park, Calif.: Sage Publications, 1992.

Garcia, Maria Cristina. *Havana USA: Cuban Exiles and Cuban Americans in South Florida*. Berkeley: University of California Press, 1996.

Garcia, Mario T. "The Californios of San Diego and the Politics of Accommodation." *Aztlán: International Journal of Chicano Studies Research* 6 (Spring 1975): 69–85.

Garcia, Richard A. *Rise of the Mexican American Middle Class: San Antonio, 1929–1941*. College Station: Texas A & M University Press, 1991.

Glazer, Nathan, and Daniel Patrick Moynihan. *Beyond the Melting Pot: The Negroes, Puerto Ricans, Jews, Italians, and Irish of New York City*. Cambridge, Mass.: MIT Press, 1963.

Gonzales, Manuel G. *The Hispanic Elite of the Southwest*. El Paso: Texas Western Press, 1989.

Iguana Dreams: New Latino Fiction, edited by Delia Poey and Virgil Suarez. New York: Harper Perennial, 1992.

Karst, Kenneth L. *Belonging to America: Equal Citizenship and the Constitution*. New Haven: Yale University Press, 1989.

Latinos and the Political System, edited by F. Chris Garcia. Notre Dame: University of Notre Dame Press, 1988.

Marquez, Benjamin. *LULAC: The Evolution of a Mexican American Political Organization*. Austin: University of Texas Press, 1993.

Olivas, Michael A. "Torching Zozobra: The Problem with Linda Chavez." *Reconstruction* 2, no. 2 (1993): 48–51.

Polinard, Jerry L., Robert D. Wrinkle, and Rodolfo O. de la Garza. "Attitudes of Mexican Americans toward Irregular Mexican Immigration." *International Migration Review* 18 (Fall 1984): 782–99.

Rieff, David. *The Exile: Cuba in the Heart of Miami.* New York: Simon & Schuster, 1993.

Rivera, Rick. *A Fabricated Mexican.* Houston: Arte Publico Press, 1995.

Rodriguez, Richard. "An American Writer." In *The Invention of Ethnicity,* edited by Werner Sollors, 3. New York: Oxford University Press, 1989.

———. *Days of Obligation: An Argument with My Mexican Father.* New York: Viking, 1992.

Sanchez, George J. *Becoming Mexican-American: Ethnicity, Culture and Identity in Chicano Los Angeles, 1900–1945.* New York: Oxford University Press, 1993.

Sollors, Werner. *Beyond Ethnicity: Consent and Dissent in American Culture.* New York: Oxford University Press, 1986.

Vasquez, Richard. *Chicano.* Garden City, N.Y.: Doubleday, 1970.

Villarreal, Carlos. "Culture in Lawmaking: A Chicano Perspective." 24 *University of California at Davis Law Review* 1193 (1991).

Villarreal, Jose Antonio. *Pocho.* New York: Doubleday, 1959.

Villasenor, Victor. *Rain of Gold.* Houston: Arte Publico Press, 1991.

Weyr, Thomas. *Hispanic U.S.A.: Breaking the Melting Pot.* New York: Harper & Row, 1988.

Part IX

Splits and Tensions within the Civil Rights Community

What is the relationship between African Americans and Latinos? Are they friends and allies in the civil rights struggle, marching hand in hand in pursuit of common objectives such as better schools, voting rights, and better civil rights enforcement? Or are they sometimes at each other's throats, battling for the few crumbs such as jobs, political appointments, and social programs that the majority society is prepared to scatter in their direction? Sometimes blacks have opposed immigration, in the belief that Latinos take jobs away from working-class blacks. Other blacks have not welcomed coalition with Latinos, seeing them as Johnnies-come-lately who first let blacks do all the work and then sought to join the civil rights movement after gains had already been made. For their part, Latinos sometimes accuse African Americans of narrow nationalism and a refusal to take seriously the needs of any group other than their own. Part IX addresses these and related issues, including whether it might not be best to get beyond race altogether.

Chapter 65

Origins of Black/Brown Conflict

Bill Piatt

Many Blacks feel that Hispanics are unfairly reaping the benefits of civil rights gains won by Blacks over centuries of struggle. On the other hand, many Hispanics feel their presence and needs have been overlooked in the Black struggle for civil rights. U.S. Senator Joseph Montoya (D-N.M.) verbalized this concern in 1972:

> We are the "invisible minority." While the Black man has made the crying needs of his Ghetto children part of the nation's known history and collective conscience, we remain unseen. . . . Our efforts are fragmented. . . . And so in fragmented disorder we remain impotent; given hand-me-down programs; counted but not taken into account; seen with hindsight but not insight; asked but not listened to; a single brown face in a sea of black and white.[1]

Hispanics note with dismay that there never have been predominantly Hispanic institutions of higher education, nor has there ever been a Hispanic Justice of the Supreme Court of the United States.

Blacks fear being displaced by Hispanics in affirmative action programs. The media feeds this fear with a drumbeat of "Hispanics Soon to be Largest Minority" articles. Members of both groups, themselves the victims of White oppression, seek to vindicate themselves, or perhaps even subconsciously curry White favor by oppressing members of the other group. It is a vicious cycle.

Sometimes the conflict explodes in violence. Miami, for example, has witnessed a horrible series of conflicts between Blacks and Hispanics, resulting, in the 1980s, in four major race riots. Antagonistic relationships between disenfranchised Blacks and a more affluent Cuban American population are seen as the source of virtually every racial confrontation.

The political tension between these groups surfaced again in June 1990. Nelson Mandela visited Miami only to be snubbed by the administration of then Miami mayor, Xavier Suarez. Mayor Suarez and other Cuban-born officials indicated unease with Mandela's leftist leanings and his communist ties. The snub infuriated

Black leaders in the Miami area who view Mandela as an icon in the worldwide struggle for Black liberation.

The tension between Blacks and Hispanics in Miami involves more than political feuding and differences. It has included bullets, rocks, and bottles. In 1989 a Hispanic Miami police officer, William Lozano, shot and killed two Black youths on a motorcycle. Rioting followed the shootings, just before the 1989 Super Bowl. Lozano was convicted, but his conviction was overturned by a Florida appeals court, which found that the threat of another riot in the event of an acquittal tainted the jury's deliberations and prevented Lozano from getting a fair trial. To the surprise of the media, no rioting broke out when the reversal was announced. Two days after the reversal was announced, however, another police shooting resulted in more rioting. On Thursday, June 27, 1991, a Miami police officer shot a Black man who the officer claimed aimed a gun at him. Some witnesses said that the man had thrown down his gun before he was shot. Black youths threw rocks and bottles, breaking windows in a city bus and in a police station, and numerous injuries were reported.

Los Angeles, too, has been the site of tremendous tension between Blacks and Hispanics. In Southgate, Hispanic parents objected to sending their children to a predominantly Black high school. In Compton, Black city officials objected to hiring more Latinos. In numerous schools in the Los Angeles area, groups of African-American and Latino students fought each other repeatedly. The Martin Luther King, Jr./Drew Medical Center in Watts was the scene of intense confrontation between Black and Hispanic county employees over hiring and promotion. Violent confrontations occurred between Blacks and Hispanics at a detention facility in the Los Angeles area.

Following the Los Angeles riots, racial tensions escalated over employment opportunities. In July 1992, a Latino group described an incident in which they claimed Latino laborers were attacked and chased off a construction site by about thirty-five Black men who were objecting to the fact that no Blacks worked there. Racial divisions between Hispanics and Blacks proved to be a problem in other phases of the post-riot rebuilding efforts. Hispanic city councilors protested to Mayor Bradley the composition of the board of "Re-Build L.A.," the post-riot renewal group. The political conflicts drew upon the anger and resentment of some Hispanics who felt that Blacks, westside liberals, and a downtown business community constituted the core of the mayor's support and interest to the exclusion of Latinos.

Washington, D.C., has also witnessed strife between Blacks and Latinos. The increasing verbal tension erupted in physical violence on July 4, 1993. On the nation's birthday, in the nation's capital, Blacks and Latinos brawled in a predominantly Black area of D.C. Economic competition, immigration concerns, language issues, and a whole host of problems seemed to spark the violence. On January 26, 1994, the owner of two Black-oriented radio stations in D.C., Kathy Hughes, complained that Hispanics have "taken over" parts of Washington, D.C. She also complained about overcrowded Hispanic apartments and Hispanic drunk drivers. This is not the first time that Hughes had angered the Hispanic population. After the 1991 disturbances in D.C.'s Mt. Pleasant section, Hughes noted that Mayor Sharon Pratt Kelly had restrained the police because the Mt. Pleasant section had a Hispanic population and "she was not on such good terms with Hispanics."[2] In a February 6, 1993, article in the *Washington Post* entitled "Treatment of D.C. Latinos Called Appalling by Panel," the authors discussed police abuse and denial of rights suffered by Latinos at the hands of Black officials. In a reversal of the Miami police shootings, the May 5, 1991 disturbances in the Mt. Pleasant area erupted after a Black police officer shot and critically injured a Hispanic man.

Variations on the theme of Black/Brown conflict have occurred throughout the country. In 1994, Latinos alleged that racist policies have kept Latinos numbers down at subsidized housing programs run by the city of Chicago, because Blacks were being given the opportunities. In New York, endless examples of cooperation and contention surfaced in recent mayoral elections. In virtually any urban area in the United States, confrontations between Blacks and Hispanics have occurred and continue to occur. Even smaller areas are not immune. In Lubbock, Texas, in 1995, two Hispanics and a White man were convicted of a federal "hate crime" offense after driving around the city shooting Black men with a shotgun. The perpetrators announced they wanted to start a "race war." Not all confrontations rise to the level of a dramatic shooting or riot; most are played out in the schools, workplaces, prisons, and marketplaces.

Even where the confrontations do not rise to a visible level, the attitudes harbored by each group about the other reflect the potential for devastating conflict. In a recent poll of Hispanic residents of Los Angeles conducted by a Spanish-language television station, respondents were asked to identify the group that "Hispanics have most trouble with." Sixty-seven percent of the respondents said Blacks were that group, while only 14 percent identified Anglos. A Louis Harris poll conducted in 1994 found many Blacks and Hispanics agreed with the negative stereotypes of each other. Forty-nine percent of Blacks said Hispanics "tend to have bigger families than they can support." Fifty-one percent of Hispanics agreed with the statement that Blacks "are more likely to commit crimes and violence."

Statements by civic leaders often add to the tensions. Jack Shakely, the president of the California Community Foundation, was quoted publicly as stating that "Latins are very, very prejudiced. The Latino is about as anti-Black as a Southern Baptist in Mississippi."[3]

How Did We Get Here?

Hispanics and Blacks arrived in what is now the United States well before non-Hispanic Europeans did. They have a long history of interaction in the western hemisphere. Like all other Americans, they are here as the result of migration, voluntary and otherwise.

Since the beginning of humankind, people have migrated in search of better living conditions. With the possible exception of a few linear descendants of the first humans who were born in Africa, virtually every human being in every country on the planet is a descendant of someone who moved or was moved to the area where he or she now lives. Even the people to whom we now refer as "Native Americans" were not native. Their ancestors entered what is now the North American continent over a land bridge from Asia somewhere between 60,000 and 40,000 B.C. By the time the Spaniards and Africans had arrived, the Native Americans had developed highly sophisticated governmental systems throughout what are now the Americas. Their achievements included well-developed trade and agriculture practices. The arts, sciences, and medicine flourished. By the time of Columbus's arrival, between 75 and 145 million "Native Americans" lived in the Americas. Somewhere between 7.5 and 18 million of these people resided in what is now the United States and Canada. By comparison, Europe's population at this time was perhaps 60 to 70 million.

Columbus's arrival in 1492 eventually led to the exploration, in 1513, by Juan Ponce de Léon of what is now Florida, although a permanent Spanish colony was not established in that area until 1565. Meanwhile, Cuba had been colonized under the Spaniard Diego Velasquez in 1511. In 1519 an army led by Hernan Cortez left Cuba for the area which is now Mexico. A brutal military campaign resulted in the conquering of the natives and the establishment of Spanish colonial rule in Mexico. From that base, in turn, other Spanish "conquistadores" explored northward into what is now the American Southwest and Midwest. Cortez's conquering entourage included Africans, though it is not certain whether they were free or enslaved. The first record of African slaves in Mexico appeared in 1523. These Africans were brought for the purpose of providing household labor as well as to work in silver mines, the textile industry, fisheries, and in the growing and harvesting of sugar. By the time slavery was abolished in Mexico in 1829, approximately 200,000 slaves had been brought from Africa to Mexico.

Juan de Oñate established what has survived as the oldest continuous European settlement in the southwestern part of the United States at Gabriel de los Españolas, near the town of Española in northern New Mexico. Santa Fe was founded in 1609 and other settlements soon followed in what is now Colorado, Arizona, and Texas. Spain established these settlements with the religious and political goals of spreading the Spanish empire, its tongue and culture, and the Catholic religion.

Africans accompanied and participated in the exploration and settlement process. As historian David Weber has noted: "Despite the enduring myth that 'Spaniards' settled the border lands, it is quite clear that the majority of the pioneers were Mexicans of mixed blood. In New Spain, the three races of mankind, Caucasian, Mongol, and Negro, blended to form an infinite variety of blood strains, and this blending continued as Mexicans settled among aborigines in the Southwest. Thus 'Mestizaje,' or racial mixture, was so common that today the vast majority of all Mexicans are of mixed blood."[4]

It is important to recognize that not only did Africans accompany the Spaniards to the New World, the Spaniards themselves carried African blood. A Muslim army from Africa invaded Spain across the Strait of Gibraltar in 711. By 719 Muslim power was supreme and the Spanish peninsula was held as a dependency of the province of North Africa, a division of the caliphate of Damascus. The caliphate eventually split into a number of independent and mutually hostile Moorish kingdoms. Subsequent Muslim sects from Africa invaded Spain in 1086 (Almoravids) and in 1145 (Almohads). Eventually, Christian kings expelled most of the Moors following a great battle fought on the plains of Toledo in 1212. However, the African Moors were not completely vanquished until 1492. Thus, for most of the seven centuries prior to Spain's arrival in the New World, Africans lived in and ruled Spain, and undoubtedly transmitted some of their blood to the Spanish conquistadores.

The Spaniards developed a nomenclature and a caste system in the New World depending upon place of birth and blood mixture. From the top of the structure reigned the Spaniards, also known as *gachupines* ("those who wear spurs") or as *peninsulares*. Next were the *criollos* (creoles), who were the white descendants of Europeans who had settled in America. The next class consisted of *mestizos,* those whose fathers were Europeans and mothers were natives, followed by *mulattoes,* those of mixed African and European percentage. Below them on the social rank were Africans, and last of all, natives. These categories were enforced by custom and by law. When only one-sixth of African or Indian blood ran in the veins of a colonist, she or he was by Spanish law given the designation *que se tenga por blanco* (white).

Creoles were generally raised in relative affluence. They were afforded privileged positions in the church, army, or the law. Because the mestizos had Spanish blood, they too were allowed a relatively favored life-style. Although often darker in skin color, mulattoes were seen as *gente de razón* ("people of reason") because of their white blood. Natives were generally regarded as the mental equivalent of children.

When the Portuguese settled Brazil they too created a caste system based on blood mixtures. In addition to categorizing mestizos and mulattoes, the Portuguese recognized a *sambo* as a person of mixed Negro and Indian blood. When a person carried mixed Portuguese, Native American, and African blood in unknown proportions, that person was referred to as a *meti.*

The Spaniards were the first but obviously not the only European colonizers in what is now the United States. Beginning with the settlement at Jamestown in 1607, the overwhelming majority of new arrivals to the areas that would become the American colonies were English-speaking Europeans. The result of this European immigration and subsequent conquest of the native populations was devastating. Europeans unleashed barbaric campaigns aimed at eliminating all native peoples. The horror of these campaigns included hanging and burning natives alive in groups of thirteen "in honor" of Christ and the twelve apostles, as was done by the Spanish. American soldiers slaughtered native women, cut off their genitals, and wore them on their hats.

Diseases carried into the New World were also devastating to the indigenous population. The net effect was the entire destruction of some Indian tribes and nations, a catastrophic population decline in the magnitude of 95 to 99 percent of Native Americans, and a total death toll of perhaps as many as 100 million.

Once much of the native population was destroyed or subdued, European colonialists established their own governmental and commercial systems. On the East Coast, English colonies rebelled in 1776, and established the United States of America. From there, the country expanded westward and into the Southwest. While the first Blacks and Hispanics arrived voluntarily in what is now the United States, the growth of the colonies and the later expansion of the nation meant that Africans and

Hispanics would be involuntarily incorporated. Africans were brought as slaves and Hispanics were made part of the country by a conquering military force.

The slave trade ended, by one conservative estimate, with at least 350,000 Africans entering the United States beginning in colonial Virginia in 1619. Many others were shipped to other parts of the New World, and still more died in the process of being captured and transported. The entire process resulted in the deaths of as many as 30 million Africans. Not all slaves remained slaves. Some escaped and fled north, where they were welcomed by various Native American tribes. United States soldiers who arrived in what is now the American West were amazed to find Black Indians—the offspring of these slaves and natives.

In 1836, Texas won its independence from Mexico following a war. In 1845, the United States annexed Texas. The boundaries, however, remained unclear. In 1846 a skirmish occurred between American and Mexican troops on the north bank of the Rio Grande, an area where both Mexico and the United States claimed sovereignty. President James Polk claimed that the United States had been invaded and obtained a congressional declaration of war. Many matters involving U.S.-Texas-Mexico relations, including the location of boundaries, interpretation of factual events, and even the factual events themselves continue to be the subject of heated dispute and disagreement. Contrary to prevailing American legend, for example, Fernando Orozco, a Mexican historian, asserts that the surviving defenders of the Alamo surrendered, were taken prisoner by Mexican forces, and were executed by firing squad on March 7, 1836. In any event, the military victory by the United States over Mexico resulted in the signing of a peace treaty between two nations: the Treaty of Guadalupe Hidalgo. Pursuant to Article VIII of the treaty, those Mexicans who preferred to remain in the territories that would now be part of the United States had the option of either retaining their status as Mexican citizens or becoming citizens of the United States. Those who remained in the territories for more than one year without having declared an intent to retain Mexican citizenship were considered to have elected to become citizens of the United States. Most of the inhabitants thus elected to become United States citizens. They were not granted citizenship until their respective states were admitted into the union. They were not immigrants; the country, instead, had come to them.

Even when these Hispanics sought to claim citizenship and statehood on a par with other peoples who had entered the Union, they ran into opposition. For example, despite many attempts, New Mexico was not admitted as a state until 1912. National commentators repeatedly and successfully urged opposition to granting statehood to a population "who haven't troubled to learn English." New Mexico's population was characterized by one writer as "half-breeds, greasers, outlaws, etc., . . . no more fit to support a proper state government than . . . to turn missionaries." Another asked whether it would be fair to place "the mixed and half-civilized people of New Mexico on a par with the people of Massachusetts and Wisconsin."[5]

Ironically, while the United States forced both Blacks and Hispanics into the Union, it soon sought to try to devise means of purging itself of most of them. From the beginning, involuntary incorporation meant death for many Blacks and Hispanics, and the resentment by Whites of those who survived and remained.

Benjamin Franklin objected to bringing Africans into the United States, asking, "Why increase the Sons of Africa by planting them in America, where we have so fair an opportunity, by excluding all Blacks and Tawneys, of increasing the lovely White and Red?"[6] In a letter to James Monroe of November 19, 1801, Thomas Jefferson objected to the presence of Africans as a "Blot or mixture on that surface" of the United States. Other White leaders, during the early years of the United States, favored the physical removal of Africans from the United States.

Similarly, throughout the history of this country and especially during this century, many have called for the removal of Hispanics. It may come as a shock to some Hispanics to learn that these calls were made by many people, including noted intellectuals, who recognized the presence of African blood in Hispanics and used that as an important indicator of the need to remove them. The best example can be seen in efforts in the 1920s to curtail Mexican immigration.

In 1921 and 1924 Congress passed immigration laws that for the first time placed numerical limits on the admission of European aliens. However, by 1925 race-conscious nativists realized that Mexico had been excluded from the numerical restrictions. Referring to unlimited immigration from Mexico, Madison Grant, one of America's most influential nativists, argued that "it is not logical to limit the number of Europeans while we throw the country open without limitation to Negroes, Indians, and half-breeds."[7] In their campaign for restriction, nativists stressed racial reasons for excluding Mexicans. Again, referring to Mexicans, Princeton economist Robert Foerster, in a study sponsored by the Department of Labor, noted that mestizo, Indian, and Black stock, that is, Mexicans, "do . . . not attain the race value of white stocks and therefore . . . tend to lower the average of the race value of the white population in the United States."[8] Foerster insisted that no rational individual could contend that immigrants from below the Rio Grande were "racially better stock" than Europeans. Therefore, "There would appear to be no valid justification for permitting such persons to continue to enter the United States. We can now, if we desire, recruit our future human seed stock from immigrants of assimilable races, who will also improve our existing hereditary family stock qualities. We can serve and improve our domestic plants and animals, why not our human seed-stock also?"[9] Historian Albert Bushnell Hart predicted that allowing Mexicans into the United States "will plague future generations very much as the South has suffered from the presence of unassimilable Negroes."[10]

Besides fearing a booming Mexican birthrate, nativists feared the possibility of miscegenation. Congressmen John C. Box and Thomas A. Jenkins argued that because Mexicans themselves were the product of intermarriage among Whites, Indians, and Blacks, they harbored a casual attitude toward interracial unions and were likely to mix freely with both Whites and Blacks in the United States. To the congressmen, "Such a situation will make the blood of all three races flow back and forth between them in a distressing process of mongrelization. No other alien race entering America, provides an easier channel for the intermixture than does the mongrel Mexican . . . their presence and intermarriage with both White and Black races . . . create the most insidious and general mixture of White, Indian and Negro blood strains ever produced in America."

Nativist Harry Laughlin warned, "If the time ever comes when men with a small fraction of colored blood can readily find mates among White women, the gates would be thrown open to a final radical race mixture of the whole population." "The perpetuity of the American race," he explained, depended entirely upon the "virtue of American women."[11] Hostility against Mexicans and Mexican Americans, fomented by Laughlin and other nativists, led to the actual deportation of American citizens of Mexican American origin during the Depression.

Of course, not all Blacks and Hispanics were involuntary arrivals in the United States. Even now, voluntary immigration, while higher among Hispanics, still accounts for a significant portion of the increase in the Black population in the United States. According to the Census Bureau, one-sixth of the increase in the Black population from 1980 to 1982 resulted from immigration. Among Hispanics, more than half of the increase during this time period occurred as the result of immigration.

It is the dramatic increase in the Hispanic population due to immigration that has led to the projections that Hispanics will soon overtake Blacks as the largest minority group in the country. By 1994, Hispanics outnumbered Blacks in four of the ten largest cities in the United States (Los Angeles, Houston, Phoenix, San Antonio) and were poised to overtake the Black population in the largest city, New York. These numbers led to the projections that the Latino population will surpass that of African Americans sometime around the year 2005.

How then did Hispanics and Blacks get here? They got here the hard way. They were placed in chains, loaded onto ships, hauled across an ocean, and turned out onto plantations. They were conquered, subjugated, and incorporated into a society that needed their labor and resented their presence. They arrived on the East Coast and in the South. They were in the Southwest and West when the Whites arrived. Now, many more of them arrive with the hope shared by all other Americans for a better life for themselves and their children. They meet each other, in increasing numbers, in urban areas throughout the nation. For the first time in hundreds of years they once again share their living and work arrangements. In the process, they are doing what White nativists feared the most: they are mixing their blood with each other, and with Whites.

NOTES

1. 118 Cong. Rec. S 26664 (1972) (statement of Sen. Montoya).

2. Howard Kurtz, "Hughes Remarks Anger Hispanics," *Washington Post,* Feb. 22, 1994, at D1.

3. Karen Bates, "Perspectives on Race Relations: Don't Muzzle the Messenger," *Los Angeles Times,* July 18, 1993, Op. Sec., at 5.

4. *Foreigners in Their Native Land: Historical Roots of the Mexican Americans* 33 (David J. Weber, ed., 1973), cited in Juan Perea, "Los Olvidados: On the Making of Invisible People," 70 *N.Y.U. L. Rev.* 965, n.52 (1995).

5. W. Beck, *New Mexico: A History of Four Centuries* (1962), at 231.

6. Benjamin Franklin, "Observations Concerning the Increase of Mankind, Peopling of Countries, etc." (1751), cited in Perea, at 34.

7. Mark Reisler, *By the Sweat of Their Brow* (1976), at 152.
8. Reisler, at 153.
9. *Id.*
10. *Id.*
11. *Id.*

Chapter 66

Beyond Black/White
The Racisms of Our Time

Elizabeth Martínez

By Way of Introduction

Let me begin by admitting that I have an axe to grind. A bell to toll, a *grito* to shout, a banner to wave. The banner was fashioned during ten years in the Black civil rights-human rights movement followed by ten years in the Chicano *movimiento*. Those years taught that liberation has similar meanings in both histories: an end to racist oppression, the birth of collective self-respect, and a dream of social justice. Those years taught that alliances among progressive people of color can and must help realize the dream.

Such alliances require a knowledge and wisdom that we have yet to attain. For the present, it remains painful to see how divide-and-conquer strategies succeed among our peoples. It is painful to see how prejudice, resentment, petty competitiveness, and sheer ignorance fester. It is positively pitiful to see how often we echo Anglo stereotypes about one another.

All this suggests that we urgently need some fresh and fearless thinking about racism at this moment in history. Fresh thinking might begin with analyzing the strong tendency among Americans to frame racial issues in strictly Black-white terms. Do such terms make sense when changing demographics point to a U.S. population that will be 32 percent Latino, Asian/Pacific American, and Native American—that is, neither Black nor white—by the year 2050? Not to mention the increasing numbers of mixed people who incorporate two, three, or more "races" or nationalities? Don't we need to imagine multiple forms of racism rather than a single, Black-white model?

Practical questions related to the fight against racism also arise. Doesn't the exclusively Black-white framework discourage perception of common interests among people of color—primarily in the working class—and thus sustain White Supremacy? Doesn't the view of institutionalized racism as a problem experienced only

Social Justice Vol. 20, Nos. 1–2: 22–34 (1993). Copyright © by *Social Justice*. Reprinted by permission of *Social Justice* magazine.

by Black people isolate them from potential allies? Doesn't the Black-white definition encourage a tendency often found among people of color to spend too much energy understanding our lives in relation to Whiteness, obsessing about what the White will think? That tendency is inevitable in some ways: the locus of power over our lives has long been white (although big shifts have recently taken place in the color of capital) and the oppressed have always survived by becoming experts on the oppressor's ways. But that can become a prison of sorts, a trap of compulsive vigilance. Let us liberate ourselves, then, from the tunnel vision of Whiteness and behold the colors around us!

To criticize the Black-white framework is not simply a resentful demand from other people of color for equal sympathy, equal funding, equal clout, equal patronage. It is not simply us-too resentment at being ignored or minimized. It is not just another round of mindless competition in the victimhood tournament. Too often we make the categories of race, class, gender, sexuality, age, physical condition, etc., contend for the title of "most oppressed." Within "race," various population groups then compete for that top spot. Instead, we need to understand that various forms and histories of oppression exist. We need to recognize that they include differences in extent and intensity. Yet pursuing some hierarchy of competing oppressions leads us down dead-end streets where we will never find the linkage between oppressions or how to overcome them.

The goal in reexamining the Black-white definition is to find an effective strategy for vanquishing an evil that has expanded rather than diminished in recent years. Three recent developments come to mind. First is the worldwide economic recession in which the increasingly grim struggle for sheer survival encourages the scapegoating of working-class people—especially immigrants, especially those of color—by other working-class people. This has become so widespread in the West that a Klan cross-burning in London's Trafalgar Square or on Paris's Champs Élysée doesn't seem hard to imagine. The globalization of racism is mounting rapidly.

Second, and relatedly, the reorganization of the international division of labor continues, with changing demands for workers that are affecting demographics everywhere. History tells us of the close relationship between capital's need for labor and racism. If that relationship changes, so may the nature of racism.

Finally, in the U.S., we have passed through a dozen years of powerful reaction against the civil-rights agenda set in the 1960s. This has combined with the recession's effects and other socioeconomic developments to make people go into a defensive, hunkering-down mode, each community on its own, at a time when we need more rather than less solidarity. Acts of racist violence now occur in communities that never saw them before (although they always could have happened). An intensification of racism is upon us.

We see it in the anti-immigrant emotions being whipped up and new divisions based on racism and nativism. We see escalating white fears of becoming the minority population, the minority power, after centuries of domination. As U.S. demographics change rapidly, as the "Latinization" of major regions and cities escalates, a cross fire of fears begins to crackle. In that climate the mass media breed both cynical hopelessness and fear. Look only at that October 1992 *Atlantic* magazine cover proclaiming "BLACKS VS. BROWNS: Immigration and the New American Dilemma" for one chilling symptom of an assumed, inevitable hostility.

Today the task of building solidarity among people of color promises to be more necessary and difficult than ever. An exclusively Black-white definition of racism makes our task all the harder. That's the banner that will be raised here: an urgent need for twenty-first-century thinking, which can move us beyond the Black/white framework without negating its central, historical role in the construction of U.S. racism. We do need much more understanding of how racism and its effects developed, not only similarly, but also differently for different peoples according to whether they were victimized by genocide, enslavement, or colonization in various forms.

Greater solidarity among peoples of color must be hammered out, painstakingly. With solidarity a prize could be won even bigger than demolishing racism. The prize could be a U.S. society whose national identity not only ceases to be white, but also advances beyond "equality"—beyond a multiculturalism that gives people of color a respect equal to whites. Toni Morrison has written eloquently in *Playing in the Dark* of this goal from an Africanist perspective: "American means white, and Africanist people struggle to make the term applicable to themselves with ethnicity and hyphen after hyphen after hyphen. . . . In the scholarship on the formation of an American character [a] . . . major item to be added to the list must be an Africanist presence—decidedly not American, decidedly other" (Morrison, 1992: 47).

We need to dream of replacing the white national identity with an identity grounded in cultures oriented to respect for all forms of life and balance rather than domination as their guiding star. Such cultures, whose roots rest in indigenous, pre-colonial societies of the Americas and Africa, can help define a new U.S. identity unshackled from the capitalist worldview. Still alive today, they color my banner bright.

Let us begin that dialogue about the exclusively Black-white model of racism and its effects with the question: does that definition prevail and, if so, why?

Alas, it does prevail. Major studies of "minorities" up to 1970 rarely contain more than a paragraph on our second largest "minority," Mexican-Americans (Blauner, 1972: 165). In two dozen books of 1960s movement history, I found inadequate treatment of the Black Civil Rights Movement, but almost total silence about the Chicano, Native American, and Asian American movements of those years (Martínez, 1989). Today, not a week goes by without a major media discussion of race and race relations that totally ignores the presence in U.S. society of Native Americans, Latinos, Asian/Pacific Americans, and Arab-Americans.

East Coast–based media and publishers are the worst offenders. Even a progressive magazine like *The Nation* can somehow publish a special issue entitled "The Assault on Equality: Race, Rights, and the New Orthodoxy" (December 9, 1991) containing only two brief phrases relating to people of color other than African-Americans in twenty-seven pages. Outbreaks of Latino unrest or social uprising, such as we saw in the Mt. Pleasant section of Washington, D.C., make little if any dent. New York, that center of ideological influence, somehow remains indifferent to the fact that in 1991, Latinos totaled 24.4 percent of its population while Asians formed 6.9 percent.

Even in California, this most multinational of the states, where Latinos have always been the most numerous population of color, it is not rare for major reports on contemporary racial issues to stay strictly inside the Black-white framework. Journalists in San Francisco, a city almost half Latino or Asian/Pacific-American, can see no need to acknowledge "This article will be about African-Americans only"—which would be quite acceptable—in articles on racial issues. At best we may hear that after-thought construction, "Blacks and other minorities."

Again, momentous events that speak to Latino experience of racist oppression fail to shake the prevailing view. Millions of Americans saw massive Latino participation in the April 1992 Los Angeles uprising on their TV screens. Studies show that, taken as a whole, the most heavily damaged areas of L.A. were 49 percent Latino, and the majority of people arrested were Latino (Pastor, 1993). Yet the mass media and most people have continued to view that event as "a Black riot."

Predominantly Anglo left forces have not been much better than the mainstream and liberals. The most consistently myopic view could be heard from the Communist Party U.S.A., which has seen the African-American experience as the only model of racism. Left groups that adopted the Black Nation thesis rarely analyzed the validity of Chicano nationalism in the Southwest, or advocated giving lands back to the Native Americans, or questioned the "model minority" myth about Asian/Pacific Americans.

A semi-contemptuous indifference toward Latinos—to focus on this one group—has emanated from institutions in the dominant society for decades. Echoing this attitude are many individual Anglos. To cite a handful of personal experiences: Anglos will admit to having made a racist remark or gesture toward an African-American much more quickly than toward a Latino. Or if you bring up some Anglo's racist action toward a Latino, they will change the subject almost instantly to racism toward a Black person. Or they may respond to an account of police brutality toward Latinos with some remark of elusive relevance about Spanish crimes against indigenous people in the Americas.

A stunning ignorance also prevails. Race-relations scholar Robert (Bob) Blauner has rightly noted that:

> Even informed Anglos know almost nothing about La Raza, its historical experience, its present situation. . . . And the average citizen doesn't have the foggiest notion that Chicanos have been lynched in the Southwest and continue to be abused by the police, that an entire population has been exploited economically, dominated politically, and raped culturally (Blauner, 1972: 166).

Above all, there seems to be little comprehension of what it means to suffer total disenfranchisement in the most literal sense. Millions of Latinos, like many Asian/Pacific Americans, lack basic political rights. They are often extremely vulnerable to oppression, and the most intense oppression occurs when people have problems of legal status. This means the borderlands, where vulnerability rests on having formal admission documents or not. Aside from South Africa's pass system, it is hard to imagine any mechanism in modern times so well designed to control, humiliate, and disempower vast numbers of workers than the border and its requirements.

Why the Black-White Framework?

Three of the reasons for the Black-white framework of racial issues seem obvious: numbers, geography, and history. African-Americans have long been the largest population of color in the U.S.; only recently has this begun to change. Also, African-Americans have long been found in sizable numbers in most of the United States, including major cities. On the other hand, Latinos—to focus on this group—are found primarily in the Southwest plus parts of the Northwest and Midwest and they have been (wrongly) perceived as a primarily rural people—therefore of less note.

Historically, it has been only 150 years since the U.S. seized half of Mexico and incorporated those lands and their peoples into this nation. The Black/white relationship, on the other hand, has long been entrenched in the nation's collective memory. White enslavement of Black people together with white genocide against Native Americans provided the original models for racism as it developed here. Slavery and the struggle against it form a central theme in this country's only civil war—a prolonged, momentous conflict—and continuing Black rebellion. Enslaved Africans in the U.S. and African-Americans have created an unmatched history of massive, persistent, dramatic, and infinitely courageous resistance, with individual leaders of worldwide note. They cracked the structure of racism in this country during the first Reconstruction and again during the second, the 1960s Civil Rights Movement, as no other people of color have done.

Interwoven with these historical factors are possible psychological explanations of the Black/white definition. In the eyes of Jefferson and other leaders, Native Americans did not arouse white sexual anxieties or seem a threat to racial purity, as did Blacks. In any case, White Supremacy's fear of Indian resistance had greatly diminished by the late 1800s as a result of relentless genocide accompanied by colonization. Black rebelliousness, on the other hand, remains an inescapable nightmare to the dominant white society. There is also the fact that contemporary Black rebellion has been urban: right in the Man's face, scary.

A relative indifference toward Mexican people developed in Occupied America in the late 1800s. Like the massacre of Indians and enslavement of Africans, the successful colonization of Mexicans in what became the Southwest was key to U.S. economic growth. One would expect to see racist institutions and ideology emerge, and so they did in certain areas. Yet even in places like the Texas borderlands, where whites have historically reviled and abused Latinos, the Mexican presence didn't arouse a high level of white sexual anxiety and other irrational fears. Today Latinos often say Anglo attitudes make them feel they are less hated than dismissed as inconsequential. "There's no Mau-Mau factor," observed a Black friend half-humorously about Latino invisibility.

Of course there may be an emergent Mau-Mau factor, called demographics. Anglo indifference to Latinos may be yielding to a new fear. The white response to anticipation of becoming a minority during one's own lifetime is often panic as well as hatred and those "hordes" at the gate are of colors other than Black. But the new frenzy has yet to show the same fear-stricken face toward Latinos—or Asian/Pacific Americans—as toward African-Americans.

Robert Blauner, an Anglo and one of the few authors on racism to have examined the Black/white framework, looks at these psychological factors as revealed in literature:

> We buy black writers, not only because they can write and have something to say, but because the white racial mind is obsessed with blackness. . . . Mexican-Americans, on the other hand, have been unseen as individuals and as a group. . . . James Baldwin has pointed to the deep mutual involvement of black and white in America. The profound ambivalence, the love-hate relationship, which Baldwin's own work expresses and dissects, does not exist in the racism that comes down on La Raza. . . . Even the racial stereotypes that plague Mexican-Americans tend to lack those positive attributes that mark antiblack fantasies—supersexuality, inborn athletic and musical power, natural rhythm. Mexicans are dirty, lazy, treacherous, thieving bandits—and revolutionaries (Blauner, 1972: 163–64).

(Not that I would want to choose between having Rhythm or Roaches.)

A final reason for the Black/white framework may be found in the general U.S. political culture, which is not only white-dominated, but also embraces an extremely stubborn form of national self-centeredness. This U.S.-centrism has meant that the political culture lacks any global vision other than relations of domination. In particular, the U.S. has consistently demonstrated contempt for Latin America, its people, their languages, and their issues. The U.S. refuses to see itself as one nation sitting on a continent with twenty others whose dominant languages are Spanish and Portuguese. That myopia has surely nurtured the Black/white framework for racism.

The Culture of Color

Color is crucial to understanding the Black/white framework of racial issues. Early in this nation's history, Benjamin Franklin perceived a tri-racial society based on skin color—"the lovely white," black, and "tawny," as Ron Takaki tells us in *Iron Cages*. Echoing this triad, we still have the saying "If you're white, you're all right; if you're Black, get back; if you're brown, stick around." As that old saying indicates, racism is experienced differently by Native Americans, African-Americans, Latinos, and Asian/Pacific Americans. In the case of Latinos, we find them somewhat more likely to be invisibilized—rendered "unseen"—than problematized (with thanks to writer/activist Linda Burnham for that concept). Color explains much of this.

The relatively light skin and "Caucasian" features of many Latinos mean they are less threatening in the eyes of white racism and can even can "pass"—unnoticed, invisible—much more often than African-Americans. Obviously this carries certain advantages in a racist society. Many Latinos would like to pass, work hard to assimilate, and succeed.

Until 1990 the U.S. Census categorized Latinos as "White," and even in that year it generated mass confusion on this issue; today the common term "Non-Hispanic Whites" certainly suggests a view of Latinos as white. At the same time, a 1992 poll of Latinos has shown an unexpectedly strong lack of self-identification as such. More than 90 percent, for example, said they did not belong to any ethnic organizations and less than 13 percent participated in any political activities organized around their national groups.

The term Hispanic (Her Panic, His Panic), whose emergence accompanied the rise of a Latino middle-class in the late 1970s to 1980s, encourages the wannabe whites/don't wannabe Indians. Always the unspoken goal has been to sidestep racist treatment, and who can be criticized for that? But we must also recognize the difference between those whom racism's obsession with color allows to try, and those with no such choice. "Passing" is an option for very few African-Americans. If it is possible for some Latinos to assimilate, one cannot say that of most African-Americans; they can only accommodate.

Latinos themselves buy into the hierarchy of color. Too often we fail to recognize the ways in which we sustain racism ideologically. We do it when we express prejudice against those among us who look *indio,* mulatto, or just Black. We do it when we favor being lighter. Such prejudice dehumanizes fellow human beings, it divides our forces in the struggle for social justice, and must be confronted.

The Devils of Dualism

The issue of color, and the entire Black/white definition, feed on a dualism that shaped the U.S. value system as it developed from the time of this nation's birth. Dualism sees reality as consisting of two irreducible elements, usually oppositional, like: good and evil, mind and body, civilized and savage. A Western, Protestant version of dualism was used by the invaders, colonizers, and enslavers of today's United States to rationalize their actions by stratifying supposed opposites along race and gender lines (e.g., mind is European and male, body is Colored and female). The uses of dualism in relation to racism, along with the Enlightenment impulse to classify for the sake of social "order," have been studied by various scholars of racial theory. One simple example tells a great deal: the U.S. insistence on classifying as Black a child with a single Black ancestor, no matter how "white" that child might otherwise be. If the child is not white, it has to be Black. If not good, then evil. And so forth.

The dread of "race-mixing" as a threat to White Supremacy enshrined dualism. Today we see that "a disdain for mixture haunts and inhibits U.S. culture. Because it does not recognize hybridism, this country's racial framework emphasizes separateness and offers no ground for mutual inclusion," as David Hayes-Bautista and Gregory Rodriguez (1993) put it. I, for one, remember growing up haunted by that crushing word "half-breed," meaning me. It was years before *mestizaje*—mixing—began to suggest to me a cultural wealth rather than a polluted bloodline. U.S. society, the Dean of Denial, still has no use for that idea, still scorns the hybrid as mysteriously "un-American."

Such disdain helps explain why the nature of Latino identity seems to baffle and frustrate so many folk in this country. The dominant culture doesn't sit happy with complex ideas or people, or dialectics of any sort. And the Latino/a must be among the most complex creatures walking this earth, biologically as well as culturally. They originated as a sixteenth-century continentwide mix of at least three "racial" groupings, which led philosopher José Vasconcelos to apply the phrase *la raza cosmica*—the cosmic people, La Raza.

In the sixteenth century they moved north, and a new *mestizaje* took place with Native Americans. The Raza took on still more dimensions with the 1846 U.S. occupation of Mexico and some intermarriage with Anglos. Then, in the early twentieth century, newly arrived Mexicans began to join those descendants of Mexicans already here. The mix continues today, ever more complex, with notable differences between first-, second-, third-, and twentieth-generation people of Mexican descent.

All this means Latinos are *not* an immigrant population and yet they are. On the one hand, they are a colonized people displaced from their ancestral homeland, with roots here that go back centuries. On the other hand, many have come to the U.S. more recently as economic refugees seeking work or as political refugees fleeing war and repression. Politically, the reality is even more dialectical: today's Chicanos were born from a process of colonization in Mexico by whites, then became colonizers themselves in what is today's Southwest, only to be colonized again by other whites!

Such complexity is too much for most Anglos and, let's face it, for some Latinos, too. Noted writer Cherríe Moraga articulates the sense of paradox:

> "*Los Estados Unidos es mi país, pero no es mi patria.*" (It is my land, but not my country.) I cannot flee the United States, my land resides beneath its borders. . . . Chicanos with memory banks like our Indian counterparts recognize that we are a nation within a nation (Moraga, 1993: 18).

We must also remember that the very word "Latino" is a monumental simplification. Chicanos/as, already multifaceted, are only one Latino people. In the U.S., we also have Puerto Ricans, Dominicans, Cubans, Central Americans, Panamanians, South Americans, and so forth. We have a broad range in terms of class status and color (a light-skinned Argentine psychiatrist, for example, has little in common with a dark Mexican tomato picker or a Black Dominican taxi driver).

The eye-opening variety and ambiguity of Latino people and experience led poet Bernice Zamora to write:

> *You insult me*
> *When you say I'm*
> *Schizophrenic.*
> *My divisions are*
> *Infinite.*

Yet dualism prefers a Black/white view in all matters, leaving no room for an in-between color like brown—much less a wildly multicolored, multilingual presence called "Latino." And so, along with being invisibilized by the dominant society, Latinos are homogenized.

The Color of Culture

If there is a culture of color in these racist United States, is it possible we also have a color of culture?

In trying to understand the Black/white construct, one might distinguish between racial oppression (derived from physical appearance, especially skin color) and national minority oppression (derived from cultural differences or nationality). According to these criteria Latinos—like Asian/Pacific Americans—would be victims of national minority rather than racial oppression. Racism itself, then, would indeed be strictly white on Black.

Does the distinction hold? Do Latinos suffer for reasons of culture and nationality, but not for their "race"?

On one hand, cultural difference (especially language) and nationality are indeed used in oppressing a colonized people like Mexicans or those of Mexican descent in the U.S. The right to speak Spanish on the job or in a school playground has been historically denied. A Spanish accent (though not a British or French accent) is a liability in many professional situations. Children are ridiculed at school for bringing Mexican lunches, their names are Anglicized by white teachers, humiliation is daily fare. Later in life, they will be treated as foreigners; citizens will be denied citizen rights and noncitizens will be denied human rights.

Culturally, Latinos are seen as *exotica,* outside the mainstream, alien. They speak a funny language, some say (the most beautiful in the world, others say), and nobody outside the *barrio* can understand their best jokes, their beloved play-on-words, or self-mocking style. This isolation largely results from tactics of self-defense: culture has provided a longstanding survival mechanism for many people of Latino origin in a hostile world. It is a mechanism whose strength has continued to flow, given the proximity of Mexico, Central America, and the Caribbean to the United States. Latino efforts to move from outside to inside have intensified in the last twenty-five years and will continue, but the sense of inhabiting a culturally distinct world remains, especially in newer generations.

Latinos are acknowledged—if at all—in a ghettoized cultural framework: as actors, film makers, musicians, and other kinds of artists; as a growing market with great promise if one caters to its cultural characteristics; perhaps as an "ethnic" electoral force—or, on the negative side, as immigrants who speak a "foreign" language and "swarm" across the border; as urban gangbangers with a culture of their own, *órale* Eddie Olmos! Even when these attitudes are not actively hostile, they are dehumanizing.

Does all this mean Latinos suffer for their culture and nationality, but not for their "race"? If we look at social conditions, at the actual experience of Latinos in the U.S., it makes more sense to conclude that the presence of national minority oppression doesn't signify the absence of racial oppression. It makes more sense to understand "racial" in terms of peoplehood and not only a supposed biology.

Social conditions affirm that combination of national, cultural, and racial oppression. The statistics for Latinos are grim: their national poverty rate (27 percent), high school drop-out rate (36 percent), and child poverty rate (42 percent) are even higher than for African-Americans, according to news reports on the 1990 Census. They are now reported to experience the most discrimination in housing markets of any U.S. population group (Lueck, 1991).

Life-endangering racism is not rare for Latinos in the Southwest, especially near the border, and especially for those who are poor and working class. For decades, Anglos in Texas, Arizona, and California have enslaved, tortured, and murdered Latinos because their victims were nonwhite "foreigners." Hundreds of Mexicans were lynched between 1847 and 1935, if not later.

On a recent visit, San Diego County in California felt to me for Mexicans and Central Americans like Mississippi felt for Blacks in the 1960s. Five years ago, in that county a pair of middle-class white youths spied two young, documented Latinos standing by the roadside; one shot them dead and later explained to the judge that he did it because he "didn't like Mexicans." Such attitudes are even more common in that county today. In urban areas Latinos number high among the victims of Los Angeles Police Department and Sheriff's Department brutality. It's far from chic to be a spic, as poet Gerardo Navarro rhymed it sardonically.

The borderlands remain the locus of the most intense oppression, for that is where Latinos are most vulnerable by virtue of nationality—with or without documents. Agents of the Border Patrol, the largest police force in the U.S., murder Latinos with impunity. Killing Latinos as they try to run back to Mexico, running them down with official vehicles, forcing them into the river to drown—all these seem to be favorite Border Patrol pastimes.

Women are among those most brutally abused at the border; their victimization has only recently attracted public attention. Officials rape and then sometimes murder Latinas trying to cross the border, at will. Latina women contracted in their home countries as housekeepers have been raped on the day of arrival here at a new job; worked fourteen to sixteen hours a day, seven days a week; never paid promised wages; and kept isolated from possible sources of assistance. What happens to young, "illegal" children has included separation from parents and being jailed.

Latino men, women, and children are victimized on the basis of nationality and culture, rendered vulnerable by their lack of documents and scant knowledge of English or of local institutions. More often than not, they are rendered additionally vulnerable by their skin color and other physical features. Nationality then combines with a nonwhite (though not Black) physical appearance to subject them to an oppression that is a form of racism. Even if a nonwhite appearance is lacking, however, nationality and culture create a separate peoplehood as the basis for oppression.

In a land where the national identity is white, nationality and race become interchangeable. We live today with a white definition of citizenship, which generates a racist dynamic. Think about our words, our codes, in the media and conversation. "Immigrants" today means only two things: Mexicans and Central Americans, or Asians. It doesn't mean French or Irish or Serbian people who have come to relocate (a nicer word than "immigrate").

A rigid line cannot be drawn between racial and national oppression when all victims are people of color. Both are racism, and in combination they generate new varieties of racism. All this suggests why we need to understand more than the Black/white model today.

Racism Evolves

Racism evolves; as editor David Goldberg points out in his book *Anatomy of Racism,* it has no single, permanently fixed set of characteristics. New forms are being born today out of global events, in particular from the new international division of labor. He writes:

> all forms of racism may be linked in terms of their exclusionary or inclusionary undertakings. A major historical shift has been from past racist forms defining and fueling expansionist colonial aims and pursuits to contemporary expressions in nationalist terms. Insistence on racial inferiority in the past fed colonial appetites and imperialist self-definition. Racism is taken now to be expressed increasingly in terms of isolationist nationalist self-image, of cultural differentiation tied to custom, tradition, and heritage, and of exclusionary immigration policies, anti-immigrant practices and criminality (Goldberg, 1990: xiv).

The increasing equation of racism with nationalism is spotlighted by the title of Paul Gilroy's provocative book, *There Ain't No Black in the Union Jack.* We need to look at that equation more closely here in the U.S. The challenge is to understand such new developments and to draw strength from our understanding. The challenge is to abandon a dead-end dualism that comprises two White Supremacist inventions: Blackness and Whiteness. The challenge is to extend a dialectical reach.

Black/white are real poles—but not the only poles. To organize against racism, as people in SNCC (the Student Nonviolent Coordinating Committee) used to say, Blackness is necessary but not sufficient. They were thinking of class, as I remember; today we can also think of other colors, other racisms. In doing so, we have to proceed with both boldness and infinite care. Talking race in these United States is an intellectual minefield; for every social observation, one can find three contradictions and four necessary qualifications. Crawling through the complexity, it helps to think: keep your eye on the prize, which is uniting against the monster.

Sitting on the porch of a Puerto Rican friend's beach cottage one warm evening about twenty years ago, my friend Jim Forman asked me the question. We had been working on his book, The Making of Black Revolutionaries, *about the years of fighting for Black civil rights and human rights. As Executive Secretary of SNCC, Jim had faced almost every danger and hardship; somehow he kept on pushing.*

With the surf crashing nearby under a million stars, Jim said: "We're all Black don't you see? African people and Mexican people and Puerto Rican people, we are all Black in the eyes of racism. So we must come together as Black."

I thought to myself: there's sense in that. But Latinos also have their particularities. They don't want to give that up, it has meant survival. So I said nothing because the truth seemed to be somewhere between my thought and his, in a hidden place we had yet to find. Today it seems clearer that Jim's words were true at heart. He spoke not from a fortress looking down, but across borders that must be breached.

REFERENCES

Blauner, Robert. 1972. *Racial Oppression in America*. New York: Harper & Row.

Goldberg, David Theo (ed.). 1990. *Anatomy of Racism*. Minneapolis: University of Minnesota Press.

Hayes-Bautista, David, and Gregory Rodriguez. 1993. "Latinos Are Redefining Notions of Racial Identity." *Los Angeles Times* (January 15).

Lueck, T. J. 1991. "U.S. Study Finds Hispanic Minority Most Often Subject to Victimization." *New York Times* (November 3).

Martínez, Elizabeth. 1989. "A Certain Absence of Color." *Social Justice* 16, no. 4.

Moraga, Cherríe. 1993. *The Last Generation*. Boston: South End Press.

Morrison, Toni. 1992. *Playing in the Dark: Whiteness and the Literary Imagination*. Cambridge: Harvard University Press.

Pastor, Manuel, Jr. 1993. *Latinos and the L.A. Uprising*. Tomás Rivera Center (TRC) Study, Occidental College, California.

Chapter 67

It's Not Just Black and White Anymore

Deborah A. Ramirez

The passage of the Civil Rights Act of 1964 marked the culmination of the African-American struggle for legal equality, ending nearly a century of legislative and judicial decisionmaking that tolerated and, at times, even mandated differential treatment of citizens solely on the basis of skin color. When courts and legislatures first created these remedies, blacks constituted approximately 10 percent of the population, and whites nearly 90 percent. Numerous other ethnic and religious groups suffered from past and present discrimination, but blacks were, for all practical purposes, the only racial minority group of significant size. Since the 1960s, however, three important demographic trends have changed the face of America and its race relations: first, the increasing percentage of persons of color; second, the increasing percentage of persons of color who are not black; and third, the increasing number of persons who consider themselves multiracial. These demographic changes affect existing color-conscious remedies in crucial ways. As the percentage of people of color in the population increases, so too will the "exclusionary" effects of affirmative action on nonminorities. According to the 1990 census, one out of four Americans views himself or herself as a person of color. Given the steady increase between 1960 and 1990, the percentage of people of color is likely to rise further in the next few decades. The increase in self-identified people of color may have important consequences for affirmative action programs and other remedial measures employing racial classifications. While 10 percent of existing slots may have been set aside for people of color in the 1960s, similar programs in the 1990s will set aside closer to 25 percent.

Furthermore, because a growing percentage of the population of color is Latino, Asian, or Native American, rather than black, the potential for interracial conflict over the benefits and burdens of race-conscious measures increases. All this threatens the political viability of race-conscious remedies as we now know them. In addition, the phenomenon of multiracial identity confounds the simplistic notion of race underlying our color-conscious remedial system.

Changed circumstances require a reexamination of our approach to the continuing problems of race, ethnicity, and discrimination. I believe two of the possible options for change—tinkering with existing, government-sponsored affirmative action or, alternatively, eliminating all racial preferences in favor of a colorblind approach—are both unacceptable. In their place, I offer a third alternative, which I call "multicultural empowerment." Multicultural empowerment acknowledges the importance of race, yet penetrates beyond race to identify and incorporate the realities of political, economic, and social problems which cannot be solved through racial preferences. A new paradigm of multicultural empowerment will benefit all groups in the population by acknowledging that race matters without limiting identity to race alone.

"Minority" Is No Longer a Synonym for "African American"

In 1960, blacks constituted 96 percent of the minority population. Today, the phenomenal growth in the Asian and Latino communities has altered the mix of people of color so that blacks now make up only about 50 percent of the population of people of color. Indeed, projections indicate that early in the twenty-first century, Latinos will be the largest group of color in the United States. As a result, affirmative action remedies originally designed to address the legacy of suffering and discrimination experienced by African Americans are increasingly benefiting other people of color. The exclusionary effect of these remedies grows at the same time their historic justification diminishes. Reserving race-conscious remedies for blacks alone may alleviate these political and conceptual problems. But the exclusion of other people of color, in turn, raises the questions whether blacks are uniquely disadvantaged historically and, if so, whether this uniqueness entitles them to exclusive remedies. If blacks are indeed uniquely disadvantaged, does the "lesser" history of discrimination against Latinos and Asians entitle them to a lesser remedy, or no remedy at all? As the number of groups and subgroups included within the concept of "people of color" grows, the risk of conflict between and among those groups escalates. For example, may an institution meet its affirmative action obligations simply by hiring Latinos, or must it also hire a certain percentage of blacks, Native Americans, and Asians?

Multiracial Minorities: Erasing the Premise of a Single Racial Identity

Another demographic trend to consider is the increasing number of Americans who are not solely black, Asian, white, Latino, or Native American. Instead, their heritage represents some combination of these racial and ethnic categories and they identify as multiracial. The emergence and increasing visibility of multiracial Americans is transforming the face of America and forcing lawmakers to reevaluate remedies and programs which rely on simplistic racial classifications. While, at some level, all individuals are racially mixed, many do not know or acknowledge their full racial and ethnic backgrounds. Historically, our multiracial heritage has been concealed by an odd, racist American institution known as the "one-drop rule," which states that even a person with only one drop of black blood must be classified as black. Thus, although many estimate that 75 to 90 percent of the black population is, in fact, multiracial, these individuals are lumped together into a monolithic black category. In contrast, the test used by the Bureau of Indian Affairs for identifying Native Americans who are eligible for certain government benefits is more restrictive. In order to be classified as Native American, an individual must have an Indian "blood quantum" of at least one-fourth.

Though aimed at blacks, the "one-drop rule" incidentally fostered a pervasive American belief that all individuals belong to one racial group or another, but not more than one. As a result, partly out of ignorance, partly out of choice, and partly because of a racist American cultural tradition, most individuals choose not to identify themselves in multiracial terms. Instead, most identify with a single racial group. Accordingly, federal and state data collection agencies, including the United States Census Bureau, compile racial and ethnic statistics on the premise that individuals identify with a single racial and ethnic group. Therefore, the creation of a multiracial category for self-identification would have far-reaching effects on society and the administration of race-conscious remedies.

Increasing Clashes among and between Minority Groups

Johnson v. De Grandy

In *De Grandy*,[1] two separate groups of Latino and black plaintiffs alleged that Florida's Senate and House redistricting plan violated the Voting Rights Act of 1965, unlawfully diluting the strength of blacks and Latinos in the Dade County area. Although the district court found violations of the Act, it was unable to fashion a Senate district remedy to accommodate both black and Latino plaintiffs. According to the court, the remedies for blacks and Latinos were mutually exclusive: The creation of a majority Latino district would dilute black voting strength, and vice versa. Unsure how to balance the competing interests of two distinct and noncohesive minority groups, the court acknowledged that in some cases minority interests would be similar and, therefore, might be aggregated; but it also declared that *De Grandy* was not such a case. The court found that Hispanics and blacks were politically cohesive intraracially, but at odds with each other interracially. Hispanics, heavily Cuban, tended to vote conservative and Republican, while blacks voted mainly liberal and Democratic. Helpless to solve the dilemma, the district court held that no remedy existed for this particular situation. It left the plan undisturbed, reasoning that "these political questions" are best resolved by the legislature.[2]

By essentially relinquishing judicial review of the legislature's gerrymandering decisions affecting two minority groups, the district court implicitly favored the minority group with superior political power even though the Act was clearly intended to empower politically weak groups. Indeed, if the weaker group had the political strength to make its voice heard, it would have obtained its voting district through the legislature and had no need for the courts. Ultimately, the Supreme Court held in *De Grandy* that Florida's 1992 state legislative plan did not violate the Voting Rights Act.[3] Thus the Court never addressed the thorny remedial issue that troubled the district court: When faced with two independent, viable claims, how does one reconcile the distinct and often mutually exclusive remedies advanced by each group?

Lowell High School

Lowell High School, a public magnet school in San Francisco, enjoys a reputation for academic excellence. In response to an NAACP lawsuit alleging racial segregation in the San Francisco public schools, a 1983 consent decree set strict racial and ethnic quotas for all San Francisco schools, including Lowell. Specifically, the decree provided that no single group could constitute more than 40 percent of the school population. The decree divided students into nine racial and ethnic categories: Spanish-surnamed, other white, black, Chinese, Japanese, Korean, Filipino, American Indian, and other nonwhite. Admission to Lowell is based on a combined grade point average and standardized test score. However, the school sets separate cutoff levels for various racial and ethnic groups in order to adhere to the decree's quotas. For example, in 1993, Chinese applicants had to score sixty-six out of a perfect sixty-nine in order to gain admission. Blacks and Spanish-surnamed children qualified with a score of fifty-six. This quota system diminishes the chances of a Chinese-American applicant in three ways. First, the quotas were based on population statistics from 1983, when the Chinese-American population in San Francisco was far lower than in 1993. Second, because the Chinese-American dropout rate is lower than that of other minority groups, fewer admits are needed to maintain a relative balance. Finally, the high academic performance of Chinese-American students necessitates a higher score than that required for other minority students to win admittance. For all these reasons, Chinese leaders in the local civil rights community filed a countersuit against the San Francisco public school system, charging that the consent decree denies their children equal access to education on the basis of race.

The Lowell High School scenario raises two fundamental issues. First, because race-conscious remedies may hurt some minority groups, they may prefer that the government limit its role to attacking discrimination and mandating colorblind decisionmaking. In this sense, proportional representation of various ethnic and racial groups acts as a restrictive ceiling rather than an inclusive floor. Second, the interracial conflict at Lowell exposes the deficiencies of current racial classifications. For admissions purposes, a multiracial person's self-identification has enormous consequences. For example, a Chinese-black student's racial classification may well determine her admission or exclusion. This determination highlights the arbitrariness of monoracial categories and reveals the potential for abuse when the consequences of multiracial individuals' self-identification are great.

Employment Set-Asides: The United States Postal Service

According to a top-ranking postal official, the United States Postal Service hires a disproportionate number of black workers, sometimes at the expense of Hispanics. The Service maintains a voluntary affirmative action plan which uses race as one criterion in evaluating prospective postal employees. In Los Angeles in 1993, blacks greatly outnumbered Latinos in the postal service even though blacks made up a much smaller percentage of the total civilian labor force. The disproportion is even greater in supervisory and managerial ranks. A study by the General Accounting Office of Postal Service employment patterns concluded that, in several major cities, "Hispanics . . . were underrepresented in the USPS workforce in comparison to their number in the nation's civilian labor force."[4]

The Postal Service scenario, like *De Grandy* and Lowell High School, illustrates the potential for interracial conflict whenever members of distinct racial and ethnic groups compete for access to limited remedies and benefits. Traditional race-based classifications and even generic "minority" categories cannot withstand the pressures of escalating conflicts within our increasingly multiracial minority population.

The changing demographics of our population is thus causing the current race-conscious remedial system to implode. Undoubtedly, public and political support will erode as increasing numbers of people of color magnify the exclusionary effects of race-based programs on nonminority groups. Not only will friction increase between minority and nonminority constituencies, but conflicts will also arise among minority groups until we learn to balance their conflicting claims. Finally, as multiracial individuals increase in number and demand recognition, our existing race-conscious framework must consider the viability of a multiracial category, as well as the consequences of allowing a person to self-define race.

Race-conscious remedies must either adapt to changing demographics or perish. I see three possible approaches to reform: First, continue government-sponsored racial preferences and affirmative action programs, but create dispute resolution mechanisms for interracial and ethnic conflict and devise a method for acknowledging multiracial identity; second, embrace a colorblind tradition, flatly prohibiting any distinctions made on the basis of race or ethnicity; third, construct policies that confront problems stemming from race without relying upon racial classifications.

I reject the traditional results-oriented affirmative action paradigm, because I believe racial classifications are no longer appropriate for our multicultural society. They exacerbate racial and ethnic balkanization, fail to acknowledge multiracial identity, and depend upon subjective data processing. The existing classification system also pits ethnic and racial groups against one another, destroying the potential for transracial and ethnic alliances. I also reject the second, process-oriented, colorblind paradigm because it disregards the reality of racial and ethnic discrimination. Although race should not matter, it does. By ignoring race, the colorblind approach fails to square with reality.

The third approach presents a new, more eclectic paradigm. Premised on a principle of nondiscrimination, it rejects the colorblind approach, recognizing that race matters too much to be ignored. However, unlike traditional affirmative action, which focuses exclusively on race, this new paradigm penetrates beyond race to identify the political, economic, and social problems at issue within specific government or institutional programs. Race may contribute to these problems, but race-conscious remedies alone offer insufficient solutions. Thus, this third paradigm establishes a more complex notion of identity, enabling individuals to define themselves by race or other factors that shape their sense of self. I call this new paradigm "multicultural empowerment." Consider four examples of this approach.

Cumulative Voting

De Grandy illustrates the pitfalls of legislatively created voting districts tailored along racial or ethnic lines. Only one representative can win in a single district. Sometimes candidates are groomed for election in a district because they match its racial or ethnic composition. However, as districts become increasingly multiracial, and still only one candidate can win, this race-based politicking engenders conflicts between minority groups. But, if we rethink the wisdom of geographic districting, recognizing that even people in the most polarized racial environments care about more than just a candidate's race, we can avoid the zero-sum game that negated a remedy in *De Grandy*.

Cumulative voting may offer such a solution. Under this scheme, individuals receive as many votes as seats up for election, and may cast as many of their votes as they wish for a single candidate. In other words, voters may "cumulate" their votes to reflect the intensity of their preferences. This proposal maximizes voter choice by reflecting not just preference, but intensity of preference. Second, it acknowledges that race matters without resorting to racial categories, permitting, but not requiring, a voter to cumulate votes to reflect racial or ethnic interests. For example, if black voters wished to ensure election of one black candidate in a race for five seats, they could multiply their electoral impact by five by casting all their votes for that black candidate. If black voters cared more about a candidate's stand on abortion than his race, they could spread their votes to reflect that preference.

Cumulative voting, however, has some formidable shortcomings. In certain elections, such as for the United States House of Representatives, cumulative voting would require a constitutional amendment. Cumulative voting also gives immense importance to voting strategy. For instance, if 20 percent of the electorate cast all five of their votes for a single candidate in a five-seat election, they could ensure his victory. While its ability to measure intensity of preference is the strength of cumulative voting, it is also its weakness, multiplying the political influence of fringe groups and rewarding polarization rather than unity. Third, cumulative voting negates one of the virtues of geographical districting: identification of a local representative from whom to seek constituent services. Finally, if cumulative voting broadens district lines, wealthy candidates who can afford television advertising will have a distinct advantage over "grass roots" candidates limited to door-to-door, local canvassing.

Nonetheless, cumulative voting is an important example of multicultural empowerment. By enabling voters to cast multiple ballots, aggregating or dispersing votes according to issues, cumulative voting constructs an individual preference profile that results from a voter's self-selected priorities, rather than his or her race. It liberates individuals from the constraints of racially drawn districts, promoting multicultural empowerment through enhanced voting power.

Affirmative Peremptory Choices

Multiracial empowerment also offers an affirmative mechanism to enhance all litigants' opportunities to select a jury of their peers. I call this mechanism affirmative peremptory choice. Currently, a litigant may strike for cause potential jurors who demonstrate an inability to consider the case fairly and impartially. If no such showing is made, prospective jurors join the qualified venire and can be removed only by one of the litigant's limited peremptory challenges. She can base a peremptory challenge on anything except the race, gender, ethnicity, and, probably, religion of the juror. But while a litigant can strike prospective jurors she dislikes, she cannot affirmatively include those she prefers. If a black defendant wants at least one black juror to hear her case, no mechanism extends to increase those chances.

I propose allocating a certain number of affirmative peremptory choices litigants could use to include peers within the qualified venire. These affirmative choices would not be assigned by race or ethnicity; rather, the litigant would personally select the characteristics by which to define a jury of her peers. In this sense, affirmative peremptory choices facilitate multicultural empowerment. These affirmative peremptory choices could be exercised for any reason, including race, gender, and religion, without explanation. Once the venire formed, both parties would then exercise their peremptory challenges in accordance with established equal protection principles. No litigant can guarantee inclusion of her selected venire members on the petit jury, but affirmative peremptory choices will increase the odds. Also, since both minority and nonminority litigants choose the criteria upon which to base their selections, affirmative peremptories mark a departure from our current race-based remedial system, signifying a progression toward multicultural empowerment.

A Hypothetical Admissions Plan

Most schools employ some form of affirmative action through admissions policies focused on race and ethnicity. If a school's goal is selecting a student body whose racial and ethnic representation is proportionate to the general population, race-based admissions categories are an indispensable tool. However, if a school's primary aim is diversity, inclusion of disadvantaged students, or education of potential role models for disadvantaged communities, then race and ethnicity may be poor and unnecessary proxies. I propose a plan that replaces race-based affirmative action measures with open-ended application questions that enable students to construct their own profile and highlight the personal qualities with which they self-identify. Such an admissions plan maximizes a school's ability to pinpoint desired qualities efficiently, and simultaneously enhances applicant autonomy through multicultural empowerment.

For example, if an admissions criterion were successful in overcoming personal obstacles, a school's reliance on race and ethnicity might be both over- and underinclusive. Instead, the admissions application might ask: "Are you from a disadvantaged background or have you overcome significant obstacles in your life? If so, please explain." Reliance on personal statements, as opposed to race-based proxies, enables all applicants to provide information not merely about their achievement, but also about their grit, determination, and resourcefulness in attaining that success. However, because race and ethnicity may be insufficient proxies for diversity as well, a school could "affirmatively include individuals from systematically excluded and disadvantaged groups, on all levels of society."[5]

Finally, the proxies of race and ethnicity may disserve a school's goal of providing resources and role models for the disadvantaged groups. Dean Paul Brest and Miranda Oshige maintain that when we educate an isolated individual, no ripples occur; whereas when we educate a member of a disadvantaged community, that individual can then return as a resource and role model, creating a "multiplier effect."[6] However, for the "multiplier effect" to work, the admissions process should identify those applicants, regardless of race or ethnicity, who actively associate with disadvantaged groups.

Community Economic Empowerment

Small businesses fuel economic prosperity and create tremendous job opportunities. However, people of color face pervasive lending discrimination when they set out as entrepreneurs. In response, standard affirmative action proposals have required banks to make a certain percentage of loans to people of color or have set aside a small percentage of state and federal contracts for firms owned by minorities or women. However, one scholar proposes coalitions of broad-based, transracial community organizations to develop targeted inner-city neighborhoods. These organizations would create five major community initiatives to revitalize the local economy.[7]

The first step is establishing small business "incubator" centers to assist business people of color who lack the training and technical expertise to meet loan documentation requirements. Incubators would provide accounting assistance, help in drafting marketing or business plans, and legal advice. In addition, these centers would offer ongoing consultations regarding finance, bookkeeping, and marketing. Second, business mentoring programs would assign successful business professionals as mentors to struggling entrepreneurs. Third, an interest subsidy program for banks lending in designated communities would encourage their assumption of higher risk ventures. Fourth, to bolster available funds, communities should encourage the Small Business Administration to guarantee 80 to 90 percent of the principal lent by participating banks or other financial institutions. Fifth, community organizations can support entrepreneurial startups and expansions with "microloans," small, shortterm loans from a revolving fund.

This model's strength lies in its reliance on the universal principle of community empowerment, advancing the interests of all members of disadvantaged communities, regardless of their race or ethnicity. Because it rejects racial classifications, community empowerment is likely to receive broader political acceptance. More importantly, the Community Development Board can unify community racial and ethnic groups in strategizing development plans and can facilitate transracial coalition building. By encouraging productive interracial dispute resolution, this model unites groups in a common struggle against the larger structural problems facing all small minority businesses.

New Approaches to De Grandy, Lowell High School, and Employment Set-Asides

If we apply the principles of multicultural empowerment to the interracial conflicts in *De Grandy*, Lowell High School, and the Postal Service, we can resolve each without using racial classifications. A federal court could satisfy both Latino and black plaintiffs in *De Grandy* by instituting cumulative voting as a remedy. Cumulative voting would be particularly effective in local elections for school boards, city councils, and the local judiciary.

The Lowell High School litigation presents a more complex problem. If San Francisco's school policy were aimed not at integration, but at maximization of educational quality for all low-income public school students, a voucher system would provide a viable alternative to race-based remedies. A school choice program offers distinct advantages over court-imposed race-based remedies. When properly funded and administered, vouchers provide all parents with more autonomy over their children's education. Because they enable parents to weigh for themselves the importance of diversity, location, and other factors, voucher programs infuse the principles of multicultural empowerment into the educational realm.

Finally, interracial conflicts resulting from employment set-asides or voluntary affirmative action programs do not require race-based remedies. Donald Munro advocates an alternative approach consistent with multicultural empowerment: One answer may be a shift away from race-based preferences altogether, and the adoption of affirmative action based on economic status and class history.[8]

Munro's proposal has several advantages. First, a class-based system of preferences aids all poor people, regardless of race or ethnicity, and thereby facilitates consensus building on civil rights issues and creates solidarity among the disenfranchised. Second, his approach is a cost-effective replacement for existing racial preferences, which may be both over- and underinclusive in terms of disadvantaged status. Third, if the alternative is eliminating affirmative action entirely, Munro's proposal of economic preferences represents a second-best remedial measure for minority groups, many of whose members will continue to qualify for benefits under the new scheme. Because this approach eliminates race and ethnicity as proxies for need, it emphasizes the reality of each individual's identity in furtherance of the goals of multicultural empowerment.

The Limits of Multicultural Empowerment

The multicultural empowerment paradigm does have its limits. I anticipate three major areas in which racial classifications may be unavoidable. First, race may be important when institutions want to achieve integration, proportional representation, or racially or ethnically balanced distribution of benefits. While a multicultural empowerment program may encourage these goals, it cannot assure them. Success may sometimes require a traditional race-based affirmative action scheme. Second, if institutions attempt to solve overtly racial or ethnic problems, minority group membership may be an essential proxy for linguistic or cultural understanding. Third, and most importantly, proven patterns of institutional bias may require racial and ethnic classifications to remedy past identified discrimination against particular groups.

Conclusion

The current system of race-conscious remedies was constructed in the 1960s for a nation that understood itself as black and white. Now, thirty years later, changing demographics have destroyed the black-and-white myth of America. Accordingly, our current color-conscious remedial system must accomplish a task for which it was never designed: balancing competing claims among people of color and finding a place for multiracial identity within the remedial scheme. Far from advocating a single, universal solution, my aim is to provide a framework for constructing future programs that will empower people of color without racial classifications. If America is to succeed as a nation, we must find ways to empower all people in society without pitting people of color against each other or the shrinking white majority.

NOTES

1. 114 S. Ct. 2647 (1994).

2. De Grandy v. Wetherell, 815 F.Supp. 1550, 1569–70, 1574, 1577–80, 1582 (N.D. Fla. 1992).

3. De Grandy, 114 S. Ct. at 2662–63.

4. U.S. General Accounting Office, Hispanic Employment at the U.S. Postal Service (No. B-252924 1993) at 1.

5. Sheila Foster, *Difference and Equality: A Critical Assessment of the Concept of "Diversity."* 1993 Wis. L. Rev. 105, 105.

6. Paul Brest & Miranda Oshige, *Affirmative Action for Whom?* 47 Stan. L. Rev. 855, 868 (1995).

7. Anthony D. Taibi, *Banking, Finance, and Community Empowerment: Structural Economic Theory, Procedural Civil Rights, and Substantive Racial Justice,* 107 Harv. L. Rev. 1465 (1994).

8. Donald Munro, *The Continuing Evolution of Affirmative Action under Title VII: New Directions after the Civil Rights Act of 1991,* 81 Va. L. Rev. (1995).

Chapter 68

Tensions and Differences within the Latino Community

Kevin R. Johnson

Tensions often flare between Latinos of different national origin groups. Recall the scene from *El Norte*,[1] a movie telling the poignant tale of two young refugees from Guatemala. One of the refugees is receiving advice before crossing the U.S.-Mexico border. Fearing arrest by the Border Patrol, he wants at all costs to avoid return to likely persecution in Guatemala. The advice given: tell them you are from Mexico and curse a lot so that they think you are Mexican. This gives an idea how some Latinos view Mexicans. Although only a small example, it suggests tensions between Latinos of different national origin groups.

Ideological and Political Differences

Ideological diversity, not infrequently tied to national origin, is an oft-ignored characteristic of the Latino community. Ideological divides among Latinos are important, in no small part, because they impair the ability to construct and promote a unified position on certain critical questions. Cuban Americans, for example, as a group are more politically conservative than Mexican Americans and Puerto Ricans. This has made it difficult at times to build a cohesive Latino political coalition.

Political differences have concrete impacts on particular issues such as assimilation, which in turn influence positions on language issues. Although Latino activists historically have strongly supported bilingual education programs and questioned the efficacy of forced assimilation, some prominent conservative Latinos, such as Linda Chavez and Richard Rodriguez, decry bilingual education and unequivocally endorse Latino assimilation into the mainstream.

Consider also the issue of immigration. Although virtually all Latinos agree on the need to curb abusive immigration enforcement, opinion is divided on the appropriate levels of legal immigration. Not all Mexican Americans, for example, support high levels of immigration from Mexico. To the contrary, believing that they compete with immigrants in the job market, some Mexican Americans express restrictionist views. Exit polls, for example, indicate that nearly 25 percent of Latino voters cast ballots *for* Proposition 187. Adding to Latino ambivalence on immigration, the Immigration and Naturalization Service has aggressively pursued affirmative action in its hiring for positions along the border, thereby making it a large employer of Mexican Americans and other minorities in some localities.

Cuban American interest in immigration tends to focus on South Florida and reflects the volatile history of U.S.-Cuba relations. The all-important immigration issue for the Cuban American community is how the United States treats persons fleeing Cuba, not how it enforces immigration law along the U.S.-Mexico border. As a leader of a Cuban American activist group in Florida observed, " '[t]he problem here on the East Coast, specifically in South Florida regarding Cuba, is a totally different issue from the Mexican problem on the West Coast.'"[2] President Clinton's announcement in 1995 of an agreement with Cuba to limit the refugee flow from Cuba to the United States received mixed responses from the Cuban American community. While this controversy brewed among the Cuban American community, many Mexican-American advocacy groups expressed concern with the heightened border enforcement efforts pursued along the Mexican border.

Physical Appearance

An infrequently analyzed Latino divide of a wholly different sort involves physical appearance. Research shows that Latinos on the average have different life experiences depending on phenotype. In essence, indigenous appearance correlates generally with lower socioeconomic status. A telling moment at a recent Lat/Crit conference occurred when a speaker asked the audience to consider how light-skinned the Latino law professors in the room were compared to the general Latino population. Physical appearance plays an important role in one's ability and, perhaps, desire to assimilate. To "look Mexican," for example, affects one's life experiences in many different ways. For example, the more "Mexican" a person looks, the more likely that he or she will be questioned by Border Patrol officers in and about the border.

Looked at differently, a significant number of Latinos do not fit the stereotype, which may promote their assimilation. This, in turn, suggests that voluntary adoption of a Latino identity among Latinos, especially offspring of mixed Anglo/Latino marriages, may be more prevalent than for other racial minorities. At the same time, Latinos who "look" Anglo may embrace false hopes of assimilation into the Anglo-Saxon mainstream. This is because Latino identity is not simply an issue of physical appearance but one of ethnicity, language, family, and religion. To be a fully assimilated Anglo may be extremely difficult for a fully-acculturated Latino, even one who has a fair complexion.

Because the social construction of Latino-ness is based on characteristics other than physical appearance, Latino identity differs from those of other racial minorities. Society constructed different races in different ways through different mechanisms for different purposes. Indeed, the, social construction of "race" may vary among different groups of Latinos. Specifically, Mexican Americans in the Southwest appear to have been socially constructed differently than Cuban Americans in South Florida and Puerto Ricans in the urban Northeast. The history of subordination of Mexican Americans differs from other Latinos, such as Puerto Ricans, for example. Although commonalities exist, such as their treatment as "foreigners," they may be "racialized" in different ways and, in effect, may be of different "races."

NOTES

1. *El Norte* (Cinecom International, 1983).
2. John Marelius, *Wilson Courts Cuban Americans,* SAN DIEGO UNION-TRIB., June 18, 1995, at A1.

Chapter 69

A Long-Standing Commitment

Linda Chavez

I am honored to be President Reagan's nominee for the position of staff director of the U.S. Commission on Civil Rights. I have a long-standing commitment to civil rights and to increasing opportunity for hispanics, blacks, and other minorities and for women. Most of my professional career has been spent working in education and in civil rights. I taught remedial English to economically disadvantaged freshmen at the University of Colorado and UCLA. I was a member of the professional staff of the Civil and Constitutional Rights Subcommittee of the House Judiciary Committee responsible for preparing for oversight hearings and for writing committee reports on civil rights enforcement in federal employment, housing, voting rights and programs receiving federal funds. I have been a lobbyist and the director of publication at the American Federation of Teachers, managing the largest staff and budget of any department in our national office. Since March 1982, I have been the assistant to the AFT president responsible for coordinating and supervising the entire professional staff of the AFT, approximately 40 persons, and have final authority over a discretionary budget of some $2 million in the area of travel and printing. I was also briefly a consultant to the President's Reorganization Project on Civil Rights in 1977 and was a special assistant to the Deputy Assistant Secretary of Health, Education, and Welfare for Education Legislation in 1977.

In each of these capacities I have been able to work to expand equal opportunity and to fight against discrimination. In my nearly fifteen-year career, I have never wavered in my commitment to civil rights. My personal beliefs, however, have sometimes led me to take positions on such issues as quotas, busing, and bilingual education that are at variance with the views of some of the organizations represented here today. For that reason I would like briefly to summarize the positions I have taken over the years on these issues and to explain why I believe as I do.

From Statement of Linda Chavez, Nominee for Staff Director, U.S. Commission on Civil Rights. "Presidential Nominations to the Civil Rights Commission," Hearings before the Committee on the Judiciary, United States Senate, 98th Congress, 1st Session, on Nomination of Morris B. Abram, John A. Bunzel, Robert A. Destro, and Linda Chavez to serve on the U.S. Commission of Civil Rights, Washington, D.C. July 13 and 26, 1983, pp. 105–7.

I believe that efforts to recruit qualified minority candidates and women for employment and educational opportunities are crucial to the legitimate goal of reversing past discrimination. However, those efforts cannot include means that would inflict a new burden of discrimination on innocent parties. The imposition of quotas to ensure that minorities or women occupy specified percentages of jobs or positions in schools or other institutions is contrary to the intent and the language of civil rights law and, moreover, flies in the face of the principles of equity and justice.

I am personally committed to the goal of integration and am gratified that fair housing will once again be the focus of congressional attention in bills before this committee. I live in an integrated neighborhood in Washington, Shepherd Park; my children attend D.C. public schools. Like most Americans, however, I have reservations about whether busing for the purpose of desegregation promotes either social harmony—one of the real values of integration—or better education for minority children. The education problems of disadvantaged children are great, but assignment to schools by race does not address those problems and may undermine the consensus for public support of education necessary if we are to begin to solve them.

Children living in the United States who cannot speak English are limited in their access to the full benefits of this society. Equal opportunity for them will be delayed so long as they cannot speak, understand, read and write English. Bilingual education is one method of helping non-English speaking children to learn English; but there are many others, including English immersion and English as a second language programs. No one method is suitable to all children or all occasions. More fundamentally, the federal government ought not to prescribe single pedagogical approaches to any subject. While I have lobbied on behalf of funding for bilingual education programs and while I believe they are a useful tool in teaching limited English proficiency children, I oppose . . . efforts . . . to mandate bilingual education for these children under proposed *Lau* regulations. Both houses of Congress in separate actions also opposed implementation of these proposed regulations, and they were withdrawn by the current Administration.

My differences with some of those testifying today center on how best to implement equal opportunity in employment and education. I sincerely believe that you cannot eliminate a history of discrimination by shifting the burden of discrimination from one group to another. I believe that so long as race determines who will be educated, who will be hired, who will be promoted, and who will be fired, we will have denied the promise of equal opportunity. Blacks, hispanics, women and others who have been victims of discrimination want the chance to compete on an equal footing. In some cases that will require extra training and preparation for those who suffer the effects of past discrimination. Individuals who are attempting to compete and who have overcome overwhelming obstacles such as poverty might be given special consideration for such programs, not because of their race, but because those personal qualities of dedication and hard work in the face of adversity deserve to be rewarded. That is not to say that certain groups are entitled to preferential consideration, however. On the contrary, group entitlements undermine individual achievements. When race, sex, and national origin replace merit in determining who will have access to which educational programs or which jobs, we will be sending a clear message to minorities and women that we have no faith that they are capable of competing. Not now—nearly twenty years after passage of the Civil Rights Act and fifteen years after affirmative action became the policy of the federal government. Perhaps not ever.

I am reminded of a reference to the landmark *Bakke* decision from a book by William Bennett and Terry Eastland called *Counting by Race:*

> To institutionalize low expectations is not to encourage motivation but to dampen it. It is to tell the minority student that less is expected of him—indeed that he is inferior to those of whom more is expected. This, of course, resurrects the doctrine of black inferiority—and the legacy of slavery. It encourages the black student to give up in the face of adversity, to think that he is a loser or that he just cannot make it; and that, if he can make it, it is only through the charity or the payoffs he can extort from the white man. This is not good teaching. And it is not true.

I think that we will have done an enormous disservice to those individual minorities and women who want to and can compete if we insist on preferential treatment. But more than that, I think we discourage young people from making the individual effort needed to succeed on their own merits once discrimination has been eliminated.

I hope as staff director of the Civil Rights Commission to work with the commissioners and the staff to assure that we are doing all that we can as a nation to make the goal of equal opportunity for all a reality. I believe that goal can be achieved by once again focusing the work of the Civil Rights Commission on discrimination—that most invidious barrier to the hopes and aspirations of all Americans.

From the Editors
Issues and Comments

How do divisions within the Latino group compare in intensity to those within the African-American or Asian-American communities?

Why are tensions between Latinos and blacks increasing?

Is the increasing number of people who identify themselves as multiracial a good or a bad thing?

Do you agree with Deborah Ramirez that neither colorblindness nor affirmative action is the answer to society's ills, but that "multicultural empowerment" is? Can you think of a better solution?

If a black supervisor or mayor prefers black workers and associates over brown ones, or vice versa, is that racism? Should it be redressable under the nation's civil rights laws just as it would be if a white supervisor were the one denying employment or a promotion?

Is the system set up so that Latinos, blacks, and Asians are constantly fighting for crumbs rather than confronting the systems of hierarchy and privilege that oppress them all? If so, is a pan-ethnic coalition the answer?

When Latinos and blacks feud, does this just play into the hands of white power, or are there sometimes genuine issues between them?

If one (say, a Latino) has been the victim of discrimination, does that make one more, or less, likely to inflict that evil on another (say, a black)? In other words, does racism "trickle down?" Does victimization predispose, or inoculate against, victimizing others in the same way?

Do blacks and Latinos experience racism at the hands of white society in the same way?

In a colloquy between Jorge Klor de Alva and Cornel West, Klor de Alva says that African Americans are Anglos—their culture more American than American. Is this so? Which group—Latinos, some of whom are light-skinned and can pass for white; or blacks, who have been here a long time and whose music, styles, and literature have influenced mainstream shopping habits and musical tastes—is more Anglo than the other?

Suggested Readings

Blacks, Latinos, and Asians in Urban America: Status and Prospects for Politics and Activism, edited by James Jennings. Westport, Conn.: Praeger, 1994.

Davis, Mike. *City of Quartz: Excavating the Future in Los Angeles*. London: Verso, 1992.

Johnson, James H., and Walter C. Farrel, Jr. "The Fire This Time: The Genesis of the Los Angeles Rebellion of 1992." 71 *North Carolina Law Review* 1403 (1993).

Lemann, Nicholas. "The Other Underclass." *Atlantic Monthly*, December 1991, 96.

Loewen, James. "Levels of Political Mobilization and Racial Bloc Voting among Latinos, Anglos, and African-Americans in New York City." 13 *Chicano Law Review* 38 (1993).

Maharidge, Dale. *The Coming White Minority: California's Eruptions and the Nation's Future*. New York: Times Books, 1996.

McDaniel, Antonio. "The Dynamic Racial Composition of the United States: An American Dilemma Revisited." *Daedalus*, January 1995, 179.

Miles, Jack. "Blacks vs. Browns: African Americans and Latinos." *Atlantic Monthly*, October 1992, 41.

Moran, Rachel F. "Getting a Foot in the Door: The Hispanic Rush for Equal Education Opportunity." 2 *Kansas Journal of Law and Public Policy* 35 (1992).

Oh, Angela E. "Race Relations in Los Angeles: 'Divide and Conquer' Is Alive and Flourishing." 66 *California Law Review* 1647 (1993).

"Our Next Race Question: The Uneasiness between Blacks and Latinos." (Colloquy with Jorge Klor de Alba, Earl Shorris, and Cornel West). *Harpers*, April 1996, 55.

Pastor, Manuel, Jr., Lisa Magana, Amalia Cabezas, and Morgan Appel. *Latinos and the Los Angeles Uprising: The Economic Context*. Claremont, Calif.: Tomás Rivera Center, 1993.

Portes, Alejandro, and Alex Stepick. *City on the Edge: The Transformation of Miami*. Berkeley: University of California Press, 1993.

Rieff, David. *Los Angeles: Capital of the Third World*. New York: Simon & Schuster, 1991.

Torres, Rodolfo D., and ChorSwang Ngin. "Racialized Boundaries, Class Relations, and Cultural Politics: The Asian-American and Latino Experience." In *Culture and Difference: Critical Perspectives on the Bicultural Experience in the United States*, edited by Antonia Darder, 55–69. New York: Bergin & Garvey, 1995.

Part X

Sex, Gender, and Class

Sure I'm a Latino, but I'm Still Different from You—How about It?

The Latino group contains not only men, but women, gays and lesbians, and children. Not all of these stand on the same footing with respect to issues like immigration, social welfare, and civil rights. Many issues that are foremost on the agenda of one subgroup, say Cuban men in Miami, may not be particularly important to Chicano single mothers in California or lesbian Puerto Rican office workers in Queens, New York. Sometimes members of one subgroup accuse others of failing to take seriously issues of concern to them, or of silencing their voices in the name of a false unity. The Latino community struggles to come to terms with "machismo," a kind of exaggerated masculine bravado, and with Marianismo, a syndrome in which women accept undue burdens and suffer in silence. As with many relatively poor communities, spousal abuse and neglect are all too common. The chapters in Part X address these issues.

Chapter 70

Mexican Gender Ideology

Adelaida R. Del Castillo

Traditionally, gender in culture has been assessed through a sex/gender dichotomy in which the former is a biological given and the latter a cultural construction. As such, gender in culture is expressed through individuals who are bearers of prescribed male/female social roles. In the past, gender roles have been identified, described, and explained by anthropologists through the observation of the patterned, recurrent, and typical, contributing to the reification of predictable and fixed gender roles. This approach offers a binary frame of reference, which posits the oppositional (he's strong, she's weak, etc.) as universal in male/female gender-based norms and relegates all other gendered possibilities to the realm of the exceptional, the unexplainable, or the deviant. For although tradition may express expected practices, beliefs, and cultural ideals, it cannot account for cultural flexibility, contradiction, and indeterminacy.

According to gender-based norms, the family in Mexico is hierarchical in structure, asymmetrical in social and gender relations, genealogical in patterns of residence, and loyal to the family in its moral economy.[1] According to the traditional ideal, men have authority over women, the husband has authority over his wife as does the brother over his sister; and while the older have authority over the younger, the father remains the ultimate authority over the household and family matters.

It is significant that Mexico's most distinguished authors and pundits (mostly males) have also had something to say about the character, status, and gender-based norms of the Mexican male and female, thus contributing to the social construction of sex/gender ideology in Mexican society.[2] Their conceptualizations cannot go unnoticed because they are probably more widely read internationally than any other literature of social scientific significance. The most notable of these authors is Nobel Prize laureate Octavio Paz. Through the use of various forms of literary license, Paz offers insights into the character and motives of the *macho* by positing a dialectical relationship between men and women whose relational duality is as "closed" is to

From *Gender and Its Discontinuities in Male/Female Domestic Relations: Mexicans in Cross-Cultural Context* by Adelaida R. Castillo, in CHICANAS/CHICANOS AT THE CROSSROADS: SOCIAL, ECONOMIC AND POLITICAL CHANGE, edited by David R. Maciel and Isidro D. Ortiz. Copyright © 1996 by the Arizona Board of Regents. Reprinted by permission of University of Arizona Press.

"open." "The ideal of manliness is never to 'crack,' never to back down. Those who 'open themselves up' are cowards. . . . Women are inferior beings because, in submitting, they open themselves up. This inferiority is constitutional and resides in their sex, their submissiveness, which is a wound that never heals."[3] For Paz, the sexual encounter itself speaks to a socio-moral asymmetry between the sexes, reified in physiology: "The *macho*, the male . . . rips open . . . the female, who is pure passivity, defenseless against the exterior world."[4] Thus, a woman who transcends passivity is a cultural anomaly representative of gender chaos. Here, also, Paz offers a portrayal of the bad woman, *la mala mujer*, which serves logocentric propositions of unchaste female behavior in a Mexican context. The *mala mujer*, he tells us, is a woman who does not conform to the traditional female ideal and assumes male attributes such as the independence of the macho. Mexican gender ideology, its observations and portrayals, expresses cultural ideals of gender-appropriate behavior which may or may not have correlations in actual behavior.

NOTES

1. Beverly Chiñas, The Isthmus Zapotecs: Women's Roles in Cultural Context (New York: Holt, Rinehart & Winston, 1973); May N. Díaz, Tonalá: Conservatism, Responsibility, and Authority in a Mexican Town (Berkeley: University of California Press, 1966); Larisa A. Lomnitz, Networks and Marginality: Life in a Mexican Shantytown (New York: Academic Press, 1977).

2. Many of these concepts have been based on Mexican psychological and family studies, including the work of María E. Bermúdez, La vida familiar del mexicano (México, D.F.: Antigua Libería Robredo, 1955); Rogelio Díaz-Guerrero, Estudios de la psicología del mexicano (México, D.F.: Editorial F. Trillas, 1967); and Samuel Ramos, Profile of Man and Culture in Mexico (Austin: University of Texas Press, 1934).

3. Octavio Paz, The Labyrinth of Solitude: Life and Thought in Mexico (New York: Grove Press, 1961), 29–30.

4. *Ibid.*, 77.

Chapter 71

Domestic Violence against Latinas by Latino Males

Jenny Rivera

> After about two months he started . . . hitting me again.
> This time I was going to do something, so I told
> Yolanda, my best friend. She said, and I'll never forget it,
> "So what, you think my boyfriend doesn't hit me? That's
> how men are." It was like I was wrong or weak because
> I wanted to do something about it. Last time he got mad
> he threatened me with a knife. That really scared me.[1]

Although the general issue of domestic violence has received tremendous attention, the specific issue of violence inflicted upon Latinas by their spouses and male partners has not been comprehensively examined within the mainstream battered women's movement or elsewhere. This specific issue deserves consideration because differences of gender, race, and national origin shape Latinas' experiences with this form of violence.

Latinas' Experiences and Expressions of Male Violence

Racial and cultural differences are critical in analyzing and responding to the crisis of domestic violence. These differences are not merely cosmetic or superficial, much less mere grounds to support demands for assistance. Differences based on race and culture are both internal[2] and external,[3] and represent primary factors affecting the experiences of violence by women of color. Latinas are best situated to describe the nature of the violence against them by their male partners. The following excerpt reflects some of these feelings of anger, fear, and isolation:

> I have never called the police here because [he] told me that they will deport us if I do.
> I've thought about learning some English, but between work and the kids there is hardly

From "Domestic Violence against Latinas by Latino Males: An Analysis of Race, National Origin, and Gender Differentials." 14 B. C. Third World L.J. 231 (1994). Originally published in the *Boston College Third World Law Journal*. Reprinted by permission.

any time. So I've never really asked anybody for help. Anyway sometimes he goes months without hurting me and I try to forget about it and just work.

Latinas are differently situated from white and black women. They experience vulnerability and helplessness because of a dearth of bilingual and bicultural services from social service providers and shelters. In addition, Latinas may experience cultural isolation. These differences have led one researcher to conclude that Latinas need support services—targeted to their specific needs—to a greater extent than other battered women. Understanding the dynamic interplay of race and ethnicity in Latinas' lives first requires an analysis that focuses on the intersection of Latina experiences and needs.

Stereotypes: "El Macho" and the Sexy Latina

Historically, Latinos have been stereotyped as violent and alien. Latino males are believed to be irrational, reactive, hot-blooded, passionate, and prone to emotional outbursts. "Macho" is the accepted—and expected—single-word description synonymous with Latino men and male culture. For their part, Latinas are presented as both innocent virgins and sexy vixens. Accustomed to a male-centered community, the Latina is constructed as docile and domestic. In order to satisfy her hot-blooded, passionate partner, however, the Latina must also be sensual and sexually responsive. One commentator succinctly summarized these caricatures as they developed through film: "[They] established and repeated other stereotypes, including the violent-tempered but ultimately ineffective Puerto Rican man; the mental inferior; the innocent, but sensual Puerto Rican beauty; and the 'loose', 'hot-blooded mama.'"[4]

Within the Latino community, Latinas' identities are defined by their roles as mothers and wives. By encouraging definitions of Latinas as interconnected with and dependent upon status within a family unit structure, the Latino patriarchy denies Latinas individuality on the basis of gender. For Latinas, cultural norms and myths of national origin intersect with these patriarchal notions of a woman's role and identity. Those within the Latino community expect Latinas to be traditional, and to exist solely within the Latino family structure. A Latina must serve as a daughter, a wife, and a parent, and must place the needs of family members above her own. She is the foundation of the family unit, treasured as a self-sacrificing woman who will always look to the needs of others before her own. The influence of Catholicism throughout Latin America solidifies this image within the community, where Latinas are expected to follow dogma and to be religious, conservative, and traditional in their beliefs. The proliferation of stereotypes, which are integral to institutionalized racism, obstructs the progress and mobility of Latinas. Assumptions about Latinas' intellectual abilities and competence are formed on the basis of stereotypes, and justified by pointing to poor educational attainment statistics. Unless these myths and misconceptions are dispelled, the reality of Latinas as targets of Latino violence will remain unexplored, and Latinas' critical problems will remain unsolved.

Legal Strategies

Many of the strategies and responses to domestic violence evidence a lack of understanding of the needs of Latinas and other women of color. When Latinas are treated differently by law enforcement officials or denied access to domestic violence shelters because of language and cultural differences, or when Latinas do not even take the first step of seeking assistance because there is no place to turn, the domestic violence movement fails.

Legislation

The effectiveness of state and local legislation that criminalizes spousal abuse and marital rape must be evaluated by considering the numerous obstacles that Latinas must surmount in order to exercise their rights to security and protection. First, state law enforcement officers and judicial personnel continue to reflect the Anglo male society. Latinos and bilingual personnel are rarely found within the legal system, and women continue to represent only a small percentage of the police force. Second, the nature of the protection or sanctions set forth in state laws notwithstanding, domestic violence legislation remains susceptible to poor enforcement by police and judicial personnel.

Law Enforcement

Law enforcement officials' failure to respond appropriately to violence against women has received harsh criticism as it affects women and efforts geared toward ending domestic violence. Discussions of appropriate techniques and mechanisms for ensuring women's protection have failed to address Latinas. Instead, the debate has focused on women as a monolithic class with similar patterns of conduct and common concerns. When women of color have been considered, they have been treated without reference to race-specific differences and experiences. The treatment of women of color has focused primarily on their economic status, and has lacked a detailed analysis of the role of race—including the entrenched racism of law enforcement institutions nationally. As a result, the different experiences and realities of women of color are not considered when designing effective guidelines on enforcement in domestic violence situations. This absence creates the risk that strategies aimed at all women will fail to address adequately the needs of Latinas.

Latinos in the United States have had a long, acrimonious history of interaction with local police and federal law enforcement agencies. This history is marked by abuse and violence suffered by the Latino community at the hands of officers and dims the prospects of success of any domestic violence enforcement strategy. For example, Latinas are suspicious of police who have acted in a violent and repressive manner toward the community at large. In addition, a Latina must decide whether to invoke assistance from an outsider who may not look like her, sound like her, speak her language, or share cultural values.

A second factor is the failure of activists to consider the role of race in police response. Officers often fail to make an arrest, minimize the seriousness of the situation, or treat the woman as if she were responsible for the violence. Battered women's activists have criticized male police officers for their sympathetic attitudes toward batterers. But they rarely consider the race of the batterer, which is a relevant factor in the police response to a domestic violence situation. The history of aggression toward Latino males by police officers cannot be ignored, nor can the police's belief that violent behavior is commonplace and acceptable within the Latino community. No definitive research examines the impact of these stereotypes on arrest patterns, yet they are important factors in patterns of arrest for domestic violence.

Against this backdrop, the first issue regarding the impact of Latinas' political status becomes clear: if a Latina decides to go beyond her community and seek assistance from persons already considered representatives of institutional oppression, the community may view her acts as a betrayal. A Latina, therefore, may tolerate abuse rather than call for outside help. This hesitance to seek assistance provides the community with an excuse for ignoring or denying violence against Latinas, as well as for trivializing and resisting Latina activists' efforts to create a community strategy to end the violence.

Second, law enforcement officials may not give adequate consideration to calls received from poor neighborhoods and neighborhoods with significant populations of people of color, believing such work either highly dangerous or unrewarding. Although a misperception, this attitude engenders a sense within the community that seeking police assistance is futile.

The Criminal Justice System

Local prosecutors and judges react differently to domestic violence cases than to other criminal cases. They often treat these cases as inconsequential or private matters, ill suited to state intervention. Gender bias in the courts therefore results in the disparate treatment of domestic violence crimes compared to other crimes of violence.

Numerous obstacles based on language and culture must be removed in order for a Latina to use the criminal justice system effectively and ensure a criminal prosecution against her batterer. First, the shortage of bilingual and bicultural personnel—prosecutors, judges, clerks, and psychologists, all of whom are crucial and can influence the ultimate outcome of a Latina's case—creates a system unprepared to address claims by Latinas. Second, Latinas have limited resources to fill the gaps in available support services to assist them. Third, Latinas face racial and ethnic barriers. Neither white women victims nor white male batterers receive discriminatory treatment on account of their race. Latinas do. Latinas are devalued and dehumanized in this process, having no connection to those who have been assigned to prosecute and adjudicate their complaints. Fourth, the "cultural defense" raised by men in response to prosecution for killing their wives represents another barrier to Latinas.[5] The defendant's theory in each of these cases is that violence against women is normal and sanctioned by the culture.

Such an approach, by requiring legal institutions to consider all relevant factors and to judge the defendant from his or her actual perspective, may initially appear inherently more fair and just. With violence against women, however, a cultural defense serves only to promote violence within the community. Even if violent actions against women are common in a particular culture in certain situations, legitimizing them only reinforces patriarchy, and exposes women to more of the same. It also runs counter to a legal system allegedly founded on the equality of all individuals.

Social Services

Social services, including counseling, assistance in securing entitlements and health coverage, and temporary or permanent housing for women who leave their homes, are especially critical for Latinas, whose access to and utilization of judicial and law enforcement remedies are also limited. Because of linguistic, cultural, and institutional barriers, Latinas have limited access to such services.

A recent study found that Latina shelter residents were the least likely to contact a friend, minister, or social service provider for assistance prior to entering the shelter. It also found that Latinas' actions comported with marital norms, which differed from those of other shelter residents. Specifically, Latinas appear bound by a norm of "loyal motherhood." They tend to get married younger, have larger families, and stay in relationships longer. They are correspondingly poorer, have completed fewer years of formal education, and suffer more extensive periods of abuse than their non-Latino counterparts. Moreover, when Latinas try to enter shelters, many are turned away because they speak little or no English. Indeed, the lack of bilingual and bicultural personnel represents a major barrier to Latinas' access to programs and shelters. Shelters without such personnel insist that they would do a disservice to Latinas by accepting them, because the language barrier would prevent personnel from providing Latinas with adequate services. Latinas are therefore denied access to shelters on the basis of national origin. Unfortunately, the shelter is often the only resource available to Latinas, thus compounding the negative impact of this exclusionary practice.

When accepted into a shelter, Latinas find themselves in foreign and unfamiliar surroundings, because a shelter rarely reflects a Latina's culture and language. For purposes of safety, women are often placed in shelters outside their community, which contributes to Latinas' sense of loneliness and isolation. Without bilingual and bicultural personnel and a familiar community environment, these shelters can provide only the barest, most temporary, services. Insensitivity based on racism or on a lack of knowledge about or exposure to other cultures, by both shelter personnel and other residents, further isolates Latinas and escalates their sense of unwelcomeness.

Nor do shelters facilitate the Latina's return to her own community. Because most lack Spanish-speaking personnel, the Latina cannot develop the skills and strengths necessary to escape the violence permanently and establish a new, independent life.

These shelters currently provide only temporary, short-term services. They can scarcely hope to ameliorate the dependency and disempowerment that brought about the Latina's predicament in the first place. Women of color should be placed at the center of feminist reform movements. The current lack of services available to Latinas reflects the consequences of failing to do so.

Responses

The Latino community has not yet begun to develop a comprehensive strategy to end violence within itself. This failure reflects more than mere oversight. Historically, activists and leaders within the community have confronted racism and national origin discrimination with clear, focused strategies. Moreover, Latinos have vehemently opposed the characterization of those in their community as violent and uneducated. This commitment to equality and civil rights stops short, however, of addressing issues such as "women's rights" that are of specific importance to Latinas. Struggles within the Latino community to recognize the pervasiveness of domestic violence and its impact upon the lives of women and their families must continue. Unfortunately, demands for a community response to the violence have been met with insistence that such issues are private matters that cause division within the community and impair the larger struggle for equality. This approach skirts the real issue: Latinas are physically, emotionally, and psychologically abused on a daily basis by the men who are closest to them. These are not private matters—just as the lack of adequate health care, education, and living wages are not.

The development of strategies to address domestic violence must be grounded in the reality and experiences of all women, recognizing that there may be tensions and conflicts associated with developing reforms. It must be accepted that Latinas face multiple barriers because of their race, national origin, and gender; that this multiple discrimination factors into how Latinas experience and respond to domestic violence; and that institutional racism and patriarchal structures are interrelated in the experience of Latinas. A reform movement that recognizes these realities and experiences will acknowledge the need to work in unison, but only from a strong base. Latino community-based organizations must be strengthened and provided with the financial and political flexibility to develop and establish domestic violence shelters and services. The Latino community must place a high priority on domestic violence initiatives. The lives of women and the well-being of an entire community depend on it.

NOTES

1. Myrna M. Zambrano, Mejor Sola Que Mal Acompanada 140 (1985).
2. Common characteristics of ethnic and racial groups—such as English as a second language—provide an example of internal differences.
3. External differences are demonstrated when the treatment accorded to particular individuals or groups is based on their membership in a racial or ethnic category.

4. Richie Perez, *From Assimilation to Annihilation: Puerto Rican Images in U.S. Films,* 2 CENTRO BULL. 8, 13 (1990).

5. Sarah Eaton & Ariella Hyman, *The Domestic Component of the New York Task Force Report on Women in the Courts: An Evaluation and Assessment of New York City Courts,* 19 FORDHAM URB. L.J. 391, 487 (1992).

Chapter 72

Maternal Power and the Deconstruction of Male Supremacy

Elizabeth M. Iglesias

Although feminism has sometimes aspired to establish the solidarity women seek as we struggle to overcome our common oppressions, feminist theory remains as much a source of conflict and misunderstanding among women as it is a source of solidarity. Thus, while sexual oppression is a common experience for most women, feminist legal struggles have floundered around two major problems that are presented most directly in the lives of straight women of color. The first is heterosexual desire, a problem engendered by the experience of female sexual desire for and emotional dependence on men. The second problem is racial and ethnic solidarity. Indeed, many Black and Third World feminists have been particularly critical of the priority given sexual oppression, claiming that this prioritization reduces feminism to gender essentialism and the specific concerns of middle-class white women.

A genuinely inclusive feminism must join the struggle against racism, cultural imperialism, and economic exploitation. In this chapter, however, I explore the problems of heterosexual desire and racial/ethnic solidarity from a different perspective. More specifically, I approach sexuality as a realm of social interaction where liberation is, indeed, a feminist issue for women of color. My perspective emphasizes the differences that culture, class, and sexual orientation can make in how women experience the struggle for and envision the objective of sexual autonomy. From this perspective, the questions feminists need to ask and answer are these: What would it take to secure every woman's right to heterosexual autonomy? How can women experience and express heterosexual desire without fear of rape, harassment, or other forms of coercion through which men attempt to appropriate our sexuality?

If the ultimate goal is to secure women's sexual autonomy, then part of the struggle is to change the way women and men think about ourselves and each other. However, just as class, culture, and sexual orientation shape how women experience the social meaning of rape, they can also affect how women respond to different images of feminine sexual identity. Understanding the feminist struggle for sexual autonomy

From "Rape, Race, and Representation: The Power of Discourse, Discourses of Power, and the Reconstruction of Heterosexuality." 49 Vand. L. Rev. 869 (1996). Originally published in the *Vanderbilt Law Review*. Reprinted by permission.

as part of a larger struggle to alter the culturally dominant images of race and sexuality highlights women's potential inter-cultural conflicts over the "feminist images" that emerge from this struggle. Nevertheless, while women may not agree on which images are more liberating, a genuinely inclusive feminism will seriously consider these differences in the struggle over the production of alternative images of motherhood and sexuality.

Images of Women: The Political Pathologies of Enacting a Feminine Identity

Feminists have long recognized that the dominant images of women represent us as mother, virgin, or whore. However, the images of mother in Black and Latin culture are very different from those of mother in white American culture. They are also very different from the images of motherhood that circulate in white discourses about Black and Latin mothers. In many of these accounts, the Black and Latin mother's culturally recognized power to direct her children and run her home is translated through the lens of white racism and patriarchal misogyny into the image of the castrating matriarch, thereby reinscribing the delusion that male power depends on female powerlessness. By contrast, Black and Latin culture offer images of motherhood that challenge the idea that men are men only if they control and subordinate women. The interpersonal practices found in the matrifocal extended family of Black and Latin culture offer women a wide variety of psycho-social resources that are simply ignored in the various discourses that portray these families as failed versions of their white, male-headed nuclear counterparts.

Mothers in Matrifocal Perspective: Powerful and Oppressed

The images of mother in Black and Latin culture reflect common elements that are directly attributable to the way motherhood is experienced in both cultures as the central element in a matrifocal network of extended familial relations. Drawing on the key elements of Stanley Kurtz's brilliant re-reading of psychoanalytic theory as applied to Hindu child-rearing practices,[1] I argue that matrifocal extended families have more potential for constructing a subject-to-subject heterosexuality than the male-headed nuclear families that are so popular in white, American patriarchy. These images of motherhood—of maternal power and agency—offer more empowering identities for women, even as the daily experience of extended family interdependence provides the building blocks for developing unappropriating sexual relationships. Motherhood does not have to eliminate effective agency, nor is it necessary for sexual intimacy to include the abdication of sexual autonomy. Motherhood is currently experienced this way because of the legal doctrines, public policies, and cultural narratives through which women's maternal identity and sexual autonomy are socially constructed.

In Latin culture, the image of the mother shares similar characteristics and resonates power: *cualquiera es padre, pero madre solo hay una.*[2] For example, in a fascinating account of the narratives of masculinity and femininity that circulate in Colombia and the Caribbean, Peter Wade writes:

> The most central concept of femininity . . . sees women as a stable force. In the Pacific region, for example, the mother is symbolized as the *guayacan de esquina*, a house corner post made from a very hard and durable tropical wood which supports the whole structure of the house.[3]

Penelope Harvey strikes a similar theme in her ethnographic study of sex and violence in the Southern Peruvian Andes:

> Images of motherhood are strong, positive and pervasive and present women as those who are most able to form close bonds with their children and take responsibility for them and the immediate environment in which they are raised. A woman shows her love for a man by having his children and bringing them up. It is motherhood that confers adult status and motherhood that places women firmly in a world of sexual differentiation and complementary agency.[4]

To be sure, patriarchal relations are embedded in these maternal images of agency and power. They invite women to assume, as mothers, the substantial burdens and personal sacrifices required to provide such stability. The image of mother as a stable force creates a space that diffuses the negative consequences of the man's lack of parental responsibility. Paternal irresponsibility, if not affirmatively condoned by the image of maternal stability and responsibility, is nevertheless rendered less threatening in cases where the mother as a stable force is an available image. Indeed, the conservative hysteria over white feminism, with its emphasis on increasing women's freedom from domestic responsibilities, presupposes that men cannot, will not, or should not assume any significant responsibility for making the home a stable, nurturing environment for children.

The Latin image of maternal strength and reliability suppresses the practices through which women enact an alternative identity of the woman as individual: the Western, capitalist, economic free agent. The positive value associated with this Latin image of mother comes at the expense of individual independence or, more precisely, of individual freedom from the obligation to respond to the needs of children, husbands, and other dependents. Nevertheless, the difference between the Latin images of mother and the dominant ones of the white mother are explained by the fact that lack of individual freedom (even from gendered obligations) is not the same as lack of power, autonomy, or agency. As Penelope Harvey writes of Latin culture in the Peruvian Andes,

> As mothers, women are responsible for the running of the home, and to be worthy of respect a woman must show herself to be hard-working in this regard. Men are not expected to display aptitude or interest in the day-to-day maintenance tasks such as serving food or cooking. This ability in women is thus seen as something worthy of respect. . . . A lively clever woman will represent the interests of her household behind the scenes in informal networks and in the subtle manipulation of the man over whom she has some influence. An ideal woman is quick-witted *(viva)*, hard-working *(trabajadora)*, tender *(carinosa)* and attractive *(simpatica)*—a quality which combines physical and moral attributes. There is no ideal of passive receptive femininity. A bad woman is one

who is not effective because she is lazy *(floja)*, stupid *(sonsa)*, or uses her abilities for anti-social purposes *(mala)*.[5]

Given these narratives, Latin children do not experience the Latin mother's lack of freedom from gendered obligations the same way the white mother appears coded in white feminist and psychoanalytic theory. Put differently, the mother's lack of agency and subjectivity independent from the superior authority of an otherwise absent father is a decidedly white, Anglo image. Indeed, many Latin daughters and sons grow up believing their mothers will have the final way, if not the final word. For example, appealing for paternal intervention in the disciplinary regimens established in the home (matters such as bedtimes, television hours, curfews, and dating) is often deemed futile and likely to backfire. Latin mothers commonly expect to set the rules for their children and expect these rules to be obeyed by their children and enforced by their husbands. Many Latin fathers readily embrace the role of background enforcer and rarely intervene of their own initiative because intervention may invite claims for continued involvement and because the narratives of Latin masculinity discourage intervention in such matters.

The practices through which Latin men enact masculine identities substantially reduce their standing to intervene or countermand the will of Latin mothers in the home. Peter Wade discusses the images of masculinity that circulate in Colombia and the Caribbean, images of *el mujeriego, el hombre parrandero,* and *el buen padre, buen marido,* which call men to fulfill competing expectations. Constructing a powerful or strong masculinity depends largely on achieving a balance among the different value systems embedded in these different masculinities. "The point is, of course, that the two realms are intimately interdependent, since a man's success as party-goer and womanizer is partly dependent on him keeping his mujer principal happy, or failing that, submissive in the domestic realm."[6]

The message is that the strong and vital man gets to have it all because, despite his philandering, he can keep his woman happy. Keeping her happy means satisfying her sexually and providing economic support for her and their children. Thus "the sex he has with his mujer principal is in fact a duty he owes her, rather than an expression of his sexual dominance."[7] An additional reading is that keeping her happy means deferring to and enforcing her authority in the home. From this perspective, male deference and respect for female authority in the home is the quid pro quo for male freedom from the home, a freedom both men and women have some interest in preserving.

Many Latin mothers are further empowered by relations of female solidarity. Like the images of Black mothers, and unlike those of white, middle-class mothers, Latin mothers enjoy the support of other women, thereby increasing their authority and the felt legitimacy of the power they exercise in the home. As Oliva Espin explains:

> Latin women experience a unique combination of power and powerlessness which is characteristic of the culture. The idea that personal problems are best discussed with women is very much part of the Hispanic culture. . . . There is a widespread belief among Latin women of all social classes that most men are undependable and are not

to be trusted. [And yet], many of these women will put up with a man's abuse because having a man around is an important source of a woman's sense of self-worth. Middle-aged and elderly Hispanic women retain important roles in their families even after their sons and daughters are married. Grandmothers are ever present and highly vocal in family affairs. Older women have much more status and power than their white American counterparts, who at this age may be suffering from depression due to what has been called the "empty-nest syndrome."[8]

The important point is that these cultural differences create a setting in which Latin children tend to view maternal power quite differently from the images projected in the psychoanalytic accounts of white motherhood. In sharp contrast to the fear some white men express of being absorbed and infantilized by maternal pampering, Latin boys, like their fathers, are routinely catered to in the home, in part, because Latin images of masculinity make male domestic labor a cultural taboo and, in part, because no Latin mother wants to raise her son to be a wimp.

Cross-cultural analyses of matrifocal kinship relations suggest that strong and positive mother/child bonds are staple features of matrifocal family structures and are formed in relation to both daughters and sons. In Latin culture, this bond is formed through the culturally pervasive practices of celebrating children, indulging their childhood, and protecting their innocence. It is commonplace for Latin children to express deep love and respect for the mothers who raised them. As adults, Latin sons continue to "respect and revere their mothers, even when they may not show much respect for their wives or other women. As adolescents they may have protected their mothers from their fathers' abuse or indifference. As adults they accord their mothers a respect that no other woman deserves, thus following their fathers' steps."[9]

Latin daughters are raised to identify with their mothers. Moreover, while daughters are encouraged and indeed compelled to serve their fathers and brothers, the psycho-social meaning of that service is ambiguously situated at the intersection of two competing discourses. As entitlements of male supremacy, these services reinforce male superiority, but, as evidence of male dependence on female capabilities, the domestic services Latin women provide men are invested with an element of female superiority not conveyed in any accounts of the white family. As a result, the Latin woman often indulges, but she does not expect to depend upon the male whom she is raised to believe is emotionally and psychologically undependable.

Stanley Kurtz offers a conceptual framework for re-examining and revaluing the psycho-cultural impact of numerous practices pervasive in Latin culture. While significant differences mark Hindu and Latin (as well as among Latin) cultures, Latin children in traditional extended families (not disrupted by revolutions, assimilation, or other social upheavals) are raised more like Hindu children than white, American children precisely because they are raised into their families, rather than into the individualistic independence of white children in American culture. Put differently, like similar Hindu practices, Latin child-rearing practices are connected to the cultural emphasis on the family and the child's membership in that group.

In white, Western psychoanalytic theory, the familial interdependence these practices produce is coded as pathological and regressive. As adults, Latin sons and daughters routinely make significant personal sacrifices in order to promote the interests or meet the needs of their parents or other family members. These sacrifices, when interpreted through the lens of American individualism, are often deemed evidence of failed individuation or excessive familial entanglement in the individual's life. One cannot properly understand or evaluate these practices, however, without taking account of the culturally specific normative commitments that define the objectives of maturation and the meaning of family in Latin culture.

Re-valuing the matrifocal extended family is a crucial step in displacing the cultural enshrinement of the nuclear male-headed sexual family in public policies. This displacement is crucial to reforming policies, like welfare eligibility rules, which make it increasingly difficult for single mothers to maintain their families as viable economic units, or legal doctrines, like "the best interests of the child," which are used to punish women for nonmarital sexual relationships. These policies and legal doctrines reflect a general pattern in which state power prefers the male-headed nuclear family and disciplines women who cannot or will not conform to this arrangement. These policies also promote women's continued dependence on individual men and thereby increase women's sexual vulnerability.

The most important objection raised against using the images of maternal power in Black and Latin culture to change the legal regulation of motherhood has been the prevalence of "machismo," particularly in Latin culture. This objection, however, reflects a failure to understand the broader significance of Kurtz's psychoanalytic analysis of the child-rearing practices in matrifocal extended families. In fact, my point is not that Black or Latin culture is any less crippled by the ideology and practices of male supremacy. Rather, it is that male supremacy cannot be so readily explained as inherent in the psycho-dynamics of female mothering precisely because male supremacy thrives in cultures where child-rearing practices are organized differently from the symbiotic one-to-one relationship of the mother and infant. This symbiotic relationship characterizes the traditional nuclear family of white, middle-class suburbia and drives the anti-mother narratives. That an ideology of male supremacy exists in both cultures despite different child-rearing practices is a crucial point for feminists to understand because it suggests that this ideology is not grounded in the mother/infant relationship. A number of insights follow from this realization.

First, that male supremacy has been explained as a defensive response to maternal power, despite the existence of machismo in cultures with very different familial structures, supports the hypothesis that male supremacy does not originate from the practice of female mothering. This observation encourages inquiries along two lines, both of which are likely to produce more fruitful trajectories for promoting women's sexual autonomy. The first is the search for alternative explanations of the psycho-cultural origins of the ideology and practices of male sexual dominance. Once we see the inadequacy of theories that explain male supremacy as a defensive reaction to maternal power, we further the search for alternative explanations. For example, it may be that machismo in Black and Latin culture is a defensive response to the economic, social, and political subordination produced by race discrimination and economic exploitation.

Rejecting the supposed link between maternal power and male supremacy also clears the way for more affirmative narratives of maternal power. These narratives provide the ideological foundation needed to secure the policies and legal doctrines that support child-rearing practices and familial arrangements that do not compel women to depend on men. Protecting motherhood from the socioeconomic imperatives that currently reinforce women's dependence on men is probably the single most important reform needed to reduce many women's sexual vulnerability and increase our sexual autonomy.

Indeed, a fuller understanding of the cultural logic of matrifocality suggests that women's subordination is not so much a product of exclusive female parenting as the social setting in which motherhood is practiced. In the cultural logic of matrifocality, exclusive female parenting is the vehicle through which women acquire and exercise power, construct and enjoy relations of female solidarity, and promote respect for and allegiance to maternal authority. From this perspective, women's autonomy, both as mothers and as sexual subjects, is much more likely to emerge from the "maternal empowerment" trajectory, which advocates reforms designed to ensure women access to the socioeconomic resources they need to raise their children independently of men, if they so choose, than from policies designed to promote gender-neutral parenthood.

Equally important, a clearer understanding of the cultural logic and psychoanalytic impact of matrifocal extended families also suggests that the maternal empowerment reform trajectory may help reconstruct the terms upon which men and women interact as heterosexual desiring subjects. This cross-cultural analysis suggests a very different account of the origin of male supremacist narratives of pornographic masculinity. In this account, fear and resentment toward women and the urge to dominate women are not so much a function of the mother's power as of her powerlessness, both as a mother and as a wife, in the male-dominated nuclear family. When women command real power in the family, maternal authority is respected and cherished. Indeed, from this perspective, rather than being the source of male supremacist ideologies and practices, maternal empowerment is a potential solution because the pornographic attack on feminine sexual beauty, maternal authority, and the devaluation of femininity are means men use to maintain the socioeconomic and coercive relations through which they continue to subordinate and dominate each other.[10]

NOTES

1. Stanley N. Kurtz, ALL THE MOTHERS ARE ONE: HINDU INDIA AND THE CULTURAL RESHAPING OF PSYCHOANALYSIS (1992).

2. Literally translated, this saying reads: "Anybody can be a father, but there is only one mother."

3. Peter Wade, *Man the Hunter: Gender and Violence in Music and Drinking in Columbia,* in SEX AND VIOLENCE: ISSUES IN REPRESENTATION AND EXPERIENCE 115, 118 (Penelope Harvey and Peter Gow eds., 1994).

4. Penelope Harvey, *Domestic Violence in the Peruvian Andes,* in SEX AND VIOLENCE at 73, 74.

5. *Id.* at 74.

6. Wade, in SEX AND VIOLENCE at 123.

7. *Id.* at 122.

8. Oliva M. Espin, *Cultural and Historical Influences on Sexuality in Hispanic/Latin Women: Implications for Psychotherapy,* in PLEASURE AND DANGER: EXPLORING FEMALE SEXUALITY 155 (Carole S. Vance ed., 2d ed., 1985).

9. *Id.* at 157.

10. To be sure, promoting cultural images and familial structures that foster maternal power is only one strategy in a much broader socio-political, legal, and cultural struggle to secure women's sexual autonomy and reduce women's vulnerability to rape. These other strategies address dysfunctions in the social construction of heterosexual desire that are directly related to ways in which female and male sexual identities are dichotomized and commodified for our collective consumption. I examine these issues more fully in the article from which this chapter is drawn.

Chapter 73

What's in a Name?
Retention and Loss of the Maternal Surname

Yvonne M. Cherena Pacheco

"Where is our history?
What are the names washed down the sewer
In the ceptic flood?
I pray to the rain
Give me back my rituals
Give back truth
Return the remnants of my identity
Bathe me in self-discovered knowledge
Identify my ancestors who have existed suppressed
Invoke their spirits with power . . ."
—Sandra Maria Esteves[1]

Consider names, the difficulties which historically have confronted and continue to confront millions of Latino citizens and residents of the United States in their attempts to gain recognition of their complete names, and the impact of the failure of those attempts upon Latinas. Human beings generally receive names within their first days of life. Traditions regarding naming vary considerably from one culture to another, reflecting ancestral, religious, or linguistic customs. In any given state, the traditional naming patterns of the dominant culture or cultures will be reflected in the laws and the official behavior of that state.

The names originally given to a child usually reflect her parentage or lineage, clan membership, place of origin, as well as individual identity. Whatever the tradition within which the child is named, her name serves as the cornerstone of her identity as she grows toward maturity. Naming issues arise when the desire of the individual to be known by a particular name comes into conflict with social practice. Naming issues have a long history in North America, dating to at least colonial times. En-

From "Latino Surnames: Formal and Informal Forces in the United States Affecting the Retention and Use of the Maternal Surname." 18 Marshall L. Rev. 1 (1992). Originally published in the *Thurgood Marshall Law Review*. Reprinted by permission.

slaved Africans routinely were renamed by those who bought them, while Native American names quickly came to be shortened, mispronounced or translated into English or French. With the dominance of Anglo-Saxon culture well established from the beginning of the republic, European immigrants from other traditions had similar experiences of renaming, particularly if they hailed from Southern or Eastern Europe. What all of the victims of these practices had in common was their relative powerlessness, and the desire of those representing the dominant culture to force them to conform.

Very little has changed over the years regarding the value that an individual places on his name. Poet Sandra Maria Esteves seeks the true names of her ancestors in order to be able to name herself as an individual. In recent decades, women inspired by the feminist movement have asserted their right to retain their birth names after marriage, or to resume their use upon divorce or widowhood. At the same time, many couples have opted to combine their surnames after marriage to form a new, hyphenated version which is then borne by their offspring.

In the case of Latinos, the principal naming conflict centers on the use or non-use of a two-part surname representing the lineages of both parents. More precisely, the question is whether, as a practical matter, an individual living in the United States who has been named in the traditional Latin American style can retain both parental surnames, or must submit to use of the father's surname only. This issue has a special poignance for the Latina, because the application of the Anglo-cultural tradition to a traditional Latin surname eradicates the maternal or female identity of the individual.

Latin American Naming Tradition: The Form and the Substance

The Latina's name is made up of one or more given names together with a two-part surname (consisting of a patronymic and a matronymic), which is more than the traditional Anglo-American first name, middle name, and single surname combination. For the Latina, both parts of the two-part surname are considered essential in making her entire family name. The involuntary dropping of either part constitutes an unwanted name change and gives rise to the Latina's name issue. Many American individuals of all traditions prefer to use their complete name—the one given at birth, or during christening or formal naming. Among these are perhaps millions of Latinas in the United States, including both those who came to the United States from Latin America (i.e., Mexico, Central America, South America, and the Caribbean) and those born on the mainland.

The Latina positions both the paternal name and maternal name, respectively, in the place generally reserved in the North American custom for the single last name. For example, if an individual's name is Maria Iris Rivera Sancho then the name is ordered as follows:

(1) Maria, the given name or *nombre;*
(2) Iris, the *segundo nombre* or "second given name," not considered a middle name;

(3) Rivera, her paternal surname, known as the *primer apellido,* which translates as the "first last name"; and

(4) Sancho, the maternal surname, known as the *segundo apellido,* the "second last name."

The positioning indicates that Maria Iris is the daughter of a father named Rivera and a mother named Sancho. Sometimes the letter 'y' (as the word 'and') separates the *primer apellido* and the *segundo apellido,* e.g. Maria Iris Rivera y Sancho. However, each surname is considered part of the family name; one is not subordinate to the other. The position of the *primer* or *segundo apellido* indicates the paternal and the maternal order respectively. The Latina's birth name is made up of two names; her complete surname is used as a unit. In fact, until about 150 years ago, Spanish women did not take their husband's name after marriage. Today some of them retain both the mother's and the father's *apellidos.* For example, Sra. Leticia Maria Riosvega de Borrero's name indicates: her *primer nombre* is Leticia, *segundo nombre* Maria; her father's surname is Rios; her mother's surname is Vega; and she is married to one named Borrero.

It is not a novelty for an individual to use both paternal and maternal surnames nor is it an attribute solely belonging to one class, ethnic or racial group. In fact, by far the dominant custom throughout all of Latin America and Spain is to use both paternal and maternal surnames. For the Latina it is important culturally that both surnames be used; they represent both families to which the individual belongs. As the family unit is central to the identity of the individual so, too, is the name that each family unit bears. By custom, the use of both surnames is essential to self-identification. The two names appear in all official documents such as birth certificates, baptismal certificates, marriage licenses, drivers' licenses, death certificates, professional licenses, etc. Not all Latinos may be interested in using both paternal and maternal surnames but my purpose is to give that choice to all Latinos.

Involuntary Name Changes: How and Why They Occur

The Latino who emigrates to the United States finds himself caught between these two naming traditions—desiring to keep his Latino tradition but facing the opposition of a different dominant practice.

Although tradition or custom is not necessarily law, the custom of using the first, middle, and surname in the United States inhibits other name usage practices or at best ignores them. The customary becomes the familiar, the expected, the appropriate, and the legitimate, even it if does not take on the full force of law. No law in the United States restricts the use of surnames or precludes the Latina's right to cling to her full, original surname. Likewise, no official policy or other formal directive consciously sheds the *segundo apellido* or requires a Latina to depart from full adherence to familial traditions. Thus, if it is customary in the United States to have one surname, then the practice is to look for one surname for identifying an individual. When a Latino chooses to use the family name, which in the United States would be considered two surnames, the situation becomes problematic.

This pattern of legislative "benign neglect" does not mean that the United States is at all hospitable to the Latino naming tradition. In fact, cultural supremacy, bureaucratic laziness, racism and simple ignorance combine to make it exceptionally difficult for the Latino, as a practical matter, to obtain recognition for both last names. The United States' tradition of one surname is so well-entrenched that any deviation from it is immediately deemed awkward and odd, and subtle—but pervasive and quite powerful—forces will operate to change it. Actions by governmental units, by large and small private business organizations, by individual people—and ultimately by the Latina herself—will tend to drop the matronymic half of the surname, squeezing the Latina into the Anglo-Saxon mold.

How does American society accomplish this? A variety of mechanisms operate simultaneously; even though no one of them in isolation could enforce the transformation, together they become nearly inescapable. Federal and state governments prefer using a single surname, despite lack of any statutory proscription against more. Administrative personnel may view those with multi-part surnames as un-American. Government forms may have insufficient space to register a complete Latino name, and the instructions and format of the form may suggest that only a single word should be entered into the place for "last name." Teachers may regularly refer to students by only a single last name. Military officers may likewise assume that a single word can suffice for a Latino soldier or sailor, as for an Anglo-Saxon, and the second last name is omitted. On alphabetical lists, on court papers, on government notices, the Latino can regularly anticipate inclusion of only the first half of his surname. No official rules require the shortening, but every Latino person in the United States has experienced it, and many have now grudgingly accepted the official system.

Even more than governmental action, the practices of private business and individuals reinforce the social norm of using a single last name. Telephone companies, banks, and credit agencies all act as if they expect every customer to adhere to the Anglo-Saxon style. If anyone objects, he could probably succeed, but many will not "rock the boat" when confronting a large, powerful organization. In applying for a job or for an apartment, a special incentive presses to conform. To the Latino, it may seem more prudent to go along with the popular culture, to acquiesce in the name change, even at the cost of cultural identity.

The Impact of Involuntary Name Changes

Although they overlap, three distinct types of problems are associated with the unwanted deletion of the second last name. Sometimes, these phenomena can be comical. But more often than not, they are serious and traumatic with long-range effects in economic, cultural, and personal terms.

Costs of Being Different

Costs are associated with simply being different, being reminded—every time some-one says or writes your name—that your heritage derives from a culture unlike that of the numerically and economically dominant groups in the country. Three separate sub-themes emerge for the Latina.

First is the economic, social, and political disadvantage in perpetuating an iden-tity at odds with the North American norm. Because peoples of British background were the principal early colonizers of the United States, a prejudice developed in fa-voring Americans with English-rooted names. Job opportunities benefited those with names that could be identified as English, and early immigrants, such as the Irish, the Italians, and the Eastern Europeans, felt the effects of discrimination in the struggle for employment. Eventually this type of discrimination lessened within the second and third generations as they have grown more homogeneous, especially socioeco-nomically. Although many immigrants kept their family names, significant numbers succumbed to the pressures of a name change.

Second, costs are associated with going in the opposite direction: attempting to conform to an Anglo-American society, assimilate into its practices, and adopt its naming patterns. When an individual simplifies or streamlines the family name, she may do so after a thorough assessment of the effects it will have on the individual and her culture. This assessment may include focusing on the origins of the family name, how the individual may see herself connected to that name, what impact changing the name or not being able to continue to use the name may have on the individual, and how the individual sees herself and therefore how she chooses to name herself.

Third, use of one's own name—and the misuse, modification, or appropriation by others—speaks volumes about "control" and "empowerment" in other aspects of one's life. An individual needs to rely on his sense of self and have the privacy that brings self-control and self-empowerment. For the individual to decide for himself what he should be named is a matter of privacy. The right as an individual to one's privacy is addressed in the term "personhood." The principle behind the term personhood, which was used by Professor Paul Freund, employs a rationale used in Justice Brandeis's dissenting opinion in *Olmstead v. United States.*[2] Brandeis points out that the makers of the Constitution were favorable to the notion of the "pursuit of happiness." They recognized the significance of man's spiritual nature, of his feelings and of his intellect. They knew that only a part of the pain, pleasure, and satisfaction of life are to be found in material things. They sought to protect Americans in their beliefs, their thoughts, their emotions, and their sensations. They conferred, as against the Government, the right to be let alone—the most comprehensive of rights and the right most valued by civilized men. To protect that right, every unjustifiable intrusion by the Government upon the privacy of the in-dividual, whatever the means employed, must be deemed a violation of the Fourth Amendment.

Costs of Not Being Accepted

The Latino and the Latino naming tradition are not merely treated as being "different" by the dominant society; they are treated as "inferior," subject to capricious, unwanted alteration to fit the expectations of mainstream society. Both racism and sexism play a role in this operation. Most members of the dominant society may respond that they are not racists, because they have never intended to treat those from the non-white races discriminatorily. However, Americans who share a common historical and cultural heritage harbor many ideas, attitudes, and beliefs that attach significance to an individual's race and induce negative feelings and opinions about non-whites.[3] Any unconscious racism or negative feelings towards Latinos may affect how members of the dominant society view the Latino name and whether or not they may "unconsciously" modify the name. By the same token, a society that has valued the male name more than the female is asked to value the way in which both the Latino and Latina prefer to use their name. In addition to the Latina, the Latino becomes a victim of sexism, when he is denied the usage of his maternal surname.

Costs of Being Compelled to Conform—Invisibility

Unfortunately, not much has been written about the plight of the women and men who have not been able to completely use the names which identify them. They have been made invisible. In Ralph Ellison's *Invisible Man,* the protagonist reflects:

> It is sometimes advantageous to be unseen, although it is most often rather wearing on the nerves. Then too, you're constantly being bumped against by those of poor vision. Or again, you often doubt if you really exist. You wonder whether you aren't simply a phantom in other people's minds. . . . It's when you feel like this that, out of resentment, you begin to bump people back.[4]

Not having her complete name recognized is part of a greater reality of not being seen, for the Latina struggles with a denial of her identity that goes far beyond the loss of a name. The Latina remains invisible each time her life experience and her input are considered inferior, when her diversity and culture are not welcomed, and when she is discriminated against because she does not belong and her opinion does not matter.

It is never easy to attempt to reform a social practice that is as widespread, as subtle, and as basic as the dominant United States practice of insisting upon single-word surnames. This form of anti-Latino repression is so elusive and insidious that few people are even aware of it. This story boasts no overt villain, no blatantly racist government actions, no xenophobic community leaders attempting to resist Latino surnames, not even very many scrupulous clerks and form-filers who object to anything out of the ordinary. Instead, the Latina naming issue presents an unusually subtle phenomenon, which will have to be dealt with through concerted action by three different sets of actions.

First, the government will have to play a role. No name-purist statutes remain on the books, but official actions are still too unfriendly to the Latino tradition. Perhaps a persuasive argument for freedom in naming is that the government has other means of identifying an individual—i.e., use of social security number and the date and place of birth, together with the use of the family name. Additionally, if the use of a complete family name causes fear of an administrative nightmare, then that argument can be countered with the upgrading of data through the use of computer rather than manual collection of journal entries in books.

Second, society as a whole will have to be more accommodating. An imperfect "melting pot," society can do more to accommodate this form of diversity. Telephone books could regularly carry two last names. Newspapers could alter their conventions, and start referring to Latinos by two last names. All of us can be more aware of the Latino's preference and more respectful of it. Finally, and most importantly, the Latina herself must take the lead in promoting use of both surnames. She must clearly indicate her name preference to the world at large, consistently adopting the full Latin tradition and requesting that others do so, too. This will require effort, patience, and persistence—and quite often she will have to educate others about the reasons for her choice.

NOTES

1. Sandra Maria Esteves, *It Is Raining Today,* in TROPICAL RAINS: A BILINGUAL DOWNPOUR 5 (1984).

2. 277 U.S. 438 (1928), overruled, Katz v. United States, 389 U.S. 347, 352–53 (1967).

3. Charles R. Lawrence, III, *The Id, the Ego, and Equal Protection: Reckoning with Unconscious Racism,* 39 STAN. L. REV. 317, 322 (1987).

4. Ralph Ellison, INVISIBLE MAN 3 (1989).

Chapter 74

A Chicana Perspective on Feminism

Beatriz M. Pesquera and Denise A. Segura

We asked Chicana informants to describe ways in which the American Women's Movement has addressed or not addressed Chicana concerns. Ninety-five women answered this question; six women did not reply. Over half of the informants indicate that Chicana concerns have been somewhat addressed (53.5 percent) by the American Women's Movement, whereas 38.6 percent feel these needs have not been addressed. Only two women feel that the American Women's Movement has addressed Chicana concerns.

Eighty-two women provided in-depth, written responses in support of their answers. Their responses range from acknowledging the importance of the American Women's Movement to forceful critiques of race-class biases. The latter sentiment prevails both among women who feel that the American Women's Movement has somewhat addressed and those who feel that it has not addressed Chicana concerns. The major difference between these two groups of women is the tenor of the critique; that is, women who feel that the movement has not addressed Chicana concerns articulate more intense antagonism, harsher criticism, and less acknowledgment of benefits gained.

Chicanas tend to portray the American Women's Movement as articulating the issues of relatively privileged, well-educated, middle- and upper-class white women. Informants argue that the social origins of movement activists hindered the development of issues relevant to women outside a narrow social milieu. For example, one respondent noted that "by its very historical origins, the movement has emphasized middle-class to upper-class concerns" (Chicana faculty member, 34 years old). This informant's criticism of the lack of diversity within the movement echoes that of other women of color and many white feminist scholars.

Informants object to what they perceive as a marked tendency within the American Women's Movement to present itself in global terms (i.e., The Women's Movement). Chicanas in Mujeres Activas en Letras y Cambio Social (MALCS) feel that

From *With Quill and Torch: A Chicana Perspective on the American Women's Movement and Feminist Theories* by Beatriz M. Pesquera and Denise A. Segura, in Chicanas/Chicanos at the Crossroads: Social, Economic and Political Change, edited by David R. Maciel and Isidro D. Ortiz. Copyright © 1996 by the Arizona Board of Regents. Reprinted by permission of University of Arizona Press.

this attitude obscures important racial/ethnic and class differences among women: "The women's movement that stands out in my mind is the 'second wave,' which occurred during the 1960s. This movement was primarily a 'white, middle-class movement' that openly called for the liberation of women. Although the movement seemed to speak in universal liberation terms (for all women), it systematically excluded the concerns of non-white women, as it failed to consider issues of race, class, and cultural oppression" (Chicana faculty member, 40 years old).

Another informant stated that "the movement has failed to adequately address classism and racism and how it impacts on women as a class and in dealing with our areas of common concern [i.e., women and the family]. I think we have been used to present a collective voice on behalf of women but have not been extended the same degree of importance in areas that concern us differently, i.e., class and race issues. In other words, white women also have to overcome their own prejudices as they try to overcome prejudice altogether" (Chicana graduate student, 24 years old). Like other women who feel that the American Women's Movement has somewhat addressed Chicana concerns, this informant recognizes that the movement often articulates issues pertinent to many women (e.g., the family). What she and others object to is the movement's failure to "adequately address" how other forms of inequality, in particular, race/ethnicity and class, condition women's lives. She and the other informants take exception to the manner in which the Women's Movement postulates stances on behalf of all women without considering these differences. Ultimately, she challenges white women to confront their own race and class privileges side-by-side with the struggle to eradicate sexism.

In general, the women who feel that the Women's Movement has somewhat addressed and those who feel that it has not addressed Chicana concerns object to an analysis of oppression that grants primacy to gender. They argue that overreliance on a gender critique inhibits the development of a more inclusive perspective sensitive to the ways in which race/ethnicity and class, as well as gender, shape the Chicana experience. As another Chicana observed, "The Anglo-American women's movement addresses the dominant culture's sexist practices but many times failed to address the development of our present economic system and how that brought about the division of labor, the social class differences, and the racist institutions" (Chicana graduate student, 32 years old). This woman acknowledges the need to eradicate sexism, but argues for the incorporation in the discussion of class and race/ethnicity as well.

Many women also voice disapproval of the "liberal-reformist" tendencies they feel predominate within the movement. They argued that the American Women's Movement should be less dedicated to finding ways to integrate women into a male-dominated world and more devoted to developing strategies to end structures of inequality and exploitation produced by American capitalism. These perceptions are captured in the response of one Chicana: "The reluctance of the dominant NOW-type feminism in the United States to face up to the reality of racism and class-based problems facing Chicanas has been the main obstacle to feminist concerns for Chicana issues. At the root of this problem is the narrow definition of feminism that is based on sex differences and not a problem of domination" (Chicana graduate student, 29 years old). This woman, like many of the informants, did not distinguish between the various segments within the American Women's Movement. While this overgeneralization may have contributed to the harsh tone of the critique, it is important to note that women who made this distinction tended to voice similar criticisms; for example, "The Women's Movement addressed the specific concerns that affect us as a race and/or class only when we demanded it, but only temporarily. There were few changes in white middle-class women's ideology and practice among the women's rights groups and women liberationists" (Chicana graduate student, 30 years old). This woman, like other informants, combines the different branches of the American Women's Movement in her critique to emphasize how the omission of Chicana concerns cuts across political and ideological alignments of feminists within the American Women's Movement.

Despite their criticism of the American Women's Movement, nearly all the informants endorse the key maxim: eradicating female subordination is essential. Many women credit the movement's critique of patriarchy with influencing their own development as Chicana feminists. They acknowledge that Chicanas benefit from the struggle against patriarchy. Despite this view, a majority feel that the gains netted from this particular struggle are inadequate and largely incidental: "All women of all races are helped when a woman, or any group of women, defies stereotypes and promotes a progressive agenda or idea. But Chicana-specific concerns are not usually what 'the larger agenda' of the Women's Movement is about" (Chicana faculty member, 39 years old). In words reminiscent of Chicana feminists in the 1960s and 1970s this woman contends that the American Women's Movement has not placed a high priority on Chicana concerns. According to this view, Chicana concerns are implicit rather than explicit within feminist agendas. Moreover, because white middle-class women tend to define the direction of this struggle, they will likely garner the greatest benefits. "The Women's Movement addresses the problems of women in general (i.e., white women because they're the leaders of the women's movement) and not those of minority women specifically. Though all women should gain from the movement, statistics show that it is white women who have gained" (Chicana graduate student, 47 years old).

Not only is the previous informant critical of the direction taken by the Women's Movement, she also questions its effectiveness to advocate for women outside the social mainstream. She, like most of the women in this study, contends that social policies to redress gender inequality have not significantly improved the life chances of most Chicanas. In general, Chicanas are poorer, less educated, and employed in the lowest-paying jobs vis-à-vis white women, as well as men. Sex discrimination in training and job access is but one barrier Chicanas face. They also experience discrimination based on their race/ethnicity and culture.

A few informants acknowledge that in recent years, the concerns of working-class and racial/ethnic women have been moving from "margin to center," to quote Hooks. Many women feel this change has resulted from the critiques and demands of women of color. As one informant states, "Over the past decade, there appears to be increased concern to address working-women's issues *and* [respondent's emphasis] to incorporate women of color into ongoing organizational efforts. Thus, incorporation in terms of issues and individuals sought out for membership in women's caucuses, organizations, etc., appears to be evolving. Mostly, there appears to be a heightened consciousness (perhaps out of guilt) among white women to address more directly the concerns of women of color" (Chicana faculty member, 37 years old).

While many women indicate that the American Women's Movement had been moving toward a more inclusive agenda, others feel that Chicana feminist efforts have been almost completely ignored. Their view is typified by the sentiment expressed by one respondent, who wrote that "women of color, particularly Chicanas themselves, have struggled as a group since the late 1960s and early 1970s to raise their/our own issues as women from an oppressed nationality group in the United States. Our fight within the predominantly white, middle-class 'women's movement' has been to address the issues of class and race, as *inextricable* [respondent's emphasis] to our gender issues" (Chicana graduate student, 27 years old). This informant articulates the widespread feeling that white feminists need to acknowledge that Chicanas have been actively challenging patriarchy and racial/ethnic and class oppression. The complexity of Chicanas' struggle requires a multidimensional approach. The term "Chicana" embraces political activism, ethnicity, and gender; therefore, Chicanas do not order their oppression hierarchically. Hence, their articulation of a triple-oppression approach that considers race/ethnicity and class, as well as gender.

Many informants assert that the American Women's Movement neglects the cultural heterogeneity of the American landscape. About one-third of the informants who feel that the movement has not addressed Chicana concerns refer to feminism's lack of cultural sensitivity and cultural awareness. "In general the WM [Women's Movement] has been an Anglo movement, not one considering the cultural heterogeneity of women" (Chicana faculty member, 65 years old).

Chicanas' critiques of the American Women's Movement led them to conclude that they should articulate their own issues: "We need to do this—as Chicanas. We can't expect the white women to understand us in a cultural sense—though they may be able to understand us sociologically in a larger sense" (Chicana faculty member, 43 years old). This woman voices a sentiment heard throughout this group—that neither white women nor Chicano men know how to liberate Chicanas. Moreover, there is no compelling reason for them to do so, inasmuch as they derive privileges from the continued subordination of Chicanas.

Feminist Theory and Chicana Concerns

In this study, many women feel that feminist theories are less relevant to Chicanas than to the American Women's Movement. Forty-eight women (47.5 percent) indicate that feminist theory/scholarship has not incorporated the particular circumstances of Chicanas, while forty-two women (41.6 percent) feel it has somewhat incorporated them. Only two women contend that feminist theory has incorporated the particular circumstances of Chicanas. Nine women did not provide information on this issue.

The women who assert that feminist theory has not incorporated and those who assert that it has somewhat incorporated the particular circumstances of Chicanas describe it as grounded in a narrow range of experiences without a global vision. Echoing the voices of early Chicana feminists, the informants also discuss a range of exclusionary practices within feminist scholarship that limits Chicana voices: "Basically, I know of no major feminist theoretical piece which dismisses Chicanas. I think there is discussion now . . . of women of color, but that is not the same as a discussion of Chicanas" (Chicana graduate student, 30 years old). While this woman acknowledges recent efforts to include women of color, she, like the majority of the informants, asserts that these discussions typically overlook Chicanas. One result of this omission is Chicanas' alienation from American feminism and antagonism toward "white" feminists, who often act as "gatekeepers," limiting access to research and publication outlets necessary to the development of Chicana feminist discourse.

Even more objectionable to Chicana feminists than their exclusion is their inclusion as an "externalized other," whose experiences are appended to theory rather than centered at its heart. As one informant states, "Feminist scholars (excluding Chicanas) rarely talk about Chicanas or care to do any research on us. When we are included in any feminist theory we are used to substantiate a theory on white women. Generally theories are designed to explain the power relations between white males and females and then the experiences of Chicanas are forced into these theoretical frameworks" (Chicana faculty member, 31 years old). This woman, like a majority of the informants, questions the validity of feminist theories that cast Chicanas' experiences into preexisting analytic frameworks. They feel that feminist scholars need to develop an integrative perspective rather than the more obvious additive approach: "Chicanas are seldom represented in feminist theory courses or feminist colloquia unless of course in a marginal sense. As an afterthought many feminist seminars offer a single session which will touch on 'women of color' in general. We have, however, reached a point in history where feminist theorists are a bit self-conscious about failing to consider the particular circumstances of Chicanas, and as a result, the latest publications, etc., have in a limited way begun to solicit Chicana feminist scholarship" (Chicana faculty member, 40 years old). This respondent, like most of the other women surveyed, speaks from personal experiences with Women's Studies courses (e.g., as student, faculty or staff member). Her words display frustration with the misrepresentation of Chicanas and their token inclusion in feminist writings.

Other informants focused attention on recent attempts by women of color to bring the theoretical and political issues to the forefront. One, for example, declared that "unfortunately, it seems that true change in the intellectual debate as well as the political territory comes about only when spearheaded by Chicanas themselves. Chicanas and U.S. Third-World women (i.e., other 'minority' women) have shifted the debate and political agendas through political action, scholarship, cultural/artistic activity, and journalism. . . . There remains, of course, all the work to do which will end only when racism and sexism (and class oppression) are obsolete" (Chicana graduate student, 27 years old). This informant emphasizes that, by and large, inclusion of women of color in feminist theory has been by women of color themselves. Their goal is a praxis addressing multidimensional forms of Chicana oppression.

Chicanas who discussed the incorporation of Chicana concerns into feminist theories voiced considerable cynicism regarding possible underlying motivations. Their view is captured in the response of one MALCS member, who observed, "I predict that it will become more 'fashionable' to hype the 'Hispanic' presence in the United States and the white feminist academics will give lip service to Chicana issues. Their appropriation of our concerns, however, will only serve their interests and diffuse our own voices" (Chicana graduate student, 36 years old). The respondent notes that research on Chicanas is becoming more popular. Yet, she and most of the informants harbor deep misgivings that research on Chicanas will be expropriated by white feminists and to a lesser extent by other non-Chicana scholars who are employed in significantly greater numbers in the academy than are Chicanas, as is noted by several scholars. Study informants fear that non-Chicana scholars will secure recognition more readily for Chicana studies research than the Chicanas who initiated this line of inquiry. This is a particularly sensitive issue for Chicanas who feel they have spent years developing research on their communities.

Consistent with this apprehension, Chicanas in this study and others report that their research is often treated with skepticism in academic departments and denied publication in established research outlets. This experience is not unique to Chicanas, but forms the backdrop for much discussion on the discourse of privilege and power currently underway among many feminist scholars of color. One consequence of this limitation is the establishment of alternative outlets (e.g., Kitchen Table Press, Third Woman Press). To advance Chicana studies, Chicana faculty and graduate students have formed groups such as MALCS and collaborative research/ writing projects to advance Chicana studies. These groups and activities are one way to empower Chicanas, as well as to provide forums wherein Chicanas struggle to navigate their academic paths.

Study informants' critiques of feminist theories reveal a myriad of ideological and political contradictions. Chicanas are caught in the contradiction of seeking a feminist praxis while experiencing alienation from feminists' theories and feminist theoreticians. They are torn between criticizing feminism's lack of theoretical synthesis while denying the ability of white feminists to capture the essence of Chicana subjectivity. Chicana feminism, then, is struggling to wrestle free of these contradictory locutions to create a discourse that speaks to their multifaceted reality.

Despite their apprehensions and criticisms, most Chicanas view feminist theories as useful building blocks to develop their scholarship. As two informants noted, "I believe feminist theory addresses the circumstances of women in general and addresses some of the circumstances of Chicanas (e.g., scholarship that deals with sexism, patriarchy, male dominance and control over women, economic and legal oppression of women)" (Chicana faculty member, 26 years old); and, "It is true that a close reading of feminist theory gives us a base from which we can develop our own theories and scholarship reflecting the Chicana/Latina reality" (Chicana graduate student, no age given). Informants value approaches analyzing the social construction/reproduction of gender, but they tend to favor broader analytic frameworks grounded on women of color outside the U.S. context: "More recent feminist scholarship, most specifically Marxist feminist scholarship, on women in Latin America, addresses some of the issues of race and sex/gender both historically and contemporaneously, and this scholarship is useful for Chicana research" (Chicana graduate student, 46 years old).

While the informants feel that Chicanas should be actively engaged in formulating theories of oppression that integrate race/ethnicity, class, and gender, they intimate that this scholarship will develop slowly. As one woman said, "Chicanas who have become participating members of institutions are barely beginning to become part of the written canon which is the only way that the particular circumstances of the Chicana reality can be incorporated into any theory/scholarship" (Chicana faculty member, 44 years old). Informants point out that there are few Chicanas in academic settings where they can develop scholarship. Their observation is supported by the available data: out of more than 57,000 tenured academics in the United States, only 255 are Hispanic women.

Given the paucity of Chicanas in the academic world, many informants express their desire to help make academic institutions more responsive to the needs of Chicanas. It is within this context that informants evaluate the effectiveness of Women's Studies programs and centers to meet the needs of Chicanas.

Women's Studies, Women's Centers, and Chicana Needs

An important facet of American feminism is the institutionalization of Women's Studies programs and women's centers at colleges and universities. These programs are typically designed to provide support for women, offer courses on women, and support research on women. The extent to which these programs and centers meet Chicana needs is largely unknown. This is important to examine, because it provides another indicator of American feminism's sensitivity to Chicanas.

We asked informants whether or not Women's Studies programs and women's centers existed on their campus and the extent to which they feel they meet the needs of Chicanas. Over three-fourths of the informants (76.2 percent) indicate that there is a Women's Studies program on the campus (10.9 percent of the informants indicated that their campus did not have a Women's Studies program; 12.9 did not reply). More than half of these women (56.4 percent) feel these programs do not meet Chicanas' needs. Only 3 percent feel Women's Studies programs meet Chicanas' needs while 16.8 percent feel these programs somewhat meet these needs. A little less than one-fourth of the women (23.8 percent) did not answer the question.

Over two-thirds of the women (69.3 percent) said their campus has a women's center (19.8 percent of the informants indicated that their campus did not have a women's center; 10.9 did not reply). Of these women, 47.5 percent feel it does not meet Chicanas' needs. Five percent of the informants said the women's center meets Chicanas' needs, 22.8 percent indicate these needs are somewhat met, and 24.8 percent did not answer the question.

The answers regarding the relevancy of Women's Studies programs and women's centers to Chicanas' needs raise serious considerations for institutionalized feminism. Only a minute proportion of the informants, 5 percent or less, feel that Women's Studies and women's centers meet their needs. If we consider the proportion of women who feel Women's Studies programs and centers somewhat meet Chicanas' needs, women's centers are more favorably evaluated.

Almost one-fourth of the informants did not answer questions on Women's Studies programs or women's centers. This implies that either they have little or no knowledge of these programs/centers, or they are not involved in either. The low number of women who feel Women's Studies programs or women's centers meet or somewhat meet Chicanas' needs corresponds with the high number of women who voice forceful criticisms of their marginality to the American Women's Movement and feminist theories.

Conclusion

Women in this study overwhelmingly criticize American feminism for failing to incorporate their concerns adequately within feminist theories, political agendas, and institutionalized programs. They oppose American feminism's tendency to "universalize" the experience of white middle-class women and to either ignore or subsume racial/ethnic, culture, and class differences among women to a general theory of women's common oppression. Many of these women acknowledge the importance of the struggle against patriarchy, but feel this addresses only one dimension of Chicana oppression.

Chicanas contend that the class privilege and racial advantage shared by white middle-class feminists often blind them to Chicana concerns. They advocate "deconstructing" American feminism, to account for ways the tripartite axes of stratification shape women's experiences and demarcate relations of power and privilege in American society.

To reiterate, Chicanas interpret reality thorough a "triple-oppression lens" rooted in their experiences as Chicanas in the United States. By a triple-oppression lens, we mean that Chicanas simultaneously experience reality as members of a historically oppressed group, with a culture distinct from that of the dominant culture. Furthermore, their location in the class structure is mediated by their racial/ethnic status. The social construction of a Chicana perspective, or worldview, is filtered through their racial/ethnic/class status. As a result, Chicanas' interests as women are distinct from and at times contradictory to those articulated within American feminism.

A general theory of the common oppression of women proposed by American feminism unravels as we consider class, race/ethnicity, and culture, as well as gender interests. A Chicana perspective is fueled by the combined effects of class, race/ethnicity, and gender on Chicanas' life chances.

Chapter 75

Three Perspectives on Workplace Harassment of Women of Color

Maria L. Ontiveros

For women of color, sexual harassment is rarely, if ever, about sex or sexism alone; it is also about race. For us, racial epithets are spoken in sexist terms, and sexual or sexist comments involve our race and or our culture. Marcia Gillespie, speaking for African-American women, but with words applicable for many other women of color, wrote,

> We say, I am a Black Woman, I cannot separate my race from my sex, cannot separate racism from sexism. They are rarely separate, never indivisible. So don't ask me to choose, I cannot; I am myself, I am not you. Nor will I let you choose for me. And I will not let you pretend that racism and sexism are not inseparable issues in all of our lives.[1]

This indivisibility was noted by early victims of workplace harassment who, when they were asked if they were filing racial or sexual harassment claims, responded that they could not tell. While everyone agrees that sexual harassment is about sexism and power, for us it is also about race and culture. From the viewpoint of the harasser, women of color appear less powerful, less likely to complain, and the embodiment of particular notions of sexuality. From the perspective of the women, attitudes in their community and lessons learned in their culture may make it more difficult for them to respond forcefully to discrimination. Finally, the judicial system's perspective on both women of color and relationships between men and women of color often influences the outcome of such cases.

The Harasser

Since workplace harassment is a power dynamic, women of color serve as likely targets because they are the least powerful participants in the workplace. Unlike white women, they are not privileged by their race. Unlike men of color, they are not priv-

From "Three Perspectives on Workplace Harassment of Women of Color." 23 Golden Gate U. L. Rev. 817 (1993). Originally published in the *Golden Gate University Law Review*. Reprinted by permission.

ileged by their gender. Although a white man might harass any woman, a man of color is not likely to feel that he has the prerogative to harass a white woman because of his lack of racial status or because he knows he could be subject to the harsh, vengeful treatment society has visited in such cases. If the harasser is a man of color, the victim is likely to be a woman of color. Harassers may also prefer those women of color, such as Latinas and Asian-American women, whom they view as more passive and less likely to complain.

Additionally, racism and sexism can blend together in the mind of the harasser and be displayed as an inseparable whole. The types of statements used and actions taken incorporate the unique characteristics of women of color, subjecting each race and ethnicity to its own cruel stereotype of sexuality. Harassment of African-American women incorporates images of slavery, degradation, sexual availability, and natural lasciviousness. In *Brooms v. Regal Tube Co.*, the defendant showed the victim several photocopies of racist pornography involving bestiality, gave her pornographic pictures depicting an interracial act of sodomy and told her that she was hired for the purposes indicated in the photograph because it showed the "talent" of a black woman.[2] In *Continental Can Co. v. Minnesota*, the harasser told his African-American victim that "he wished slavery days would return so that he could sexually train her and she would be his bitch."[3]

A parallel stereotype portrays Asian-American women as exotic, submissive, and naturally erotic. This attitude most likely grows out of the 1870s racist portrayal of all Asian women as prostitutes, seeking to enter the United States to engage in "criminal and demoralizing purposes."[4] Unfortunately, several examples illustrate that these historical stereotypes still exist and affect women today. Hearings on sexual harassment sponsored by the California Women's Caucus included the testimony of an "Asian construction worker whose co-workers shoved a hammer between her legs, who was taunted with racial slurs, who was repeatedly grabbed on her breasts while installing overhead fixtures, and who was asked whether it was true that Asian women's vaginas were sideways."[5]

In another case, a young Japanese-American receptionist's harasser told her he had a foot fetish, stroked and kissed her feet, and kissed the nape of her neck. He told her, "I thought Oriental women get aroused by kissing the back of the neck."[6] Finally, a Taiwanese-American banking executive won a settlement from a Los Angeles bank because, among other things, a co-worker said that she was best suited to a job as a "high-class call girl" and the bank's president once introduced her as "vice president in the real estate and sex department."[7]

Like African-American and Asian-American women, society considers Latinas naturally sexual, in this instance evoking the image of the "hot-blooded" Latin. In addition, Latinas are often perceived as readily available and accessible for sexual use, with few recriminations for abusing them. Sonoma County District Attorney Gene Tunney has seen this perception become reality. In commenting on one case which typifies this situation, he stated, "[W]e've become aware of people who have imported Mexican women, usually from rural villages in the middle of nowhere, and brought them here for sexual reasons. My suspicion is there is a lot of it going on."[8]

Women of Color as Members of the Minority Community

The community in which a woman lives and the culture in which she was raised influence her reaction to workplace harassment. For example, some women of color have been raised to become passive, defer to men, and not bring attention to themselves. This may be particularly true in the traditional Asian value system that includes obedience, familial interest, fatalism, and self-control, and which tends to foster submissiveness, passivity, pessimism, timidness, inhibition, and adaptiveness. Similar barriers may face Latinas growing up in a "macho" culture. For these women to resist an act aggressively or to pursue a legal remedy, these cultural issues must first be confronted. Additionally, many women wrestle with feelings that they will be blamed for the harassment. For Asian-American women, philosophies like "Shikata ga nai"[9] and "If something happens to you, it is your fault for putting yourself in that position" exacerbate the guilt and self-doubt felt by any victim. One Mexican immigrant victim of harassment, when asked why she did not report it earlier, told a rape counselor that "a woman who is raped in Mexico is the one at fault, maybe because her parents didn't watch her."[10] Upon learning of the harassment, her husband denounced her as a permanent shame to her family.

Immigrant or illegal status and a lack of understanding of their legal rights further handicap women of color. Marie DeSantis, a community advocate for Sonoma County Women Against Rape, notes that immigrant women are often victims of what she terms "rape by duress."[11] They do not report such crimes because they are too intimidated by their fear of deportation, ignorance of their legal rights, and presumed power of their employers. One Mexican housekeeper explained that because she was here illegally and was paid by her employer, she had no place else to go. She worried that "He could have cut me up in a million pieces, and no one would have known."[12]

The inability to understand the situation is further compounded by the differing ideas of sexuality which permeate different cultures. Sex is discussed less frequently and openly by Asian-American women; sexual harassment is therefore not something to be discussed either. In fact, no words for "sexual harassment" exist in Japanese, Mandarin, or Cantonese. In cultures that do not even have words to encompass the concept of sexual harassment, it is predictable that many women in those cultures are less likely to recognize harassing behavior when it occurs. Finally, victims recognize that accusations of workplace harassment will reflect badly on their cultures and likely bring adverse community response. For example, one Latina community worker was urged by two female co-workers (who had also been harassed and remained silent) not to report an incident of harassment "for fear that exposing the perpetrators would undermine their movement and embarrass the Latino community."[13] This adverse community response may be especially painful for women of color, to whom community is particularly important.

The Legal System

Once an incident of workplace harassment becomes a lawsuit, the legal system provides the final construct of the event in at least three ways: judges and juries may tend to disbelieve what the women of color say; the dominant culture's construct of their sexuality influences the cases' outcomes; and the entire justice system misperceives relationships between men and women of color, thereby excusing discriminatory acts by men of color.

The story of a Mexican immigrant woman evidences the credibility problem. She told the Sonoma District Attorney that she believed her employer was "a doctor . . . and that is a title of some esteem and high position in Mexico. . . . If you're a peasant girl, and it's your word against his, you don't have a chance."[14] African-American women also have a hard time convincing the legal system that they are telling the truth. Judges have been known to tell jurors to take a black woman's testimony "with a grain of salt."[15] A recent study of jury members in rape trials indicated the lack of credibility given black women's testimony. One juror said of black rape victims, "you can't believe everything they say; they're known to exaggerate the truth."[16]

Penalties are affected because women of color are believed to have been "asking for it," to not be greatly affected by the abuse, or simply to not be worthy of the same legal protection given to the rest of society. One study concluded that defendants who assault African-American women are less likely to receive jail time than those who assaulted white women. Another found that assailants of African-American women receive an average sentence of two years, compared to one of ten years for defendants who assault white women. One juror, sitting in the case of a rape of a black pre-teen, stated "being from that neighborhood she probably wasn't a virgin anyway."[17]

A final problem occurs when the legal system misinterprets relationships between men and women of color. The so-called "cultural defense" has been used by people of color to explain why their action is understandable and even excusable in their culture, even when it offends American values. In *People v. Chen*,[18] a Chinese man, after learning of his wife's adultery, killed her by hitting her on the head eight times with a hammer. The defense argued that, in traditional Chinese culture, a man is often driven to violence upon hearing of his wife's infidelity, but, unlike this defendant, is stopped by someone in the community before he can actually hurt her. The court took this defense into account and sentenced him to five years probation. In another case, two Korean youths were acquitted on the charge of rape after arguing that the victim, a Korean woman, tacitly consented to the rape because her visit to bars with the men would communicate consent in Korea.[19] Although many protested that these rulings misinterpreted Chinese and Korean social norms and views of justice, the legal system accepted them, thereby devaluing women of color in the process.

Following the Hill-Thomas hearings, the issue of sexual harassment has, justifiably, been raised in the collective consciousness of our society. Unfortunately, sexual harassment only describes part of what happened to Anita Hill and continues to happen to many other women. Race or national origin affects the way she is perceived by the harasser, her ability to respond to the incident, and the judicial system's eventual resolution of the matter. We need to reconstruct our perception of sexual harassment to face the issue of workplace harassment of women of color. This transformation must take place because the elements of a sexual harassment case are different from and more onerous than those in a racial harassment case. Treating these cases as sexual harassment, then, not only misstates the dynamic but further disadvantages these women. Such a solution could be reached either by modifying the rules governing sexual harassment or by creating a new cause of action prohibiting discrimination against women of color as such.

This reform would address some of the problems discussed here, but true solutions are not so simple because the problems and interrelationships are so complex. Deeply held notions of race, gender, identity, sexuality, and power must be examined and reevaluated. Furthermore, this discovery must take place both within and across cultural and class boundaries. Only in this way will we be able to answer the challenges raised by the Hill-Thomas hearings and, as Marcia Gillespie said, no longer pretend that racism and sexism are not inseparable issues in all of our lives.

NOTES

1. Marcia A. Gillespie, *We Speak in Tongues,* Ms., Jan.–Feb., 1992, at 41–42.
2. 881 F.2d 412, 417 (7th Cir.1989).
3. 297 N.W.2d 241, 246 (1980).
4. Sucheta Mazumdar, *General Introduction: A Woman-Centered Perspective on Asian American History,* in Making Waves: An Anthology of Writings by and about Asian American Women 1, 2–3 (1989).
5. Kimberlè Crenshaw, *Race, Gender and Sexual Harassment,* 65 S. Cal. L. Rev. 1467, 1474 (1992).
6. California Dept. of Fair Employment and Housing v. Guill, et al., (1989) FEHC Oct. No. 89-15 (CEB 11). Modified on remand, (1991) FEHC Feb. No. 91-16 (CEB 10).
7. Kim Murphy, *Bank Will Pay $400,000 in Sexual Harassment Suit,* L.A. Times, Oct. 7, 1986, Part 2, at 1.
8. Carla Marinucci, *Despair Drove Her to Come Forward,* S.F. Examiner, Jan. 10, 1993, at A11.
9. Japanese for "it can't be helped."
10. Marinucci.
11. *Id.*
12. *Id.*
13. Crenshaw, at 1474.
14. Marinucci.
15. Crenshaw, at 1470.
16. *Id.*
17. *Id.*
18. No. 87-7774 (N.Y. Sup. Ct. Mar. 21, 1989).
19. Melissa Spatz, *A "Lesser" Crime: A Comparative Study of Legal Defenses for Men Who Kill Their Wives,* 24 Colum. J.L. & Soc. Probs., 597, 625 n.200 (1991).

Chapter 76

Culture and Economic Violence

Berta Esperanza Hernández-Truyol

Much of the economic violence that is perpetrated on, and experienced by, Latinas as a group is a result of, and is perpetuated by, gendered cultural norms. Latinas are acculturated to be secondary, subordinate beings. *Marianismo*—a construct in which the Virgin Mary is the aspirational model—demands that a Latina must be *la buena mujer* ("the good woman"), and requires of women self-sacrifice, self-effacement, and self-subordination. The notion of *familismo* (family comes first) also keeps Latinas, right here within our own *fronteras* (borders), hiding behind the proverbial privacy closet door of family. Familismo results in the expectation of Latinas to take the blows from husbands and fathers alike, and never to complain. Of course, many who are undocumented immigrants will not report violence against them, because they fear deportation for themselves or their families. As a result, they learn to suffer indignities and tolerate physical, sexual, and economic violence at the hands of their husbands and underground employers. Latinas endure such violence in their own homes, as well as in the homes of those for whom they work as nannies, housekeepers, and maids, because they are afraid that if they complain about or reject the sexual harassment, the underpayments, the humiliation, the rapes, and the insults that they suffer, they will be deported.

Economics and culture often clash in the demands they make of Latinas. Consider the complex, paradoxical messages given daily to all women in poverty. Society expects women to stay home and care for children, family and spouses, but the very same society demonizes them for the very same conduct if they happen to be in poverty and accept financial assistance from the state. The same conduct of stay-at-home care-taker goes from glorified to condemned and demonized depending on who is signing the paycheck, all the time for doing their jobs as mothers. This, too, is everyday economic violence.

The international community must re/vision "violence" so that it offers women greater protection in the twenty-first century. Recognizing the close nexus between economic dependence and marginalization to physical victimization, I propose that

From "Sex, Culture, and Rights: A Re/Conception of Violence for the Twenty-First Century." 60 Alb. L. Rev. 607. Originally published in the *Albany Law Review*. Reprinted by permission.

the conceptualization of violence be developed, expanded, and transformed to embrace the indivisibility and interdependence of human rights. Such a re/conceptualization must embrace all three "generations" of rights: (1) civil and political rights (first generation); (2) social, cultural, and economic rights (second generation); and (3) solidarity rights (third generation).

As a prologue to re/constituting and re/conceptualizing violence, one useful blueprint/model to make the transition from the "A hit B" or "A shot B" to the less physically forceful but equally damaging forms of violence is the evolution (revolution) that transmogrified domestic violence from a private to a public act. In the past (and in some cultures in the present), it was believed that what happens between or among family members is a "private" matter. If a spouse hit his or her spouse or child, it was not a crime, but rather, business as usual within the family structure. Not too long ago, it was acceptable for a husband to keep his wife in line by using force. Courts even permitted a husband to beat his wife with a stick so long as it was no bigger than his thumb, the so-called "rule of thumb." It was believed that wives, like children, needed to be disciplined, controlled, and supervised not only physically, but also economically. Women were not allowed to deal in their own property. Municipal systems of law would not get into the business of forbidding violence in the home so as not to intrude in this private sphere of life. As a result, it was considered to be well outside the realm of the international legal system to reach such private individual conduct. In fact, until recently, states alone were subjects of international law; individuals were simply objects, and not subjects of it.

Recently, however, the United Nations has recognized that women's unequal status transcends the social and family spheres. Women's global disadvantages and marginalization also result from lack of access to economic development opportunities (in both the private and public sectors), denial of educational opportunities, and restriction from social and political participation. Scrutiny of women's condition reveals that their less-than-full citizenship status can be traced to both physical and economic violence. Such violence is often widely accepted, and even embraced, under the pretext of cultural normativity. Consequently, before women can achieve social and economic equality and engage in full political participation, societies world-wide must re/conceptualize the notion of violence. This reconceptualization must include all forms of injustice for women, including injustice beyond the hitting-or-shooting paradigm. It must include economic marginalization and acts of violence justified on the grounds of culture or traditional practices. Indeed, such a framework will facilitate and permit the recognition and understanding of the many intersections of the physical abuse and economic deprivation components in the construction of violence.

Thus, here are my suggestions on how to reconceptualize violence. On any matter, always ask the woman question: can or does the policy/practice/standard effect, facilitate, promote, or ignore violent consequences to women? This inquiry must recognize that such violent consequences can be direct or indirect, and physical as well as economic, emotional, psychological, social, educational, or political. Such a model requires women's comprehensive participation in the consideration of the consequences of the specific rules and practices. Indeed, in order to ensure that this model is truly inclusive, women must participate in the drafting process. In addition, the drafter must ask women if the proposal has an impact on their real lives. Indeed, women must participate in the process as both inquirers and inquired. The only effective way to eradicate violence against women is to understand its overt and subtle forms by deconstructing its causes and manifestations so that violence can be detected at the outset.

In looking at violence, we must expand our view from guns and fists to jobs and dignity. We need to ask those at the bottom of the economic ladder, the educational ladder, the health ladder and at the margins of the cultural borders what their needs are and how such needs can best be met. We must ask those who are not represented what their needs are. We must give a voice and render visible those who are unseen and unheard. We need to give the vote to those who have been denied access to the ballot box, and we must give dignity to the second sex—women of all races, colors, religions, sexualities, languages, national origins, and classes. A re/constructed paradigm must ask the necessary questions to bring those at the margins to the center of human rights talk. All this can be achieved through a re/conceptualization of violence that truly recognizes the needs of women around the world.

Chapter 77

Gendered Inequality

Elvia R. Arriola

In the late nineteenth century American society drastically changed. At this time, the Court declared the commonplace and accepted act of distinguishing people on the basis of race unconstitutional. A simple message emerged from this period: certain kinds of personal and governmental classifications of people would be viewed as illegal. Furthermore, the federal courts would play a special role in ensuring that particular classifications, such as race-based distinctions, would never be reinstated. By extending "equal protection" to people regardless of the color of their skin, the principle of equality affirmed a fragile, yet clear, notion of the individual's inherent moral worth.

Despite this new emphasis on equal protection, a series of Reconstruction era Supreme Court decisions reflected society's continued tolerance of racial classifications. This tolerance was epitomized by the view that a racial classification is constitutional as long as each class is treated "equally"—a view that persisted for over fifty years. The infamous *Plessy v. Ferguson* articulated this vision of group-based equality.[1]

Another version of group-based equality emerged several decades later, in the now famous footnote four to *United States v. Carolene Products Co.*[2] While the Court in *Carolene* upheld a "reasonable" piece of state legislation, it warned that courts might, on occasion, have to exercise an antimajoritarian check on legislative powers when a law discriminates against "discrete and insular minorities."[3]

The rhetoric surrounding the group-based model often obscures the public policy that undergirds its close relative, the individual-regarding or "irrelevancy" model of equality. The irrelevancy model reminds individuals and governments that under the Constitution certain personal traits are not legitimate classifying criteria. To this end, the rhetoric of irrelevancy argues that equality means never considering one's race, sex, religion, or national origin for classification purposes. This model thus contains two considerations. First, as human beings who are identified by several personal traits, such as age and race, we are also a member of a larger class of "all persons"

From "GENDERED INEQUALITY: LESBIANS, GAYS, AND FEMINIST LEGAL THEORY." 9 BERKELEY WOMEN'S L.J. 103 (1994). Originally published in the *Berkeley Women's Law Journal*. Reprinted by permission.

or individuals. Second, given one's membership in the class of all persons, the law demands that all class members be accordingly treated as equals. The second consideration contains an idealized notion of personal equality, and declares that certain personal traits, such as skin color, are irrelevant to the process of deciding whether to grant or deny a right, privilege, or benefit.

The group-based model embraces the principle of the individual-regarding model by recognizing that although an individual may suffer personal discrimination, the source of the harm is often a group-based generalization about that individual. However, despite the relationship between the two models of equality, a dichotomous rhetoric has developed which pits the individual-regarding model against the group-based one. This rhetoric incorrectly implies that there can be only one true version of equality.

The strength of the irrelevancy model is that it brings to the foreground an underlying assumption of the group-based model: our personhood—or respect for the total individual—is important. Arbitrary labels and categories should not define our identity or provide the basis for depriving (or granting) a job or other benefit. In its most idealistic phrasing, the individual-regarding model echoes Justice Harlan's dissent in *Plessy v. Ferguson,* asserting that the Constitution is colorblind.[4]

This strength notwithstanding, the individual-regarding model cannot be the sole criterion for meaningful equality because, although the Constitution is colorblind, people are not. In other words, in some situations, social justice is unattainable without an exploration of unconscious social attitudes—the vestiges of systems of overt discrimination—that perpetuate inequality.

Constructing a Holistic/Irrelevancy Model of Equality

Governing paradigms encourage legal analysts to make a number of problematic assumptions. First, the various characteristics of one's identity, such as sexual orientation, gender, and race, are always disconnected. Second, these characteristics carry fixed and clear meanings. Third, the various aspects of one's identity may be ranked so that, for example, race may be prioritized over gender. Fourth, some characteristics, such as class, do not provide a relevant basis for discrimination claims. Finally, these paradigms create false dichotomies and false power relationships and promote limited visions of equality. They obscure whether or how discrimination occurs, what remedy to use, or why conflict has arisen.

Under a "holistic/irrelevancy" model, courts would recognize that a person's identity is rarely limited to a singular characteristic. Instead, identity represents the confluence of an infinite number of factors. Those can include race, religion, sexual orientation, nationality, ethnicity, age, class, ideology, and profession. The components of an individual identity constantly shift, some becoming more prominent in certain settings than others. I arrive at this conclusion through an understanding that no single trait defines my own identity. Rather, my being Mexican, Catholic, a woman who is lesbian-identified, a feminist lawyer, professor, and yogin, are all important aspects of my identity.

Addressing Categorization

Although numerous factors comprise an individual identity, others may identify that individual on the basis of a single trait. The trait which becomes prominent, or even legally relevant, is seldom predictable. While a single trait may become prominent and legally relevant, discrimination in fact stems from stereotypes about a person's entire identity. Thus, models that fail to acknowledge that people move in and out of communities and that categories never match reality cannot adequately reveal how multiple unconscious attitudes motivate acts of discrimination.

My holistic/irrelevancy model rejects both the individual's and the law's tendency to choose their own preferred and accepted categories or to see them as necessarily separate and unrelated. Courts should acknowledge the multiple forms of oppression that are often facilitated by stereotypes of various social identities. This would reveal the complexity of social identities currently rendered invisible under traditional frameworks. At the same time it would avoid the categorization promoted and perpetuated by other responses to this invisibility, such as lesbian legal theory. With this end in mind, I encourage the reader to consider the following hypotheticals which illustrate the complexity of personal identities and discrimination.

Suppose, for example, that an employer pays all women the same wage. However, he places white women in the front office jobs because the clientele is mostly white, and relegates blacks and hispanics to the back room. Meanwhile, he sexually harasses the white women. Would a black woman denied a front office job have any right to challenge the employer on the basis of racism, or sexism, or both? What about a white woman? Is one issue more important than the other?

In another hypothetical, an Asian employer prefers to hire hispanics and Asians over blacks or whites. How do we assess this kind of preferential treatment when our standard paradigms of analysis usually see whites as oppressors and all minorities as victims? Is this a case of the so-called problem of reverse discrimination? What about when an employer hires Mexican nationals over Mexican-Americans because the latter are more likely to question working conditions and wages?

Finally, suppose that a white male employer fires a black lesbian after she rebuffs his sexual advances. Is this discrimination on the basis of race, gender, or sexual identity, or some combination of the three? Claims of discrimination brought by lesbians of color face two obstacles under current discrimination analysis. First, the categories of race and gender may be viewed as distinct and separate. Second, the category of sexual identity is not even recognized as a basis of legally remediable discrimination. Faced with a claim by a woman of color, a court could determine that although the categories of race and sex apply, these categories have not been shown to bear any clear relationship to each other. This type of determination was made in *Munford v. James T. Barnes, Inc.,*[5] a case brought by a black woman whose white male supervisor demanded that she have sex with him. She repeatedly refused. The sexual harassment carried racial overtones. Limited by conventional legal reasoning, the court in *Munford* failed to see how racism and sexism intersected in this case. It held instead that the race discrimination claim was "far removed" from the sexual harassment claim.[6]

For a lesbian of color, the same methodology that fails to recognize a claim of racialized sexual harassment, or gendered racial harassment, also denies her claims of homophobic sexism. The firing of a black lesbian, as illustrated in the hypothetical above, presents a complex picture of identity and discrimination. Yet, the source of the problem is not complex; it is simple, though subtle—she is being fired because she has defied white male supremacy, and is a victim of anti-lesbian sexism.

The holistic/irrelevancy model recognizes the role of unconscious attitudes and the ways that interrelated factors create unique, compounded patterns of discrimination and affect special social identities. In doing so, it rejects the idea of arbitrarily separating out categories to address discrimination in our society. Instead, this model understands discrimination as a problem that arises when multiple traits and the stereotypes constructed around them converge in a specific harmful act. Traditional categories then become points of departure for a deeper, more subtle analysis that explores the historical relationships between certain social groups, as well as an individual's experience within each of these groups.

This model is holistic because it looks to the whole harm, the total identity. It is an irrelevancy perspective because it assumes that one trait or several traits operating together create unfair and irrelevant bases of treatment. Thus, under a holistic/irrelevancy model, the theory and practice of non-discrimination law become tools for mediating social conflict by challenging the power of deeply ingrained cultural attitudes that perpetuate cycles of oppression for certain social groups.

We need new models that acknowledge the reality of identity and personhood, notwithstanding that an individual may not fit rigid, dichotomized categories such as "masculine" or "feminine." The governing paradigms encourage the courts to ignore social reality and to refuse to extend existing and relevant legal protections to lesbians and gays. Courts have refused to extend these protections to lesbian and gay litigants because anti-gay discrimination merges questions of conduct with identity. The courts' refusal reflects the legal culture's insistence that discrimination occurs within distinct and separate categories. This categorization denies the complexity of individual identity, thereby preventing society from embracing the richness of its cultural diversity. Discrimination harms not only the individual but society as a whole. Equality theorists should recognize the public policy underlying existing paradigms: respect for one's total identity. This public policy demands respect for traits such as gender, sexuality, race, class, age, and ethnicity. Each trait is important to one's moral worth, yet none provides justification for the denial of equal rights under the law.

NOTES

1. 163 U.S. 537 (1896).
2. 304 U.S. 144, 152–53 n.4 (1938).
3. *Id.* at 152–53.
4. 163 U.S. 537, 559 (1896) (Harlan, J., dissenting).
5. 441 F.Supp. 459 (E.D. Mich. 1977).
6. *Id.* at 466–67.

Chapter 78

Notes on the Conflation of Sex, Gender, and Sexual Orientation

A QueerCrit and LatCrit Perspective

Francisco Valdes

Because sex, gender, and sexual orientation are central concepts in our society's sex/gender system, their histories and meanings are significant and complex. However, the conflation of this trio, and its effects, have gone largely unnoticed both in law and society. The conflation comprises three constructs: sex, gender, and sexual orientation. The first leg of this triangle is the conflation of sex and gender; the second, that of gender and sexual orientation. The third is the conflation of sex and sexual orientation.

The first leg, conflating sex and gender, holds that every person's sex is also that person's gender. This leg, or its disruption, produces "sissies" and "tomboys." The second leg, conflating sex-derived gender and sexual orientation, is less familiar, at least initially. This leg is the generally recognizable linkage between "queers" and "sissies" on the one hand, and "dykes" and "tomboys" on the other, suggesting that some correlation between sex-determined gender and sexual orientation *is* at work.

The conflation's third leg may be the least familiar, but is discernible and demonstrable nonetheless. The conflation of sex and sexual orientation is shown by the way in which sexual orientation is directly surmised by the sameness or difference of sex(es) within a coupling: a sameness of sex within a coupling results directly in conclusions of homosexual orientation for each participant whereas a difference of sexes within a coupling produces conclusions of heterosexual orientation.

In this conflationary scheme, "sex" refers to external genitalia, usually as observed at birth, while "gender" signifies the composite of personal appearance and social behaviors, characteristics and roles imputed to all persons at birth on the basis of sex. These attributes are organized into an active/male and passive/female paradigm that extends both to social *and* sexual identities. In other words, the conflationary manifestation or performance of sex-determined gender, in the form of "ac-

From "Queers, Sissies, Dykes, and Tomboys: Deconstructing the Conflation of 'Sex,' 'Gender,' and 'Sexual Orientation' in Euro-American Law and Society." 83 Calif. L. Rev. 1 (1995). Originally published in the *California Law Review*. Reprinted by permission.

tive/male" or "passive/female" personality, is expected and demanded in both social ("public") settings as well as in sexual ("private") relations. In this scheme, "sexual orientation" effectively represents the sexual dimension or performance of gender: sexual orientation denotes the sense and enactment of erotic desire or personality, which is cast as either "active" or "passive" under the sexed and gendered dictates of the active/passive paradigm. Moreover, in the active/passive hierarchy of this scheme, masculinity structurally is valorized over femininity and cross-sex couplings structurally are valorized over same-sex couplings. The conflation's sex/gender ideology therefore is heteropatriarchy—the intertwining of androsexism and heterosexism to validate malecentric and heterocentric biases.

As these socio-legal definitions indicate, the conflation of the three constructs begins with and pivots on "sex," and on its assignment at birth. And because gender is deduced from and fixed by sex, this conflationary scheme constructs the social and sexual dimensions of "gender" as both deductive and intransitive. It bears emphasis that these basic definitions, and their anchoring to active/passive ideology, are entrenched in Euro-American history, and they continue to prevail in the United States as a matter of clinical practice, cultural custom and legal doctrine.[1]

The courts have faced these conflations in several modern cases. In one, *Strailey v. Happy Times Nursery Sch., Inc.*,[2] the Ninth Circuit confronted all three legs at once. In that case, Strailey alleged that he "was fired by Defendants in September 1975 because he [was] a homosexual and failed to present a proper male image," and that this action violated Title VII. He further alleged that his employer "refuse[d] to employ anyone it [knew to be a] homosexual, including persons it believed[d] [did] not present a proper male (or female) image, despite their abilities to teach and to deal with children effectively."[3] As such, the claim asserted that the school maintained a "policy and practice of denying equal employment opportunities to homosexual applicants and employees because of their sex and sexual orientation."[4] This framing linguistically used "sex" when meaning "gender" because conceptually this claim sought to describe effeminacy—the social display of "female" gender by a person of a "male" sex. Strailey's effeminacy/"sissy" and homosexuality/"queer" claims thus invoked the conflation's first and second legs, respectively.

Further, Strailey asserted that "[d]iscrimination based on sexual orientation is based upon the gender of the plaintiffs as well as that of their sexual partners, just as discrimination based on hetero-racial relationships is based upon the race of each party to such relationships."[5] Conversely, this framing linguistically used "gender" when meaning "sex" because conceptually this claim sought to analogize homo-sexual couplings to hetero-racial ones. Without directly implicating gender, this claim characterized discrimination against same-sex couples as based on "sex" in the same way that discrimination against cross-race couples is based on "race."

In support of this claim, Strailey relied on cases decided during the 1960s that had invalidated anti-miscegenation statutes. Defenders of those statutes had argued then that because the prohibition against cross-race relations applied "equally" to both races, the laws did not "discriminate" on the basis of race. The courts resolutely rejected that reasoning, discerning that the anti-miscegenation statutes were intended and employed as a means of preserving racial hierarchies that subordinated minority races. Thus, judicial rejection of this sophistry in the miscegenation setting was based on a recognition that the abstract equality on the face of the statutes masked and perpetuated race-based inequalities in practice.

In effect, Strailey's third claim advanced and presaged an analogy between sex and race: since Strailey's framing and assertion of this claim, this "miscegenation analogy" has received scholarly attention and development. Here, as in the subsequent scholarship, this analogy was employed to train the court(s) on the direct, unmediated inter-connection between sex and sexual orientation in order to obtain judicial recognition of sexual orientation discrimination as a sub-set of sex-based discrimination. This claim, and the analogy as later developed, thus introduce Leg Three of the conflation into the sex/gender record of legal culture.

In this vein, Strailey's brief went on to analogize this claim to EEOC decisions dealing with discrimination based on an employee's "associations" with persons of another race. Specifically, it referred to a 1971 decision in which the EEOC considered the claim of a white employee who had been discharged, in the former employee's words, "because of her friends."[6] The EEOC in that case had concluded that the discharge was based unlawfully on the employee's "interracial dating," an association that was "clearly protected by Title VII."[7]

Unfortunately, the *Strailey* court's response to this analogizing disregarded the reasoning of precedent, and was as strained and superficial as the rest of its opinion. The court asserted that Strailey's analogy had not claimed that his employer would "terminate anyone with a male (or female) friend."[8] Rather, the court maintained, Strailey had claimed that his employer "discriminated[d] against employees who have a certain type of relationship—i.e., homosexual relationship—with certain friends."[9] This distinction—presumably between "friends" on the one hand and "certain relationships . . . with certain friends" on the other—seems slippery, and is incongruent with the statute's anti-discrimination principles because it serves to license rather than to limit bigotry.

Still, even as reformulated by the court, Strailey's associational claim seems precisely analogous to cross-race intimacy. Anti-miscegenation statutes, as well as the discharge of employees who had "friends" of other races, discriminated against persons who had a certain type of relationship—i.e., a hetero-racial relationship—with certain friends. In each instance, the discrimination sought to regulate intimate interactions with sexual or affectional partners. In each instance the discrimination was calculated to subordinate minority groups. Finally, in each instance the discrimination succeeded in doing just that (and nothing else).

The conflation today remains as firmly entrenched in sexual minority communities as it is in mainstream American society and its legal culture. This entrenchment is exemplified by the continuing sway of identifications like "butch" or "femme" or "queen" that project various conflationary configurations of sex, gender, and sexual orientation. And, though the butch-femme debate is often most directly associated with lesbian identity, its sex/gender issues extend to gay male identity as well because both female and male same-sex couples necessarily confront male/husband and female/wife roles and issues defined by traditionalist active/passive standards.

For instance, both female and male same-sex couples frequently encounter queries from friends, relatives, or acquaintances in the sexual majority asking, "Who plays the 'wife's' role?" This query, in effect, seeks to determine who is the "butch" and who is the "femme"; in other words, who conforms and who does not—who is socially *and* sexually gender typical and who is socially *and* sexually gender atypical. Of course, this query effectively signals underlying confusion (or incredulity) over the possibility that sex-determined gender and sexual orientation are not necessarily correlated or conflated either socially/publicly or sexually/privately.

Perhaps the most familiar example of the butch-femme issue in specifically gay male subculture might be the still-ubiquitous "drag" shows that glorify cross-dressing and other social gender-bending affectations as a means of representing sexual orientation to the audience. Much as we saw in the 1982 film, *Victor, Victoria,* these shows feature lip-sync impersonations of hyper-glamorous female performers, replete with wigs, makeup, gowns, and gestures. Major cities often have at least one establishment specializing in the presentation of this type of activity, and many other bars or lounges across the country include such fare in their regular entertainment schedules. Literally and normatively, these shows place gender squarely at center stage in the cultural life of communities apparently defined by sexual orientation, and thereby project active/passive traditions represented and reproduced jointly by the first and second legs of the conflation.

The ongoing butch-femme debate in lesbian communities, which contests the pros and cons of acting out sex-based gender roles socially and/or sexually within an all-female coupling, likewise attests to the conflation's hardiness. For example, JoAnn Loulan's groundbreaking surveys of lesbians throughout the country illustrate the phenomenon well: her most recent data, from 1989–90, show 44 percent of the 589 lesbians interviewed electing to adopt a socially and/or sexually gendered role within the relationship, with 19 percent identifying themselves as butch (the male role) and 25 percent as femme (the female role). The conflation thus persists among sizable segments of lesbian communities, coexisting with the growing recognition that butch-femme categorizing often serves to perpetuate androsexist as well as heterosexist images. In short, under the first and second legs of the conflation, internalized active/passive traditions regarding sex and gender continue to drive, at least in part, the personal(ized) constructions of sexual orientation among many lesbians living today.

In both male and female same-sex settings, the butch/femme/queen discourse manifests an awareness of and an acquiescence to official active/passive sex/gender themes and traditions, even when "bending" them. Among both the men and the women, sex is viewed as gender's determinant. Among both sexes, gender is understood to comprise social/public and sexual/private personality. Among both gay men and lesbians, social gender atypicality is associated with sexual gender atypicality. Thus, Leg One and Leg Two of the conflation remain jointly in place among both male and female segments of sexual minority communities.

In like vein, sexual minorities of color continue to live the conflation in much the same way that Eric Garber depicted in his study of early-to-mid-1900s Harlem. Indeed, the costumed events that Garber described now have evolved into the highly stylized recent innovation known as "voguing." Popularized by Madonna's 1990 pop music hit single, *Vogue,* this activity involves "striking a pose" which, more often than not, amounts to glamorized and exaggerated social gender posturing; the voguing balls of today, as with their earlier equivalents, are characterized by flamboyant social gender regalia and props.

The popularity of voguing and balls among African-American and Latino sexual minorities in New York City was depicted in movingly graphic detail in the 1990 film *Paris Is Burning.* The film documents the "houses" that play central roles in the production of balls; each is headed by a "mother" who directs his/her house's participation in the events. Participants compete in categories such as "Butch Queen," "Pretty Girl," and "Miss Cheesecake." One set of categories, "Realness," focuses on the ability of the competitors to emulate the subjects of the category; for instance, "Looking Like a Girl Going to School" or "Executive Man." In an especially revealing comment on these categories of competition, one participant explains that the object of the latter category is to "look like a real man, a straight man." Indeed, under the conflation's configuration and depiction of active/passive human identities and personalities, "real" men (and women) are "straight" men (and women).

Not surprisingly, then, social/public gender affectations provide much of the film's thematic centerpiece, attesting to the continuing vitality of the conflation's first and second legs even among youngsters unequipped to (re)cognize them: throughout the film, we repeatedly encounter young males in interviews and escapades who self-identify as gay, and who uniformly conceive and articulate that sexual identity by adopting in both outlandish and discreet ways the social/public attributes associated with femininity. This film, in fact, portrays individuals for whom sex-determined gender and sexual orientation are indistinguishable, and who live their lives *today* on that basis; these are persons who today define themselves as sexually and therefore socially cross-gendered, or vice versa, and who thereby apply to their beings and lives the active/passive dictates corresponding both to the first and to the second leg of the conflation.

Finally, there is Jacob's story. As an African American growing up in the southeast just as the integration of public schools was getting underway, Jacob was a star student who excelled both in academics and in extracurricular activities.[10] Fearful that his "effeminate mannerisms" (coupled with his apparent lack of interest in girls) and general timidity toward sports might label him as gay, Jacob used his studies and activities to insulate himself from suspicion: he deflected any questioning of his closeted (homo)sexuality by raising his "bookworm" persona as a shield. Additionally, he steered clear of any association with the "hard-core faggots" in his high school, characterizing the group as "very effeminate acting." As Jacob's story indicates, for him as well as for his peers among both the "faggots" and nonfaggots, social effeminacy (in the form of mannerisms, activities, or talents) stood for, and therefore was interpreted as, same-sex desire. Social effeminacy, in other words, signaled and was tantamount to sexual effeminacy, and vice versa.

To avoid identification with the latter attribute of his personality, Jacob strategically deployed and disguised the former attributes of his personality. In doing so, Jacob displayed an intuitive understanding of the way(s) in which active/passive sex/gender traditions under the conflation's first and second legs operate(d) in tandem to shape his peers' and his family's (mis)perceptions of him, both socially and sexually. He intuited that society officially and culturally regards gender as deductive and intransitive; in turn, Jacob understood that his personal survival and prosperity depended on deflecting suspicion over his sexual/private personality which, by his own account, he consciously set out to do by disguising his apparently atypical or cross-gendered social/public personality.

Confirming this intuition, Jacob's calculated disguises succeeded. Though he engaged in same-sex liaisons throughout his high school years, Jacob was able to "pass for straight" in the eyes of both friends and family. In this way, Jacob enabled himself to avoid (some of) the stigma and prejudice heaped on persons who somehow—socially, sexually, or both—are deemed cross-gendered; persons who are devalued or denigrated because they personify the violation or disruption of one or more of the conflation's legs.

Both voguing and Jacob display yet again the way(s) in which contemporary sexual minorities—including those living in communities of color—comply with traditionalist sex/gender conceptions, even as they bend or break official or cultural sex/gender rules accompanying those conceptions. In both instances, sex was understood to fix gender. In both instances, gender was understood to encompass both social/public and sexual/private components. In both instances, gender transitivity that was social was associated with the sexual version. And, in both instances, society's problematization of gender atypicality socially and/or sexually was intuitively, if not intellectually, understood. Thus, while indulging, both socially and sexually, in various forbidden cross-gender attributes or activities, the individuals in these instances clearly were aware of—and accepted and accommodated—the official premises and the cultural power of the first and second legs of the conflation.

Although the history of the conflation in modern Euro-American culture presented above is necessarily oversimplified, it points to the inescapable conclusion that the conflation of sex, gender, and sexual orientation envelops our intellectual and attitudinal environment and shapes our personal and collective sensibilities. The conflation's embodiment and enforcement of active/passive sex/gender themes and traditions are so pervasive, so ingrained, so institutionalized, so internalized, that even our children unknowingly collect epithets like "queer," "sissy," "dyke," and "tomboy" in single, automatic breaths. These epithets, in turn, display how heteropatriarchy is imprinted in the collective psyche of each generation.

In short, this nation's sex/gender system is designed, built, and maintained precisely along the conflation's traditionalist active/passive fault lines, both socially and sexually. These official and cultural fault lines do not operate randomly: in practice, they operate to secure the social/public and sexual/private intransitivity of deductive gender, and thereby to secure the hierarchical imperatives that underlie and drive the Euro-American sex/gender system and its heteropatriarchal ideology. Unthinking schoolyard comments only reflect and confirm the conflationary system's continuing grip on the nation's senses, while underscoring traditionalist fear and loathing of social or sexual challenges to conflationary arrangements that (might) disrupt the sex/gender status quo.

In Latina/o cultures or settings, both within and beyond the United States, this conflationary dynamic and its sex/gender ideology are also present, and perhaps even more virulently so due to the prevalence of a strong "machismo" norm. Terms like "marimacha" and "maricon"—meaning dyke and queer, respectively—reflect and reify the conflation's sway over Latina/o sex/gender norms and sexual orientation identities: the former connotes a mannish female, the latter an effeminate man. Both are devalued because they enact nonconforming combinations of sex, gender, and sexuality. Thus, as in Euro-American contexts, all three legs of the conflation operate, and in combination construct social and sexual identifications: sex establishes gender expectations, and gender a/typically is construed and mis/treated as homo/heterosexual orientation. As in Euro-American culture, social or sexual disruption of any leg is censured. Moreover, as these terms imply, Latina/o sex/gender hierarchies are not only heterocentric, they also are androcentric. Thus, as in the Euro-American sex/gender system, Latina/o ideals and values instill and demand conformity to the conflation's active/passive heteropatriarchal bent.

Accordingly, resistance to this conflation and its ideology must be recognized as central to the anti-subordination strategy of Queer legal theory. But this strategy also must guard against our prior internalization of conflationary beliefs or associations. In particular, concerns over gay male androsexism, and the dangers that it poses for Queer theorizing, should serve constructively to heighten our individual and collective vigilance against the potential for a wholesale or creeping influence of androsexism within Queer critiques. Because it counters the tradition of male supremacy that has run through Western history, this heightened vigilance may not come easily, but it is also not impossible. Indeed, by definition, the term "Queer" reflects and invokes this type of heightened awareness for sex/gender egalitarianism and against sex/gender imperialism. The key, then, is to live up to the standards of the term, and the challenge is to join in the fulfillment of the ideals underlying this commitment.

However, to do so we also must take into account other issues raised by Queer legal theory. American culture employs "queer" to denigrate persons suspected of being gay, but in recent years "Queer," has come to signify principally a rebellious resistance to heterosexist customs and precepts. As a result, "Queer" like "queer," tends to indicate minority "sexual orientation." But it need (and should) not be so: "Queer" is a description of consciousness regarding sexuality and its relationship to one's self and to one's culture.[11] Thus, even though most persons who self-identify as Queer today probably are gay, lesbian, bisexual, or trans/bi-gendered, one *can* be gay or lesbian or bisexual or trans/bi-gendered without being Queer; Queer consciousness is neither innate nor uniform among sexual minorities. Likewise, Queer subjectivity may be articulated from a sexual majority position.

Queer legal theory likewise must and can avoid the similar danger of carelessly (or intentionally) reiterating the racist biases that, like androsexism, pervade our social and legal environments. The vigilance of Queer legal theory against racism is again especially important due to our cultural backdrop: the larger Queer social movement already has experienced problems with racial (dis)harmony because it has not (fully) excised racist overtones and undertones from its ranks. This failure excludes people of color from Queer venues, replicating and compounding the race divisions of the sexual majority. This failure thus demonstrates how deeply we are mired in acculturation, and how crucial it is for Queer legal theory to intercede during these formative times on behalf of Queers of color. Queer as legal theory, using Queer cultural politics and studies as its point of departure, has the opportunity and obligation to discontinue, interrupt, and condemn the replication of racism both in sexual minority cultural venues and legal projects.

This opportunity is also an obligation because the exclusion or marginalization of people of color within Queer settings is antithetical to the inclusiveness and expansiveness that is definitive and constitutive of Queerness. As in the case of androsexism, Queer undertakings proactively must show and apply a heightened sensitivity to, and an uncompromising opposition against, the omission of race, ethnicity, and class from Queer critiques. Queer as legal theory cannot tolerate or ignore any show of wholesale or creeping racism, ethnocentrism, or classism. The inclusiveness and egalitarianism of Queerness demand that Queer legal theory not ignore the lives and presence of Queers of color, of varying ethnic backgrounds, or of (dis)advantaged economic backgrounds: to do so would be to lend support to the oppression that subordinates groups based on race, ethnicity, or class more generally. As legal theory, the Queer enterprise must take a proactive stance toward race, ethnicity, and class, toward their particularized intersections with (homo/bi)sexuality, and toward their broader intertwining with sex/gender issues.

At the threshold—where we stand today—this concern therefore necessitates nothing less than a sustained effort to make the historic and unfinished fight against racism, ethnocentrism, and classism integral to Queer critiques of the law. This effort in turn requires an affirmative interrogation of why and how Queerness plays differently in different racial, ethnic, or class contexts, as much as it requires an interrogation of where and when racism, ethnocentrism, and classism—perhaps even of the unconscious type—confine Queer theorizing in arbitrary or unproductive ways. From the outset, Queer legal critiques therefore must take the time and make the effort expressly to discuss and expose the role of race, ethnicity, and class in the (mis)fortunes visited by the law on Queer (and other) lives. In this way, "Queer" as legal theory can avoid importing the assumed and imposed whiteness of "queer" as cultural epithet and also align itself with the greater anti-subordination civil rights movement for equality in color and class relations.

Finally, these notes make plain that the conflation's androcentric and heterocentric prejudice is replicated and disseminated not only through Anglo, but also through Hispanic, norms. For Latinas/os in the United States, and especially for those who identify as lesbian, gay, bisexual or trans/bi-gendered, this social combination is a "double whammy." In other words, Latina/o members of sexual minorities in the United States are socially and legally marginalized through the conflationary precepts and practices of the two systems that constitute our beings and structure our environments.

These notes thus make plain that this conflation concerns more than Queer legal theory; the conflation's impact specifically on Latina/o sexual minority communities implicates LatCrit theory as well. The conflation's heteropatriarchal biases are directly relevant to the anti-subordination mission of LatCrit theory because the Lat-

Crit enterprise is explicitly and self-consciously dedicated to the cause of social justice for *all* Latinas/os; LatCrit theory insistently embraces and celebrates the multiple diversities of "Latinas/os," rejecting both single-axis analyses that essentialize Latinas/os as well as internal and external ideologies of subordination.[12] Because the conflation's promotion of androsexism and heterosexism subordinates many Latinas/os, these notes suggest that LatCrit theory and Queer legal theory share a common interest in the transformation of today's sex/gender system, a transformation that unites the QueerCrit and LatCrit goals of a just post-subordination society. These notes, in sum, invite LatCrit interrogation of this conflation, an interrogation that properly is deemed integral to the LatCrit anti-subordination agenda.

NOTES

1. Francisco Valdes, *Queers, Sissies, Dykes and Tomboys: Deconstructing the Conflation of "Sex," "Gender," and "Sexual Orientation" in Euro-American Law and Society,* 83 Calif. L. Rev. 1, 36–55 (1995).

2. 608 F.2d 327 (9th Cir. 1979).

3. Complaint at 3, Strailey v. Happy Times Nursery Sch., Inc. (N.D. Cal.) (Civil Action No. 76-1088).

4. *Id.*

5. Complaint at 3–4.

6. EEOC Decision No. 71-1902, 3 Fair Empl. Prac. Cas. (BNA) 1244, 1244–45 (1971).

7. *Id.*

8. *Strailey,* 608 F.2d at 331.

9. *Id.*

10. James T. Sears, Growing Up Gay in the South: Race, Gender, and Journeys of the Spirit 117–29 (1991).

11. *See generally* Lauren Berlant & Elizabeth Freeman, *Queer Nationality,* in Queer Planet: Queer Politics and Social Theory (Michael Warner ed., 1993) at 193.

12. *See generally* Symposium, *LatCrit Theory: Naming and Launching a New Discourse of Critical Legal Scholarship,* 2 Harv. Latino L. Rev. 1 (1997); Symposium, *LatCrit Theory: Latinas/os and the Law,* 85 Calif. L. Rev. (forthcoming 1998).

From the Editors
Issues and Comments

Do black and Latina women suffer a "double whammy," or is their status sometimes an advantage in that employers reap a two-for-one benefit in hiring them and also view them as less threatening than men of their group?

Is a black or Latina woman essentially a woman, or a member of her minority group? That is, which affiliation is more vital to her identity, or is the answer neither?

Do women, especially women of color, suffer forms of violence that we simply do not call by that name?

Is it racism if a government official, agency, or the phone book discourages Latino double surnames? Is it sexism in that the name invariably cut is that of the mother?

Why do some Latino men affect a super-macho persona or stance? Why do some majoritarian stereotypes of minority people—for example, the sexless Mammy or hapless Mexican clown or buffoon—depict them as desexed neuters? Are the reasons possibly related?

Is Latino or black culture homophobic and even harder on gays and lesbians than white culture is? If so, why?

Are women of color disadvantaged in the marriage marketplace because of prevailing standards of beauty, such as, light skin, straight nose, and blond hair? Why is this not true also of minority men? (Or is it?)

If a practice would be sexual harassment in one culture but not another, should the law punish the practice anyway?

Are illegal immigrants at increased risk of sexual oppression because of their fear that reporting the crime could lead to deportation? If so, is the solution to provide that the police overlook their illegal status when they report a crime against them?

Do you think that those who have suffered discrimination of one kind (say racial) are less likely to discriminate on another basis (say sex) because they know the pain and hardship that it causes? Or do you think they are more likely to discriminate against others in order to feel above some other groups?

You are a Latina. An expedition of Space Traders offers you one of two pills, which introduced into the water system will solve either racism or sexism permanently and completely. Which practice of victimization causes you more misery, and which pill would you choose? If you were a Latino, which pill would you choose?

Suggested Readings

Between Borders: Essays on Mexicana/Chicana History, edited by Adelaida R. Del Castillo. Encino, Calif.: Floricanto Press, 1990.

Beyond Stereotypes: The Critical Analysis of Chicana Literature, edited by María Herrera-Sobek. Binghamton, N.Y.: Bilingual Press, 1985.

Blackwelder, Julia Kirk. *Women of the Depression: Caste and Culture in San Antonio, 1929–1939*. College Station: Texas A & M University Press, 1984.

Bonilla-Santiago, Gloria. *Breaking Ground and Barriers: Hispanic Women Developing Effective Leadership*. San Diego: Marin Publications, 1992.

Building with Our Hands: New Directions in Chicana Studies, edited by Adela de la Torre and Beatriz M. Pesquera. Berkeley: University of California Press, 1993.

Castillo, Ana. *The Mixquiahuala Letters*. Binghamton, N.Y.: Bilingual Review Press, 1986.

Cervantes, Lorna Dee. *Emplumada*. Pittsburgh: University of Pittsburgh Press, 1981.

Chabram-Dernersesian, Angie. "I Throw Punches for My Race, but I Don't Want to Be a Man: Writing Us—Chica-nos (Girl Us)/Chicanas—into the Movement Script." In *Cultural Studies*, edited by Lawrence Grossberg, Cary Nelson, and Paula Treichler, 81. New York: Routledge, 1992.

Chicana Creativity and Criticism: New Frontiers in American Literature, edited by María Herrera-Sobek and Helena María Viramontes. Rev. ed. Albuquerque: University of New Mexico Press, 1996.

Chicana Critical Issues, edited by Norma Alarcon et al. Berkeley: Third Woman Press, 1993.

Chicana Lesbians: The Girls Our Mothers Warned Us About, edited by Carla Trujillo. Berkeley: Third Woman Press, 1991.

Chicana Voices: Intersections of Class, Race, and Gender, edited by Teresa Cordova et al. Austin: Center for Mexican American Studies, University of Texas, 1990.

Chicana (W)rites on Word and Film, edited by María Herrera-Sobek and Helena María Viramontes. Berkeley: Third Woman Press, 1995.

Chicanas in the 80's: Unsettled Issues, edited by Mujers en Marcha. Berkeley: Chicano Studies Library Publications Unit, University of California, 1983.

Compañeras: Latina Lesbians, An Anthology, edited by Juanita Ramos. New York: Routledge, 1994.

Delgado, Richard. "Rodrigo's Sixth Chronicle: Intersections, Essences and the Dilemma of Social Reform." 68 *New York University Law Review* 639 (1993).

Deutsch, Sarah. *No Separate Refuge: Culture, Class, and Gender on an Anglo-Hispanic Frontier in the American Southwest, 1880–1940*. New York: Oxford University Press, 1987.

Diaz-Cotto, Juanita. *Gender, Ethnicity, and the State: Latina and Latino Prison Politics*. Albany: State University of New York Press, 1996.

García, Alma M. "The Development of Chicana Feminist Discourse, 1970–1980." *Gender and Society* 3 (1989): 217–38.

Gil, Rosa Maria, and Carmen Inoa Vazquez. *The Maria Paradox: How Latinas Can Merge Old World Traditions with New World Self-Esteem.* New York: G. P. Putnam's Sons, 1996.

Gonzalez, Deena J. "Chicana Identity Matters." In *Culture and Difference: Critical Perspectives on the Bicultural Experience in the United States,* edited by Antonia Darder, 41–53. New York: Bergin & Garvey, 1995.

Gonzalez, Rosalinda M. "Chicanas and Mexican Immigrant Families 1920–1940: Women's Subordination and Family Exploitation." In *Decades of Discontent: The Women's Movement, 1920–1940,* edited by Lois Scharf and Joan M. Jensen, 59+. Westport, Conn.: Greenwood Press, 1983.

Gonzalez, Rudolfo "Corky." *I Am Joaquin. Yo Soy Joaquin.* Toronto: Bantam Books, 1972.

Grillo, Trina. "Anti-Essentialism and Intersectionality: Tools to Dismantle the Master's House." 10 *Berkeley Women's Law Journal* 16 (1995).

Gutiérrez, Ramón A. *When Jesus Came, the Corn Mothers Went Away: Marriage, Sexuality, and Power in New Mexico, 1500–1846.* Stanford: Stanford University Press, 1991.

Herrera-Sobek, María. *The Mexican Corrido: A Feminist Analysis.* Bloomington: Indiana University Press, 1990.

Hondagneu-Sotelo, Pierrette. *Gendered Transitions: Mexican Experiences of Immigration.* Berkeley: University of California Press, 1994.

Iglesias, Elizabeth M. "Structures of Subordination: Women of Color at the Intersection of Title VII and the NLRA. Not!" 28 *Harvard Civil Rights–Civil Liberties Law Review* 395 (1993).

Johnson, Kevin R. "Racial Restrictions on Naturalization: The Recurring Intersection of Race and Gender in Immigration and Citizenship Law." 11 *Berkeley Women's Law Journal* 142 (1996).

Lebell, Sharon. *Naming Ourselves, Naming Our Children: Resolving the Last Name Dilemma.* Freedom, Calif.: Crossing Press, 1988.

Lionnet, Françoise. *Autobiographical Voices: Race, Gender, Self-Portraiture.* Ithaca, N.Y.: Cornell University Press, 1989.

Making Face, Making Soul=Haciendo Caras: Creative and Critical Perspectives by Women of Color, edited by Gloria Anzaldúa. San Francisco: Aunt Lute Foundation Books, 1990.

Mirande, Alfredo. *Hombres y Machos: Masculinity and Latino Culture.* Boulder, Colo.: Westview Press, 1997.

Mirande, Alfredo, and Evangelina Enriquez. *La Chicana: The Mexican American Woman.* Chicago: University of Chicago Press, 1979.

Now the Volcano: An Anthology of Latin American Gay Literature, edited by Winston Leyland. San Francisco: Gay Sunshine Press, 1979.

Ontiveros, Maria L. "Fictionalizing Harassment—Disclosing the Truth." 93 *Michigan Law Review* 1373 (1995).

———. "Rosa Lopez, David Letterman, Christopher Darden, and Me: Issues of Gender, Ethnicity, and Class in Evaluating Witness Credibility." 6 *Hastings Women's Law Journal* 135 (1995).

Pesquera, Beatriz M., and Denise Segura. "There Is No Going Back: Chicanas and Feminism." In *Chicana Critical Issues: Mujeres Activas En Letras Y Cambio Social,* edited by Norma Alarcon. Berkeley: Third Woman Press, 1993.

The Puerto Rican Woman: Perspectives on Culture, History and Society, edited by Edna Acosta-Bélen and Barbara R. Sjostrom. New York: Praeger, 1986.

Rechy, John. *City of Night*. New York: Grove Press, 1963.

Rivera, Jenny. "The Politics of Invisibility." 3 *Georgetown Journal on Fighting Poverty* 61 (1995).

———. "The Violence against Women Act and the Construction of Multiple Consciousness in the Civil Rights and Feminist Movements." 4 *Journal of Law and Policy* 463 (1996).

Romany, Celina. "Ain't I a Feminist." 4 *Yale Journal of Law and Feminism* 23 (1991).

———. "Women as *Aliens*: A Feminist Critique of the Public/Private Distinction in International Human Rights Law." 6 *Harvard Human Rights Journal* 87 (1993).

Ruiz, Vicki L. "By the Day or Week: Mexicana Domestic Workers in El Paso. In *"To Toil the Livelong Day"*: *America's Women at Work, 1780–1980,* edited by Carol Groneman and Mary Beth Norton, 269. Ithaca, N.Y.: Cornell University Press, 1987.

Sanchez, George F. "'Go after the Women': Americanization and the Mexican Immigrant Woman, 1915–1929." In *Unequal Sisters: A Multicultural Reader in U.S. Women's History,* edited by Ellen C. DuBois and Vicki L. Ruiz, 250. New York: Routledge, 1990.

The Sexuality of Latinas, edited by Norma Alarcon, Ana Castillo, and Cherríe Moraga. Berkeley: Third Woman Press, 1993.

Symposium on the Feminization of Poverty: The Hispanic Perspective. Co-sponsored by the New York State Division for Women and the National Conference of Puerto Rican Women, Inc., June 1986.

This Bridge Called My Back: Writings by Radical Women of Color. edited by Cherríe Moraga and Gloria Anzaldúa. 2d ed. New York: Kitchen Table, Women of Color Press, 1983.

English-Only, Bilingualism, Interpreters
You Mean I Can't Speak Spanish?

Latinos are perhaps more attached to their language than is any other non-English-speaking immigrant or minority group. Why is this so, and how legitimate is the desire to maintain the mother language in a country whose dominant language is English? The right to speak Spanish arises in schools, criminal and civil courtrooms, and in the workplace. Part XI contains essays addressing the role of court interpreters; school boards and other authorities charged with offering bilingual instruction; legal witnesses who speak or do not speak English or Spanish; and English-only laws that would forbid the speaking of Spanish or other foreign languages in connection with certain official functions. Authors also address the United States' history as a multilingual nation, showing that our society in many eras has tolerated and given official sanction to the speaking of foreign languages such as French and German.

Chapter 79

Hold Your Tongue

James Crawford

There is nothing new about ethnic intolerance. But beginning in the United States of the 1980s, it assumed a guise we had not seen before: the politics of English Only.

Traditionally taken for granted, our national tongue emerged as a cause célèbre, a civic passion touching nearly every state house, the U.S. Congress, and numerous municipalities. The fervor was not so much *for* English as *against* the growing prominence of other languages. "Bilingualism" had arrived, to the dismay of many monolingual Americans. Some claimed it was now easier to function in English when traveling abroad than in the immigrant ghettos of U.S. cities. Apparently today's newcomers, unlike their predecessors, felt no obligation to learn our language. Did they expect us to learn Spanish? shocked Anglo-Americans wanted to know. Whose country was this, after all? Most amazing, government was pursuing policies that seemed to discourage English acquisition: bilingual schooling, bilingual driver's tests, bilingual welfare forms, even bilingual assistance in the voting booth. Could we afford to accommodate millions of new Americans—literally scores of different language groups—each in their own tongue? Would Congress soon be translating its proceedings, United Nations–style, with every member listening through a headset? Where would it end?

Such anxieties and resentments have given rise to a movement to declare English the nation's official language. While the objective may seem innocuous, the proposed means are not. A constitutional English Language Amendment seeks to prohibit most uses of other tongues by government (federal, state, and local) and, in some circumstances, by individuals. Whether it would achieve these aims no one can say with certainty. But, if adopted, the measure would jeopardize a wide range of rights and services now available to non-English speakers, from bilingual clerks at city hall to the freedom of speech itself. At a symbolic level, Official English would be a way of telling newcomers, "Conform or get out." Indeed, that message has already been conveyed by the current agitation, polarizing several communities where Hispanics or Asians have settled.

Americans are not accustomed to quarreling over language. Earlier generations of nativists were usually too preoccupied with immigrants' race or religion to worry whether their English skills were up to snuff. Contrary to melting-pot mythology, newcomers often maintained their native tongues for generations on U.S. soil. Many fought for and, depending on their political clout, won concessions like bilingual public education, which was commonplace in nineteenth-century "German America." Moreover, this country has a kind of libertarian tradition where language is concerned—a democracy is not supposed to tell its citizens how to talk—which may explain the Founders' "oversight" when it came to mandating an official tongue.

This is not to say the tradition has been consistent. At various points in our history, linguistic minorities have faced policies of exclusion or coercive assimilation or both. Yet, unlike today's campaigns, these were normally aimed at particular groups for particular purposes—for example, in the 1880s, when federal authorities decided that "the first step . . . toward teaching the Indians the mischief and folly of continuing in their barbarous practices" was to force their children to attend English-only boarding schools; or in 1897, when Pennsylvania enacted an English-proficiency requirement for miners, seeking to bar Italians and Slavs from the coal fields; or in 1921, when Republicans in New York pushed through an English literacy test for voting, hoping to disfranchise one million Yiddish speakers who had an annoying habit of electing Democrats.[1]

What distinguishes today's English Only phenomenon is the apocalyptic nature of its fears: that the American language is "threatened" and, with it, the basis of American nationhood. We are warned that unless action is taken to halt our "mindless drift toward a bilingual society," the United States will soon be balkanized, divided, at war with itself.[2] Ostensibly to defend "the primacy of English," a new cadre of zealots is working to restrict speech in other tongues. And there is a real chance that such proposals could become law; in several states, they already have.

Worries about the slipping status of English in the United States come, ironically, at a time when English continues to spread as a world language, the undisputed medium of international business, science, and statecraft. To be sure, this country is more diverse, linguistically and otherwise, than it was a generation ago. Immigration is the major reason. Exotic cultural enclaves have appeared not only in coastal cities, but throughout the heartland. In 1960, how many citizens of Fort Smith, Arkansas, or Garden City, Kansas, would have foreseen a Vietnamese community in their midst? (How many had even heard of Vietnam?) Just as in the past, the newcomers find it natural to preserve remnants of their homelands—food, customs, religion, and language—that some Americans find jarring. The number of U.S. residents who speak a minority tongue at home increased by 41 percent during the 1980s.[3] Yet at the same time, all available evidence shows that today's immigrants are learning English faster than ever before. By objective measures, bilingualism is no more prevalent now than in several earlier periods of U.S. history.

So what accounts for the new English Only mentality? Some say bigotry. It is no coincidence that the targets of antibilingual campaigns are frequently racial as well as linguistic minorities. Leaders of U.S. English, the major lobby promoting an English Language Amendment, have expressed an animus toward Hispanics in particular. This organization is an outgrowth of the immigration restriction movement. One of its founders has warned that Spanish speakers may use their "greater reproductive powers" to seize political control in the United States. ("Perhaps this is the first instance in which those with their pants up are going to get caught by those with their pants down!")[4] A similar group, English First, complains: "Tragically, many immigrants these days refuse to learn English! They never become productive members of American society. They remain stuck in a linguistic and economic ghetto, many living off welfare and costing working Americans millions of tax dollars each year." It goes on to claim that "radical activists have been caught sneaking illegal aliens to the polls on election day and using bilingual ballots to cast fraudulent votes." The fact that U.S. English and English First have raised millions of dollars with such appeals suggests a sizable nativist constituency.

Nevertheless, it is a mistake to assume that enthusiasm for Official English is driven solely, or even primarily, by such prejudices. According to opinion polls and election results, about three Americans in four are inclined to endorse the idea. Many ask: Shouldn't newcomers be expected to learn English, for their own good and the country's? What's racist about that? Nothing whatsoever. Bilingual accommodations are the issue. Should government be able to provide them, as needed, to ease immigrants' transition into this society? Should there be an affirmative *right* to certain services in minority tongues? Or should public-sector bilingualism be banned by law? When Congress passed the Bilingual Education Act of 1968 and the bilingual voting rights amendments of 1975, it galloped headlong into this arena with little foresight and almost no public discussion. Such an abrupt turn in policy was bound to provoke debate sooner or later. At last, language issues are beginning to receive some needed attention. It is only unfortunate that vital programs, for example, the schooling of limited-English-proficient children, are now held hostage to symbolic politics.

English Only flows from feelings of insecurity. Now that demographic changes of all kinds—greater mobility, nontraditional families, mass culture—are disrupting Americans' sense of community, there is a renewed search for unifying institutions. With ethnic warfare spreading in eastern Europe, many are wondering when it will reach our shores. Already there is talk of "tribalism" and "the disuniting of America" from those who fear that common ties are being frayed by group claims of all descriptions. Many fair-minded people, who otherwise cherish individual rights and cultural pluralism, are beginning to wonder whether the national tongue may be an exceptional case. Perhaps "unilingualism" is our best hope of managing diversity, the one bond that might keep us together. If so, it becomes too precious to risk and legislating conformity becomes justifiable.

It is my aim to show how mistaken, how shortsighted, and how disastrous that view can be.

NOTES

1. Arnold H. Leibowitz, *English Literacy: Legal Sanction for Discrimination,* NOTRE DAME LAWYER 45, no. 7 (1969), pp. 34–35.

2. Gerda Bikales, Presentation to Georgetown University Round Table on Languages and Linguistics, March 12, 1987.

3. Current Population Survey, Nov. 1989, cited in *Numbers and Needs* 2, no. 1 (1992), pp. 2–4.

4. John Tanton, "Memorandum to WITAN IV Attendees," Oct. 10, 1986.

Chapter 80

A Bilingual-Education Initiative as a Prop. 187 in Disguise?

Ruben Navarrette, Jr.

Bilingual education is back in the news. The Orange Unified School Board has voted unanimously to seek permission from the state to terminate its bilingual education program and replace it with English immersion. Ruben Zacarias, superintendent of the L.A. Unified School District, wants to limit the number of years a student remains on a bilingual track. And new polling data suggest that a majority of Latino parents, notably in Orange County, are worried that their children will become mired in bilingual education; they strongly believe in early English proficiency. Come June 1998, all California may be pulled into the bilingual fray if the English Language Education for Immigrant Children Initiative qualifies for the ballot.

At first glance, the measure appears to be the latest embodiment of the sort of anti-immigrant and anti-Latino prejudice enshrined in Proposition 187. But that oversimplification may mischaracterize the proposed initiative as harmful, when it may be helpful.

The initiative would require that all students be placed in English-language classrooms, provide students classified as "English learners" (limited English proficient in current parlance) with a one-year transition period of "sheltered immersion" in which instruction is in English but the curriculum and presentation are designed for non-English speakers, allow students' parents, under certain conditions, to opt for bilingual education, and annually appropriate $50 million for English-language instruction classes for parents who pledge to provide students with "English language tutoring."

The initiative, sponsored by former gubernatorial candidate Ron Unz and teacher Gloria Matta Tuchman, is based on a number of suppositions. One, that bilingual education has failed. Two, that school bureaucracies addicted to the additional funding provided for bilingual students ignore complaints of parents who want their children taught in English. And finally, since schools have shirked their "moral obliga-

From L.A. Times, July 6, 1997, Sec. M, p. 6. Originally published in the *Los Angeles Times*. Reprinted by permission.

tion" to leave students with the skills necessary to be successful, including English proficiency, more power should be returned to parents.

The English for the Children initiative will no doubt run afoul of extremists on both right and left. Cultural purists, nativists and those resentful of financing bilingual education in California will balk at either the prospect of paying an additional $50 million to teach English to parents or the idea of allowing those parent to opt for bilingual education. The pro-bilingual crowd, on the other hand, will bristle at the idea of putting all children in English-language classrooms and will, on the heels of Proposition 187 and 209, decry the initiative as the third assault in as many elections on California's growing Latino population.

One wild card in all this will be younger Mexican Americans. They opposed Proposition 187 because it blocked access to education. They were conflicted over Proposition 209 because it seemed both to limit opportunity and reward merit. On bilingual education, how will they line up? For the MTV generation, at ease with English, there are no historical scars, no romantic connection to bilingual education as rectifier of linguistic wrongs, no hang-ups over "the way it used to be" in public schools, no hostility toward English and no reluctance to scrutinize the motivations of interest groups. Within a generation that struggles with Spanish and answers its Mexican *abuelita*'s questions in English it may prove difficult to whip up hysteria over an end to government-subsidized bilingualism.

Along the way, these young, more open-minded Mexican Americans may be joined by immigrant parents. Early last year, at the Ninth Street School in downtown Los Angeles, where nine of ten students do not speak English and where only 1 percent of students master enough English to test out of the bilingual program, dozens of parents, calling themselves Las Familias del Pueblo, revolted against bilingual education, demanding that the school eliminate it and re-emphasize learning English. School officials dismissed their wishes.

A few months later, a survey of 600 Latino parents, by the Washington-based Center for Equal Opportunity, found that 81.3 percent preferred that their children's courses be taught in English, while only 12.2 percent chose Spanish. Those figures are consistent with a 1988 Department of Education study, which revealed that 78 percent of Mexican parents opposed teaching language-minority children in a non-English language if "it meant less time teaching them English." They also mesh with more recent findings in a *Los Angeles Times* poll, which found that 83 percent of Latino parents in Orange County favor English-language instruction as soon as their children begin school, while only 17 percent support native-language instruction.

Presented with such figures, school officials and defenders of bilingual education have, up to now, held their ground, contending that parents are "uninformed," "misguided," and asserting that schools know how best to educate their children.

This old refrain hearkens back to 1968, at the height of the modern Chicano Movement. That was also the year that Congress pushed through the Bilingual Education Act—and sparked thirty years of intermittent debate. It was also the year when thousands of Mexican American students, protesting what they considered to be an inferior education designed by mostly white school officials, walked out of five high schools in the L.A. Unified School District. At school board meetings, the students' parents rose and spoke in support of their children. The school officials' response: They knew better.

That story is a poignant reminder of just how far those who profess to advocate for Latinos have, in thirty years, strayed from their own ideals. Today, advocacy groups, in circling the wagons to preserve besieged programs like bilingual education, no longer ask themselves tough questions about whether such programs are worth preserving in the first place. As a result, Latino parents who have taken a stand against bilingual education have stood alone, at odds with the very groups that are supposed to be their champions.

Meanwhile, the national education system claims, from the beginning, to have used bilingual education to give non-English-speaking students a voice. How ironic that now, in ignoring growing opposition to the program, that same system should deny a voice to their parents.

Chapter 81

American Languages, Cultural Pluralism, and Official English

Juan F. Perea

The demand for bilingual education dates back to the inception of our nation. In 1787, the German college at Lancaster was established to provide bilingual education in German and in English. In 1837, the Pennsylvania legislature authorized the founding of German-language schools on an equal basis with English-language schools, both at public expense. Louisiana, prior to 1864 and after 1879, provided for public education in English and French. Many schools of this time, and earlier, were monolingual in languages other than English. Whatever the merits of the current debate about bilingual education, it has existed as a legitimate, state-supported form of education since our nation's beginning. The statement that this is a demand "never voiced by immigrants before" is simply false for two reasons: false, because bilingual education, at least in German and French, has been a feature of our educational landscape literally for centuries; and false, because Hispanic populations have lived within the current borders of the United States since before this nation existed. The Hispanic population is both a colonial population with ancient ties to this country, in the same sense as the English colonists, and an immigrant population, with reference to current immigrants. To refer to the entire Hispanic population, and particularly the Mexican-American population of the Southwest and California, as "immigrants" denies the longevity of the Hispanic populations of this country.

American nativism and racism have, of course, targeted many groups throughout our history. Native Americans, African Americans, Mexican Americans, and Asian Americans, among other groups, have been subjected to unequal treatment and oppression because of their differences from the majority culture. This chapter discusses the restrictive use of literacy and language requirements in our immigration laws, describes the official English movement and its use of language to exclude certain Americans from political participation, and concludes with an evaluation of official English.

From "DEMOGRAPHY AND DISTRUST: AN ESSAY ON AMERICAN LANGUAGES, CULTURAL PLURALISM, AND OFFICIAL ENGLISH." 77 MINN. L. REV. 269 (1992). Originally published in the *Minnesota Law Review*. Reprinted by permission.

Despite the absence of federal laws declaring English the official language, a number of federal laws do, in effect, produce this result. Our current federal immigration and naturalization laws require English literacy for naturalized citizenship and a literacy requirement for admission to the United States. In addition, the Immigration Reform and Control Act of 1986 required aliens newly legalized under its amnesty provision to demonstrate "minimal understanding of ordinary English" in order to become permanent resident aliens.[1]

The English-literacy requirement for citizenship is of tremendous symbolic importance. It is an important expression of federal policy in favor of English. It is through our naturalization laws that, in clearest form, the nation spells out the criteria that must be met by those who would join the American nation. English literacy has not, however, always been a requirement for citizenship. Nor has literacy always been a requirement for initial admission to the nation. The evolution of the English-language literacy requirement further demonstrates that nativism finds expression through language restrictions.

A strong popular movement favoring coerced assimilation occurred for the first time near the beginning of the twentieth century. Until around 1880, immigration to the United States had been open and unrestricted. Most assumed that American society would simply assimilate new immigrants. Indeed, because most of the immigrants until this time were from northwestern Europe, and especially from Great Britain, Germany, and Scandinavia, traditional sources of the American population, their racial and cultural characteristics matched those of the existing population relatively well, allowing them to assimilate with relatively little friction.

By 1890, immigrants from these countries began to be outnumbered by ones from southern and eastern Europe: Italy, Poland, and the Austro-Hungarian empire. These new immigrants brought with them their distinctive cultural traits. In response, a strong popular movement, fueled by American nativism, developed in favor of restrictions on immigration to the United States. The first goal of proponents of restricted immigration was a literacy test for immigrants that, in theory, would exclude a large proportion of those seeking admission to the United States. The test, "though ostensibly selective in theory, would prove restrictive in operation."[2] The purpose was clear: to exclude people whose ethnicity differed from that of the majority. Advocates hoped the test would reduce immigration by 25 percent.[3]

Opponents of the new European immigration tried three times, without success, to enact legislation that included a literacy requirement in some language for admission to the United States. Such legislation passed the Congress on three occasions. It was consistently vetoed by successive presidents because it was such a departure from prior, liberal immigration policy. Congress, however, enacted a provision requiring a literacy test over President Wilson's veto in 1917, on the eve of America's entry into World War I. The literacy test excluded "[a]ll aliens over sixteen years of age, physically capable of reading, who can not read the English language, or some other language or dialect, including Hebrew or Yiddish."[4] Increasing literacy rates in southern Europe and the postwar migration of educated Europeans, however, made a simple literacy test ineffective as an exclusionary device.

When this failure became apparent, new legislation established numerical quotas for immigrants. The prevailing idea among advocates of quota restrictions was that national unity depended on racial "homogeneity," which appeared to mean preservation of the existing racial character of the country. This illustrates the theme, repeated throughout our history, that our national identity, unity, and loyalty to our government depend on uniformity—sometimes racial, sometimes linguistic. "Foreign influences," persons whose ethnicity differs from that of the majority, are perceived as a threat to the nation. An identical theme underlies the official English movement's claim that national unity depends on linguistic uniformity or purity.

The controversy over inclusion of a literacy test for admission to the United States illustrates two of the principal themes of this chapter. First, the repeated exchanges between several presidents and several Congresses illustrate the tension between the perception of America that would accommodate pluralism and a view of America based on a need to restrict difference and encourage conformity. These exchanges illustrate the dialectic between plurality and conformism. The repeated presidential vetoes of legislation including the literacy test drew from the tradition of liberty that includes freedom for ethnically different peoples within our shores. By reaffirming the view of America as a land of opportunity for different peoples, these presidents reaffirmed the view of America as a pluralistic society. Congress, in contrast, responded to a strong popular movement supporting coerced assimilation, or increased conformity to some image of the desirable American. During this period, pressures for conformity within American society ran strong. Second, the controversy over the literacy tests illustrates the use of language as a proxy for the exclusion of immigrants on the basis of national origin. The literacy test, in effect, operated as an indirect, disguised device for exclusion. The first statutory requirement of English ability for naturalized citizenship appeared in 1906. The rationale for the statute was that a requirement of ability to speak English would improve the "quality" of naturalized citizens. The Commission on Naturalization of 1905 expressed the prevailing view: "[T]he proposition is incontrovertible that no man is a desirable citizen of the United States who does not know the English language."[5]

The initial requirement was that an applicant be able to speak English. Some courts, however, added a gloss requiring literacy to the statutory provision. For example, in *Petition of Katz*, the federal district court found that a successful Polish immigrant, unable to read English, could not fulfill the statutory requirement of attachment "to the principles of the Constitution of the United States."[6] The Nationality Act of 1940 also contained the requirement that an applicant for citizenship speak English. Section 304 of the Act stated: "No person . . . shall hereafter be naturalized as a citizen of the United States upon his own petition who cannot speak the English language."[7]

In 1950, at the height of hysteria over communism, Congress stiffened the language requirements for naturalization. The Subversive Activities Control Act of 1950 amended section 304 to demand full literacy in English. The provisions of the naturalization statute remain essentially the same today.

The symbolic importance of an English literacy requirement for naturalization should not be underestimated. It is in the naturalization laws that the criteria for belonging to America, for participating in its government, are most clearly set out. As one leading commentator put it, "[a]n English literacy requirement . . . establishes the fact that the United States is an English culture and that its citizens will have to learn English in order to participate fully in it. The very existence of a literacy test establishes the 'official' character of the language."[8] To date, this represents the maximum degree to which English is officially and legally recognized as the language of the United States.

From the panorama of the legal treatment of ethnicity and language several distinctive features of nativist movements stand out. Nativism tends to grow and flourish at times of national stress, often in response to unwelcome immigration or wartime. Nativism triggers restrictive laws aimed at persons whose ethnicity differs from that of the core culture, ostensibly to serve the goals of national unity or national security. Nativist movements seek to reinforce their narrow view of American cultural identity by restricting cultural traits deemed "foreign." They also strive to disenfranchise certain Americans, or to impede the naturalization of aspiring Americans, because of their difference from the core culture.

The official English movement of the 1980s is part of this ignoble tradition. Former Senator S. I. Hayakawa, acting through U.S. English, an organization he founded with Dr. John Tanton, sought an amendment to the Constitution making English the official language of the United States. Subcommittees of the Senate Judiciary Committee, in 1984, and the House Judiciary Committee, in 1988, conducted hearings on proposed official English amendments. Despite persistent efforts and publicity, proponents of official English have not yet succeeded in achieving a federal constitutional amendment.

The official English movement now appears to have a two-fold strategy: first, to obtain official English laws or constitutional amendments in the states, and, second, to enact a federal statute making English the official language of the federal government. Since the movement's ultimate goal is still a federal constitutional amendment, it appears that official English proponents will attempt to strengthen their position by arguing that the presence of many state laws and a possible federal statute increases or proves the necessity for a federal constitutional amendment.

The official English movement has been quite successful at the state level. Seventeen states now have laws declaring English to be the official language within their borders. These laws have usually been enacted by direct popular votes on referenda by overwhelming margins. Moreover, a federal statute to codify English as the official language of the federal government was introduced in 1990 and 1991. These legislative efforts of U.S. English continue unabated.

The official English movement belongs squarely within the matrix of American nativism, in modern form. The cause of the official English movement is the immigration of people unpopular in the eyes of the majority. Its manifestations are those of earlier nativist movements: a desire to restrict immigration; an appeal to national unity or, conversely, the familiar spectre of national disunity and the disintegration of American culture caused by new immigration; and, most important, the desire to disenfranchise certain Americans.

Many commentators agree that the cause of the official English movement is the large, and largely unwelcome, immigration of many Hispanics and Southeast Asians during recent decades. Since the repeal of national origin quotas in 1965, increasing numbers of immigrants have come from non-European countries, thus changing the racial and cultural balance carefully preserved by the prior quota system. In addition to legal immigration, a large influx of aliens from Latin America arrived, many of whom subsequently were legalized during the amnesty offered in 1987 and 1988. According to one estimate, 300,000 Hispanic immigrants a year flow into the southern and western regions of the United States. Like all other such groups, these immigrants have brought with them their native languages. The influx of Spanish-speaking Hispanic immigrants has antagonized many Americans. Immigrants from Southeast Asia have also encountered hostility, violence, and language restriction. The racial and cultural differences of recent immigrants from the core culture have not gone unnoticed.

Part of U.S. English's original program was to "control immigration so that it does not reinforce trends toward language segregation."[9] The organization intended to lobby for legislation to restrict immigration that would reinforce the maintenance of certain languages, particularly Spanish, which, after English, is the second most-used language in this country. This means limiting the immigration of Hispanics, who are depicted as advocates of "language segregation." Its original emphasis on restricting immigration is not surprising. This has been a long-time goal of Dr. John Tanton, founder and former chairman of U.S. English.

The official English movement renews the claim that national unity depends on ethnic purity—really conformity with the Anglo core culture—this time in the form of language. This perceived threat to the English language, however, is not supported by fact. English is ubiquitous. Between 94 and 96 percent of the American population is English-speaking. Fully 85 percent of the population claims English as its mother tongue. Furthermore, English enjoys virtual hegemony as an international language of business, commerce, and interaction between nations. The unparalleled international status of English as "the world's most prestigious, most effective, and most sought-after vehicle of communication" only reinforces its importance.[10] Given the national and international status of English, concerns about its submergence, echoed throughout our history, are greatly overstated. Since fact does not support claims of deterioration of the English language, nor of national disunity, something else must be going on.

Voting

Since its inception, one of the official English movement's principal goals has been to eliminate bilingual, or more correctly, multilingual voting ballots. This can be accomplished only through the Congress's repeal, or refusal to extend, provisions in the 1975 amendments to the Voting Rights Act. Proponents of official English argue that

English-only ballots create incentives for citizens to learn English and to realize that they cannot enjoy full participation in American life without learning English. Furthermore, multilingual ballots supposedly impair the political process because they make some voters dependent on "interpreters or go-betweens," because they preserve "minority voting blocks," and because voters whose primary language is not English will not be "as fully informed as possible" when they go to the polls.[11] Proponents of official English thus charge that multilingual ballots reduce political participation, an assertion glaringly at odds with the obvious access to political participation that multilingual ballots provide to non-English speakers.

These arguments deserve brief response. First, English-only ballots create no meaningful incentive to learn English, particularly given the overwhelming social and economic incentives to learn English. English-only ballots disenfranchise citizens who, for various reasons, have retained a language other than English. Second, voters who rely on American newspapers printed in languages other than English, such as Miami's main newspaper, the *Miami Herald*, which is published daily in both Spanish and English editions, can be fully informed about the issues in an election. The movement's concern about "minority voting blocs" defined by language both expresses fear of the political power of Hispanics and the offensive assumption that minority group members think and vote alike. If proponents of official English are truly concerned about ethnic voting blocs, they should also be equally concerned about English-speaking ethnic voting blocs. Their concern, however, is only about ethnicity, Hispanic or Asian, different from that of the core culture.

Language as Symbol

The historical record demonstrates both the significant legal recognition and protection given to different languages and the nativist restrictions imposed through the law on language. While many aspects of this history are virtually unknown within the legal academy, scholars of language and politics and sociolinguistics have long been aware of the political significance of language. The work of scholars in these disciplines provides a framework within which to assess the current meaning and symbolism of the official English movement.

Language is both our principal means of communication and a social symbol, malleable and capable of manipulation for the achievement of social or political goals. For this reason a study of context, for our purposes the history of the legal treatment of ethnicity and different American languages, is fundamental for an understanding of the symbolic meaning of language. The context contains many components, social and legal. In America we have (and always have had) many languages coexisting, with English dominant. Spanish, for example, is the second most-used American language. Sociolinguists sometimes refer to this situation as diglossia, defined as "[a] situation where two languages coexist in the same speech community but differ in domains of use, attitudes toward each, and patterns of acquisition and proficiency."[12] As we can infer from this definition, coexistence does not imply equal dominance, prestige, or spheres of influence.

Discussions of different languages and other aspects of ethnicity are discussions of human differences. And "it is almost an axiom of human society that . . . [h]ierarchy is found everywhere superimposed upon difference."[13] So it is with languages. Different languages have very different prestige values in our society. These differences manifest themselves through bias, conscious or unconscious, for or against certain languages. The perceived intelligibility, for example, of languages is influenced by these prestige rankings. For instance, if the people who speak a particular language have prestige and power, people perceive their language as easy to understand. Conversely, the languages of groups perceived as lacking in prestige and power, or groups who are the objects of prejudice, are often perceived as difficult to understand.

Discourse itself, the expression of ideas, and the ordering of discourse, who gets to express ideas, who gets to express them first, and which ideas get expressed, also reflect hierarchy and relationships of power in society. As Michel Foucault wrote, "as history constantly teaches us, discourse is not simply that which translates struggles or systems of domination, but is the thing for which and by which there is struggle. . . . [D]iscourse is the power which is to be seized."[14] For example, access to public forums or the press is an ample power indeed. The presence or absence of certain languages, their encouragement within or elimination from certain public forums, like the ballot in public elections, reflect the results of this struggle and the presence or absence of domination. Furthermore, discourse and the order of discourse are governed by ritual, and are thus endowed with social significance. Accordingly, we pay more attention to those discourses made significant through rituals with social sanction than to others.

Given the symbolic and psychological values attached to language, important consequences attend governmental intervention and establishment of language policies. In a democracy, the attitudes and feelings of "government" are those of the majority or its representatives. Thus the majority can manipulate language and language laws to express its approval or disapproval of favored or disfavored groups within the society. Often in our society favored and disfavored groups are defined by their ethnicity: race, national origin, religion, ancestry, and language. Language often has been the basis for discrimination against groups whose language is not English. Language is a fundamental symbol of ethnicity. This is just as true of English as of Spanish or any other language. English is a crucial symbol of the ethnicity of America's dominant core culture. Language can be a symbol of group status, a symbol of dominance, and a symbol of participation in or exclusion from the political process. Campaigns to make a language standard or official can thus be seen as attempts to create or reinforce the dominance of the culture of which the language forms an integral part.

As we have seen, legal history demonstrates that many American languages have co-existed within these borders. Yet, different languages have never threatened the unity of the nation. Indeed, even if one accepts the assumption that other languages somehow threaten the dominance of English, then the threat to English is currently at its minimum point, given the unprecedented domestic and international prestige and influence the English language holds.

The official English movement appears to be, then, another round in the "dialectic of plurality and conformism," the paradox generated by the confrontation of American cultural pluralism with the demand for conformity to core culture. Official English is the demand for national identity through linguistic homogeneity, a homogeneity that has never existed in America's people. It is a demand for unity based on conformity, a demand clearly at odds with pluralism and core principles of American liberty.

Our country, and its government, must include all who belong. Cultural pluralism need not lead to distrust. To disenfranchise Americans, or to exclude Americans "symbolically" because of the language they speak, is an old wrong of exclusion. Rather than repeat this wrong, we must expand the concept of "American" to include the full measure, linguistic, racial, and cultural, of Americans.

NOTES

1. See Immigration Reform and Control Act of 1986, Pub. L. No. 99-603, 100 Stat. 3359, 3394 (codified at 8 U.S.C. § 1255a(b)(1)(D)(i) (1987 & Supp. 1992)).

2. Robert Divine, American Immigration Policy, 1924–1952 at 4 (1957).

3. *Id.* at 5; Denis Baron, The English-Only Question 57 (1990).

4. Immigration Act of 1917, ch. 29, § 3, 39 Stat. 874, 877 (repealed 1952).

5. Commission on Naturalization, *Report to the President* (Nov. 8, 1905), Reprinted In H.R. Doc. No. 46, 59th Cong., 1st. Sess. 11 (1905).

6. 21 F.2d 867, 868 (E.D. Mich. 1927).

7. Nationality Act of 1940, ch. 876, § 304, 54 Stat. 1140 (repealed 1952).

8. Arnold H. Leibowitz, *English Literacy: Legal Sanction for Discrimination*, 45 Notre Dame L. 7, 14 (1969).

9. Guy Wright, *U.S. English*, S.F. Chron., Mar. 20, 1983, at B3.

10. Joshua A. Fishman, *"English Only": Its Ghosts, Myths, and Dangers*, 74 Int'l. J. Soc. Language 125, 129 (1988) (citing Joshua A. Fishman, et al., The Rise and Fall of the Ethnic Revival (1985)).

11. The English Language Amendment: Hearing on S.J. Res. 167 Before the Subcomm. on the Constitution of the Senate Comm. on the Judiciary, 98th Cong., 2d Sess., at 20 (testimony of Sen. Huddleston).

12. Joan Rubin, *Language and Politics from a Sociolinguistic Point of View*, in Language and Politics, 389 (William O'Barr and Jean O'Barr eds., 1976).

13. William O'Barr, *Boundaries, Strategies, and Power Relations*, in Language and Politics, at 405, 415.

14. Michel Foucault, *The Order of Discourse*, in Language and Politics 108, 110 (Michael J. Shapiro ed., 1984).

Chapter 82

Law and Language(s)

Margaret E. Montoya

For many Chicanas and Chicanos, language introduced us to law, providing the earliest point of intersection with official rules, official regulations, and official prohibitions. The use of Spanish in the schools throughout the Southwest was widely prohibited and routinely punished. My father tells of being beaten in kindergarten for speaking Spanish. In *Culture and Truth*,[1] Renato Rosaldo remembers his Tucson junior high school where students were made to grab their ankles while they were swatted for the crime of speaking Spanish. One of my University of New Mexico colleagues recalls that in a New Mexico town during the 1950s, if a student were overheard speaking Spanish, he/she would be forced to stand on tiptoes as the teacher drew a circle at the height of his/her nose. The student would be made to stand with his/her nose in the circle for the required length of time, enduring pain and humiliation for speaking Spanish.

Stories like these have normative consequences. As time passes, the necessity for creative cruel punishment attenuates. Our parents encourage us to speak English. Accomplished English speakers listen for and correct our accents. We hear and sometimes laugh at jokes about fractured English or comedy routines featuring Jose Jimenez, Speedy Gonzales, Paul Rodriguez, or Cheech Marin. We receive praise from teachers for speaking the over-corrected speech of the over-achiever. We learn to value the syntax, the cadence, and the accent of the monolingual English speaker. Over time these stories constrain our behavior, mold our values, and create our preferences. Over time Spanish, our mother tongue, becomes an "outlaw" language. Spanish joins other languages, dialects, and patois that have been devalued and prohibited. Being obliged to abandon your mother tongue, to surrender your primary language, to give up the language that you first learned as a baby, forces a rupture with your family, your community, and your history. Being obliged to surrender a language is akin to losing parts of your senses.

Although bilingual when I arrived at law school, I had been well trained in my carefully accented and polysyllabic English. English was my public language. My

From "Law and Language(s): Image, Integration, and Innovation." 7 La Raza L.J. 147 (1994). Originally published in the *La Raza Law Journal*. Reprinted by permission.

memories from law school begin with one of the first cases I ever read. On page one of my criminal law casebook I met the only Chicana or Latina I would ever hear about during my law school education. The case dealing with infanticide was entitled *People of the State of California v. Josephine Chavez.*[2] In addition to the appellate opinion, the casebook included copies of the actual Chavez Complaint, Warrant of Arrest, Jury Instructions, Verdict and Judgment, news reports of the Chavez arrest and trial from *The Fresno Bee,* the local newspaper, the relevant sections of the California Penal Code, and the author's commentary and analysis.

Josephine Chavez gave birth one night over the toilet in her mother's home without waking her year-and-a-half-old son, her brothers, sisters, or mother. She delivered, in the words of the opinion, with "the doors open and no lights . . . turned on."[3] The baby dropped into the toilet and Josephine cut the umbilical cord with a razor blade. She recovered the body of the baby, wrapped it in newspapers and hid it underneath the bathtub. She attended a carnival that evening and then ran away. Later she turned herself in to her probation officer.

The class wrestled with the legal issue: whether the baby had been born alive and was therefore subject to being killed by its mother. Finally, on the third day, I broke my silence and interjected what I thought were other equally relevant facts, her youth, her poverty, her fear of the pregnancy, her delivery in silence and in darkness.

My vivid recollection is that the classroom discussion about the Chavez case, like the appellate court opinion, was oblivious to the cultural, linguistic, or socio-economic context of the alleged crime. Perhaps this oblivion is not surprising for an opinion written in 1947, nor even perhaps for a law school discussion in the mid-1970s. However, I am sure that, even today, a classroom discussion of this case or others dealing with Outsider experiences would not emphasize the contextual information, especially if that contextualization required a language other than English.

So how are we today to make sense of this story? Can these tragic events be understood from the traditional perspective—a perspective that is monolingual and monocultural? How do we effectively explore Josephine Chavez's criminal intent, mens rea, diminished capacity, or examine the legal personhood of this dead baby unless we are prepared to draw on knowledge that is embedded in the life experiences of those who have been historically silenced? The linguistic and socio-cultural norms that control legal discussion, particularly within the classroom, impede the introduction of information about the experiences of subordinated groups. These norms impoverish the discussion within the classroom and stunt the creativity that can be brought to bear on the legal issues presented by the client's complex story. These constraints have legal and representational ramifications.

The effective representation of a bicultural client such as Josephine Chavez requires that we tell her story using language and knowledge that has been taboo in the traditional law school classroom. Our understanding of Josephine Chavez's motives and behavior is enhanced if we import words and concepts from Spanish into our analysis. Her story implicates information about *familia,* about *verguenza,* about *respeto.* The familial and cultural matrices that encode meaning are different in the two languages. The networks embedded in the words *familia* and family are defined differently and experienced differently. *Verguenza* may translate into shame but *ver-*

guenza is experienced as more than shame. *Respeto* has different cultural parameters than the meaning we give to respect.

In other words, the effective legal representation of the bicultural and bilingual client requires the re-presentation of her reality—what the Mauritian literary critic Françoise Lionnet has called "metissage."[4] The term "metissage," originally used to refer to racial and cultural mixing or creolization, is here used to describe the literary criticism technique which borrows insights from various disciplines to examine the interreferential nature of the writings of post-colonial cultures.[5] Lionnet uses metissage to describe the autobiographical story that is told in the dominant language but which draws from the dominated language.

Metissage urges us to eschew race- or gender-imbued concepts that distort or demean our lived experiences. It propels us to seize language, reinvent it, redefine it to give meaning and value to our lives. Metissage creates discursive space for the telling of stories from the vantage point and in the words of the subordinated. It brings authenticity to our stories. By appropriating public space for stories that combine the dominant language with the "outlaw" language, we can give a voice to parts of our lives that have been silenced.

Metissage means more than autobiographical narratives. The linguistic code-switching that characterizes metissage enhances our ability to teach our students to understand their client's stories. A central task in lawyering is to take the client's story and translate it into legal parlance. An appreciation of metissage, of creating a new story by valuing and respecting both the client's version and the lawyer's jargon, allows the lawyer to choose from different linguistic systems and from varying identities for the client and for the lawyer herself.

I have found that telling personal stories establishes a climate of trust with students. Reciprocity in self-disclosures creates an environment of safety for storytelling. So I work to incorporate narrative formats into my classroom and clinical teaching. I use narratives to teach students to listen to and interpret client stories, and, at times, tell their own stories. For example, I have taped a mock interview that demonstrates metissage and raises cultural and linguistic as well as ethical issues for discussion by law students in my clinical course. In the interview I play a Latina lawyer with limited facility in Spanish. The client Miguel "Caballo" Grado has suffered a back injury and is seeking assistance with an SSI claim. Soon after the interview begins, the client asks about my family background:

Client: Did you say it was Montoya?
Lawyer: . . . my name is Margaret Montoya.
Client: Donde . . . Where are you from?
Lawyer: Well, my dad's family, Los Montoya, is from the southern part of the state and my mother's family is from the northern part of the state.
Client: What's your dad's name?
Lawyer: Ricardo Montoya and, you know, they're from, he was from Santa Rita.
Client: Hmm, I knew a bunch of Montoyas who were all from Silver City, and I think the family was from Santa Rita.
Lawyer: Well, my grandfather's name was Felix Montoya . . .
Client: No.

Lawyer: . . . and my grandmother's name was Refugio Sierra.

Client: Hmm, that's interesting. Did . . . You're telling me they're from Santa Rita, but did they live in Silver City too? Because I know *este* Modesto Montoya, Modesto Montoya there in Silver.

Lawyer: Oh, you know, Mr. Grado, I don't know a lot about, you know I know my dad's brothers and sisters, but . . . I don't really know those one generation back, so I don't really know if there would have been . . .

As I proceed to share information about my family, the client attempts to locate me within his framework of names and geographic associations. In fact, the client and I spend over three minutes of the taped interview discussing my family connections. As the interview goes on, the client provides relevant information about his family's financial affairs. In a subsequent interview, after displaying some concern about providing this information, the client tells me that he has been treated by a *curandera*, a medicine woman who has given him massages and herbal tea medications.

Client: You know, I don't know how the Social Security is going to look at it, but I've been seeing a *curandera.*

Lawyer: Hmm.

Client: . . . and uh, she's been doing wonderful stuff for my back—at least it lasts more than the pill does. Ah, she helps me with the massages and she does other things for me, gives me some potions if you will, and ah, they've been pretty effective so that I could get to bed at night.

Lawyer: I need to get more information . . . the *curandera* is, hmm . . . so she, does she do other things than give you a massage? You said that she gives you . . .

Client: Well, she gives me some teas.

Lawyer: And what kind of teas does she . . .

Client: Ah, various kinds of bark . . . I know that I was having some problems with my bladder one time and she gave me some *popotillo* and then she gave me some *yerba buena.*

Lawyer: Yeah . . . I don't know *popotillo. Yerba buena* is mint tea. Uh, I don't know *popotillo.*

Client: It's a . . . It's a wild herb that grows out there and, ah, it's good for bladder infections and stuff like that and it really works great. It cleans your whole system out.

Lawyer: And you have told Dr. Fox [the treating physician] that in fact you're . . .

Client: Umm, uh.

Lawyer: It's alright if you haven't. It's that I'm going to have to figure out how we use this information.

Client: Well, you know . . . It's traditional to seek a *curandera.* There's nothing wrong with it. I really haven't mentioned it to him too much. Uh, I do not know how he would take it.

Lawyer: Sure.

Client: I don't know how up here, but down there, it's just, ah, you know anything that has to do with our culture and stuff is frowned upon . . .

The purpose of this simulated interview is to explore the following issues through the use of metissage: the impropriety of attorney disclosures when interacting with clients; client expectations about attorney behavior; techniques for gaining access to and interpreting legally relevant information that is culturally coded; and interviewing and counseling techniques for intra- and intercultural interactions. The deliberate and extended use of Spanish and English in the simulation and the interjection of details from the everyday lives of poor Latinos/as has yielded rich discussions about the representation and re-presentation of clients from subordinated populations.

When I consider who we are as legal educators and why we do what we do—my answers to those questions are based on what I learned from the Josephine Chavez case. The Josephine Chavez story impels us to transgress the traditional linguistic norms that constrain legal analyses and cabin legal discourse.

Claiming the right to use Spanish in academic discourse is an important form of resistance against cultural and linguistic domination. Reclaiming these "outlaw" languages, taboo knowledge, and devalued discourses is a stand against cultural hegemony. Telling stories through the language of the master and the language of the subversive subaltern (in Gita Rajan's phrase)[6] allows us to examine how language can be regenerative of meaning.

The Josephine Chavez case has long had a grip on me because in the same way that I couldn't fully tell her story without resorting to Spanish, I couldn't then, and can't now, tell my story either. As a Latina, weaving meaning from both English and Spanish is a necessary process in the understanding of my subjectivities. To the extent that my identity is socially constructed, that identity is encoded through two linguistic codes. Reflecting on my subjectivities, de/constructing the forces that have acted to create my multiple identities, requires decoding through Spanish and English. [For more on Josephine Chavez, see chapter 39—Eds.]

Gloria Anzaldúa has written about the psychological, sexual, and spiritual borderlands "physically present wherever two or more cultures edge each other, where people of different races occupy the same territory, where under, lower, middle, and upper classes touch, where the space between two individuals shrinks with intimacy."[7] My contribution to academic discourse is my ability to extract meaning from the aesthetic, linguistic, and cultural borderlands of my existence and blend that meaning with traditional legal analysis. Indeed, this is the challenge for legal educators who identify with subordinated communities. It is time that we reclaim Spanish and other outlaw languages for use in the classroom and in legal scholarship and seize the opportunities these languages offer for pedagogical innovation.

NOTES

1. Renato Rosaldo, CULTURE AND TRUTH: THE REMAKING OF SOCIAL ANALYSIS 149 (1989).

2. People v. Josephine Chavez, 77 Cal. App. 2d 621 (1947).

3. *Id.* at 622–23.

4. *Metis* is the French word for half-breed. But *metis* is also cloth woven from cotton and hemp. *Metis* describes a new product from two different inputs.

5. Françoise Lionnet, AUTOBIOGRAPHICAL VOICES: RACE, GENDER, SELF-PORTRAITURE 8 (1989).

6. See Gita Rajan, *Subversive-Subaltern Identity: Indira Gandhi as the Speaking Subject,* in DE/COLONIZING THE SUBJECT: THE POLITICS OF GENDER IN WOMEN'S AUTOBIOGRAPHY 196 (Sidonie Smith & Julia Watson eds., 1992).

7. See Gloria Anzaldúa, BORDERLANDS/*La Frontera:* THE NEW MESTIZA (1987), at unpaginated preface.

Chapter 83

How the García Cousins Lost Their Accents

Christopher David Ruiz Cameron

This is the story of how the federal law of equal opportunity failed to protect three bilingual, distant cousins, each of whom bears the family name García, when they spoke Spanish in the workplace.

The first cousin is Hector García, "a native-born American of Mexican descent."[1] He was employed as a salesman by Gloor Lumber and Supply, Inc., at its retail store in Brownsville, Texas. Mr. García was among the seven of eight Gloor salesmen who were "Hispanic"—a business decision perhaps influenced by the fact that three-quarters of the company's customer base is also Latino "and many of Gloor's customers wish to be waited on by a salesman who speaks Spanish."[2]

Mr. García, who speaks English perfectly but prefers Spanish because that is the language spoken *en casa,* was hired by Gloor "precisely because he was bilingual."[3] Eventually, he was fired for the same reason. This happened after Gloor adopted a work rule forbidding any on-duty employee from speaking a language other than English unless he was waiting on a non-English-speaking customer. Soon thereafter Mr. García was asked a question by another Mexican-American employee about an item sought by a customer. Mr. García replied "in Spanish that the article was not available."[4] Alton Gloor, a company officer and stockholder, overheard the conversation; Mr. García was promptly discharged.

The second cousin is Priscilla García, "a fully bilingual" employee of the Spun Steak Company of South San Francisco, California.[5] Of Spun Steak's thirty-three employees, Ms. García is among the twenty-four who speak Spanish, "virtually all of whom are 'Hispanic.'"[6] As a production line worker, she stands in front of a conveyor belt and places poultry and other meats into packages for resale. The company's production line workers have little contact with the general public, and "Spun Steak has never required job applicants to speak or to understand English as a condition of employment."[7]

From "How the García Cousins Lost Their Accents: Understanding the Language of Title VII Decisions Approving English-Only Rules as the Product of Racial Dualism, Latino Invisibility, and Legal Indeterminacy." Copyright © 1997 by Christopher David Ruiz Cameron. Used by permission of the author. Publication forthcoming in the *California Law Review.*

Ms. García's production line *compañera*, Maricela Buitrago, is also "fully bilingual," but the two prefer communicating with one another in Spanish. Two co-workers, one African American and the other Chinese American, who apparently did not
understand Spanish, nevertheless complained that García and Buitrago had made
"derogatory, racist comments in Spanish."[8] The company's president, Kenneth Ber-
telsen, formulated a new workplace rule, mandating that employees communicate
only in English "in connection with work."[9] The rule permits conversation in languages other than English when speaking in situations outside the work setting, such
as at lunch and on breaks. After catching Ms. García and Ms. Buitrago speaking in
Spanish while working, the company issued warning letters and prohibited the pair
from working next to each other for two months. The workers' union unsuccessfully
filed suit, charging that Spun Steak's English-only policy violates Title VII of the Civil
Rights Act of 1964.

The third cousin is Yolanda García de la Torre, a fictional American poet who as
a young girl emigrated from the Dominican Republic to New York with her parents
and sisters Carla, Sandra, and Sofía. The lifelong adventures of the Misses García de
la Torre are brought to life by novelist and literature professor Julia Alvarez in her
novel *How the García Girls Lost Their Accents*.[10] Although Professor Alvarez
weaves the García family tapestry in all its intricate and variegated splendor, the singular thread in the life of each girl—and especially the poet Yolanda, or "Yo"—is her
transformation from a comfortable Spanish-speaking immigrant child into an unsure
bilingual American adult, who in struggling with her dual identity cannot help but
keep one foot firmly planted in the Old Country and the other in the New.

Soon after their move to the United States, several incidents with a neighbor introduce the Misses García to America's resistance toward biculturalism—and, by extension, bilingualism. *La Bruja*, the old woman "with a helmet of beauty parlor blue
hair" who lives in the apartment below them, has been complaining to the building
superintendent since the day the family moved in that the Garcías should be evicted.
Their food smells. They speak loudly and not in English. The kids sound like a herd
of wild burros. One day *La Bruja* stops Mrs. García and the four girls in the lobby
and spits out that ugly word the kids in school sometimes used: "Spics! Go back to
where you came from!"[11]

The stories of the three cousins García are unremarkable merely because they are,
or could be, true. Even in what we sometimes suppose to be these enlightened times,
tales of overt discrimination against American citizens and legal residents who look,
speak, or act in a manner that the Anglo cultural majority considers "foreign" could
be told by all too many folks, whether native-born or immigrant, professional or
campesino, Latino or non-Latino. Rather, the Garcías' stories are remarkable because, according to the leading federal appellate decisions, none of them states a
claim for illegal national-origin discrimination.

In the real-life cases of Hector and Priscilla, the United States Court of Appeals for
the Fifth and Ninth Circuits, respectively, each held that a private employer's English-only rule could not be considered discriminatory. The Garcías, these courts reasoned, are bilingual and therefore can "easily comply" with the directive.[12] Under the
law, neither García has the right to speak Spanish while on duty—to supervisors, co-

workers, or even customers—unless communicating with somebody else who speaks Spanish only. So Mr. García stays fired, and Ms. García remains segregated from her Spanish-speaking *compañera* for as long as her boss sees fit.

Even in the fictional case of Yolanda García, were the super to placate *La Bruja* by putting the García family out on the street, a legal challenge might well fail. In the eyes of the law, the family's ancestry, and especially its bilingualism, is more of a liability than an asset. Nearly twenty-five years ago, the United States Supreme Court held that Title VII's ban on "national origin" discrimination does not mean what it appears to say, thereby permitting an employer to deny a job to a lawful resident alien from Mexico based solely upon her alienage.[13] Unfortunately for the García family, Title VIII of the Civil Rights Act of 1968, which purports to outlaw "national origin" discrimination in public housing, contains language similar to that found in Title VII and is practically indistinguishable.

Under Title VII, a work rule whose adverse effects fall exclusively upon the most widely accepted class of protected workers—African-American men—ordinarily would raise a prima facie violation of the statute. In most of our courts, an attempt to defend such a rule by claiming it could easily be complied with would be rejected, if not mocked, as the equivalent of telling an African American that she may lawfully be "required to sit at the back of a bus" because she could easily do so. How, then, can a work rule which effectively requires a bilingual employee "to sit at the back of the bus" escape the grasp of the employment discrimination laws?

That English-only rules have a discriminatory impact on Latinos ought to be beyond rational debate. The Spanish language is central to Latino identity. People whose primary language is Spanish constitute a cognizable group—a "discrete and insular minority"—who historically have been, and continue to be, subject to discrimination. Therefore, English-only policies that appear to be neutral workplace regulations are actually language discrimination against bilingual employees, including Spanish-speakers. This is illegal national-origin discrimination, as so many commentators have persuasively argued.

The question, then, is not *whether* English-only rules are national-origin discrimination, but why courts have consistently refused to find them so. I believe the explanation lies in the tendency of judges toward "racial dualism"—the tendency to view civil rights discourse in terms of Blacks and Whites only. Racial dualism is a world view that infects judicial decision making, as reflected in the reported opinions of cases dealing with challenges to English-only rules brought under Title VII. This view embraces, among other things, reliance on false dichotomies, such as the traditional jurisprudential distinction between "mutable" and "immutable" personal characteristics. Decisions approving English-only rules in the workplace are based largely on judges' limited understandings of the forms that national-origin discrimination can take: after all, for a bilingual employee, isn't the ability to speak Spanish a mutable characteristic, changeable without causing serious inconvenience?

Racial dualism is problematic not only because it limits judges' understanding of national-origin claims but also because it makes Latinos and their problems in the workplace invisible. If racial dualism were a coin, then its flip side would be blank.

When culture allows only two ways of seeing things—Black or White—other colors, such as Brown, are bound to remain hidden from view.

Finally, racial dualism and invisibility are often submerged, and thereby left unexamined, in the texts of judicial decisions. This happens because the jurisprudential tools of legal reasoning are constructed so as to conform to pre-existing world views. That is, legal rules, and nowhere more so than in the realm of national-origin discrimination, are indeterminate—making it not only possible but also easy to reach results that make English-only policies seem benign to the decision makers who consider them.

By their use of language—phraseology, choice of metaphor, or silence—parties and judges offer insights into why the bilingual population receives a second-class (if any) form of protected status. These insights yield a rich harvest of information about their, and our, belief systems respecting the treatment of minority cultures in the workplace. By confronting these values and prejudices, combatants and courts alike may begin to change them and accord victims of national-origin discrimination the respect they truly deserve.

NOTES

1. García v. Gloor, 618 F.2d 264, 266 (5th Cir. 1980) *(García I)*.

2. *Id.* at 267.

3. *Id.* at 269.

4. *Id.* at 266. Precisely what the offending Spanish words or phrases were does not appear in the decision—a remarkable omission in itself since uttering them got Mr. García fired.

5. García v. Spun Steak Co., 998 F.2d 1480 (9th Cir. 1993) *(García II)*. The opinion does not specify Ms. García's ancestry, other than to suggest she is "Hispanic."

6. *Id.* at 1483.

7. *Id.*

8. *Id.*

9. *Id.*

10. Julia Alvarez, How the García Girls Lost Their Accents (1991).

11. *Id.* at 171.

12. *See García I,* 618 F.2d at 270; *García II,* 998 F.2d at 1487–88.

13. Espinoza v. Farah Mfg. Co., 414 U.S. 86, 95 (1973).

Chapter 84

Death by English

Juan F. Perea

In his recent book, *Latinos,* Earl Shorris poignantly describes Bienvenida Petion, a Jewish Latino immigrant, who clings to her language and culture "as if they were life itself."[1] When Bienvenida dies, it is "not of illness, but of English."[2] Bienvenida dies of English when she is confined to a nursing home where no one speaks Spanish, an environment in which she cannot communicate and in which no one cares about her language and culture.

"Death by English" is a death of the spirit, the slow death that occurs when one's own identity is replaced, reconfigured, overwhelmed, or rejected by a more powerful, dominant identity. For Latinos, illness by English of varying degree, even death by English, is a common affliction, without known cure. It may be identified, however, by some of its symptoms.

The mere sound of Spanish offends and frightens many English-only speakers, who sense in the language a loss of control over what they regard as "their" country. Spanish also frightens many Latinos, for it proclaims their identity as Latinos, for all to hear. The Latino's fear is rational. Spanish may subject Latinos to the harsh price of difference in the United States: the loss of a job, instant scapegoating, and identification as an outsider. Giving in to this fear and denying one's own identity as a Latino is, perhaps, to begin to die of English.

Latino invisibility is the principal cause of illness by English. When I write of Latino invisibility, I mean a relative lack of positive public identity and legitimacy. Invisibility in this sense is created in several ways. Sometimes we are rendered invisible through the absence of public recognition and portrayal. Sometimes we are silenced through prohibitions on the use of Spanish. Sometimes we are rendered politically invisible, or nearly so, through the attribution of foreignness, what I shall call "symbolic deportation." I do not maintain that Latinos are the only people rendered invisible in America. In many respects the processes of invisibility have more general application. In this chapter, however, I shall discuss only the invisibility I know best:

From "*Los Olvidados:* On the Making of Invisible People." 70 N.Y.U. L. Rev. 965 (1995). Originally published in the *New York University Law Review.* Reprinted by permission.

How American culture, history, and laws make "invisible people" out of American Latinos who arrived before the English.[3]

The Media Presentation of the Los Angeles Riots and the Creation of Latino Invisibility

The media presentation of the Los Angeles riots in the spring of 1992 illustrates Latino invisibility by omission. The riots have been characterized as the worst of this century. Over fifty persons died, and over 2,400 were injured. Estimates of the value of property destroyed or damaged run in the billions of dollars.

I identify three images that emerged from the riots as perhaps the most compelling. First is the horrifying image of organized police brutality and violence inflicted upon Rodney King, fortuitously videotaped and then broadcast nationally. The videotaped images resonate with centuries of similar violence suffered by African Americans at the hands of armed whites intent on brutalizing them. Without the fortuitous videotape as witness and testimony to King's beating, I am confident that he would have been an invisible victim of police violence.

The second image is the horrible violence inflicted upon Reginald Denny, also captured and widely broadcast on videotape. Many commentators and journalists presented this image as a kind of symbolic counterpoint to the violence against Rodney King, as though both events were comparable. Reginald Denny's beating created possibilities for certain artificial and misleading symmetries: Even if the Los Angeles police were out of control, so were the black rioters; a black victim is matched by a paired white victim.

A third image from the Los Angeles riots is that of Korean or Korean-American merchants protecting their stores with firearms. The media covered the riots as if they were the outcome of simmering conflict between Korean Americans and African Americans, casting conflict as an ethnic and racial one between two minority groups—one good, one bad. Koreans were the good ethnics, "model minority members"—hardworking, quiet, law-abiding property owners striving to climb the ladder of the American dream. Blacks were the bad—violent, criminal, and out of control. The good minority versus bad minority oppositional pairing disguises our traditional racial hierarchy and racism by displacing it onto two oppressed minority groups.

Now a fourth image: groups of Latino-looking people rushing from a storefront, arms laden with stolen merchandise. While images like this were broadcast frequently, they were treated as incidental in public discussion of the Los Angeles riots. Yet this image contains a remarkably important part of the story. Most of the early victims of crowd violence were Latinos; one-third of the dead were Latino; between 20 and 40 percent of the businesses damaged were Latino owned; and one-half of those arrested were Latino. Particularly by the beginning of the second day, the Los Angeles riots were heavily Latino, not black-white riots.

The story of the Los Angeles riots is, therefore, largely a Latino story too. This makes perfect sense because half of the population of South Central Los Angeles was

Latino, mostly Mexican American with more recent Mexican and other Central American immigrants. Yet neither the stories of Latino victimization nor Latino criminality entered public debate about the riots at all. Despite widespread Latino anger at conditions in South Central Los Angeles similar to those faced by African Americans, the needs of the Latino community in South Central were neither seen nor discussed publicly. The dominant images that emerged from the Los Angeles riots suggest the persistence of a cultural lens which focuses primarily, if not exclusively, on images of conflict between blacks and whites. It is a severely distorted lens, however, for it ignores roughly half the picture and fully half of the story.

Searching for Latinos in the Bookstores

When I travel, I spend a lot of time in bookstores searching for books on Latino life and history. It is hard to find such books. Not that they do not exist, as I own many dozens, perhaps hundreds, of books about Latinos. Yet I have never found a bookstore with a section on Latinos. There must be at least one, somewhere, but I have not found it yet. Since bookstores never have a section of books on Latinos, I have to search through many categories to find what I want. A typical search includes perusing sections on Native American studies, Latin American studies (which usually refers to South or Central, not North, American studies), anthropology, sociology, and occasionally United States history or "Americana," the catch-all section. A few really good bookstores have an "ethnic studies" section, which is usually a treasure trove of books about Latinos, Latino history, and the histories of other ethnic groups.

The absence of a Latino or Hispanic studies section in most bookstores demonstrates a point about racial and ethnic categories in popular and scholarly culture. The need to roam across various subjects to find books on Latinos is caused by ignorance that Latinos constitute an important subject about which many books have been written. The absence of a section on Latino studies and the fairly random sprinkling of books on Latinos throughout sections of varying relevance to Latinos is a metaphor for our denied identity, our absence from the popular imagination. To place books on United States Latinos in the Latin American studies section is to place us outside the borders of the United States—again, symbolic deportation.

The Framers' Plan for a White America

According to its English conquerors, America was always meant to belong to white Englishmen. In 1788, John Jay, writing in the Federalist Number 2, declared, "Providence has been pleased to give this one connected country to one united people—a people descended from the same ancestors, speaking the same language, professing the same religion, attached to the same principles of government, very similar in their manners and customs."[4] Although Jay's statement was wrong—early American society was remarkably diverse—his wish that America be a homogeneous, white, English-speaking Anglo society was widely shared by the Framers of the Constitution and other prominent leaders.

Early on, Benjamin Franklin expressed his distaste for the Germans in Pennsylvania who, by 1790, accounted for over one-third of the citizens of that state.[5] The presence of German colonists and their different language, in Franklin's eyes, threatened the English and their government. In his "Observations Concerning the Increase of Mankind," written in 1751, Franklin lamented the presence of Germans, other Europeans, and Africans who would render impure or darken the "lovely White and Red" complexion of the English in America.[6] Regarding the Germans, Franklin wrote:

> [W]hy should the *Palatine Boors* be suffered to swarm into our Settlements and, by herding together, establish their Language and Manners, to the Exclusion of ours? Why should *Pennsylvania,* founded by the *English,* become a Colony of *Aliens,* who will shortly be so numerous as to Germanize us instead of our Anglifying them, and will never adopt our Language or Customs any more than they can acquire our Complexion?

Interestingly, Franklin thought that Germans and other Europeans had a "swarthy complexion," different and inferior to the "lovely White and Red"[7] of the English. Franklin attributed racial differences in skin color to the Germans, differences that would probably not be perceptible today, because of his hostility toward their ethnic differences: the assignment of an inferior position to a disliked other.

With respect to Africans, Franklin pronounced that "[a]ll *Africa* is black or tawny." He asked, rhetorically: "Why the Sons of *Africa,* by planting them in *America,* when we have so fair an Opportunity, by excluding all Blacks and Tawneys, of increasing the lovely White and Red?" Franklin's design for a white America called for excluding others of a different complexion, so that America might not darken its people.[8]

Like Franklin and Jay, Thomas Jefferson was also preoccupied with creating a homogeneous and white nation. In 1801, Jefferson wrote that

> it is impossible not to look forward to distant times, when our rapid multiplication will expand itself . . . & cover the whole northern, if not the southern continent, with a people speaking the same language, governed in similar forms, by similar laws; *nor can we contemplate with satisfaction either blot or mixture on that surface.*[9]

The "blot or mixture" that concerned him was the presence of Africans in the United States. Jefferson worried that the black "blot" would lead to "mixture" and the "staining" of "the fine mixture of red and white."[10] Jefferson's solution was expulsion: the African was "to be removed beyond the reach of mixture," perhaps to Santo Domingo or perhaps back to Africa as a last resort.[11] For Jefferson, the lovely white, homogeneous republic must not allow its people to be stained and to become a nation of mulattoes.

Benjamin Rush, signer of the Declaration of Independence and leading educator and physician of his time, saw blackness as a disease, like leprosy, which was curable with proper treatment. Rush wanted to cure blacks of their blackness. While they re-covered from their blackness, Rush proposed isolating and segregating blacks in in-ternal domestic colonies, black farming communities, rather than expelling them from the country.[12]

Whites were no more willing to include Native Americans in their society than they were to accept Africans. White hatred of the Indian was perhaps best personi-fied by President Andrew Jackson, who viewed Indians as impulsive and lacking in discipline. He also feared Indian men as sexual threats to white women. Jackson de-scribed Indians as "savage bloodhounds" and "blood thirsty barbarians." He urged their extermination, encouraging his troops to commit acts of great cruelty and bru-tality against them. As President, Jackson was most responsible for the removal of Indians from their desirable lands in the eastern United States and their relocation west of the Mississippi.[13]

As different American leaders implemented their visions of a homogeneous white nation, peoples of color were inconvenient obstacles to be managed by any of sev-eral means: expulsion, isolation, removal, enslavement, even extermination. How, then, would the white nation deal with its Latinos—a hybrid people, a tiny portion part-Spanish, mostly Indian, many part-African, speaking Spanish, and embodying the very "blot and mixture" the Framers had thought so necessary to expel?[14]

The Early Conflict between White America and Indians

As historian David Weber has written:

> Despite the enduring myth that "Spaniards" settled the borderlands, it is quite clear that the majority of the pioneers were Mexicans of mixed blood. In New Spain, the three races of mankind, Caucasian, Mongol, and Negro, blended to form an infinite variety of blood strains, and this blending continued as Mexicans settled among aborigines [In-dians] in the Southwest. Thus *mestizaje,* or racial mixture, was so common that today the vast majority of all Mexicans are of mixed blood.[15]

The imperative of establishing and preserving a pure white government still ran strong when Anglos first encountered Mexicans. Senator John Calhoun opposed United States annexation of Mexican land on racial grounds.

> I know further, sir, that we have never dreamt of incorporating into our Union any but the Caucasian race—the free white race. To incorporate Mexico, would be the very first instance of the kind of incorporating an Indian race. . . . I protest against such a union as that! *Ours, sir, is the Government of a white race.*[16]

Both before and after the conquest of Mexico in 1846, the ideological stage had been set for the mutual dislike that Mexicans and white Americans had for each other. As David Weber has written: "American visitors to the Mexican frontier were nearly unanimous in commenting on the dark skin of Mexican mestizos who, it was generally agreed, had inherited the worst qualities of Spaniards and Indians to pro-duce a 'race' still more despicable than that of either parent."[17] Rufus B. Sage, newspaperman and Rocky Mountain trapper, expressed the common view, describing residents of New Mexico in 1846:

> There are no people on the continent of America, whether civilized, with one or two exceptions, more miserable in condition or despicable in morals than the mongrel race inhabiting New Mexico. . . .
>
> To manage them successfully, they must needs be held in continual restraint, and kept in their place by force, if necessary—else they will become haughty and insolent.
>
> As servants, they are excellent, when properly trained, but are worse than useless if left to themselves.[18]

Lest one think this kind of thinking is a thing of the distant past, consider the views of historian Walter Prescott Webb, writing in 1935:

> The Mexican nation arises from the heterogeneous mixture of races that compose it. The Indian blood—but not Plains Indian blood—predominates, but in it is a mixture of European, largely Latin. The result is a conglomerate with all gradations from pure Spanish to pure Indian. There are corresponding social gradations with grandees at the top and peons at the bottom. The language is Spanish, or Mexican, the religion Catholic, the temperament volatile and mercurial.[19]

Both writers appear obsessed with the racial "blot and mixture" that so preoccupied white Americans, Framers, frontiersmen, and historians alike. Interestingly, in Webb's writing, the historian imposes racial hierarchy according to the relative amounts of "Spanish" (i.e., quasi-white) and Native American ancestry exhibited by Mexicans.

Today, an important part of the public image of the Latino is the Latino as alien: an immigrant, a recent arrival, a foreigner not really belonging to, or in, America. The irony and the proof of falsity in this public image are found in history. The Spanish language was introduced into Mexico in 1519 when explorers and conquerors claimed Mexico for the Spanish crown. The presence of the largest group of people we now call Latinos, Mexican Americans, has been continuous in the Southwest since the sixteenth century.

Of course, Mexicans formulated their own views of the Anglos that began entering their territories in Texas, New Mexico, and California. José Maria Sanchez, writing in 1828, described the living conditions of Anglos settled in Villa de Austin, on the Texas frontier:

> Its population is nearly two hundred persons, of which only ten are Mexicans, for the balance are all Americans from the North with an occasional European. Two wretched little stores supply the inhabitants of the colony: one sells only whiskey, rum, sugar, and coffee; the other, rice, flour, lard, and cheap cloth. . . . The Americans from the North, at least the greater part of those I have seen, eat only salted meat, bread made by themselves out of corn meal, coffee, and homemade cheese. To these the greater part of those who live in the village add strong liquor, for they are in general, in my opinion, lazy people of vicious character. Some of them cultivate their small farms by planting corn; but this task they usually entrust to their negro slaves, whom they treat with considerable harshness.[20]

Juan Seguin, former mayor of San Antonio, was forced to flee Texas because of a huge influx of Anglo Americans. In 1858, he described the painful irony of his new powerlessness at the hands of the new Anglo rulers of San Antonio: "A victim to the wickedness of a few men, whose imposture was favored by their origin, and recent domination over the country; a foreigner in my native land; could I be expected stoically to endure their outrages and insults?"[21] Anglo Americans thus turned Latinos into foreigners in their own lands.

White America and the English Language

The Framers' white America also had to be a predominantly English-speaking America in the words of John Jay and later echoed by Thomas Jefferson. Benjamin Franklin's dislike of the German language was palpable. I will use two examples to illustrate the perceived need for a white and English-speaking America.

In 1807, Jefferson proposed the resettlement, at government expense, of thirty thousand presumably English-speaking Americans in Louisiana in order to "make the majority American, [and] make it an American instead of French State."[22] The first governor of Louisiana, William Claiborne, unsuccessfully attempted to require that all the laws of Louisiana be published in English.

The saga of New Mexico's admission to statehood also illustrates the perceived need for a white and English-speaking America. Despite repeated attempts beginning in 1850, New Mexico did not become a state until 1912, when a majority of its population was English-speaking for the first time. Statehood was withheld from New Mexico for over sixty years because of Congress's unwillingness to grant statehood to a predominantly Spanish-speaking territory populated by Mexican people.

Our Multilingual Heritage

A tremendous disparity, of course, separated the country the Framers desired and the one they came to possess. The country was composed of many groups, of different hues and speaking different languages. Several examples of governmental recognition of American multilingualism illustrate my point. The Continental Congress, hoping to communicate with and win the allegiance of American peoples whose language was different from English, published many significant documents in German and French. After the Revolutionary War, the Articles of Confederation were published in official English, German, and French editions.

Particularly during much of the nineteenth century, several states had rich legal histories of official bilingualism, by which I mean statutory or constitutional recognition of languages other than English: Pennsylvania was officially bilingual in German and English; California and New Mexico were officially bilingual in Spanish and English; and Louisiana was officially bilingual in French and English. The implementation of official bilingualism in these several states shared common features.

All of the laws of those states were required to be published in more than one language. Although this state-sponsored bilingualism mostly died out during the nineteenth century, New Mexico's official bilingualism was remarkably long-lived. New Mexico was officially bilingual between 1846 and early 1953, over one hundred years.

Most people are not aware of the existence and the extent of American multilingualism and its official, state-sponsored character. I am not aware of any United States history text that includes this material. Nor will you find it in any legal history text. This raises a fundamental question that must be asked of historians: Why have historians left all this material out of the telling of history?

The "National Origin" Concept and the Creation of Latino Invisibility

Historians have produced Latino invisibility by omission. Lawmakers have produced it through the attribution of stigmatizing foreignness. This form of invisibility also has its genesis in the Framers' vision of a pure, white America. This vision of America was implemented in our earliest naturalization statutes. The first condition for naturalized citizenship under both the Naturalization Laws of 1790 and 1795 was that an alien be a " free white person."[23] Much later, in 1924, Congress attempted to preserve the predominantly white society by restricting immigration through national origin quotas for immigrants. These quotas, defined by the countries of origin of prospective immigrants, limited immigration so that the demographic composition of immigrants matched the predominantly white, northern European composition of the extant American population. Thus the statutory language of "national origin" began in this century as a concept meant to preserve the existing racial character of American society. It was a concept meant to exclude immigrants who varied too much from white America.

Today the statutory phrase "national origin" appears most prominently in Title VII of the Civil Rights Act of 1964, which prohibits discrimination in employment because of national origin. At first glance, the current "national origin" concept appears to include and protect ethnically different Americans. I believe, however, that true to its origins in the immigration laws, today's "national origin" concept operates to exclude ethnically different Americans in a way similar to the way in which the national origin quotas excluded undesirable immigrants.

The Failure of Title VII to Prohibit Discrimination Because of Latino Ethnicity

How well, then, does the "national origin" language of Title VII protect against discrimination because of perceptible aspects of Latino ethnicity? Not very well. Our system of law provides no meaningful protection against discrimination based on the ethnicity of Latinos. This is a surprising statement, because the Equal Employment

Opportunity Commission (EEOC) has issued extensive guidelines which largely prohibit employment discrimination because of ethnic characteristics. The courts, however, including the Supreme Court, routinely ignore the EEOC's expert agency guidelines, thus rendering them largely ineffectual. The guidelines, at present, offer a false promise of protection that is useless in the courts.

To understand why this is the case, one must understand that, to date, there has been no serious commitment to protect against discrimination because of ethnicity or ethnic traits. Congress's principal purpose in enacting Title VII was to prohibit employment discrimination because of race or color. Despite its parallel status and equal longevity in Title VII, the prohibition against national origin discrimination remains remarkably undeveloped and ineffective. In a legislative history spanning literally thousands of pages of the *Congressional Record,* consideration of the "national origin" term was limited to a few unilluminating paragraphs of House debate. Congress gave no serious thought to the content of the national origin term nor to its proper scope.

Since that time, there has been a remarkable scarcity of analysis and commentary regarding the "national origin" term and whether it remains adequate for the forms of discrimination common today. In the thirty years since Title VII was enacted, only one Supreme Court decision interprets the "national origin" term, the 1973 decision in *Espinoza v. Farah Manufacturing Co.*[24] The Court has denied certiorari in national origin cases many times. This contrasts sharply with myriad Court decisions developing the law of race and sex discrimination. Law reviews and casebooks have also been remarkably silent about problems of national origin discrimination. A casual review of most employment discrimination casebooks will reveal many cases and many pages discussing issues of race and sex discrimination but very few discussing discrimination because of national origin or ethnicity. Together, legislators, the courts, commentators, and casebooks have created Latino, and more generally, ethnic invisibility by silence.

The Judicial Creation and Enforcement of a Normative American Identity

Because Congress never considered the question of national origin or ethnicity seriously, judges are left with enormous discretion to decide which, if any, aspects of ethnic identity will be protected by the prohibition of discrimination due to national origin. This discretion manifests itself in the threshold judicial decisions regarding whether a trait may function at all as a proxy for national origin, and, if so, whether it is a close enough proxy to merit protection. Judges are free to impose their own value preferences, consciously or unconsciously, according to their views of the consistency of particular traits with their notions of American identity. Judges thus have the discretion to create or reproduce a normative American identity through Title VII and like statutes.

Courts have acted consistently with the Framers' wish for an English-speaking America and have helped enforce that wish. For example, in *García v. Gloor,*[25] Hector García was fired for asking a co-worker a job-related question in Spanish. He was doing his job at the time he was fired; he was summarily dismissed because he did his job in Spanish. The United States Court of Appeals for the Fifth Circuit ruled that García's dismissal did not constitute national origin discrimination, since "national origin" was not the same as language and because, for a bilingual person, language is not immutable. The original opinion, however, contained language suggesting that the judges were simply reinforcing their view of the proper dominance of English:

> *An employer does not accord his employees a privilege of conversing in English. English, spoken well or badly, is the language of our Constitution, statutes, Congress, courts and the vast majority of our nation's people.* . . . [I]f the employer engages a bilingual person, that person is granted neither right nor privilege by the statute to use the language of his personal preference.[26]

Thus only English is consistent with our laws and culture, according to this court, and Spanish may be silenced. This opinion was later withdrawn and replaced by an opinion identical in all respects except that the italicized language I quoted above had been deleted. Perhaps someone made the judges aware of the blatant Anglocentrism of the now-missing passage.

Many courts, because of their own biases, favor results that support the English language and ignore the claims of plaintiffs alleging discrimination because of language. More generally, courts enforce mainstream notions of American identity and deny protection to other expressions of ethnic and racial identity. This is the judicial enforcement of a normative, English-speaking American identity. It is also the judicial silencing of the Latino voice, the judicial reinforcement of Latino invisibility.

The "National Origin" Concept and the Problem of "Symbolic Deportation"

So the "national origin" concept serves as a vehicle for judicial imposition of dominant norms of American identity. As legal rhetoric, the "national origin" concept also has revealing and troubling social meanings. A plaintiff discriminated against because of some aspect of her ethnicity (other than race or color) must claim protection under the "national origin" language of Title VII. She must claim to be of some distinguishable national origin as a preliminary matter. The "national origin" language of the statute thus forces many, probably most, plaintiffs to plead a fiction about themselves and a truth about their ancestors that is also true for virtually everyone in the country. Assuming that most plaintiffs in "national origin" discrimination cases are United States citizens by birth, the fiction is that their national origin is someplace other than the United States. With respect to ancestry, and with the exception of Native Americans, the truth is that every American has an ancestry, traced far enough back in time, that began in another place or nation. When brought by citizens, then, most national origin discrimination claims require emphasizing the ancestry of parents or some earlier ancestor to find a national origin, a country of birth, different from the United States.

Because of its focus on a fictional difference in national origin and on ancestry, the "national origin" concept forces plaintiffs to define themselves as outsiders, belonging to some other country or place of birth and, correspondingly, outside the scope of American identity. By reinforcing the notion of "foreign" national origin even among American-born citizens, at least two negative consequences result. First, United States citizens who constitute part of the American polity and part of American identity must define themselves as having a foreign national origin and as outsiders not belonging to the American community. This is a false, statutory, and Court-created outsider status, since Americans born here all have equal claim to American national origin and to equal citizenship as a birth right under the Fourteenth Amendment. Second, the operation of the "national origin" concept reinforces unstated norms of "true" American identity and reinforces an underinclusive conception of American identity. By making ancestry the significant concept in claiming statutory protection, the statute excludes many ethnic traits of United States citizens, including different languages, accents, and names, from the legal and cultural conception of United States identity.

The "national origin" concept thus perpetuates false beliefs about what is and what is not American. The falsity lies in the concept that Americans who differ ethnically from unstated norms of American identity are from a different place than the United States. Ethnically different Americans are marginalized because of their ethnic differences, which are made attributable to fictional foreign origins which further remove these Americans and their traits to a periphery outside American national identity. Thus the "national origin" concept, now meant to protect Americans from discrimination, in fact operates to exclude ethnically different Americans, at times overtly in court decisions and at times surreptitiously in the meaning and use of the term "national origin." This is symbolic deportation outside the borders of the United States.

Latinos are made invisible and foreign, therefore, in several contexts: in the reporting of significant racial events, in the bookstores, in the historical conception of America as a white and English-speaking nation, and in the operation of the "national origin" concept. We are made invisible and foreign, despite our longtime presence, substance, and citizenship. Latinos must be recognized as full and equal members of our community. This equality I describe is an equality of respect and of dignity for the full identity and personhood of Latino people. It is an equality and respect for the similarities we share with our fellow Americans. It is also an equality and respect for the differences we contribute to American identity. In 1883, Walt Whitman complained that the states "showed too much of the British and German influence. . . . To that composite American identity of the future," Whitman wrote, "Spanish character will supply some of the most needed parts."[27] Our Mexican and Latino character continues to supply some of our most needed parts.

NOTES

1. Earl Shorris, Latinos: A Biography of the People 3 (1992).

2. *Id.*

3. Latino people began migrating northward into what is now the Southwestern United States soon after Spanish conquerors arrived in 1519. Charles Gibson, SPAIN IN AMERICA 25 (1966); A. Curtis Wilgus, THE DEVELOPMENT OF HISPANIC AMERICA 89 (1941). Spanish was the first European language to be introduced into America. The first English-speaking colonization began almost a century later in Virginia in 1607. SETTLEMENTS TO SOCIETY 1607–1763: A DOCUMENTARY HISTORY OF COLONIAL AMERICA 1–2 (Jack P. Greene ed., 1975).

4. THE FEDERALIST No. 2, at 91 (John Jay) (Isaac Kramnick ed., 1988).

5. 2 Albert B. Faust, THE GERMAN ELEMENT IN THE UNITED STATES 14 (1909).

6. Benjamin Franklin, *Observations Concerning the Increase of Mankind, Peopling of Countries, Etc.* (1751), in 3 THE WRITINGS OF BENJAMIN FRANKLIN 63, 73 (Albert H. Smyth ed., 1905).

7. *Id.* at 72–73.

8. See *id.* at 72–73. These observations, including the comments on Germans, were deleted from all editions of Franklin's essay that appeared during his lifetime except the first edition. *Id.* at 63 n.1, 72 n.1.

9. Thomas Jefferson, Letter to James Monroe (Nov. 24, 1801), in THOMAS JEFFERSON: WRITINGS 1096, 1097 (Merrill D. Peterson ed., 1984) (emphasis added).

10. Thomas Jefferson, *Notes on the State of Virginia*, Query XIV (1844), reprinted in THOMAS JEFFERSON: WRITINGS, at 264–65.

11. *Id.* at 270; see also Ronald Takaki, IRON CAGES: RACE AND CULTURE IN NINETEENTH-CENTURY AMERICA 49–50 (1979) (describing Jefferson's thoughts about dealing with America's African population).

12. See Takaki, at 33–35.

13. *Id.* at 95–97.

14. It is an understatement to note, as Judge Higginbotham wrote, that the English colonists had "difficulties in fostering a sense of community in a colony [Virginia] populated by Portuguese, Spanish, French, Turks, Dutch, blacks, and Indians." A. Leon Higginbotham, Jr., IN THE MATTER OF COLOR: RACE AND THE LEGAL PROCESS 29 (1978).

15. FOREIGNERS IN THEIR NATIVE LAND: HISTORICAL ROOTS OF THE MEXICAN AMERICANS 33 (Daniel J. Weber ed., 1973).

16. *Cong. Globe*, 30th Cong., 1st Sess., 98 (1848) (remarks of Sen. Calhoun), excerpted in FOREIGNERS IN THEIR NATIVE LAND, at 135 (emphasis added).

17. FOREIGNERS IN THEIR NATIVE LAND, at 59–60.

18. 2 RUFUS B. SAGE: HIS LETTERS AND PAPERS, 1836–1847, at 82–87 (LeRoy R. Hafen & Ann W. Hafen eds., 1956), excerpted in FOREIGNERS IN THEIR NATIVE LAND, at 72, 74.

19. Walter P. Webb, THE TEXAS RANGERS: A CENTURY OF FRONTIER DEFENSE 13–14 (2d ed. 1965), excerpted in FOREIGNERS IN THEIR NATIVE LAND, at 77.

20. José M. Sanchez, *A Trip to Texas in 1828*, 29 SW. HIST. Q., Apr. 1926, at 270–71 (Carlos E. Castañeda trans.), excerpted in FOREIGNERS IN THEIR NATIVE LAND, at 81–82.

21. Juan N. Seguin, PERSONAL MEMOIRS OF JOHN N. SEGUIN: FROM THE YEAR 1834 TO THE RETREAT OF GENERAL WOLL FROM THE CITY OF SAN ANTONIO, 1842, at iii–iv, 18–32 (1858), excerpted in FOREIGNERS IN THEIR NATIVE LAND, at 178.

22. Letter from Thomas Jefferson to John Dickinson (Jan. 13, 1807), in THOMAS JEFFERSON: WRITINGS, at 1169, 1169–70.

23. Act of Mar. 26, 1790, ch. III, s 1, 1 Stat. 103 (establishing conditions and procedures for naturalization); Act of Jan. 29, 1795, ch. xx, s 1, 1 Stat. 414 (repealing and revising conditions set forth in act of 1790).

24. 414 U.S. 86 (1973).

25. 609 F.2d 156 (5th Cir.), withdrawn, 618 F.2d 264 (5th Cir. 1980), cert. denied, 449 U.S. 1113 (1981).

26. *Garcia*, 609 F.2d at 161.

27. Carey McWilliams, NORTH FROM MEXICO: THE SPANISH-SPEAKING PEOPLE OF THE UNITED STATES 10 (1968) (quoting Walt Whitman).

Chapter 85

Lawyers, Linguists, Story-tellers, and Limited English-Speaking Witnesses

Miguel A. Méndez

How serious is the problem of interpretation in American courts? Data on America's changing demography suggest that the problem is profound and worsening. A recent study estimated that in 1990 the number of home speakers of non-English languages in the United States was nearly thirty-two million, or about 13 percent of the United States population. Of these, over half (17.3 million) spoke Spanish at home. More than half of the Spanish home speakers (9.8 million) resided in the border states of Arizona, California, New Mexico, and Texas.

The implications for court proceedings in California, New Mexico, and Texas are especially serious. Home speakers of Spanish comprise 18 percent of California's population, 25 percent of New Mexico's population, and 20 percent of Texas's population. Since speakers of other languages who reside in these and other states also speak some English, the potential number of limited English speakers who may be called to give testimony in state and federal courts is high.

A Lawyer's View of Courtroom Story-telling

Evidentiary Constraints

Evidentiary concerns impose limits on how events from the past can be described in the courtroom. The general rule in American courts is that witnesses may only speak in response to questions.

Direct Examination. In the absence of compelling circumstances, witnesses may not relate their testimony in the form of a narrative.[1] Thus, to tell their stories, witnesses must refrain from telling stories. The result on direct examination is a fragmented account in which the witness is expected to respond only to the examining attorney's questions. Answers that do not respond to the examiner's questions may be stricken

From "Lawyers, Linguists, Story-Tellers, and Limited English-Speaking Witnesses." 27 N.M L. Rev. 1 (1997). Originally published in the *New Mexico Law Review*. Reprinted by permission.

upon motion by the examining party as "unresponsive."[2] Responsive answers, even when considered as a whole, are unlikely to resemble the story which the witness would have related in another less formal setting—her living room, for example. The answers, moreover, will contain much information which the witness would not have provided, but which the examining lawyer considers important.

The limitation on direct examination testimony is justified by the need to diminish the risk that witnesses will relate matters which the rules of evidence deem inadmissible for a variety of reasons. Only by forcing the witness to answer specific questions posed by the direct examiner will the opposing lawyer have an opportunity to raise objections before the witness answers. Simply asking witnesses to relate all they know about a specific event defeats this goal.

Cross-Examination. Cross-examination poses even more severe challenges than direct examination to lay notions of how witnesses should relate their stories. In commonplace story-telling, the listeners may or may not voice their disagreements with the story-teller's account. Common rules of courtesy discourage listeners from interrupting or discrediting the story-teller. In courtroom story-telling, however, the party opposing the witness is expressly given permission to discredit the story-teller's account. The cross-examiner, for example, may challenge the witness's perceptual powers—"You weren't wearing your glasses, were you?"—or veracity—"Just last year, you were convicted of perjury, were you not?"

A good cross-examiner, moreover, utilizes a form of examination that is alien to story-telling. When we tell a story, *we* get to tell the story. We select the words and phrases that convey the desired information. But, as demonstrated by the above two examples, cross-examiners use questions that are designed to limit the witness to "yes" or "no" answers. The last thing a cross-examiner wants is for the witness to repeat any damaging answers given on direct examination. That risk is diminished by asking the witness "leading questions" on cross-examination. The rules of evidence assume that leading questions are among the most effective means for exposing flaws in perception, recollection, narration, and sincerity. Modern codes of evidence expressly allow the use of such questions on cross-examination.

Other Non-conventional Story-Telling Courtroom Practices. Other aspects of courtroom practice distinguish testimony from conventional story-telling. When we tell stories in our own homes, no one stands between us and the listeners. The listeners know their cognitive needs and may ask clarifying questions if they wish. In the courtroom, however, the attorneys comprise a special class of listeners. As a rule, only they get to ask questions, including follow-up ones. Jurors are usually passive players. Their cognitive needs, if addressed at all, must be anticipated by the lawyers.

The restraints on testimony, moreover, make witnesses a special class of storytellers. As a result of pretrial preparation, witnesses know that they are not free to relate their recollection of the events in question with the same freedom enjoyed by conventional story-tellers. Witnesses also know that whatever they say on direct examination can be challenged on cross-examination and under circumstances far removed from those attending living-room conversations. And, unlike conventional story-tellers, witnesses can be subjected to perjury prosecutions for knowingly making false statements under oath.

Strategic and Tactical Concerns

The rules of evidence are not the only force shaping courtroom story-telling. Strategic concerns of lawyers play an equally important role. Preparing witnesses to tell a convincing story that complies with the rules of evidence will be of no avail if lawyers fail to get their case-in-chief to the jury. Unless lawyers produce some evidence of each element of their claims or affirmative defenses, their cases, generally, will be nonsuited at the conclusion of their case-in-chief.

This harsh reality forces lawyers to approach litigation along two simultaneous tracks. The first, less obvious, track is technical in nature. The lawyers must make sure that they have presented some evidence of each element of their case's claim or defense by the conclusion of their case-in-chief. That is the subject of procedure. The second, more obvious track, requires lawyers to plan their presentation of the evidence in the fashion most likely to be accepted by the fact-finder(s)—making sure, for example, that a lawyer's witnesses tell a credible story in response to the lawyer's questions on direct examination. That is the subject of trial advocacy.

Though procedural and advocacy goals are not necessarily inconsistent, complying with the procedural requirements may require eliciting information from witnesses which they would not ordinarily provide when retelling their stories in their homes. In criminal cases, for example, prosecutors will elicit from some witnesses information about where the offense took place. The fact that an offense took place in Palo Alto and that Palo Alto is in Santa Clara County and that Santa Clara County is in the State of California could hardly matter to a jury hearing a murder case where the killing occurred in Palo Alto. But the procedural rules require the prosecution to establish the Santa Clara County Superior Court's jurisdiction to hear the case.

Tactical concerns can play an even greater role than technical ones in shaping courtroom story-telling. Tactical considerations include an assessment of the credibility of the witnesses to be called by each side.

> Trial lawyers know that the outcome of a trial will be determined in [most] cases by which witnesses the juro[rs] choose[] to believe and which [ones they] decide[] to ignore. Telling jurors which witnesses to believe or disbelieve is thus a crucial part of a closing argument. But such an appeal will not be [well-received by the jurors] unless the lawyer can give [them] reasons rooted in the evidence about why a witness's testimony should be accepted or rejected. This inescapable dynamic of jury trials encourages lawyers to produce the most favorable evidence about the credibility of their witnesses and the most unfavorable about their opponents.[3]

In theory, lawyers develop their witness lists and the order and structure of their witness examinations with one goal in mind—presenting the information in the form most likely to be accepted by the fact-finder. In an ideal world, a lawyer would lead with a strong witness, one who can grab the jurors' attention, and end with an equally strong one, a witness who could tug the jurors' hearts hard enough so that their minds, in the form of a favorable verdict, would follow. This goal may well require the lawyer to abandon a convention that shapes most story-telling, developing the story chronologically. Instead, a lawyer might otherwise begin with an ending and end with what might be considered a beginning of a narrative.

Irrespective of the steps lawyers take to support the credibility of their witnesses on direct examination (or to attack the credibility of the opposing party's witnesses on cross-examination), one thing is clear—the telling of the whole story will be affected in ways that do not intrude in everyday story-telling. The production as a whole may not resemble a chronicle, as in traditional story-telling; themes, rather than discrete events occurring over time, may be the dominant features. Individual witnesses may not be given opportunities to share their narratives, and even the stories they do get to tell may be disrupted with side-trips bearing on their credibility.

In sum, the rules for taking testimony handicap witnesses in ways which are of little or no concern to conventional story-tellers. Rules of evidence and trial tactics shift the story-teller's concern from transmitting important information to worries about whether the story-teller is complying with the rules of the forum.

The Example of *Gonzalez v. United States*

Witnesses are not entitled to use interpreters just because they say they need them. Judges make this determination.[4] Whether an interpreter should be appointed is left to judicial discretion. What standards do judges employ when a witness claims some limited English-speaking ability?

Gonzalez v. United States,[5] an interpreter proceedings case, illustrates the limitations of the common law's approach. Miguel Angel Gonzalez sought to overturn his convictions for drug offenses on the ground that the district court judge failed to appoint an interpreter for him at the time he pleaded guilty. Gonzalez claimed that his limited English-speaking ability prevented him from understanding the nature of the charges against him and the potential consequences of a guilty plea.

Two of three appellate judges concluded that the district court judge did not abuse his discretion in finding that Gonzalez's language difficulties did not present a "major" problem. They emphasized that at the time the plea was taken the district court judge "knew that Gonzalez had lived in Oregon for ten years, was buying his own home, and worked in the auto and truck sales business. In addition, the two judges paid particular attention to the following colloquy which took place between the district court judge and Gonzalez at the change of plea hearing:

> *Court:* What did you do? Did you work with other people to buy drugs and sell them?
> *Gonzalez:* I used the telephone.
> *Court:* In addition to using the phone, what did you do?
> *Gonzalez:* I worked with Forcelledo.
> *Court:* Did you sell drugs to people?
> *Gonzalez:* Yes. . . .
> *Court:* Was that drug cocaine?
> *Gonzalez:* Yes. . . .

Court: Where did you get the drugs you sold?
Linstedt [Gonzalez's lawyer]: You worked for Forcelledo?
Gonzalez: Right.
Court: Did you ever sell cocaine to somebody?
Gonzalez: Yes.
Court: Where did you get that cocaine?
Gonzalez: Get [*sic*] it from Forcelledo.[6]

The two affirming judges also focused on the district court judge's observations:

The record should reflect that [Gonzalez] has been in court when other defendants have entered a plea of guilty and that he has been assisted by competent counsel who has fully advised him of his rights and that he has also been assisted also [*sic*] by his wife who is able to assist the attorney in explaining these matters to him.[7]

However, looking at the same colloquy, the dissenting judge found that Gonzalez was capable of responding to the judge's questions only when they required "yes" or "no" answers. Other parts of the colloquy not considered by the majority led the dissenting judge to conclude that "whenever the district court asked a question requiring a slightly more-complicated answer, Gonzalez's answers were non-responsive, even when coached by his lawyer."[8] The dissenting judge cited the following examples:

District Judge: Would you tell me what your understanding of Count I of the indictment is; that is, the conspiracy charge? What do you think they are charging you with by alleging you participated in the conspiracy?
Gonzalez's Lawyer: He is asking you on the conspiracy what does that mean [*sic*]. What are you charged with? What did you do?
Gonzalez: With the telephone call? . . .
District Judge: What did you do? Did you work with other people to buy drugs and sell them?
Gonzalez: I used the telephone.[9]

The dissenting judge was not impressed by the fact that Gonzalez's wife may have assisted him in understanding the proceedings. "The district court had no evidence that Gonzalez's wife was an accurate or impartial interpreter [as required by the federal Court Interpreters Act[10] and noted by the accompanying House of Representatives Report;][11] to the contrary, the fact that she was a *codefendant* in the case render[ed] her involvement highly questionable."[12]

A linguist would be astonished by the Ninth Circuit's explanations. To a linguist the question would not be whether the trial judge abused his discretion in making the linguistic call. Rather, it would be whether a linguistically defensible call could be made on the basis of the information available to the judge. A linguist would be interested primarily in assessing Gonzalez's linguistic competency in English and then in determining whether, given his competency level, he would most likely understand what would be demanded of him at a change of plea hearing. In assessing Gonzalez's English proficiency, a linguist decidedly would not ask the type of leading questions used at times by the district court judge. Instead, a linguist, like dissenting Judge Reinhardt in *Gonzalez,* would take the use of leading questions into account in determining whether the trial judge made a linguistically sound determination in light of the available information.

The Statutory Response

Congress and some state legislatures have responded to the dramatic increase in recent years of the non-English-speaking population by enacting statutes providing for court interpreters. Courts have increasingly relied on these enactments in assessing claims of error grounded on a trial judge's failure to appoint an interpreter. However, both the federal and state measures have inadequately addressed the problem faced by limited English-speaking witnesses and litigants. . . .

The disadvantages and costs of the use of interpreters makes their use unattractive. But the alternative, erroneously withholding interpreters from limited English-speaking witnesses, is even less attractive. The use of interpreters cannot be avoided so long as witnesses with little or no command of English are called to the stand because they possess information that is vital to the resolution of a case. Trial judges will have to rule on whether a particular witness should be assisted by an interpreter. Until reliable and easily applied language assessment tests are developed and employed, trial judges will have no choice but to continue to make ad hoc and untrained guesses about the linguistic competency of limited English-speaking witnesses.

NOTES

1. See Miguel A. Méndez, California Evidence § 1.04, at 10 (1993).

2. See Méndez § 1.04, at 12–13. In California, unresponsive answers *must* be stricken on the motion of *any* party, not just the examining party.

3. Méndez, § 15.01, at 260.

4. See, e.g., Fed. R. Evid. 604, 706.

5. 33 F.3d 1047 (9th Cir. 1994).

6. *Id.* at 1050. Gonzalez's *lawyer* also stated that he believed that Gonzalez's plea was an "understanding plea."

7. *Id.* at 1050–51.

8. *Id.*

9. *Id.* at 1053–54 n.3.

10. 28 U.S.C. § 1827 (1994). The Court Interpreters Act mandates the provision of qualified and impartial interpreters to criminal defendants who are language impaired. See *id.*; see also *Gonzalez,* 33 F.3d at 1054 (Reinhardt, J., dissenting).

11. H.R. Rept. No. 95-1687, at 5 (1978), *reprinted in* 1978 U.S.C.C.A.N. 4652, 4656.

12. *Gonzalez,* 33 F.3d at 1054 (Reinhardt, J., dissenting).

Chapter 86

Hernandez
The Wrong Message at the Wrong Time

Miguel A. Méndez

In *Hernandez v. New York,*[1] the United States Supreme Court dealt a serious blow to the cause of bilingualism and equal access to jury service. In that case, the Court confronted the question of whether prosecutors could eliminate from jury service bilingual persons whom they "feel" might not abide by the official interpretation of the testimony of non-English-speaking witnesses. A plurality of the Court held that unless the accused persuades the trial judge that the prosecutor removed these prospective jurors, known as venirepersons, on account of their race or ethnicity, their removal would not violate the Equal Protection Clause.

The Court's holding prescribes the wrong remedy for correcting inaccuracies by court interpreters. Disqualifying from jury service individuals who can call attention to such inaccuracies defeats the truth-seeking function of a jury trial. It also reinforces a deeply embedded fear that retaining a language in addition to English might undo the fragile bonds of our society. The United States is one of the few developed nations which views the mastery of a foreign language with suspicion. This is especially true if the speakers acquired their foreign language skills from their families rather than through formal study. To these speakers, the Court's decision is but another painful reminder of how proficiency in another language is a liability, not an asset. As even the plurality concedes, "It is a harsh paradox that one may become proficient enough in English to participate in a trial . . . only to encounter disqualification because he knows a second language as well."[2]

Finally, the Court's standard guarantees that most defendants will be unsuccessful in challenging the State's use of peremptories to exclude bilingual venirepersons who happen to know the language spoken by non-English-speaking witnesses. Since many, if not most, of these venirepersons will be members of minority groups, the Court's holding will ensure the disproportionate exclusion of members of these groups from participating in determining the guilt or innocence of those charged with crimes.

From "*Hernandez:* The Wrong Message at the Wrong Time." 4 Stan. L. and Pol'y Rev. 193 (1993). Originally published in the *Stanford Law and Policy Review*. Reprinted by permission.

Presumably, the justification for *Hernandez* is that jurors should employ a common fund of information to arrive at their verdict. Under our adversary system, the parties bring all helpful information to the trier of fact, while the judge, upon motion of the opposing party, deletes inadmissible data from the information presented. Such a process helps ensure that all jurors reach a verdict based on the same facts. The court routinely instructs jurors to draw from this common nucleus of information. They are routinely told to avoid news accounts of the trial and to refrain from discussing the case with anyone until they begin deliberations, during which they are to discuss the case only with their fellow jurors. In addition, if they have heard about the case prior to trial, they are instructed to set aside any pre-formed impressions about the case. Underlying the common fund view is the assumption that in an adversary system it is the parties who challenge and test the information upon which the jury will rely. Jurors who use information "outside the record" become untested evidentiary sources.

Jurors who rely on their own interpretation of what a non-English-speaking witness says pose a serious challenge to the concept of maintaining a shared source of information. Seemingly, bilingual persons who insist on relying on their own interpretation should not serve on the jury since they have announced their intention not to abide by the evidence presented in the case. That, however, was not the situation presented in *Hernandez*. In response to the prosecutor's questions, the venirepersons said that they "would try" to abide by the official interpretation.[3] When questioned by the judge, they said that they "could."[4] The prosecutor nonetheless struck them peremptorily because he "just felt from the hesitancy in their answers and their lack of eye contact that they would not be able to do it."[5] Yet, as defense counsel pointed out, any honest venireperson would have answered the prosecutor's questions in the same way. Without knowing anything about the interpreter's ability to interpret accurately, they could only promise to try to abide by the official interpretation.

But, if a bilingual juror believes that an official interpretation is incorrect, why should the presumed error be ignored? If in fact the interpreter is wrong, *Hernandez* would require the bilingual juror to ignore the error and refrain from bringing it to the attention of the other jurors. Accurate fact-finding would dictate a different rule: one that would not disfavor the selection of bilingual jurors who can bring serious errors in interpretation to the judge's attention. Indeed, Justice Stevens advocated such a rule in his *Hernandez* dissent.[6]

In *Hernandez*, the accused argued that because Spanish-language ability bears a close relationship to ethnicity, the peremptory removal of bilingual venirepersons was tantamount to removal on account of ethnicity. The Court declined to address this argument. It did concede, however, that removal of bilingual venirepersons whom the prosecutor felt would not abide by the official English translation "might well result" in the disproportionate removal of Latino venirepersons. But it concluded that such disproportionate effects would not violate the Equal Protection Clause of the Constitution unless the accused proved that the prosecutor's true motive was to prevent bilingual Latinos from serving on the jury. Thus, even if foreign language proficiency correlated perfectly with ethnicity, this would be of scant use to the accused. The problem, then, is not the degree of correlation, but the Court's use of standards far removed from the realities of the courtroom.

Precise data on the number of adult bilinguals who may be subject to exclusion under *Hernandez* are unavailable. Preliminary 1990 Census data indicate that approximately 17.3 million persons over the age of five speak Spanish in the home. Of these, approximately two-thirds are bilingual. If the same proportion of Latinos eighteen and over are also bilingual, then roughly 66 percent of Latinos who qualify for jury duty may be excludable under *Hernandez*. Countless others who speak English and some other language are also subject to exclusion. Many, if not most, bilinguals claim an ethnic background that qualifies for protection under the Equal Protection Clause. The actual number subject to removal, while lower, cannot be known. Available data do not show the probability that an ethnic bilingual will be called for jury service; the percentage of ethnic bilinguals who would meet jurisdictional requirements for jury service; the probability that in a given trial a non- English speaker will be called as a witness; or whether an ethnic bilingual called for jury service will understand the language spoken by a non-English-speaking witness. The point, though, is not the difficulty in arriving at precise figures. Members of ethnic groups who happen to know or understand the language of a non-English-speaking witness are, by reason of that knowledge, excludable from jury service.

Hernandez exacts other costs as well. It reinforces a provincial American view that the retention of languages other than English is bad. We admire the multilingual abilities of Europeans but view American children who start school knowing only a foreign language as a problem. Rather than help them retain this asset, we immerse them in programs designed to convert them into monolingual English speakers and thinkers in the shortest time possible. In the process, we strip them not only of an asset but of a sense of self that would benefit them and society as well. We are a multicultural, multilingual society that draws much of its strength from its diversity. Exploiting this strength fully will require a respect and tolerance for our differences, which we have yet to achieve.

NOTES

1. 111 S.Ct. 1859 (1991).
2. *Id.* at 1872.
3. *Id.* at 1865.
4. *Id.*
5. *Id.*
6. *Id.* at 1877 (Stevens, J., dissenting).

Chapter 87

Attorney as Interpreter

Bill Piatt

Should an attorney serve as an interpreter for a non-English-speaking client in a criminal prosecution? Out of an apparent sense of duty to the court or client, some bilingual attorneys have been willing to assume that role. Moreover, trial courts which have imposed such an obligation upon counsel have generally been upheld on appeal. This chapter examines the potential harm to the client, counsel, and the administration of justice when an attorney acts as an interpreter for a client in litigation.

As with other language rights issues, problems with interpreters develop because courts and counsel seem not to understand the significance of the interests at stake. The lack of a coherent recognition of language rights in this country and the absence of any United States Supreme Court decision defining the right to court interpreters add to the uncertainty. Yet, the use of interpreters is becoming increasingly important to the administration of justice. For example, in 1986, interpreted proceedings constituted 6 percent of all federal court hearings.[1] Examining the issues that arise when an attorney is called upon to interpret for a client first requires some understanding of the nature of the right to an interpreter. An understanding of the extent to which an attorney-interpreter fulfills the obligation of zealous advocacy is also required.

Through the middle of the twentieth century, courts generally held that appointment of an interpreter in a criminal proceeding rested solely in the trial court's discretion. Even after a provision was enacted for the appointment of interpreters in criminal proceedings in the federal courts, such an appointment was still considered to be a matter of discretion. However, in 1970, the Second Circuit Court of Appeals in *United States* ex rel. *Negron v. New York,* determined that the sixth amendment's confrontation clause, made applicable to the states through the fourteenth amendment's due process clause, requires that non-English-speaking defendants be informed of their right to simultaneous interpretation of proceedings at the government's expense.[2] Otherwise, the trial would be a "babble of voices,"[3] the defendant

From "ATTORNEY AS INTERPRETER: A RETURN TO BABBLE." 20 N.M. L. REV. 1 (1990). Originally published in the *New Mexico Law Review*. Reprinted by permission.

would not understand the testimony against him, and counsel would be hampered in effective cross-examination.

The right to an interpreter in the federal courts was expanded by enactment of the Court Interpreters Act in 1978.[4] The Act requires judges to employ competent interpreters in criminal or civil actions initiated by the government in a United States district court. An interpreter must be appointed when a party or witness speaks only or primarily in a language other than English or suffers from a hearing impairment, so as to inhibit the person's comprehension of the proceedings. The Director of the Administrative Office of the United States Courts is required to prescribe, determine, and certify the qualifications of persons who may serve as interpreters. The Director maintains a list of interpreters and prescribes a fee schedule for their use.

Courts have repeatedly determined that no constitutional right guarantees an interpreter in civil or administrative proceedings. However, various state constitutional and legislative provisions do so, in most cases leaving the determination to the trial court's discretion. Under traditional views of zealous advocacy, counsel for a party with a language barrier should be ethically required to urge the Court to exercise its discretion in a manner favorable to that client regarding these interpretation issues. Before turning to a discussion of counsel as interpreter, it is important to consider how counsel who is not also required to serve as an interpreter should ordinarily proceed regarding interpretation issues in litigation.

The first issue is whether a client is entitled to an interpreter. Courts will ordinarily not appoint one in the absence of a request to do so, but the failure of an attorney to request an interpreter for a qualifying client has been held to constitute ineffective assistance of counsel. A client need not be totally ignorant of the English language in order to be entitled to an interpreter. The federal test is basically whether the client speaks only or primarily a language other than English. Thus, even though a client may be able to function in English in a social conversation, he or she may still be entitled to an interpreter in litigation. Zealous advocacy would seem to require counsel to seek an interpreter when a language barrier may inhibit his or her client's comprehension of the proceedings or interfere with presentation of evidence on the client's behalf.

Counsel must also ensure that the interpreter is qualified. In the federal system, the Director of the Administrative Office of the United States Courts examines and maintains lists of certified interpreters; some states do as well. In the absence of such certification, an attorney should require the interpreter to demonstrate sufficient education, training, or experience to satisfy the trial judge that he or she can make a competent translation. Although interpreters with obvious conflicts of interest, such as a family relationship to a witness, may be allowed to serve, opposing counsel should identify such conflicts and object, in order to preserve a record for appeal.

Assuming the court appoints a competent, unbiased interpreter, counsel's work is still not done. Counsel should ordinarily insist on a simultaneous translation. Because the court reporter only transcribes the English dialogue, counsel should insist on a "first-person" translation to avoid a garbled record. Further, counsel should adamantly insist on having two interpreters in the courtroom. One would translate witness testimony and proceedings for the record. The other would facilitate communication between counsel and client, and advise counsel of any translation errors made by the first, or "court" interpreter. Finally, counsel should insist that testimony be tape-recorded where an interpreter is used, for correcting errors at trial or for transmission with the record on appeal if necessary.

In some pre-*Negron* cases, courts encountered no difficulty in finding that the right to confront witnesses in a criminal proceeding was satisfied where defense counsel was bilingual, or understood the testimony even though the defendant did not. Thus, the presence of counsel who could communicate with their respective clients in French, Italian, or Polish, as well as Spanish, was held to obviate the need for the appointment of an interpreter. The "bald assertion" that an attorney who was forced to act as the client's interpreter could not thereby function effectively as counsel was found to be without merit in a case with a Spanish-speaking defendant and bilingual counsel.[5] As a further variation on this theme, the presence of a bilingual judge was held to satisfy the constitutional right of a Spanish-speaking defendant to confront witnesses in a criminal proceeding.[6]

The failure of courts to consider these issues can produce potentially severe consequences. Language minority clients may be convicted without the traditional safeguards afforded to English-speaking clients. Bilingual attorneys can be subjected to state-imposed sanctions for participation without objection in the process. Constitutional ramifications may come into play, as well. Even though the Supreme Court has never recognized a constitutional right to an interpreter, and although lower courts have reached contradictory conclusions on the subject, the Supreme Court has found a due process right to state-furnished "basic tools," including psychiatric experts on behalf of indigents. Similarly, a showing of particularized need for an interpreter coupled with a showing as to why a bilingual attorney cannot fulfill the need should lead to a conclusion that the failure to appoint a separate interpreter violates due process. In addition, *Negron* teaches that confrontation clause and due process violations occur when a language minority client does not have an interpreter to confront adverse witnesses. *Negron* also refers to a standard of "simple humaneness."[7] Counsel should invoke these concerns as well in resisting the dual appointment as attorney and interpreter.

Equal protection considerations also come to the fore. The only apparent reason why courts require counsel to also serve as interpreters is to save the money which would otherwise be paid by the court to independent interpreters. Assuming that such a scheme effectively deprives the client of either the attorney or the interpreter to which the client would otherwise be entitled, the situation appears analogous to equal protection problems identified by the Supreme Court where state court schemes denied indigent defendants appellate transcripts.[8]

Moreover, even though trial courts have been given wide discretion to appoint as interpreters persons with obvious bias, inherent conflict issues stemming from the attorney-client relationship loom large. For example, the attorney who interprets for a client at trial may well end up testifying against the client on appeal if an issue as to the adequacy of the translation is raised. Even though the issue of effective assistance of trial counsel is occasionally raised in criminal appeals, no good reason argues for counsel to agree to inject an additional potential area of conflict between themselves and clients.

These concerns are not limited to the attorney-client relationship at trial. For example, the entry of a guilty plea has traditionally been viewed as the waiver of constitutionally protected rights. These rights include the privilege against self-incrimination, the right to trial by jury, as well as the right to confront witnesses. Waiver of these rights cannot be presumed from a silent record. The waiver traditionally can only be made by the defendant personally and not by counsel. When a bilingual attorney agrees to interpret for his or her client at this stage of the proceedings, the attorney runs the risk of effectively testifying against his client if the issue on appeal is whether, because of the language barrier, the client made a knowing and intelligent waiver of the rights set forth above. In such an appeal, the client would be arguing no waiver could have occurred because the "interpreter," who had not been certified as such, did not effectively communicate to the defendant a sufficient understanding of the interests at stake to constitute a waiver. Upholding the plea in such a circumstance is tantamount to our courts, with the approval and participation of defense counsel, telling language minority defendants:

1. You have a right to confront your accusers;
2. That right is not lost if you can't understand your accusers;
3. That right is lost if you can't understand this inquiry as to whether you wish to waive the right to confront your accusers, because of interpretation errors by your own counsel.

Given the many serious problems that surface when counsel serve as interpreters for their own clients, one cannot help but wonder why the situation has continued. Monolingual judges may have been unaware of the inherent difficulties in the understanding of courtroom testimony and the presentation of an effective case in the presence of a language barrier. The lack of any United States Supreme Court decision defining and applying the right to an interpreter undoubtedly adds to uncertainties as to the exact nature and parameters of the right. Viewing the situation somewhat less charitably, judges may have been aware of the difficulties, but chosen not to rectify them because of the same fear, apprehension, and hostility monolingual people exhibit toward a language and speakers they do not understand.

Whatever the motivations of court and counsel, it should now appear obvious that it is unfair to the client when his or her attorney must serve as interpreter in court. The client, obviously, cannot enter his or her own objection because of a lack of understanding of the language and the process. Thus it becomes incumbent upon counsel and the courts to protect the due process and confrontation rights of clients who are not fluent in English.

NOTES

1. H.R. Rep. No. 100-889, 100th Cong., 2d Sess., reprinted in 1988 U.S. Code Cong. & Admin. News 6018, 6019. Spanish is by far the most widely used language in these proceed-

ings. Interpreted proceedings utilizing languages other than Spanish accounted for only one-third of 1 percent of all federal court hearings in 1986.

2. United States *ex rel.* Negron v. New York, 434 F.2d 386, 390–91 (2d Cir.1970).

3. *Id.* at 388.

4. 28 U.S.C. § 1827 (1988).

5. United States v. Paroutian, 299 F.2d 486, 490 (2d. Cir. 1962).

6. United States v. Sosa, 379 F.2d 525, 527 (7th Cir.), cert. denied, 389 U.S. 895 (1967).

7. 434 F.2d, at 390.

8. Griffin v. Illinois, 351 U.S. 12 (1956).

Chapter 88

The Politics of Discretion
Federal Intervention in Bilingual Education

Rachel F. Moran

Historically, state and local educators have exercised considerable discretion in designing the school curriculum. Only boards of education, which typically represent the values of an electoral majority, traditionally have had authority to constrain that discretion. Beginning with the challenge to segregation in the schools, however, minority communities began to express growing dissatisfaction with pedagogical discretion restrained only by majority will. In keeping with these developments, the federal government during the late 1960s began to take a more active role in formulating bilingual education policy. Advocates of federal intervention initially focused on the need to include linguistic minorities fully in the educational system in the face of local prejudice. Upon discovering that state and local educators had failed to meet the needs of linguistic minority students, however, congressional policymakers recast the problem in terms of pedagogical effectiveness rather than civil rights. In light of the uncertainties associated with educating these students, federal policymakers stressed the importance of designing and implementing adequate instructional programs.

Eventually, the federal government endorsed programs that rely heavily on native-language instruction, such as transitional bilingual education (TBE and bilingual-bicultural programs.) TBE programs employ subject-matter instruction in a student's native language until the child is sufficiently proficient in English to participate in a regular classroom. Bilingual-bicultural education programs not only promote mastery of English but also foster native-language proficiency and preserve respect for a child's cultural heritage.

Critics have increasingly questioned these programs. Some have expressed doubts about their pedagogical effectiveness; others have argued that the programs fail to socialize children to speak English and acquire "American" values. Opponents of TBE and bilingual-bicultural education programs have urged greater federal support for alternative techniques that emphasize the use of English. One such approach is

From "The Politics of Discretion: Federal Intervention in Bilingual Education." 76 Calif. L. Rev. 1249 (1988). Originally published by the *California Law Review*. Reprinted by permission.

an English-as-a-Second-Language (ESL) program in which linguistic minority students spend most of the day in regular classes but receive intensive English instruction as well. Another is a structured immersion program in which teachers primarily use English for subject-matter instruction but structure the curriculum in a way that does not assume extensive familiarity with English.

This chapter will demonstrate that despite efforts to frame the bilingual education debate as a scientific argument about the appropriate content of the curriculum for linguistic minority students, the controversy actually reflects a battle over the allocation of discretion to make educational policy. The chapter first sets forth a framework for analyzing disputes over discretion and describes the parties challenging the discretionary authority of state and local educators. Then it shows how different justifications for federal intervention in bilingual education colored conclusions about the appropriate role of state and local discretion. Finally, it suggests ways in which federal policymakers can strike a better balance between state and local discretionary prerogatives and the requirements of effective bilingual education policy.

Traditionally, state and local officials have enjoyed broad discretion in designing and implementing the educational curriculum. Policymakers have justified vesting considerable discretion in state and local officials on the ground that these officials' experience uniquely equips them to formulate the school curriculum. Their experience includes not just a technical understanding of how children learn but also a sensitivity to local conditions. This sensitivity results from being familiar with the special characteristics of the student body and the surrounding community as well as with budgetary and political constraints.

Nevertheless, the perceived failure of state and local authorities to meet linguistic minority students' needs eventually led to federal intervention. Since the federal government first became engaged in bilingual education policymaking in 1968, four major groups have challenged state and local educators' discretionary prerogatives in developing curricula for non-English-proficient (NEP) and limited-English-proficient (LEP) students: (1) linguistic minority parents and community leaders; (2) educational experts; (3) federal officials, especially administrators and judges; and (4) English-only reformers seeking to promote socialization into the American way of life. Each of these groups has shaped federal bilingual education policy. Because each characterized the problems involved in bilingual education differently, each has offered distinctive justifications for federal intervention and accordingly favored different methods of constraining state and local discretion.

Linguistic Minority Parents and Community Leaders

Linguistic minority parents and community leaders have typically argued that the insensitivity, indifference, or hostility of state and local educators has prevented NEP and LEP children from benefiting fully from the school curriculum. These parents and their representatives contend that the failure of state and local officials to educate linguistic minority students, as evidenced by low achievement and high drop-out rates, warrants federal intervention to divest these educators of some de-cisionmaking prerogatives. While linguistic minority parents and community lead-ers have agreed that past discrimination necessitates federal incursions on state and local discretion, they differ over how federal policy can best redress their griev-ances. Some seek greater participation by linguistic minority parents and commu-nity leaders in decisions that affect the education of NEP and LEP students. By ex-panding parental and community input into the decisionmaking process, they hope to limit the ability of school officials to impose curricular choices that are unre-sponsive to linguistic minority students' needs. Supporters of this view argue that direct participation by parents and community representatives not only would im-prove the instructional process but also would empower a previously excluded community. This empowerment could confer self-esteem, respect, and dignity on linguistic minority groups.

Other parents and community leaders prefer to delegate responsibility for polic-ing school districts to the federal government. Perhaps recognizing that linguistic mi-nority communities command limited resources, these parents and leaders are less in-terested in a direct role in educational decisionmaking. Instead, they demand that federal agencies and courts devote sufficient resources to ensure that school districts meet NEP and LEP students' needs. They advocate limiting state and local discretion through federal regulations that restrict the instructional options available to school districts. They also seek strict standards for federal review of state and local deci-sionmaking. These parents and leaders have been less concerned with the long-term, indirect benefits of empowerment than with the immediate, direct benefits of strong federal enforcement.

Educational Experts

Educational experts have justified federal intervention in state and local decision-making on grounds of competence. These experts have questioned local officials' ability to make sound curricular decisions regarding NEP and LEP students because school personnel lack sufficient information about the ways in which these children learn. In their view, school districts are apt to be unable or unwilling to undertake the experimentation necessary to overcome pedagogical uncertainties. Moreover, school districts that conduct experiments often do so improperly, analyze the find-ings incorrectly, or fail to disseminate their results. Accordingly, educational experts believe that the federal government must intervene to promote experimentation, co-ordinate research, and share information.

Nevertheless, experts disagree over the proper scope of the federal role. Those who see the federal government as merely facilitating bilingual education research do not favor restricting state and local decisionmakers' prerogatives. Federal experi-mentation, they suggest, should supplement, not supplant, state and local decision-making by giving school districts more information about program effectiveness. Other educational experts support a more intrusive federal role. They advocate using federally sponsored studies as a means of forcing school districts to meet the needs of NEP and LEP students. Federal studies would form the basis for external review, permitting evaluators to scrutinize a district's decision after the fact. Federal policymakers could use these findings to assess not only a program's effectiveness but also the adequacy of state and local decisionmaking processes. Still others urge that once educational experts decide upon an appropriate means of meeting linguistic minority students' needs, the federal government should mandate adoption of such methods. According to this view, a school official's disregard of definitive expert findings is necessarily an abuse of discretion; under such circumstances, the federal government may dictate curricular choices without infringing on legitimate state and local discretion.

Federal Officials

In arguing that school districts should be divested of some of their discretion, some federal officials contend that national decisionmaking processes are superior to those of state and local governments. These officials note that state and local school administrators have systematically neglected NEP and LEP students' needs and claim that the federal government is likely to be more responsive to these concerns. In their view, federal decisionmakers are less susceptible than school districts to pressures exerted by local majorities, making them better able to protect linguistic minorities from biased treatment. Moreover, federal decisionmakers have greater access than state and local educators to top educational experts. Therefore, federal officials are better able to amass the technical information necessary to make sound educational policy for NEP and LEP students.

Those who understand the federal role as protecting linguistic minorities from discrimination have sought to expand the existing framework of civil rights protections to accommodate NEP and LEP students. This framework employs, in part, centralized control to restrict the options available to state and local decisionmakers. For example, federal law prohibits schools from employing discriminatory techniques that segregate racial and ethnic minorities. Some federal decisionmakers have sought to extend this enforcement regime's protection to linguistic minority students. These officials have urged that federal agencies and courts apply the same demanding scrutiny to decisions disadvantaging linguistic minorities as they do to those adversely affecting racial and ethnic minorities.[1]

Others who concentrate on amassing pedagogical expertise recommend expanding the national educational bureaucracy, rather than federal civil rights agencies. The federal educational bureaucracy focuses on enhancing the resources available to state and local officials, with whom it has cultivated cooperative, ongoing relationships. Proponents of this approach hope to increase federal funding of programs for NEP and LEP students, coordinate school districts' efforts to provide programs, promote research and experimentation, and disseminate information about effective instructional techniques. The federal educational bureaucracy thus can assume a leadership role without seriously jeopardizing the prerogatives of state and local officials or straining long-term working relationships.

English-Only Reformers

English-only reformers demand reallocation of discretion because they believe that schools have not properly inculcated English language skills and "American" values in linguistic minority schoolchildren. These reformers fear that the federal government has capitulated to advocates of linguistic and cultural pluralism. In their view, federal endorsement of TBE and bilingual-bicultural education programs threatens the preeminence of the English language and the American way of life. Some even contend that federal support of these programs jeopardizes national unity by encouraging the "balkanization" of language groups and fomenting separatism.

English-only reformers have thus supported federal laws that encourage programs with a heavy emphasis on English acquisition, such as ESL and structured immersion. English-only reformers do not wish merely to widen the range of instructional techniques available to local educators, thereby resurrecting state and local discretion. They too favor limiting the options available to state and local officials. Indeed, they want to amend the Constitution to establish English as the official language of the United States. The proposed amendment is designed not only to prohibit federal support of linguistic and cultural pluralism but also to constrain school districts' use of programs that detract from the status of English. After failing to win support for the amendment at the federal level, English-only reformers have turned to state legislation, municipal ordinances, and popular referenda to restrict pedagogical discretion. Thus, rather than protecting state and local discretion, their attempts to limit schools' choices in socializing students represent a significant incursion on state and local educators' decisionmaking prerogatives.

Models for Allocating Discretion and the Politics of Bilingual Education

The battle over the allocation of discretion to structure the curriculum for linguistic minority students has reflected three distinctive approaches: (1) constraining the discretion of state and local educators in order to remedy past abuses; (2) enabling state and local educators to exercise their discretion more satisfactorily; and (3) limiting the discretion of bilingual educators who promote bilingualism and biculturalism. Linguistic minority parents and community leaders, federal officials in the civil rights bureaucracy, and educational experts convinced of the superiority of TBE and bilingual-bicultural education programs have favored the first approach. State and local educators, federal officials in the traditional educational bureaucracy, and educational experts concerned about conflicting evidence of pedagogical effectiveness have supported the second view. English-only reformers fearful of threats to a sense of national identity have adopted the third method to ensure assimilation and prevent the balkanization of language groups.

Let us now examine the assumptions underlying these three approaches and assess how they have shaped proposals for federal intervention. The analysis will focus on perceptions of uncertainty in educational decisionmaking about NEP and LEP students, characterizations of state and local failures as either isolated instances of official misconduct or systemic deficiencies, and choices between retrospective relief and prospective reform.

For state and local educators to exercise their discretion properly, they must be both willing and able to make sound decisions. Those who believe that constraints on state and local discretion are necessary to remedy abuses have assumed that these officials are unwilling to engage in judicious decisionmaking to meet NEP and LEP students' needs. Linguistic minority parents and community leaders, federal civil rights officials, and experts advocating native-language instruction—all have questioned the good faith and sensitivity of state and local educators. These groups have assumed that abuses of discretion are readily identifiable, that instances of misconduct arise through official malfeasance in an otherwise adequate school system, and that such wrongs can be ameliorated after the fact by limiting discretion. Under this view, discretion must be curbed to achieve corrective justice; that is, the wrongdoer must be punished and the victim's harm rectified through the constraints imposed.

Title VI and the EEOA have served as the primary vehicles for advancing the corrective justice rationale. Both Title VI and the EEOA are civil rights statutes designed to punish state and local educational agencies that discriminate against minority students on the basis of race or ethnicity by cutting off federal funds or subjecting the offending school districts to pervasive regulation and extensive monitoring. The harshness of the potential sanctions reflects the moral egregiousness of the wrong. School officials are not being punished for a mere lapse of judgment; they are guilty of a serious abuse of discretion.

The corrective justice rationale underlying Title VI and the EEOA creates several difficulties in formulating appropriate bilingual education policy. First, the corrective justice perspective presumes sufficient certainty about effective teaching techniques for NEP and LEP students to label some curricular choices as an abuse of discretion. Yet, because of ambiguity regarding the purposes of bilingual education and conflicting evidence on program effectiveness, it is often difficult to classify decisions as improper.

Second, the corrective justice approach emphasizes that bias or insensitivity has tainted school policy and practices in ways that have impaired the education of linguistic minority students. Proponents of the corrective justice rationale contend that because discrimination against minority students is pervasive, federal intervention is justified. This implies, however, that state and local discretion would be appropriate in a school system free of invidious prejudice. Thus, the proponents fail to consider whether even unbiased state and local decisionmaking processes exhibit systemic deficiencies that disadvantage NEP and LEP students.

Third, a corrective justice model narrowly focuses on retrospective reforms. This approach does not explicitly acknowledge the need for prospective policies to improve decisionmaking; rather, constraints are imposed only after past discrimination has been demonstrated and are intended to rectify some instance of official wrongdoing. Each of these shortcomings has created problems in applying the corrective justice perspective to bilingual education policymaking.

Those who seek to constrain state and local discretion have assumed that school officials are unwilling to address fully NEP and LEP students' problems. By contrast, those who want to facilitate the exercise of state and local discretion have assumed that these officials are willing but unable to meet linguistic minority children's needs. Receptive to state and local educators' concerns about pedagogical uncertainties, some experts and federal officials in the educational bureaucracy have contended that school districts cannot work scholastic miracles with inadequate information, funding, and personnel. Under their view, devising a curriculum for NEP and LEP students requires school officials to weigh competing purposes and conflicting evidence about program effectiveness; state and local educators must inevitably exercise considerable discretion in fashioning a program. Precisely because the task is complex, decisionmakers need ample resources; yet, school districts often lack the data, financial support, and staff necessary to exercise discretion effectively. The federal government can provide resources to alleviate these impediments. The object of federal intervention under this revitalization rationale is not to do corrective justice, but to facilitate wise state and local policymaking.

Although some civil rights advocates have tried to cast the Bilingual Education Act as a corrective measure intended to constrain state and local discretion, many of the Act's features reflect the revitalization perspective. The Act originally provided grants-in-aid to school districts for research and experimentation in the field of bilingual education.[2] Later, the Act funded teacher training, technical assistance, and resource centers.[3] Grants under the Act have been designed to develop state and local capacity to deliver sound educational services to NEP and LEP students. Federal grants have therefore been treated as short-term investments, rather than as long-term commitments.[4]

This goal of state and local revitalization stands in marked contrast to the corrective justice perspective. The corrective justice model presumes sufficient certainty to identify an abuse of discretion, but the revitalization approach asserts that there is so little certainty about the impact of bilingual education programs that it is counterproductive to promulgate hard-and-fast rules to limit state and local discretion. Moreover, while a corrective justice model treats instances of discrimination as particularized wrongdoing, a revitalization orientation treats resource limitations as a systemic problem for state and local officials. Finally, the corrective justice perspective adopts a retrospective orientation designed to remedy past wrongs; in contrast, the revitalization approach seeks prospective improvement of state and local decisionmaking processes. Nevertheless, the assumptions underlying the revitalization perspective also pose problems that distort the formulation of bilingual education law. Because the revitalization perspective does not attempt to resolve uncertainties about the pedagogical benefits of various programs, policymakers have no way to evaluate independently the soundness of local program choices. In addition, this approach never tackles the underlying, systemic reasons for state and local educational agencies' tendency to underfund programs for NEP and LEP students.

English-only reformers have sought to constrain the discretion of bilingual educators as well as that of federal officials who support TBE and bilingual-bicultural education programs. In their view, these educators and officials have embraced a vision of bilingualism and biculturalism that undermines the stature of English as the national language. These reformers believe that there is sufficient agreement about the propriety of keeping English preeminent in the schools to conclude that implementation of programs that rely heavily on native-language instruction is an abuse of discretion. English-only reformers have alleged that such abuses are widespread enough to threaten national unity and foment separatist tendencies. As a consequence, the English-only movement has advocated prospective, system-wide changes in the curriculum that would reestablish the singular importance of English and the American way of life.

English-only reformers have proposed an English language amendment to the Constitution to accomplish their goals. The amendment would declare English the official language and prohibit governmental action inconsistent with its status. State and local educators would thus be obligated to respect the importance of English in devising programs for NEP and LEP students. Like proponents of a corrective justice paradigm, English-only reformers believe that abuses of discretion are identifiable. Like advocates of a revitalization perspective, they have concluded that the problems of educating NEP and LEP students are generalized and require prospective reform. Like both the corrective justice and revitalization models, the assumptions underlying the English-only approach have produced shortcomings in fashioning federal policy initiatives. Support for English-acquisition as a program goal does not provide a clearcut way to choose among a range of programs, all of which are designed to help children learn English. In light of ongoing pedagogical uncertainty, there seems to be little basis for allegations of bad faith and abuse of discretion in using native-language instruction.

In sum, then, each of the models used to justify federal intervention in bilingual education has made different assumptions about the nature of state and local decisionmaking regarding NEP and LEP students. These contrasting assumptions have yielded distinct policy recommendations. Unfortunately, however, all three models suffer from serious flaws in converting a theory of state and local failure into a concrete agenda for federal reform. To fashion effective bilingual education policy, federal officials must understand the reasons for these persistent shortcomings.

Coming to Grips with Discretion: The Future of Federal Bilingual Education Policy

Advocates of the corrective justice paradigm, the revitalization perspective, and the English-only approach have to surmount the federal government's traditional reluctance to intervene in state and local educational decisionmaking. Federal policymakers generally presume that state and local educators are uniquely able to respond to students' needs in a flexible, innovative way. To overcome this presumption in favor of state and local competency, the corrective justice paradigm, the revitalization perspective, and the English-only approach all have provided competing explanations for the failure to meet NEP and LEP students' needs. Each model has tailored federal intervention to address these presumed sources of failure while otherwise leaving state and local discretion intact. To win federal support, each model has evoked a monolithic, compelling image of deficient educational decisionmaking; consequently, these models have ignored the diversity of problems that school districts confront and the richness of their organizational structures. This oversight has undermined the prospects for successful implementation of federal reforms designed to constrain state and local discretion.

Deference to state and local discretion is a significant feature of all of the federal government's bilingual education policy initiatives. The corrective justice paradigm defers to state and local autonomy by confining federal intervention to instances in which officials have abused their discretion. Where an abuse of discretion has been stringently defined by requiring proof of discriminatory intent, the corrective justice rationale imposes a high threshold for federal intervention. To the extent, however, that the definition of an abuse of discretion allows plaintiffs to rely on a showing of adverse effects, this check on federal intervention is weakened.

The revitalization perspective constrains the federal role by characterizing it as passively supportive, rather than aggressively reformist. However, attaching conditions to the provision of federal aid can substantially undermine this restriction on potential federal overreaching. Not surprisingly, the more elaborate the conditions, the more vehemently state and local decisionmakers have attacked the provisions as an assault on their autonomy.

At present, the English-only perspective has raised the fewest concerns about excessive federal involvement. Most importantly, the proposed English language amendment has enjoyed little success at the federal level. Instead, similar reforms have been promulgated in states and municipalities through majoritarian political measures, such as legislative resolutions, initiatives, and referenda. At present, there is little reason to believe that an English language amendment will be adopted at the federal level. If the federal government eventually were to embrace such a proposal, its endorsement could be explained as nothing more than an acknowledgement of burgeoning state and local support. Moreover, given the vague wording of English language amendments preferred to date, a similarly general federal provision would be unlikely to pose any significant threat to state and local discretion. However, if the English-only perspective did manage to generate all-inclusive, rigid constraints on schools' decisions regarding the inculcation of language and culture, it could pose a greater threat to state and local autonomy than either the corrective justice paradigm or the revitalization perspective.

Whatever the approach adopted, national policymakers worry about the trade-off between the preservation of state and local autonomy and effective federal intervention on behalf of NEP and LEP students. Although federal policymakers have questioned the soundness of state and local decisionmaking regarding linguistic minority students, two important considerations have prompted them to be cautious about abrogating state and local discretion. First, state and local educators' sympathy for linguistic minority claims is typically secondary to a concern for their own decisionmaking prerogatives. They view their autonomy to structure curricula as important not only for NEP and LEP students but for all students. Moreover, these state and local educators are well-organized, command considerable resources, and have established ongoing relationships with federal officials. By contrast, linguistic minority communities tend to be politically disorganized with low rates of voter registration and turn-out; they are also socioeconomically disadvantaged with comparatively low levels of education and income. Consequently, the relative political pressures exerted by the two groups most directly affected by federal intervention generally work in favor of preserving state and local educators' prerogatives.

Second, federal decisionmakers are more certain about the measures needed to preserve state and local autonomy than they are about those necessary to promote linguistic minority students' educational achievement. Academics, lawyers, and government officials have long debated the merits of different approaches to federalism, and they consider themselves experts on how policy proposals will affect state and local autonomy. Decisionmakers have been less successful in assessing the characteristics of effective bilingual education policy; indeed, the energy devoted to this subject has produced a frustrating array of conflicting pedagogical opinions. Thus, federal decisionmakers may be tempted to accord greater weight to the traditionally valued preservation of state and local discretion than to the formulation of an educational agenda that at most promises highly speculative benefits.

To appreciate fully the trade-off between protecting state and local discretion and advancing the interests of linguistic minority students, federal decisionmakers must understand the nature of particular policy problems and the extent of federal intervention required. In justifying federal intervention, however, the corrective justice paradigm, the revitalization perspective, and the English-only approach have constructed unique (and often conflicting) images of school districts that fail to meet NEP and LEP students' needs. Although these monolithic images may be necessary to win federal support, they simultaneously hinder a proper analysis of implementation problems. To better address implementation concerns, federal policymakers must consider the variability of tasks that school districts face and the resulting richness of their bureaucratic structures. In this way, federal reformers can tailor both the degree and method of restricting local discretion to the particular characteristics of the problem addressed.

As noted earlier, federal policymakers have frequently affirmed the value of linguistic minority parents' participation in state and local educational decisionmaking. To promote parental participation, Congress has established parental advisory councils and parental notice requirements under the Bilingual Education Act. These reforms often have yielded little more than formalistic parental participation. The approach set forth here suggests the need for flexibility in the implementation of parental participation programs, rather than a uniform program for all districts.

Attempts to increase parental participation in the educational decisionmaking process are complicated by the diverse situations that school districts face. Teachers and administrators have different attitudes toward parental engagement, and school decisionmaking processes operate in distinctive ways. Under these circumstances, the federal government should not promulgate rigid requirements regarding parental participation but should experiment with different procedural reforms tailored to the characteristics of different school districts. The federal government should facilitate state and local efforts to enhance parental participation by providing supplementary resources and disseminating information about successful programs. Where state and local educational agencies generally have established policies conducive to parental participation, the federal government can provide incentives to principals and teachers to include linguistic minority parents fully in the decisionmaking process. Federal agencies can also provide teachers and school administrators with training to improve the solicitation of parental input. Finally, federal resources can assist state and local policy elites to construct effective systems for monitoring and evaluating parental participation programs.

In selecting reform initiatives, federal officials should consider how intrusive they will appear to state and local decisionmakers. If federal reforms greatly enhance parents' ability to participate but fail to allay school officials' doubts about parental engagement, state and local educators will object that these reforms undermine the exercise of their professional judgment. To avoid such resistance, federal policymakers should build an official consensus about the value of parental participation while cultivating parents' capacity to get involved.

In sum, then, even if a national consensus about the value of parental participation exists, there is no simple answer to how the federal government should promote such participation. Federal policymakers must undertake a closer analysis of the characteristics of school districts and the linguistic minority populations they serve to determine what types of measures are most likely to succeed.

This chapter has discussed how the corrective justice paradigm, the revitalization perspective, and the English-only approach have influenced ongoing debates over the allocation of discretion in bilingual education. Based on deficiencies in each of these approaches, I suggested an alternative framework that carefully examines the nature of the task, the organizational structure of schools, and the necessary comprehensiveness of reforms. Applying this framework will demand a significant investment of time, money, and thought. Its effective utilization will also depend on flexibility and candor in dealing with linguistic minority students' problems.

The chances that such an approach will emerge in the federal policy arena are hampered by the polarization of the bilingual education debate. Participants hoping to influence federal policy have often been intent on finding villains to explain the plight of NEP and LEP children. Proponents of a corrective justice perspective have cited the insensitivity and hostility of school administrators and teachers; English-only reformers have impugned the motives of those who advocate TBE and bilingual-bicultural education programs. Unfortunately, pointing fingers does not help solve NEP and LEP students' problems.

Amid the charges and countercharges, it may be difficult to assert that problems can exist without villains, and that even when villains are ferreted out, solutions will not necessarily be forthcoming. The more polarized the decisionmaking process, the less likely that those involved will be sufficiently flexible and forthright to engage in effective policy formulation. Hopefully, for the sake of linguistic minority children, partisans will set aside some of their differences to engage in a more fruitful dialogue that produces responsive bilingual education policy.

NOTES

1. See Jeremy A. Rabkin, *Office for Civil Rights,* in The Politics of Regulation 331–32, 338–40 (J. Wilson ed., 1980).

2. Susan G. Schneider, Revolution, Reaction or Reform: The 1974 Bilingual Education Act (1976); Bilingual Education Act of 1968, § 702, 81 Stat. at 816. The Senate Committee Report indicated that the Act did not mandate any specific type of program because of the need for extensive research. S. Rep. No. 726, 90th Cong., 1st Sess. 50, reprinted in 1967 U.S. Code Cong. & Admin. News 2730, 2781.

3. 20 U.S.C. § 3223(a)(6) (Supp. IV 1986), amended by Bilingual Education Act of 1988, Pub. L. No. 100-297, 102 Stat. 274 (1988).

4. *Id.* § 3242(e) (Supp. IV 1986).

From the Editors
Issues and Comments

Is the English language the tie (or a tie) that holds the United States together? Or, on the contrary, are English-only laws insulting and racist? Suppose that in 150 years, Latinos are a majority of the U.S. population; could they then impose a Spanish-only regime in order to unify the nation?

Does bilingual instruction slow the ability of immigrant schoolchildren to acquire the English they will need to survive and flourish in the United States? Who should decide the answer to this question?

What is wrong with a bilingual juror's hearing testimony in a foreign language and giving it as much weight as the official translation by a court interpreter?

Should government make special efforts to employ emergency personnel—police, firefighters, paramedics—who speak foreign languages? Is this a form of affirmative action?

Can a non-Anglo culture survive in an English-only environment, or is culture inextricably tied with language, so that loss of the language eventually causes the culture to wither?

If Puerto Rico joins the United States as the fifty-first state, will its official language (now Spanish) have to change, or will the United States have to tolerate a Spanish-speaking state?

Suggested Readings

Alvarez, Julia. *How the García Girls Lost Their Accents*. Chapel Hill, N.C.: Algonquin Books, 1991.

Baron, Denis. *The English-Only Question: An Official Language for Americans?* New Haven: Yale University Press, 1990.

Bender, Steven W. "Consumer Protection for Latinos: Overcoming Language Fraud and English-Only in the Marketplace." 45 *American University Law Review* 1027 (1996).

Berk-Seligson, Susan. "The Importance of Linguistics in Court Interpreting." 2 *La Raza Law Journal* 14 (1988).

Califa, Antonio J. "Declaring English the Official Language: Prejudice Spoken Here." 24 *Harvard Civil Rights–Civil Liberties Law Review* 293 (1989).

Crawford, James. *Bilingual Education: History, Politics, Theory and Practice*. 2d ed. Los Angeles: Bilingual Educational Services, 1991.

Hayakawa, S. I. *One Nation . . . Indivisible? The English Language Amendment*. Washington, D.C.: Washington Institute for Values in Public Policy, 1985.

Jacobson, Rodolfo. "The Social Implications of Intra-Sentenial Code-Switching." In *New Directions in Chicano Scholarship,* edited by Richard Romo and Raymond Paredes, 227. La Jolla: Chicano Studies Program, University of California, San Diego, 1978.

Kloss, Heinz. *The American Bilingual Tradition*. Rowley, Mass.: Newbury House, 1977.

Language Loyalties: A Source Book on the Official English Controversy, edited by James Crawford. Chicago: University of Chicago Press, 1992.

Matsuda, Mari J. "Voices of America: Accent, Antidiscrimination Law, and a Jurisprudence for the Last Reconstruction." 100 *Yale Law Journal* 1329 (1991).

Mirande, Alfredo "'*En la Tierra del Ciego, el Tuerto Es Rey*' ('In the Land of the Blind, the One-Eyed Person Is King'): Bilingualism as a Disability." 26 *New Mexico Law Review* 75 (1996).

———. "'Now That I Speak English, *No Me Dejan Hablar*' ('I'm Not Allowed to Speak'): The Implications of *Hernandez v. New York*." 18 *Chicano-Latino Law Review* 115 (1996).

Moran, Rachel F. "Bilingual Education as a Status Conflict." 75 *California Law Review* 321 (1987).

———. "Of Democracy, Devaluation, and Bilingual Education." 26 *Creighton Law Review* 255 (1993).

Perea, Juan F. "English-Only Rules and the Right to Speak One's Primary Language in the Workplace." 23 *University of Michigan Journal of Law Reform* 265 (1990).

———. "Ethnicity and Prejudice: Reevaluating 'National Origin' Discrimination Under Title VII." 35 *William and Mary Law Review* 805 (1994).

———. "Ethnicity and the Constitution: Beyond the Black White Binary Constitution." 36 *William and Mary Law Review* 571 (1995).

———. "*Hernandez v. New York:* Courts, Prosecutors, and the Fear of Spanish." 21 *Hofstra Law Review* 1 (1992).

Piatt, Bill. *Language on the Job: Balancing Business Needs and Employee Rights.* Albuquerque: University of New Mexico Press, 1993.

———. *¿Only English? Law and Language Policy in the United States.* Albuquerque: University of New Mexico Press, 1990.

———. "Toward Domestic Recognition of a Human Right to Language." 23 *Houston Law Review* 885 (1986).

Porter, Rosalie Pedalino. *Forked Tongue: The Politics of Bilingual Education.* New York: Basic Books, 1990.

Ramirez, Deborah A. "Excluded Voices: The Disenfranchisemnt of Ethnic Groups from Jury Service." 1993 *Wisconsin Law Review* 761.

Valdez, Guadalupe. "The Language Situation of Mexican Americans." In *Language Diversity, Problem or Resource? A Social and Educational Perspective on Language Minorities in the United States,* edited by Sandra L. McKay and Sau-Ling C. Wong, 111. Cambridge, Mass.: Newbury House, 1988.

Walsh, Catherine E. *Pedagogy and the Struggle for Voice: Issues of Language, Power, and Schooling for Puerto Ricans.* South Hadley, Mass.: Bergin & Garvey, 1991.

Part XII

The Border as Metaphor

What Border Theory Tells Us about Culture

Borders are important to many Latinos in a physical, literal sense, since as an immigrant group they must sometimes cross them to obtain work, reunite with their families, or for other purposes. Border regions, such as those along the Texas-Mexico border, show the influence of both cultures, with Spanish and English existing side by side and shops, restaurants, and other businesses catering to both sets of tastes. Recently, a group of scholars in literature, history, and law have been pointing out that the border is also a powerful metaphor. Focusing on the intersection of words, meanings, concepts, and cultures shows how we may benefit from inhabiting two or more spheres at once. In Part XII, distinguished Latino writers and social scientists address issues of mixture, overlap, and the braiding of narratives and cultures.

Chapter 89

Borderlands

Gloria Anzaldúa

The actual physical borderland that I'm dealing with is the Texas–U.S. Southwest/Mexican border. The psychological borderlands, the sexual borderlands, and the spiritual borderlands are not particular to the Southwest. In fact, the Borderlands are physically present wherever two or more cultures edge each other, where people of different races occupy the same territory, where under, lower, middle and upper classes touch, where the space between two individuals shrinks with intimacy.

I am a border woman. I grew up between two cultures, the Mexican (with a heavy Indian influence) and the Anglo (as a member of a colonized people in our own territory). I have been straddling that *Tejas*-Mexican border, and others, all my life. It's not a comfortable territory to live in, this place of contradictions. Hatred, anger, and exploitation are the prominent features of this landscape.

However, there have been compensations for this *mestiza,* and certain joys. Living on borders and in margins, keeping intact one's shifting and multiple identity and integrity, is like trying to swim in a new element, an "alien" element. There is an exhilaration in being a participant in the further evolution of humankind, in being "worked" on. I have the sense that certain "faculties"— not just in me but in every border resident, colored or noncolored—and dormant areas of consciousness are being activated, awakened. Strange, huh? And yes, the "alien" element has become familiar—never comfortable, not with society's clamor to uphold the old, to rejoin the flock, to go with the herd. No, not comfortable but home.

This book, then, speaks of my existence. My preoccupations with the inner life of the Self, and with the struggle of that Self amidst adversity and violation; with the confluence of primordial images; with the unique positionings consciousness takes at these confluent streams; and with my almost instinctive urge to communicate, to speak, to write about life on the borders, life in the shadows. . . .

El otro México/The Homeland, Aztlán

This is my home
this thin edge of
barbwire.
But the skin of the earth is seamless.
The sea cannot be fenced,
el mar does not stop at borders.
To show the white man what she thought of his
arrogance,
Yemaya blew that wire fence down.

This land was Mexican once,
was Indian always
and is.
And will be again.

Yo soy un puente tendido
del mundo gabacho al del mojado,
lo pasado me estirá pa' 'trás
y lo presente pa' 'delante.
Que la Virgen de Guadalupe me cuide
Ay ay ay, soy mexicana de este lado.

The U.S.-Mexican border *es una herida abierta* [an open wound—*Eds.*] where the Third World grates against the first and bleeds. And before a scab forms it hemorrhages again, the lifeblood of two worlds merging to form a third country—a border culture. Borders are set up to define the places that are safe and unsafe, to distinguish *us* from *them*. A border is a dividing line, a narrow strip along a steep edge. A borderland is a vague and undetermined place created by the emotional residue of an unnatural boundary. It is in a constant state of transition. The prohibited and forbidden are its inhabitants. *Los atravesados* live here: the squint-eyed, the perverse, the queer, the troublesome, the mongrel, the mulato, the half-breed, the half dead; in short, those who cross over, pass over, or go through the confines of the "normal." Gringos in the U.S. Southwest consider the inhabitants of the borderlands transgressors, aliens—whether they possess documents or not, whether they're Chicanos, Indians, or Blacks. Do not enter, trespassers will be raped, maimed, strangled, gassed, shot. The only "legitimate" inhabitants are those in power, the whites and those who align themselves with whites. Tension grips the inhabitants of the borderlands like a virus. Ambivalence and unrest reside there and death is no stranger.

In the fields, la migra. *My aunt saying,* "No corran, *don't run. They'll think you're* del otro lao." *In the confusion, Pedro ran, terrified of being caught. He couldn't speak English, couldn't tell them he was fifth generation American.* Sin papeles—*he did not carry his birth certificate to work in the fields.* La migra *took him away while we watched.* Se lo llevaron. *He tried to smile when he looked back at us, to raise his fist. But I saw the shame pushing his head down, I saw the terrible weight of shame hunch his shoulders. They deported him to Guadalajara by plane. The furthest he'd ever been to Mexico was Reynosa, a small border town opposite Hidalgo, Texas, not far from McAllen. Pedro walked all the way to the Valley.* Se lo llevaron sin un centavo al pobre. Se vino andando desde Guadalajara.

During the original peopling of the Americas, the first inhabitants migrated across the Bering Straits and walked south across the continent. The oldest evidence of humankind in the U.S.—the Chicanos' ancient Indian ancestors—was found in Texas and has been dated to 35,000 B.C.[1] In the Southwest United States archeologists have found 20,000-year-old campsites of the Indians who migrated through, or permanently occupied, the Southwest, Aztlán—land of the herons, land of whiteness, the Edenic place of origin of the Azteca. . . .

La Conciencia de la Mestiza/Towards a New Consciousness

Numerous possibilities leave *la mestiza* floundering in uncharted seas. In perceiving conflicting information and points of view, she is subjected to a swamping of her psychological borders. She has discovered that she can't hold concepts or ideas in rigid boundaries. The borders and walls that are supposed to keep the undesirable ideas out are entrenched habits and patterns of behavior; these habits and patterns are the enemy within. Rigidity means death. Only by remaining flexible is she able to stretch the psyche horizontally and vertically. *La mestiza* constantly has to shift out of habitual formations; from convergent thinking, analytical reasoning that tends to use rationality to move toward a single goal (a Western mode), to divergent thinking,[2] characterized by movement away from set patterns and goals and toward a more whole perspective, one that includes rather than excludes.

The new *mestiza* copes by developing a tolerance for contradictions, a tolerance for ambiguity. She learns to be an Indian in Mexican culture, to be Mexican from an Anglo point of view. She learns to juggle cultures. She has a plural personality, she operates in a pluralistic mode—nothing is thrust out, the good the bad and the ugly, nothing rejected, nothing abandoned. Not only does she sustain contradictions, she turns the ambivalence into something else.

She can be jarred out of ambivalence by an intense, and often painful, emotional event which inverts or resolves the ambivalence. I'm not sure exactly how. The work takes place underground—subconsciously. It is work that the soul performs. That focal point or fulcrum, that juncture where the *mestiza* stands, is where phenomena tend to collide. It is where the possibility of uniting all that is separate occurs. This assembly is not one where severed or separated pieces merely come together. Nor is it a balancing of opposing powers. In attempting to work out a synthesis, the self has added a third element which is greater than the sum of its severed parts. That third element is a new consciousness—a *mestiza* consciousness—and though it is a source of intense pain, its energy comes from continual creative motion that keeps breaking down the unitary aspect of each new paradigm.

En unas pocas centurias, the future will belong to the *mestiza.* Because the future depends on the breaking down of paradigms, it depends on the straddling of two or more cultures. By creating a new mythos—that is, a change in the way we perceive reality, the way we see ourselves, and the ways we behave—*la mestiza* creates a new consciousness.

The work of *mestiza* consciousness is to break down the subject-object duality that keeps her a prisoner and to show in the flesh and through the images in her work how duality is transcended. The answer to the problem between the white race and the colored, between males and females, lies in healing the split that originates in the very foundation of our lives, our culture, our languages, our thoughts. A massive uprooting of dualistic thinking in the individual and collective consciousness is the beginning of a long struggle, but one that could, in our best hopes, bring us to the end of rape, of violence, of war.

NOTES

1. John R. Chavez, The Lost Land: The Chicano Images of the Southwest (Albuquerque: University of New Mexico Press, 1984), 9.

2. Robert Plant Armstrong, The Powers of Presence: Consciousness, Myth, and Affecting Presence (Philadelphia: University of Pennsylvania Press, 1981), 4.

Chapter 90

Surveying Law and Borders

Renato Rosaldo

Let me begin with poetry from Gloria Anzaldúa's 1987 book called *Borderlands/La Frontera: The New Mestiza*. Her poetry does two rather remarkable things. She describes the border, the literal U.S/Mexico border as well as her metaphorical borders, as a

> 1,950 mile-long open wound
> dividing a pueblo, a culture,
> running down the length of my body,
> staking fence rods in my flesh,
> splits me splits me
> *me raja me raja*
> This is my home
> this thin edge of
> barbwire.[1]

She calls the border "una herida abierta," an open wound, yet she gets accused of seeing borders as playthings or sights of creativity or an aesthetic site in the mind. But *una herida abierta* conveys the sense, I think, of borders as sites of violence, at one and the same time symbolic and material.

The other remarkable aspect of her poetry is that she describes her own self and the site of the border as zones of crossing, indeed as crossroads:

> To live in the Borderlands means
> the mill with the razor white teeth wants to shred off
> your olive-red skin, crush out the kernel, your heart
> pound you pinch you roll you out
> smelling like white bread but dead;
> To survive the Borderlands
> you must live *sin fronteras*
> be a crossroads.[2]

From "Surveying Law and Borders." 48 Stan. L. Rev. 1037 (1996). Originally published in the *Stanford Law Review*. Copyright © 1996 by the Board of Trustees of the Leland Stanford Junior University. Reprinted by permission.

When she conceives herself, she becomes an intersection of different kinds: social identities that include but are more complicated than the standard list of class, race, gender, sexuality. Such differently inscribed identities emerge from personal history in idiosyncratic ways. Anzaldúa offers us a methodology for creating subjectivities capable of a politics of difference and coalition. Hers is a fresh vision of a more inclusive social whole.

The open wound, *la herida abierta,* is but one side of the coin whose other side is personal and collective survival as a border crossroads. In other words, Anzaldúa argues that multiple identities intersect in the individual, rather than there being a singular, coherent individual identity. She enumerates certain standard identities: Chicano, Anglo, Indian. She sees all these identities as strongly present in her, alongside lesbian and woman. The stereotype of identity politics as a separatist monolithic group that isolates itself from other groups could not be further from what she proposes. Instead, she offers us a vision of a politics of difference and coalition, a politics where no person is trapped within a singular identity. Each person encompasses idiosyncratic, personal, historical, biographical identities that intersect in the person and create lines of alliance, lines of connection with other kinds of people. Contrary to the notions of identity politics as fundamentalism or ethnic absolutism propounded by thinkers both on the left and the right, Anzaldúa argues that the intersection of multiple identities in the individual breeds participation and connection, and that in this context each singular identity is self-dissolving, and not monolithic. Such identity politics do not create divisiveness but actually radiate lines with potential for connection and broader coalition.

This notion is not new. Consider, for example, Emile Durkheim's social division of labor as an enabling condition for the creation of social solidarity.[3] If the model of social union were based on solidarity, one could argue that in fact differences can create solidarity greater than the kind of consensus generated by similarities between persons. Durkheim, of course, speaks of the solidarity that emerges from the social division of labor. The person who grows wheat needs the person who sells bread, and the person who sells bread needs the person who grows wheat, and that sense of mutual need produces solidarity.

The differences created by boundaries also give rise to family solidarity. The abstract nuclear family, the favorite example of many politicians, represents perhaps the opposite notion of unity, a fundamental building block with unity based on sameness. The nuclear family is usually presented as a monolithic unit or a biological unit. But to the extent that family solidarity exists (an urgent question in itself), one could argue that the basis of that solidarity emerges from differences within the group, and not from a biological or sociological sameness. It is difficult, for example, to imagine a family made up of male age-mates. We might call such a unit a brotherhood, or the Marine Corps, but not a nuclear family.

How do people conceive social identities and their boundaries? Sometimes they are regarded as emergent from external circumstances, such as social movements. Stuart Hall and David Held pointed out in *Citizens and Citizenship* that social identities are based on dissident traditions that have long histories, such as women's suffrage and anti-slavery movements in the nineteenth century as predecessors for present-day feminism and civil rights movements.[4] These dissident traditions empower people because they have long been legitimate and effective. Does anyone, for example, think that many people would, in this day and age, seriously say, "Let's restore slavery," or "Let's take the vote away from women"? Neither sounds like a winning proposition. Thus a number of identities in political play today have emerged from social movements that make claims and seek resources from the state, from corporations, or from neighborhood organizations.

The view of borders that I would support opposes the notion of monolithic closed human groups that has been variously called fundamentalism, ethnic absolutism, or purity. I would argue against the history that Arthur Schlesinger proposes where he talks about "our" history versus "their" history—men's history versus women's history, white history versus people of color history.[5] What Schlesinger would take as his model of what it is to be an American, or good citizen of the United States, is that one arrives from Europe, casts aside the old culture as if it were so much excess baggage, and becomes a new man in the new world. His model is assimilation. Perhaps it could be called coercive conformity. Schlesinger supposes that union, or national unity, requires a sense of sameness and consensus that derives from shared language, culture, and territory. He and I disagree. Where he advocates the new man and sameness as the basics of unity, all the while imagining that race does not matter, I would propose leavening sameness with the recognition that solidarity can emerge through difference and coalition.

When someone speaks, as I have, about identities and politics, one often hears, "Well, it all boils down to subjectivity," or "this is all too subjective." At such a juncture one must remember the solidity of the ancient concepts such as hegemony, dominant ideologies, state formations, the things that Althusser spoke about as the ideological state apparatus and the repressive state apparatus.[6] Advanced capitalism and local corporate capital are also very powerful forces to keep in mind when considering issues in the borderlands. In thinking about borderlands one does not want to dissolve everything into subjectivities or personal identities.

Yet, I would caution against uncritical use of the concept of counterhegemony. Counterhegemony argues from the perspective of a dominant ideology and studies movements against hegemonic forces. My caution is that the analyst's main identification resides with the dominant and not the subordinate group and resistance movements too easily become merely reactive to whatever is dominant. The analyst in this mode too easily looks down from on high. What one should seek out is an analytical position that's mobile and capable of seeing what's happening on high, what dominant ideologies are, but at the same time is capable of moving to groups that are not on high, to subordinate groups. Otherwise subordinate groups become reactive, rather than having their own dissident traditions of thought. They often try to achieve certain goals that are quite different from being merely counterhegemonic. People of course do react to what's coming down on them, but it's reductive to see all their aspirations and political action as if they were all response and no challenge.

My stance is in part an anthropologist's predilection—to look at subordinate groups, to actually live among them and then try to get a sense of their perspectives and practices. If the analytical differences were less central, one could chalk it all up to a matter of disciplinary taste and nothing more. One place to find an example of this scholarship is Paul Gilroy's work. In his recent book, *The Black Atlantic,* Gilroy suggests that if one were to move beyond the canonical texts and study English history in a manner that encompasses blacks as well as whites, one's vision of the whole would be transformed.[7] Gilroy also considers the notion of Englishness put forward by thinkers on both the left and the right. What, he asks, if one were to consider that venerable institution, the English navy. Who made up the English navy? What was its ethnic and racial composition? Gilroy critiques Raymond Williams's subtle, rather anthropological notions of Englishness that involve a range of customs and mores that take a lifetime, if not several generations, to acquire.[8] Gilroy notices not who is included, but those excluded from being properly English and the resulting denial of participation in the nation and status as a full citizen.

Gilroy thus argues that the concepts of history, identity, and nation need to be broadened. The whole of national history can be reenvisioned by taking seriously subordinated and excluded groups in much the manner Anzaldúa does for the United States. These histories—black and white, Chicano, Indian, and Anglo—are so interconnected as to be often inseparable, much in the way that a pertinent context can change the text or yellow placed next to blue will change both colors. The sense of the whole will change as the borders between ethnic and national histories are crossed and in certain respects dissolved. When one moves beyond Schlesinger's notion of our history and their history and sees instead interconnected histories that interact and mutually shape one another, subordinated histories and dissident traditions become a pathway, not to separatism and fundamentalism, but to a renewed vision of national histories. The inclusion of excluded and marginalized histories offers a vision of the social whole.

Let me now turn from the figurative to the literal and physical border. Consideration of the literal U.S.-Mexico border also requires a discussion of social boundaries and social space. One should, I think, see physical borders and social boundaries in time and in space, and, I would add, as theater. For example, in January 1991, on the eve of the Gulf War, I happened to be on the U.S.-Mexico border. While in Tijuana for a conference, I went with the conference organizers to see the fence that divides the two nations. The border was what literary theorist Mary Louise Pratt would call a contact zone, a place where differences and inequalities come together.[9] As it turned out, I came to witness *teatro de la frontera,* border theater. What I saw there was not what I expected. I expected to see the Border Patrol, a fence with guards marching up and down. What I saw instead was groups of Mexicans buying tacos from stands next to holes in the fence. I saw no guard, no cops, nothing of the policing I expected. Instead, people were waiting for signs that were mysterious and invisible to me. The signs, however, were known to the people along the fence, or at least to their guides, and they conveyed a message: "Now's the time to run across the border." The Mexicans along the fence were sitting and waiting patiently until the sign announced something like, "Agribusiness in the Central Valley needs you today." Or "Strawberries are ripe and we need somebody to pick them."

Far from being sealed, the fence was policed by a Border Patrol more like a faucet than an iron curtain. The point was to regulate the flow. Nothing was being shut down, contrary to what the media claimed. I crossed the border the day that the Gulf War started. I was nervous, even afraid; willy-nilly I had become a bit player in the border theater and I anxiously wondered what the script, authored elsewhere, had in store for me. What, five years later, do we now see on the border? We now see that the border is policed. We see that there's escalating violence on the border. We see that the border faucet is being shut down. Questions we can ask about borders in general are: Are they open or closed? Who is policing them and with what degree of violence? One thinks of California's recession and the loss of its defense contracts. One thinks of cynical politicians who succeed in winning votes, never mind the *herida abierta,* the open wound, they leave as their enduring mark. The anthropologist sees a politics that plays on fear and a sense of threat. Fear and threat require cultural analysis. What, after all, is there to fear from unarmed people trying to cross the border in search of work? What fear can possibly justify today's border theater with the high-tech weapons, the declaration that this is a DMZ zone, and the building of walls? The theater has many actors, so that on the border in Nogales, Arizona the walls were extended, and Mexicans simply walked further to get around them.

Analytically, the job is to notice that the border theater is simultaneously symbolic and material, constructed and violent. That is, the ammunition is live and the high-tech surveillance is real. But one must also notice the reverse. Simply because it's material and simply because there's violence, doesn't mean that it's not also laced with meaning and symbolic dimensions. Border theater appeals to certain audiences for certain kinds of reasons. That's how it has been designed.

The art of interpreting the literal border today involves the simultaneous analysis of the theater and its symbolic dimensions as well as the actual violence. One should not reduce one to the other, not become so constructivist as not to notice that people are being killed, not look so closely at the violence as not to notice its symbolic dimensions. Holding seeming opposites together is easy to say, but hard to do in practice.

Finally, I'd like to say a few words about social position, social space, and social boundaries. Much of this could be called point of view. Let me quickly enumerate some examples to convey a sense of what point of view or social position, social boundaries, and social space might be. First, I remember going with a lawyer to interview people at Stanford's Webb Ranch. The lawyer immediately said, "What is going on here? What have they done about your electricity? Do you have the letter from the. . . ." And I said, "Holy cow." "Do you," the lawyer went on, "have the letter? Does it have the letterhead?" He kept going on like that. His opening questions were antithetical to anthropological sensibilities and practices. We just kind of go in and have our two methods: hanging out, method one; asking questions, method two. We wait and try to see what's going on for a long time before we ask questions. We try to figure out what people's lives are like and what their issues are. One thing to think about in this area is the social position of the analyst. If we don't notice what it's like to be in our own shoes, it's hard to determine what it's like to be in somebody else's shoes. The methodology of the interview can be remarkably different from person to person and from discipline to discipline. The lawyerly interview is quite different from the anthropological one.

Second, try shouting "Police" in a suburban neighborhood. People come and say, "Gee, can I help?" "What's going on?" Now try shouting "Police" in the barrio or the ghetto. People run for cover. One thus notices social context, social boundary, and social position.

Third, think of the way people sometimes look at urban space. They look at it from the point of view of the architect or the city planner. Suppose, now, that one goes to a park in San Jose. What the city planners would say about the park I'm not sure, but what one sees there are mainly Japanese Americans playing tennis, recent Mexican and Central American arrivals playing soccer, older arrivals from Mexico and Central America playing baseball, mainly Italians and Portuguese doing lawn bowling, and an ethnically very mixed group of mainly women with children in the sand pool. Further away one used to see the homeless out on the lawn. For all groups there's a daily cycle in the park, times when they are more and less present or absent. From the point of view of the urban planner one learns little about how the space is actually used as opposed to how it was designed to be used on the drawing board.

Fourth, in *City of Quartz*, Mike Davis's admirable book,[10] the author fails to distinguish his viewpoint from that of city planners, and from the views of people who use urban space. One of the most remarkable things about the book is that it suggests an analysis of urban space and social boundaries as motivated by an underanalyzed cultural politics. Fear and a sense of threat motivate the policing and the placing of locked walls around suburban neighborhoods; they invite the creation of rounded park benches designed to discourage "loitering" and social gatherings in public spaces. The vivid examples in Davis's work are myriad. The fear is thus architecturally concretized in gates, guards, security devices, and so on, but it's not explored at the level of what people have to say about it—their fantasies, dreams, and speech. The cultural shape of the fear is more often regarded as transparent common sense already familiar to all observant readers rather than being a problem, a set of questions begging for analysis.

When Davis talks about the panoptican mall, it becomes evident that he feels about the mall just about the way I do—uncomfortable and out of place in consumerland. He writes as the alienated intellectual in the mall. But talk to teenagers, any group of teenagers, and ask them about their favorite spaces: "Where do you feel most comfortable? Where do you feel most at home? What space do you like most?" "The mall," they usually say. It is at the top of the list. We've interviewed over the past six years on social space in San Jose; we've talked with Vietnamese, Native Americans, European Americans, Chicanos, and new immigrants, especially from Mexico and Central America. Across the board we have found that far from being panoptican-phobic intellectuals, the teenagers describe something like a Mexican *paseo* where the boys walk in one direction and the girls walk in the other. They are in a safe space where they greet their numerous friends as if they were queens and kings of the mall. They know everybody and they know that nobody's going to get hurt because the malls are guarded.

All of us, including Mike Davis, need to think about point of view. Whose viewpoint is represented by the phrase "panoptican mall"? There are a number of distinct malls. Think of the people who live to shop 'til they drop, the teenage queens and kings of the mall, and, yes, those who feel alienated from the panoptican mall. The perceptions and practices of the mall are, among other things, generationally strati-fied and they produce remarkably different mall experiences.

Fifth, consider a poem by a Chicana poet from nearby San Jose, Lorna Dee Cervantes: "Poem for the Young White Man Who Asked Me How I, an Intelligent, Well-Read Person, Could Believe in the War between Races." The Young White Man says:

> In my land there are no distinctions.
> The barbed wire politics of oppression
> have been torn down long ago. The only reminder
> of past battles, lost or won, is a slight
> rutting in the fertile fields
> In my land
> people write poems about love,
> full of nothing but contented childlike syllables.[11]

The Chicana poet replies:

> I believe in revolution
> because everywhere the crosses are burning,
> sharp-shooting goose-steppers round every corner,
> there are snipers in the schools . . .
> (I know you don't believe this.
> You think this is nothing but an exaggeration. But they
> are not shooting at you.)[12]

The key difference in perception derives from whether or not you happen to be one of those being shot at. In this case point of view means that the "same" world can be experienced as remarkably different depending on one's social position.

In considering social space and borders one must, I think, consider the viewpoints of differently positioned subjects. Let me end with another poem that gives a sense of point of view. The poem says, "To Dad and Quetzalcoatl." Quetzalcoatl is an Aztec divinity of peace and order in urban spaces. The poem was written to me as I was leaving to give a talk the eve of the unveiling of the statue of Quetzalcoatl in San Jose. The statue was vigorously opposed by evangelical Christians who were also anti-abortion activists. I was apprehensive about what could happen when I spoke there, so my daughter Olivia wrote me a poem and handed it to me as I walked out the door. "Remember," her poem says:

> Remember,
> who, how. Remember who you are.
> How did I get here?
> Remember your descendants.
> Remember your language.
> Remember who you are.
> even when there's prejudice of who you are.
> and what you are
> Remember.

NOTES

1. Gloria Anzaldúa, *El otro Mexico*, in Borderlands/*La Frontera:* The New Mestiza 1, 2–3 (1987).

2. Gloria Anzaldúa, *To Live in the Borderlands Means You,* in Borderlands/*La Frontera,* at 194, 195.

3. See Emile Durkheim, The Division of Labor in Society (George Simpson trans., 1933).

4. See Stuart Hall & David Held, *Citizens and Citizenship,* in New Times: The Changing Face of Politics in the 1990s 173, 187 (Stuart Hall & Martin Jacques eds., 1989).

5. See Arthur M. Schlesinger, Jr., The Disuniting of America (1992).

6. See Louis Althusser, *Ideology and Ideological State Apparatuses*, in Lenin and Philosophy and Other Essays 142–70 (Ben Brewster trans., 1971).

7. Paul Gilroy, The Black Atlantic: Modernity and Double Consciousness (1993).

8. See Raymond Williams, Towards 2000 (1983); see also Paul Gilroy, There Ain't No Black in the Union Jack 49 (1987).

9. See Mary Louise Pratt, Arts of the Contact Zone, Profession 91, at 33, 33–40 (1991).

10. Mike Davis, City of Quartz: Excavating the Future in Los Angeles (1990).

11. Lorna Dee Cervantes, *Poem for the Young White Man Who Asked Me How I, an Intelligent, Well-Read Person, Could Believe in the War between the Races*, in Emplumada 35 (1981).

12. *Id.*

Chapter 91

Border Crossings

Margaret E. Montoya

This volume is appearing at a time when immigration, free trade, illicit drugs, affirmative action for Latinos, and the English-only movement have pushed relations with Mexico, Mexicanos, and Chicanos to the fore. But concerns about transborder movement of people, goods, capital, languages, and accompanying legal claims are not just national, but global. People throughout the globe are moving from the southern regions with their relative poverty into the northern countries in search of employment and political stability. Within this current political environment borders become embedded with symbolic meaning about national sovereignty, a desired clarity about who "belongs" and who does not, and employment security. Border crossers become media symbols and political scapegoats. The border, in short, becomes a metaphor for large social forces. Let us see how this happens.

The Border

The U.S./Mexico border was defined, as many international borders have been, by war, political intrigue, and river morphology. The 1848 Treaty of Guadalupe Hidalgo ended the United States' war with Mexico and established the Rio Grande as the border from the Gulf of Mexico to El Paso. Moving west, the Gila River that runs from New Mexico through Arizona at a point above Tucson and into the Colorado River was the negotiated boundary. From the Colorado River, a straight line was drawn to the Pacific Ocean at a point just below San Diego.

By 1853, Mexico, and its President Santa Ana, had land and needed money; the United States had money and wanted land for a transcontinental railroad system. So James Gadsden, the minister to Mexico, bargained to have the United States buy large portions of northern Mexico. Originally hoping for Baja California and parts of Sonora and Chihuahua, he eventually settled for a smaller section of land, approximately 30,000 acres for which the United States paid $10 million. With the so-

From "Border Crossings in an Age of Border Patrols: *Cruzando Fronteras Metaforicas*." 26 N.M. L. Rev. 1 (1996). Originally published in the *New Mexico Law Review*. Reprinted by permission.

called Gadsden Purchase, the border was now drawn below Nogales and Douglas, Arizona.

What has characterized the border for most of its 150-year history has been the lack of open hostility among the people who inhabit the territory along the border. According to historians, the process of cultural lending and borrowing began almost immediately with the flows of people, capital, and ideas largely disregarding the political boundary.

During most of the past century, the United States actively encouraged the movement of workers from Mexico. In the late 1800s, miners were recruited from Sonora and Jalisco, and those immigrant laborers were responsible for the feasibility and profitability of open-pit copper mines in Arizona and New Mexico. Later, as the Imperial and Mesilla Valleys were irrigated, farm labor from Mexico became critical for the planting, weeding, and harvesting of crops. Immigration laws were specifically drafted to protect the Mexican labor supply for agribusiness in California and elsewhere.

Much of the current political debate centers on the "violations" and "transgressions" of the border by undocumented workers who cross to work in the United States or who overstay their visas. This debate stands in sharp contrast to the original desire of the two countries to facilitate transborder interactions. A series of "sister-cities" were established along the border—Mexicali and Calexico; Nogales, Arizona, and Nogales, Sonora; El Paso, Texas, and El Paso del Norte (now Ciudad Juarez); Laredo, Texas, and Nuevo Laredo, Tamaulipas—with the explicit intent, at the time, to create a population along the border with facility in both cultures, a borderlands in which both languages would be spoken and goods, labor, and capital would move fairly freely. These hopes have largely been realized. Current proposals to fortify the border by building impenetrable concrete walls, electrified fences, or a human fence of border guards fail to take into account the considerable advantages of these historic connections, especially those offered by a hybrid population that navigates easily through both societies.

Rep. Duncan Hunter (R–El Cajon, Calif.) has proposed the building of a triple fence along the fourteen-mile stretch of border from the Pacific Ocean to Otay Mesa, known colloquially as "Smugglers Alley." According to the *Los Angeles Times*, the idea for the fence is based on a study prepared by the Sandia National Laboratory in New Mexico, which "concluded that if one fence was good, three fences were better."[1] The triple fence idea is opposed by nearly everyone, the Clinton administration, both senators from California, the Immigration and Naturalization Service, the labor union for the Border Patrol, and even the conservative San Diego newspaper, the *Union-Tribune*. Nevertheless, the border continues to serve the political fortunes of jingoistic politicians.

Border as Metaphor

More recently, the border has been imbedded with metaphoric and tropic meanings. Applicable to disciplinary, cultural, and epistemological spaces, the border is seen as site, intersection, bridge, and membrane. Borders have been transformed from bilateral national boundaries to cultural and epistemic sites of contestation.

Gloria Anzaldúa has transformed the concept of the "border" from geographic and physical spaces to a series of psychological, sexual, and spiritual sites, "present wherever two or more cultures edge each other, where people of different races occupy the same territory, where under, lower, middle, and upper classes touch, where the space between two individuals shrinks with intimacy."[2] Renato Rosaldo observes:

> [O]ur everyday lives are crisscrossed by border zones, pockets and eruptions of all kinds. Social borders frequently become salient around such lines as sexual orientation, gender, class, race, ethnicity, nationality, age, politics, dress, food or taste. Along with "our" supposedly transparent cultural selves, such borderlands should be regarded not as analytically empty transitional zones but as sites of creative cultural production that require investigation.[3]

Dwight Conquergood extended the notion of contested sites to the self, exploring the reframing of borders for purposes of epistemology and identity formation:

> Borders bleed, as much as they contain. Instead of dividing lines to be patrolled or transgressed, boundaries are now understood as crisscrossing sites inside the post-modern subject. Difference is resituated within, instead of beyond, the self. Inside and outside distinctions, like genres, blur and wobble.[4]

Finally, consider Ruth Behar's centerpiece story about an indigenous Mexican woman. Behar speaks partly in her ethnographic voice, but the multilayered translation of Esperanza's story requires Behar to tell her own story. Here the border is integral to the identities of both the Cuban ethnographer and her Indian informant, but, more importantly, both Behar and Esperanza use their relation to the border to create their identity, to name themselves as illegal, as "literary wetbacks," thereby robbing the popular discourse of its power to define epithets, to construct identities, and to stigmatize experience:

> Esperanza has given me her story to smuggle across the border. Just as Mexican laborers export their bodies for labor on American soil, Esperanza has given me her story for export only. Her story, she realizes, is a kind of commodity that will have a value on the other side that it doesn't have at home—why else would I be "using up" my life to write about her life? She has chosen to be a literary wetback, and I am to act as her literary broker, the border crosser who will take her story to the other side and make it be heard in translation. The question will be whether I can act as literary broker without becoming the worst kind of *coyote*, getting her across, but only by exploiting her lack of power to make it to *el otro lado* any other way. . . .
>
> [T]here is a special burden that authorship carries if you have ever occupied a borderland place in the dominant culture, especially if you were told at some point in your life that you didn't have what it takes to be an authority on, an author of, anything. It means writing as a "literary wetback," as the Chicana poet Alicia Gaspar de Alba puts it, without "the 'right' credentials . . . to get across."
>
> It is not just Esperanza, then who is a literary wetback. Even though I have borne her story across to this side of the border, I recognize that I, too, in a quite different way, am

a literary wetback in the world of academic letters, a wetback despite the papers that tell me I'm okay, I'm in, I'm a legal alien.[5]

Policing the southern border of the United States became a central issue in the political agenda of both the Democratic and Republican parties in the presidential campaigns of 1996. The House considered and passed sweeping new immigration legislation, further restricting legal immigration and adding 5,000 new border patrol agents. In California, the Riverside police were videotaped in a high-speed chase that ended with their vicious billy-clubbing of Enrique Funes Flores and Alicia Sotero, two Mexican nationals who put up no resistance when caught. The Mexican male driver had been transporting some twenty Mexican undocumented workers in the bed of a dilapidated truck.

> And while the Mexicans were stereotyped as lazy, shiftless, passive siesta seekers, people who patronized *mañana*, those who knew them realized that just the opposite was true. The Mexican was one of the hardest working individuals on earth, and [s]he proved it just to get into the United States. [Sh]e walked for weary weeks, forded muddy and violent rivers, clung to the tenuous underside of trucks and trains, stuffed him[/her]self into the sizzling engine compartment of automobiles, slipped through and over jagged fences, risked being murdered by his own people, flattened by traffic as [s]he darted across the freeway, suffocated in tightly enclosed vans and railroad cars, arrested by the Border Patrol, all so [s]he could earn minimum wages toiling with a short hoe from dawn to dusk. If [s]he wasn't an illegal, [s]he would surely have deserved commendation for bravery, perseverance, and endurance. Such are the people whom we expel from our borders.[6]

As Peter McLaren reminds us, "Some people cross borders willingly, some people are forced to cross them, and others are shot in their attempts at crossing."[7] So as we deploy the border as a metaphor, we need to remember that for many people throughout the world crossing borders is not cognitive or rhetorical; border crossings can be life-risking and life-losing endeavors.

We engage in disciplinary and discursive border crossings to ally ourselves with the millions in their diasporic searches for new homelands with their unfulfilled promise of work, food, security, and opportunity. We engage in disciplinary and discursive border crossings to construct new, more fluid, more complex identities, and in doing so we turn our gaze southward towards our ancestral homes. We engage in disciplinary and discursive border crossings to destabilize the meanings and inscriptions that the superordinate cultures, the Euro/Anglo/North American cultures with their Border Patrols, place on borders.

NOTES

1. Tony Perry, *Rep. Hunter Defends Plan to Erect Triple Fence Along Mexican Border*, L.A. TIMES, May 5, 1996 at A22.
2. See Preface to Gloria Anzaldúa, BORDERLANDS / *La Frontera*: THE NEW MESTIZA (1987).
3. Renato Rosaldo, CULTURE AND TRUTH: THE REMAKING OF SOCIAL ANALYSIS 207–08 (1989).
4. Dwight Conquergood, *Rethinking Ethnography: Towards a Critical Cultural Politics*,

58 COMMUNICATION MONOGRAPHS 179, 184 (1991) (citing Stephen A. Tyler, THE UNSPEAKABLE DISCOURSE, DIALOGUE, AND RHETORIC IN THE POSTMODERN WORLD 151 (1987) and quoting Thi Minhha Trinh, WOMAN, NATIVE, OTHER: WRITING POSTCOLONIALITY AND FEMINISM 94 (1989).

5. Ruth Behar, TRANSLATED WOMAN: CROSSING THE BORDER WITH ESPERANZA=S STORY (1993).

6. Leon C. Metz, BORDER, THE U.S.-MEXICO LINE 395–96 (1989).

7. Peter McLaren, CRITICAL PEDAGOGY AND PREDATORY CULTURE: OPPOSITIONAL POLITICS IN A POSTMODERN ERA 113 (1995).

Chapter 92

Sandra Cisneros
The Fading of the Warrior Hero

Renato Rosaldo

The author of *The House on Mango Street,* Sandra Cisneros, is a young woman who grew up in the Mexican community of Chicago. A writer and a teacher, she graduated from the Iowa Writers Workshop, and she has taught creative writing at an alternative school for dropouts in Chicago. For her, writing is a craft and a form of empowerment. At once widely accessible and unobtrusively bilingual, her writing reflects concerns at once Chicana, feminist, and broadly political.

Cisneros's work grows out of a wider movement. During the 1980s, the most creative modes of imagining Chicano identity have emerged less often from social thinkers than from creative writers, particularly from short-story cycles authored by women. It is no accident that a marginal genre, such as the short story, should become a site for political innovation and cultural creativity. Literary theorist Mary Louise Pratt has argued, for example, that the short-story cycle's formal marginality (as compared with the novel) makes it a particularly likely arena for experimentation, for the development of alternative moral visions, and for the introduction of women and teenagers as central protagonists.[1] In the case at hand, young Chicana authors have written against earlier versions of cultural authenticity that idealized patriarchal cultural regimes that appeared autonomous, homogeneous, and unchanging.

Esperanza, the central protagonist of *The House on Mango Street,* tells a gender-specific coming-of-age story that develops a distinct strand of her cultural heritage. More matriarchal than patriarchal, her vision reaches back to her great-grandmother and forward to herself. Yet her constant play, her deceptively childlike patter, subverts oppressive patriarchal points of cultural coherence and fixity.

Esperanza does not orient to a remembered ancestral homeland in Mexico or anywhere else. Unlike the works of [Américo] Paredes and [Ernesto] Galarza [earlier twentieth-century writer-activists—*Eds.*], Cisneros's narrative invokes neither a primordial pastoral patriarchy nor a primeval tropical village. If Esperanza has a cul-

From CULTURE & TRUTH: THE REMAKING OF SOCIAL ANALYSIS by Renato Rosaldo. Copyright © 1989, 1993 by Renato Rosaldo. Reprinted by permission of Beacon Press, Boston.

tural anchor, an Edenic reference point, it is the house of her dreams, paradoxically tucked away in a future that never arrives. "I knew then," she says, "I had to have a house. A real house. One I could point to. But this isn't it. The house on Mango Street isn't it. For the time being, Mama said. Temporary, said Papa. But I know how those things go" (p. 9). The bilingualism of this prose is subtle enough to be ignored by Anglo readers. In her own public readings, however, Cisneros pronounces mango with the "a" of "all," not that of "hat," and she accents Mama and Papa on the second syllable, not the first. Even life in the *barrio* appears not as near-documentary portraits of grinding poverty but as Esperanza's oblique statement that the American Dream has eluded her; she has no home, not even a room, of her own, and in her childhood she never will.

In one of her short stories, she plays with themes of the warrior hero—the horseman, the name shouted in combat, and the *corrido* which sings of his deeds— destabilizing each as she goes. Let me illustrate by citing "My Name" in its entirety:

> In English my name means hope. In Spanish it means too many letters. It means sadness, it means waiting. It is like the number nine. A muddy color. It is the Mexican records my father plays on Sunday mornings when he is shaving, songs like sobbing.
>
> It was my great-grandmother's name and now it is mine. She was a horse woman too, born like me in the Chinese year of the horse—which is supposed to be bad luck if you're born female—but I think this is a Chinese lie because the Chinese, like the Mexicans, don't like their women strong.
>
> My great-grandmother. I would've liked to have known her, a wild horse of a woman, so wild she wouldn't marry until my great-grandfather threw a sack over her head and carried her off just like that, as if she were a fancy chandelier. That's the way he did it.
>
> And the story goes she never forgave him. She looked out the window all her life, the way so many women sit their sadness on an elbow. I wonder if she made the best with what she got or was she sorry because she couldn't be all the things she wanted to be. Esperanza. I have inherited her name, but I don't want to inherit her place by the window.
>
> At school they say my name funny as if the syllables were made out of tin and hurt the roof of your mouth. But in Spanish my name is made out of a softer something like silver, not quite as thick as sister's name Magdalena which is uglier than mine. Magdalena who at least can come home and become Nenny. But I am always Esperanza.
>
> I would like to baptize myself under a new name, a name more like the real me, the one nobody sees. Esperanza as Lisandra or Maritza or Zeze the X. Yes. Something like Zeze the X will do. [pp. 12–13]

Esperanza inhabits a border zone crisscrossed by a plurality of languages and cultures. Multiple subjectivities intersect in her own person, where they coexist, not in a zone of free play but each with its own gravity and density. Moving between English and Spanish, her name shifts in length (from four letters to nine), in meaning (from hope to sadness and waiting), and in sound (from being as cutting as tin to as soft as silver). In contrast to Gregorio Cortez, she does not stand in one place, looking straight ahead, and shout, "Yo soy Esperanza."

Like her grandmother, Esperanza is a horse woman, but not a female imitation of the *hidalgo,* the male warrior horseman. No, she was born, of all things, in the *Chinese* year of the horse; in her heterogeneous cultural world, the Chinese and the Chicano readily come into play together. Both Chinese and Mexicans agree, she says, because neither culture likes its women strong. Her narrative moves, as if along links in a chain of free associations, and great-grandmother Esperanza undergoes a metamorphosis from a rider, the horse woman, to the beast itself, a wild horse of a woman.

Her patrimony, the *corrido,* has been reduced to Mexican records that sound like sobbing. Although she accepts her matronymy (that is, her name), Esperanza refuses to assume her great-grandmother's place by the window. As she concludes the tale, Esperanza yet again turns things topsy-turvy by baptizing her invisible, real self: Zeze the X. Nothing stands still, especially not her name.

Near poems, the short stories evoke twin threats to her person in the form of sexuality and physical danger. Yet the power of these threats deceptively appears in the patter of "childlike" diction that often imitates nursery rhymes:

> Across the street in front of the tavern a bum man on the stoop.
>
> Do you like these shoes?
>
> Bum man says, Yes, little girl. Your little lemon shoes are so beautiful. But come closer. I can't see very well. Come closer. Please.
>
> You are a pretty girl, bum man continues. What's your name, pretty girl?
>
> And Rachel says Rachel, just like that.
>
> Now you know to talk to drunks is crazy and to tell them your name is worse, but who can blame her. She is young and dizzy to hear so many sweet things in one day, even if it is a bum man's whiskey words saying them.
>
> Rachel, you are prettier than a yellow taxi cab. You know that.
>
> But we don't like it. We got to go, Lucy says.
>
> If I give you a dollar will you kiss me? How about a dollar? [p. 39]

That this is a Chicana version of "Little Red Riding Hood" becomes evident as the bum man asks her to draw nearer, virtually saying, "The better to see you, my dear." His threatening presence echoes the cliched warning of parents who say to their children, " Don't take candy from strangers." Instead of candy, the bum man offers saccharine words, calls her a pretty girl, praises her shoes, compares her with a yellow cab, and, in the end, offers a dollar for her kiss.

Esperanza depicts her sexual awakening as a process at once sensuous and dangerous. The story entitled "Hips" plays back and forth, metaphorically, between her suddenly present hips and a brand new Buick: "One day you wake up and there they [your hips] are. Ready and waiting like a new Buick with the keys in the ignition. Ready to take you where?" (p. 47). In a later story, she is bursting: "Everything is holding its breath inside me. Everything is waiting to explode like Christmas. I want to be all new and shiny. I want to sit out bad at night, a boy around my neck and the wind under my skirt" (p. 70). Esperanza interweaves her sexuality, her rounding hips, and images of automobiles. Not unlike a car, she is polished and ready to go (where?). In being "bad," she moves toward the sensuous, pleasurable, threatening edges of her world.

In this play of desire and threat, Esperanza meets dangers by gracefully moving on. If her sexuality resembles a new car, her grace is danced. "And uncle," she says, "spins me and my skinny arms bend the way he taught me and my mother watches and my little cousins watch and the boy who is my cousin by first communion watches and everyone says, wow, who are those two who dance like in the movies, until I forget that I am wearing only ordinary shoes, brown and white, the kind my mother buys each year for school" (p. 46). Her grace resides in her person, not in her ordinary shoes. Never standing in one place, she uses the dance to counter male violence and efforts to confine and subordinate her. She just moves on, in her dance of life.

Cisneros opens fresh vistas in what Américo Paredes saw as the inextricably intertwined realms of culture and politics. In her narrative analysis, the concept of culture undergoes a metamorphosis. The warrior hero has seen better days. No longer can he serve as the "unified subject" around which Chicano sagas of masculine heroics revolve. Yet what the concept of culture loses in purity and authenticity, it gains in range and engagement. As embodied in Cisneros's short-story cycle, Chicano culture moves toward the borderlands, the spaces that readily include blacks, Anglos, mundane happenings of everyday life, and heterogeneous changing neighborhoods. Certain border crossings involve literal immigration, in which a number of people move in and out of the neighborhood, or a "wetback" with no last name dies anonymously in an accident, or a fat woman who speaks no English sits by the window and plays homesick songs. Others appear as more figurative border dances through which Esperanza makes her way in a world of desire and threat, budding sexuality and dangerous male violence.

In trying new narrative forms, Cisneros has developed a fresh vision of self and society; she has opened an alternative cultural space, a heterogeneous world, within which her protagonists no longer act as "unified subjects," yet remain confident of their identities. Esperanza's name itself twists and twirls until it reaches the end of its alphabet, "Zeze the X." In moving through a world laced with poverty, violence, and danger, Esperanza acts at once assertive and playful. She thrives, not just survives, as she dances through her unpredictable world with grace and wit. For all her grace, however, Esperanza does not just take on personas and remove them, as if they were so many old shoes; unlike the less encumbered French literary theorist Roland Barthes, Esperanza feels the weight of the multiple identities that intersect through her person.

On a more reflexive note, I should like to conclude by underscoring the analytical import of the interplay between "their" (Anglo-American) narratives and "ours" (Chicano). In the case at hand, the implications of Sandra Cisneros's short-story cycle came to me quite gradually. It took time—from initially conceiving my article "Grief and a Headhunter's Rage" onward—for the concept of a multiplex personal identity to move in alongside its predecessor, the "unified subject," and for the notion of culture as multiple border zones to find a place next to its predecessor, the "homogeneous community." Yet it would be difficult to exaggerate the major role played by the narrative analyses of Paredes, Galarza, and Cisneros in my charting a path for renewing the anthropologist's search for meaning.

NOTES

1. Mary Louise Pratt, *The Short Story: The Long and the Short of It,* Poetics 10 (1981): 175–94.

Chapter 93

Voices/*Voces* in the Borderlands

Melissa Harrison and Margaret E. Montoya

While derided as the bane of the Western intellectual tradition and a threat to the most noble of human achievements, multiculturalism (or postmodernism dressed in grunge) has settled with a shrug into the pages of the Spiegel catalog. Listen, as we are cajoled that:

> [I]n a perfect world, it would be out to tell anyone what's in. In the meantime, a few ideas seemed important to us. Diversity. A home should be as surprising as its owner. Integrity. There's a reason some things are called classics. Efficiency. If it isn't smart, it's stupid. Other than that, our advice is to do what you want. Be who you are. Make yourself at home.[1]

In a section called "News," prominent hues of browns and black are set off by animal prints. The products "mix contemporary style with primitive overtones."[2] Page after page of discreetly encoded descriptions: "The 'Genoa' chair . . . the Kalibo floor screen . . . the Mexican lion vase . . . the zephyr chair . . . the Cagayan floor lamp," and a "vase with an attitude: [E]xotic!"[3] We are exhorted to "[r]aise some cane in the library." But relax, it's only a coy play on words, the "cane" being referred to is in "[t]he 'Plantation' chair, originally designed during British Colonial times to enjoy an evening's viewing of the sky," "stir[ring] up images of a tropical retreat."[4]

In the next section, the words "NEW SIMPLICITY" are overlaid with "Good design knows no boundaries. . . ."[5] This visually mixed message is followed by: "The shape of things to come. . . ."[6] "Mixing cultures is only natural. . . ."[7] "The freedom of neutrality. . . ."[8] Then, new themes are introduced: "Home Country";[9] "Americana. An at-ease attitude. Freedom of expression. The more mixed, the better. Where opportunities are endless."[10] "The New Frontier. There's more to Rustic than 'Cowboys and Indians.' Expand your horizons with ethnic looks from around the world."[11]

Juxtapose Spiegel's celebratory excursion into cultural diversity with the Ralph Lauren lay-outs running each Sunday in the *New York Times Magazine,* depicting in-your-face scenes of money, privilege, and apartheid.

From "VOICES/*VOCES* IN THE BORDERLANDS: A COLLOQUY ON RE/CONSTRUCTIONG IDENTITIES IN RE/CONSTRUCTED LEGAL SPACES." 6 COLUM. J. GENDER & L. 387 (1996). Originally published in the *Columbia Journal of Gender and Law.* Reprinted by permission.

"Plantations" and "colonies" cease being sites of enslavement, oppression, and degradation and become instead bucolic and nostalgic memories of sunset-colored retreats. The "primitive" and the "exotic" are broken from their histories of subordination. The coded images and mantras of the political Right: "Americana," "neutrality," "freedom of expression," and "endless opportunities" are insouciantly juxtaposed with "Diversity" and its hues of browns and black. Cultural and racial hybridity with their "mixing of cultures" and "ethnic looks" are stripped of their search and yearning for political and economic re/location and instead, fetishized, commodified, and re-defined as "natural," "better," and "at ease."

Advertising squeezes out old meanings of words, investing them with new associations. Commercial-speak suctions out pejorative representations, replacing them with acceptable and seductive ones. Subtly but inexorably, the language of commerce affects perceptions, alters attitudes, and reframes understanding. Capitalism's need to expand markets and increase sales coopts images, vocabulary, and historical experience. This cooptation can be critiqued from the perspective of the Right as well as that of Progressives. To the dismay of the Right, diversity is portrayed as elegant, chic, and desirable; to the dismay of the Progressives, it emerges historically transparent and ideologically neutral.

Advertising and other types of popular culture form, deform, reform, and conform what they represent. Are all identities up for grabs? Is it useful to search for the relationship between popular culture's construction of identities and its creation of desire and meaning, or the construction of identities of studied peoples by ethnographers, or, more directly for our purposes, the construction of identities of clients by lawyers during the process of legal re/presentation? How does legal discourse resemble and emulate commercial-speak in masking historic forms of subordination? Like Spiegel's manipulation of plantation imagery and signification, does legal discourse also supplant the odious with invented memories, replacing and displacing the obvious with the oblique? Or do lawyers obfuscate by eschewing the playful and the foolish, abjuring any lampooning of their tools, techniques, and vocabularies? Do such questions bear on the lawyer's tasks of speaking for clients and representing them? Isn't a lawyer's or law student's understanding of the dynamism of racial identities and the attendant complexity of client relations informed as much, if not more, by popular culture as by critical theory? Can we link the "reading" of popular culture and the deciphering of its encoded messages with the lawyer's need to "read" the culture of her client?

Students enter law school steeped in messages such as these, multilayered messages in which racist and neocolonialist attitudes merge into the everyday familiarity of objects offered for sale, the real blending with the ersatz. Yet, upon entering law school, students are confronted with legal materials and legal language that seem curiously ignorant of the rhetoric and the vocabularies of contemporary public speech. Were the nineteenth-century colonizers, who packed their plantation cane chairs with their imperialism and headed for Africa, India, Mexico, and the so-called Wild West, to appear today, we fear that many law school classes would be astonishingly familiar to them. Looking around, they would likely be surprised to see women and people with skin in shades of tan to black. But looking down at their casebook they would recognize the measured words and the syllogistic patterns of the appellate judges, writing in what some would describe as expository English, the language of the profession perceived as "normal" in its monolinguality, monoculturalism, and transparent in its representation of reality. Looking forward, this imaginary colonizer might even see a woman of color teaching the class. We posit that all too frequently she or we or I would sound alarmingly like our predecessors from a bygone era.

Just compare the imagery, vocabulary, playfulness, and cultural diversity deployed by popular culture with those that typify traditional legal pedagogy. The schism between the discourse and semiotics of the marketplace and television (to say nothing of hip-hop videos or rap lyrics) and our classrooms contributes to the persistent and pernicious separation between the personal and professional lives of the lawyer. We model this separation for students in and out of the classroom, inculcating them with what we already know to be an unsatisfying and ineffective way of leading our lives. We recognize that students have diverse backgrounds and perspectives, as well as varying stakes in cultural debates, and this makes our pedagogical tasks immensely more interesting and more challenging as well. Many students, and our daughters and sons, are already considerably adept at deciphering popular culture. We seek to make them our allies in constructing pedagogical spaces where together we can attenuate the assaults on our sensibilities and our spirits by fashioning new individual and collective identities within new myths, narratives, and ethics.

The Borderlands as Metaphor

We begin by using the concepts of essentialism and anti-essentialism as our theoretical backdrop. We then examine borderland theories as a way out of this dichotomy. We offer the borderland as a liminal space filled with potentiality. For some students it may represent a place to invent and construct new identities, or to re/member lost ones. For other students the borderlands is a way station, a periphery where the norms of the dominant culture can be learned and practiced, but also a place that can be left behind in order to return to one's home community. We discuss strategies of transculturation mapped along "literal and figurative borders where a 'person' is crisscrossed by multiple identities."[12] The border metaphor, with its imbedded notions of multiple nationalities, cultures, and languages, motivates us to consider methodologies drawn from ethnography and literary translation. We propose the concept of the Malinche Paradox to problematize the roles of Outsiders who seek to deploy the discursive tools and tactics of the dominant culture, only to produce unexpected and, at times, unwanted outcomes.

Our purpose is to use interdisciplinary materials to identify techniques that can be used to ameliorate our own and the student's "cultural dyslexia," a term meaning "the inability to read the alien, cultural worlds of other people."[13] In this way we can maintain fluidity and connectedness in our personal and professional identities, as well as a synergy between our scholarship and our pedagogical agendas. We propose two techniques to diminish cultural dyslexia: slow-motion reading and resonance.

Slow-motion reading is a methodology proposed decades ago by the French feminist lawyer and literary critic Claudine Herrmann as a way of using our personal experience to interpret what we read, a way of listening to our internal voice interrogate the text. The concept of resonance was developed by the Norwegian anthropologist Unni Wikan to increase cross-cultural understanding and appreciation by applying both feeling and thought; this concept of "feeling-thought" is one she borrows from the Balinese.

We find the concept of borderlands useful in thinking about essentialism and anti-essentialism because the very concept challenges the idea of a single perspective. A borderland can refer to the actual physical border between two geographic entities. However, we refer to psychic borderlands—"physically present wherever two or more cultures edge each other, where people of different races occupy the same territory, where under, lower, middle and upper classes touch, where the space between two individuals shrinks with intimacy"[14]—and "border writing" as that which "emphasizes the differences in reference codes between two or more cultures and depicts, therefore, a kind of realism that approaches the experience of border crossers, those who live in a bilingual, bicultural, biconceptual reality."[15]

By this same token, we may consider "border identities" as "created out of empathy for others by means of a passionate connection through difference. Such a connection is furthered by a narrative imagination which enables critical linkages to be made between our own stories and the stories of cultural others."[16] One scholar theorizes that border identities are both one and the Other as the border crosser is both self and other. This awareness of the Other and of the blurring of identities is dislocating. This may mean that we look for conflict rather than consensus. This may mean "that we need to learn to theorize, to deliberate, to make collective decisions, to resolve disputes, in new, probably time-consuming and awkward ways."[17] The full implications of being constantly aware of difference is that we treat diversity as central, not incidental.

What does it mean to live in the borderlands or with a border consciousness? It feels extremely disruptive and insecure. "[T]he abject is that which 'beckons the subject ever closer to its edge.' . . . Edges—boundaries, borderlands, margins—are places where a plethora of postmodernist and feminist writers and writers of color engaged with comparative cultural studies remember, reconstruct and construct anew the imaginative power of cultures and identities."[18] Thus, abjection is about boundary loss. The borderlands, then, are a place of abjection and exhilaration; a place where the person is "crisscrossed by multiple identities,"[19] where we are a "plural self, one that thrives on ambiguity and multiplicity."[20] The image of borderlands—with its implicit recognition of both difference and commonality—illuminates a tension for feminists: how do we "attempt to talk about all women in terms of something we have in common [while not] undermin[ing] attempts to . . . [acknowledge] the differences among us, and vice versa?"[21] How can we make sure that voices are not silenced and that we do not assume to speak inappropriately for others while claiming that social critiques of patriarchy can be made?

We propose borderlands as a way to theorize and dissolve the tension between essentialism and anti-essentialism. Essentialism, in the general philosophical sense, is "understood as a belief in the real, true essence of things, the invariable and fixed properties which define the 'whatness' of a given entity."[22] The category "woman" has been used by men to essentialize women's nature and then as the starting point of, and justification for, the oppression of women. Constructionism, on the other hand, insists that essence itself is a historical construction, not a naturally occurring phenomenon. Constructionists, for example, insist that "woman" is a category created by society, not an immutable essence.

Awareness of the borderlands can help students interact with a wide range of clients, some of whom may be very different from the students themselves. The concept of borderlands is useful because it challenges the idea of a single perspective. Students can resist essentialism by being constantly aware of different cultures, classes, genders, races, and sexual orientations inhabiting the same space. The borderlands exhort students to be constantly aware of difference. They promote better lawyering by encouraging "empathy for others by means of a passionate connection through difference."[23] They enable students and lawyers to make "critical linkages" between their "stories and the stories of cultural others."[24] After proposing the borderlands as a construct to enable one to resist essentialism, the next task is to fashion specific techniques which can help students to bring the borderlands into their lawyering.

Can We Speak for / Re/Present AnOther?

> While the lawyer speaks for the client, the goal of translation is not for lawyer and client to "speak with one voice." Rather, the goal is for the lawyer to position the client's voice within the legal proceeding, to evoke rather than re-present the client's narratives.[25]

Speaking on behalf of another is an important aspect of lawyering. In a variety of venues, lawyers are expected to speak for their clients. In adversarial dispute resolution, for example, the lawyer's speaking for the client is at the heart of the advocacy. But, can we successfully speak for another? Or, more importantly for purposes of this chapter, can we speak for an Other while being mindful of the lessons of the essentialism debates?

To answer this question, we must examine questions being raised within other disciplines about essentialism and anti-essentialism. To do so, we begin by examining scholarship that integrates translation and ethnographic techniques into lawyering practices. Then, we listen to feminists, phenomenologists, ethnographers, and translators who have questioned the ability of one person to speak for another, particularly when the speaker is situated within the hierarchical structures of the academy or the legal system, and is speaking about persons who do not share the speaker's characteristics of race, class, sexual orientation, gender, language, or nationality. To reiterate, we are using these characteristics as proxies for certain life experiences that result in some loosely defined collective perspective, as markers of positionality.

The role of the translator offers insights into the lawyer/client relationship and into the lawyer's task of translating the client's story into legal parlance. Translation, according to James Boyd White, is a "useful way of thinking and talking about excellence in law,"[26] a way "forcing us to respect the other—the other language, the other person, the other text."[27] But even as Professor White recognizes the potential that translation practices have for reframing the relationship between the lawyer and her client, he describes the difficulty of "carrying over" the meaning from one text to a new one articulated in the language of the translator/lawyer. White elucidates why it isn't possible to "say" in one language what has been "said" in another.

The lawyer in pursuit of techniques to enhance communications with clients can learn from White's descriptions of language as well as from the process of translation. White also appropriately focuses us on the potential of translation practices for helping lawyers to "provide a place in which unheard voices can be heard and responded to."[28] White beckons to lawyers to hear the voices of the dispossessed, the subordinated.

But does ethnography, coupled with White's ethic of translation, provide insight like that claimed by Outsiders, those who deploy multiple consciousness? We believe the answer is both yes and no. We are persuaded that close and careful listening, coupled with scrutinized and repeated readings of the client's story, can assist one in better understanding the nuances of another's experience.

Some cultural and historical context would make this point from a different perspective. In the early sixteenth century, Hernan Cortés landed in the Americas. He was met by Maya and Tlazcala Peoples (known today because of a curious misnaming as "Indians"). Cortés was presented with many gifts, including a group of young women. Before being given to Cortés and his men, the women were baptized. One of the young women, given the name Marina, knew at least two indigenous languages (Nahuatl and Maya). Her value was quickly recognized by Cortés and she was taken as his translator. Because of her language ability, she quickly learned Spanish and thus eliminated the need for multiple translators. She was known as Doña Marina to the Spaniards, which was then translated as Malintzin in Nahuatl and then mispronounced in Spanish as Malinche.

In a painting done contemporaneously with the events, Marina is shown translating for Cortés and a group of Tlaxcalan nobles. The chronicler, Bernal Díaz, writes that "the Indians called Cortés 'Malinche' because of the inseparableness of the capitán and his Nahuatl interpreter."[29]

Let us think about her for a moment. At the time she was given to Cortés, she had already been given away on two other occasions. After Marina bore Cortés a son, he gave her to one of his lieutenants with whom she had several children. She was repeatedly treated as property, as chattel to be disposed of at the whim of her owners. Nonetheless, it appears that she had considerable latitude in her translation activities and provided Cortés with information to allow the Spaniards to quell counter-rebellions at great suffering to the Indians.

Today, La Malinche maintains a place of ambiguous prominence in Mexico, revered by some but reviled by many.[30] Her name, which once included titles of respect in two languages (Doña and -tzin), is now used by some as an epithet. Many Mexicans see her as the betrayer of a hemisphere, a traitor to her people and a col-

laborator with the conquistadores. Without her or someone who served as language and cultural translator for the Spaniards, Montezuma and the Aztecs could not have been conquered.

Dicen que los espanoles no hubieran conquistado America sin la Malinche. Traduccion y traicion estan enredados en la mentalidad mexicana. Translation from the point of view of the Mexican is embedded with betrayal. So, is la Malinche an archetype or an historical antecedent? Are lawyers only modern-day Cortés/Malinches subordinating the client/indigene? Is she godmother to those of us in the academy tentatively and ambivalently engaged in language and cultural translations? Does she peer over my shoulder with a knowing half-smile on her face? How are we to understand her agency or lack of agency? What does our understanding of her actions say to us about our subjectification/subjugation and about how we participate in the subjectification/subjugation of others?

How does the "native" lawyer come to the undertaking of legal ethnography? The anthropologist Sarah Williams has written an ethnographic representation which she calls "silhouettes, not representations of objective reality." The story tells of an academic meeting at which postmodern anthropological practice is being discussed. At one point, a question is asked about who will read the paper being presented:

[T]he moderator interrupts and jokes about more Trobriand Islanders reading Malinowski to determine who they are.

Sitting in the seminar room, I see the student who is a Trobriand Islander. Am I to envision this Trobriand Islander dangling another anthropological simulacrum . . . ? Or is the moderator being dangled by Malinowski, who from his grave literally (that is, textually) does dangle "the Trobriand Islander?" . . . The department is supposedly proud to be training the first native Trobriand Islander anthropologist. Furthermore, this student's principal adviser is a Malinowski expert. Is this would-be native anthropologist of the Trobriand Islands reading the texts of Malinowski to determine his identity? Or is he reading Malinowski to learn how anthropologists have represented his culture? Is there a difference? Does it matter?[31]

The Trobriander identity—at least the identity/ies known through anthropological texts—is named into existence, is constructed by Malinowski, the ethnographer extraordinaire. In much the same way, the client's identity *qua* client emerges as the lawyer's construction. How many of our clients would recognize their stories in the legal narratives we construct for them? How many of our clients would recognize themselves as we contruct them as clients?

A different aspect of forced silencing and its companion loss of words has been described by Claudine Herrmann. In her now-classic book *Les Voleuses de Langue* [The Tongue Snatchers], published in 1976, she states that women are oppressed through language and that those women who desire to free themselves must "steal (or snatch)" language. She contends that the

woman who wants to become educated is forced to let a little man grow inside of her.
. . . But it takes enormous energy to let a man who reasons as a man in the world of men

cohabit, in the depths of one's self, with a woman who refuses to abjure her own judgments and uses them to gauge the alternatives proposed to her.

The woman who makes this effort is necessarily schizoid. . . . She knows how wide
the gap is between what is lived and what is expressed; she soon understands that the
whole culture has been colonized.

However, there is no choice; it is necessary to learn, and with the tools at our disposal: a colonized body of language and an adulterated language.[32]

Herrmann's metaphor of the little man inside the educated woman is essentialist,
i.e., written from the point of view of a white woman as though it encompasses the
experience of all women; it thus fails to consider characteristics other than gender
with respect to both her educated woman and her little man. Such analyses can be
criticized for being at best only partially accurate because they ascribe excessive importance to language of the dominant culture, while ignoring the power that resides
in the discourses of the subordinated, including their silences.

We should not, however, quickly discount the power of Herrmann's metaphor and
her point that public language has been created within a context that excluded, devalued, and oppressed women of all backgrounds, classes, and colors. Her observation about the colonized quality of language has validity with respect to how we
speak about gender relations and how we speak for ourselves. It has even greater
force when we think about speaking for others. "You are led to reflect on how particular translations become constructed. What gets lost, what is gained, what and
how altered, in the passage from one language to the next?"[33]

What is of salience as we consider the colonization of language is that the client's
story passes through a series of adulterated languages: from the language of the
story's origin to the lawyer's language to legal parlance. Concepts such as the borderlands can help us as we speak for clients who are situated differently from us. The
borderlands are where common parlances and legal languages can be examined for
their contamination by subordinating influences.

Today, however, a substantial body of scholarship examines the role of the translator and that of the ethnographer in the process of colonization. For women, especially women of color in the legal academy, scholarship from disciplines other than
law poses difficult questions because we are forced to acknowledge the close similarity between progressive lawyering and translation as both exhibit potential for reproducing subordination.

Concerns about the interrelationship of power and knowledge and about asymmetries in power between the translator and the translated and between the researcher and the subject have been appearing with increasing frequency in ethnographic literature. Feminist fieldworkers and others have problematized not only
ethnographic scholarship and its privileging of written over oral texts, but have focused also on the luxury and privilege associated with the production of such academic work in a context of global colonialism and political hegemony maintained
through racist and sexist violence.

Like the lawyer who relies on the client, the ethnographer depends on disclosures
from the research subject. But, as we borrow from anthropological discourses, we
should be mindful of categories such as the "primitive," an analytical device that per-

vaded ethnography through the colonial period into "decolonization."[34] Anthropology's links to colonialism have been debated from the early 1960s until the present. These intra-disciplinary concerns about the subordinating effects of ethnography are not settled questions of the past. What is at stake here is the representation of the colonized, who need to be produced in such a manner as to justify neocolonial domination.

Concerns expressed from within various disciplines about the asymmetries and the historicity of the practices of translation and ethnography should force us to confront our participation as lawyers in the normalization of neocolonial practices. When you/we set out to borrow insights and methodologies from other disciplines in order to increase your/our understanding of Outsiders, it is incumbent upon you/us to seek out the literature written from the Outsider perspective critiquing such insights and methodologies. Are we likely to hear the muffled voices of clients if we don't hear the voices of those speaking from inside the academy saying that ethnography, translation, and law, perforce, are all discourses and sites through which the neocolonial subject (as represented by our clients) is constructed?

Slow-Motion Reading/Listening

In the mid-1970s, Claudine Herrmann wrote an essay in which she decried Evelyn Wood-type techniques for speed reading.[35] She described speed reading as a danse macabre, a dance with the dead. What she saw as dead were the texts, the linguistic constructions vitiated by a reader intent on getting through and getting out of the text. Herrmann exhorted us to engage in what she called "slow-motion reading," listening to our inner voice enter into an interrogation of the text.[36] "Slow-motion reading" invites us to disrupt disciplinary boundaries, to weave together different languages, to look at Spiegel catalogs with the eye of the postmodern critic. "Slow-motion" interpretation can be deployed with oral texts as well. "Slow-motion listening" prompts us to listen on several levels to our clients, our friends, and our families.

Using slow-motion techniques, especially when they include non-verbal elements a person is likely to be unaware of, can be disconcerting, and care must be taken not to offend. However, non-verbal communication is highly ambiguous and examining one's interpretation of paralanguage sounds and gestures can be instructive for both the sender and receiver of the encoded messages.

Slow-motion reading and slow-motion listening are techniques that we can teach and use with our students and our children. It is likely that they already have at least a nascent understanding of the multiple meanings of their language(s). Many students, especially the Outsiders—students of color, gays, lesbians, dis/abled, the different, and the alienated—are attuned to the encoding of messages through the *metissage* of rap music and the hybridity of slick advertising with all its dangers and allure. Students are thus likely to understand the stereographic and stereophonic nature of messages and may be using slow-motion listening to decode cultural messages. The transferability of this skill to the listening of their clients' stories, however, may not be obvious.

Slow-motion reading with an appreciation for the polylingualism of language is only one technique to treat our cultural dyslexia. This slow-motion interplay between our inner voice and the client's story can be informed by the work of Dan Sperber,[37] who draws a distinction between the translation or interpretation of, on the one hand, individual words and thoughts and, on the other hand, collective representations attributed to a whole social group ("The So-and-So believe that . . .").[38] This distinction between individual words and cultural facts can be employed with students in discussions about essentialism. The client's communication as collective representation or, conversely, the lawyer's framing of the client's individual experience in collective terms, can provide a moment for the lawyer and the client to decide together whether a re-communication, a re-presentation, of the cultural fact is strategic as well as consistent with the purposes of both the lawyer and the client.

Resonance

How can the lawyer speak for an/Other without constructing and representing the client as alien and exotic? How can the lawyer employ the techniques of ethnography and translation without embracing the attitude implicit in the essentialistic and racist device of the "primitive"?

The Norwegian anthropologist Unni Wikan uses the term "resonance" to describe an approach to intercultural communication.

> Resonance thus seems akin to an attitude which we might label sympathy, empathy or understanding. Whether it is "the same" or "different," I cannot say. Balinese see as critical that it entails using one's feelings as well as and at once with one's thoughts. Only this enables appreciation—which is more than just understanding.[39]

Resonance, particularly in the context of anthropological fieldwork, requires both parties to "try to grasp, respectively convey, meanings that reside neither in words, 'facts,' nor text, but are evoked in the meeting of one experiencing subject with another."[40] Relying on the work of Donald Davidson, Richard Rorty, and Balinese epistemologists, Wikan explains, using the words of a Balinese colleague, that resonance "fosters empathy or compassion . . . by apply[ing] both feeling and thought."[41] Resonance challenges anthropology's (and, by extension, the law's) "romance with words, concepts, symbols, text and discourse."[42] The necessity of transcending words while attending to the speaker's intention is inherent in "the maxim of interpretive charity," which has also been called "the co-operative principle."[43] Wikan writes that too often we come to our work with a critical frame of mind instead of a charitable one. Too much, she argues, has been made of *critical* thinking. . . .

Wikan cautions us that *"the quest for meaning blinds us to what life is all about. It entices us to get lost in words, and lose sight of the larger issues."*[44] Wikan admonishes her fellow anthropologists intent upon gathering, writing, and publishing their ethnographic texts. It is an undertaking that she describes as a "'freedom from urgency, from necessity'; our anthropological observation-point is 'founded upon the neutralisation of practical interests and practical stakes.'"[45] How much more compelling is it for the poverty lawyer to learn to "attend" to people's complaints, joys, and tribulations? Such a lawyer, unlike the ethnographer in the safety of her academic department, usually can't neutralize the practical interests and practical stakes.

In short, we seek to ally ourselves with our students in creating pedagogical spaces where difference can be explored. To do so, we use popular culture to introduce the notion that messages are encoded with layered and ambiguous meanings. The pages of the Spiegel catalog cunningly lace together the imagery and verbal codes of neo-colonialist liberalism with those of postmodern cultural hybridity as though the significations of the two are indistinguishable. "Plantation chairs" and "Rustic Cowboys and Indians" are juxtaposed with "Americana," "Freedom of expression" and "Home Country" where "mixing cultures is only natural" and one is free to "expand horizons with ethnic looks."[46] We can be, and are, co-opted through our consumption rituals into a silent complicity with racist commercialism. But how do we resist? We suggest that in learning to decode such messages, we begin to see the connections between "reading" pop culture and "reading" the culture of one's client. Understanding multivalent meanings and engaging in code-switching is a skill that is transferrable, a technique for the home, the classroom, and the courthouse.

We also offer the borderlands as a trope for understanding the process of rendering oneself vulnerable but open to opposing perspectives, new voices, and different worlds. We have employed the notion of the border to propose new ways of thinking about and teaching about a culturally diverse society where law students must be adept at interacting with a wide range of clients, peers, and present and future colleagues. Cross-cultural learning is possible only in tandem with others. It is a journey that cannot be taken alone. The borderlands are places of collaboration, of interactivity, of shared as well as opposing values, of exposed and juxtaposed weaknesses, and of ignorance, unmasked and remasked. Borderlands beckon to risk takers, meaning awakers, and vision makers.

NOTES

1.   SPIEGEL CATALOG, Fall/Winter 1994, at 276.

2.   *Id.* at 278, Item H.

3.   *Id.* at 278, 286.

4.   *Id.* at 292, Item D.

5.   *Id.* at 328–29.

6.   *Id.* at 330.

7.   *Id.* at 332.

8.   *Id.* at 334.

9.   *Id.* at 336.

10.   *Id.* at 337.

11.   *Id.* at 352.

12.   Renato Rosaldo, CULTURE & TRUTH: THE REMAKING OF SOCIAL ANALYSIS 216 (1993).

13.   Gisli Pálsson, *Introduction: Beyond Boundaries,* in BEYOND BOUNDARIES: UNDERSTANDING, TRANSLATION AND ANTHROPOLOGICAL DISCOURSE 1, 23 (Gisli Pálsson ed., 1993).

14.   Gloria Anzaldúa, BORDERLANDS/*La Frontera:* THE NEW MESTIZA, at Preface (1987).

15. D. Emily Hicks, *Deterritorialization and Border Writing,* in Ethics/Aesthetics: Post-Modern Positions 47, 49 (Robert Merrill ed., 1988).

16. Peter McLaren, Critical Pedagogy and Predatory Culture: Oppositional Politics in a Post-Modern Era 106 (1995).

17. Jennifer Nedelsky, *The Challenges of Multiplicity,* 89 Mich. L. Rev. 1591, 1608 (1991).

18. Sarah Williams, *Abjection and Anthropological Praxis,* 66 Anthropological Q. 67, 74 (1993).

19. Rosaldo, at 216.

20. Françoise Lionnet, Autobiographical Voices: Race, Gender, Self-Portraiture 16 (1989).

21. See Elizabeth V. Spelman, Inessential Woman: Problems of Exclusion in Feminist Thought 3 (1988).

22. Diana Fuss, Essentially Speaking: Feminism, Nature and Difference, xi (1989).

23. McLaren, at 106.

24. *Id.*

25. Christopher P. Gilkerson, *Poverty Law Narratives: The Critical Practice and Theory of Receiving and Translating Client Stories,* 43 Hastings L. J. 861, 916–17 (1992).

26. James B. White, Justice as Translation: An Essay in Cultural and Legal Criticism xvii (1990).

27. *Id.*

28. *Id.* at 267.

29. Frances Karttunen, Between Worlds: Interpreters, Guides and Survivors 9 (1994).

30. See generally Sandra Messinger Cypess, *La Malinche,* in Mexican Literature: From History to Myth (1991).

31. Williams, at 71–72.

32. See Nancy Kline, *Translator's Introduction* to Claudine Herrmann, The Tongue Snatchers at 6–7 (Nancy Kline trans., 1989).

33. Nicole Ward Jouve, White Woman Speaks with Forked Tongue 47 (1991).

34. Pálsson, at 8–9.

35. See Kline, at xii (citing Claudine Herrmann, *In Favor of Slow Motion Reading,* 20 B.U. J. 2, 2 (Nancy Kline trans. 1972)).

36. *Id.*

37. Dan Sperber, *Interpreting and Explaining Cultural Representations,* in Beyond Boundaries, at 162, 165.

38. *Id.* at 165.

39. Unni Wikan, *Beyond Boundaries: The Power of Resonance,* in Beyond Boundaries, at 184, 194.

40. See Wikan, at 190.

41. *Id.* at 189.

42. *Id.* at 193.

43. Wikan credits Stanley Tambiah with the term "the maxim of interpretive charity," and Dan Sperber and Deidre Wilson with "the co-operative principle." *Id.* at 193.

44. *Id.* at 207 (emphasis in text).

45. *Id.* at 206.

46. Spiegel Catalog, at 292, 336–37, 352.

Chapter 94

Street Vendors
The Battle over Cultural Interpretation

David R. Diaz

The recent controversy regarding street vending in Los Angeles has become a flash point for racist anti-immigrant sentiment (Martinez, 1991; Moffat, 1991). The underlying issue of street vending is not the most important aspect of this raging debate. The key concern focuses on the future of the city and who will control urban cultural patterning in Los Angeles. Street vending has been conducted throughout the city's history. Vendors have sold various types of products since the city's early history (Martinez, 1991). As this community was transformed into a Latino enclave, the practice of street vending remained a mainstay of everyday life. Vendors, shop owners, and consumers coexisted in a social relationship that viewed each as part of a whole.

When U.S. Cold War policies influenced the civil wars in Central America, Los Angeles became the *de facto* second city of Nicaragua, El Salvador, and other nations. Refugees fleeing persecution entered the city anticipating a certain level of opportunity and job security (Lopez-Garza, 1989). What existed was a region in the initial phase of deindustrialization experiencing a decimation of low-wage jobs. Many immigrants had few options from poverty and low-wage injustice. A number of Central Americans joined immigrant Mexicans and established street vending as a major component of the city's informal economy. The result, by the mid-1980s, was a burgeoning street culture dominated by Latinos—vendors and consumers—which was dramatically transforming the cultural landscape of Los Angeles.

The elite barons of culture and white suburbanites initiated a vehement opposition to the looming transition of urban Los Angeles into a city with a vibrant street culture dominated by bicultural communities (Lopez, 1993). The independent-minded street vendors became the most visible target to those social and economic sectors aghast at the cultural changes occurring in everyday life, changes over which they had minimal control or understanding. Los Angeles became a cultural target of both internal and external critics decrying the transition from a European-dominated society into a culturally diverse city increasingly characterized by a constant street culture that Euro-Americans had abandoned for the suburbs two decades earlier (Rieff, 1991).

The battle to eliminate street vendors is in reality a site of confrontation to regain control over areas that suburbanites had ignored and avoided for years (Moffat, 1991). The downtown establishment, appalled by their apparent lack of control over what was occurring below their high-rise offices, joined in this attempt to reinstitute a suburbanite symbolism to city streets. Why they wanted to regain political control had more to do with their revulsion to a new spatial transformation manifested in street culture than any challenge to the independent and free-market spirit of the street vendors (Beyette, 1990). Thus, the real battle over spatial relations in Los Angeles and other cities is over who will control new cultural patterns and new cultural groups.

The active intervention of a mass of social actors connected to everyday space is being characterized as a social phenomenon to be feared and eliminated (Martinez, 1991). The power elite have spent a small fortune in a foolish assumption that money can buy street culture and a civic center filled with active street users. When ethnically diverse daily consumers of space appeared and the streets were reincarnated as essential components of an ethnically diverse city, revisionists raged with disdain. The "wrong people" were transforming the streets. The massive redevelopment subsidies had failed to reinvent a middle-class urban civic center. Something had to be done to reverse the flow of users of space (predominantly Latino, Asian, and African American) in defense of middle-class cultural symbolism and economic power. When the street vendors ask, "What's wrong with selling *fruta, aguas, maize* or a *paleta?*" the answer is, "Nothing is wrong with the concept, it's just all those people" who are constantly on the street creating the demand. The street vendors have become the target of a strategy designed to reverse the infusion of a new and vibrant street culture that is controlled by everyday people of the city. Street vending is not a problem; people walking is not a problem. The racialization of the people involved in this liberating activity is at the crux of the controversy.

Crossroads of Everyday Space

Street culture is free. There is no price of admission. Yet, the elites of the city view free space in sterile economic terms and how daily consumers fit a socioeconomic profile conforming to a specified function of the built environment (Gottdiener, 1986). In downtown Los Angeles, the vertical expansion of the financial center was programmed to be mirrored by a horizontal expansion of white-collar professionals. Built on an assumption that function follows form, the city invested millions to attract steel and glass towers, with an expectation that it would be followed by people with high expendable incomes. Tax subsidies and super economic zones were established in part to "recreate" urban culture. Los Angeles's self-image was deficient in comparison to London, New York, Paris, and Tokyo. There was a perceived dearth of people and activity in the financial district. When this economic catalyst worked to attract a new immigrant populace during the 1980s, the streets of the city were transformed. However, bicultural communities tended to patronize neighborhood space and carefree zones of daily consumption. East Los Angeles, Westlake, Chinatown, Santee Alley in the garment district, and selected suburban thoroughfares patronized by Latinos assumed a character reflective of this emerging street culture. The city's streets became a site of experimentation in which new interpretations of old world traditions of street culture reconstructed daily life (Roseman & Vigil, 1993). While ethnic communities engaged in liberating social public space, an "alienated" car culture hurriedly rolled up its collective windows and stepped on the gas pedal.

The social landscape of the city is in the process of a permanent transformation directed by bicultural communities intent on retaining patterns of cultural interaction transferred from previous life experiences onto the city's existing social milieu. The "Crossroads of Space" (Rieff, 1991) are being redefined through the simple act of walking as a major form of daily commerce and social networking. In a real sense, "the street and the demonstration (are the) primary symbols of modern life" (Berman, 1984). The irony of this renewed period of the social reconstruction of spatial relations is that the physical form of Los Angeles is horribly ill-suited for a high level of pedestrian activity. Sidewalks are narrow; there are few public plazas; the city caters to cars, not people; the city's elite has destroyed much public park space; and open air cafes are a nouveau (1980s) development. In spite of this city's regressive history of planning for concrete and steel in abeyance of the needs of daily social actors, the streets have come alive in the last ten years. In diverse geographic districts, urban and suburban, the use of public space has dramatically intensified. The rebirth of the historic Broadway commercial zone is among the most notable examples of how immigrant Latinos have reintroduced an active street culture into a built environment which had remained obdurate since the 1920s and 1930s (Roseman & Vigil, 1993). The reappropriation of public space by bicultural communities now is the most influential signifier of urban culture in this city.

In this era of new interpretations of older cultural traditions, the reconstruction of a new civic culture has refocused attention on who is appropriating and reappropriating urban space. The focus on *who* are the users of public space—not the fact that use of this space is a desirable attribute or characteristic—has become the political battleground of the l990s. What is occurring is a desperate attempt to superimpose a revisionist value system, reflective of a disappeared past, designed to restore an illusionary cultural hegemony (Lefebvre, 1991a; de Certeau, 1984, p. 201). Instead of celebrating users of space, the dominant culture decries the loss of cultural control and their lack of power to force-feed a narrow interpretation of culture into an economically driven self-concept of daily social life.

Having abandoned the inner city and ignored its decline for decades, a nervous middle class is demanding a revisionist reincarnation of its value system to be superimposed on bicultural neighborhoods (McDonnell & Jacobs, 1993). Apparently, economic and political hegemony has proven an insufficient advantage in the contest over the future of cultural and spatial relations. The raging controversy concerning immigrants is not solely how laws should be interpreted or enforced, it is how to limit the infusion of different cultural symbols and practices that influence public space and everyday life. . . .

Social transformation is inherently connected to the creative capacity of everyday life, language, and space which serve to reconstruct social relations (Lefebvre, 1991b). Within this framework, reappropriation of space is understood as a fundamental challenge to the cultural hegemony of Euro-Americans. Space is political; it is not a scientific object removed from ideology or politics; it has always been political and strategic (Lefebvre, 1976). The influence of bicultural communities on urban culture extends into both the economic and political arenas. In the midst of contemporary controversy and racist reactions against bicultural communities, new actors and new struggles are taking shape in which social conflicts and cultural achievements are reconstructing social life (Touraine, 1981). A reflected view from the barrio to the high rises crystallizes the basic contention over who is really experiencing everyday life.

At the level of everyday street culture, a new urban culture has already arrived. What has not been resolved is the avoidance and detachment from daily life of a middle-class ideology based on social consumption in which the consumer is the one who is consumed (Lefebvre, 1971). Active street culture directly contradicts this middle-class social construction of urban space. Bicultural communities, in reestablishing the streets as the focus of everyday life, are returning a basic political and social function to social actors, and are thereby gaining control over their lives.

"Casual time . . . is the actual discourse of the city" (de Certeau, 1984, p. 203). Indeterminate interaction within places and random social practices articulate the fabric of community. Space, in a growing number of neighborhoods dominated by bicultural actors, is becoming liberated on a human scale and in celebration of community. Walking down the street, touching people, seeing neighbors, feeling communal space is a liberating experience. That's an alienating thought in a "postmodern" society.

REFERENCES

Berman, M. (1984). "The signs and the street." *New Left Review* (144) (March–April).
Beyette, B. (1990). "Vendors vs. the law." *Los Angeles Times* (June 27).
de Certeau, M. (1984). *The practice of everyday life.* Berkeley: University of California Press.
Gottdiener, M. (1986). "Culture, ideology, and the sign of the city," in M. Gottdiener & A. P. Lagopoulous (eds.), *The city and the sign.* New York: Columbia University Press.
Lefebvre, H. (1971). *Everyday life in the modern world.* London: Allen Lane.
———. (1976). "Reflections on the politics of space." *Antipode, 8*(2).
———. (1991a). *Critique of everyday life.* London: Verso.
———. (1991b). *The production of space.* Oxford, Eng.: Basil Blackwell.
Lopez, R. J. (1993). "Pushcart power." *Los Angeles Times* (July 25).
Lopez-Garza, M. (1989). "Immigration and economic restructuring: Introduction." *California Sociologist, 12*(2).
Martinez, R. (1991). "Sidewalk wars: Why LA's street vendors won't be swept away." *LA Weekly* (December 6–12).

McDonnell, P. J. & P. Jacobs. (1993). "FAIR at forefront of push to reduce immigration." *Los Angeles Times* (November 24).

Moffat, S. (1991). "Vendors bring new way of life to Los Angeles streets." *Los Angeles Times* (December 25).

Rieff, D. (1991). *Los Angeles: Capital of the third world*. New York: Simon and Schuster.

Roseman, C. C. & J. D. Vigil. (1993). "From Broadway to Latinoway." *Places, 8*(3).

Touraine, A. (1981). *The voice and the eye*. Cambridge, Mass.: Cambridge University Press.

From the Editors
Issues and Comments

What borders are you most familiar with in your life? Are they physical ones? Linguistic? Cultural? Something else?

When you visualize national borders, are they places of barbed wire and machine guns, or ones where trade and cultural exchange flourish?

Does border-crossing in the cultural sense encourage understanding of outsider groups, or does it simply allow the dominant culture to coopt and redefine the outsider experience?

Are borders dangerous places, "open wounds"?

Is everyone a border person in the sense of having an identity criss-crossed by many strands, such as race, ethnicity, age, class, financial status, and sexual orientation? Are borders the only place where you can be yourself—that is, be represented fully and understood?

What borders do you routinely cross? Is the crossing an empowering, "voice-finding" experience or a risky, self-exposing one?

Do concepts, words, meanings—categories of all kinds—always shade off into each other, like a border region (e.g., southern Texas), or do some have well-defined boundaries, like the one between your property and that of your neighbor?

Suggested Readings

Across Boundaries: Transborder Interaction in Comparative Perspective, edited by Oscar J. Martinez. El Paso: Texas Western Press and the Center for Inter-American and Border Studies, University of Texas at El Paso, 1986.

Behar, Ruth. *Translated Woman: Crossing the Border with Esperanza's Story.* Boston: Beacon Press, 1993.

Breaking Boundaries: Latina Writing and Critical Readings, edited by Asunción Horno-Delgado et al. Amherst: University of Massachusetts Press, 1989.

Cheyfitz, Eric. *The Poetics of Imperialism: Translation and Colonization from the Tempest to Tarzan.* Expanded ed. Philadelphia: University of Pennsylvania Press, 1991.

Clifford, James. *The Predicament of Culture: Twentieth-Century Ethnography, Literature, and Art.* Cambridge, Mass.: Harvard University Press, 1988.

Criticism in the Borderlands: Studies in Chicano Literature, Culture, and Ideology, edited by Héctor Calderón and José David Saldívar. Durham, N.C.: Duke University Press, 1991.

Cunningham, Clark D. "The Lawyer as Translator, Representation as Text: Towards an Ethnography of Legal Discourse." 77 *Cornell Law Review* 1298 (1992).

Cypess, Sandra Messinger. *La Malinche in Mexican Literature: From History to Myth.* Austin: University of Texas Press, 1991.

Fernandez Retamar, Roberto. "Caliban: Notes toward a Discussion of Culture in Our America." *Massachusetts Review* 15, nos. 1–2 (Winter-Spring 1974): 7–72.

Gilkerson, Christopher P. "Poverty Law Narratives: The Critical Practice and Theory of Receiving and Translating Client Stories." 43 *Hastings Law Journal* 861 (1992).

Gómez-Peña, Guillermo. *The New World Border: Prophecies, Poems, and Loqueras for the End of the Century.* San Francisco: City Lights, 1996.

———. *Warrior for Gringostroika: Essays, Performance Texts, and Poetry.* St. Paul, Minn.: Graywolf Press, 1993.

Gordon, Deborah. "Writing Culture, Writing Feminism: The Poetics and Politics of Experimental Ethnography." *Inscriptions,* nos. 3–4, 1988.

Gutierrez-Jones, Carl. *Rethinking the Borderlands: Between Chicano Culture and Legal Discourse.* Berkeley: University of California Press, 1995.

Harris, Charles H., III, and Louis R. Sadler. *The Border and the Revolution.* Las Cruces: New Mexico Center for Latin American Studies/Joint Border Research Institute, New Mexico State University, 1988.

Herrmann, Claudine. *The Tongue Snatchers,* translated by Nancy Kline. Lincoln: University of Nebraska Press, 1989.

Hicks, D. Emily. *Border Writing: The Multidimensional Text.* Minneapolis: University of Minnesota Press, 1991.

Hinojosa, Gilberto Miguel. *A Borderlands Town in Transition: Laredo, Texas, 1755–1870.* College Station: Texas A & M University Press, 1983.

Hoffman, Eva. *Lost in Translation: A Life in a New Language.* New York: E. P. Dutton, 1989.

Karttunen, Frances. *Between Worlds: Interpreters, Guides and Survivors.* New Brunswick, N.J.: Rutgers University Press, 1994.

Lessig, Lawrence. "Fidelity in Translation." 71 *Texas Law Review* 1165 (1993).

Martinez, Oscar J. *Border People: Life and Society in the U.S.-Mexico Borderlands.* Tucson: University of Arizona Press, 1994.

———. *Troublesome Border.* Tuscon: University of Arizona Press, 1988.

McLaren, Peter. "Border Disputes: Multicultural Narrative, Identity Formation, and Critical Pedagogy in Postmodern America." In *Naming Silenced Lives: Personal Narratives and the Process of Educational Change,* edited by Daniel McLaughlin and William G. Tierney, 201. New York: Routledge, 1993.

———. *Critical Pedagogy and Predatory Culture: Oppositional Politics in a Postmodern Era.* New York: Routledge, 1995.

Metz, Leon Claire. *Border: The U.S.-Mexico Line.* El Paso: Mangan Books, 1989.

Palsson, Gisli. "Introduction: Beyond Boundaries." In *Beyond Boundaries: Understanding, Translation and Anthropological Discourse,* edited by Gisli Palsson. Oxford, Eng.: Berg, 1993.

Salazar, Ruben. *Border Correspondent: Selected Writings, 1955–1970,* edited by Mario T. García. Berkeley: University of California Press, 1995.

Todorov, Tzvetan. *The Conquest of America: The Question of the Other.* New York: Harper & Row, 1982.

U.S.-Mexico Borderlands: Historical and Contemporary Perspectives, edited by Oscar J. Martinez. Wilmington, Del.: Scholarly Resources, 1996.

Wikan, Unni. "Beyond Boundaries: The Power of Resonance." In *Beyond Boundaries: Understanding, Translation and Anthropological Discourse,* edited by Gisli Palsson. Oxford, Eng.: Berg, 1993.

Williams, Sarah. "Abjection and Anthropological Praxis." *Anthropological Quarterly* 66 (1993): 67

Writing Culture: The Poetics and Politics of Ethnography, edited by James Clifford and George Marcus. Berkeley: University of California Press, 1986.

Bibliography

Abalos, David T. *Latinos in the United States: The Sacred and the Political.* Notre Dame: University of Notre Dame Press, 1986.

Acosta, Oscar "Zeta." *The Autobiography of a Brown Buffalo.* 2d ed. New York: Vintage, 1989.

———. *The Revolt of the Cockroach People.* 2d ed. New York: Vintage, 1989.

———. *The Uncollected Works,* edited by Ilan Stavans. Houston: Arte Publico Press, 1996.

Across Boundaries: Transborder Interaction in Comparative Perspective, edited by Oscar J. Martinez. El Paso: Texas Western Press and the Center for Inter-American and Border Studies, University of Texas at El Paso, 1986.

Acuña, Rodolfo F. *Anything but Mexican: Chicanos in Contemporary Los Angeles.* London: Verso, 1996.

———. *A Community under Siege: A Chronicle of Chicanos East of the Los Angeles River 1945–1975.* Los Angeles: Chicano Studies Research Center, University of California at Los Angeles, 1984.

———. *Occupied America: A History of Chicanos.* 3rd ed. New York: Harper & Row, 1988.

———. *Occupied America: The Chicano's Struggle Toward Liberation.* San Francisco: Canfield Press, 1970.

Allsup, Carl. *The American G.I. Forum: Origins and Evolution.* University of Texas Center for Mexican American Studies Monograph, no. 6. Austin: University of Texas Press, 1982.

Almaguer, Tomás. *Racial Fault Lines: The Historical Origins of White Supremacy in California.* Berkeley: University of California Press, 1994.

Alvarez, Julia. *How the García Girls Lost Their Accents.* Chapel Hill, N.C.: Algonquin Books, 1991.

American Committee for the Protection of the Foreign Born. *Our Badge of Infamy: A Petition to the United Nations on the Treatment of the Mexican Immigrant.* N.p., 1959. Reprinted in *The Mexican American and the Law,* edited by Carlos Cortes. New York: Arno Press, 1974.

American G.I. Forum of Texas and Texas State Federation of Labor. *What Price Wetbacks?* Austin: G.I. Forum of Texas, 1954. Reprinted in *Mexican Migration to the United States,* edited by Carlos Cortes. New York: Arno Press, 1976.

Anaya, Rudolfo A. *Heart of Aztlán.* Berkeley: Justa Publications, 1976.

Anzaldúa, Gloria. *Borderlands/La Frontera: The New Mestiza.* San Francisco: Spinsters/Aunt Lute, 1987.

Arce, Carlos H., et al. "Phenotype and Life Chances among Chicanos." *Hispanic Journal of Behavioral Science* 9 (1987): 19.

Arce, Carlos H., and Aida Hurtado. "Mexicans, Chicanos, Mexican Americans, or Pochos . . . Que Somos? The Impact of Language and Nativity on Ethnic Labeling." *Aztlán: A Journal of Chicano Studies* 17 (1987): 103–30.

Arriola, Elvia R. "Faeries, Marimachas, Queens and Lezzies: The Construction of Homosexuality before the 1969 Stonewall Riots." 5 *Columbia Journal of Gender and Law* 33 (1995).

———. "Gendered Inequality: Lesbians, Gays, and Feminist Legal Theory." 9 *Berkeley Women's Law Journal* 103 (1994).

———. "LatCrit Theory, International Human Rights, Popular Culture, and the Faces of Despair in INS Raids." 28 *University of Miami Inter-American Law Review* 245 (1997).

———. "'What's the Big Deal?' Women in New York City Construction Industry and Sexual Harassment Law, 1970–1985." 22 *Columbia Human Rights Law Review* 21 (1990).

Austin, Regina, and Michael Schill. "Black, Brown, Poor and Poisoned: Minority Grassroots Environmentalism and the Quest for Eco-Justice." 1 *Kansas Journal of Law and Public Policy* 69 (1991).

Aztlán: An Anthology of Mexican American Literature, edited by Luis Valdez and Stan Steiner. New York: Knopf, 1972.

Aztlán: Essays on the Chicano Homeland, edited by Rudolfo A. Anaya and Francisco A. Lomeli. Albuquerque: Academia/El Norte Publications, 1989.

Balderrama, Francisco E. *In Defense of La Raza: The Los Angeles Mexican Consulate and the Mexican Community, 1929 to 1936*. Tucson: University of Arizona Press, 1982.

Balderrama, Francisco E., and Raymond Rodriguez. *Decade of Betrayal: Mexican Repatriation in the 1930s*. Albuquerque: University of New Mexico Press, 1995.

Baron, Denis. *The English-Only Question: An Official Language for Americans?* New Haven: Yale University Press, 1990.

Baron, Jane B. "Resistance to Stories." 67 *Southern California Law Review* 255 (1994).

Barrera, Mario. *Beyond Aztlán: Ethnic Autonomy in Comparative Perspective*. New York: Praeger, 1988.

———. "The Historical Evolution of Chicano Ethnic Goals: A Bibliographic Essay." *Sage Race Relations Abstracts* 10 (February 1985): 1–48.

———. *Race and Class in the Southwest: A Theory of Racial Inequality*. Notre Dame: University of Notre Dame Press, 1979.

Barrera, Mario, Carlos Muñoz, Jr., and Charles Ornelas. "The Barrio as an Internal Colony." In *People and Politics in Urban Society*, edited by Harlan Hahn, 465–98. Urban Affairs Annual Reviews, no. 6. Beverly Hills: Sage Publications, 1972.

Barrio, Raymond. *The Plum Pickers*. Sunnyvale, Calif.: Ventura Press, 1969.

Bean, Frank D., and Marta Tienda. *The Hispanic Population of the United States*. New York: Russell Sage Foundation, 1987.

Behar, Ruth. *Translated Woman: Crossing the Border with Esperanza's Story*. Boston: Beacon Press, 1993.

Bender, Steven W. "Consumer Protection for Latinos: Overcoming Language Fraud and English-Only in the Marketplace." 45 *American University Law Review* 1027 (1996).

Bennett, David H. *The Party of Fear: From Nativist Movements to the New Right in American History*. Chapel Hill: University of North Carolina Press, 1988.

Berg, Charles Ramírez. "Images and Counterimages of the Hispanic in Hollywood." *Tonantzin* 6 (November 1988): 12–13.

———. "Immigrants, Aliens, and Extraterrestrials: Science Fiction's Alien 'Other' as (among Other Things) New Hispanic Imagery." *CineAction!* 18 (Fall 1989): 3–17.

———. "Stereotyping in Films in General and of Hispanics in Particular." *Howard Journal of Communications* 2 (Summer 1990): 286–300.

Berk-Seligson, Susan. *The Bilingual Courtroom: Court Interpreters in the Judicial Process.* Chicago: University of Chicago Press, 1990.

———. "The Importance of Linguistics in Court Interpreting." 2 *La Raza Law Journal* 14 (1988).

Between Borders: Essays on Mexicana/Chicana History, edited by Adelaida R. Del Castillo. Encino, Calif.: Floricanto Press, 1990.

Beyond Stereotypes: The Critical Analysis of Chicana Literature, edited by María Herrera-Sobek. Binghamton, N.Y.: Bilingual Press, 1985.

Blacks, Latinos, and Asians in Urban America: Status and Prospects for Politics and Activism, edited by James Jennings. Westport, Conn.: Praeger, 1994.

Blackwelder, Julia Kirk. *Women of the Depression: Caste and Culture in San Antonio, 1929–1939.* College Station: Texas A & M University Press, 1984.

Blauner, Robert. *Racial Oppression in America.* New York: Harper & Row, 1972.

Bonilla-Santiago, Gloria. *Breaking Ground and Barriers: Hispanic Women Developing Effective Leadership.* San Diego: Marin Publications, 1992.

Bosniak, Linda S. "Exclusion and Membership: The Dual Identity of the Undocumented Worker under United States Law." 1988 *Wisconsin Law Review* 955.

———. "Opposing Prop. 187: Undocumented Immigrants and the National Imagination." 28 *Connecticut Law Review* 555 (1996).

Boswell, Richard A. "Restrictions on Non-Citizens' Access to Public Benefits: Flawed Premise, Unnecessary Response." 42 *UCLA Law Review* 1475 (1995).

Bracamonte, José A. "Foreword: Minority Critiques of the Critical Legal Studies Movement." 22 *Harvard Civil Rights–Civil Liberties Law Review* 297 (1987).

———. "The National Labor Relations Act and Undocumented Workers: The De-Alienation of American Labor." 21 *San Diego Law Review* 29 (1983).

Breaking Boundaries: Latina Writing and Critical Readings, edited by Asunción Horno-Delgado et al. Amherst: University of Massachusetts Press, 1989.

Brest, Paul, and Miranda Oshige. "Affirmative Action for Whom?" 47 *Stanford Law Review* 855 (1995).

Brimelow, Peter. *Alien Nation: Common Sense about America's Immigration Disaster.* New York: Random House, 1995.

Bruce-Novoa, Juan. *Retrospace: Collected Essays on Chicano Literature, Theory and History.* Houston: Arte Publico Press, 1990.

Building with Our Hands: New Directions in Chicana Studies, edited by Adela de la Torre and Beatriz M. Pesquera. Berkeley: University of California Press, 1993.

Burciaga, José Antonio. *Drink Cultura: Chicanismo.* Santa Barbara, Calif.: Joshua Odell Editions, 1993.

Butler, R. E. "Rusty." *On Creating a Hispanic America: A Nation within a Nation?* Washington, D.C.: Council for Inter-American Security, 1985.

Cabranes, José A. "Citizenship and the American Empire." 127 *University of Pennsylvania Law Review* 391 (1978).

Calavita, Kitty. *Inside the State: The Bracero Program, Immigration, and the I.N.S.* New York: Routledge, 1992.

Calderón, José. "'Hispanic' and 'Latino': The Viability of Categories for Panethnic Unity." *Latin American Perspectives* 19 (Fall 1992): 37–44.

Califa, Antonio J. "Declaring English the Official Language: Prejudice Spoken Here." 24 *Harvard Civil Rights–Civil Liberties Law Review* 293 (1989).

Camarillo, Albert M. *Chicanos in a Changing Society: From Mexican Pueblos to American Barrios in Santa Barbara and Southern California, 1848–1930.* Cambridge, Mass.: Harvard University Press, 1979.

———. *Chicanos in California: A History of Mexican Americans in California.* San Francisco: Boyd & Fraser Publishing Co., 1984.

———. *Latinos in the United States: A Historical Bibliography.* Santa Barbara, Calif.: ABC-Clio, 1986.

Cameron, Christopher David Ruiz. "How the Garcia Cousins Lost Their Accents: Understanding the Language of Title VII Decisions Approving Speak-English-Only Rules as the Product of Racial Dualism, Latino Invisibility, and Legal Indeterminacy." 85 *California Law Review* (1998).

Cardoso, Lawrence A. *Mexican Emigration to the United States, 1897–1931.* Tucson: University of Arizona Press, 1980.

Carens, Joseph H. "Aliens and Citizens: The Case for Open Borders." *Review of Politics* 49 (1987): 251

Carleton, Don E. *Red Scare! Right Wing Hysteria, Fifties Fanaticism, and Their Legacy in Texas.* Austin: Texas Monthly Press, 1985.

Carrasco, Enrique R. "Collective Recognition as a Communitarian Device: Or, Of Course We Want to Be Role Models!" 9 *La Raza Law Journal* 81 (1996).

Castillo, Ana. *The Mixquiahuala Letters.* Binghamton, N.Y.: Bilingual Review Press, 1986.

Cervantes, Lorna Dee. *Emplumada.* Pittsburgh: University of Pittsburgh Press, 1981.

Chabram-Dernersesian, Angie. "I Throw Punches for My Race, but I Don't Want to Be a Man: Writing Us—Chica-nos (Girl Us)/Chicanas—into the Movement Script." In *Cultural Studies,* edited by Lawrence Grossberg, Cary Nelson, and Paula Treichler, 81. New York: Routledge, 1992.

Chavez, Cesar. "The California Farm Workers' Struggle." *Black Scholar* 7 (June 1976): 16–19.

Chavez, John. *The Lost Land: The Chicano Image of the Southwest.* Albuquerque: University of New Mexico Press, 1984.

Chavez, Leo R. "The Power of the Imagined Community: The Settlement of Undocumented Mexicans and Central Americans in the United States." *American Anthropologist* 96 (1994): 52

———. "Settlers and Sojourners: The Case of Mexicans in the United States." *Human Organization* 47 (1988): 95

———. *Shadowed Lives: Undocumented Immigrants in American Society.* 2d ed. Fort Worth: Harcourt Brace, 1998.

Chavez, Linda. *Out of the Barrio: Toward a New Politics of Hispanic Assimilation.* New York: Basic Books, 1991.

Cherena Pacheco, Yvonne M. "Latino Surnames: Formal and Informal Forces in the United States Affecting the Retention and Use of the Maternal Surname." 18 *Thurgood Marshall Law Review* 1 (1992).

Cheyfitz, Eric. *The Poetics of Imperialism: Translation and Colonization from the Tempest to Tarzan.* Expanded ed. Philadelphia: University of Pennsylvania Press, 1991.

Chicana Creativity and Criticism: New Frontiers in American Literature, edited by María Herrera-Sobek and Helena María Viramontes. Rev. ed. Albuquerque: University of New Mexico Press, 1996.

Chicana Critical Issues, edited by Norma Alarcon et al. Berkeley: Third Woman Press, 1993.

Chicana Lesbians: The Girls Our Mothers Warned Us About, edited by Carla Trujillo. Berkeley: Third Woman Press, 1991.

Chicana Voices: Intersections of Class, Race, and Gender, edited by Teresa Cordova et al. Austin: Center for Mexican American Studies, University of Texas, 1990.

Chicana (W)rites on Word and Film, edited by María Herrera-Sobek and Helena María Viramontes. Berkeley: Third Woman Press, 1995.

Chicanas in the 80's: Unsettled Issues, edited by Mujers en Marcha. Berkeley: Chicano Studies Library Publications Unit, University of California, 1983.

Chicanas/Chicanos at the Crossroads: Social, Economic, and Political Change, edited by David R. Maciel and Isidro D. Ortiz. Tucson: University of Arizona Press, 1996.

Chicano: The Evolution of a People, compiled by Renato Rosaldo, Robert A. Calvert, and Gustav L. Seligmann, Jr. 2d ed. Malabar, Fla.: Krieger, 1982.

Chicano Cinema: Research, Review, and Resources, edited by Gary D. Keller. Binghamton, N.Y.: Bilingual Review/Bilingual Press, 1985.

Chicanos and Film: Representation and Resistance, edited by Chon A. Noriega. Minneapolis, University of Minnesota Press, 1992.

Clark, Juan M. *The 1980 Mariel Exodus: An Analysis and Prospect.* Washington, D.C.: Council for Inter-American Security, 1981.

Clifford, James. *The Predicament of Culture: Twentieth-Century Ethnography, Literature, and Art.* Cambridge, Mass.: Harvard University Press, 1988.

Clopper, J. C. "Journal of J. C. Clopper, 1828." *Southwestern Historical Quarterly* 13 (July 1909): 44–80.

Coles, Robert. *The Old Ones of New Mexico.* With photographs by Alex Harris. Rev. ed. Albuquerque: University of New Mexico Press, 1975.

Colker, Ruth. *Hybrid: Bisexuals, Multiracials, and Other Misfits under American Law.* New York: New York University Press, 1996.

Colloquium: "International Law, Human Rights, and LatCrit Theory." 28 *University of Miami Inter-American Law Review* 177 (1997).

Colloquium: "LatCrit Theory: Naming and Launching a New Discourse of Critical Legal Scholarship." 2 *Harvard Latino Law Review* 1 (1998).

Colloquium: "Representing Latina/o Communities: Critical Race Theory and Practice." 9 *La Raza Law Journal* 1 (1996).

Community Research Associates. *Undocumented Immigrants: Their Impact on the County of San Diego.* San Diego: Community Research Associates, Inc., for the County of San Diego, 1980.

Compañeras: Latina Lesbians, an Anthology, edited by Juanita Ramos. New York: Routledge, 1994.

Conover, Ted. *Coyotes: A Journey through the Secret World of America's Illegal Aliens.* New York: Vintage, 1987.

Controlling Immigration: A Global Perspective, edited by Wayne A. Cornelius, Philip L. Martin, and James F. Hollifield. Stanford: Stanford University Press, 1994.

Cornelius, Wayne A. *America in the Era of Limits: Migrants, Nativists, and the Future of U.S.-Mexican Relations.* La Jolla: Center for U.S.-Mexican Studies, University of California, San Diego, 1982.

———. *The Future of Mexican Immigrants in California: A New Perspective for Public Policy.* La Jolla: Program in United States-Mexican Studies, University of California, San Diego, 1981.

A Cotton Picker Finds Justice! The Saga of the Hernandez Case, edited by Ruben Munguia. N.p., 1954.

Crawford, James. *Bilingual Education: History, Politics, Theory and Practice.* 2d ed. Los Angeles: Bilingual Educational Services, 1991.

———. *Hold Your Tongue: Bilingualism and the Politics of "English Only."* Reading, Mass.: Addison-Wesley, 1992.

Criticism in the Borderlands: Studies in Chicano Literature, Culture, and Ideology, edited by Héctor Calderón and José David Saldívar. Durham, N.C.: Duke University Press, 1991.

Cunningham, Clark D. "The Lawyer as Translator, Representation as Text: Towards an Ethnography of Legal Discourse." 77 *Cornell Law Review* 1298 (1992).

Cypess, Sandra Messinger. *La Malinche in Mexican Literature: From History to Myth.* Austin: University of Texas Press, 1991.

Dana, Richard Henry. *Two Years before the Mast.* Boston: Houghton Mifflin, 1911.

Daniel, Cletus E. *Bitter Harvest: A History of California Farm Workers, 1870–1941.* Ithaca, N.Y.: Cornell University Press, 1981.

———. *Chicano Workers and the Politics of Fairness: The FEPC in the Southwest, 1941–1945.* Austin: University of Texas Press, 1991.

Darder, Antonia. "The Politics of Biculturalism: Culture and Difference in the Formation of *Warriors for Gringostroika* and *The New Mestizas.*" In *Culture and Difference: Critical Perspectives on the Bicultural Experience in the United States,* edited by Antonia Darder, 1–20. New York: Bergin & Garvey, 1995.

Davis, Adrienne D. "Identity Notes Part One: Playing in the Light." 45 *American University Law Review* 695 (1996).

Davis, Marilyn. *Mexican Voices/American Dreams: An Oral History of Mexican Immigration to the United States.* New York: Henry Holt, 1990.

Davis, Mike. *City of Quartz: Excavating the Future in Los Angeles.* London: Verso, 1992.

de la Garza, Rodolfo O. *Chicano Elite Perceptions of the Undocumented Worker: An Empirical Analysis.* Working Papers in U.S.-Mexican Studies, no. 31. La Jolla: Center for U.S.-Mexican Studies, University of California, San Diego, 1981.

de la Garza, Rodolfo O., et al. *Latino Voices: Mexican, Puerto Rican and Cuban Perspectives on American Politics.* Boulder, Colo.: Westview Press, 1992.

De León, Arnoldo. *Ethnicity in the Sunbelt: A History of Mexican Americans in Houston.* Houston: University of Houston Press, 1989.

———. *The Tejano Community, 1836–1900.* Albuquerque: University of New Mexico Press, 1982.

———. *They Called Them Greasers: Anglo Attitudes toward Mexicans in Texas, 1821–1900.* Austin: University of Texas Press, 1983.

De León, Arnoldo, and Kenneth L. Stewart. *Tejanos and the Numbers Game: A Socio-Historical Interpretation from the Federal Censuses, 1850–1900.* Albuquerque: University of New Mexico Press, 1989.

Delgado, Richard. "Affirmative Action as a Majoritarian Device: Or, Do You Really Want to Be a Role Model?" 89 *Michigan Law Review* 1222 (1991).

———. "Brewer's Plea: Critical Thoughts on Common Cause." 44 *Vanderbilt Law Review* 1 (1991).

———. "Campus Antiracism Rules: Constitutional Narratives in Collision." 85 *Northwestern University Law Review* 343 (1991).

———. *The Coming Race War? And Other Apocalyptic Tales after Affirmative Action and Welfare.* New York: New York University Press, 1996.

———. "The Ethereal Scholar: Does Critical Legal Studies Have What Minorities Want?" 22 *Harvard Civil Rights-Civil Liberties Law Review* 301 (1987).

———. "The Imperial Scholar: Reflections on a Review of Civil Rights Literature." 132 *University of Pennsylvania Law Review* 561 (1984).

———. "The Imperial Scholar Revisited: How to Marginalize Outsider Writing, Ten Years Later." 140 *University of Pennsylvania Law Review* 1349 (1992).

———. "Left-Right Parallels in Recent Writing about Race." 91 *Columbia Law Review* 1547 (1991).

———. "Minority Law Professors' Lives: The Bell-Delgado Survey." 24 *Harvard Civil Rights-Civil Liberties Law Review* 349 (1989).

———. "Recasting the American Race Problem." 79 *California Law Review* 1389 (1991).

———. *The Rodrigo Chronicles: Conversations about America and Race.* New York: New York University Press, 1995.

———. "Rodrigo's Chronicle." 101 *Yale Law Journal* 1357 (1992).

———. "Rodrigo's Fifteenth Chronicle: Racial Mixture, Latino-Critical Scholarship, and the Black-White Binary." 75 *Texas Law Review* 1181 (1997).

———. "Rodrigo's Fourteenth Chronicle: American Apocalypse." 32 *Harvard Civil Rights–Civil Liberties Law Review* 275 (1997).

———. "Rodrigo's Sixth Chronicle: Intersections, Essences and the Dilemma of Social Reform." 68 *New York University Law Review* 639 (1993).

———. "Rodrigo's Twelfth Chronicle: The Problem of the Shanty." 85 *Georgetown Law Journal* 667 (1997).

———. "When a Story Is Just a Story: Does Voice Really Matter?" 76 *Virginia Law Review* 95 (1990).

———. "Words That Wound: A Tort Action for Racial Insults, Epithets, and Name-Calling." 17 *Harvard Civil Rights–Civil Liberties Law Review* 133 (1982).

Delgado, Richard, and Vicky Palacios. "Mexican Americans as a Legally Cognizable Class under Rule 23 and the Equal Protection Clause." 50 *Notre Dame Lawyer* 393 (1975).

Delgado, Richard, and Jean Stefancic. "Images of the Outsider in American Law and Culture: Can Free Expression Remedy Systemic Social Ills?" 77 *Cornell Law Review* 1258 (1992).

———. "Norms and Narratives: Can Judges Avoid Serious Moral Error?" 69 *Texas Law Review* 1929 (1991).

Delpar, Helen. "Mexico, the MPPDA, and Derogatory Films, 1922–1926." *Journal of Popular Film and Television* 12 (Spring 1984): 34–41.

Deutsch, Sarah. *No Separate Refuge: Culture, Class, and Gender on an Anglo-Hispanic Frontier in the American Southwest, 1880–1940.* New York: Oxford University Press, 1987.

Diaz-Cotto, Juanita. *Gender, Ethnicity, and the State: Latina and Latino Prison Politics.* Albany: State University of New York Press, 1996.

"Directive No. 15, Race and Ethnic Standards for Federal Statistics and Administrative Reporting." 43 *Federal Register* 19,260. Washington, D.C.: National Archives and Records Administration, 1978.

Divine, Robert A. *American Immigration Policy, 1924–1952.* New Haven: Yale University Press, 1957.

Dossick, Jesse J. *Cuba, Cubans, and Cuban-Americans, 1902–1991: A Bibliography.* Coral Gables, Fla.: North-South Center, University of Miami, 1992.

Dunn, Timothy J. *The Militarization of the U.S.-Mexican Border, 1978–1992: Low-Intensity Conflict Doctrine Comes Home.* Austin: CMAS Books, University of Texas, 1996.

Durkee, Ellen. "Special Problems of Custody for Unaccompanied Refugee Children in the United States." In *Michigan Yearbook of International Legal Studies* 203 (1982).

Espinoza, Leslie G. "The LSAT: Narrative and Bias." 1 *American University Journal of Gender and Law* 121 (1993).

———. "Masks and Other Disguises: Exposing Legal Academia." 103 *Harvard Law Review* 1878 (1990).

———. "Multi-Identity: Community and Culture," 2 *Virginia Journal of Social Policy and Law* 23 (1994).

Ethnic Identity: Formation and Transformation among Hispanics and Other Minorities, edited by Martha E. Bernal and George P. Knight. Albany: State University of New York, 1993.

Ethnicity: Theory and Experience, edited by Nathan Glazer and Daniel Moynihan. Cambridge, Mass.: Harvard University Press, 1975.

Fan, Stephen Shie-Wei. "Immigration Law and the Promise of Critical Race Theory: Opening the Academy to the Voices of Aliens and Immigrants." 97 *Columbia Law Review* 1202 (1997).

Farber, Daniel A., and Suzanna Sherry. "Telling Stories out of School: An Essay on Legal Narratives." 45 *Stanford Law Review* 807 (1993).

Farnham, Thomas Jefferson. *Life, Adventures, and Travel in California*. New York: Nafis & Cornish, 1847.

Fernandez, Carlos A. "La Raza and the Melting Pot: A Comparative Look at Multiethnicity." In *Racially Mixed People in America*, edited by Maria P. P. Root, 126. Newbury Park, Calif.: Sage Publications, 1992.

Fernandez Retamar, Roberto. "Caliban: Notes toward a Discussion of Culture in Our America." *Massachusetts Review* 15, nos. 1–2 (Winter-Spring 1974): 7–72.

Fiscal Impact of Undocumented Aliens: Selected Estimates for Seven States. New York: Urban Institute, 1994.

Fix, Michael, and Jeffrey S. Passel. *Immigration and Immigrants: Setting the Record Straight*. New York: Urban Institute, 1994.

Foreigners in Their Native Land: Historical Roots of the Mexican Americans, edited by David J. Weber. Albuquerque: University of New Mexico Press, 1973.

Freeman, Alan D. "Legitimizing Racial Discrimination through Antidiscrimination Law: A Critical Review of Supreme Court Doctrine." 62 *Minnesota Law Review* 1049 (1978).

Fregoso, Rosa Linda. "*Born in East L.A.* and the Politics of Representation." *Cultural Studies* 4 (October 1990): 264–80.

Fusco, Coco. "The Latino 'Boom' in American Film." *Centro Bulletin* 2 (1990): 48

Galarza, Ernesto. *Barrio Boy*. Notre Dame: University of Notre Dame Press, 1971.

———. *Farmworkers and Agribusiness in California, 1947–1977*. Notre Dame: University of Notre Dame Press, 1977.

———. *Merchants of Labor: The Mexican Bracero Story, an Account of the Managed Migration of Mexican Farm Workers in California, 1942–1960*. Charlotte, N.C.: McNally & Loften, 1964.

Galarza, Ernesto, Herman Gallegos, and Julian Samora. *Mexican Americans in the Southwest*. Santa Barbara, Calif.: McNally & Loftin, 1969.

Galería de la Raza. *Cactus Hearts/Barbed Wire Dreams: Media, Myths, and Mexicans*, art exhibition curated by Yolanda Lopez (1988).

Gamio, Manuel. *The Life Story of the Mexican Immigrant: Autobiographical Documents*. Chicago: University of Chicago Press, 1931. Reprint, New York: Dover Publications, 1971.

———. *Mexican Immigration to the United States: A Study of Human Migration and Adjustment*. Chicago: University of Chicago Press, 1930. Reprint, New York: Dover Publications, 1971.

García, Alma M. "The Development of Chicana Feminist Discourse, 1970–1980." *Gender and Society* 3 (1989): 217–38.

García, F. Chris, and Rodolfo O. de la Garza. *The Chicano Political Experience: Three Perspectives*. North Scituate, Mass.: Duxbury Press, 1977.

García, Ignacio M. *United We Win: The Rise and Fall of La Raza Unida Party*. Tucson: Mexican American Studies and Research Center, University of Arizona, 1989.

García, Juan Ramon. "Hollywood and the West: Mexican Images in American Films." In *Old Southwest/New Southwest: Essays on a Region and Its Literature*, edited by Judy Nolte Lensink, 75. Tuscon: Tuscon Public Library (distributed by University of Arizona Press), 1987.

———. *Operation Wetback: The Mass Deportation of Mexican Undocumented Workers in 1954*. Westport, Conn.: Greenwood Press, 1980.

García, Maria Cristina. *Havana USA: Cuban Exiles and Cuban Americans in South Florida, 1959–1994*. Berkeley: University of California Press, 1996.

García, Mario T. "The Californios of San Diego and the Politics of Accommodation." *Aztlán: International Journal of Chicano Studies Research* 6 (Spring 1975): 69–85.

———. *Desert Immigrants: The Mexicans of El Paso, 1880–1920*. New Haven: Yale University Press, 1981.

———. *Memories of Chicano History: The Life and Narrative of Bert Corona*. Berkeley: University of California Press, 1994.

———. *Mexican Americans: Leadership, Ideology, and Identity, 1930–1960*. New Haven: Yale University Press, 1989.

García, Richard A. *Rise of the Mexican American Middle Class: San Antonio, 1929–1941*. College Station: Texas A & M University Press, 1991.

García, Ruben J. "Critical Race Theory and Proposition 187: The Racial Politics of Immigration Law." 17 *Chicano-Latino Law Review* 118 (1995).

Garza, Edward D. *LULAC: The League of United Latin American Citizens*. San Francisco: R & E Research Associates, 1972.

Gaspar de Alba, Alicia. "The Alter-Native Grain: Theorizing Chicano/a Popular Culture." In *Culture and Difference: Critical Perspectives on the Bicultural Experience in the United States*, edited by Antonia Darder, 103–22. New York: Bergin & Garvey, 1995.

Gil, Rosa Maria, and Carmen Inoa Vazquez. *The Maria Paradox: How Latinas Can Merge Old World Traditions with New World Self-Esteem*. New York: G. P. Putnam's Sons, 1996.

Gilkerson, Christopher P. "Poverty Law Narratives: The Critical Practice and Theory of Receiving and Translating Client Stories." 43 *Hastings Law Journal* 861 (1992).

Giménez, Martha E. "'Latino/Hispanic'—Who Needs a Name? The Case against a Standardized Terminology." *International Journal of Health Services* 19 (1989): 557–71.

Glazer, Nathan, and Daniel Patrick Moynihan. *Beyond the Melting Pot: The Negroes, Puerto Ricans, Jews, Italians, and Irish of New York City*. Cambridge, Mass.: MIT Press, 1963.

Golden, Renny, and Michael McConnell. *Sanctuary: The New Underground Railroad*. Maryknoll, N.Y.: Orbis Books, 1986.

Gomez, David F. *Somos Chicanos: Strangers in Our Own Land*. Boston: Beacon Press, 1973.

Gomez, Laura E. "The Birth of the 'Hispanic' Generation: Attitudes of Mexican-American Political Elites toward the Hispanic Label." *Latin American Perspectives* 19 (Fall 1992): 45

Gómez-Peña, Guillermo. *The New World Border: Prophecies, Poems, and Loqueras for the End of the Century*. San Francisco: City Lights, 1996.

———. *Warrior for Gringostroika: Essays, Performance Texts, and Poetry*. St. Paul, Minn.: Graywolf Press, 1993.

Gómez-Quiñones, Juan. *Chicano Politics: Reality and Promise, 1940–1990*. Albuquerque: University of New Mexico Press, 1990.

———. *Mexican-American Labor, 1790–1990*. Albuquerque: University of New Mexico Press, 1994.

————. *Mexican Students por La Raza: The Chicano Student Movement in Southern California, 1967–1977.* Santa Barbara, Calif.: Editorial La Causa, 1978.

————. *Roots of Chicano Politics, 1600–1940.* Albuquerque: University of New Mexico Press, 1994.

Gonzales, Manuel G. *The Hispanic Elite of the Southwest.* El Paso: Texas Western Press, 1989.

Gonzalez, Deena J. "Chicana Identity Matters." In *Culture and Difference: Critical Perspectives on the Bicultural Experience in the United States,* edited by Antonia Darder, 41–53. New York: Bergin & Garvey, 1995.

Gonzalez, Gilbert G. *Chicano Education in the Era of Segregation.* Philadelphia: Balch Institute, 1990.

Gonzalez, Rodolfo "Corky." "Chicano Nationalism: The Key to Unity for La Raza." In *A Documentary History of the Mexican Americans,* edited by Wayne Moquin, 488–93. New York: Bantam Books, 1972.

————. *I Am Joaquin. Yo Soy Joaquin.* Toronto; New York: Bantam Books, 1972.

Gonzalez, Rosalinda M. "Chicanas and Mexican Immigrant Families 1920–1940: Women's Subordination and Family Exploitation." In *Decades of Discontent: The Women's Movement, 1920–1940,* edited by Lois Scharf and Joan M. Jensen, 59. Westport, Conn: Greenwood Press, 1983.

Gordon, Deborah. "Writing Culture, Writing Feminism: The Poetics and Politics of Experimental Ethnography." *Inscriptions,* nos. 3–4, 1988.

Grant, Lindsey, and John H. Tanton. *Immigration and the American Conscience.* Washington, D.C.: Environmental Fund, 1982.

Grebler, Leo. *Mexican Immigration to the United States: The Record and Its Implications.* Los Angeles: Division of Research, Graduate School of Business Administration, University of California, 1965.

Grebler, Leo, Joan Moore, and Ralph Guzman. *The Mexican American People: The Nation's Second Largest Minority.* New York: Free Press, 1970.

Greenfield, Alice. *The Sleepy Lagoon Case: A Pageant of Prejudice.* Los Angeles: Citizen's Committee for the Defense of the Mexican-American Youth, 1942.

Greenfield, Gary A., and Don B. Kates, Jr. "Mexican Americans, Racial Discrimination, and the Civil Rights Act of 1866." 63 *California Law Review* 662 (1975).

Griffith, Beatrice. *American Me.* Boston: Houghton Mifflin Co., 1948.

Grillo, Trina. "Anti-Essentialism and Intersectionality: Tools to Dismantle the Master's House." 10 *Berkeley Women's Law Journal* 16 (1995).

————. "The Mediation Alternative: Process Dangers for Women." 100 *Yale Law Journal* 1545 (1991).

Griswold del Castillo, Richard. *The Los Angeles Barrio, 1850–1890: A Social History.* Berkeley: University of California Press, 1979.

————. *The Treaty of Guadalupe Hidalgo: A Legacy of Conflict.* Norman: University of Oklahoma Press, 1990.

Gutiérrez, David G. *Walls and Mirrors: Mexican Americans, Mexican Immigrants, and the Politics of Ethnicity.* Berkeley: University of California Press, 1995.

Gutiérrez, Ramón A. *When Jesus Came, the Corn Mothers Went Away: Marriage, Sexuality, and Power in New Mexico, 1500–1846.* Stanford: Stanford University Press, 1991.

Gutiérrez-Jones, Carl. *Rethinking the Borderlands: Between Chicano Culture and Legal Discourse.* Berkeley: University of California Press, 1995.

Guzman, Ralph C. *The Political Socialization of the Mexican American People.* New York: Arno Press, 1976.

Hacker, Andrew. *Two Nations: Black and White, Separate, Hostile, Unequal.* New York: Scribner's, 1992.

Hammerback, John C., Richard J. Jensen, and José Ángel Gutiérrez. *A War of Words: Chicano Protest in the 1960s and 1970s.* Westport, Conn.: Greenwood Press, 1985.

Haney López, Ian F. "Community Ties, Race, and Faculty Hiring: The Case for Professors Who Don't Think White." *Reconstruction* 1, no. 3 (1991): 46.

———. "Race, Ethnicity, and Erasure: The Salience of Race to LatCrit Theory." 85 *California Law Review* (1998).

———. "The Social Construction of Race: Some Observations on Illusion, Fabrication, and Choice." 29 *Harvard Civil Rights–Civil Liberties Law Review* 1 (1994).

———. *White by Law: The Legal Construction of Race.* New York: New York University Press, 1996.

Harris, Angela. "Foreword: The Jurisprudence of Reconstruction." 82 *California Law Review* 741 (1994).

Harrison, Melissa, and Margaret E. Montoya. "Voices/*Voces* in the Borderlands: A Colloquy on Re/Constructing Identities in Re/Constructed Legal Spaces." 6 *Columbia Journal of Gender and Law* 387 (1996).

Hart, James D. *American Images of Spanish California.* Berkeley: Friends of the Bancroft Library, University of California, 1960.

Hart, John M. *Anarchism and the Mexican Working Class, 1860–1931.* Austin: University of Texas Press, 1978.

Hayakawa, S. I. *One Nation . . . Indivisible? The English Language Amendment.* Washington, D.C.: Washington Institute for Values in Public Policy, 1985.

Hayes-Bautista, David. *The Burden of Support: Young Latinos in an Aging Society.* Stanford: Stanford University Press, 1988.

———. "Identifying 'Hispanic' Populations: The Influence of Research Methodology on Public Policy." *American Journal of Public Health* 70 (1980): 353

Hayes-Bautista, David, and Jorge Chapa. "Latino Terminology: Conceptual Bases for Standardized Terminology." *American Journal of Public Health* 77 (1987): 61

Heizer, Robert F., and Alan J. Almquist. *The Other Californians: Prejudice and Discrimination under Spain, Mexico, and the United States to 1920.* Berkeley: University of California Press, 1971.

Hernández-Truyol, Berta Esperanza. "Building Bridges—Latinas and Latinos at the Crossroads: Realities, Rhetoric, and Replacement." 25 *Columbia Human Rights Law Review* 369 (1994).

———. "Natives, Newcomers and Nativism: A Human Rights Model for the Twenty-First Century." 23 *Fordham Urban Law Journal* 1075 (1996).

———. "Sex, Culture, and Rights: A Re/conceptualization of Violence for the Twenty-First Century." 60 *Albany Law Review* 607 (1997).

———. "Women's Rights as Human Rights—Rules, Realities and the Role of Culture: A Formula for Reform." 21 *Brooklyn Journal of International Law* 605 (1996).

Herrera-Sobek, María. *The Bracero Experience: Elitelore versus Folklore.* Los Angeles: UCLA Latin American Center Publications, University of California, 1979.

———. *The Mexican Corrido: A Feminist Analysis.* Bloomington: Indiana University Press, 1990.

Herrmann, Claudine. *The Tongue Snatchers,* translated by Nancy Kline. Lincoln: University of Nebraska Press, 1989.

Hicks, D. Emily. *Border Writing: The Multidimensional Text.* Minneapolis: University of Minnesota Press, 1991.

Higham, John. *Strangers in the Land: Patterns of American Nativism 1860–1925.* 2d ed. New Brunswick, N.J.: Rutgers University Press, 1988.

Hing, Bill Ong. "Beyond the Rhetoric of Assimilation and Cultural Pluralism: Addressing the Tension of Separatism and Conflict in an Immigration-Driven Multiracial Society." 81 *California Law Review* 863 (1993).

Hinojosa, Gilberto Miguel. *A Borderlands Town in Transition: Laredo, Texas, 1755–1870.* College Station: Texas A & M University Press, 1983.

The Hispanic American Almanac: From Columbus to Corporate America, edited by Nicolas Kanellos. Detroit: Invisible Ink, 1993.

Hispanic Migration and the United States, edited by Gaston Fernandez, Beverly Nagel, and Leon Narvaez. Bristol, Ind.: Wyndham Hall Press, 1987.

Hoffman, Abraham. *Unwanted Mexican Americans in the Great Depression: Repatriation Pressures, 1929–1939.* Tucson: University of Arizona Press, 1974.

Hoffman, Eva. *Lost in Translation: A Life in a New Language.* New York: E. P. Dutton, 1989.

Hogeland, Chris, and Karen Rosen. *Dreams Lost, Dreams Found: Undocumented Women in the Land of Opportunity: A Survey Research Project of Chinese, Filipina, and Latina Undocumented Women.* San Francisco: The Coalition, 1991.

Hollinger, David A. *Postethnic America: Beyond Multiculturalism.* New York: Basic Books, 1995.

Hondagneu-Sotelo, Pierrette. *Gendered Transitions: Mexican Experiences of Immigration.* Berkeley: University of California Press, 1994.

Horsman, Reginald. *Race and Manifest Destiny: The Origins of American Racial Anglo-Saxonism.* Cambridge, Mass.: Harvard University Press, 1981.

Huerta, Dolores. "Dolores Huerta Talks: About Republicans, Cesar, Her Children and Her Home Town." *Regeneración* 2 (1975): 20–24.

Human Rights and the Mexico-U.S. Border. Philadelphia: American Friends Service Committee, Immigration Law Enforcement Project, 1990.

Iglesias, Elizabeth M. "Rape, Race and Representation: The Power of Discourse, Discourses of Power, and the Reconstruction of Heterosexuality." 49 *Vanderbilt Law Review* 869 (1996).

———. "Structures of Subordination: Women of Color at the Intersection of Title VII and the NLRA. Not!" 28 *Harvard Civil Rights–Civil Liberties Law Review* 395 (1993).

Iguana Dreams: New Latino Fiction, edited by Delia Poey and Virgil Suarez. New York: Harper Perennial, 1992.

Images of Mexico in the United States, edited by John H. Coatsworth and Carlos Rico. San Diego: Center for U.S.-Mexican Studies, University of California, San Diego, 1989.

Immigrants Out! The New Nativism and the Anti-Immigrant Impulse in the United States, edited by Juan F. Perea. New York: New York University Press, 1996.

Infinite Divisions: An Anthology of Chicana Literature, edited by Tey Diana Rebolledo and Eliana S. Rivero. Tucson: University of Arizona Press, 1993.

Jackson, Helen Hunt. *Ramona.* Boston: Robert Bros., 1884.

Jacobson, Rodolfo. "The Social Implications of Intra-Sentenial Code-Switching." In *New Directions in Chicano Scholarship,* edited by Richard Romo and Raymond Paredes, 227. La Jolla: Chicano Studies Program, University of California, San Diego, 1978.

Jankowski, Martin Sanchez. *City Bound: Urban Life and Political Attitudes among Chicano Youth*. Albuquerque: University of New Mexico Press, 1986.

Jenkins, J. Craig. *The Politics of Insurgency: The Farm Worker Movement in the 1960s*. New York: Columbia University Press, 1985.

Johannsen, Albert. *The House of Beadle and Adams and Its Dime and Nickel Novels: The Story of a Vanished Literature*. 3 vols. Norman: University of Oklahoma Press, 1950–1962.

Johnson, James H., and Walter C. Farrel, Jr. "The Fire This Time: The Genesis of the Los Angeles Rebellion of 1992." 71 *North Carolina Law Review* 1403 (1993).

Johnson, Kevin R. "Civil Rights and Immigration: Challenges for the Latino Community in the Twenty-First Century." 8 *La Raza Law Journal* 42 (1995).

———. "An Essay on Immigration Politics, Popular Democracy, and California's Proposition 187: The Political Relevance and Legal Irrelevance of Race." 70 *Washington Law Review* 629 (1995).

———. "Fear of an 'Alien Nation': Race, Immigration, and Immigrants." 7 *Stanford Law and Policy Review* 111 (1996).

———. "Free Trade and Closed Borders: NAFTA and Mexican Immigration to the United States." 27 *University of California at Davis Law Review* 937 (1994).

———. "*Los Olvidados:* Images of the Immigrant, Political Power of Noncitizens, and Immigration Law and Enforcement." 1993 *Brigham Young University Law Review* 1139 (1993).

———. "'Melting Pot' or 'Ring of Fire'? Assimilation and the Mexican-American Experience." 85 *California Law Review* (1998).

———. "Public Benefits and Immigration: The Intersection of Immigration Status, Ethnicity, Gender, and Class." 42 *UCLA Law Review* 1509 (1995).

———. "Racial Restrictions on Naturalization: The Recurring Intersection of Race and Gender in Immigration and Citizenship Law." 11 *Berkeley Women's Law Journal* 142 (1996).

———. "Some Thoughts on the Future of Latino/a Legal Scholarship." 2 *Harvard Latino Law Review* (1998).

———. "Why Alienage Jurisdiction? Historical Foundations and Modern Justifications for Federal Jurisdiction over Disputes Involving Noncitizens." 21 *Yale Journal of International Law* 1 (1996).

Karst, Kenneth L. *Belonging to America: Equal Citizenship and the Constitution*. New Haven: Yale University Press, 1989.

Karttunen, Frances. *Between Worlds: Interpreters, Guides and Survivors*. New Brunswick, N.J.: Rutgers University Press, 1994.

Keefe, Susan E., and Amado M. Padilla. *Chicano Ethnicity*. Albuquerque: University of New Mexico Press, 1987.

Kennedy, Randall L. "Racial Critiques of Legal Academia." 102 *Harvard Law Review* 1745 (1989).

Kibbe, Pauline. *Latin Americans in Texas*. Albuquerque: University of New Mexico Press, 1946.

Klor de Alva, J. Jorge. "Telling Hispanics Apart: Latino Sociocultural Diversity." In *The Hispanic Experience in the United States: Contemporary Issues and Perspectives,* edited by Edna Acosta-Belén and Barabara R. Sjostrom, 107–36. New York: Praeger, 1988.

Kloss, Heinz. *The American Bilingual Tradition*. Rowley, Mass.: Newbury House, 1977.

La Raza: Forgotten Americans, edited by Julian Samora. Notre Dame: University of Notre Dame Press, 1966.

Lacy, James M. "New Mexican Women in Early American Writings." *New Mexico History Review* 34 (1959): 1

Lamb, Blaine P. "The Convenient Villain: The Early Cinema Views the Mexican-American." *Journal of the West* 14 (1975): 75

Lamm, Richard D., and Gary Imhoff. *The Immigration Time Bomb: The Fragmenting of America*. New York: Truman Tallet Books, E. P. Dutton, 1985.

Language Loyalties: A Source Book on the Official English Controversy, edited by James Crawford. Chicago: University of Chicago Press, 1992.

Langum, David J. "Californios and the Image of Indolence." *Western Historical Quarterly* 9 (April 1978): 181–96.

Larson, Jane E. "Free Markets Deep in the Heart of Texas." 84 *Georgetown Law Journal* 179 (1995).

Latham, Francis S. *Travels in Texas, 1842*. Edited by Gerald S. Pierce. Austin, Tex.: Encino Press, 1971.

The Latino Encyclopedia, edited by Richard Chabrán and Rafael Chabrán. New York: Marshall Cavendish, 1996.

Latinos and the Political System, edited by F. Chris García. Notre Dame: University of Notre Dame Press, 1988.

Latinos in the United States: History, Law and Perspective, edited by Antoinette Sedillo Lopez. 6 vols. New York: Garland Publishing Co., 1995.

Laughlin, Harry H. *Conquest by Immigration: A Report of the Special Committee on Immigration and Naturalization*. New York: Chamber of Commerce of the State of New York, 1939.

Lebell, Sharon. *Naming Ourselves, Naming Our Children: Resolving the Last Name Dilemma*. Freedom, Calif.: Crossing Press, 1988.

Lee, Sharon M. "Racial Classifications in the U.S. Census: 1890–1990." *Ethnic and Racial Studies* 16 (1993): 75

Lemann, Nicholas. "The Other Underclass." *Atlantic Monthly*, December 1991, 96.

Lessig, Lawrence. "Fidelity in Translation." 71 *Texas Law Review* 1165 (1993).

Levy, Jacques. *Cesar Chavez: An Autobiography of La Causa*. New York: W. W. Norton, 1975.

Lind, Michael. *The Next American Nation: The New Nationalism and the Fourth American Revolution*. New York: Free Press, 1995.

Lionnet, Françoise. *Autobiographical Voices: Race, Gender, Self-Portraiture*. Ithaca, N.Y.: Cornell University Press, 1989.

Loewen, James. "Levels of Political Mobilization and Racial Bloc Voting among Latinos, Anglos, and African-Americans in New York City." 13 *Chicano Law Review* 38 (1993).

López, Gerald P. "The Idea of a Constitution in the Chicano Tradition." 37 *Journal of Legal Education* 162 (1987).

———. "Lay Lawyering." 32 *UCLA Law Review* 1 (1984).

———. *Rebellious Lawyering: One Chicano's Vision of Progressive Law Practice*. Boulder, Colo.: Westview Press, 1992.

———. "Reconceiving Civil Rights Practice: Seven Weeks in the Life of a Rebellious Collaboration." 77 *Georgetown Law Journal* 1603 (1989).

———. "Training Future Lawyers to Work with the Politically and Socially Subordinated: Anti-Generic Legal Education." 91 *West Virginia Law Review* 305 (1989).

———. "Undocumented Mexican Migration: In Search of a Just Immigration Law and Policy." 28 *UCLA Law Review* 615 (1981).

———. "The Work We Know So Little About." 42 *Stanford Law Review* 1 (1989).

Luna, Guadalupe T. "'Agricultural Underdogs' and International Agreements: The Legal Context of Agricultural Workers within the Rural Economy." 26 *New Mexico Law Review* 9 (1996).

Maciel, David R. "The Celluloid Frontier: The U.S.-Mexico Border in Contemporary Cinema, 1970–1988." *Renato Rosaldo Lecture Series Monograph* 5 (1989): 1–34.

———. *El Norte: The U.S.-Mexican Border in Contemporary Cinema.* San Diego: Institute for Regional Studies of the Californias, San Diego State University, 1990.

Maharidge, Dale. *The Coming White Minority: California's Eruptions and the Nation's Future.* New York: Times Books, 1996.

Making Face, Making Soul=Haciendo Caras: *Creative and Critical Perspectives by Women of Color,* edited by Gloria Anzaldúa. San Francisco: Aunt Lute Foundation Books, 1990.

Marin, Christine. *A Spokesman of the Mexican American Movement: Rodolfo "Corky" Gonzalez and the Fight for Chicano Liberation, 1966–1972.* San Francisco: R & E Research Associates, 1977.

Marquez, Benjamin. *LULAC: The Evolution of a Mexican American Political Organization.* Austin: University of Texas Press, 1993.

Martínez, Elizabeth. "Beyond Black/White: The Racisms of Our Time." *Social Justice* 20, nos. 1–2 (1993): 22–34.

———. "Histories of 'the Sixties': A Certain Absence of Color." *Social Justice* 16 (Winter 1989): 175–84.

Martinez, George A. "The Legal Construction of Race: Mexican Americans and Whiteness." 2 *Harvard Latino Law Review* (1998).

———. "Legal Indeterminacy, Judicial Discretion and the Mexican-American Litigation Experience: 1930–1980." 27 *University of California at Davis Law Review* 555 (1994).

Martinez, John. "Trivializing Diversity: The Problem of Overinclusion in Affirmative Action Programs." 12 *Harvard BlackLetter Law Journal* 49 (1995).

Martinez, Oscar J. *Border People: Life and Society in the U.S.-Mexico Borderlands.* Tucson: University of Arizona Press, 1994.

———. *Troublesome Border.* Tuscon: University of Arizona Press, 1988.

Martinez, Ruben. *The Other Side: Fault Lines, Guerrilla Saints, and the True Heart of Rock and Roll.* London: Verso, 1992.

Matsuda, Mari J. "Voices of America: Accent, Antidiscrimination Law, and a Jurisprudence for the Last Reconstruction." 100 *Yale Law Journal* 1329 (1991).

Matthiessen, Peter. *Sal Si Puedes: Cesar Chavez and the New American Revolution.* New York: Random House, 1969.

Mazon, Mauricio. *The Zoot-Suit Riots: The Psychology of Symbolic Annihilation.* Austin: University of Texas Press, 1984.

McDaniel, Antonio. "The Dynamic Racial Composition of the United States: An American Dilemma Revisited." *Daedalus,* January 1995, 179.

McLaren, Peter. "Border Disputes: Multicultural Narrative, Identity Formation, and Critical Pedagogy in Postmodern America." In *Naming Silenced Lives: Personal Narratives and the Process of Educational Change,* edited by Daniel McLaughlin and William G. Tierney, 201. New York: Routledge, 1993.

———. *Critical Pedagogy and Predatory Culture: Oppositional Politics in a Postmodern Era.* New York: Routledge, 1995.

McWilliams, Carey. *Factories in the Fields: The Story of Migratory Farm Labor in California.* Boston: Little, Brown, 1939.

———. *North from Mexico: The Spanish-Speaking People of the United States.* New ed., updated by Matt S. Meier. New York: Greenwood Press, 1990.

———. *Southern California: An Island on the Land*. Santa Barbara, Calif.: Peregrine Smith, 1988.

Meier, Matt S. *Mexican American Biographies: A Historical Dictionary, 1836–1987*. Westport, Conn.: Greenwood Press, 1988.

Meier, Matt S., and Feliciano Rivera. *The Chicanos: A History of Mexican Americans*. New York: Hill & Wang, 1972.

Menchaca, Martha. "Chicano Indianism: A Historical Account of Racial Repression in the United States." *American Ethnologist* 20 (1993): 583–603.

———. *The Mexican Outsiders: A Community History of Marginalization and Discrimination in California*. Austin: University of Texas Press, 1995.

Méndez, Miguel A. "*Hernandez:* The Wrong Message at the Wrong Time." 4 *Stanford Law and Policy Review* 193 (1993).

———. "Lawyers, Linguists, Story-Tellers and Limited English-Speaking Witnesses." 27 *New Mexico Law Review* 1 (1997).

Metz, Leon Claire. *Border: The U.S.-Mexico Line*. El Paso: Mangan Books, 1989.

The Mexican American Experience: An Interdisciplinary Anthology, edited by Rodolfo O. de la Garza, Frank D. Bean, Charles M. Bonjean, Ricardo Romo, and Rodolfo Alvarez. Austin: University of Texas Press, 1985.

Mexican Immigrants and Mexican Americans: An Evolving Relationship, edited by Harley L. Browning and Rodolfo O. de la Garza. Austin: Center for Mexican American Studies Publications, University of Texas, Austin, 1984.

Miles, Jack. "Blacks vs. Browns: African Americans and Latinos." *Atlantic Monthly,* October 1992, 41.

Mirande, Alfredo. *The Chicano Experience: An Alternative Perspective*. Notre Dame: University of Notre Dame Press, 1985.

———. "'*En la Tierra del Ciego, el Tuerto Es Rey*' ('In the Land of the Blind, the One-Eyed Person Is King'): Bilingualism as a Disability." 26 *New Mexico Law Review* 75 (1996).

———. *Gringo Justice*. Notre Dame: University of Notre Dame Press, 1987.

———. *Hombres y Machos: Masculinity and Latino Culture*. Boulder, Colo.: Westview Press, 1997.

———. "'Now That I Speak English, *No Me Dejan Hablar*' ('I'm Not Allowed to Speak'): The Implications of *Hernandez v. New York*." 18 *Chicano-Latino Law Review* 115 (1996).

Mirande, Alfredo, and Evangelina Enriquez. *La Chicana: The Mexican American Woman*. Chicago: University of Chicago Press, 1979.

Missions in Conflict: Essays on U.S.-Mexican Relations and Chicano Culture, edited by Renate von Bardeleben, Dietrich Briesemeister, and Juan Bruce-Novoa. Tübingen: G. Marr, 1986.

Montejano, David. *Anglos and Mexicans in the Making of Texas, 1836–1986*. Austin: University of Texas Press, 1987.

Montoya, Margaret E. "Law and Language(s): Image, Integration and Innovation." 7 *La Raza Law Journal* 147 (1994).

———. "Mascaras, Trenzas, y Grenas: Un/masking the Self While Un/braiding Latina Stories and Legal Discourse." 17 *Harvard Women's Law Journal* 185 (1994), concurrently published in 15 *Chicano-Latino Law Review* 1 (1994).

Moore, Joan W. *Homeboys: Gangs, Drugs, and Prison in the Barrios of Los Angeles*. Philadelphia: Temple University Press, 1978.

Moore, Joan W., with Alfredo Cuellar. *Mexican Americans*. Englewood Cliffs, N.J.: Prentice-Hall, 1970.

Moraga, Cherríe. *The Last Generation*. Boston: South End Press, 1993.

———. *Loving in the War Years*: *Lo Que Nunca Paso por Sus Labios*. Boston: South End Press, 1983.

Moran, Rachel F. "Bilingual Education as a Status Conflict." 75 *California Law Review* 321 (1987).

———. "Demography and Distrust: The Latino Challenge to Civil Rights and Immigration Policy in the 1990s and Beyond." 8 *La Raza Law Journal* 1 (1995).

———. "Getting a Foot in the Door: The Hispanic Rush for Equal Education Opportunity." 2 *Kansas Journal of Law and Public Policy* 35 (1992).

———. "Of Democracy, Devaluation, and Bilingual Education." 26 *Creighton Law Review* 255 (1993).

———. "The Politics of Discretion: Federal Intervention in Bilingual Education." 76 *California Law Review* 1249 (1988).

———. "Unrepresented." *Representations* 55 (1996): 139.

Morgan, Patricia. *Shame of a Nation: A Documented Story of Police-State Terror against Mexican Americans in the U.S.A.* Los Angeles: Los Angeles Committee for the Protection of the Foreign Born, 1954.

Morin, Raul. *Among the Valiant: Mexican Americans in WWII and Korea*. Alhambra, Calif.: Borden Publishing Co., 1966.

Mueller, Jerry E. *Restless River: International Law and the Behavior of the Rio Grande*. El Paso: Texas Western Press, 1975.

Muñoz, Carlos, Jr. *Youth, Identity, Power: The Chicano Movement*. London: Verso, 1989.

Muñoz, Carlos, Jr., and Mario Barrera. "La Raza Unida Party and the Chicano Student Movement in California." *Social Science Journal* 19 (April 1982): 101–20.

Murguia, Edward. "On Latino/Hispanic Ethnic Identity." *Latino Studies Journal* 2, no. 3 (September 1991): 8–18.

Nabakov, Peter. *Tijerina and the Courthouse Raid*. Albuquerque: University of New Mexico Press, 1969.

Navarrette, Ruben, Jr. *A Darker Shade of Crimson: Odyssey of a Harvard Chicano*. New York: Bantam Books, 1993.

Neuman, Gerald L. "Aliens as Outlaws: Government Services, Proposition 187, and the Structure of Equal Protection Doctrine." 42 *UCLA Law Review* 1425 (1995).

Noriega, Chon A. "Citizen Chicano: The Trials and Titillations of Ethnicity in the American Cinema, 1935–1962." *Social Research: An International Quarterly of the Social Sciences* 58 (Summer 1991): 413–38.

Now the Volcano: An Anthology of Latin American Gay Literature, edited by Winston Leyland. San Francisco: Gay Sunshine Press, 1979.

Oboler, Suzanne. *Ethnic Labels, Latino Lives: Identity and the Politics of (Re)Presentation in the United States*. Minneapolis: University of Minnesota Press, 1995.

Oh, Angela E. "Race Relations in Los Angeles: 'Divide and Conquer' Is Alive and Flourishing." 66 *California Law Review* 1647 (1993).

Olivas, Michael A. "'Breaking the Law' on Principle: An Essay on Lawyers' Dilemmas, Unpopular Causes, and Legal Regimes." 52 *University of Pittsburgh Law Review* 815 (1991).

———. "*The Chronicles*, My Grandfather's Stories, and Immigration Law: The Slave Traders as Racial History." 34 *St. Louis University Law Journal* 425 (1990).

———. "The Education of Latino Lawyers: An Essay on Crop Cultivation." 14 *Chicano-Latino Law Review* 117 (1994).

———. "Legal Norms in Law School Admissions: An Essay on Parallel Universes." 42 *Journal of Legal Education* 103 (1992).

————. "Torching Zozobra: The Problem with Linda Chavez." *Reconstruction* 2, no. 2 (1993): 48–51.

————. "Unaccompanied Refugee Children: Detention, Due Process, and Disgrace." 1 *Stanford Law and Policy Review* 159 (1990).

Olmstead, Frederick Law. *A Journey through Texas: Or, A Saddle-Trip on the Southwestern Frontier, with a Statistical Abstract.* New York: Dix, Edwards & Co., 1857. Reprint, Austin: University of Texas Press, 1978.

Ontiveros, Maria L. "Fictionalizing Harassment—Disclosing the Truth." 93 *Michigan Law Review* 1373 (1995).

————. "Rosa Lopez, David Letterman, Christopher Darden, and Me: Issues of Gender, Ethnicity, and Class in Evaluating Witness Credibility." 6 *Hastings Women's Law Journal* 135 (1995).

————. "Three Perspectives on Workplace Harassment of Women of Color." 23 *Golden Gate University Law Review* 817 (1993).

————. "To Help Those Most in Need: Undocumented Workers' Rights and Remedies under Title VII." 20 *N.Y.U. Review of Law and Social Change* 607 (1993–94).

Oppenheimer, David Benjamin. "Understanding Affirmative Action." 23 *Hastings Constitutional Law Quarterly* 921 (1996).

Oquendo, Angel R. "Re-Imagining the Latino/a Race." 12 *Harvard BlackLetter Law Journal* 93 (1995).

"Our Next Race Question: The Uneasiness between Blacks and Latinos" (Colloquy with Jorge Klor de Alva, Earl Shorris, and Cornel West). *Harpers,* April 1996, 55.

Padilla, Felix M. *Latino Ethnic Consciousness: The Case of Mexican Americans and Puerto Ricans in Chicago.* Notre Dame: University of Notre Dame Press, 1985.

————. *Puerto Rican Chicago.* Notre Dame: University of Notre Dame Press, 1987.

Pálsson, Gisli. "Introduction: Beyond Boundaries." In *Beyond Boundaries: Understanding, Translation and Anthropological Discourse,* edited by Gisli Palsson. Oxford, Eng.: Berg, 1993.

Paredes, Américo. "On 'Gringo,' 'Greaser,' and Other Neighborly Names." In *Singers and Storytellers,* edited by Mody C. Boatright et al. Dallas: Southern Methodist University Press, 1961.

————. *"With His Pistol in His Hand": A Border Ballad and Its Hero.* Austin: University of Texas Press, 1958.

Paredes, Raymund A. "The Mexican Image in American Travel Literature, 1813–1869." *New Mexico Historical Review* 52 (January 1977): 5–29.

————. "The Origin of Anti-Mexican Sentiment in the United States." *New Scholar* 6 (1977): 130–65.

Pastor, Manuel, Jr., Lisa Magana, Amalia Cabezas, and Morgan Appel. *Latinos and the Los Angeles Uprising: The Economic Context.* Claremont, Calif.: Tomás Rivera Center, 1993.

Payson, Kenneth R. "Comment, Check the Box: Reconsidering Directive No. 15 and the Classification of Mixed-Race People." 84 *California Law Review* 1233 (1996).

Paz, Octavio. *The Labyrinth of Solitude.* New York: Grove Press, 1961.

Peller, Gary. "Race Consciousness." 1990 *Duke Law Journal* 758.

Perea, Juan F. "The Black/White Binary Paradigm of Race: The 'Normal Science' of American Racial Thought." 85 *California Law Review* (1998).

————. "Demography and Distrust: An Essay on American Languages, Cultural Pluralism, and Official English." 77 *Minnesota Law Review* 269 (1992).

————. "English-Only Rules and the Right to Speak One's Primary Language in the Workplace." 23 *University of Michigan Journal of Law Reform* 265 (1990).

———. "Ethnicity and Prejudice: Reevaluating 'National Origin' Discrimination Under Title VII." 35 *William and Mary Law Review* 805 (1994).

———. "Ethnicity and the Constitution: Beyond the Black White Binary Constitution." 36 *William and Mary Law Review* 571 (1995).

———. "*Hernandez v. New York:* Courts, Prosecutors, and the Fear of Spanish." 21 *Hofstra Law Review* 1 (1992).

———. "*Los Olvidados:* On the Making of Invisible People." 70 *N.Y.U. Law Review* 965 (1995).

Perez, Richie. "From Assimilation to Annihilation: Puerto Rican Images in U.S. Films." *Centro Bulletin* 2 (1990): 8

Pesquera, Beatriz M., and Denise Segura. "There Is No Going Back: Chicanas and Feminism." In *Chicana Critical Issues: Mujeres Activas En Letras Y Cambio Social,* edited by Norma Alarcon. Berkeley: Third Woman Press, 1993.

Peterson, Richard H. "Anti-Mexican Nativism in California, 1848–1853: A Study in Cultural Conflict." *Southern California Quarterly* 62 (Winter 1980): 309–28.

Pettit, Arthur G. *Images of the Mexican American in Fiction and Film.* College Station: Texas A & M University Press, 1980.

Piatt, Bill. "Attorney as Interpreter: A Return to Babble." 20 *New Mexico Law Review* 1 (1990).

———. *Black and Brown in America: The Case for Cooperation.* New York: New York University Press, 1997.

———. "Born as Second Class Citizens in the U.S.A.: Children of Undocumented Parents." 63 *Notre Dame Law Review* 35 (1988).

———. *Language on the Job: Balancing Business Needs and Employee Rights.* Albuquerque: University of New Mexico Press, 1993.

———. *¿Only English? Law and Language Policy in the United States.* Albuquerque: University of New Mexico Press, 1990.

———. "Toward Domestic Recognition of a Human Right to Language." 23 *Houston Law Review* 885 (1986).

Pitt, Leonard. *The Decline of the Californios: A Social History of the Spanish Speaking Californians, 1846–1890.* Berkeley: University of California Press, 1966.

Polinard, Jerry L., Robert D. Wrinkle, and Rodolfo O. de la Garza. "Attitudes of Mexican Americans toward Irregular Mexican Immigration." *International Migration Review* 18 (Fall 1984): 782–99.

Porter, Rosalie Pedalino. *Forked Tongue: The Politics of Bilingual Education.* New York: Basic Books, 1990.

Portes, Alejandro. "From South of the Border: Hispanic Minorities in the United States." In *Immigration Reconsidered,* edited by Virginia Yans-McLaughlin, 160. New York: Oxford University Press, 1990.

Portes, Alejandro, and Robert L. Bach. *Latin Journey: Cuban and Mexican Immigrants in the United States.* Berkeley: University of California Press, 1985.

Portes, Alejandro, and Alex Stepick. *City on the Edge: The Transformation of Miami.* Berkeley: University of California Press, 1993.

Preston, William, Jr. *Aliens and Dissenters: Federal Suppression of Radicals, 1903–1933.* Cambridge, Mass.: Harvard University Press, 1963.

The Puerto Rican Woman: Perspectives on Culture, History and Society, edited by Edna Acosta-Belén and Barbara R. Sjostrom. New York: Praeger, 1986.

Raat, W. Dirk. *Revoltosos: Mexico's Rebels in the United States, 1903–1923.* College Station: Texas A & M University Press, 1985.

Racially Mixed People in America, edited by Maria P. P. Root. Newbury Park, Calif.: Sage Publications, 1992.

Ramirez, Deborah A. "Excluded Voices: The Disenfranchisemnt of Ethnic Groups from Jury Service." 1993 *Wisconsin Law Review* 761.

———. "The Mixed Jury and the Ancient Custom of Trial by Jury *De Medietate Linguae:* A History and a Proposal for Change." 74 *Boston University Law Review* 777 (1994).

———. "Multicultural Empowerment: It's Not Just Black and White Anymore." 47 *Stanford Law Review* 957 (1995).

Rangel, Jorge C., and Carlos M. Alcala. "Project Report: De Jure Segregation of Chicanos in Texas Schools." 7 *Harvard Civil Rights–Civil Liberties Law Review* 307 (1972).

Rechy, John. *City of Night.* New York: Grove Press, 1963.

Recovering the U.S. Hispanic Literature Heritage, edited by Ramón A. Gutiérrez and Genaro Padilla. Houston: Arte Publico Press, 1993.

Reid, John C. *Reid's Tramp: Or, A Journal of the Incidents of Ten Months' Travel . . .* Selma, Ala.: J. Hardy Co., 1858. Reprint, Austin, Tex.: Steck Co., 1935.

Reisler, Mark. *By the Sweat of Their Brow: Mexican Immigrant Labor in the United States, 1900–1940.* Westport, Conn.: Greenwood Press, 1976.

Rendon, Armando B. *Chicano Manifesto.* New York: Collier Books, 1972.

Ressler, Everett, Neil Boothby, and Daniel Steinbock. *Unaccompanied Children: Care and Protection in Wars, Natural Disasters, and Refugee Movements.* New York: Oxford University Press, 1988.

Rieff, David. *The Exile: Cuba in the Heart of Miami.* New York: Simon & Schuster, 1993.

———. *Los Angeles: Capital of the Third World.* New York: Simon & Schuster, 1991.

Rivera, Edward. *Family Installments: Memories of Growing Up Hispanic.* New York: Morrow, 1982.

Rivera, Jenny. "Domestic Violence against Latinas by Latino Males: An Analysis of Race, National Origin, and Gender Differentials." 14 *Boston College Third World Law Journal* 231 (1994).

———. "The Politics of Invisibility." 3 *Georgetown Journal on Fighting Poverty* 61 (1995).

———. "The Violence against Women Act and the Construction of Multiple Consciousness in the Civil Rights and Feminist Movements." 4 *Journal of Law and Policy* 463 (1996).

Rivera, Rick. *A Fabricated Mexican.* Houston: Arte Publico Press, 1995.

Rivera, Tomás. *—y no se lo tragó la tierra [And the Earch Did Not Devour Him].* Houston: Arte Público Press, 1987.

Robinson, Cecil. *Mexico and the Hispanic Southwest in American Literature.* Revised from *With the Ears of Strangers: The Mexican in American Literature.* Tucson: University of Arizona Press, 1977.

Rodriguez, Clara E. *Puerto Ricans: Born in the U.S.A.* Boston: Unwin Hyman, 1989.

Rodriguez, Clara E., Aida Castro, Oscar Garcia, and Analisa Torres. "Latino Racial Identity: In the Eye of the Beholder?" *Latino Studies Journal* 2, no. 3 (September 1991): 33–48.

Rodriguez, Luis J. *Always Running: La Vida Loca—Gang Days in L.A.* Willimantic, Conn.: Curbstone Press, 1993.

Rodriguez, Richard. "An American Writer." In *The Invention of Ethnicity,* edited by Werner Sollors, 3. New York: Oxford University Press, 1989.

———. *Days of Obligation: An Argument with My Mexican Father.* New York: Viking, 1992.

———. *Hunger of Memory: The Education of Richard Rodriguez.* Boston: David R. Godine, 1981.

Roeder, George H., Jr. *Mexicans in the Movies: The Image of Mexicans in American Films, 1894–1947.* Unpublished manuscript, University of Wisconsin, 1971.

Rogg, Eleanor. *The Assimilation of Cuban Exiles: The Role of Community and Class*. New York: Aberdeen Press, 1974.

Romany, Celina. "Ain't I a Feminist." 4 *Yale Journal of Law and Feminism* 23 (1991).

———. "Women as *Aliens:* A Feminist Critique of the Public/Private Distinction in International Human Rights Law." 6 *Harvard Human Rights Journal* 87 (1993).

Romero, Leo, Richard Delgado, and Cruz Reynoso. "The Legal Education of Chicano Students: A Study in Mutual Accommodation and Cultural Conflict." 5 *New Mexico Law Review* 177 (1975).

Romo, Ricardo. *East Los Angeles: History of a Barrio*. Austin: University of Texas Press, 1983.

———. "Responses to Mexican Immigration 1910–1930." *Aztlán: International Journal of Chicano Studies Research* 6 (1975): 173

———. "Southern California and the Origins of Latino Civil-Rights Activism." *Western Legal History* 3 (1990): 379

Rosaldo, Renato. *Culture & Truth: The Remaking of Social Analysis*. Boston: Beacon Press, 1993.

———. "Surveying Law and Borders." 48 *Stamford Law Review* 1037 (1996).

Rosales, Francisco Arturo. *Chicano! The History of the Mexican American Civil Rights Movement*. Houston: Arte Publico Press, 1996.

Rosenbaum, Robert J. *Mexicano Resistance in the Southwest: "The Sacred Right of Self-Preservation."* Austin: University of Texas Press, 1981.

Ruiz, Vicki L. "By the Day or Week: Mexicana Domestic Workers in El Paso." In *"To Toil the Livelong Day": America's Women at Work, 1780–1980*, edited by Carol Groneman and Mary Beth Norton, 269. Ithaca, N.Y.: Cornell University Press, 1987.

Salazar, Ruben. *Border Correspondent: Selected Writings, 1955–1970*, edited by Mario T. García. Berkeley: University of California Press, 1995.

Saldívar, José David. *The Dialectics of Our America: Genealogy, Cultural Critique, and Literary History*. Durham, N.C.: Duke University Press, 1991.

Saldivar, Ramon. *Chicano Narrative: The Dialectics of Difference*. Madison: University of Wisconsin Press, 1990.

Salinas, Guadalupe. "Mexican-Americans and the Desegregation of Schools in the Southwest." 8 *Houston Law Review* 929 (1971).

Samora, Julian, Joe Bernal, and Albert Pena. *Gunpowder Justice: A Reassessment of the Texas Rangers*. Notre Dame: University of Notre Dame Press. 1979.

Samora, Julian, with Jorge A. Bustamente and Gilbert Cardenas. *Los Mojados: The Wetback Story*. Notre Dame: University of Notre Dame Press, 1971.

Samora, Julian, and Patricia Vandel Simon. *A History of the Mexican-American People*. Rev. ed. Notre Dame: University of Notre Dame Press, 1993.

San Miguel, Guadalupe. *"Let All of Them Take Heed": Mexican Americans and the Campaign for Educational Equality in Texas, 1910–1981*. Austin: University of Texas Press, 1987.

Sanchez, George F. "'Go after the Women': Americanization and the Mexican Immigrant Woman, 1915–1929." In *Unequal Sisters: A Multicultural Reader in U.S. Women's History*, edited by Ellen C. DuBois and Vicki L. Ruiz, 250. New York: Routledge, 1990.

Sanchez, George Isidore. *Forgotten People: A Study of New Mexicans*. Albuquerque: University of New Mexico Press, 1967.

Sanchez, George J. *Becoming Mexican-American: Ethnicity, Culture and Identity in Chicano Los Angeles, 1900–1945*. New York: Oxford University Press, 1993.

Santos, Boaventura de Sousa. *Toward a New Common Sense: Law, Science and Politics in the Paradigmatic Transition*. New York: Routledge, 1995.

Saragoza, Alex M. "Mexican Cinema in the United States, 1940–1952." In *History, Culture, and Society: Chicano Studies in the 1980s*, issued by National Association of Chicano Studies. Ypsilanti, Mich.: Bilingual Press/Editorial Bilingue, 1983.

Saragoza, Alex M., Concepción R. Juarez, Abel Valenzuela, Jr., and Oscar Gonzalez. "History and Public Policy: Title VII and the Use of the Hispanic Classification." 5 *La Raza Law Journal* 1 (1992).

Saunders, Myra K. "California Legal History: A Review of Spanish and Mexican Legal Institutions." 87 *Law Library Journal* 487 (1995).

Schlesinger, Arthur M., Jr. *The Disuniting of America*. New York: W. W. Norton, 1992.

Schuck, Peter H. "Alien Rumination." 105 *Yale Law Journal* 1963 (1996).

Schuck, Peter H., and Rogers M. Smith. *Citizenship without Consent: Illegal Aliens in the American Polity*. New Haven: Yale University Press, 1985.

Sealing Our Borders: The Human Toll. Philadelphia: American Friends Service Committee, 1992.

Seguin, Juan N. *Personal Memoirs of John N. Seguin: From the Year 1834 to the Retreat of General Woll from the City of San Antonio*. San Antonio, Tex.: Printed at the Ledger Book and Job Office, 1858.

The Sexuality of Latinas, edited by Norma Alarcon, Ana Castillo, and Cherríe Moraga. Berkeley: Third Woman Press, 1993.

Shirley, Dame. *The Shirley Letters from the California Mines, 1851–1852*. New York: Knopf, 1949.

Shorris, Earl. *Latinos: A Biography of the People*. New York: W. W. Norton, 1992.

Simon, Lisette E. "Hispanics: Not a Cognizable Ethnic Group." 63 *University of Cincinnati Law Review* 497 (1994).

Skerry, Peter. *Mexican Americans: The Ambivalent Minority*. New York: Free Press, 1993.

Sleepy Lagoon Defense Committee. *The Sleepy Lagoon Case*. Los Angeles: The Committee, 1944.

Sollors, Werner. *Beyond Ethnicity: Consent and Dissent in American Culture*. New York: Oxford University Press, 1986.

"Standards for the Classification of Federal Data on Race and Ethnicity: Advance Notice of Proposed Review and Possible Revision of OMB's Statistical Policy Directive No. 15." 59 *Federal Register* 29,831, 29,832. Washington, D.C.: National Archives and Records Administration, 1994.

Starr, Kevin. *Americans and the California Dream, 1850–1915*. New York: Oxford University Press, 1973.

Stavans, Ilan. *Bandido: Oscar "Zeta" Acosta and the Chicano Experience*. New York: HarperCollins, 1995.

———. *The Hispanic Condition: Reflections on Culture and Identity in America*. New York: HarperCollins, 1995.

Stefancic, Jean. "Latino and Latina Critical Theory: An Annotated Bibliography." 85 *California Law Review* (1998).

Steinberg, Stephen. *The Ethnic Myth: Race, Ethnicity, and Class in America*. Updated and expanded ed. Boston: Beacon Press, 1989.

Steiner, Stan. *La Raza: The Mexican American*. New York: Harper & Row, 1970.

Sterne, Adolphus. *Hurrah for Texas! The Diary of Adolphus Sterne*. Edited by Archie P. McDonald. Waco, Tex.: Texian Press, 1969.

Symposium: "Latinos and the Law: Twenty Years of Legal Advocacy and Lessons for Advancement." 14 *Chicano-Latino Law Review* 1 (1994).

Symposium on the Feminization of Poverty: The Hispanic Perspective. Co-sponsored by the New York State Division for Women and the National Conference of Puerto Rican Women, Inc., June 1986.

Takaki, Ronald T. *A Different Mirror: A History of Multicultural America.* Boston: Little Brown, 1993.

Tamayo, William R. "When the 'Coloreds' Are Neither Black nor Citizens: The United States Civil Rights Movement and Global Migration." 2 *Asian Law Journal* 7 (1995).

Tanton, John H. *Rethinking Immigration Policy.* Washington, D.C.: Federation for American Immigration Reform, 1978.

Taylor, Paul S. *An American Mexican Frontier: Nueces County, Texas.* Chapel Hill: University of North Carolina Press, 1934.

Taylor, Ronald B. *Chavez and the Farm Workers.* Boston: Beacon Press, 1975.

Telles, Edward E., and Edward Murguia. "Phenotypic Discrimination and Income Differences among Mexican Americans." *Social Science Quarterly* 17 (1990): 682

This Bridge Called My Back: Writings by Radical Women of Color, edited by Cherríe Moraga and Gloria Anzaldúa. 2d ed. New York: Kitchen Table, Women of Color Press, 1983.

Thomas, Piri. *Down These Mean Streets.* New York: Knopf, 1967.

Todorov, Tzvetan. *The Conquest of America: The Question of the Other.* New York: Harper & Row, 1982.

Toro, Luis Angel. "'A People Distinct from Others': Race and Identity in Federal Indian Law and the Hispanic Classification in OMB Directive No. 15." 26 *Texas Tech. Law Review* 1219 (1995).

Torres, Gerald. "Critical Race Theory: The Decline of the Universalist Ideal and the Hope of Plural Justice—Some Observations and Questions of an Emerging Phenomenon." 75 *Minnesota Law Review* 993 (1991).

———. "Local Knowledge, Local Color: Critical Legal Studies and the Law of Race Relations." 25 *San Diego Law Review* 1043 (1988).

Torres, Luis R. "The Chicano Image in Film." *Caminos* 3 (November 1982): 8.

———. "Distortions in Celluloid: Hispanics and Film." *Agenda: A Journal of Hispanic Issues* 11 (May-June 1981): 37–40.

———. "Hollywood and the Homeboys: The Studios Discover Barrio Gangs." *Nuestro* 3 (April 1979): 27–30.

Torres, Rodolfo D., and ChorSwang Ngin. "Racialized Boundaries, Class Relations, and Cultural Politics: The Asian-American and Latino Experience." In *Culture and Difference: Critical Perspectives on the Bicultural Experience in the United States,* edited by Antonia Darder, 55–69. New York: Bergin & Garvey, 1995.

Trevino, Jesus Salvador. "Latino Portrayals in Film and Television." *Jump Cut* 30 (March 1985): 14–16.

———. "Latinos and Public Broadcasting: The 2% Factor." *Jump Cut* 28 (1983): 65.

Trulio, Beverly. "Anglo-American Attitudes toward New Mexican Women." *Journal of the West* 12 (1973): 229.

Undocumented Migration to the United States: IRCA and the Experience of the 1980s, edited by Frank D. Bean et al. Santa Monica, Calif.: Rand Corp.; Washington, D.C.: Urban Institute Press, 1990.

U.S. Commission on Civil Rights. *Mexican American Education Study: Ethnic Isolation of Mexican Americans in the Public Schools of the Southwest.* Washington, D.C.: Government Printing Office, 1971.

————. *Mexican Americans and the Administration of Justice in the Southwest.* Washington, D.C.: Government Printing Office, 1970.

U.S. Mexico Borderlands: Historical and Contemporary Perspectives, edited by Oscar J. Martinez. Wilmington, Del.: Scholarly Resources, 1996.

Valdes, Francisco. "Diversity and Discrimination in Our Midst: Musings on Constitutional Schizophrenia, Cultural Conflict, and 'Interculturalism' at the Threshold of a New Century." 5 *St. Thomas Law Review* 293 (1993).

————. "Queers, Sissies, Dykes, and Tomboys: Deconstructing the Conflation of 'Sex,' 'Gender,' and 'Sexual Orientation' in Euro-American Law and Society." 83 *California Law Review* 1 (1995).

————. "Unpacking Hetero-Patriarchy: Tracing the Conflation of Sex, Gender and Sexual Orientation to Its Origins." 8 *Yale Journal of Law and Humanities* 161 (1996).

Valdez, Guadalupe. "The Language Situation of Mexican Americans." In *Language Diversity, Problem or Resource? A Social and Educational Perspective on Language Minorities in the United States,* edited by Sandra L. McKay and Sau-Ling C. Wong, 111. Cambridge, Mass.: Newbury House, 1988.

Valdez, Luis. *Zoot Suit and Other Plays.* Houston: Arte Publico Press, 1992.

Valle, Victor, and Rodolfo D. Torres. "The Idea of Mestizaje and the 'Race' Problematic: Racialized Media Discourse in a Post-Fordist Landscape." In *Culture and Difference: Critical Perspectives on the Bicultural Experience in the United States,* edited by Antonia Darder, 139–53. New York: Bergin & Garvey, 1995.

Vasquez, Richard. *Chicano.* Garden City, N.Y.: Doubleday, 1970.

Vigil, James Diego. *Barrio Gangs: Streetlife and Identity in Southern California.* Austin: University of Texas Press, 1988.

Villarreal, Carlos. "Culture in Lawmaking: A Chicano Perspective." 24 *University of California at Davis Law Review* 1193 (1991).

————. "Limits on Lawmaking: A Chicano Perspective." 10 *St. Louis University Public Law Review* 65 (1991).

Villarreal, Jose Antonio. *Clemente Chacon.* Binghamton, N.Y.: Bilingual Press, 1984.

————. *Pocho.* New York: Doubleday, 1959.

Villasenor, Victor. *Rain of Gold.* Houston: Arte Publico Press, 1991.

————. *Wild Steps of Heaven.* New York: Delacorte Press, 1996.

Viramontes, Helena María. *Under the Feet of Jesus.* New York: Dutton, 1995.

Walsh, Catherine E. *Pedagogy and the Struggle for Voice: Issues of Language, Power, and Schooling for Puerto Ricans.* South Hadley, Mass.: Bergin & Garvey, 1991.

Walzer, Michael. *Spheres of Justice: A Defense of Pluralism and Equality.* New York: Basic Books, 1983.

Waters, Mary C. *Ethnic Options: Choosing Identities in America.* Berkeley: University of California Press, 1990.

Webb, Walter Prescott. *The Texas Rangers: A Century of Frontier Defense.* 2d ed. Austin: University of Texas Press, 1965.

Weber, David J. "Here Rests Juan Espinoza: Toward a Clearer Look at the Image of the 'Indolent' Californios." *Western Historical Quarterly* 1 (January 1979): 61–68.

————. *The Mexican Frontier, 1821–1846: The American Southwest under Mexico.* Albuquerque: University of New Mexico Press, 1982.

————. "Stereotyping of Mexico's Far Northern Frontier." In *An Awakened Minority: The Mexican American,* edited by Manuel P. Servin, 18–24. 2d ed. Beverly Hills, Calif.: Glencoe Press, 1974.

Weyr, Thomas. *Hispanic U.S.A.: Breaking the Melting Pot.* New York: Harper & Row, 1988.

Wikan, Unni. "Beyond Boundaries: The Power of Resonance." In *Beyond Boundaries: Understanding, Translation and Anthropological Discourse,* edited by Gisli Pálsson. Oxford, Eng.: Berg, 1993.

Williams, Linda. "Type and Stereotype : Chicano Images in Film." *Frontiers 5* (Summer 1980): 14–17.

Williams, Robert A., Jr. "Taking Rights Aggressively: The Perils and Promise of Critical Legal Theory for Peoples of Color." *5 Law and Inequality Journal* 103 (1987).

Williams, Sarah. "Abjection and Anthropological Praxis." *Anthropological Quarterly* 66 (1993): 67

Woll, Allen L. "Bandits and Lovers: Hispanic Images in American Film." In *The Kaleidoscopic Lens: How Hollywood Views Ethnic Groups,* edited by Randall M. Miller. Englewood, N.J.: Jerome S. Ozer, 1980.

———. *The Latin Image in American Film.* Los Angeles: UCLA Latin American Center Publications, [1977] 1980.

Woll, Allen L., and Randall M. Miller. "Hispanic Americans." In *Ethnic and Racial Images in American Film and Television: Historical Essays and Bibliography,* edited by Allen W. Woll and Randall M. Miller. New York: Garland Publishing, 1987.

Wright, Luther, Jr. "Who's Black, Who's White, and Who Cares: Reconceptualizing the United States' Definition of Race and Racial Classifications." *48 Vanderbilt Law Review* 513 (1995).

Writing Culture: The Poetics and Politics of Ethnography, edited by James Clifford and George Marcus. Berkeley: University of California Press, 1986.

Yankauer, Alfred. "Hispanic/Latino—What's in a Name?" *American Journal of Public Health* 77 (1987): 15

Young, Robert. *White Mythologies: Writing History and the West.* New York: Routledge, 1990.

Zamora, Emilio. *The World of the Mexican Worker in Texas.* College Station: Texas A & M University Press, 1993.

Contributors

Oscar "Zeta" Acosta was born in El Paso, Texas. After serving as a legal aid attorney, he became a political activist in the Chicano community in Los Angeles. He unsuccessfully campaigned for sheriff of Los Angeles County in 1970, then traveled through the West with the writer Hunter Thompson and wrote *The Autobiography of a Brown Buffalo* and *The Revolt of the Cockroach People*. He disappeared during a journey to Mazatlán, Mexico, in 1973.

Rodolfo Acuña is professor of Chicano studies at California State University at Northridge. His widely acclaimed work, *Occupied America*, is now in its third edition. One of America's leading scholar-activists, Professor Acuña has been instrumental in establishing Chicano Studies programs at several universities, and in articulating the histories and voices of the oppressed. Featured in the TV series "Chicano: History of the Mexican American Civil Rights Movement," Professor Acuña has lectured and commented extensively on issues of racial justice in the popular media.

Tomás Almaguer, professor of American culture and sociology at the University of Michigan, is also the Director of the Center for Latino Studies there. He specializes in the areas of Chicano studies, race relations, social stratification, and gay and lesbian studies.

Gloria Anzaldúa is a poet, essayist, fiction writer, editor, and feminist critic. The anthology *This Bridge Called My Back: Writings by Radical Women of Color,* coedited with Cherríe Moraga, won the Before Columbus Foundation American Book Award in 1983. Since then, she has published the autobiographical *Borderlands/La Frontera: The New Mestiza,* as well as *Making Face, Making Soul=Haciendo Caras,* an anthology of critical writings by women of color.

Elvia R. Arriola, assistant professor at the University of Texas School of Law, received her J.D. from Boalt Hall School of Law, University of California at Berkeley, and her M.A. from New York University. A onetime Karpatkin Fellow at the ACLU, her main areas of scholarship and teaching are civil rights, employment discrimination, and gender in the law.

Charles Ramírez Berg, Distinguished Teaching Professor in the Department of Radio-Television-Film, is also on the faculty of the Center for Mexican American

Studies, both at the University of Texas at Austin. Author of *Cinema of Solitude: A Critical Study of Mexican Film, 1967–1983,* as well as numerous articles on film and communications, he has served on the Executive Council of the Society for Cinema Studies and writes screenplays, fiction, and poetry.

Linda S. Bosniak is professor of law at the Rutgers School of Law, Camden, where she teaches immigration law, employment discrimination, and administrative law. She has written extensively on immigration policy, the status of aliens, and nationalism.

Christopher David Ruiz Cameron serves as professor and director of externships at Southwestern University School of Law, where he teaches employment law and civil procedure. A graduate of Harvard Law School, where he served as an editor of the *Harvard Law Review,* Professor Cameron clerked for the Honorable Harry Pregerson of the U.S. Court of Appeals, Ninth Circuit, and practiced law in Los Angeles before entering teaching.

Gilbert Paul Carrasco, professor of law at Villanova University School of Law, teaches constitutional law and immigration law. An author of casebooks on immigration law and civil rights, he has served on the Council of Legal Advisors to the U.N. High Commissioner for Refugees, and as Consultant to the U.S. Department of Justice's Office of Immigration Related Unfair Employment Practices.

Linda Chavez is president of the Center for Equal Opportunity, a Washington, D.C., think tank, and a former Senior Fellow at the Manhattan Institute. During the Reagan Administration, she was director of the U.S. Commission on Civil Rights. As a former president of U.S. English, Chavez fought against excesses of multiculturalism and bilingualism. She is a columnist for *USA Today* and a frequent guest on CNN and National Public Radio. The author of *Out of the Barrio: Toward a New Politics of Hispanic Assimilation,* Chavez is currently at work on a second book, *A House Divided: Race and the Politics of Multiculturalism.*

Yvonne M. Cherena Pacheco, associate dean at St. Mary's University School of Law, received her J.D. from CUNY at Queens and LL.M. from Georgetown. Her subjects include clinical teaching, jurisprudence, and legal method.

James Crawford, a Washington-based journalist, has been the Washington editor of *Education Week,* as well as the author of *Bilingual Education* and the editor of *Language Loyalties: A Source Book on the Official English Controversy.*

Arnoldo De León, professor of history at Angelo State University in San Angelo, Texas, has also written *The Tejano Community, 1836–1900,* and specializes in the history of Mexican Americans in Texas.

Adelaida R. Del Castillo, assistant professor in the Department of Mexican American Studies at San Diego State University, where she received the Timeos outstanding teaching award, is also the editor of *Between Borders: Essays on Mexicana/Chicana History.*

Richard Delgado is Jean Lindsley Professor of Law at the University of Colorado School of Law. Author of numerous articles and books, including *The Rodrigo Chronicles,* he is also one of the founders of critical race theory. Winner of several book awards and prizes, he is also considered a pioneer of narrative theory and legal storytelling.

David R. Diaz earned his M.A. in city and regional planning at the University of California at Berkeley and his Ph.D. in the Urban Planning Program at the University of California at Los Angeles. He has held positions in both the private and the public sectors.

Leslie G. Espinoza, clinical professor of law at Boston College, teaches civil law clinic, health-care law, trusts and estates, and women and the law. Author of leading articles on race, ethnicity, and higher education, she also serves as an officer or member of several committees devoted to community and minority affairs and law school governance.

Ruben J. Garcia received his J.D. from the University of California at Los Angeles School of Law. He currently practices union-side labor law at Rothner, Segall, Bahan & Greenstone in Pasadena, California.

Alicia Gaspar De Alba, assistant professor of Chicano/a Studies at the University of California at Los Angeles, is the author of a collection of short fiction, *The Mystery of Survival and Other Stories,* which received the Premio Aztlan for 1994. Her literary work focuses on borders of identity, sexuality, and language.

Oscar Gonzalez attended Cornell University and served as a research intern in the Summer Graduate Program at the University of California at Berkeley.

David G. Gutiérrez, associate professor of History at the University of California at San Diego, received his Ph.D. from Stanford University. Voted Academic Senate Distinguished Teacher, his work focuses on Chicano history, comparative immigration, ethnicity, and the history of the Southwest.

Ian F. Haney López is acting professor of law at Boalt Hall School of Law, University of California at Berkeley, where he teaches and writes in the areas of race relations law and critical theory. The author of *White by Law: The Legal Construction of Race,* he served as a Rockefeller Fellow in Law and Humanities at Stanford University during the 1994–95 academic year.

Melissa Harrison, professor of law at the University of Montana, earned her B.A. at the University of the South and her J.D. at Vanderbilt. After serving as assistant district attorney in New York and assistant U.S. attorney in Nashville, she entered teaching in 1991, specializing in criminal law and procedure, sentencing, and white-collar crime.

Berta Esperanza Hernández-Truyol, a much sought-after speaker, is professor of law at St. John's University School of Law, where she writes and teaches in the areas of international law, race and gender in the law, and employment discrimination. The author of many leading articles on international human rights laws, Professor Hernández was born in Cuba, grew up in Puerto Rico, and attended university and law school in the United States.

Reginald Horsman, professor of history at the University of Wisconsin at Milwaukee, is the author of ten books, most recently *Dr. Nott of Mobile: Southerner, Physician, and Racial Theorist*. A native of Leeds, England, he specializes in American history, with an emphasis on the early national period, westward expansion, and racial attitudes, and is the recipient of distinguished teaching awards. His 1981 book *Race and Manifest Destiny* is considered a milestone in the development of critical studies of whiteness.

Elizabeth M. Iglesias is professor of law and codirector of the Center for Hispanic and Caribbean Legal Studies at the University of Miami School of Law, where she teaches criminal procedure, individual employment relations, and international economic law. After receiving her J.D. from Yale, she worked as a research associate with the Center for Criminal Justice at Harvard Law School on law reform in Guatemala.

Kevin R. Johnson is professor of law at the University of California at Davis School of Law. After receiving his J.D. from Harvard, he clerked for the Honorable Stephen Reinhardt of the U.S. Court of Appeals, Ninth Circuit, Los Angeles, and practiced law in San Francisco. He has written extensively on immigration law and policy, including California's Proposition 187. His work has focused on the influence of race on U.S. immigration laws. He is currently writing a book about life as a white-brown person.

Concepción R. Juarez is a graduate student in the Department of Ethnic Studies at the University of California at Berkeley.

Gerald P. López is professor of law at the University of California at Los Angeles School of Law, where he teaches local economic development, community outreach, education and organizing, and civil rights litigation. His book *Rebellious Lawyering: One Chicano's Vision of Progressive Law Practice* develops perspectives on lawyering that he pioneered as an activist and as cofounder of both the new Program in Public Interest Law and Policy at UCLA and the former Lawyering for Social Change Concentration at Stanford Law School. He continues to work with a wide range of people, employing innovative strategies to tackle diverse social problems.

David R. Maciel teaches courses on Chicano history, Mexico, modern Latin America, and the U.S. Southwest at the University of New Mexico, where he is professor of history. In addition to visiting professorships at a number of universities, including the National Autonomous University of Mexico (UNAM), he has received teaching and research fellowships from the Ford Foundation and the National Endowment for the Humanities.

Elizabeth Martínez, a longtime veteran of the civil rights movement, is the author of five books, including the bilingual work *500 Years of Chicano History in Pictures*. In 1968, she helped found the Chicano movement newspaper *El Grito del Norte*, and she presently writes a column on Latino issues in *Z* magazine. She lives in the San Francisco Bay Area, where she serves on the editorial board of *Social Justice* and teaches ethnic studies in the California State University system.

George A. Martinez, associate professor at Southern Methodist University School of Law, teaches jurisprudence, federal courts, civil rights, civil procedure, and complex litigation, and serves as deputy editor-in-chief of *NAFTA: Law and Business Review of the Americas*. After receiving an M.A. in philosophy from the University of Michigan and a J.D. from Harvard, he practiced law in San Francisco before entering teaching.

Carey McWilliams served as editor of *The Nation*, 1951–1975, and wrote *Ambrose Bierce, Factories in the Field, Ill Fares the Land, Brothers under the Skin, Prejudice, Southern California Country, California: The Great Exception, A Mask for Privilege, Witch Hunt*, and *The Education of Carey McWilliams*. A leading figure on the history of disempowered people in the United States, he also practiced law.

Martha Menchaca, an anthropologist at the University of Texas, received her Ph.D. from Stanford University. Born in Mexico, she was raised in the biracial agrarian community of Santa Paula in Ventura County, California. Her recent book *The Mexican Outsiders: A Community History of Marginalization and Discrimination in California* explores social segregation in that community.

Miguel A. Méndez holds the Adelbert H. Sweet Professorship at Stanford Law School. After a distinguished career as a public interest lawyer, Professor Méndez entered teaching in 1977, first at Santa Clara University School of Law and then at Stanford, where he teaches clinical courses, criminal law, and evidence. He is the author of numerous law review articles and materials for practicing lawyers.

Margaret E. Montoya, associate professor at the University of New Mexico Law School, teaches clinical law, employment law, and critical race feminism. After earning a J.D. from Harvard, she served as assistant to the president at Potsdam College and as associate university counsel at the University of New Mexico. An active participant in many civic causes, she has also been named to the National Advisory Organization for the NAFTA labor side agreement. The mother of two daughters, she frequently draws on mothering experiences in her academic writing.

Rachel F. Moran is a professor at the Boalt Hall School of Law, University of California at Berkeley. After receiving her J.D. from Yale, she clerked for the Honorable Wilfred Feinberg, chief judge of the U.S. Court of Appeals, Second Circuit, New York City. Prior to her teaching career, she was an associate at Heller, Ehrman, White & McAuliffe in San Francisco. In 1995 she won a distinguished teaching award at Berkeley, where she teaches bilingualism and the law, torts, and law and education.

Ruben Navarrette, Jr., is a freelance writer and columnist at the *Arizona Republic.* A graduate of Harvard, Navarrette has served the College Board as a consultant for Latino student affairs, worked as a legal assistant to the California Attorney General's Office, served as an extern to the Honorable Alex Kosinski of the Ninth Circuit Court of Appeals, and taught at the elementary, secondary, and university level.

Suzanne Oboler, a Peruvian American, teaches Latino/Latina studies and Latin American literature and culture at Brown University, where she is an assistant professor in the Department of American Civilization. Formerly a teacher at the New School for Social Research and the Institute for Puerto Rican Urban Studies, she has also directed worker education programs in New York City and taught literature to adult education classes in Brazil.

Michael A. Olivas holds the William B. Bates Professorship of Law at the University of Houston Law Center, where he also serves as director of the Institute for Higher Education Law and Governance and formerly served as associate dean for research. In addition to his J.D. from Georgetown University Law Center, he earned a Ph.D. in higher education from Ohio State University. The author of numerous books and articles on immigration law, higher education law, and civil rights, he serves as general counsel of the American Association of University Professors.

Maria L. Ontiveros, associate professor at Golden Gate University School of Law, teaches courses in employment discrimination, evidence, and labor law. After receiving her J.D. from Harvard, she earned an M.A. in Industrial and Labor Relations from Cornell and a J.S.D. from Stanford Law School. Her teaching is enriched by five years of practice in the field of labor and employment. She serves on the board of directors for the ACLU, as well as the National Advisory Committee for the North American Agreement on Labor Cooperation.

Angel R. Oquendo, associate professor at the University of Connecticut School of Law, teaches civil procedure, comparative law, and jurisprudence. Born in Puerto Rico, Professor Oquendo earned a Ph.D. from Harvard and served as senior editor of the *Yale Law Journal* where he earned his J.D. After graduating he clerked for the Honorable Stephen Reinhardt of the U.S. Court of Appeals, Ninth Circuit, Los Angeles.

Vicky Palacios, associate professor of law at Southern Methodist University School of Law, received her J.D. from Nebraska, after which she served as Hastie Fellow at the University of Wisconsin Law School. After teaching for six years at the University of Utah School of Law, she accepted the position of chair of the State of Utah Parole Board, returning to teaching in 1990 at Notre Dame. Her areas of scholarship include sentencing and the death penalty, and civil rights.

Juan F. Perea is professor of law at the University of Florida College of Law, where he teaches constitutional law, employment law, and law and pluralism. Before entering teaching he clerked for the Honorable Bruce M. Selya, U.S. Court of Appeals, First Circuit, and practiced law in Boston at Ropes & Gray. He has written extensively on American language policy, nativism, and ethnic identity, and is the editor of *Immigrants Out! The New Nativism and the Anti-Immigrant Impulse in the United States*. He is currently writing a book on the black/white binary paradigm and the Latino struggle for civil rights.

Beatriz M. Pesquera, associate professor and director of the Chicana/Chicano Studies Program at the University of California at Davis, has published articles on Chicanas' employment and familial experiences and on Chicana feminism. A 1990–1991 Rockefeller Humanist-in-Residence at the Southwest Institute for Research on Women at the University of Arizona, she is coeditor of *Building with Our Hands: New Directions in Chicana Studies*.

Bill Piatt is J. Hadley Edgar Professor of Law at Texas Tech University and author of *¿Only English? Law and Language Policy in the United States* and *Language on the Job: Balancing Business Needs and Employee Rights*. His many areas of expertise include immigration law, law and language policy, corporations, and family law.

Deborah A. Ramirez, professor of law, teaches criminal justice, criminal procedure, and evidence at the Northeastern University School of Law. Before entering teaching she served as U.S. Attorney in the Department of Justice. Professor Ramirez has written on courts, juries, and bias.

Jenny Rivera, assistant professor at Suffolk University Law School, teaches property, administrative law, and state and local government law. After earning a J.D. from New York University and an LL.M. from Columbia, Professor Rivera clerked for Judge Sonia Sotomayor of the U.S. District Court, Southern District of New York. Before entering teaching, she worked as staff attorney for the Homeless Family Rights Project of the Legal Aid Society in New York and as associate counsel for the Puerto Rican Legal Defense and Education Fund.

Richard Rodriguez is an editor at Pacific News Service and a contributing editor for *Harper's Magazine, U.S. News & World Report*, and the Sunday "Opinion" section of the *Los Angeles Times*. In addition to his two widely acclaimed books, *Hunger of Memory* and *Days of Obligation: An Argument with My Mexican Father*, he has written documentaries for the BBC and published numerous articles in newspapers and periodicals. A distinguished lecturer, he has received awards from the National Endowment for the Humanities and the World Affairs Council of California.

Renato Rosaldo, Lucie Stern Professor of Anthropology at Stanford University, is the author of the prizewinning *Ilongot Headhunting, 1883–1974: A Study in Society and History*. A member of the American Academy of Arts and Sciences, his research interests include history, society, the islands of Southeast Asia, U.S. Latinos, and Latin America.

Alex M. Saragoza is associate professor in the Ethnic studies/Chicano studies program at the University of California at Berkeley, where he is also chair of the Center for Latin American Studies. His research and writing, focusing on Mexico and the United States, includes *The Monterrey Elite and the Mexican State.*

Denise A. Segura, associate professor of sociology at the University of California, Santa Barbara, has published articles on Chicanas and Mexican immigrant women workers, Chicano education, and Chicana feminism. A 1991–1992 Ford Foundation Postdoctoral Fellow, she is currently coauthoring a book on the contemporary and historical dimensions of Chicana feminism.

Earl Shorris, a former advertising executive and consultant to corporations, serves as a contributing editor for *Harper's Magazine*. He is the author of ten books, including the widely acclaimed *Latinos: A Biography of the People.*

Ilan Stavans was born in Mexico City, received his Ph.D. from Columbia University, and teaches at Amherst College. His many publications include the widely acclaimed *Imagining Columbus: The Literary Voyage; Talia in Heaven,* a novel for which he won the Latino Literature Prize; *Growing Up Latino,* a coedited anthology with Harold Augenbraum; and *The Hispanic Condition.*

Jean Stefancic, research associate at the University of Colorado School of Law, is the author of numerous articles and books on civil rights and critical theory, including *No Mercy: How Conservative Think Tanks and Foundations Changed America's Social Agenda.* In 1993, she was co-recipient of a Rockefeller Bellagio award to write a book about law and social change, *Failed Revolutions.*

Ronald Takaki, grandson of Japanese immigrant plantation laborers in Hawaii, holds a Ph.D. in American history from the University of California at Berkeley, where he has served as professor of ethnic studies for over two decades. Author of the critically acclaimed *Iron Cages* and the prizewinning *Strangers from a Different Shore,* he has won numerous teaching awards and university honors and is a nationally recognized scholar of multicultural studies.

Luis Angel Toro, after earning his J.D. at the Boalt Hall School of Law, University of California at Berkeley, taught legal process at the McGeorge School of Law. He also served as clerk to the Honorable Carlos F. Lucero of the U.S. Court of Appeals, Tenth Circuit. He currently practices law at the firm of Senn, Lewis, Viciano & Strahle in Denver.

Francisco Valdes, professor of law at the University of Miami School of Law, teaches constitutional law; Latinos/as and the law; and law, race, and sexuality. His areas of scholarship include the social construction of sexuality and of race, subjects on which he is currently writing a book.

Abel Valenzuela, Jr., received his Ph.D. from M.I.T. in urban and regional studies and is assistant professor of urban planning and Chicano studies at the University of California at Los Angeles. He publishes and teaches courses on urban poverty and public policy, planning issues in minority communities, urban labor markets, and immigration. His research focuses on the social status and impact of recent immigrants, Latinos, African Americans, and Asian Americans.

Index

ABA. *See* American Bar Association

acculturation, 438–41. *See also* assimilation

Acosta, Oscar "Zeta," life of, 327–29

advertising, 650

affirmative action, 44–45, 432–33; and African Americans, 479; and conservatives, 291–99; Hispanic critics of, 50; proposal for, 402

African American(s). *See* black(s)

African Americans: as a reference point for civil rights. *See* black/white binary

African(s): in Spain, 461; slaves, in Mexico, 460

Afro-Antillean ethos, 65

aggregation of Latino subgroups, 49–50

Agricultural Workers Organizing Committee (AWOC), 316

Alarcón, Arthur, 337

Alien Nation (Brimelow), 198

alienage, 103, 126–30, 140; classifications, 115–16

alienation, 450–51. *See also* bicultural conflict

Alvarez, Julia, 580

Always Running: La Vida Loca, Gang Days in L.A. (Rodriguez), 439–40

American Bar Association (ABA): inspection team, and detained aliens, 323

American national imagination about community, 99–104

American women's movement, 523–30

Americanization institutes, 196

ancestry, 9–13; and Chicanos, 285

Anglo-Saxonism, 150, 183

Anglo-Saxons, and Mexicans, 149–51, 183

angry diner story, 125

anti-Mexican sentiment, 199–200, 661; in Texas, 422–23

Anzaldúa, Gloria, 38, 39, 578, 631–32, 641

Appiah, Anthony, 69, 189

argument: and meaning, 272; and relationship to storytelling, 273–74

Asian immigrants, in California, 166

assimilate, failure to, 198–99

assimilation, 170, 185, 419–20, 423–26, 431–34, 442–43; difficulty of Latino, 445–46; of European immigrants, 444; limits of, 427–30; narrative, in film, 215–16; utopian view of, 366

assimilationism, rhetoric of, 121–22

asylum process, 321–24

attorney as interpreter: disadvantages of, to clients, 605–8

autobiography, and legal scholarship, 38–42

Autobiography of a Brown Buffalo, The (Acosta), 327

AWOC. *See* Agricultural Workers Organizing Committee

Ayres, Lt. Ed Duran, and Ayres report, 311

Aztlán, 34, 69, 333, 335, 628–29

Badillo, Con. Herman (N.Y. State Assembly), 58

Bamba, La (film), 218

barrio clubs, 310

Bataan Death March. *See* World War II, and Mexican Americans

Behar, Ruth, 641–42

Bell, Derrick, 28, 255, 258

Beyond the Melting Pot (Glazer and Moynihan), 126

bicultural behavior, 281, 440–41

bicultural conflict, 419–20, 442–43, 450–51

bilingual education, 138, 563–65, 566; policy debate about, 610–20

Bilingual Education Act of 1968, 561, 564, 616

bilingual jurors, 21–22; disqualification of, from service, 602–4. *See also* juror(s)

bilingualism, official, 589–90

Biltmore Six, 336–37

binary paradigm of race, 361–67

biological view of race. *See* race(s), biological view of

birth names. *See* surnames, Latina

Black Atlantic, The (Gilroy), 634

black/brown conflict. *See* tensions, between Latinos and blacks

Blackmun, Justice Harry, 383

black(s): in California, 166; and the civil rights movement, 432–33; Hispanics, 60; racial identity of, 9–15

black/white binary, 28–29, 45, 47–48, 53, 60, 68–69, 138–39, 180; and Chicanos, 284–90; effect of, 480–83; history of, 361–67; and mixed race people, 364; and racism, 466–76; reasons for, 470–71; and reproduction of inequality, 369–75

705